Assessment of Children and Youth with Special Needs

THIRD EDITION

Libby G. Cohen
The Spurwink Institute

Loraine J. Spenciner
University of Maine at Farmington

Boston   New York   San Francisco
Mexico City   Montreal   Toronto   London   Madrid   Munich   Paris
Hong Kong   Singapore   Tokyo   Cape Town   Sydney

Executive Editor: Virginia Lanigan
Editorial Assistant: Matthew Buchholz
Marketing Manager: Kris Ellis-Levy
Production Editor: Janet Domingo
Editorial-Production Service: Walsh & Associates, Inc.
Composition Buyer: Linda Cox
Manufacturing Buyer: Linda Morris
Electronic Composition: Omegatype Typography, Inc.
Interior Design: Omegatype Typography, Inc.
Photo Researcher: Annie Pickert
Cover Administrator: Kristina Mose-Libon

For related titles and support materials, visit our online catalog at www.ablongman.com.

Between the time website information is gathered and then published, it is not unusual for some sites to have closed. Also, the transcription of URLs can result in typographical errors. The publisher would appreciate notification where these errors occur so that they may be corrected in subsequent editions.

Library of Congress Cataloging-in-Publication Data

Cohen, Libby G.
  Assessment of children and youth with special needs / Libby G. Cohen, Loraine J. Spenciner.—3rd ed.
    p. cm.
  Includes bibliographical references and index.
    ISBN 0-205-49353-X
    1. Psychological tests for children. 2. Child development—Testing. 3. Youth—Psychological testing. 4. Adolescence. 5. Behavioral assessment of children. 6. Behavioral assessment of teenagers. 7. Educational tests and measurements. I. Spenciner, Loraine J. II. Title.

BF722.C638 2006
371.26—dc22

                                                          2006041621

Printed in the United States of America

10 9 8 7 6 5 4 3 2 1   10 09 08 07 06

Contents

chapter **3**   # Reliability and Validity   37

chapter **4**   # Developing Technical Skills   50

chapter **5** | **Observing, Interviewing, and Conferencing   70**

chapter **6**   # Performance-Based, Authentic, and Portfolio Assessments   106 chapter **7** | **Test Interpretation and Report Writing   134**

chapter **8** | Achievement: Overall Performance   156

chapter **9** | **Reading   184**

chapter **10** | **Written Language   209**

chapter **13** | Cognitive Development   271

chapter **14** | Adaptive Behavior   299

chapter **15** | Behavior in the Classroom   313

chapter **16** Implementing Program Evaluation   **339**

chapter **17** Involving Families   **351**

chapter **18**   # Assessment of Young Children   373

chapter **19**   # Youth in Transition   388

Preface

The purpose of this book is to provide future and experienced educators and other professionals with a fundamental understanding of traditional and contemporary perspectives on the assessment of children and youth, ages 3 through 21. New developments in cognitive psychology and school reform and research on teaching and learning have had an impact on current thinking about assessment.

Features

This book features broad coverage of traditional and contemporary assessment approaches. The text discusses individual tests at length and explains various assessment approaches in detail. Research-based practices and the views of practitioners are conveyed. Links to professional standards are emphasized.

Major topics covered in this revised edition are:

- Individuals with Disabilities Education Act of 2004 (IDEA)
- No Child Left Behind legislation
- Research-based practices
- Practitioner snapshots
- Description of professional standards
- Accommodations and modifications
- Assistive technology
- The role of families in the assessment process
- Students how have diverse cultural and linguistic backgrounds
- Assessment of the physical, learning, and social environments
- Observation techniques
- Functional behavioral assessment
- Performance-based, authentic, and portfolio assessment
- Standardized instruments, with recent updates
- Criterion-referenced testing
- Curriculum-based assessment
- Informal assessment
- Contemporary approaches to the assessment of mathematics and literacy
- Transition assessment
- The role of technology in gathering, synthesizing, interpreting, and reporting information
- Interpreting tests and writing reports
- Program evaluation

Organization

Several themes are common throughout the book. Each chapter begins with a set of objectives. We hope that the reader will use these objectives as guideposts in learning. Each chapter contains an "Overview" section that discusses theories, perspectives, and conceptual frameworks; "TESTS-at-a-Glance" provide brief information about specific standardized assessment instruments; "Snapshots" examine individual students so that the reader may deepen understandings; "What Works!" provides an in-depth look at effective classroom assessment practices; "Research-Based Practices" describe research findings; and "Responding to Diversity" considers issues of sensitivity and responsiveness to students and the uniqueness of their families. Key points from each chapter are summarized.

Companion Website

This text is accompanied by a website (http://www.ablongman.com/cohen3e) that provides students and instructors with numerous activities and ideas to extend learning along with information about the book and its authors. The site consists of a student area and an instructor area.

In the student area, students can select Web-based activities and links, locate chapter objectives, and check word meanings in the glossary. These Web-based activities:

- Relate to each chapter of the textbook.
- Describe problems for individuals or small group of students to solve by finding information on the Web.
- Provide students with opportunities to apply concepts discussed in the text and to locate assessment information related to actual questions that might arise in the classroom.

In the links area, students can continue to build Web-based resources by following links related to individual chapters or through awareness activities designed by the instructor.

The instructor area provides a place for instructors to post a course syllabus, quizzes, and tests.

Acknowledgments

We dedicate this book to current and future teachers—we admire and respect you for your dedication to improving the lives of children and youth. We extend our sincere appreciation to the many people who helped and supported us in the development of this book. Special thanks to Virginia Lanigan of Allyn and Bacon for her support of this third edition.

We extend grateful appreciation to the manuscript reviewers who provided us with thoughtful and insightful reviews for this edition: J. Patrick Brennan II, Armstrong Atlantic State University; Kimberly Fields, Albany State University; Cecil Fore, University of Georgia; Arlene Hall, Murray State University; Robert Ives, University of Nevada, Reno; Sharon Piety-Nowell, Bethune-Cookman College; and Marcee Steele, University of North Carolina, Wilmington.

Libby extends a special thank you to ALLTech staff members who have supported and nurtured her work over the years: Dale Blanchard, John Bott, Cynthia Curry, Deb Dimmick, Doug Kahill, Suzanne Johnson, Nancy Lightbody, Rick Mills, Andrea Norwood, Lisa Smith, Jessica Sumner, and Rich Vaglia. You are the best!

Loraine dedicates this work to her many students and colleagues who have helped to enhance this book. A special thank you to Sharon Adams, Deb Albert, Kelly Asselin, Naomi Shardlow, Barb Williams, and Dolores Appl.

We are especially grateful to our families, Les, Seth, Jay, Amy, Dave, and Dina—we appreciate your continued support and good humor.

1 Foundations of Assessment

Chapter Objectives

After completing this chapter, you should be able to:

- Explain the general requirements for assessment as mandated by federal laws.
- Discuss professional knowledge and skills related to assessing students with disabilities.

Key Terms

Assessment
Assessment approach
Individuals with Disabilities Education Improvement Act (IDEA) of 2004
Response to intervention (RTI)
IEP team
Accommodations

Modifications
Individualized education program (IEP)
Alternative assessments
Developmental delay
Individualized family service plan (IFSP)
Transition services

Due process
Informed consent
No Child Left Behind Act (NCLB) of 2001
Adequate yearly progress
Family Educational Rights and Privacy Act (FERPA)

Overview

A teacher shares concerns with another teacher about a new student in the classroom. A mother calls to discuss questions that were raised during a meeting about her child. Teachers and other professionals who work with students with disabilities not only raise questions but must work with others to respond to concerns and make decisions about students. They must be able to observe, collect, record, and interpret information about students with disabilities. As members of a school team, they plan, monitor, and evaluate individualized education programs.

This chapter discusses federal laws that relate to the assessment of children and youth with disabilities. Federal legislation has had profound effects on assessment practices and the education of students with disabilities. Since this is an area that continues to change, we will examine resources that regularly provide updated information.

Sections of this chapter begin themes that you will learn more about throughout this book. Each chapter contains an "Overview" section, which discusses theories, perspectives, and conceptual frameworks; "Tests-at-a-Glance" provide brief information

▶ You can find out more about the Council for Exceptional Children and standards for special educators at http://www.cec.sped.org/

about specific standardized assessment instruments; "Snapshots" examine individual students so that you may deepen understandings; "What Works!" provides an in-depth look at effective classroom assessment practices; "Research-Based Practices" describe research findings; and "Responding to Diversity" considers issues of sensitivity and responsiveness to students and the uniqueness of their families. Throughout the chapters, you'll find references to the knowledge and skills that beginning special education teachers need to know about assessment. These references are based on the standards developed by the Council for Exceptional Children, a professional organization for special educators, in the text *What Every Special Educator Must Know*.

Why Do Teachers Assess?

Assessment is a global term for observing, gathering, recording, and interpreting information to answer questions and make legal and instructional decisions about students. Assessment is an integral aspect of instruction: It enables educators to gather and interpret information about students and to make decisions and provide information about what individual students can and cannot do, know and do not know. Schoolwide assessments help administrators and school board members determine the success of school programs and the progress of students.

Assessment is a major focal point in education today. The term **assessment approach** describes the way information is collected for making an educational decision. In addition to quizzes, tests, and exams, teachers use other assessment approaches such as portfolios or authentic assessments to provide regular feedback to students regarding their performance and to give them opportunities to improve. Teachers connect instruction with assessment and use this information to change, modify, and evaluate teaching and learning activities.

Teachers also use assessment approaches to answer questions regarding student achievement, abilities, behavior, development, and skills. Is there a possibility that the student has a disability? Should the student be referred for further assessment? By observing, collecting, and recording information, classroom teachers work with other educators and school personnel to interpret the information, answer questions, and make decisions about students. Some of these students may have disabilities.

Questions about students with disabilities bring assessment to another level. Assessment in the field of special education involves not only these general assessment aspects but legal aspects as well. Does the student have a disability? Federal and state laws specify assessment requirements that must be followed. The following section examines the federal mandates regarding assessment practices. These mandates address the assessment process that will be conducted. Special educators and other personnel working with students with disabilities must comply with these requirements.

Individuals with Disabilities Education Improvement Act (IDEA) of 2004

Children and youth with disabilities have been able to receive special education services in their local schools from the time of the passage of federal legislation (PL 94-142) in 1975. Since then, IDEA has been revised and reauthorized several times. In 2004, the reauthorization (PL 108-446) was known as the **Individuals with Disabilities Education Improvement Act of 2004**, or **IDEA**. Sometimes this acronym is written to include the term "improvement": IDEiA.

The revised law provides new emphasis on improving results for students with disabilities. IDEA specifies special education services for children and youth ages 3 through 21 and early intervention services for infants and toddlers, birth through age

2. IDEA ensures that all children with disabilities have available to them a free and appropriate public education (FAPE) that emphasizes special education and related services designed to meet their unique needs and prepare them for further education, employment, and independent living (20 USC Sec. 602(d)(1)(A)).

IDEA includes mandated requirements relating to the assessment process that teachers and test examiners must know and understand. These requirements form the legal basis for identifying and providing services to children and youth with disabilities.

▶ **CEC Common Core Knowledge and Skills.** The beginning special educator should understand legal provisions and ethical principles regarding assessment of individuals (CC8K2).

Who Is Eligible for Special Education?

During the assessment process, students are identified as being eligible for special education using criteria outlined in IDEA. IDEA guarantees that children and youth with disabilities have the right to special education services if their disability adversely affects their educational performance and if these special services would allow them to benefit from the education program. Students who receive special education services must meet the eligibility description of one of the categories of disability identified in IDEA and listed in Figure 1.1.

To address possible overidentification of students, IDEA encourages schools to provide effective teaching strategies and positive behavioral interventions to prevent misidentification. IDEA offers alternatives for identifying students with high incidence disabilities, such as learning disabilities, that go beyond simply looking at the discrepancy between intelligence and achievement. This federal mandate encourages schools to consider new ways of identifying students by examining each student's response to intervention.

Response to Intervention (RTI)

Response to intervention (RTI) is a prereferral activity that occurs prior to a referral for special education services. By identifying students who are experiencing difficulties early in their school career and providing them with specific intervention to address areas of difficulty, the focus of RTI is to catch children before they fail.

Response to intervention involves a multistep process, beginning with a clear assessment of a student's abilities. Next, a teacher selects and implements a research-based approach to intervention. During this time, the student's progress is monitored closely. Teachers may try more than one research-based approach if the student does not respond to the first. For many students, intervention will be successful, and they will make progress. If a student does not respond to the intervention, then the student will be referred for additional assessment. The lack of progress despite two or more interventions would be added to documentation of a student's possible need for special education services, and the student is referred to a multidisciplinary team.

Multidisciplinary Teams

As members of a multidisciplinary team, teachers and other professionals who assess children and youth suspected of having disabilities represent various disciplines, depending on the needs of the student. For example, individuals may come from the fields of medicine, occupational therapy, physical therapy, psychology, social work, speech and language pathology, or therapeutic recreation in addition to general education and special education. A

Autism
Hearing impairments (including deafness)
Mental retardation
Orthopedic impairments
Other health impairments
Serious emotional disturbance (referred to as emotional disturbance)
Specific learning disabilities
Speech or language impairments
Traumatic brain injury
Visual impairments (including blindness)

FIGURE 1.1 • Disabilities and Impairments Qualifying Children and Youth for Special Education and Related Services

Source: 20 USC Sec. 3(A).

student's parent(s) also provide important information to the assessment process. A multidisciplinary team consisting of the parents, school personnel, and, when possible, the student, that is responsible for planning, developing, monitoring, and evaluating specialized instruction and related services for a student with a disability is often referred to as an **IEP team.** This team may be known as the special services team or other term as defined by state regulation. As a result of assessments, the multidisciplinary team will determine if the student has a disability.

When the student's IEP team meets, there must be an individual who can interpret the instructional implications of assessment results (20 USC Sec.(d)). Professionals involved in the assessment of students with disabilities should be knowledgeable of the general requirements of assessment (Figure 1.2).

Another function of the IEP team is to determine if the child or youth needs accommodations or modifications to be successfully involved and make progress in the general curriculum and to achieve IEP goals. **Accommodations** are changes to the education program and assessment procedures and materials that do not substantially alter the instructional level, the content of the curriculum, or the assessment criteria. An accommodation for a writing assessment, for example, might consist of changes in the format of materials, such as using a laptop computer instead of paper and pencil.

Accommodations also include changes to the classroom arrangement, scheduling, or timing; for example, giving a student extra time to complete the assessment. On the other hand, **modifications** refer to changes or adaptations made to the educational program or assessment that alter the level, content, and/or assessment criteria. For example, a modification to an assessment might include reading a condensed version of the paragraph or completing half of the assessment items.

Assessment procedures must be fair and equitable for all children and youth. Educators must:

- Use a variety of assessment tools and strategies to gather relevant functional, developmental, and academic information, including information provided by the parent, that may assist in determining whether the child has a disability; and determine the content of the child's individualized education program, including information related to enabling the child to be involved in and progress in the general education curriculum, or, for preschool children, to participate in appropriate activities.

- Not use any single measure or assessment as the sole criterion for determining whether a child has a disability or determining an appropriate educational program for the child.

- Use technically sound instruments that may assess the relative contribution of cognitive and behavioral factors, in addition to physical or developmental factors.

- Select and administer assessments and other evaluation materials so as not to be discriminatory on a racial or cultural basis.

- Select assessment and other evaluation materials in the language and form most likely to yield accurate information on what the child knows and can do academically, developmentally, and functionally, unless it is not feasible to so.

- Use assessments for purposes for which the assessments or measures are valid and reliable.

- Ensure that assessments are administered by trained and knowledgeable personnel; and are administered in accordance with any instructions provided by the publisher.

- Assess the student in all areas of suspected disability.

- Provide assessment tools and strategies that provide relevant information that directly assists persons in determining the educational needs of the child

- Ensure that assessments of children with disabilities who transfer from one school district to another school district in the same academic year are coordinated with such children's prior and subsequent schools, as necessary and as expeditiously as possible, to ensure prompt completion of full evaluations.

FIGURE 1.2 ● General Requirements for Assessments

Source: 20 USC Sec. 614(b)(2).

The purpose of making accommodations and modifications is to reduce the impact that certain student characteristics, such as distractibility or short-term memory deficits, have on test performance. Accommodations and modifications should respond to the needs of the student, and test administrators should document and describe them in the testing report. Although two students may have the same disability, such as a learning disability, the accommodations and modifications each student may need can differ.

When the IEP team determines that a student needs an accommodation or modification, this is written into the student's individualized education program (IEP). When a student receives accommodations or modifications during the instructional program, the student also is eligible to receive similar accommodations or modifications during assessments. However, even when the IEP team recommends an accommodation or a modification, not all accommodations or modifications are permitted on state assessments. Each state develops a state list of acceptable accommodations allowable, and these vary from state to state (McCardle, Mele-McCarthy, & Leos, 2005, p. 69). Table 1.1 describes frequently used accommodations and modifications.

▶ **CEC Common Core Knowledge and Skills.** The beginning special educator will understand national, state or provincial, and local accommodations and modifications (CC8K5).

▶ Download a helpful guide, *Students with Disabilities Performance Assignments Accommodations Reference Guide* at http://www.cresst96.cse.ucla.edu/resources/justforteachers/ACCOMMODATIONS.pdf Review this document and discuss the ways that you have seen educators make accommodations during instruction and assessment.

TABLE 1.1 ● Frequently Used Accommodations and Modifications

Type of Accommodation or Modification	Example of Accommodations	Examples of Modifications
Presentation mode	• Test is administered individually rather than administered in a group. • Examiner reads items out loud (except when student is tested in reading). • Student takes a computer-administered form of the test. • Large print forms are used. • Braille form of the test is used. • Test directions and items are signed. • A specific examiner may be chosen who is able to develop (or who already has) rapport with the student.	• Examiner uses prompts or cues.
Location of the test administration	• Test is administered in an area with reduced distractions. • Test is administered while student is using special furniture. • Test is administered in space that has special lighting.	
Response mode	• Teacher or helper marks the responses as indicated by the student. • Student indicates responses on paper that has lines or grid. • Student uses a communication device. • Time limits for responding are extended or modified.	• Student is allowed to use a calculator for mathematics calculation. • Examiner accepts key word responses instead of complete sentences required by the test. • Student is allowed to use a spell checker, specialized software, or dictionary for writing test.
Test content	• Number of items per page is reduced but student completes all test items. • Use of bilingual glossaries and dictionaries (for English language learners).	• Fewer test items are presented
Test format	• Test items are magnified.	• Key words in the test directions are highlighted or color coded. • Test items are reworded. • Pictures or graphics are substituted for words.

The Individualized Education Program

Each child or youth who receives services must have an **individualized education program (IEP).** An IEP team develops the written document from a comprehensive assessment and includes annual goals that the student will meet. For students who will be working toward alternate achievement standards and who will be taking alternative assessments, the IEP includes short-term objectives, or benchmarks. **Alternative assessments** enable students with persistent academic problems and students with severe or significant disabilities to participate in general large-scale assessments.

The IEP team conducts a reevaluation not more frequently than once a year, unless the parent and school personnel agree otherwise, and at least once every three years, unless the parent and school personnel agree that a reevaluation is unnecessary (20 USC Sec. 614(a)(2)). The team begins by reviewing existing assessment information. Using the review and input from the parents, the team determines what additional assessment is needed. Figure 1.3 illustrates the assessment information required on the IEP.

▶ Does your state department of education allow multi-year IEPs?

---

(1) A statement of the child's present levels of academic achievement and functional performance, including how the child's disability affects the child's involvement and progress in the general education curriculum.
   (a) For preschool children, as appropriate, how the disability affects the child's participation in appropriate activities.
   (b) For children with disabilities who take alternate assessments aligned to alternate achievement standards, a description of benchmarks or short-term objectives.
(2) A statement of measurable annual goals, including academic and functional goals, designed to—
   (a) Meet the child's needs that result from the child's disability to enable the child to be involved in and make progress in the general education curriculum.
   (b) Meet each of the child's other educational needs that result from the child's disability.
(3) A description of how the child's progress toward meeting the annual goals described in subclause (2) will be measured and when periodic reports on the progress the child is making toward meeting the annual goals (such as through the use of quarterly or other periodic reports, concurrent with the issuance of report cards) will be provided.
(4) A statement of the special education and related services and supplementary aids and services, based on peer-reviewed research to the extent practicable, to be provided to the child, or on behalf of the child, and a statement of the program modifications or supports for school personnel that will be provided for the child—
   (a) To advance appropriately toward attaining the annual goals.
   (b) To be involved in and make progress in the general education curriculum in accordance with subclause (1) and to participate in extracurricular and other nonacademic activities.
   (c) To be educated and participate with other children with disabilities and nondisabled children in the activities described in this subparagraph.
(5) An explanation of the extent, if any, to which the child will not participate with nondisabled children in the regular class and in the activities described in subclause (4)(c).
(6) A statement of any individual appropriate accommodations that are necessary to measure the academic achievement and functional performance of the child on state- and districtwide assessments consistent with section 612(a)(16)(A); and if the IEP team determines that the child shall take an alternate assessment on a particular state- or districtwide assessment of student achievement, a statement of why—
   (a) The child cannot participate in the regular assessment.
   (b) The particular alternate assessment selected is appropriate for the child.
(7) The projected date for the beginning of the services and modifications described in subclause (4) and the anticipated frequency, location, and duration of those services and modifications.

FIGURE 1.3 ● Assessment Information Required in the IEP

Source: 20 USC Sec. 614(d)(1).

To help reduce paperwork, IDEA offers states an opportunity to develop multi-year IEPs. This allows IEP teams to engage in long-term planning by developing an IEP, not to exceed three years, that is designed to coincide with natural transition points for the student (20 USC Sec. 614(a)(d)). Schools must provide informed consent to parents and assurances that a multi-year IEP is optional.

Special Considerations for Young Children

Over the years, teachers and professional organizations have voiced concerns over (1) the potential detrimental effects of labeling a child at a young age, (2) the lack of adequate assessment tools for young children, and (3) the belief that some of the disability categories used with older children may not be appropriate (Figure 1.1). IDEA allows state personnel to include the term **developmental delay** in state regulations so that children ages 3 through 9 can receive special education and related services without being labeled according to specific disability category (Figure 1.4). Although young children vary greatly in their rate of development, this term reflects a significant delay in one or more areas of development, including physical, cognitive, communication, social or emotional, or adaptive development.

Early childhood multidisciplinary teams focus on children with disabilities from birth through age 2. In some states, teams cover children from birth to school-age 5. The early childhood multidisciplinary team includes parents, the family service coordinator, and other team members from various disciplines. This team assesses, implements, and evaluates early childhood intervention services. The early childhood multidisciplinary team writes an **individualized family service plan (IFSP)** for children age birth through age 2. Children may continue to be served under an IFSP until entry into kindergarten as long as (1) the IFSP is consistent with state policy, and (2) the parents concur (20 USC Sec. 635 (C); *Federal Register,* 1999, sec. 300.342(c)). Similar to an IEP, the individualized family service plan includes information about the child's level of functioning, the goals or outcomes for the child, and the services the child and family will receive.

Transition Services

When a student with a disability reaches age 16, or earlier if the IEP team determines the need, preparation for transition begins. The IEP team discusses and begins planning the **transition services** (Figure 1.5) that the student will need during the transition

A child aged 3 through 9 (or any subset of that age range, including ages 3 through 5) may, at the discretion of the state and the local educational agency, include a child—

(i) experiencing developmental delays, as defined by the State and as measured by appropriate diagnostic instruments and procedures, in one or more of the following areas: physical development; cognitive development; communication development; social or emotional development; or adaptive development; and

(ii) who, by reason thereof, needs special education and related services.

FIGURE 1.4 ● Definition of Developmental Delay

Source: 20 USC Sec 3(B); *Federal Register,* 1999, Sec. 300.7(b)(1).

Transition services means a coordinated set of activities for a child with a disability that—

• Is designed to be within a results-oriented process that is focused on improving the academic and functional achievement of the child with a disability to facilitate the child's movement from school to post-school activities, including post-secondary education, vocational education, integrated employment (including supported employment), continuing and adult education, adult services, independent living, or community participation;

• Is based on the individual child's needs, taking into account the child's strengths, preferences, and interests; and

• Includes instruction, related services, community experiences, the development of employment and other post-school adult living objectives, and, when appropriate, acquisition of daily living skills and functional vocational evaluation.

FIGURE 1.5 ● Definition of Transition Services

Source: 20 USC Sec. 602(34).

to postsecondary education or employment and community living. Transition needs are based on the individual student, taking into account the student's preferences and interests. Beginning no later than the first IEP that is in effect when the child is 16 (or younger, if determined appropriate by the IEP team), the team writes a statement of transition service needs. From this point forward, the IEP must include:

- Appropriate measurable postsecondary goals based upon age-appropriate transition assessments related to training, education, employment and independent living skills, where appropriate;
- Transition services needed to assist the child in reaching those goals, including courses of study; and
- Beginning not later than one year before the child reaches the age of majority under state law, a statement that the child has been informed of the child's rights under this title, if any, that will transfer to the child on reaching the age of majority under Section 615(m). (20 USC Sec. 614(d)(1)(A)VIII)

Transition services and assessment are further described in Chapter 19.

Procedures for Ensuring the Rights of Students and Families

IDEA specifies procedures that ensure the protection of parents' and children's rights during the assessment process and the delivery of services. These procedures, called **due process** requirements, specify that:

- Parents must receive written notice whenever there is a proposal to initiate or change the identification, evaluation, or educational placement of their child.
- Parents have the right to review their child's records regarding the assessment and educational placement.
- Parents may obtain an independent evaluation of their child by a qualified examiner who is not employed by the school. The evaluation is at no cost to the parent and is paid for by the public school.
- Due process also ensures that parents, schools, or agencies have a right to an impartial hearing conducted by a hearing officer when disagreements occur. A hearing can be requested by either a parent or a school district.

IDEA requires the school to obtain informed consent from the parent before his or her child is assessed. **Informed consent** is a process that involves (1) presenting information so that it can be easily understood, (2) providing alternatives, (3) identifying risks and benefits, and (4) accepting or consenting to the information proposed. Figure 1.6 illustrates a school district form for obtaining parent consent. Informed consent is also required before the team develops a comprehensive multi-year IEP. The only exceptions to these requirements are if the school can demonstrate that it had taken reasonable measures to obtain parent consent and the student's parent has failed to respond, if the parental rights have been terminated, or if the whereabouts of the parents are unknown.

No Child Left Behind Act (NCLB) of 2001

The **No Child Left Behind Act (NCLB) of 2001** created many changes with the goals of improving academic performance for ALL students. This act stressed accountability through scientifically based research practices and regular and ongoing assessment of student progress. Even before NCLB, educators working with professional organizations

Point Street School District

CONSENT TO CONDUCT INDIVIDUAL ASSESSMENT(S)

Name: _Loren Sinkinson_   Date of Birth: _2/21/xx_

School: _Point Street_   Grade: _7_

Date: _September 12, xxxx_

The following is a description of the methods to be used to evaluate your child. You will be notified and given the opportunity to review and obtain copies of evaluation summaries or other reports to be discussed at the multidisciplinary team meeting. At this meeting, we will explain the results of the evaluation and discuss its significance to your child's education program. If you have any questions about these procedures, please call the special education director at 111-1111, and we will discuss them with you.

Description of Evaluation

☑ 1. *Academic testing* is designed to determine what the student's academic progress is within specific academic areas. The student's achievement will be compared to the achievement of students in this school and students throughout the country. Commonly used tests include: Wechsler Individual Achievement Test-Second Edition (WIAT-II), Woodcock-Johnson Test of Achievement-III, and curriculum-based assessments. Other: _____

☐ 2. *Intellectual testing* involves the individual administration of intelligence tests. These tests are designed to measure different types of abilities such as what the student can do. Commonly used tests include: Wechsler Intelligence Scale for Children IV (WISC- IV) and the Kaufman Assessment Battery for Children, Second Edition. Other: _____

☑ 3. *Observation* is designed to assist the team in relating test data to the student's classroom performance in academic, social, and behavioral areas as compared to others in the classroom.

☐ 4. *Speech/language testing* is designed to determine the student's communication skills in articulation, voice, fluency, expressive language, and receptive language. Commonly used test include Clinical Evaluations of Language Fundamentals-4 (CELF-4), Goldman Fristoe Test of Articulation, Peabody Picture Vocabulary Test III, Expressive Vocabulary Test, and the Oral and Written Language Assessment (OWLS). Other: _____

☐ 5. *Psychological evaluation* is designed to assess cognitive, personality, and/or behavioral function. Commonly used evaluation methods include parent and child interviews, personality inventories, and projective tests. Other: _____

☑ 6. *Additional assessments* are designed to collect essential information on health, social, or developmental history; behavior (may be completed by an interview with the parents, school personnel, or the child); sensory assessments in vision or hearing. Commonly used instruments include: Adaptive Behavior Scale, Motor Development and Behavior Rating scale. Other: _____

I understand the nature of, and the reasons for, the evaluations checked above as well as the statement of procedural safeguards attached to this consent form. I further understand the additional testing areas not indicated on this form will require prior written notice before administration.

A withdrawal of parental consent after the initial evaluation or initial placement in special education shall be considered a request to change the student's program and placement. As such, the IEP Team shall convene and consider the parent's request. If the IEP Team disagrees with the parent's request, Point Street School District may use the mediation process or initiate a hearing to override the parent's withdrawal of consent.

I do give consent for such evaluations: _Janet Sinkinson_
Parent Signature

September 17, xxxx
Date

FIGURE 1.6 ● School District Form: Consent to Conduct Individual Assessment(s)

developed content standards across each academic area, including English language arts, mathematics, science and technology, social studies, modern and classical languages, visual and performing arts, and health and physical education. Within each academic area, performance indicators describe what students should know and be able to do at each grade level. Before NCLB, many students were already taking state- and districtwide assessments to demonstrate their achievement. These assessments, aligned with content standards, provide valuable information to educators regarding student progress and instruction. When assessment information indicates that one or more students are having difficulties, educators can modify or provide supplemental instruction.

Assessment Requirements

NCLB overlapped assessment activities in some states with additional requirements. These requirements specified that schools were required to annually assess student achievement in reading/language arts and math for student in grades 3 through 8 and at least once during grades 10 through 12. Beginning in 2007–2008, states must assess science achievement at least once in grades 3 through 5, 6 through 9, and 10 through 12. Assessments must be aligned with state content and achievement standards. Students with disabilities must have reasonable accommodations, when appropriate.

When the IEP is developed, the team identifies how the student will be assessed. Most students with disabilities participate in the regular assessment, or they take the regular assessment with accommodations. When the IEP team determines that a student with a disability is unable to participate in the state- and districtwide assessments, the student must take an alternative assessment.

Alternative Assessments

Alternate assessments are based on modified achievement standards for students with "persistent academic disabilities." These students are not likely to reach grade-level achievement standards at the same pace as students without disabilities because of their disability. NCLB caps the number of students with disabilities who can take these alternative assessments at 2 percent of the total student population. For students with significant cognitive disabilities, NCLB requires states to develop additional alternative assessments for alternative achievement standards. NCLB allows an additional 1 percent of the total school population to use alternative assessments for students with significant cognitive disabilities.

The IEP team makes decisions on the abilities of each individual student. A student may take a grade-level assessment in mathematics, for example, yet need to take an alternative assessment in reading. Decisions must be based on individual student needs, not the type of disability or the setting where the student receives special education services. Each year, the IEP team reviews assessment and accommodation options. If the student takes an alternative assessment, the IEP must identify the alternative assessment and include a statement describing why the student cannot participate in the regular assessment (with appropriate accommodations). Depending on state requirements, the IEP team must document the alternate assessment decision-making process (Figure 1.7)

▶ Check with your state department of education. What accommodations for students with disabilities are permitted for state- and districtwide assessments? What types of alternative assessments allow students with disabilities to demonstrate their achievement?

For students with disabilities, providing alternative assessment options based on modified achievement standards allows students to demonstrate their achievement. However, some educators fear that students who do not need them may be given alternative assessments based on modified achievement standards. Furthermore, students not held to the same high grade-level achievement standards may become part of a cycle of low expectations. What do you think?

**Vermont Alternate Assessment Decision-Making Process:
Matching Students to Assessment Options**

Student: _____   Grade Level (at testing time): _____

School: _____   Meeting Date: _____

Directions: Use the sequence of questions below to (a) document that required eligibility procedures have been followed, (b) certify that the student is eligible for an alternate assessment, and (c) determine which of three alternate assessment options is most appropriate. Begin with the questions in Section 1 and continue through the question sequence until the directions at a particular "decision point" indicate that the correct option has been determined. Specify below the assessments in which the student will be required to participate:

❏ **Vermont—Developmental Reading Assessment** (grade 2)
❏ **NECAP Reading** (grades 3, 4, 5, 6, 7, & 8)
❏ **NECAP Math** (grades 3, 4, 5, 6, 7, & 8)
❏ **NECAP Writing** (grades 5 & 8)
❏ **NSRE English/Language Arts** (grade 10)
❏ **NSRE Math** (grade 10)

Section 1—General Questions

This section documents that the required process and procedural guidelines have been followed. Process and procedural guidelines include provisions for a team process, parent participation, and analysis of information relevant to the student's potential for participation in the general statewide assessment.

1. Was the decision to use an alternate assessment made by the student's planning team? **One of the following plans, which includes current levels of performance, must be attached to this form in order for approval to be considered!** IEP ❏ 504 ❏ EST ❏ Other (specify) _____	☐ Yes	☐ No
2. Was parent involvement provided through one of the following? (Please indicate): ❏ Parents participated in the decision-making process by attending a meeting or by providing input before a final decision was made. -Or- ❏ If parents were unable to participate, they were informed of the team's decision and reasons.	☐ Yes	☐ No
3. Were at least two of the following methods used to evaluate the student's potential to participate in the general statewide assessment? (Check all that apply): ❏ Consideration of the standard accommodations ❏ Comparison of student achievement levels to Grade Level Expectations (GLEs) ❏ Results of practice tests/released tasks ❏ Discussion concerning the student's prior experiences with similar tests ❏ Consultation with district Alternate Assessment Mentor ❏ Consultation with Vermont Department of Education ❏ Other (specify): _____	☐ Yes	☐ No

Decision Point #1
If the answer to ANY Section 1 question is NO, then STOP!
Process and procedures are INSUFFICIENT to determine eligibility.
If the answers to ALL Section 1 questions are YES, then proceed to SECTION 2.

FIGURE 1.7 • Alternate Assessment Decision-Making Process

(continued)

Section 2—Modified Assessment

Modified assessments are appropriate for students who participate in the same classroom activities as classmates and are working at essentially the same performance or difficulty levels as classmates. However, these students are unable to participate in the regular statewide assessment because existing accommodations or test formats do not allow reasonable access to the general assessment.

1. Is the student working toward the *same* standards and grade level expectations as grade level classmates? ☐ Yes ☐ No

2. Is the student working at the *same* performance levels as grade level classmates? ☐ Yes ☐ No

3. Is the student unable to participate in the general assessment for any of the following reasons? (Please indicate): ☐ Yes ☐ No

   ❏ The student is blind or visually impaired and the allowable accommodation tables indicate that a Braille version of the test is not available or that Braille is not appropriate; or

   ❏ The student is deaf or hearing impaired and the allowable accommodation tables indicate that it is not appropriate to translate assessment information into American Sign Language or other primary mode of communication; or

   ❏ In general, the student needs a specific accommodation that the allowable accommodation tables indicate is not appropriate for the assessment because the accommodations would change the nature or difficulty of assessment items or tasks; or

   ❏ The student is emotionally unable to participate in the general assessment.

4. Were at least two of the following methods used to determine that no specifed standard accommodations are available that would permit the student to participate in the general statewide assessment? (Check all that apply): ☐ Yes ☐ No

   ❏ Consideration of the standard accommodations ❏ Results of practice tests ❏ Results of released tasks ❏ Discussion concerning the student's prior experiences with similar tests ❏ Consultation with district Alternate Assessment Mentor ❏ Consultation with Vermont Department of Education ❏ Other (specify): _____

DECISION POINT #2

If the answers to ALL Section 2 questions are YES, then STOP!
The student is ELIGIBLE for a MODIFIED ASSESSMENT.
If the answer to ANY Section 2 question is NO, then proceed to SECTION 3.

FIGURE 1.7 • Continued

Section 3—Adapted Assessment

Adapted assessments are appropriate for students who are working on the same skills or standards as classmates, but at significantly lower performance or difficulty levels. On statewide assessments, even the easiest items or tasks would very likely be above the student's current capabilities. (Adapted assessments are not available for the VT -DRA).

1. Is the student working toward the *same* standards and grade level expectations as grade level classmates? (A "**NO**" response indicates that the student is working toward "*alternate achievement standards.*" Please go directly to question #3.)	☐ **Yes** ☐ **No**
2. Are the student's current performance levels significantly lower than those measured by the general assessment? If **Yes**, please indicate a more appropriate assessment level, based on the student's instructional levels. NECAP Reading: ❏ 6th grade ❏ 5th grade ❏ 4th grade ❏ 3rd grade ❏ K–2nd grade (Stanford) NECAP Math: ❏ 6th grade ❏ 5th grade ❏ 4th grade ❏ 3rd grade ❏ K–2nd grade (Stanford) NECAP Writing: ❏ 5th grade ❏ K–2nd grade (Stanford) NSRE E/LA: ❏ 8th grade ❏ 4th grade ❏ K–2nd grade NSRE MATH: ❏ 8th grade ❏ 4th grade ❏ K–2nd grade **IEPs or student plans attached to this form MUST include *current* levels of performance that substantiate the need for a replacement test in order for an adapted assessment to be approved for AYP!**	☐ **Yes** ☐ **No**

3. Were any two of the following methods used to make this decision? (Check all that apply):
  ❏ Consideration of the standard accommodations ❏ Results of practice tests
  ❏ Results of released tasks ❏ Discussion concerning the student's prior experiences with similar tests ❏ Consultation with district Alternate Assessment Mentor ❏ Consultation with Vermont Department of Education
  ❏ Other (specify): _____
	☐ **Yes** ☐ **No**

DECISION POINT #3

If the answers to ALL Section 3 questions are YES, then STOP!
The student is ELIGIBLE for an ADAPTED ASSESSMENT.
If the answer to ANY Section 3 question is NO, then proceed to SECTION 4.

FIGURE 1.7 • Continued

(continued)

Section 4—Lifeskills Assessment

Lifeskills assessments are appropriate for students working toward alternate achievement standards, at individually determined performance or difficulty levels. Students who are eligible for the Lifeskills assessment represent less than 1 percent of all students. These students will typically have IEPs that focus on functional lifeskills goals and content that are not measured by the general assessment.

1. Does the student have an educational plan that focuses on lifeskills such as basic communication, personal management, social skills, home/school/community, recreation, and vocational skills?	☐ Yes	☐ No
2. Does the majority of the student's program address skills and standards that are not measured by the general assessment?	☐ Yes	☐ No
3. Does the student's level of cognitive ability and adaptive skills prevent achievement of the standards designated for classmates who do not have disabilities?	☐ Yes	☐ No

DECISION POINT #4

**If the answers to ALL Section 4 questions are YES, then STOP!
The student is ELIGIBLE for a LIFESKILLS ASSESSMENT.
If the answer to ANY Section 4 question is NO, then GO BACK!**

As a team, reconsider accommodations, modifications, or adaptations.

NEXT STEP:

After determining the most appropriate assessment for the student, please complete the *Documentation of Eligibility for Alternate Assessment* form (4/1/05) and submit it with an IEP or student plan, listing current levels of performance to:

Vermont Dept of Education

FIGURE 1.7 • Continued

Source: Reprinted with permission of the Vermont Department of Education.

For all English language learners, NCLB requires that accommodations include native-language tests. Once students have been in school in the United States for three years in a row, they must be tested in English. Additionally, states are required to test the English proficiency of these students.

Because NCLB requires accountability for demonstrating achievement, each school district is required to produce an annual report called a *report card* that includes information on how all students performed on the districtwide tests. Three levels of student performance are used to indicate achievement level: basic, proficient, and advanced. In the report card, a district also must break out student achievement data by the following subgroups: low-income status, disability, English language proficiency, migrant status, race, ethnicity, and gender.

The report cards must indicate if a school is meeting state standards of **"adequate yearly progress" (AYP).** When a school does not meet AYP, the state identifies the school as needing improvement, corrective action, or restructuring. The school district must make its report card available to parents at the beginning of each school year. Additionally, it must notify parents if their child's school is identified as needing improvement, correction action, or restructuring.

Family Educational Rights and Privacy Act (FERPA)

The **Family Educational Rights and Privacy Act (FERPA)** (PL 93-380), commonly referred to as the "Buckley amendment," states that no educational agency may release student information without written consent from the student's parents. This consent specifies which records to release, the reasons for such release, and to whom. The agency should then send a copy of the released records to the student's parents.

FERPA allows families and students over 18 years of age access to and the right to inspect any of their records from any education institution, including preschool, elementary and secondary schools, community colleges, and colleges and universities that accept federal money. Parents also have the right to challenge and correct any information contained in these records. Professionals will want to ensure that they file only materials relevant to the student in the student's folder. Irrelevant information about the personal lives of families or information that is at best subjective and impressionistic has no place in a family's record.

▶ FERPA applies to any student who attends a school that receives federal funds. How do these regulations apply to your college or university?

Court Decisions Affecting Assessment Practices

In addition to federal legislation, assessment practices also are influenced by court decisions. Litigation has involved the misuse of intelligence tests and culturally biased assessments. Even though these decisions were made many years ago, they are important

How It Works! **Assessing Student Achievement in Mathematics at Highlands Middle School**

Tad Farnsworth is a special educator at Highlands Middle School and is part of the seventh-grade math team along with three seventh-grade mathematics teachers. The team has been meeting weekly to discuss student progress and plan instruction. Several of the students have IEPs. Sal Springer, a 12-year-old, has a learning disability. When the IEP team met for Sal's annual review, they discussed his progress and continuing needs. His parents provided their input and observations, too. The team decided that he would participate in the regular math class with additional support from the resource room. Next, the IEP team discussed the state- and districtwide assessments that would be administered this year and discussed what type of assessment Sal should take, as well as the need for any appropriate accommoda-

tion(s).The team agreed that he should take the grade-level assessments with accommodations. His IEP includes the following description of accommodations that Sal needs for assessments. *"Sal will take the District Assessment in a quiet room and will be allowed two additional breaks beyond those allowed for other students."*

His teacher, Tad Farnsworth, has been providing additional special education instruction in the resource room to Sal and the other students with learning disabilities. They have been working on using tables and graphs to represent relationships and to communicate information to supplement the ongoing instruction in this area in the regular classroom. Later this month, Sal will come down to the resource room to take the district assessment. One of the questions from the exam is listed on the following pages (Figure 1.8).

(continued)

How It Works!
continued

5–8 Mathematics
Structured Response

Canoes for Rent (4/04) 1
G1. Patterns, Functions, Relations
K2.Mathematical Communication

CANOES FOR RENT

You and your friend Marion want to rent a canoe and spend the day paddling around the lake. There are two canoe companies that you can rent from.

- The first company, Canoes-R-US, charges a $3 flat fee plus $1.50/hour.
- The second company, Paddles Away, charges $2/hour, with no flat fee.

Marion immediately says that you should rent form Paddles Away because their price is a better deal. You are not sure if you agree and want to do a few math calculations before you decide.

1. Based on the number of hours, make a table that compares the cost of renting from Canoes-R-Us to the cost of renting from Paddles Away. Asume a full day rental is 8 hours.

Local Assessment Development • Final Draft
Maine Department of Eduction • Maine Mathematics & Science Alliance

FIGURE 1.8 • Example from a Districtwide Assessment

Source: http://www.mainegov-images.informe.org/education/lsalt/LAD/Tasks/Math5-8/CanoesForRent.pdf. Reprinted with permission of the Maine Department of Education.

5–8 Mathematics
Structured Response

Canoes for Rent (4/04) 2
G1. Patterns, Functions, Relations
K2. Mathematical Communication

2. Make a graph showing the relationship between hours and cost for rental for both companies. Make sure to attach your graph paper to this sheet and that your graph is labeled.

3. Using only one variable, write an expression for how much if would cost to rent a canoe for a given number of hours from Canoes-R-Us. Let n represent the number of hours.

• Using only one variable, write an expression for how much it would cost to rent a canoe for a given number of hours from Paddles Away. Let n represent the number of hours.

> **To Exceed Standards:** Write an equation for each canoe company in slope intercept form. Explain what each equation represents in relation to the graph you drew.

4. Write an explanation using your table, graph, **and** expressions to convince Marion that you agree or disagree with her decision. **Make sure you refer specifically to the data from your table, graph, AND expressions.**

Local Assessment Development • Final Draft
Maine Department of Eduction • Maine Mathematics & Science Alliance

FIGURE 1.8 • Continued

TABLE 1.2 • Major Court Cases and Assessment Practices		
Date	Court Case	Implication for Assessment Practices
1967	*Hobson v. Hansen,* Washington, DC	Tracking of students based on intelligence test scores is unconstitutional.
1970	*Diana v. Board of Education,* CA	Students cannot be placed in special education on the basis of culturally biased tests or tests given in other than the student's native language.
1979	*Larry P. v. Riles,* CA	IQ tests cannot be used as the sole basis for placing students in special classes.
1988	*Honig v. Doe,* CA	Students with disabilities cannot be excluded from school for any misbehavior that is disability-related.

▶ **CEC Common Core Knowledge and Skills.** The beginning special educator should understand historical foundations, classic studies, major contributors, major legislation, and current issues related to knowledge and practice (GC1K3).

to study today so that injustices will not be repeated. Table 1.2 identifies the major cases and discusses implications for assessment practices.

Responding to Diversity

Students and their families have diverse cultural, ethnic, racial, and linguistic backgrounds and come from different geographic regions of origin and from different gender, disability, and economic groups. They bring with them various perspectives, values, knowledge of native languages, and attitudes about the roles and responsibilities of the family, society, education, and professionals. The perspectives and values that students bring to the assessment situation can affect the student's attitudes toward the testing environment and performance, the examiner, and the purposes of the assessment (Sattler, 2001).

Sometimes perspectives and school expectations seem to work in opposing directions. For example, educational expectations of the classroom developed by members of the majority culture may tend to focus on the individual work of the student, whereas the educational expectations held by some families place an importance on group affiliation rather than individual accomplishment. These diverse perspectives also may conflict with aspects of special education services and assessment practices in which assessment focuses on building student independence and individualizing intervention services.

To address these concerns, special educators must develop expertise in assessment. For example, assessing English language learners takes special skills on the part of the educator conducting assessment. The teacher must consider the student's native language and proficiency in English. In selecting testing materials and procedures the teacher must examine for appropriateness.

IDEA specifies assessment requirements to ensure that assessment procedures are fair for children who are English language learners (Table 1.3). Teachers and other professionals should be aware that translating a test into another language does not mean that its content, difficulty, reliability, and validity are the same. A word in one language can have a different meaning, a different frequency of use, and a different difficulty level when translated into another language (American Educational Research Association, American Psychological Association, and National Council on Measurement in Education, 1999).

▶ **CEC Common Core Knowledge and Skills.** The beginning special educator should understand cultural perspectives influencing the relationships among families, schools, and communities as related to instruction (CC3K4).

Research-Based Practices: What's to Know?

IDEA describes using scientifically based research practices with students with disabilities including early identification and referral and prereferral procedures. In addition, IDEA describes the use of research-based interventions, curricula, and practices. Sometimes professionals refer to scientifically based research practices as "evidence-based practices." Whichever term you use describes best practice, providing educators with assurance of the effectiveness of what they do. Finding out about research-based practices can involve a search of your university library databases, such as ERIC or Academic Search Premier.

Many websites also maintain information on research-based practices. You might begin with one or more of the following:

- What Works Clearinghouse [http://www.w-w-c.org/] identifies current research studies on effective practices and intervention.

- ERIC/OSEP Special Project [http://www.ericec.org/osep-sp.html#recon] disseminates federally funded special education research at this website.

- The Center for Innovations in Education [http://www.cise.missouri.edu/links/research-ep-links.html] located at the University of Missouri-Columbia, maintains links to research-based practices leading to effective instruction.

▶ Use "prereferral" as a key term to search one or more databases. Compare your results. Which search was more useful, do you think?

TABLE 1.3 • Assessment Requirements for an English Language Learner Who Has a Disability or Is Suspected of Having a Disability

Planning the Assessment

What is the student's native language? Native language refers to the language normally used by the student, or, in the case of a child, the language normally used by the parents of the child.

During the Assessment Procedure

Assessment materials or procedures are selected and administered in the child's native language or other mode of communication, unless it is clearly not feasible to do so. No single procedure should be the sole criterion for determining an appropriate educational program for a child. Any standardized tests that the child takes must:

(i)   have been validated for the specific purpose for which they are used;

(ii) be administered by trained and knowledgeable personnel; and

(iii) be administered in accordance with any instructions provided by the producer of such tests.

Materials and procedures used to assess a child with limited English proficiency are selected and administered to ensure that they measure the extent to which the child has a disability and needs special education, rather than measure the child's English language skills.

IEP Meeting

The IEP team must consider the language needs of the student as those needs relate to the child's IEP.

The school must take whatever action is necessary to ensure that the parent understands the proceedings at the IEP meeting, including arranging for an interpreter for parents who are deaf or whose native language is other than English.

Source: 20 USC Sec. 602; 612.

Summary

- A course in assessment involves learning a new set of terminology related to the assessment process.

- Knowledge of federal mandates provides the basis for requirements for assessing students with disabilities.

- The perspectives and values that students bring affect the results of assessment process.

REFERENCES

American Educational Research Association, American Psychological Association, and National Council on Measurement in Education. (1999). *Standards for educational and psychological testing.* Washington, DC: American Educational Research Association.

Federal Register (Vol. 64, No. 48, pp. 12418–12536). Washington, DC: U.S. Government Printing Office, March 12, 1999.

Individuals with Disabilities Education Improvement Act of 2004 (20 USC).

McCardle, P., Mele-McCarthy, J., & Leos, K. (2005). English language learners and learning disabilities: Research agenda and implications for practice. *Learning Disabilities Research & Practice, 20*(1), 68–78.

Sattler, J. (2001). *Assessment of children: Cognitive applications* (4th ed.). La Mesa, CA: Author.

2 Assessment Framework

Chapter Objectives

After completing this chapter, you should be able to:

- Identify assessment questions and describe the different steps and purposes for assessment.
- Describe how to administer an assessment instrument.
- Describe how to determine a student's needs for assistive technology.
- Discuss interpreting assessments with accommodations or modifications.
- Apply professional standards and ethical considerations.

Key Terms

Screening	Determining eligibility	Assistive technology
Child Find	Program planning	Assistive technology service
Student assistance team	Monitoring individual progress	Assessment strategies
Referral	Program evaluation	Universal design

Overview

This chapter introduces assessment questions that guide the process of collecting information and the steps and purposes of the assessment process. Selecting assessment approaches, or ways of assessing student skills and knowledge, begins with a careful consideration of the assessment questions and purposes. Throughout the chapters in this book, you will find detailed discussions of specific assessment questions, purposes, and approaches.

Learning how to administer assessments appropriately is an essential skill. Assessments can focus on answering questions regarding academic or behavior concerns and physical or developmental factors. Special educators must be able to observe, collect, record, and interpret information about students with disabilities. As members of a school team, they plan, monitor, and evaluate individualized education programs. When the IEP team discusses whether a student needs assistive technology to access the general education curriculum, an assessment will focus on the student and the type of assistive technology that would be most appropriate.

▶ Discussions of professional standards and ethical considerations developed by the Council for Exceptional Children and the American Psychological Association provide a foundation for assessment later in this chapter. These standards will serve to guide your work with students and their families.

Assessment Questions, Steps, and Purposes

Assessment Questions

Chapter 1 defined *assessment* as a global term for observing, gathering, recording, and interpreting information to answer questions and make legal and instructional decisions about students. What types of questions do teachers and parents have? Teachers of young children and parents wonder if the child is developing typically in one or more of the following developmental areas:

Communication development. Should Jaleh be talking more now that she is 4 years old?

Cognitive development. Is Katie experiencing difficulty performing many activities that the other children can do quite easily?

Physical development. Does Sammy have difficulty seeing? Hearing? Does he have problems with fine and gross motor activities?

Adaptive development. Should Luis be able to feed himself and take care of toileting needs?

Social-emotional development. Sonia has difficulty getting along with other children. Will she "outgrow" this?

Teachers and parents of older children frequently have questions about a student's achievement, ability, or skills in one or more areas:

Academic area. Does Elliot have a reading problem?

Overall achievement. Why doesn't Bill do better in school?

General intelligence. Will Joy be able to learn how to compute a math problem?

Transition. What transition service needs does Cristoforo have?

Social-emotional status. Daryl has difficulty making friends. How can he be helped? Sabrina seems sad and depressed. What is causing this behavior?

Vision, hearing, or motor ability. Can Norweeta hear students speaking during class discussions? Joey frequently walks on tiptoes. Does this indicate a problem?

Communication. Bradley can hear the speaker but doesn't seem to understand. What could be the cause of his difficulty?

Assessment Steps and Purposes

In working with students with disabilities or who may have disabilities, professionals ask questions and make decisions during each of the assessment steps: screening, referral, determining eligibility, program planning, program monitoring, and program evaluation. As Figure 2.1 illustrates, the steps are sequential and progressive. Decision points allow the team to use the information to make decisions regarding the needs of the student.

Step 1. Screening

Identifying children and youth who need special education services is a collaborative effort among teachers in the schools and personnel who work in agencies that serve children and families. The assessment question focuses on "Is there a possibility that the student may have a disability?" The purpose of **screening** is to determine whether students may have disabilities and to refer them for further assessment. Screening is designed to assess large numbers of students efficiently and economically. Based on the information collected during screening, evaluators decide whether to refer the student to the team for further assessment. Screening approaches differ, depending on whether the student is a preschooler or of school age.

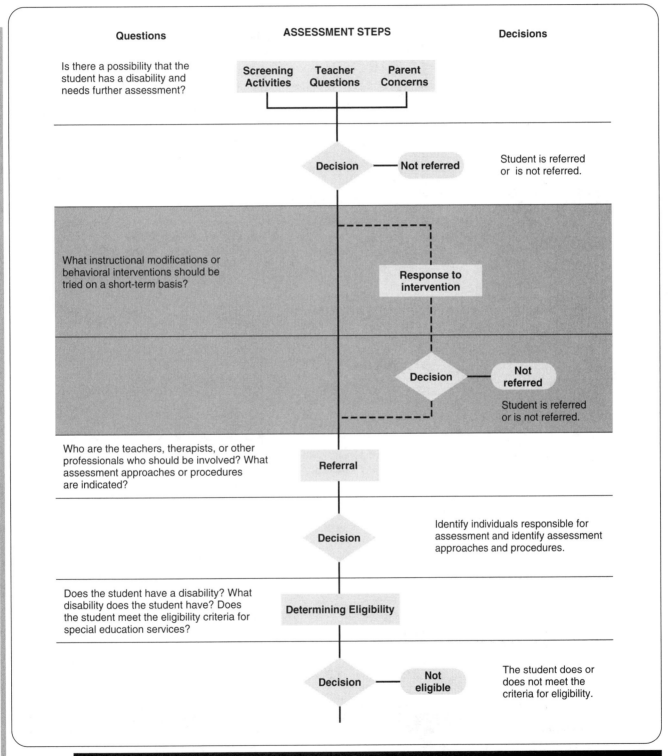

FIGURE 2.1 • The Steps in the Assessment Process

(continued)

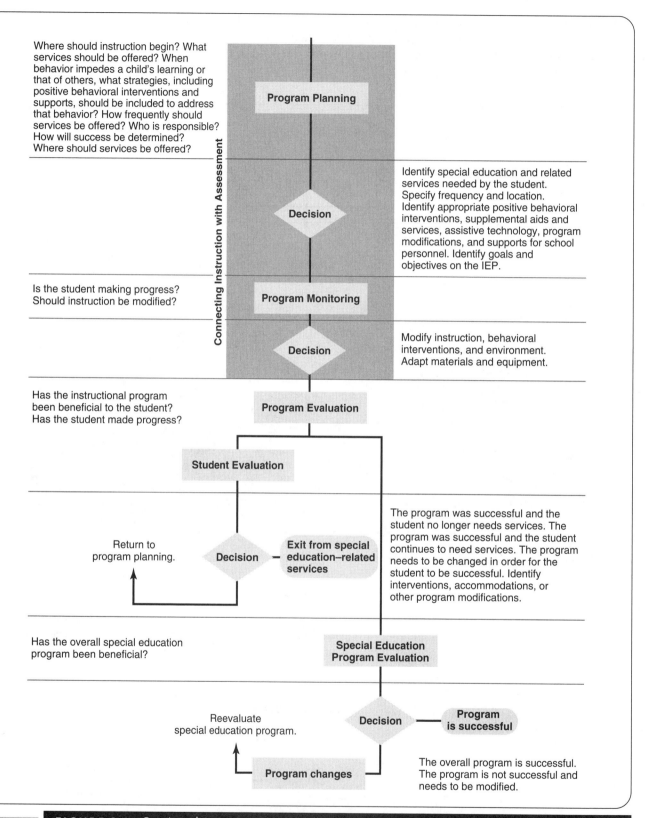

Where should instruction begin? What services should be offered? When behavior impedes a child's learning or that of others, what strategies, including positive behavioral interventions and supports, should be included to address that behavior? How frequently should services be offered? Who is responsible? How will success be determined? Where should services be offered?

Connecting Instruction with Assessment

Program Planning

Decision

Identify special education and related services needed by the student. Specify frequency and location. Identify appropriate positive behavioral interventions, supplemental aids and services, assistive technology, program modifications, and supports for school personnel. Identify goals and objectives on the IEP.

Is the student making progress? Should instruction be modified?

Program Monitoring

Decision

Modify instruction, behavioral interventions, and environment. Adapt materials and equipment.

Has the instructional program been beneficial to the student? Has the student made progress?

Program Evaluation

Student Evaluation

Return to program planning.

Decision — **Exit from special education–related services**

The program was successful and the student no longer needs services. The program was successful and the student continues to need services. The program needs to be changed in order for the student to be successful. Identify interventions, accommodations, or other program modifications.

Has the overall special education program been beneficial?

Special Education Program Evaluation

Reevaluate special education program.

Decision — **Program is successful**

Program changes

The overall program is successful. The program is not successful and needs to be modified.

FIGURE 2.1 • Continued

PRESCHOOL CHILDREN In many communities, children under age 6 come to the assessment process as a result of **Child Find** activities. Child Find directs parents to screening services in their community that are open to infants, toddlers, and preschoolers and that are free of charge.

Comprehensive screening of young children includes several components: parent concerns; medical history (often given through parental reports or completed by parents using a checklist); vision and hearing tests; and the use of commercial screening instruments and observation reports in the areas of general development, abilities, and skills. Screening instruments are generally inexpensive and are designed so they may be completed in a short amount of time, 30 minutes or less. Chapter 18 discusses specific screening instruments for young children.

SCHOOL-AGE STUDENTS Children who are entering public school for the first time or transferring to a new school require screening. One or more individuals, such as the special education teacher or general education teacher, conduct the screening, which involves various approaches. An educator often begins by reviewing past work and test scores of the incoming student or by asking the new student a set of questions. In the classroom, teachers observe and collect information about the student's work and performance. Teachers may observe that the student is having trouble seeing a computer screen, understanding and following directions, working with others, reading, or comprehending. Parents utilize screening approaches, too. They may have concerns about their child when they see their child in relation to other children in the neighborhood or when they compare their child to their knowledge about growth and development.

School personnel conduct a variety of other screening activities. The school nurse arranges for students to have regular vision and hearing screenings. Educators review student attendance records and follow up on students who are not attending school on a regular basis. Classroom teachers administer group tests of school achievement and screen student scores to identify those students who show they are having difficulty. When screening flags children, the process moves to the next step.

> ▶ **CEC Common Core Knowledge and Skills.** The beginning special educator should understand screening, prereferral, referral, and classification procedures (CC8K3).

Step 2. Making a Referral

PREREFERRAL DECISIONS Questions about a student are referred to an assistance team, which usually comprises regular classroom teachers and special educators in the school building. The team may be a **student assistance team** (SAT), teacher assistance team, or intervention assistance team. In addition to questions about individual student behaviors or academic work, this team enables teachers, both regular and special education, to help one another with general academic or discipline concerns including making accommodations to instruction and assessment. During this stage, response to intervention (RTI) activities, discussed in Chapter 1, usually occur, depending on the student's needs. When interventions are not successful, teachers document the interventions tried and the student responses in a written **referral** (Figure 2.2).

REFERRAL DECISIONS The IEP team, which is different from the assistance team, receives the written referral form. Based on the referral information about the student, the team recommends specific assessment approaches or assessment instruments to be used in **determining eligibility.**

Step 3. Determining Eligibility

To determine student eligibility for special education services, the assessment questions focus on "Does the student have a disability? What disability does the student have? Does the student meet the criteria for services?" The purpose of this step is to examine the assessment information to make a determination regarding the student's eligibility

SNAPSHOT

Cory

Cory is a fifth-grade student at Memorial School. Although he has never been referred for special education services, Cory has had some difficulty in past years. Even though school has been in session only a few weeks this fall, his teacher, Joanne Leslie, has become increasingly concerned about his lack of academic progress and his difficulty in organizing his work. Cory is very distractible in class and has a short attention span. Because his reading, language arts, and math skills are weak, he has difficulty in keeping up with assignments.

From a meeting with last year's teacher, Ms. Leslie knew that Cory had participated in small group intensive interventions for both reading and mathematics instruction. According

to the teachers, his distractibility and short attention span continued to interfere with his achievement and Cory showed little progress, in spite of the intense interventions. Ms. Leslie examined the documentation of Cory's interventions and learned that the teacher felt he should be referred for further assessment. Ms. Leslie also examined his most recent achievement scores. Compared to other students in fifth grade, Cory's reading and math scores were low. After consulting with Cory's parents, she completed a referral form for special education services (see Figure 2.2)

▶ If you were a member of Cory's IEP team, what additional information would you want to know?

Memorial School
Referral Form

Student's name: ___Cory Young___ Date of Birth: ___9/17/xx___

Grade: ___5___ Teacher: ___Ms. Leslie___

Parent/guardian: ___Joseph Davis___ Other parent/guardian: _____

Address: ___Harris Lane___ Phone: ___222-2222___

___Columbia___

Person making referral/position: ___Joanne Leslie, Classroom Teacher___

Person accepting referral/position: ___Crystal Kane, Special Education Administrator___

Date of consent for evaluation received: ___September 10, xxxx___

1. Described below are the reasons for the referral (attach separate page if necessary):

   Cory has a lot of difficulty organizing his work and he is highly distractible. His reading and math skills are below grade level. His written work is weak—mechanics, storyline, and topic development below average.

2. Described below are the interventions that were implemented and the student's response to the intervention.

   Last spring Cory participated in intensive small group instruction in corrective reading and in corrective mathematics. His distractibility and short attention span interfered with his achievement and at the end of the year Cory showed little progress.

3. Describe below are other alternative strategies that were implemented and why they were not successful.

   Cory was assigned alternative seating, near the teacher; this placement seemed to agitate him.

4. Described below are the procedures, tests, records or reports that were used as part of the basis for this referral.

   Iowa Tests of Basic Skills: Reading 3.0, Language arts 2.8, Spelling 2.5, Mathematics 3.1. A portfolio of Cory's work is available for review.

5. Described below are any other factors that are relevant to this referral and/or other school personnel knowledgeable about this referral (principal, nurse, social worker, school counselor, Title I teacher, etc.)

   Cory wears glasses inconsistently. Cory's family is proud of their Native American heritage and speaks their native language in the home.

FIGURE 2.2 ● Cory's Referral Form

for special education and related services according to state and federal (IDEA) guidelines for children and youth.

As specified in IDEA, a multidisciplinary team conducts assessment for the purposes of eligibility. Thus, a student's assessment covers all areas related to the suspected disability including, if appropriate, health, vision, hearing, social and emotional status, general intelligence, academic performance, communication, and motor abilities. For example, a student who is nonverbal may have a multidisciplinary evaluation that includes meeting with (1) an audiologist to determine the extent, if any, of a hearing loss; (2) a speech and language pathologist to assess understanding of language (receptive language) and communication skills; (3) a special educator to assess academic and functional skills; (4) a vocational rehabilitation counselor to identify interests and abilities; and (5) a psychologist to determine intellectual functioning. The team will use various approaches, including, for example, observations, norm-referenced instruments, and performance assessments. The team will ask the student's parent(s) to provide information, too. All of these individuals work together to view and analyze the assessment information, with all contributing expertise from their respective disciplines.

▶ **CEC Common Core Knowledge and Skills.** The beginning special educator should understand types and importance of information concerning individuals with disabilities available from families and public agencies (GC8K3).

Team members share the assessment information during the IEP meeting and determine the student's eligibility to receive special education and related services. As active members of the team, parents may have questions and collect various types of information such as medical records or developmental history.

Because the team bases its decisions on assessment information and data, they must choose and use appropriate assessment approaches carefully. Evaluators must have appropriate training, take responsibility in evaluating the adequacy of the approach, follow professional standards and ethical principles, and be knowledgeable about the limitations of specific approaches. In the chapters that follow we will discuss these approaches in more detail.

▶ **CEC Common Core Knowledge and Skills.** The beginning special educator should understand laws and policies regarding referral and placement procedures for individuals with disabilities (GC8K2).

Step 4. Program Planning

In **program planning,** the assessment questions focus on "What should be included in the student's individualized program? If behavior impedes learning, what strategies, including positive behavioral interventions, should the team write in the plan? What supplemental aids, services, and assistive technology does the student need? What types of accommodations and/or modifications should team members make to the curriculum? Where should instruction begin? What supports for school personnel does the student need?" The purposes are to (1) determine the student's current level of functioning and (2) plan the instructional program. Much of the information gathered in Step 4 will be useful in planning the instruction and developing realistic goals.

WHAT SHOULD PROGRAM PLANNING INCLUDE? Program planning includes assessing the student's current level of functioning and determining where instruction should begin. Members of the IEP team identify the special education and related services they will include in the student's program. The team plans accommodations and/or modifications to the curriculum and to the classroom environment. Team members utilize commercially published norm-referenced and criterion-referenced tests, checklists, observations, or curriculum-based assessments, as well as other assessment approaches.

CONNECTING ASSESSMENT WITH INSTRUCTION Connecting assessment with instruction is part of both program planning and Step 5, **monitoring individual progress.** Connecting assessment with instruction provides rich, ongoing information about a student's current level of achievement, which allows the teacher to make informed decisions regarding the student's instructional program. A teacher uses this type of assessment in planning daily teaching and learning activities to address the special needs of students. "Good classroom assessment tells us more than 'Knows it; doesn't know it.' It also tells us why" (Shepard, 1996). Connecting assessment with instruction is one of the most important aspects of the assessment process. In later chapters we will examine a variety of assessment approaches that link instruction with assessment.

Step 5. Monitoring Individual Progress

The purposes of this step are to determine (1) if the student is making progress and (2) whether to modify instruction if the student is not making progress. Teachers should assess the student's progress frequently. Information from this assessment step allows the IEP team members to modify interventions, teaching procedures, or materials if the student's progress is lagging.

Step 6. Evaluating the Program

Program evaluation is a process used to assess (1) the progress the student has made and (2) the overall quality of the school program. To evaluate the student's progress, the IEP team focuses on the student's IEP. They ask, "Is the student meeting the goals of the individualized education program?"

To address the overall evaluation of special education services, the questions focus on the achievement, as a group, that students accomplish in the program; the degree of satisfaction with the program as expressed by teachers, administrators, and parents; and the effectiveness of the program. The following section examines these two types of evaluation questions in more detail.

STUDENT EVALUATION This type of assessment helps evaluators make decisions about the success of the instructional program for individual students. The IEP team reviews the student's IEP at least annually to address any lack of expected progress, the results of any reevaluation, information about the student provided to or by the parents, or the student's anticipated needs (20 USC Sec. 614(d)). For children receiving services under an IFSP, family and evaluators must review the program every six months (or more frequently, if appropriate) and conduct the full evaluation annually.

IDEA requires a reevaluation of the student's performance and educational needs at least every three years, or more frequently if conditions warrant a reevaluation or if the child's parent or teacher requests a reevaluation. The team reviews existing assessment information including (1) evaluations and information provided by the parent; (2) current classroom-based, local, or state assessments and classroom-based observations; and (3) observations by teachers and related services providers (20 USC Sec. 614(c)) and considers the following questions: "Does the student continue to need special education and related services? What is the student's present level of performance and educational need? Does the student need any additions or modifications to the special education and related services to meet the annual goals?" On the basis of the review, and with input from the student's parents, the team decides what additional information it needs and what assessment approaches to use.

PROGRAM EVALUATION Program evaluation involves evaluating the overall services provided to groups of students or programs. Educators need to examine the success of programs offered to students, to replicate strong programs, and to refine or change programs that are not effective. Evaluation questions include: "Is the program successful? Are goals being met? Do parents feel satisfied with the services?" Information is collected in a variety of ways including aggregating assessment results of students who participate or have participated in the program; asking teachers, students, and parents to complete checklists or rating scales; interviewing current students in the program and their parents; or asking graduates of the school or program and their employers to complete questionnaires. We will study program evaluation in more detail in Chapter 16.

Assessment Approaches

Educators use a variety of assessment approaches to gather information about the student and about the classroom environment. A teacher may administer a test that consists of a set of questions to a student to determine the individual's knowledge or skill(s). The teacher reports the results in one or more types of scores. However, testing of students is only one approach. Some approaches can answer many different questions about a student, while other approaches are useful for gathering information for a specific purpose. Be sure that the approach will yield the type of information that you need.

Figure 2.3 illustrates the assessment questions, steps, and purposes that we have just discussed, in addition to some of the assessment approaches team members use. The assessment questions guide each of the steps and purposes during the assessment process. Various assessment approaches can be used to gather information, depending on the assessment questions.

▶ Make a list of various assessment approaches that you have experienced. Which approaches were the most effective for you? Why?

Assessment of Assistive Technology Needs

Some students with disabilities need devices, such as assistive technology, to learn successfully and to demonstrate their knowledge and skills. IDEA defines **assistive technology** as ". . . any item, piece of equipment, or product system, whether acquired commercially off the shelf, modified, or customized, that is used to increase, maintain, or improve functional capabilities of a child with a disability" (20 USC Sec. 602(1)). According to IDEA, a student can receive assistive technology devices and services if specifically included in the IEP.

Assistive technology encompasses a wide range of low-tech to high-tech devices to assist students in instructional and assessment activities. For example, the use of graph paper helps a student with a learning disability keep proper place value during a math assessment. Another student uses a laptop and text to speech to listen to his exam. Assistive technology can improve students' learning, independence, self-esteem, functional life skills, communication, and quality of life (Reed & Lahm, 2005).

An **assistive technology service** assists students with disabilities in selecting, acquiring, and using assistive technology devices. Assistive technology services can include evaluation of assistive technology needs; purchase or lease of assistive technology devices; selection, design, and customization; coordination of other services and therapies with assistive technology; training for students, family members, educators, and others in using assistive technology; and the use of assistive technology in students' home if the IEP determines that assistive technology is needed in order to receive the benefits of appropriate education (20 USC Sec. 602(2)).

▶ **CEC Common Core Knowledge and Skills.** The beginning special educator should know how to use technology to conduct assessment (CC8S3).

Approaches to Assistive Technology Assessment

Although a number approaches have been developed to guide the assistive technology assessment process (Lenker & Paquet, 2003), research in this area is evolving. Three approaches are described in this section: the Students, Environment, Tasks, and Tools (SETT) framework, the Matching Person & Technology (MPT) process, and the Wisconsin Assistive Technology Initiative (WATI) checklist.

SETT Framework

The SETT and ReSETT frameworks (Zabala, 1995, 2005) focus on the determination of a match between the settings in which individuals use assistive technology and tasks in which individuals are engaged. Assessment of technology needs is viewed as a

Screening	Eligibility	Program Planning	Program Monitoring	Program Evaluation
• To determine whether a student may have a disability and should be referred for further assessment	• To determine if there is a disability • To compare the student's performance with the performance of the peer group • To determine specific strength and weaknesses • To understand why the student is having difficulty	• To understand what the student knows and does not know • To plan the student's program • To determine instructional approaches • To plan for any assistive technology needs	• To understand the pace of instruction • To understand what the student knows prior to and after instruction • To understand the strategies and concepts the student uses • To monitor the student's progress • To monitor assistive technology needs and progress	• To determine whether the IEP goals have been met • To determine whether the goals of the program have been met • To evaluate program effectiveness • To evaluate assistive technology implementation
Assessment Question • Is there a possibility of a disability	**Assessment Question** • Does the student have a disability? • What disability does the student have? • Does the student meet criteria for services? • What are the strengths and weaknesses? • In what areas is the student having difficulty?	**Assessment Question** • What is the student not able to do? • What is the student not able to understand? • Where should instruction begin? • Should assistive technology be considered?	**Assessment Question** • What is the student not able to do? • What is the student not able to understand? • Where should instruction begin? • Should assistive technology be considered?	**Assessment Question** • Has the student met the IEP goals? • Has the instructional program been successful? • Has the student made progress? • Has the instructional program achieved its goals?
Assessment Approaches to Gather Assessment Data • Norm-referenced instruments • Curriculum-based assessments • Criterion-referenced instruments • Observations • Checklists	**Assessment Approaches to Gather Assessment Data** • Norm-referenced instruments • Curriculum-based assessments • Criterion-referenced instruments • Observations • Checklists • Probes • Error analysis • Interviews • Performance assessments	**Assessment Approaches to Gather Assessment Data** • Norm-referenced instruments • Curriculum-based assessments • Criterion-referenced instruments • Observations • Checklists • Probes • Error analysis • Interviews • Performance assessments	**Assessment Approaches to Gather Assessment Data** • Norm-referenced instruments • Curriculum-based assessments • Criterion-referenced instruments • Observations • Checklists • Probes • Error analysis • Interviews • Performance assessments	**Assessment Approaches to Gather Assessment Data** • Norm-referenced instruments • Curriculum-based assessments • Criterion-referenced instruments • Observations • Checklists • Probes • Error analysis • Interviews • Performance assessments • Surveys

Decision

Does not meet screening criteria **STOP**

Meets screening criteria **PROCEED**

Decision

Does not meet eligibility criteria **STOP**

Meets eligibility criteria **PROCEED**

Decisions

Does not meet eligibility criteria **EXITS** special education

Meets eligibility criteria **CONTINUES** to need secial education services

FIGURE 2.3 • Assessment Framework

continuous process. Students' technology needs change over time as school and vocational demands increase and as technology develops. In determining the correspondence between the student, environmental settings, tasks, and tools, Zabala (1995, 2005) suggested key questions that can be used to gather information, make decisions, and implement technology as seen in Figure 2.4.

Matching Person & Technology (MPT)

The MPT approach is similar to the SETT framework because MPT also considers a match between the environment and individual needs. However, MPT includes an additional consideration that relates to the function and features of the technology (Scherer & Craddock, 2002). The MPT process consists of six steps and related questions

Focus Area	Questions	Focus Area	Questions
Student	What new learning should the student be able to do? What skills should the student be able to acquire in order to achieve operational, functional, strategic, and social competence? What does the student need to do? What are the student's needs? What are the student's abilities?	Tasks	What specific tasks will be targeted for support? What are the barriers? What tools are needed to eliminate the barriers? What strategies should be implemented? How will tools be used? What activities will take place? What activities will support the student's learning? How can activities be modified? How can technology support the student's active participation?
Environment	What environmental changes should be made in order to support student change?	Change	How can changes be supported? In what areas should changes occur? What are the criteria for success? What types of evidence will be collected? Who will collect the data? When? Where? Who will make the revisions, if appropriate?
	Questions about the Student What specific technology skills will the student need to learn? How much training is required? What types of direct supervision and support will the student need? Who will provide the training and support?		
	Questions about Equipment Who will provide devices, tools, and supplies? How will the device be made available in each environment? Where will the device be located? Who will be responsible for maintaining the device, making repairs, updating the device, and ordering supplies?	Evaluation	Who will revisit the AT process to ensure that the student is successful and that implementation has been achieved? What updates should be made? What changes should be made to tasks, tools, and environments?
	Questions about the Environment Are changes necessary in order to achieve accessibility? Are additional supports necessary?		

FIGURE 2.4 ● Questions to Gather Information, Make Decisions, and Implement Assistive Technology

that are collaboratively answered by students and assistive technology experts in writing or through an interview. The six steps are:

1. Determination of initial and alternative goals.
2. Identification of technologies used in the past, levels of satisfaction, and desired technologies.
3. Assistive technology considerations.
4. Acceptance of and appropriate uses of assistive technology.
5. Implementation of interventions and strategies.
6. Development of written recommendations for assistive technology and supporting strategies.

Wisconsin Assistive Technology Initiative (WATI)

The WATI has developed a comprehensive assessment process for the consideration of assistive technology needs. During the process, problems are identified, solutions are generated, technology is tried, technology implementation is planned, and follow-up steps are specified. The major elements of WATI's AT decision-making process are:

- *Problem identification.* Problems and identified and defined.
- *Solution generation.* Suggested solutions are proposed.
- *Solution selection.* Various solutions are identified and selected; an action plan is developed.
- *Implementation.* The AT plan is implemented.
- *Follow-up.* AT implementation is evaluated periodically.

Preparing to Administer Assessments

Preparing to administer assessments begins with careful planning. This means that much is involved in getting ready to administer an assessment, knowing steps to remember during the administration, and understanding responsibilities to complete once the assessment is over.

Before the Testing Begins

Before the testing session begins, the examiner should:

1. Understand the purpose(s) of the assessment (as stated in the test manual).
2. Read the test manual thoroughly.
3. Carefully review the test items.
4. Know the administrative procedures. Some examiners find that it is helpful to mark the different sections in the manual with a paper clip or self-stick note for easy reference.
5. Organize the necessary materials and check to see that none are missing.
6. Reexamine the scoring procedures to verify that answers can be recorded correctly. Recording student responses accurately will ensure a reliable test administration.

When the Student Arrives

The following section details some of the most important **assessment strategies** to follow. Assessment strategies, individualized activities or routines that the teacher follows, assist students to demonstrate their best effort. When the student arrives, the examiner should:

1. Establish and maintain rapport. Some students may be nervous and anxious about the testing; other students may have little motivation to participate or to do their

▶ Compare one or more approaches to assistive technology assessment. What are the similarities? Which areas would you change?

best. Plan to spend enough time in making students feel comfortable before beginning the session.

2. Convey a sense of confidence about the student's performance and avoid statements such as, "This is going to be a difficult test." The examiner can say, for example, "This test may have some items that you will find easy and some items that will be more difficult."

3. Be aware of changes in lighting or noise level once the testing begins. Watch for signs of student fatigue or hunger. Some students may need a test break or an additional test session.

4. Maintain neutrality during the testing. Be careful about providing the student with information about the correctness of responses. Remember that not only words but facial expressions and other body language convey information. Students might ask if an answer is correct. Phrases such as "I see that you are trying hard" provide encouragement to students without violating testing procedures.

5. Carefully record student responses in the appropriate spaces on the test form.

6. Be sensitive to the needs of the student. Some students may need more time to explore test materials or share an interesting thought that has nothing to do with the test items!

▶ **CEC Common Core Knowledge and Skills.** The beginning special educator should know how to develop or modify individualized assessment strategies (CC8S4).

After the Testing Is Completed

After the testing session is ended:

1. Thank the student for participating.
2. Finish recording any additional information. Note any observations of the student.
3. Compute scores.
4. Interpret results.
5. Write reports.

Interpreting Assessments with Accommodations or Modifications

In Chapter 1 we discussed how accommodations do not alter the content of the assessment in a significant way; however, modifications mean changes or adaptations in a test. Both accommodations and modifications involve a nonstandard administration of the test.

Test manuals should describe appropriate accommodations and modifications and provide evidence of the validity of the test when examiners implement them. When evidence about the effects of accommodations and modifications on test performance is lacking, examiners should interpret tests cautiously.

Despite the practice of modifying tests for students with disabilities, there are several major problems to consider. Many experts believe that unless test developers norm a test using specific modifications, the test is invalid. Very few research studies demonstrate the effects of accommodations and modifications on test performance. Because of technical considerations relating to test development, it is difficult to equate the performance of students who have various accommodations or modifications with the performance of students who do not have accommodations or modifications. A test accommodation or modification may change the underlying construct of the test (American Educational Research Association et al., 1999). For example, a test of written language may become a test of spoken language if the student is permitted to dictate the response rather than writing it.

A concern of the reporting of test scores or test performance is whether to report the accommodation or modification. Some experts believe that not identifying modifications is misleading. Persons with disabilities have countered that modifying test procedures provides opportunities to demonstrate their abilities and that not modifying test procedures is unfair. Further, flagging or identifying accommodations or modifications can lead to discrimination and stigmatization (American Educational Research Association et al., 1999).

▶ What do you think?

Professional Standards

Special educators not only hold high standards for their students but also adhere to high professional standards for themselves. For teachers entering the field of special education for the first time, the Council for Exceptional Children developed a set of knowledge and skill standards. Many colleges and universities expect teacher candidates to be able to demonstrate their work toward the CEC standards. As we mentioned in Chapter 1, you will find many of these standards, which relate to information discussed in this book, indicated in the margin of the text. Other organizations such as the Interstate New Teacher Assessment and Support Consortium (INTASC) also have released standards for new teachers. The INTASC standards address what beginning general education teachers and special education teachers need to know and be able to do in teaching students with disabilities.

▶ You can read more about INTASC standards at http://www.ccsso.org/intasc.html

▶ **CEC Common Core Knowledge and Skills.** The beginning special educator should understand legal provisions and ethical principles regarding assessment of individuals (CC8K2).

In addition to demonstrating knowledge and skill standards, special educators develop a high level of competence and integrity as they engage in professional activities. They use objective professional judgment and demonstrate ethical practices.

Individuals who conduct assessments must know and understand these professional standards. According to authorities in the field (American Educational Research Association et al., 1999; Bredekamp & Rosegrant, 1995), educators and test examiners who administer tests should have the training and experience necessary and should follow professional standards and ethical procedures. Educators and examiners should not attempt to evaluate students whose age, disability, linguistic, or cultural backgrounds are outside the range of their academic training or supervised experience.

Confidentiality

Professionals who are involved with the gathering of information about a student have both a legal and an ethical responsibility to maintain the information and use it appropriately. These individuals need to agree that the shared information is for the purposes of enabling the family and assisting the student through individualized educational services. Information about a particular student should be discussed only with those professionals who have a legitimate interest in the information and with whom the parent has consented to share information.

Responding to Diversity

Sensitivity involves concern and respect for others; it begins by learning about yourself, your beliefs, and your family heritage. Sensitivity grows by meeting other people, listening to who they are, and discovering their traditions, beliefs, and values. In working with families, there should be a balance between knowledge and an appreciation for that particular family, its experience of culture, its levels of acculturation, and the changing nature of culture itself (Dennis & Giangreco, 1996).

▶ Make a list of ways that have been helpful to you in developing sensitivity toward others and identify the ways that have been most effective. Share your list and discuss your findings with the class.

Avoiding Assessment Bias

Assessment approaches are considered biased if they ". . . project only predominant values and attitudes and do not reflect the linguistic and cultural experiences of minority groups" (Padilla & Medina, 1996, p. 6). For example, students from some cultures may be less familiar with testing and less test-wise than other students. Student perspectives may depend on group cohesiveness rather than demonstration of individual skills and knowledge.

Research-Based Practices: English Language Learners and Learning Disabilities

Identifying learning disabilities in English language learners is a complex and difficult task. Peggy McCardle and colleagues (2005) write about this multifaceted area and provide insights into the current situation, where little research has been done. With over- and underreferral problems of students with learning disabilities in schools today, these authors feel that children are not being accurately identified. Among other recommendations, they write that classroom-based assessments need to be developed or adapted for teachers to monitor student progress, and clear guidelines need to be developed for when and in what languages assessments should be conducted. Cognitive and linguistic assessment tools must be validated for use with students who are English language learners. Typical accommodations, such as extended time, simplifying the English language, and the use of bilingual glossaries, as well as more effective accommodations, also need to be identified. They recommend that (1) teachers should assess students in their first language as well as in English (if they speak English) and (2) teachers should become familiar with the cultural norms of students with whom they work.

How It Works! Assessment Practices in Action

Rose Martinez works at a high-performing K–8 elementary school in southern California. Over 80 percent of the students are eligible for free/reduced price lunches, and students who are English language learners comprise 31 percent of the students. In spite of these challenges, the teachers and administration are dedicated to helping all students reach high levels of achievement.

Rose and other special educators along with regular educators belong to grade-level teams and meet regularly to ensure that all students are working toward meeting curriculum standards. The teachers hold themselves accountable to identify and address inadequate student performance. In-class instruction and intensive interventions are designed to meet the needs of individual students. When a student with a disability has difficulty accessing the general education curriculum in spite of classroom accommodations, the IEP team discusses the student's possible needs for assistive technology. An AT assessment is conducted by several members of the team who may then recommend specific AT for the student.

Assessment is an ongoing process. Teachers use various methods of monitoring student performance in the classroom. For example, in the lower grades students use white boards to write their responses and then hold up the boards to indicate their answers. This gives teachers the opportunity to immediately address student confusion. Older students use "clickers," individual handheld devices, to register their responses to teacher questions. Dana, a student with cerebral palsy, uses an assistive technology device to enter his answers. Rather than using the small keypad, he taps his response on the switch mounted to the side of his desk. Student responses are visible on the data projector. The teacher uses the technology to help keep student attention and to check for understanding, modifying instruction based on how students respond. All assessment data is imported into a database. This allows information to be shared with teachers, students, and parents in a timely fashion.

Source: Adapted from Bay Area School Reform Collaboration (2004).

Emerging Practices: Universal Design

The emerging concept of **universal design** opens new horizons for people with disabilities. According to IDEA and the Assistive Technology Act of 2004, "The term 'universal design' means a concept or philosophy for designing and delivering products and services that are usable by people with the widest possible range of functional capabilities, which include products and services that are directly usable (without requiring assistive technologies) and products and services that are made usable with assistive technologies" (20 USC Sec. 602(35); 29 USC Sec. 3002). IDEA supports the use of the principles of universal design in developing and administering assessments and instruction. In developing assessments, such as classroom-based assessments, teachers would consider the flexibility of materials, ways that students could demonstrate achievement, and the responses required of students. Although this is an evolving concept, universal design in assessment practices offers ways for students to demonstrate achievement without needing accommodations or modification.

Summary

- The examiner needs to understand a variety of assessment approaches and must be able to select those approaches that are appropriate for each of the purposes in the assessment process.

- The examiner must use only those approaches in which the examiner has received thorough training in administering and interpreting and must follow ethical procedures, adhering to the highest professional standards.

REFERENCES

American Educational Research Association, American Psychological Association, and National Council on Measurement in Education. (1999). *Standards for educational and psychological testing.* Washington, DC: American Educational Research Association.

Bredekamp, S., & Rosegrant, T. (Eds.). (1995). *Reaching potentials: Transforming early childhood curriculum and assessment.* Vol. 2. Washington, DC: National Association for the Education of Young Children.

Bay Area School Reform Collaboration. (2004). *California "Best Practices" Study: Hudson Elementary School, Long Beach Unified School District.* Long Beach, CA. Retrieved June 15, 2005 from http://www.just4kids.org/bestpractice/files/State/California/Hudson%20Case%20Study.pdf

Dennis, R. E., & Giangreco, M. F. (1996). Creating conversation: Reflections on cultural sensitivity in family interviewing. *Exceptional Children, 63*(1), 103–116.

Individuals with Disabilities Education Improvement Act of 2004, (20 USC).

Lenker, J., & Paquet, V. (2003). A review of conceptual models for assistive technology outcomes research and practice. *Assistive Technology, 15,* 1–15.

McCardle, P., Mele-McCarthy, J., & Leos, K. (2005). English language learners and learning disabilities: Research agenda and implications for practice. *Learning Disabilities Research & Practice, 20*(1), 68–78.

Padilla, A. M., & Medina, A. (1996). Cross-cultural sensitivity in assessment: Using tests in culturally appropriate ways. In L. A. Suzuki, P. J. Meller, & J. G. Ponterotto (Eds.), *Handbook of multicultural assessment.* San Francisco: Jossey-Bass.

Reed, P., & Lahm, E. (2005). *A resource guide for teachers and administrators about assistive technology.* Oshkosh, WI: Wisconsin Assistive Technology Initiative.

Scherer, M., & Craddock, G. (2002). Matching person & technology (MPT) assessment process. *Technology and Disability, 14,* 125–131.

Shepard, L. (1996, April). *Classroom testing and external accountability.* Paper presented at the annual meeting of the American Educational Research Association. New York, NY.

Zabala, J. (1995, March). *The SETT framework.* Paper presented at the Florida Assistive Technology Impact Conference and Technology and Media Division of the Council for Exceptional Children, Orlando, FL (ERIC Document Reproduction Service No. ED 381962).

Zabala, J. (2005, January). SETT and ReSETT: Concepts for AT implementation. *Closing the Gap, 23*(5), 1, 10–11.

3

Reliability and Validity

Chapter Objectives

After completing this chapter, you should be able to:

- Define reliability and validity.
- Describe the application of the concepts of types of reliability and validity.
- Explain why assessment approaches should be responsive to diversity.

Key Terms

Reliability
Correlation
Correlation coefficient
Test-retest reliability
Alternate form reliability
Split-half reliability
Internal consistency reliability
Interscorer/interrater/interob-
    server reliability

Standard error of measurement
Cut score
Item response theory
Validity
Content validity
Norm-referenced test
Criterion-related validity
Concurrent validity
Predictive validity

Construct validity
Consequential validity
Out-of-level testing
Language dominance
Language proficiency

▶ **CEC Common Core Knowledge and Skills.** The beginning teacher should understand basic terminology used in assessment (CC8K1).

Overview

Reliability and validity, two closely related concepts, are central to an understanding of assessment. This chapter continues the discussion on responding to diversity. Being responsive to diversity means that assessment procedures are fair. Fairness in assessment indicates that assessment methods are equitable, free of bias, adapted for students with disabilities, sensitive to diverse groups of students, and considerate of contemporary views of growth and development, aptitude, cognition, learning, behavior, and personality.

Reliability

Reliability indicates the consistency or stability of test performance and is one of the most important considerations when selecting tests and other assessment tools. A test must be constructed so that examiners can administer the test with minimal errors and can interpret the performance of students with confidence.

The assessment process is subject to error from many sources. Errors in measurement can stem from the testing environment, the student, the test, and the examiner. Sources of error in the testing environment include:

- Noise distractions
- Poor lighting
- Uncomfortable room temperature

Sources of error associated with the student include:

- Hunger
- Fatigue
- Illness
- Difficulty in understanding test instructions
- Difficulty in understanding or interpreting language used

Sources of error stemming from the test include:

- Ambiguously worded questions
- Biased questions
- Different interpretations of the wording of test questions

An examiner who is not prepared or who incorrectly interprets administration or scoring guidelines contributes to measurement errors. Sources of error associated with test administration include:

- Unclear directions
- Difficulty in achieving rapport
- Insensitivity to student's culture, language, preferences, or other characteristics
- Ambiguous scoring
- Errors associated with recording information about the student

▶ What additional sources of error can you identify?

Reliability information that is reported in test manuals should be carefully considered. While there are some books and journal articles that report evaluations of tests, tests are not given "seals of approval." To be useful, they must meet certain standards. Three professional organizations, the American Educational Research Association, the American Psychological Association, and the National Council on Measurement in Education (1999) have published *Standards for Educational and Psychological Testing,* which provide criteria for evaluating tests, testing practices, and the effects of test use on individuals. The 1999 edition of *Standards for Educational and Psychological Testing* describes reliability and provides a departure from more traditional thinking about reliability. In this edition, reliability refers to the "scoring procedure that enables the examiner to quantify, evaluate, and interpret behavior or work samples. Reliability refers to the consistency of such measurements when the testing procedure is repeated on a population of individuals or groups" (p. 25).

Test developers convey reliability of assessment instruments in various ways. They are responsible for reporting evidence of reliability. Test users and consumers must use this evidence in deciding the suitability of various assessment instruments. While no one approach is preferred, educators should be familiar with all of the approaches in order to judge the usefulness of instruments. These approaches are: (1) one or more correlation coefficients, (2) variances or standard deviations of measurement errors, and (3) technical information about tests known as IRT (item response theory).

Approach 1: Using Correlation Coefficients

Traditionally, reliability has been described as the stability or consistency of test performance. The teacher needs to know that a student's test performance is stable over time and over different test items that have similar objectives. Of course, it is impractical and unnecessary for a student to take a test every day. If a teacher administers a test to a student on a given day, that teacher wants to have some assurance that the student, if retested on the following day, will score about the same on both tests. Or, if a student takes one form or version of a test, the teacher needs to know that the test scores of the student, if taking a similar form of a test, will be about the same.

This type of reliability also provides an estimate of the consistency of test results when administering a test under similar conditions. This consistency or agreement is described by means of a correlation coefficient. Some test manuals use the term reliability coefficient in place of the term correlation coefficient. In order to understand this type of reliability, it is useful to know about the concepts of correlation and correlation coefficients.

Correlation

A **correlation** indicates the extent to which two or more scores vary together. It measures the degree to which a change in one score has a relationship with a change in another score. For example, in general, the higher a student's intelligence score, the higher will be the student's score on a vocabulary test. Usually, students with higher intelligence quotient (IQ) scores tend to have higher vocabulary scores and students with lower IQ scores will probably have lower vocabulary test scores. IQ and vocabulary level correlate with each other. However, examiners must use caution when interpreting relationships—just because two scores correlate does not mean that one score causes a change in the other score. The correlation between shoe size and reading achievement is an example of a strong correlation but lack of causation. As shoe size increases, reading achievement may also increase, but this is pure coincidence—a person's shoe size has nothing to do with how well that person reads.

Correlation Coefficient

A **correlation coefficient** measures the correlation, or relationship, between tests, test items, scoring procedures, observations, or behavior ratings. A correlation coefficient quantifies a relationship and provides information about whether there is a relationship, strength of the relationship, and the direction of the relationship. The symbol for correlation coefficient is a lowercase "r." Test developers conduct research studies to determine correlation coefficients and report these coefficients in test manuals.

Strength of a Relationship

The value of a correlation coefficient can vary from +1.00 to –1.00. The closer the correlation coefficient is to 1.00, either +1.00 or –1.00, the stronger the relationship. The closer the correlation coefficient is to 0.00, the weaker the relationship. For example, a coefficient of .89 is stronger than a coefficient of .15 because .89 is closer to 1.00, just as a coefficient of –.54 is stronger than a coefficient of –.45 because –.54 is closer to –1.00.

Direction of a Relationship

The presence of a plus (+) or minus (–) sign determines the direction of a correlation. A plus sign indicates that a relationship is positive; and a negative (minus) sign indicates that a relationship is negative. When positive correlation coefficients are written, the plus sign is usually omitted. When one test score increases as another test score increases, the relationship is positive. In a positive relationship, the scores either increase together or decrease together. However, when one test score decreases while the other test score increases, the relationship is negative. The relationship between IQ and vocabulary achievement is a positive relationship, because both of these variables usually increase together.

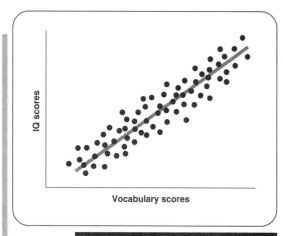

FIGURE 3.1 ● Scatter Plot of a Positive Relationship

Positive Relationship

If there were a perfect relationship between IQ level and vocabulary achievement, the correlation would be expressed as either +1.00 or 1.00. If for every increase in IQ score there is a corresponding increase in vocabulary scores, the relationship between IQ and vocabulary level would be perfect and the resulting correlation coefficient would be 1.00. However, because there are so many other variables that influence both IQ and vocabulary achievement, this relationship will never be a perfect 1.00. Figure 3.1 illustrates this relationship.

Negative Relationship

A perfect negative relationship is indicated by –1.00. The relationship between level of achievement and the number of errors made is a negative relationship. As the achievement increases, the number of errors that an individual makes decreases. Figure 3.2 illustrates this relationship.

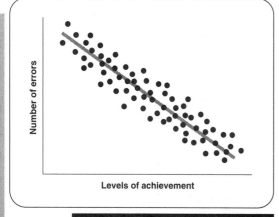

FIGURE 3.2 ● Scatter Plot of a Negative Relationship

Zero Relationship

The relationship between an individual's score on an intelligence test and the height of that individual is zero. When arranged on a scatter plot, most of the intelligence test scores and the height measurements are not associated with each other; the scores do not vary with each other. Figure 3.3 illustrates this relationship.

Applying Correlation Coefficients to Reliability

In test manuals, a lowercase r designates a reliability or correlation coefficient. For example, when a test manual reports that r = .92, the reliability for the test is .92. Because .92 is close to a perfect correlation coefficient of 1.00, a teacher can have confidence that the test has adequate reliability. For guidance in evaluating correlation coefficients, Nitko (2003) recommends that when making major educational decisions, a reliability coefficient of at least .90 is the pre ferred standard.

Types of Reliability That Involve Correlation Coefficients

The traditional view of reliability conceptualizes five types of reliability: test-retest, alternate form, split-half, internal consistency, and interscorer/interobserver/interrater reliability. For these types of reliability, it is incumbent upon test publishers to report information fully in test manuals. Test publishers should tell how they ob-

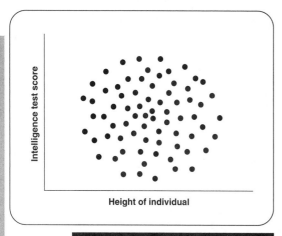

FIGURE 3.3 ● Scatter Plot of a Zero Relationship

tained the samples of students, individuals, or observations from which they determine their reliability coefficients. Interpretations of total test scores, subscores, or combinations of scores should include stated relevant reliabilities. Similarly, when tests have both long and short versions, test publishers must report reliabilities of each version based on separate independent administrations of each version.

▶ **CEC Common Core Knowledge and Skills.** The beginning special educator understands specialized terminology used in the assessment of individuals with disabilities (GC8K1).

TEST-RETEST RELIABILITY **Test-retest reliability** can be obtained when administering the same test to the same student twice by correlating the scores on the first and second administrations and obtaining a reliability coefficient. This coefficient is a measure of the stability of the test score. Because the same test is administered twice, test developers need to state the time interval between the two administrations of the test. Too short an interval will inflate the reliability coefficient. When the time interval is too long, a student may experience developmental changes that will affect the reliability coefficient.

There are several drawbacks to this type of reliability. Having seen the test items and the directions for taking the test over two test administrations, the student may obtain a higher test score on the second testing.

ALTERNATE FORM RELIABILITY **Alternate form reliability** is also known as equivalent form or parallel form reliability. Frequently, there is a need for two forms of a test that contain different test items but that evaluate the same knowledge and skills. This procedure is especially useful when pretesting and posttesting students. The two forms have different designations. For example, some forms are designated A and B; others may be labeled X and Y or L and M.

Like test-retest reliability, alternate form reliability has several disadvantages. It is difficult to develop two parallel forms of a test. In addition, as with test-retest reliability, a shorter interval between test administrations can inflate the reliability coefficient and the effect of practice on similar test items.

SPLIT-HALF RELIABILITY **Split-half reliability** is measured by administering a test to a group of students, dividing the total number of test items in half to form two tests and correlating the scores on the two halves of the test. For example, suppose a test has 20 items. We could administer the entire test to a group of students and then divide the test into two halves, each containing 10 items. We can use different methods to break a test into two halves: by separating the first half from the second half or by separating the even-numbered items from the odd-numbered items. We can then correlate the items on the two halves to determine the relationship between the scores from the first half of the test and the scores from the second half.

Dividing a test into a first half and a second half can cause problems in determining the reliability. Fatigue, practice effect, failure to complete the test, and print quality can all affect the reliability coefficient (DeVellis, 1991). Assuming random order of the test items, we could divide the test by odd-even items or by balancing the halves. Balancing halves could involve item length, response type, or another characteristic that is appropriate for the test. The most appropriate method of splitting the halves of a test will depend on the test and the testing situation (DeVellis, 1991).

With the split-half procedure, the test is administered only once. Therefore, this procedure gives reliability coefficients that are a measure of internal consistency, not of the temporal stability of test performance.

INTERNAL CONSISTENCY RELIABILITY **Internal consistency reliability** is similar to the split-half method. Internal consistency reliability is an estimate of the homogeneity or interrelatedness of responses to test items. Students take this test only once. Usually

Prentice Dillon and Erin Gates

After all the students left school for the day, Prentice Dillon, a special education teacher, decided that he needed to review the test manual for a recently purchased school test. He read the initial chapters in the manual that described the test and the administration procedures. Okay so far. Dillon began the chapter that described the reliability of the test. The section that described internal consistency reliability said, "The reliability coefficient for the composite scores was described as r = .92. This is greater than the reliability coefficients for the subtest scores." Prentice asked himself, "Why were the reliability coefficients of the composite scores higher than the reliability coefficients of the individual subtests?" Prentice decided to see what Erin Gates, the other special educator in his building, knew about this test.

After reading the reliability section of the manual, Erin explained that it was not unusual for composite scores to have higher reliability coefficients than individual subtests because test developers use more test items to calculate the reliability coefficients associated with composite scores than with individual subtests. Composite scores, in general, show higher reliability coefficients than do individual subtests.

test developers use one of the Kuder-Richardson formulas to find the average coefficient by calculating all the possible split-half coefficients. The more similar the test items are to each other, the higher will be the reliability coefficient. Like split-half reliability, internal consistency reliability does not provide an estimate of the stability of the test over time.

The advantage of using internal consistency instead of the split-half method is that internal consistency provides the average of all split-half correlations—all possible ways of dividing the test into two halves. The split-half method allows only one division of the test in half. The Snapshot of Prentice Dillon and Erin Gates illustrates how teachers consider this type of reliability.

INTERSCORER/INTEROBSERVER/INTERRATER RELIABILITY Interscorer/interobserver/interrater reliability is a measure of the extent to which two or more scorers, observers, or raters agree on how to score a test. **Interscorer/interobserver/interrater reliability** is important when errors in scoring or differences in judgment can affect the test outcomes. This type of reliability should be reported when:

1. There is a possibility that errors can be made in computing the test score(s).
2. A test item can have more than one answer.
3. A response to a question can have more than one interpretation.
4. Observations are made about the behaviors of one or more students.
5. Interviews are used to collect information.

Approach 2: Variances or Standard Deviations of Measurement Errors

The true score is the score an individual would obtain on a test if there were no measurement errors. The obtained score is the actual score that a student obtains on a test. This is the best estimate we have of a student's performance.

If all testing conditions were perfect and there were no errors of measurement, the obtained score and the true score would be the same. But, since error is always present, the true score cannot be known. However, an individual's true score can be measured by using the formula $X = T + E$ where the student's obtained or observed score, X, equals the true score, T, plus the errors that are associated with measurement, represented by E, the error score. Standard errors of measurement are especially important when evaluators need to make immediate decisions with limited information.

Examiners should report the **standard error of measurement (SEM)** for derived scores including standard scores, grade or age equivalents, and percentile ranks. SEM is of special concern when using cut scores.

Cut scores are prespecified scores that determine how to select or classify students. Typically, evaluators may select or classify students who score at or below a prespecified cut score, such as 30, for special education or labeling. When using cut scores, test publishers must specify the measurement error associated with each cut score. Standard errors of measurement are also important to consider when making score comparisons such as between achievement and ability and when interpreting score profiles.

Approach 3: Item Response Theory (IRT)

Technical information about tests is known as **item response theory** (IRT). IRT involves a statistical calculation that determines how well the instrument differentiates between individuals at various levels of measured abilities or characteristics. If test publishers, authors, and researchers choose to demonstrate reliability using IRT, they should provide sufficient information in test manuals. Test publishers should clearly and comprehensively describe the procedures they used to determine reliability.

Factors That Influence Reliability

Several factors can affect the reliability of a test (Mehrens & Lehmann, 1991; Sattler, 2001):

1. Test length. Generally, the longer a test is, the more reliable it is.
2. Speed. When a test is a speed test, reliability can be problematic. It is inappropriate to estimate reliability using internal consistency, test-retest, or alternate form methods. This is because not every student is able to complete all of the items in a speed test. In contrast, a power test is a test in which every student is able to complete all the items.
3. Group homogeneity. In general, the more heterogeneous the group of students who take the test, the more reliable the measure will be.
4. Item difficulty. When there is little variability among test scores, the reliability will be low. Thus, reliability will be low if a test is so easy that every student gets most or all of the items correct or so difficult that every student gets most or all of the items wrong.
5. Objectivity. Objectively scored tests, rather than subjectively scored tests, show a higher reliability.
6. Test-retest interval. The shorter the time interval between two administrations of a test, the less likely that changes will occur and the higher the reliability will be.
7. Variation with the testing situation. Errors in the testing situation (e.g., students misunderstanding or misreading test directions, noise level, distractions, and sickness) can cause test scores to vary.

Validity

Validity is the most important consideration when developing, evaluating, and interpreting tests. Reliability is a prerequisite of validity. A test must demonstrate reliability before test developers or test users can consider evidence of validity. A test that is reliable is not necessarily valid. According to *Standards for Educational and Psychological Testing* (American Educational Research Association et al., 1999), "Validity refers to the degree to which evidence and theory support the interpretations of test scores entailed by the proposed tests" (p. 9).

In order to establish validity of a test and of test interpretations, test developers usually gather evidence in multiple forms over a period of time. The determination of validity is the obligation of both the test developer and test user. Test developers should provide information about validity in test manuals. Ultimately, it is incumbent upon the test user to review the evidence and determine the extent to which a test is valid and the interpretations of the test are valid. The test user should consider the process used to construct the instrument, the score reliability, test administration procedures, scoring procedures, the standards-setting process, and the extent to which the test is fair. We describe fairness in detail later in this chapter.

Traditionally, validity has several aspects: content, criterion-related (which includes concurrent and predictive validity), and construct. A correlation coefficient (r) commonly represents criterion-related and construct validity. From our discussion of reliability, you will recall that r is also a measure of reliability. Therefore, it is important that users pay attention to whether the r values refer to reliability or validity.

Content Validity

Content validity measures the extent to which the test items reflect the content domain of a test. Content validity is the most important type of validity for achievement tests because achievement tests typically measure content knowledge such as reading, writing, mathematics, science, and social studies.

An estimate of the content validity of a test is obtained by thoroughly and systematically examining the test items to determine the extent to which they reflect and do not reflect the content domain. In general, a panel composed of curriculum experts and specialists in tests and measurements evaluate content validity by determining the extent to which the test items reflect the test objectives. Test developers should provide information about the experts who reviewed the test content.

> ▶ Working with a small group of other students, review a test manual. Identify the types of reliability and validity the manual reports. Explain the meaning of these two terms, using your own words.

Most norm-referenced tests represent the curricula that are taught in various geographic regions of the United States. A **norm-referenced test (NRT)** is a measure that compares a student's test performance with that of similar students who have taken the same test. In addition, scores from standardized tests can be used to make interpretations about an individual student's performance on several tests. Because these tests are so broad, they may inadequately represent the curricula in many schools. Thus, as a rule, test users must ensure the content validity of norm-referenced tests before a test user can be confident that a particular test is appropriate in this respect.

Criterion-Related Validity

Criterion-related validity refers to the extent to which scores from one test, instrument, or measure relate to scores from another test, instrument, or measure. When determining criterion-related validity, test developers compare their test with another outcome or criterion: another test, school grades, or observations. If test developers use this type of validity, they should report their findings in the test manuals.

When assessing the criterion-related validity of a test, it is important to verify the criterion measure's validity as well. Concurrent and predictive validity are two types of criterion-related validity.

Concurrent Validity

Concurrent validity is the extent to which the results of two different tests administered at about the same time correlate with each other. To obtain concurrent validity, test developers administer two different tests within a brief interval and calculate the correlation between the scores from the tests. This method of estimating validity is especially useful when constructing a new test.

Suppose a test publisher wanted to develop a new way to test the hearing abilities of students. The publisher would administer this new test and also a standard hearing test. Next, the publisher would establish concurrent validity by examining the relationship between the scores from the two tests. The test publisher wants to know the extent to which a known instrument and a new test measure the same objectives. If the new test correlates highly with the established instrument, the test publisher can conclude that the new test is valid and that it has an acceptable level of concurrent validity.

Predictive Validity

How accurately can current performance predict future performance or behavior? **Predictive validity** is the standard for forecasting student performance or behavior from a test score.

Be careful not to confuse concurrent validity with predictive validity. There are some important differences. While concurrent validity is a measure of the extent to which two sets of test scores relate to each other, predictive validity is an estimate of the extent to which one test accurately predicts future performance or behavior. When scores on one test accurately predict performance on another test or criterion, we can say that there is high predictive validity.

Construct Validity

Construct validity is the extent to which a test measures a particular trait, construct, or psychological characteristic. Examples of constructs include reasoning ability, spatial visualization, reading comprehension, sociability, and introversion.

Construct validity is the most difficult type of validity to establish. Test developers need a long period of time and numerous research studies before verifying construct validity for a particular test. Zeller (1988) compares the establishment of construct validity to a detective's search for clues, accumulating evidence bit by bit. The clues assist the test developer in determining the consistency of the evidence in the interpretation of construct validity. If the evidence falls into a systematic pattern, then test developers and test examiners can have confidence in the validity of the construct. Prentice Dillon and Erin Gates continue their conversation in the Snapshot.

Validity of Test Interpretations

The interpretation of test results can have profound consequences for students, families, and educators. Thus, test publishers should provide validity information for each proposed interpretation and use of test scores, subtests, subscores, score differences, and test profiles (American Educational Research Association et al., 1999). Test publishers should also provide evidence of validity, including the statistics they used to conduct analyses, composition of samples they used to collect the data, and conditions under which they collected the data, for each proposed interpretation.

Test users should evaluate the evidence in order to determine the extent of support for the proposed interpretations. If evidence is

▶ The director of testing has asked you to evaluate the reliability and validity of a test that is being considered for purchase. What standards of reliability and validity will you use when evaluating this measure?

SNAPSHOT
Prentice Dillon and Erin Gates

Prentice continued reading the manual of the new test that his school had purchased. After finishing the reliability section, he decided to turn to the validity section. The manual said, "The achievement subtests were correlated with the cognitive subtests, and the coefficients ranged from .20 to .65." Prentice knew that coefficients that approach 1.00 indicate that there is a very close relationship. But, when evaluating the validity of a test, what did correlations between .20 and .65 mean?

Erin Gates was still in her classroom when Prentice asked if she could help him understand validity. Erin explained that the authors of the test manual were presenting evidence for the construct validity of their test. Construct validity is the extent to which a test measures a particular trait, construct, or psychological characteristic, such as achievement and cognitive ability. In determining construct validity, the test author describes the construct, indicating how it differs from other constructs.

Erin told Prentice that the correlations between .20 and .65 indicate that there is, in fact, some relationship between achievement and cognitive ability because achievement and cognitive ability are actually two different, but not totally separate, constructs. In fact, if the correlations were close to 1.00, for example, .90, .93, or .95, it would mean that the achievement subtests and the cognitive subtests were too closely related and that they were measuring the same constructs!

unavailable or inconsistent, test publishers should disclose this information to test users. Similarly, if a test user would like to use a test in a way for which validity evidence is lacking, the user should refrain from using the test until publishers can provide sufficient evidence.

Consequential Validity

Consequential validity describes the extent to which an assessment instrument promotes the intended consequences (Linn & Baker, 1996). Test publishers use consequential validity to describe performance-based assessments. Performance-based assessment, which we discuss in Chapter 6, provides information about how a student can apply knowledge in real-life, real-world settings rather than simply accumulating isolated bits of knowledge. Domains such as dance and music have long used performance-based assessments to evaluate students. Performances are far more appropriate for evaluating how students dance or play musical instruments than are multiple-choice questions.

One of the primary reasons for using performance-based assessments is to improve student learning. Consequential validity reflects the extent to which performance-based assessment improves student learning. Factors that can affect student learning positively, and thus impact consequential validity, include school improvement activities, instructional improvements, staff development activities, levels of student achievement, and accountability systems (Linn & Baker, 1996).

Participation of Students with Disabilities in State- and Districtwide Assessments

IDEA and No Child Left Behind require that an accountability system be in place to evaluate the progress that students with disabilities make toward the established general education performance goals and indicators that apply to all students. State- and districtwide assessments must include all students with disabilities. Students with disabilities convicted as adults under state law and incarcerated in adult prisons are the only students who are exempted from participation in general state- and districtwide assessments (Heumann & Warlick, 2000).

Since laws require that all students with disabilities participate in state- and districtwide assessments, the IEP team does not determine whether students with disabilities will participate. However, the IEP team can determine how students with disabilities participate. The IEP team determines whether accommodations or modifications should be made to the test or to the procedures used in test administration so that the student can participate. Test accommodations do not mean adaptations or changes to the test but rather to the test's format, response, setting, timing, or scheduling. These changes should not significantly alter the way examiners make test interpretations or comparisons (Heumann & Warlick, 2000).

Alternate Assessment

Some students with severe or significant disabilities are unable to participate in large-scale assessments even when accommodations and modifications are made. Alternate assessments enable students with severe or significant disabilities to participate in general large-scale assessments. Alternate assessments must align with the same curriculum standards that all students use. States and local education agencies and districts must, by law, develop guidelines for alternate assessments.

Out-of-Level Testing

Out-of-level testing occurs when examiners assess students in one grade level using tests that were designed for students in other, usually lower, grade levels. IDEA does not specifically prohibit out-of-level testing; however, out-of-level testing should be discouraged for the following reasons (Heumann & Warlick, 2000):

1. Out-of-level testing may not assess the same grade-level content areas as the large-scale assessment that the majority of students in the state or district take.
2. Out-of-level testing may lower expectations for students with disabilities.
3. Scores from out-of-level testing are difficult to aggregate or group together with scores from students taking the general, large-scale assessment.
4. Scores from out-of-level testing are difficult to compare with scores from students taking the general, large-scale assessment.
5. Out-of-level testing may provide inadequate or insufficient information about how students with disabilities perform on the established goals and standards that apply to all students in the state or district.

Responding to Diversity: Fairness in Assessment

Assessment has a great influence on curriculum, instruction, classroom, and school organization, and on educational and career opportunities for students. Fairness in assessment means that all assessment approaches, including standardized tests, performance assessment, portfolio assessment, and informal measures, are free from bias and that methods of student assessment are equitable and sensitive to diverse student populations. Assessment should be fair to all students so as not to limit students' present education and their future opportunities (National Forum on Assessment, 1995). Fairness in assessment means that assessment methods reflect the following:

- Equity
- Nonbiased assessment
- Linguistic diversity
- Accommodations and modifications for students with disabilities
- Sensitivity to diverse student populations
- Consideration of contemporary views of growth and development, aptitude, cognition, learning, behavior, and personality
- Availability and use of assistive technology
- Consideration of possible adverse consequences of any applicable assessments to students

Equity

Differences in test results may be due to differences in educational opportunities, resources, or cultural expectations. This is especially true when considerations about culture, ethnicity, race, language, geographic region of origin, gender, disability, or economic status are a concern. Equity in assessment means that assessment is approached in a fair, impartial, and just manner. Assessment tools must be more than reliable and valid. Valid assessments arise only when the assessment is fair. Fair assessments mean that all students have access to and can participate in a variety of assessment approaches.

Nonbiased Assessment

Assessment tools must be nonbiased. When groups know approximately the same amount of material but one group scores consistently higher than other groups on a test, it may indicate test bias. For example, a test may portray individuals in stereotypic ways in test problems that contain references applying to only males, to only middle-class individuals, to only a particular culture, or to topics that carry status with only those groups. When evaluating student behavior in such tests, some behaviors considered aberrant for one group may be proper for another group.

Linguistic Diversity

There are important considerations when testing students who are nonnative speakers of English or who speak languages other than English. Translation of an assessment tool or use of an interpreter is not always appropriate (American Educational Research Association et al., 1999).

Translation alone does not ensure that an assessment procedure is comparable in content, difficulty level, reliability, or validity to the original version. Both the language dominance and language proficiency of test takers should be considered (American Educational Research Association et al., 1999). **Language dominance** refers to the individual's preferred language. **Language proficiency** refers to level of expertise in a language. A student who may be bilingual, or even trilingual, may have different levels of proficiency in speaking, reading, and writing. Test administrators should determine the language proficiency of the students and administer tests in the language in which the student is most proficient.

When recommending a test for use with linguistically diverse test takers, test developers and publishers should provide the information for appropriate test use and interpretation. When translating a test from one language or dialect to another, test administrators need to establish the test's reliability and validity for the uses intended in the linguistic groups they will test.

Consideration of Adverse Consequences

Some students do not perform well on assessments simply because they lack the background or experiences with certain methods of assessment. Teachers can try to ameliorate this by providing all students with instruction and practice in the assessment approaches that are used in evaluations.

Assessment developers and users must actively avoid assessment approaches, instruments, and techniques that may have adverse consequences on groups that currently are targets of discrimination or have previously been the targets of discrimination. Proper assessment assists in providing learning opportunities for students rather than in placing students in tracks or limiting educational opportunities (National Forum on Assessment, 1995).

▶ Farah, who recently moved to this country from Somalia, may have a learning disability. What must the teacher and test examiner consider when deciding which tests to use when assessing Farah?

Summary

- Test manuals provide information about reliability and validity.

- Teachers, test examiners, and administrators should review tests and test manuals and satisfy themselves that each test has acceptable levels of reliability and validity.

- Test users must be skilled examiners as well as informed consumers of tests.

- Fairness in assessment means that teachers use only those assessment approaches judged to be reliable and valid.

- Fairness also means that bias has been minimized, that the assessment is equitable, and that the measures are sensitive to diverse populations.

REFERENCES

American Educational Research Association, American Psychological Association, and National Council on Measurement in Education. (1999). *Standards for educational and psychological testing.* Washington, DC: American Educational Research Association.

DeVellis, R. F. (1991). *Scale development.* Newbury Park, CA: Sage.

Heumann, J., & Warlick, K. R. (2000). *Memorandum: Questions and answers about provisions in the Individuals with Disabilities Education Act amendments of 1997 related to students with disabilities and state and district-wide assessments.* Office of Special Education and Rehabilitative Services, Office of Special Education Programs, August 24.

Linn, R. L., & Baker, E. L. (1996). Can performance-based student assessments be psychometrically sound? In J. B. Baron & D. P. Wolf (Eds.), *Performance-based student assessment: Challenges and possibilities* (pp. 84–103.) Chicago: University of Chicago Press.

Mehrens, W. A., & Lehmann, I. J. (1991). *Measurement and evaluation in education and psychology.* Fort Worth, TX: Holt, Rinehart & Winston.

National Forum on Assessment. (1995). *Principles and indicators for student assessment systems.* Cambridge, MA: National Center for Fair and Open Testing.

Nitko, A. J. (2003). *Educational assessment of students* (4th ed.). Upper Saddle River, NJ: Prentice-Hall.

Sattler, J. M. (2001). *Assessment of children: Cognitive applications.* La Mesa, CA: Author.

Zeller, R. A. (1988). Validity. In J. P. Keeves (Ed.), *Educational research, methodology, and measurement: An international handbook* (pp. 322–330). Oxford, UK: Pergamon Press.

4

Developing Technical Skills

Chapter Objectives

After completing this chapter, you should be able to:

- Describe norm-referenced and criterion-referenced assessment.
- Discuss the advantages and disadvantages of using different types of test scores when interpreting test performance.
- Compare different ways of presenting and interpreting test scores.
- Describe how to evaluate the usefulness of tests.

Key Terms

Standardized test
Standardization sample
Population
Norm-referenced test
Criterion-referenced test
Nominal scale
Ordinal scale
Interval scale
Ratio scale
Frequency distribution
Normal curve
Skewed distribution

Mean
Median
Mode
Standard deviation
Raw score
Percentage score
Derived score
Developmental score
Interpolation
Extrapolation
Developmental quotient
Percentile rank

Standard score
Deviation IQ score
Normal curve equivalent
Stanines
Basal level
Ceiling level
True score
Standard error of measurement
Confidence interval
Chronological age

Overview

This chapter discusses scoring, interpreting, and reporting test performance and describes standardized assessment tests, scores, scoring procedures, and norms. In the following chapters we will return to these topics and discuss their application to assessment strategies and approaches.

Standardized Tests

Standardized tests are tests in which a test manual prescribes administration, scoring, and interpretation procedures that must be strictly followed by the test examiner. Examiners must follow exact administration procedures when using standardized tests. Failure to follow these procedures compromises the reliability, validity, and interpretation of the test results. Standardized norm-referenced tests can be both individual and group administered. Examples of standardized norm-referenced tests include the *Iowa Tests of Educational Development, Terra Nova®,* and the *Stanford Achievement Test Series*.

▶ **CEC Common Core Knowledge and Skills.** The beginning special educator should understand basic terminology used in assessment (CC8K1).

Standardization Sample

When a norm-referenced test is administered to a student, the teacher can compare the performance of that student with the scores obtained by the sample of students who participated in the normative sample during the development of the test. A **standardization sample** is a subgroup of a large group that is representative of the large group. When test publishers develop a test, it is this subgroup that is actually tested. The **population** is the larger group from which the sample of individuals is selected and to which individual comparisons are made regarding test performance. *Normative sample* or *norm sample* are other terms for the standardization sample.

The standardization sample must represent the population of students who will be taking the test. The standardization sample should include, in appropriate proportion, students from various geographic regions of the country; males and females; students who represent various racial, ethnic, cultural, and linguistic populations; and students from various economic strata. Information may even include the occupational categories and educational levels of the parents of the students.

The best way for a test publisher to determine the appropriate proportions of representative groups (e.g., males, females, race, ethnicity, native language) that should be included in the standardization sample is to refer to the most recent census data and base the selection of the standardization sample on those percentages. For example, a test that is to be used with students from Cambodia or from Central America should include appropriate samples of these student groups in the standardization group. If they intend to administer the test to students who are nonnative speakers of English and who come from various backgrounds, the test publisher must provide appropriate information concerning the administration and interpretation of test performance (American Educational Research Association, American Psychological Association, and National Council on Measurement in Education, 1999). Figure 4.1 shows how one test publisher illustrated the communities in the United States that participated in a national standardization of the test.

▶ Obtain two or more test manuals and read the sections pertaining to the standardization samples. Compare and contrast the development of two tests, based on these descriptions. How closely does the norm sample of each test represent students in the community in which you live? What conclusions can you make?

Norm-Referenced Tests

A **norm-referenced test** is a standardized test that compares a student's test performance with that of a sample of similar students who have taken the same test. After constructing a test, the test developers administer it to a standardization sample of students using the same administration and scoring procedures for all students. This makes the administration and scoring "standardized." The test scores of the standardization sample are called *norms,* which include a variety of types of scores. Norms are the scores obtained by the standardization sample and are the scores to which students are compared when they are administered a test.

Once test developers standardize a norm-referenced test, examiners can administer it to students with similar characteristics to the norm group and can compare the

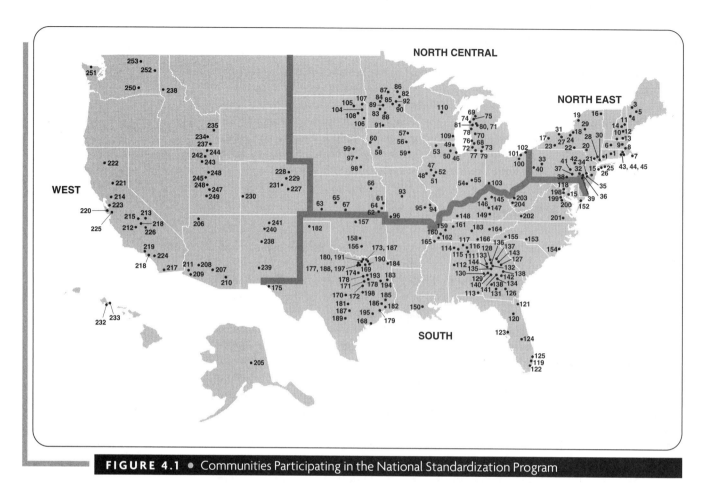

FIGURE 4.1 • Communities Participating in the National Standardization Program

Source: From Kaufman, A., & Kaufman, N. (2004). *K-ABC-II manual.* Circle Pines, MN: AGS. Reprinted with permission.

▶ What are the advantages of using norm-referenced tests?

scores of these students with those of the norm group. Norm-referenced standardized tests can use local, state, or national norms as a base. Because of the comparison of scores between a norm group and other groups of students, a norm-referenced test provides information on the relative standing of students.

When assessing students with disabilities, evaluators should employ caution before making comparisons or interpretations stemming from established norms. It is possible to use typical norms when making interpretations that draw from the relative performance of the students with disabilities and from the general population of students. However, when making comparisons or interpretations that use level or degree of disability, normative data should come from the sample population to which comparisons are made.

Test manuals should provide sufficient details about the normative group so that test users can make informed judgments about the appropriateness of the norm sample (American Educational Research Association et al., 1999).

Criterion-Referenced Tests

Instead of comparing a student's performance to a norm group, criterion-referenced tests measure a student's performance with respect to a well-defined domain such as reading or mathematics. While norm-referenced tests discriminate between the performance of individual students on specific test items, **criterion-referenced tests** provide a description of a student's knowledge, skills, or behavior in a specific range of test items. This specific range is referred to as a *domain*. Test items on criterion-referenced tests frequently correspond to well-defined instructional objectives.

Criterion-referenced tests, instead of using norms, provide information on the performance of a student with respect to specific test items. The results of criterion-referenced tests are not dependent on the performance of other students, as are norm-referenced tests. An example of a criterion-referenced test is the *BRIGANCE®Diagnostic Inventory of Essential Skills–Revised.*

Distinguishing Norm-Referenced Tests from Criterion-Referenced Tests

There are several characteristics that distinguish norm-referenced tests from criterion-referenced tests. Performance on a criterion-referenced test provides information on whether the student has attained a predetermined achievement, behavioral, or social criterion. While it is possible for a test to be both norm-referenced and criterion-referenced, professionals must use caution when interpreting the results of these tests, because it is difficult to combine both types of tests in one instrument.

Another distinction is the breadth of the content domain the test covers (Mehrens & Lehmann, 1991). Typical norm-referenced tests survey a broad domain, while criterion-referenced tests usually have fewer domains but more items in each domain. Criterion-referenced tests typically sample the domain more thoroughly than norm-referenced tests (Mehrens & Lehmann, 1991).

Criterion-referenced tests are very helpful in making instructional planning decisions. Since criterion-referenced tests frequently cover a more restricted range of content than norm-referenced tests, they can provide more information about a student's level of performance.

Scales of Measurement

Evaluators can estimate student performance using test scores based on different types of measurement scales. The description of a student's performance depends on the test's measurement scale. There are four different measurement scales: nominal, ordinal, interval, and ratio.

Nominal Scale

A **nominal scale** represents the lowest level of measurement. It is a naming scale. Each value on the scale is a name, and the name does not have any innate or inherent value. Hair color, students' names, and numbers on football jerseys are all examples of nominal scales. Although there are numerals on football uniforms, there is no inherent rank or value to the numerals. A numeral is just associated with the name of the football player. A teacher may use a nominal scale to distinguish between groups 1, 2, and 3. The numbers 1, 2, and 3 have no intrinsic value; they are simply labels for the groups. Because nominal scales merely represent names, they have limited usefulness. They cannot be added, subtracted, multiplied, or divided. They are rarely used in reporting test performance.

Ordinal Scale

An **ordinal scale** is the next level of measurement. An ordinal scale orders items in a scale or continuum. Ordering students according to class rank is an example of an ordinal scale (Table 4.1). The Snapshot "Activity Levels" also provides an example of an ordinal scale.

▶ **CEC Common Core Knowledge and Skills.** The beginning special educator will understand specialized terminology used in the assessment of individuals with disabilities (GC8K1).

TABLE 4.1 • Ordinal Scale

Student	Rank
Jean	10
Mia	9
Mura	8
Melissa	7
Chris	6
Ruth	5
Lisa	4
Mei	3
Dan	2
David	1

Activity Levels

Suppose a teacher is observing a student with a high activity level. The teacher wants to rank the activity level of the student from 1 to 10, with 10 being the most active and 1 the least active, like this:

Activity level	1	2	3	4	5	6	7	8	9	10
Classroom										
Playground										

The distance between each of the ranks 1, 2, 3, and so forth is not equal. That is, the same increase in activity may not be required, in the teacher's judgment, to raise a ranking from 3 to 4 as from 7 to 8. Because of this limitation, ordinal scales cannot be added, subtracted, multiplied, or divided.

Interval Scale

An **interval scale** is similar to an ordinal scale but it has several important advantages. Interval scales order items on a scale or continuum, as do ordinal scales, but unlike ordinal scales, the distance between the items is equal. Because of this characteristic, interval scales can be added, subtracted, multiplied, and divided.

Interval scales have another interesting characteristic. Interval scales may include a zero point but do not have a true or rational zero. For example, a Fahrenheit scale is an equal interval scale; there is an equal distance between the degrees of temperature. The zero point, however, was arbitrarily established by Daniel Fahrenheit when he developed the temperature scale. Intelligence quotient tests also base their scores on equal interval scales. Although there is an equal distance between the scores, an IQ of zero cannot be measured. Another example of a test that uses an interval scale is the Scholastic Aptitude Test (SAT). SAT scores range from 200 to 800 points. There is no zero!

Ratio Scale

A **ratio scale** has all the characteristics of ordinal and interval scales and, in addition, it has an absolute zero. Height and weight measurements are examples of ratio scales. Teacher-developed tests, such as classroom spelling or arithmetic tests, frequently use the ratio scale as a base. The total number of test items that a student answers correctly, or the raw score, is based on a ratio scale. Some observation and rating scales are also ratio scales. Because the ratio scale has an absolute zero, the scores adapt to mathematical operations. If we are recording the number of times students raise their hands, we may conclude that one student exhibits this behavior two or three times more than another student.

Frequency Distribution

A **frequency distribution** is a way of organizing test scores according to how often they occur. To create a frequency distribution, arrange the test scores in a column from high to low. Next to each test score, record the number of individuals who received that score on the test (Table 4.2). Next, construct a graph (Figure 4.2).

TABLE 4.2 ● Frequency Distribution

Score	Frequency Distribution
100	3
90	2
80	5
70	4
60	6
50	5
40	2
30	1

Total number of students: 28

Normal Curve

Frequency distributions can have different shapes. The shape represents groupings of students' scores. In a **normal curve** most scores fall in the middle, and fewer scores occur at the ends of the distribution. The normal curve is a symmetrical, bell-shaped curve (Figure 4.3).

There has been considerable debate about whether human characteristics are distributed in a normal curve. While there is some evidence that physical characteristics such as height and weight are distributed normally, there has been active discussion about whether other characteristics, such as intelligence, development, and achievement, are normally distributed. While it is less likely that the performance of small groups of children will distribute normally on a specific characteristic, the test results from large norm samples will probably be more normal in appearance (Mehrens & Lehmann, 1991).

Skewed Distributions

Sometimes, the majority of scores occur at one end of the curve. These scores show **skewed distribution.** Positively skewed distributions contain only a few high scores, with the majority of scores occurring at the low end. Negatively skewed distributions have few scores at the low end and a majority of scores at the high end. When distributions are either positively or negatively skewed, the measures of central tendency—that is, the mean, median, and mode—shift. Figure 4.4 shows the placement of the mean, median, and mode in skewed distributions.

Measures of Central Tendency

Measures of central tendency describe the typical test performance of a group of students using a single number. The number that results from the calculation of a measure of central tendency represents the typical score obtained by the group of students. The mean, mode, and median are measures of central tendency. In the Snapshot, teachers Brendan Strout and Ken Brown decide when to use measures of central tendency.

Mean

The **mean**, or the average score, is the most frequently used measure of central tendency. To compute the mean, add all of the scores and divide by the total number of scores (Table 4.3). Because all the scores in a distribution are taken into account when the mean is calculated, extreme scores affect the mean.

Median

Another measure of central tendency is the median. It is the point on a scale above which and below which 50 percent of the cases occur. The **median** is an excellent

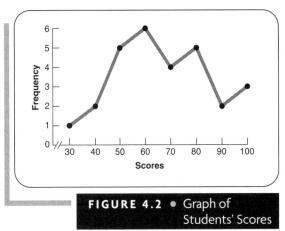

FIGURE 4.2 • Graph of Students' Scores

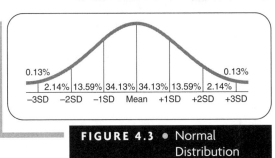

FIGURE 4.3 • Normal Distribution

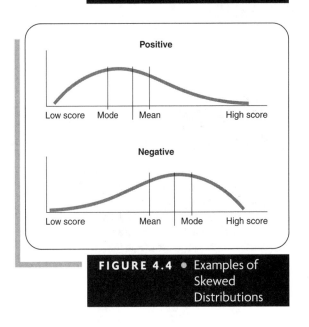

FIGURE 4.4 • Examples of Skewed Distributions

TABLE 4.3 ● Finding the Average (Mean)

Score	Frequency	Frequency × Score
100	1	100
98	2	196
90	2	180
85	4	340
70	6	420
50	5	250
42	3	126
30	2	60
25	1	25

Number of scores: 26   Sum of scores: 1697

$$\frac{\text{Sum of scores}}{\text{Number of scores}} = \text{Mean}$$

$$\frac{1697}{26} = \text{Mean}$$

$$\text{Mean} = 65.26$$

measure of central tendency when most of the scores cluster together but a few scores lie at the extreme ends of a distribution. The median score in Table 4.3 is 70.

Mode

The **mode** is the score that occurs most frequently. In a distribution of scores, the mode is the most commonly occurring score. However, a distribution of test scores can have more than one mode. If a teacher wants to know which test or test item students most frequently answer correctly, the teacher would look at the mode. However, educators use the mode infrequently because it is not very helpful when describing the performance of an individual child or of a group of students. In a normal distribution, the mean, median, and mode all occur at the same point (Figure 4.3).

Standard Deviation

The **standard deviation** (SD) tells the degree to which various scores deviate from the mean. It is a unit of measurement, just as an inch and a foot are units of measurement. Scores can be expressed by the number of standard deviation units that they deviate from the mean.

The standard deviation is useful when comparing several sets of scores. It can be helpful when interpreting the test performance of one student or a group of students. When comparing scores, the larger the standard deviation, the more variable is the performance; the smaller the standard deviation, the less variable is the performance of the students. In a normal distribution, the percentage of scores that can be expected to

SNAPSHOT
Deciding When to Use Measures of Central Tendency

Brendan Strout, the special education consultant at Washington School, was preparing to meet with Ken Brown, a sixth-grade classroom teacher. Brendan was examining the test scores of a group of students from Ken's classroom. Brendan wanted to be able to describe the performance of the students in order to assist Ken in making instructional decisions. Here are the scores of Ken's students:

90
82
81
80
79
75
75
75
20

Brendan summarized the scores in three ways:

1. By calculated the mean, or average, by adding up all of the scores and dividing by 9, the total number of scores.

90
82
81
80
79 Median
75
75 Mode
75
20

657 ÷ 9 = 73. This is the mean, or average score.

2. Next, Brendan arranged the scores from high to low and found the score that separates the top 50 percent of students who took the test from the bottom 50 percent of students. This score is 79 and is the median.

3. Finally, Brendan found the score that occurred the most often in the group of scores. This score is 75 and is the mode.

Which measure of central tendency—the mean, median, or mode—should Brendan use in his discussion with Ken? (The answer can be found on page 69.)

fall within the first, second, and third standard deviations above or below the mean are shown in Figure 4.3. For example, when a group of scores distributes normally, 34.13 percent of the scores can be expected to occur between the mean and the +1 SD, and 34.13 percent of the scores also occur between the mean and –1 SD. Approximately 13.59 percent of the scores fall between the +1 SD and +2 SD, and 13.59 percent of the scores fall between the –1 SD and –2 SD. Just over 2 percent (2.14) of the scores occur between the second and third standard deviations and 0.13 percent of the scores occur beyond the third standard deviation.

For most tests, publishers provide information about the mean and the standard deviation in test manuals. You will not have to calculate the standard deviation. For example, the manual for the third edition of the *Wechsler Intelligence Scale for Children–III (WISC–III)* reports that this test has a mean of 100 and a standard deviation of 15. This represents that approximately 34.13 percent of students have intelligence quotients (IQs) between 100 and 115. Similarly, approximately 68.26 percent of students have IQs between 85 and 115. Many states mandate specific guidelines for identification and placement of students. For example, some states may require that school-age students who are labeled with mental retardation have IQs that are at least 2 standard deviations below the mean. In this example, you will have to subtract 30 (2 times the standard deviation of 15) from 100 to obtain an IQ of 70.

Types of Scores

There are many ways of reporting test performance. A variety of scores can be used when interpreting students' test performance.

Raw Scores

The **raw score** is the number of items a student answers correctly without adjustment for guessing. For example, if there are 15 problems on an arithmetic test, and a student answers 11 correctly, then the raw score is 11. Raw scores, however, do not provide us with enough information to describe student performance.

Percentage Scores

A **percentage score** is the percent of test items answered correctly. These scores can be useful when describing a student's performance on a teacher-made test or on a criterion-referenced test. However, percentage scores have a major disadvantage: We have no way of comparing the percentage correct on one test with the percentage correct on another test. Suppose a child earned a score of 85 percent correct on one test and 55 percent correct on another test. The interpretation of the score is related to the difficulty level of the test items on each test. Because each test has a different or unique level of difficulty, we have no common way to interpret these scores; there is no frame of reference.

To interpret raw scores and percentage-correct scores, it is necessary to change the raw or percentage score to a different type of score in order to make comparisons. Evaluators rarely use raw scores and percentage-correct scores when interpreting performance because it is difficult to compare one student's scores on several tests or the performance of several students on several tests.

Derived Scores

Derived scores are a family of scores that allow us to make comparisons between test scores. Raw scores are transformed to derived scores. Developmental scores and scores of relative standing are two types of derived scores. Scores of relative standing include percentiles, standard scores, and stanines.

Developmental Scores

Sometimes called age and grade equivalents, **developmental scores** are scores that have been transformed from raw scores and reflect the average performance at age and grade levels. Thus, the student's raw score (number of items correct) is the same as the average raw score for students of a specific age or grade. Age equivalents are written with a hyphen between years and months (e.g., 12–4 means that the age equivalent is 12 years, 4 months old). A decimal point is used between the grade and month in grade equivalents (e.g., 1.2 is the first grade, second month).

Developmental scores can be useful (McLean, Bailey, & Wolery, 1996; Sattler, 2001). Parents and professionals easily interpret them and place the performance of students within a context. Because of the ease of misinterpretation of these scores, parents and professionals should approach them with extreme caution. There are a number of reasons for criticizing these scores.

For a student who is 6 years old and in the first grade, grade and age equivalents presume that for each month of first grade an equal amount of learning occurs. But, from our knowledge of child growth and development and theories about learning, we know that neither growth nor learning occurs in equal monthly intervals. Age and grade equivalents do not take into consideration the variation in individual growth and learning.

Teachers should not expect that students will gain a grade equivalent or age equivalent of one year for each year that they are in school. For example, suppose a child earned a grade equivalent of 1.5, first grade, fifth month, at the end of first grade. To assume that at the end of second grade the child should obtain a grade equivalent of 2.5, second grade, fifth month, is not good practice. This assumption is incorrect for two reasons: (1) The grade and age equivalent norms should not be confused with performance standards, and (2) a gain of 1.0 grade equivalent is representative only of students who are in the average range for their grade. Students who are above average will gain more than 1.0 grade equivalent a year, and students who are below average will progress less than 1.0 grade equivalent a year (Gronlund & Linn, 1990).

A second criticism of developmental scores is the underlying idea that because two students obtain the same score on a test they are comparable and will display the same thinking, behavior, and skill patterns. For example, a student who is in second grade earned a grade equivalent score of 4.6 on a test of reading achievement. This does not mean that the second grader understands the reading process as it is taught in the fourth grade. Rather, this student just performed at a superior level for a student who is in second grade. It is incorrect to compare the second grader to a child who is in fourth grade; the comparison should be made to other students who are in second grade (Sattler, 2001).

A third criticism of developmental scores is that age and grade equivalents encourage the use of false standards. A second-grade teacher should not expect all students in the class to perform at the second-grade level on a reading test. Differences between students within a grade mean that the range of achievement actually spans several grades. In addition, developmental scores are calculated so that half of the scores fall below the median and half fall above the median. Age and grade equivalents are not standards of performance.

A fourth criticism of age and grade equivalents is that they promote typological thinking. The use of age and grade equivalents causes us to think in terms of a typical kindergartner or a typical 10-year-old. In reality, students vary in their abilities and levels of performance. Developmental scores do not take these variations into account.

A fifth criticism is that most developmental scores are interpolated and extrapolated. A normed test includes students of specific ages and grades—not all ages and grades—in the norming sample. **Interpolation** is the process of estimating the scores of students within the ages and grades of the norming sample. **Extrapolation** is the process of estimating the performance of students outside the ages and grades of the normative sample.

DEVELOPMENTAL QUOTIENT A **developmental quotient** is an estimate of the rate of development. If we know a student's developmental age and chronological age, it is possible to calculate a developmental quotient. For example, suppose a student's developmental age is 12 years (12 years × 12 months in a year = 144 months) and the chronological age is also 12 years, or 144 months. Using the following formula, we arrive at a developmental quotient of 100.

$$\frac{\text{Developmental age 144 months}}{\text{Chronological age 144 months}} \times 100 = 100$$

$$\frac{144}{144} \times 100 =$$

$$\frac{1}{1} \times 100 =$$

$$1 \times 100 = 100$$

But, suppose another student's chronological age is also 144 months and that the developmental age is 108 months. Using the formula, this student would have a developmental quotient of 75.

$$\frac{\text{Developmental age 108 months}}{\text{Chronological age 144 months}} \times 100 = 75$$

$$\frac{108}{144} \times 100 = 75$$

Developmental quotients have all of the drawbacks associated with age and grade equivalents. In addition, they may be misleading because developmental age may not keep pace with chronological age as the individual gets older. Consequently, the gap between developmental age and chronological age becomes larger as the student gets older.

Scores of Relative Standing

PERCENTILE RANKS A **percentile rank** is the point in a distribution at or below which the scores of a given percentage of students fall. Percentiles provide information about the relative standing of students when compared with the standardization sample. Look at the following test scores and their corresponding percentile ranks.

Student	Score	Percentile Rank
Delia	96	84
Jana	93	81
Pete	90	79
Marcus	86	75

Jana's score of 93 has a percentile rank of 81. This means that 81 percent of the students who took the test scored 93 or lower. Said another way, Jana scored as well as or better than 81 percent of the students who took the test.

A percentile rank of 50 represents average performance. In a normal distribution, both the mean and the median fall at the 50th percentile. Half the students fall above the 50th percentile and half fall below. Percentiles can be divided into quartiles. A quartile contains 25 percentiles or 25 percent of the scores in a distribution. The 25th and the 75th percentiles are the first and the third quartiles. In addition, percentiles can be divided into groups of 10 known as deciles. A decile contains 10 percentiles. Beginning at the bottom of a group of students, the first 10 percent are known as the first decile, the second 10 percent are known as the second decile, and so on.

The position of percentiles in a normal curve is shown in Figure 4.5. Despite their ease of interpretation, percentiles have several problems. First, the intervals they represent are unequal, especially at the lower and upper ends of the distribution. A difference of a few percentile points at the extreme ends of the distribution is more serious than a difference of a few points in the middle of the distribution. Second, percentiles do not apply to mathematical calculations (Gronlund & Linn, 1990). Last, percentile scores are reported in one-hundredths. But, because of errors associated with measurement, they are only accurate to the nearest 0.06 (six one-hundredths) (Rudner, Conoley, & Plake, 1989). These limitations require the use of caution when interpreting percentile ranks. Confidence intervals, which are discussed later in this chapter, are useful when interpreting percentile scores.

STANDARD SCORES   Another type of derived score is a **standard score**. Standard score is the name given to a group or category of scores. Each specific type of standard score within this group has the same mean and the same standard deviation. Because each

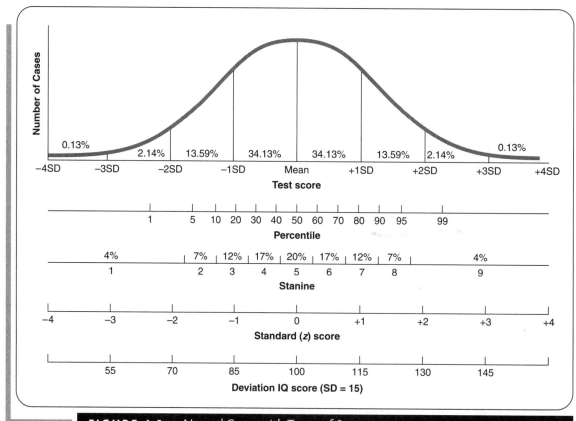

FIGURE 4.5 ● Normal Curve with Types of Scores

type of standard score has the same mean and the same standard deviation, standard scores are an excellent way of representing a child's performance. Standard scores allow us to compare a child's performance on several tests and to compare one child's performance to the performance of other students. Unlike percentile scores, standard scores function in mathematical operations. For instance, standard scores can be averaged. In the Snapshot, teachers Lincoln Bates and Sari Andrews discuss test scores. Figure 4.5 compares standard scores with the other types of scores we have discussed. As is apparent, standard scores are equal interval scores. The different types of standard scores, some of which we discuss in the following subsections, are:

1. z-scores: have a mean of 0 and a standard deviation of 1.
2. T-scores: have a mean of 50 and a standard deviation of 10.
3. Deviation IQ scores: have a mean of 100 and a standard deviation of 15 or 16.
4. Normal curve equivalents: have a mean of 50 and a standard deviation of 21.06.
5. Stanines: standard score bands divide a distribution of scores into nine parts.
6. Percentile ranks: point in a distribution at or below which the scores of a given percentage of students fall.

DEVIATION IQ SCORES **Deviation IQ** scores are frequently used to report the performance of students on norm-referenced standardized tests. The deviation scores of the *Wechsler Intelligence Scale for Children–III* and the *Wechsler Individual Achievement Test–II* have a mean of 100 and a standard deviation of 15, while the *Stanford-Binet Intelligence Scale–IV* has a mean of 100 and a standard deviation of 16. Many test manuals provide tables that allow conversion of raw scores to deviation IQ scores.

NORMAL CURVE EQUIVALENTS **Normal curve equivalents** (NCEs) are a type of standard score with a mean of 50 and a standard deviation of 21.06. When the baseline of

SNAPSHOT

A Conversation between Lincoln Bates and Sari Andrew

Just after school started in September, Lincoln Bates, a seventh-grade teacher of mathematics, reviewed last spring's test results for Karen Anderson, one of his students. He noticed that the results were reported using several types of scores:

Student's Name: Karen Anderson

Age: 13 years, 5 months

Teacher: J. Plante

Grade: 6

Subtest	Grade Equivalent	Age Equivalent	Percentile Rank
Mathematics	4.1	9–6	9
Reading Comprehension	10.2	13–0	75
Spelling	6.4	12–0	45

Lincoln was unsure how to interpret Karen's scores on the mathematics achievement subtest. He decided to ask Sari Andrews, the school's test examiner. Lincoln said, "I'm not sure how to interpret the age equivalent and grade equivalent scores. Even though I used to teach fourth grade, I don't think that Karen approaches mathematics in the same way that a typical fourth grader does."

Sari explained, "Just because Karen earned a grade equivalent of 4.1 in mathematics does not mean that her thinking, behavior, and skill patterns are the same as other students who are in the fourth grade. The same holds true for her age equivalent score of 9–6. Age and grade equivalent scores can be misleading. I prefer to use percentile rank or standard scores as a way of interpreting her performance." What do you think?

the normal curve is divided into 99 equal units, the percentile ranks of 1, 50, and 99 are the same as NCE units (Lyman, 1986). One test that does report NCEs is the *Battelle Developmental Inventory-2*. However, NCEs are not reported for some tests.

STANINES **Stanines** are bands of standard scores that have a mean of 5 and a standard deviation of 2. As illustrated in Figure 4.5, stanines range from 1 to 9. Despite their relative ease of interpretation, stanines have several disadvantages. A change in just a few raw score points can move a student from one stanine to another. Also, because stanines are a general way of interpreting test performance, caution is necessary when making classification and placement decisions. As an aid in interpreting stanines, evaluators can assign descriptors to each of the 9 values:

> 9—very superior
> 8—superior
> 7—very good
> 6—good
> 5—average
> 4—below average
> 3—considerably below average
> 2—poor
> 1—very poor

▶ Several different types of test scores are discussed in this chapter. Which ones do you prefer to use? Why?

Basal and Ceiling Levels

Many tests, because test authors construct them for students of differing abilities, contain more items than are necessary. To determine the starting and stopping points for administering a test, test authors designate basal and ceiling levels. (Although these are really not types of scores, basal and ceiling levels are sometimes called rules or scores.) The **basal level** is the point below which the examiner assumes that the student could obtain all correct responses and, therefore, it is the point at which the examiner begins testing.

The test manual will designate the point at which testing should begin. For example, a test manual states, "Students who are 13 years old should begin with item 12. Continue testing when three items in a row have been answered correctly. If three items in a row are not answered correctly, the examiner should drop back a level." This is the basal level.

Let's look at the example of the student who is 9 years old. Although the examiner begins testing at the 9-year-old level, the student fails to answer correctly three in a row. Thus, the examiner is unable to establish a basal level at the suggested beginning point. Many manuals instruct the examiner to continue testing backward, dropping back one item at a time, until the student correctly answers three items. Some test manuals instruct examiners to drop back an entire level, for instance, to age 8, and begin testing. When computing the student's raw score, the examiner includes items below the basal point as items answered correctly. Thus, the raw score includes all the items the student answered correctly plus the test items below the basal point. The **ceiling level** is the point above which the examiner assumes that the student would obtain all incorrect responses if the testing were to continue; it is, therefore, the point at which the examiner stops testing. "To determine a ceiling," a manual may read, "discontinue testing when three items in a row have been missed."

A false ceiling can be reached if the examiner does not carefully follow directions for determining the ceiling level. Some tests require students to complete a page of test items to establish the ceiling level.

Standard Error of Measurement and Confidence Intervals

Standard Error of Measurement

The administration of a test is subject to many errors: Errors can occur in the testing environment, the examiner may make errors, the examinee may not be exhibiting the best performance, and the test itself may not able to evoke the best performance from the examinee. All these errors contribute to lowering the reliability of a test.

The standard error of measurement (SEM) is related to reliability and is very useful in the interpretation of test performance. The standard error of measurement is the amount of error associated with individual test scores, test items, item samples, and test times. A **true score** is the score an individual would obtain on a test if there were no measurement errors. (The obtained score is the score that a student gets on a test.) Figure 4.6 hows the distribution of the SEM around the estimated true score.

If examiners expect that the reliability or the **standard error of measurement** will differ for different populations, SEMs should be reported for each population taking the test.

When the SEM is small, we can be more confident of a score; when the SEM is large, there is less confidence in the score. Thus, it follows that the more reliable a test is, the smaller the SEM and the more confidence we can have. The less reliable a test, the larger the SEM, and the more uncertainty we have in a score.

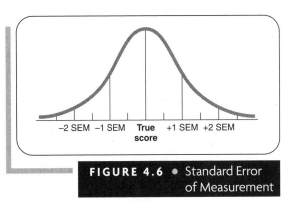

FIGURE 4.6 • Standard Error of Measurement

▶ Annie received a score of 64 and a confidence interval of ±4 on an achievement test. How can the special education teacher use the concept of confidence intervals to explain Annie's performance to her family?

Confidence Intervals

Although educators can never know a student's true score, we can use the concept of **confidence intervals** to give us a range within which the true score can be found. Because it is inadvisable to present a student's score as an exact point, the concept of confidence intervals is an important one to use when reporting a student's test score.

We can determine the probability that a student's score will fall within a particular range. Three equivalent terms can describe this range: band of error, confidence interval, and confidence band. Table 4.4 shows an example of how confidence intervals are used on one test. The higher the probability level, the more confidence we can have that a student's score falls within a specific range. The lower the probability, the less confidence we have that a score falls within a particular range. For instance, we can be 50, 68, 90, 95, 98, or 99 percent confident that a student's true score can be found within a range of scores. The percent of confidence that is chosen depends on the preference of the test examiner. However, we prefer to use 90 percent level or higher. In the Snapshot, teacher Gayle Aker explains a student's test performance using confidence intervals.

TABLE 4.4 • Example of Grade-Based Confidence Intervals from the Wechsler Individual Achievement Test-II (WIAT) (PsychCorp., 2005)

Subtest	95% Confidence Level	90% Confidence Level
Grade 1		
Word Reading	± 4	± 4
Numerical Operations	±15	±13
Reading Comprehension	± 9	± 8
Total	± 4	± 4
Grade 8		
Word Reading	± 6	± 5
Numerical Operations	± 8	± 7
Reading Comprehension	± 7	± 6
Total	± 4	± 3

Confidence Intervals

Gayle Aker, the special education consultant, had just finished administering the Comprehensive Form of the *Kaufman Test of Educational Achievement (K-TEA/NU)* to Cindy, a 7-year-old who was suspected of having a learning disability. After Gayle had marked the raw scores and the standard scores on the front of the Comprehensive Form (Figure 4.7), she was ready to write down the confidence interval. Gayle decided to use the 90 percent level of confidence. Like many tests, the developers of the *K-TEA/NU* have calculated the confidence bands so that test administrators do not need to make the calculations themselves. Gayle, using the *K-TEA/NU* manual,

found the tables that listed the bands of confidence for Cindy's standard scores.

When Gayle met with Cindy's family she was able to report her scores in this way: "I am very confident when I say that Cindy's performance on the Battery Composite on the *K-TEA/NU* showed that her score was 86 ±3. This means that her true score is between 83 and 89. It is more accurate to report her performance within a range of scores because test scores tend to fluctuate or change. There may be small changes in her scores if I were to retest her within a short time interval."

▶ Imagine that you are the director of testing for a school district and that you will be giving a one-day workshop to your staff. What topics should you discuss relating to the technical adequacy of tests? Why did you choose each of these topics?

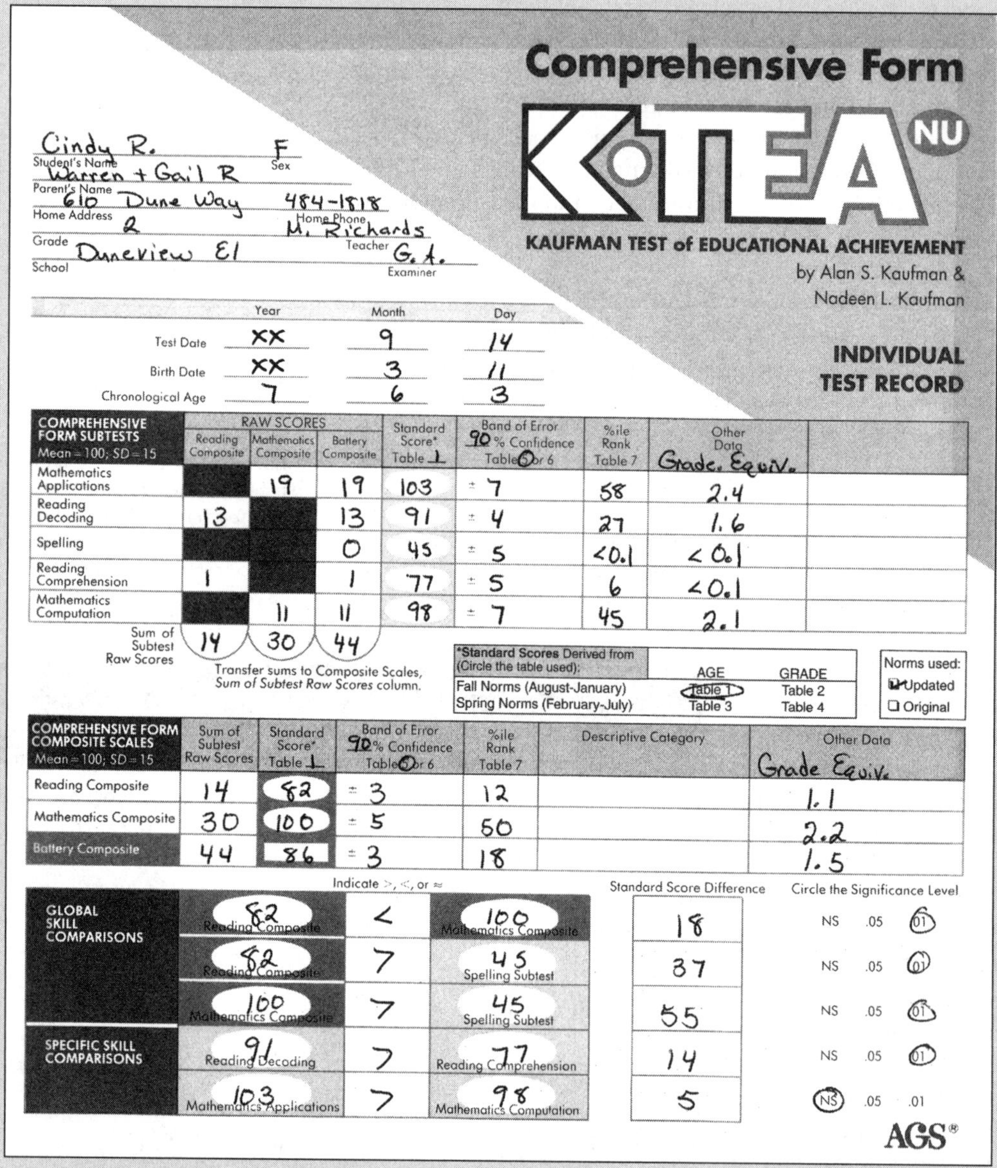

FIGURE 4.7 • Comprehensive Form from Kaufman Test of Educational Achievement

Source: *Kaufman Test of Educational Achievement Normative Update (K-TEA/NU).* Individual Test Record summary page by Alan S. Kaufman and Nadeen L. Kaufmann © 1985 American Guidance Service, Inc., 4201 Woodland Road, Circle Pines, Minnesota 55014-1796. Reproduced with permission of publisher. All rights reserved. www.agsnet.com

Scoring Guidelines

After you have administered the test, you must carefully score it. If you have used a standardized test, you must use the specific procedures for scoring described in the test manual. Score the test as soon as possible after you have administered it. Be sure to allot sufficient time so that you do not feel rushed. Scoring must be accurate. Check all calculations carefully. Many tests have computer programs that will calculate the test scores for you. These can be very helpful in avoiding errors in computation.

Completing the Test Record Form

Biographical Information

The test record form contains a section for the examiner to complete biographical information about the student (Figure 4.7). Usually, this section is on the front of the test record form. The form, in general, asks for the following information: student's name, gender, name(s) of parent(s), home address, home telephone, grade in school, age when tested, date of birth, student's homeroom teacher, name of school, and examiner's name. If the student needs to use corrective lenses or a hearing aid, the examiner should note this also.

Chronological Age

Often it is necessary to calculate the student's **chronological age**, the precise age of the student in years and months. If testing took place over several days, use the first test date to calculate the chronological age. Figure 4.8 shows the steps in calculating chronological age.

Calculating Raw Scores

The raw scores are the number of items that the student answered correctly. Directions for computing the raw score may vary from one test to another. Within each subtest you will need to add the total number of items the student answered correctly. Each test will have its own system for indicating the student's correct and incorrect answers. Following the directions given in the test manual or on the test record form, the examiner will designate the correct answers by marking either a plus sign (+) or by designating points (e.g., 1, 2, or 3 points) for each correct answer. When calculating the raw score, the examiner will need to follow the test manual directions for calculating basal and ceiling scores.

After calculating the raw scores, the examiner writes these scores on the test form and transfers them to the section that summarizes the student's scores. For many test forms, this section is on the front of the test form.

Transforming Raw Scores to Derived Scores

Calculating derived scores allows educators to make comparisons between test scores. Developmental scores and scores of relative standing are two types of derived scores. We prefer to use scores of relative standing: percentiles, standard scores, and stanines. Test manuals have norm tables that allow the examiner to convert raw scores to one or more types of derived scores. Some test manuals contain tables for age and grade norms for tests conducted during the fall, winter, or spring; other test manuals will have norm

Example 1

Begin with the right column and subtract days, then months, and finally years. In this example no borrowing is required.

	Year	Month	Day
Test Date	2006	6	15
Birthdate	1991	3	13
Chronological Age	15	3	2

Example 2

If the day for the test date is smaller than the day for the birthdate, it is necessary to borrow one month (30 days) from the month column and add the 30 days to the day column. When borrowing one month, always borrow 30 days.

	Year	Month	Day
Test Date	2006	~~6~~	~~3~~
	2006	5	33
Birthdate	1991	3	13
Chronological Age	15	2	20

Example 3

If the month for the test date is smaller than the month for the birth date, it is necessary to borrow one year (12 months) from the year column and add the 12 months to the month column.

	Year	Month	Day
Test Date	~~2006~~	~~2~~	15
	2005	14	15
Birthdate	1991	3	13
Chronological Age	14	11	2

In general, chronological age is reported in days and months. If the number of days exceeds 15, add 1 month. If the number of days is equal to or is smaller than 15, do not change the months.

FIGURE 4.8 • Three Examples of Calculating Chronological Age

tables for tests administered at any time during the year. You may need to use more than one of the norm tables in the test manual. The section of the test form that summarizes the student's scores will indicate which type of derived score to use.

Graphing Scores

Many test record forms allow the examiner to plot a graph or profile of the student's test scores. A graph allows the examiner to depict test scores visually and assists in the interpretation of test performance. To develop a graph, the examiner transfers the student's scores to the designated section of the test record form, connects the points, and creates a graph. Some record forms also allow bands of error to be plotted.

Interpreting Test Performance

Conclusions and interpretations about a student's performance based on the results of one test, measure, or observation are limited. A student's performance on only one measure indicates a narrow slice of information about the student. Because many sources of variability and error are present in any assessment situation and because many of the assessment approaches have limitations, we recommend that examiners use several different sources of assessment data. Sources of assessment data include standardized measures; portfolio assessment; performance-based assessment; interviews with family members, teachers, and the student; and observations in classrooms, playground, cafeteria, and the student's home, if appropriate.

When making interpretations about a student's performance, include observations of the behavior of the student and observations of the environment. Chapter 7 provides an in-depth discussion about the test interpretation process.

Behavioral Observations

In this section, the the student's behavior during formal and informal testing is described. The examiner will want to note whether the student was cooperative, distractible, attentive, tired, shy, or exhibited other behaviors. What was the student's behavior at the beginning of the testing? during the testing? at the end? To a certain extent the testing situation is artificial, and examiners must consider this when drawing conclusions about a child's behavior (Sattler, 2001). A child's behavior can vary in different settings and with different examiners. Systematic observations, as discussed in Chapter 5, can be important sources of information. The following list of behaviors is a starting point for discussion (Sattler, 2001):

- Physical appearance
- Reactions to test session and to the examiner
- General behavior
- Typical mode of relating to the examiner
- Language style
- General response style
- Response to failures
- Response to successes
- Response to encouragement
- Activity level
- Attitude toward self
- Attitude toward the examiner and the testing process
- Visual-motor ability
- Unusual habits, mannerisms, or verbalizations
- Examiner's reaction to the child

Observations of the Environment

Note any factors in the environment such as interruptions, excessive noise, or unusual temperature that may affect the student's test performance and behavior. Approaches to assessing the environment will be discussed in Chapter 5.

Discussion of Results

When reporting the results of standardized tests, use the same types of scores throughout. Most professionals prefer standard scores, percentiles, or stanines. Report two or more types of scores, such as standard scores and percentiles. If a graph of the student's performance is available, be sure to use it.

How Should Assessment Approaches Be Evaluated?

We have discussed many concepts in this chapter. It is important for you to understand these concepts when using a test. Table 4.5 can be helpful when determining the adequacy of assessment approaches.

Before using individual tests, professionals would do well to consult independent reviews. There are numerous resources available that provide independent evaluations of tests. *The Mental Measurements Yearbooks* (MMY) and *Tests in Print*, which are

---

TABLE 4.5 • Evaluation of a Test or Other Assessment Approach

Name of Assessment Test or Approach _____

Author(s) _____

Publisher _____ Date of Publication _____

About the Assessment Test or Approach

1. Purpose(s) (according to the manual)
2. Extent to which individual items or tasks match the purpose(s)
3. Length of time for test administration
4. Group or individual

About Administration Requirements

1. Education and experience of examiner requirements
2. Additional training requirements

About the Student

1. Considerations/adaptations for disability
2. Considerations/adaptations for language
3. Considerations/adaptations for culture/race/ethnicity

About the Technical Aspects

1. Norms, goals, standards, outcomes. If relevant, indicate:
   a. Type
   b. Age, grade, language, culture, gender
   c. Representativeness
   d. Relevance of sample to student(s) tested
   e. Method of selection of sample
   f. Date of development of norms, goals, standards, outcomes
2. Reliability. What are the coefficients and how were they determined?
   a. Test-retest
   b. Alternate form
   c. Split-half
   d. Internal consistency
   e. Interscorer/interrater/interobserver

3. Validity. What is the justification for each type of validity?
   a. Content
   b. Concurrent
   c. Predictive
   d. Construct
   e. Consequential validity

About the Results and Aids to Interpretation

1. Types of scores
2. Interpretation aids

About Fairness

1. Is the norm or comparison group appropriate?
2. Are considerations made for race, culture, gender, language, socioeconomic status, or disability?

About the Usefulness of This Test or Approach

1. Is it appropriate for the student(s)?
2. Is it fair?
3. Is it technically adequate?
4. Report from an independent source (*The Mental Measurements Yearbooks, Tests in Print, Test Critiques,* journal article, or Internet)

Conclusions

1. Overall strengths
2. Overall weaknesses
3. Summary and recommendations

About References

1. List of references consulted
2. List of other sources consulted

---

published by the Buros Institute of Mental Measurements at the University of Nebraska–Lincoln (University of Nebraska at Lincoln, Lincoln, NE 68588), are probably the best-known sources of test reviews. *Test Critiques,* published by the Test Corporation of America (4050 Pennsylvania, Suite 310, Kansas City, MO 64112), is another source. The Internet provides a wealth of information. The website of the ERIC Clearinghouse on Assessment and Evaluation provides information and access to the ERIC database on tests and measurement, newsletters on tests and measurement, descriptions of tests, information on locating tests and test reviews, research studies and essays, and links to numerous Internet resources on tests and measurement. The Buros Institute of Mental

Measurements website has information on locating tests and test reviews. Other Internet resources include the United States Department of Education; the National Center for Research on Evaluation, Standards, and Student Teaching (CRESST); and the National Association of Test Directors.

Many journals contain reviews of tests. Journals that may be of particular interest to special educators include: *Diagnostique, Exceptional Children, Journal of Early Intervention, Journal of Learning Disabilities, Journal of Reading, Journal of School Psychology, Journal of Special Education, Mental Retardation, Remedial and Special Education,* and *Topics in Early Childhood Special Education.*

Finally, test publishers provide catalogues that describe their products. Catalogues provide overviews of tests as well as information about how to purchase tests, record forms, and technical materials. Remember that the primary goal of test publishers is to sell tests. It is essential that professionals examine independent reviews of tests, such as those contained in *MMY, Tests in Print, Test Critiques,* and various journals.

Summary

- When using standardized, norm-referenced tests, educators must determine whether they are measuring consistent student performance and whether tests measure what the authors describe as the purpose of the tests.

- Test manuals provide information about technical aspects of tests, including the development of norms and test scores.

- Teachers, test examiners, and administrators need to carefully review tests before using them to satisfy themselves that each test has acceptable levels of reliability and validity.

- Professionals should apply the technical concepts we have discussed in this and previous chapters to the assessment approaches, procedures, and techniques.

Answer to Question in Snapshot: On p. 56 we asked: *Which measure of central tendency—the mean, median, or mode—should Brendan use in his discussion with Ken? Answer:* Brendan should use the median score of 79 because most of the scores in the class cluster around this score. The score represents the division between the top 50 percent of students and the bottom 50 percent of students. The mean score of 73 should not be used. Notice how this score was strongly influenced by the bottom score of 20.)

REFERENCES

American Educational Research Association, American Psychological Association, and National Council on Measurement in Education. (1999). *Standards for educational and psychological testing.* Washington, DC: American Educational Research Association.

Gronlund, N. E., & R. L. Linn (1990). *Measurement and evaluation in teaching.* New York: Macmillan.

Kaufman, A., & Kaufman, N. L. (1988). *Kaufman test of educational achievement/Normative update* (K-TEA/ NU). Circle Pines, MN: American Guidance Service.

Lyman, H. (1986). *Test scores and what they mean* (4th ed.). Englewood Cliffs, NJ: Prentice-Hall.

McLean, M., Bailey, D. B., & Wolery, M. (1996). *Assessing infants and preschoolers with handicaps.* Columbus, OH: Merrill.

Mehrens, W. A., & Lehmann, I. J. (1991). *Measurement and evaluation in education and psychology.* Fort Worth, TX: Holt, Rinehart & Winston.

PsychCorp. (2005). *Scoring and normative supplement for grades preK–12 update 2005.* San Antonio, TX: Author.

Rudner, L. M., Conoley, J. C., & Plake, B. S. (1989). *Understanding achievement tests: A guide for school administrators.* Washington, DC: Eric Clearinghouse on Assessment and Education. (ERIC Document Reproduction Service No. ED 314 426).

Sattler, J. (2001). *Assessment of students*: LaMesa, CA: Author.

Observing, Interviewing, and Conferencing

Chapter Objectives

After completing this chapter, you should be able to:

- Provide a rationale for planning and conducting observations.

- Compare and contrast the use of various recording methods, including anecdotal records, running records, event recordings, duration recordings, intensity recordings, latency recordings, interval recordings, category recordings, rating scales, checklists, and questionnaires.

- Plan and conduct observations of students.

- Describe concerns relating to reliability and validity.

- Describe the process for planning and conducting interviews.

- Identify skills in conferencing and collaborating with others.

Key Terms

Observation
Anecdotal record
Running record
Event recording
Duration recording
Percentage duration rate
Intensity recording
Latency recording

Interval recording
Category recording
Rating scale
Descriptors
Errors of omission
Errors of commission
Errors of transmission
Observer drift

Predetermined expectation
Reactivity
Checklist
Questionnaire
Conferencing
Collaborating

Overview

This chapter focuses on several informal ways by which special educators gather information to help answer assessment questions. By observing and recording a student's behavior, the teacher collects valuable information about the student's functioning. Observing the classroom environment provides insight about the physical, learning, and social environment. Some approaches, such as conferencing and collaborating, use face-to-face meetings in which participants share information, concerns, and ideas. Even though these assessment approaches are considered informal, each involves careful preparation and a high degree of skill.

Why Observe?

Observing students and their environments allows educators to gather information to answer such questions as: How independently is the student functioning? Does the student use age-appropriate skills? Does the student socialize with students without disabilities in a nonstructured setting? What factors in the classroom environment provide guidelines for appropriate behavior? Does the learning environment support the student's special needs? How does the classroom environment encourage collaboration and a feeling of well-being among students?

As an assessment approach, **observation** involves a systematic process of gathering information by looking at students and their environments. The observer may record student behaviors, language, or responses of peers or teachers, for example. Observations may be conducted by special educators and general educators, as well as parents, therapists, and other related services providers.

For students with or at risk for disability, IDEA requires observations as part of an initial assessment and as part of any reevaluation of the student. In fact, observations of the student and the environment provide valuable information in helping to answer the questions during each of the steps in the assessment process:

1. Screening
   - Is there a possibility of a disability?
2. Determining eligibility
   - Does the student have a disability?
   - What disability does the student have?
   - Does the student meet criteria for services?
   - What are the strengths and weaknesses?
   - In what areas is the student having difficulty?
3. Program planning
   - What is the student not able to do?
   - What is the student not able to understand?
   - Where should instruction begin?
   - Should assistive technology be considered?
4. Monitoring progress
   - To understand the pace of instruction
   - To understand what the student knows prior to and after instruction
   - To understand the strategies and concepts the student uses
   - To monitor the student's program
5. Conducting evaluations
   - Has the student met the IEP goals?
   - Has the instructional program been successful?
   - Has the student made progress?
   - Has the instructional program achieved its goals?

Information can be collected on student achievement levels, growth, development, characteristics, social skills, and behaviors.

In addition to gathering information about students, observers can gather information about the environment. This information can be useful in answering questions about the physical arrangement or other aspects of the classroom. Using a systematic process, an observer can collect information about the use of student groupings, teacher expectations, classroom procedures, and many other aspects of the learning and social environments.

Planning Observations

Planning observations involves identifying the assessment question(s), defining the event or behavior to be observed, specifying the location(s) for the observations, and deciding the method to use in recording observation data. In addition, one must consider what steps to take to ensure that the information being collected is accurate and is representative of the student. A good observation actually consists of a series of several observations of the student over a period of a few days. Finally, one must think about how to synthesize the observation information with other assessment information. The following section examines each of these areas in more detail.

Observation Questions

Observations can help answer assessment questions during each of the steps of the assessment process. The observation may focus on the environment or on one or more students. Since there are many activities going on in a classroom at one time, the observer needs to have a clear focus on what information will be collected. One or more observation questions identified before the observations occur permit the observer to focus on the key areas. The questions should be stated clearly, in terms that can be observed. For example, using the question "How independently is Tia functioning in the regular education classroom?", the observer records the times that Tia completes her work without assistance. Or another question might ask "How much time does Ricardo actually work during math class?", the observer records when Ricardo is engaged.

Defining an Event or Behavior

Defining an event or behavior in observable terms helps the observer know when to record an observation. A detailed definition helps ensure that the recordings are reliable. For example, we'll define Tia's independent functioning as "behaviors that require only a verbal prompt." For Ricardo, we'll define his engagement as "looking at the teacher, responding to class discussions, using math materials, or completing a worksheet."

Teachers need to collect observation information over a period of time; that is, observations should take place on several different occasions. Frequency increases reliability and, as the information is synthesized, trends become apparent.

Location

Observations take place in the classroom, cafeteria, playground, other school settings, or in the home. Teachers and parents can usually observe students without disrupting routines. However, when an observer is not typically part of the setting, the presence of the outsider can change aspects of the environment or of the students' behavior. Additional equipment, such as a video camera, also can adversely affect the results of the observations.

Recording

There are many different ways of recording information: anecdotal records, running records, event recording, duration recording, intensity recording, latency recording, interval recording, category recording, rating scales, checklists, and questionnaires. During the planning stage teachers carefully select the recording method that will be the most effective one in answering the assessment question(s). Later sections of this chapter examine each of these methods.

Accuracy

Recording information takes skill and practice. Some of the important considerations include: Are your observations accurate? Are your findings consistent with what you might observe tomorrow? Do your findings agree with others who conduct the same observation? Other sections of this chapter discuss methods of ensuring accuracy and consistency when using observation assessments.

Integration

Observation data will need to be integrated with other assessment information that has been gathered. This involves carefully reviewing all the assessment information and synthesizing the results. Chapter 7 describes a process for integrating assessment information.

Observing the Student: Responding to Diversity

Conducting observations of a student is one of the best methods for obtaining specific information regarding that student's behavior. For the observer who is sensitive and responsive to diversity, these observations create a picture of the uniqueness of the student. Some of the areas to consider in planning an observation include:

Work Habits

- Time
    How long does it take the student to get started?
    How long is the student able to stay on task?
- Levels of assistance needed
    What can the student do independently?
    How frequently does the student need prompting?
    What types of prompts are helpful (physical, verbal, gestural)?
- Reinforcements used
    What types of reinforcement are effective?
    How does the student react to the reinforcement?

Interactions with Others

- Other students
    Does the student have a variety of ways to communicate?
    Do other students communicate with the student?
    Does the student socialize with other students?
- Teacher
    Does the student have a variety of ways to communicate?
    Can the teacher communicate with the student?
    Is the student given opportunities to demonstrate competence?

Facial Expression and Affect

- Eye contact: Does the student make eye contact with others?
- Affect: Does the student have appropriate affect?

Body Movements

- Independent skills: Does the student have independent mobility skills?
- Quality of movement: Is the quality of gross and fine motor responses refined (not jerky)?

Adaptive Skills

- Independent skills
  Can the student eat independently?
- Appropriate skills
  Does the student use appropriate grooming skills?
  Does the student dress in an age-appropriate manner?

Participation in Play and Games

- Level of participation
  Does the student participate in unorganized play (free time, recess)?
  Does the student understand the rules of the game?
  Does the student play cooperatively?

Recording Methods

▶ **CEC Common Core Knowledge and Skills.** The beginning special educator will understand basic terminology used in assessment (CC8K1).

There are a number of methods from which to choose in planning observations. These methods allow for collecting and recording data in various formats. The assessment question influences the method special educators choose (Table 5.1). Let's examine some typical assessment questions and methods of recording observation data. In our discussions we'll also look at some of the advantages as well as disadvantages of these various approaches.

Anecdotal Record

An **anecdotal record** is a brief narrative description of an event or events that the observer felt was important to record. Anecdotal records are recorded after the events have occurred, usually in the form of notes. The writer records the date, time, and place of the event and, as accurately as possible, describes the event as it took place, including verbal and nonverbal cues and direct quotations. The observation should be as objective as possible, describing only what the observer saw and heard. Interpretive comments should not be part of the description of the episode.

Let's consider a question that came before a student assistance team: Leo's parent had contacted the school to inquire whether the classroom teacher would observe any changes in behavior over the next two weeks. The physician planned to change Leo's level of medication and wanted to monitor any effects, both at home and at school. The student assistance team met to plan aspects of the observation. The team decided that the classroom teacher should complete a daily anecdotal record. Figure 5.1 is an example of the anecdotal record that Leo's classroom teacher logged.

There are several advantages to maintaining anecdotal records:

1. The method requires little special training.
2. Observers can record unanticipated events.
3. Observations record actual behavior in a natural setting.
4. The method provides a check on other types of assessment.

TABLE 5.1 ● Assessment Questions and Methods of Observation

Assessment Question	Recording Methods
How independently is the student functioning?	Anecdotal record
	Latency recording
	Category recording
	Rating scale
	Checklist
How does the student communicate with peers?	Anecdotal record
	Running record
	Duration recording
	Rating scale
	Checklist
Does the student socialize with students without disabilities in a nonstructured setting?	Running record
	Event recording
	Interval recording
	Category recording

Date: October 15   Time Period: 1:00–1:50

Student: Leo B.   Class activity: Science

Leo worked in a small group with two other students for the first part of the period. The group used the classroom computer in locating information about bats for their presentation next week. Leo typed in much of the search information on the computer and worked well with the other two students. However, when they returned to their desks, he had trouble settling down. He asked to go to the bathroom twice, broke his pencil three times, and then spent the remainder of the class period with his head on the desk.

Comment:
L. seems to be very interested in this topic. Today was the first time he has worked for a steady 20 minutes. Is it the topic or use of computer? Or medication change?

Tomorrow I'll try having his group use other materials for searching for information.

FIGURE 5.1 • An Anecdotal Record

However, there are several disadvantages to this technique:

1. The recording of anecdotal records is dependent on the memory of the observer.
2. Bias may occur if the observer selects only certain aspects or incidents to record.
3. The technique may not completely describe specific behaviors.
4. There are difficulties associated with validating narrative recordings.
5. The recording of the behavior can be time-consuming.
6. Records of several anecdotal observations may be difficult to summarize (Beaty, 2002; Gronlund & Linn, 2000; Sattler, 2001).

Table 5.2 provides tips for recording anecdotal records.

TABLE 5.2 • Tips for Recording Anecdotal Records

Complete your anecdotal record as soon as possible.

Record only what you observed.

Don't forget to record:

- Any unexpected or unusual behaviors
- Events leading up to the behavior
- Events that followed the behavior

Complete multiple observations before drawing conclusions.

Running Record

A **running record**, sometimes called a continuous record, is a description of events written as they occur. Unlike an anecdotal record in which the observer records events sometime after they occur, a running record describes events while they are taking place. A running record provides a rich description of events and is helpful in analyzing the behavior of students. Unlike the anecdotal record, which is a selective record of events, the running record includes everything that is observed; it is a comprehensive, detailed account of events.

Let's examine an example: A special education teacher was gathering information about Sami's progress in preparation for the annual IEP meeting. One of the questions that the team was likely to raise was how Sami functioned in homeroom. The special education teacher decided to use a running record to gather information about Sami's interactions with other students during this time (Figure 5.2).

When recording information, the observer must carefully describe the events. It is much better to provide a factual, detailed account than to be judgmental. Factual

Date: **May 10**   Student: **Sami G.**

Period: **Homeroom**   Focus: **Sami's interactions with other students during free time**

7:45   Sami enters the room with two other students. One student grabs Sami's hat and turns it around backward. Sami grins and says "haaay."

Observer comments:
Students entering the classroom. Several students seated; about 15 students standing around.

7:47   Sami wanders toward the back of the classroom and stops at JR's desk.

7:48   JR asks "How's the man?"

7:49   Sami gives him a high five.

7:50   The homeroom teacher enters and asks everyone to take their seats.

7:52   Sami heads for his desk but stops to watch Joe and Mark arm wrestle.

About 7 of the 25 students are milling around. Sami is the only student not in his seat.

7:55   The teacher again asks everyone to take their seats.

7:56   Sami makes his way to his desk and sits down. He looks at Jen (sitting to his left) and asks her if she watched HBO last night.

7:59   The teacher takes attendance and asks students to indicate if they are taking hot lunch. Sami raises his hand.

8:05   Bell for first period rings.

FIGURE 5.2 • A Running Record

accounts are less likely to be influenced by observer bias. The observer strives to write not only accurate but detailed descriptions of the observed events. Instead of simply recording, "the student sat in his seat," the observer can write "squirmed in his seat"; "slumped in the chair"; or "sat rigidly."

Beaty (2002) describes several disadvantages of running records:

1. Writing a running record can be time-consuming.
2. Recording all observable events is difficult; some details may be overlooked.
3. This technique is useful when observing individual students but is difficult when observing a group or groups of students.

► **CEC Common Core Knowledge and Skills.** The beginning special educator will know how to elect, adapt, and modify assessments to accommodate the unique abilities and needs of individuals with disabilities (GC8S3).

One of the major disadvantages of anecdotal records and running records is that they are subject to observer bias and judgment. In addition, while they can provide rich descriptions of events, it is difficult to quantify behaviors. For these reasons, other types of recording systems have been developed.

Event Recording

Event recording, or frequency recording, is a procedure in which the observer records a behavior each time it occurs during a given period. For example, if an observation lasts for 20 minutes, the observer records each occurrence of the behavior during the

20-minute period. The observer must pay close attention to the student and precisely tally the number of times that the behavior occurs. Before beginning event recording, the observer must carefully define the behavior to be observed, including a description of the beginning of the behavior and the end of the behavior so that there is no ambiguity about whether the behavior occurred. Event recording is useful for behaviors that occur very frequently or very infrequently. Event recording is sometimes referred to as event sampling.

Several different procedures are effective for recording events. The simplest one is a tally. Each time the behavior occurs a line is drawn on the page and then the number of lines are totaled:

$$\text{卌 卌 | |}$$

Observers use event recording to answer questions about students with disabilities. For example, an IEP team wondered if accommodations to the classroom environment had helped Pedrico feel more comfortable in volunteering in class. An event recording was used to gather this information (Figure 5.3). The first observation occurred during a 20-minute period when the class was discussing a book that they had been reading. During this time, Pedrico volunteered by raising his hand on four different occasions. According to the observer's comments, Pedrico loses interest and becomes distracted when the teacher does not call on him. We might recommend that in conducting subsequent observations, the observer plan to include a comparison child. This would provide allow a comparison of Pedrico's performance with that of another student to see if his behavior is typical of same-age peers.

Date: December 1   **Student:** Pedrico G.

Observation questions: Does Pedrico participate in class discussions?

Class activity: Reading   **Behavior observed:** Volunteers by raising his hand or by responding to teacher-directed questions

Observer: Jake Orone

Time	Frequency	Comments
:00		Beginning of class discussion.
:05	I	P. immediately raises hand and teacher calls on P. After P's comment, teacher says, "That's an interesting idea about why the author chose to open the story with a flashback. What do other people think?"
:10		P. stares out the window. Is he distracted by the noise of the dump truck outside?
:15	IIII	P. raises his hand to each of the next four questions but teacher does not call on him.
:20		P. plays with pencil, doodling on paper.

FIGURE 5.3 • An Event Recording: Pedrico's Participation in Class Discussion

In monitoring another student's individualized education program, the IEP team wondered to what degree the regular classroom environment was providing opportunities for Tia to communicate with her peers. The teacher aide completed event recordings over a period of 10 days to document Tia's communication with peers during her daily schedule (Figure 5.4).

Sometimes teachers wish to know the rate of behavior over time. With event recording, they can calculate the rate of occurrences of the behavior. This is helpful when observation times vary, when evaluating behaviors before and after an intervention, or when comparing the behaviors of various students. For example, suppose the teacher is using a teaching strategy to decrease Stacy's disruptiveness in class and wants to judge its effectiveness. Two months ago, an observer counted that Stacy engaged in shouting 30 times during a 15-minute period. To obtain a rate of occurrence, divide the number of occurrences of the behavior by the length of time observed. The calculation follows:

$$N/T = \text{Rate of occurrence}$$

where N = the number of occurrences of the behavior
T = the length of time of the observation

30 occurrences/15 minutes = 2 occurrences of shouting per minute

In a recent observation, Stacy engaged in shouting 15 times during a 10-minute observation. What is the rate of occurrence? Would you say that there has been an improvement in Stacy's behavior? See page 105 to find the answer.

Student: Tia B.

Date: Weeks of September 5 through September 16

Assessment question: Is the general education classroom providing opportunities for Tia to communicate with her peers?

Behavior: Communication (verbal communication)

Observer: T. Morrill, personal aide

Schedule	Time	9/5	9/6	9/7	9/8	9/9	9/12	9/13	9/14	9/15	9/16
*Homeroom	7:30–7:45	0	0	0	1	1	0	2	0	1	0
*Art/music rotation	7:50–9:00	1	0	0	0	1	1	0	0	1	2
Functional life skills	9:10–10:20	3	0	1	2	1	0	1	3	2	0
*Physical education	10:30–11:40	2	1	3	1	2	3	3	0	2	3
*Cafeteria/lunch	11:50–12:20	0	0	1	2	1	0	2	2	1	1
Vocational training	12:30–1:50	2	0	1	2	3	1	1	3	2	2
Leisure	2:00–2:20	1	0	0	1	1	1	2	1	2	2
Prepare for departure/Bus	2:30–2:45	1	1	2	3	2	0	3	2	3	3

*General education settings

FIGURE 5.4 ● An Event Recording: Tia's Communication with Peers

Event recording has several advantages (Beaty, 2002; Sattler, 2001):

1. The behavior or event remains intact, thus facilitating analysis.
2. It is possible to monitor behaviors that occur infrequently.
3. It is possible to record changes in behavior over a period of time.

Despite the advantages, event recording also has several disadvantages (Beaty, 2002; Sattler, 2001):

1. Because the event is taken out of context, it may be difficult to analyze events that preceded the behavior.
2. Patterns of behavior may remain undetected.
3. The method cannot record behaviors that are difficult to define.
4. Reliability between observers is difficult to establish.
5. Unless the length of the observation periods across the sessions is constant, it is difficult to make generalizations.

Duration Recording

Duration recording is a measure of the length of time a specific event or behavior persists. For example, in developing instructional goals, the teacher wants to know how long a tantrum lasts or how long a student works independently. Duration recording is an effective method to use when it is important to know the length of time the behavior or event lasted rather than whether it occurred.

Before the observer begins a duration recording, precise definitions for the beginning and ending of the behaviors must be set. For example, the definition of when independent work begins could be when the student begins to look at the material, when the student picks up the pencil, or when the student actually touches the laptop keyboard. Once the observer has determined how to define the beginning and ending of a behavior or event, a stopwatch can time the length of the behavior.

Besides simply recording the duration of a behavior or event, teachers may wish to further analyze the data. The observer can determine the percentage of time a behavior or event occurs or calculate the average length of the behavior or event. Finding the percent of time that the behavior or event occurs is called the **percentage duration rate.** To calculate the percentage duration rate, the observer divides the total duration of the behavior or event by the total time of the observation and multiplies this answer by 100 to obtain a percentage.

$$d/t \times 100$$

where   d = the total duration of the behavior or event
t = the total length of the observation period

Let's see how Ian's special educator used percentage duration rate to help in planning his program. One of Ian's IEP goals was to increase his ability to work independently. The special educator, using a stopwatch, watched Ian for a 30-minute interval and recorded the information (Figure 5.5). The duration recording showed that Ian worked independently during two time periods of 8 minutes and 4 minutes for a total duration of 12 minutes.

Date: October 12   Class:

Student: Ian B.   Observer:

Purpose: To observe Ian working independently

Time: Comments:

10:00–10:08   works independently

10:08   asks for help in reading paragraph

10:15   returns to seat

10:16   drops pencil, gets up to sharpen pencil

10:20   returns to seat

10:22   starts working

10:23–10:27   works independently

10:28–10:30   glances around room

FIGURE 5.5 ● A Duration Recording

To calculate the percent of time Ian worked independently during this time period, the numbers are inserted into the formula:

$$12/30 \times 100 = 40\% \text{ of the observation period}$$

This observation data indicates that during a 30-minute period, Ian worked independently 40 percent of the time. Ian's special education teacher finds this information helpful in planning and monitoring instruction. After completing several other observations with similar results, his teacher decides to give Ian a choice of which work to complete first. After several weeks, the teacher will complete additional observations to see if this strategy increased Ian's ability to work independently.

▶ Do you agree with the explanation of the observation data on Ian? What other suggestions could you offer his teacher?

Intensity Recording

Intensity recording is a measure of the degree of a behavior. Since the degrees are usually defined as high, medium, or low, the observer's judgment can be very subjective and unreliable. Before using an intensity recording, the teacher must specify the ways in which the various levels differentiate. For example, Carlos's IEP team wanted to know if the teaching strategies for including students with and without disabilities were enabling him to generalize the skills to other settings. The team asked the special education teacher to observe Carlos's behavior on the playground during informal play and games. The teacher decided not to use event recording because the information needed (level of involvement) went beyond whether Carlos simply participated in outdoor games with students without disabilities. The teacher defined the degrees of involvement in the following ways:

High involvement: The target student participated fully in the activity and showed great interest through interactions with other students, body language, and general overall affect.

Medium involvement: The target student joined the other students in the activity but showed little interest in the progression of the activity, either by lack of interactions or affect.

Low involvement: The target student primarily watched the other students, occasionally shouting words of encouragement or adding comments to the activity.

No involvement: The target student ignored the activity.

Using these descriptors, the teacher was able to complete an accurate, reliable recording.

▶ Can you design a form to help a teacher collect information about the intensity of a student's behavior?

Latency Recording

Latency recording is a measure of the amount of time between a behavior or event (or request to begin the behavior) and the beginning of the prespecified or target behavior. For example, suppose we wanted to know the length of time that elapsed between the moment Darcy was encouraged to use a switch to select an activity and when she depressed the switch. Using a stopwatch, the observer can determine the amount of time that elapses between the initiation of the request and when Darcy begins the requested behavior.

Latency recording can be difficult to measure. The observer must carefully define the stimulus behavior (the behavior that actually signals the request to initiate behavior), the beginning of the target behavior, and the end of the target behavior. In a variation of latency recording, instead of recording the time it takes to begin the requested behavior, the observer can record the time between the initial request and the completion of the behavior (Alessi & Kaye, 1983).

▶ What other assessment questions might be answered by using a latency recording?

Interval Recording

Interval recording is an observational method that involves the recording of specific events or behaviors during a prespecified time interval. Interval recording is effective for behaviors that are visible and occur frequently. The period of observation is divided into equal time segments, and in each time slot the observer records the presence or absence of the behavior. Generally, the length of the time interval ranges from 5 seconds to 30 seconds. During each interval the observer records whether the behavior has occurred. The observer proceeds from one interval to the next until the end of the observation period.

An easy way to set up interval recording is to indicate time intervals on graph paper. For example, intervals of 30 seconds each can be drawn on graph paper using a ruler. If the observer will be watching for 10 minutes, there will be twenty 30-second intervals; for a 20-minute observation period, there will be forty 30-second intervals.

Generally, educators should use a combination of interval and event recording for behaviors that occur frequently. Let's examine why a teacher might select this method. The top section of Figure 5.6 illustrates an interval-event recording during fifteen 1-minute time intervals to collect information about a student's disruptive behavior, defined as "poking others with a pencil, name-calling, and swearing." Here the educator recorded the number of disruptive behaviors (events) that the target student, Sheena, and a typical student, Angela, displayed during each minute (interval) of the 15-minute observation period. The bottom section of Figure 5.6 shows the same information scored as an interval-only recording. By looking at both of these recordings one can see that interval-only scoring does not provide information about the increase in disruptive behaviors during the latter part of the observation period—only the presence of the behavior. By examining the interval-event recording, one can see a sudden increase in the behaviors after 9 minutes. Likewise, the interval-only recording is not as

One-Minute Intervals																Total number of disruptive behaviors during observation period
Student	1	2	3	4	5	6	7	8	9	10	11	12	13	14	15	
Sheena	0	0	//	/	///	/	/	/	//	////	////	///	////	////	///	33
Angela	0	0	0	0	0	0	/	0	0	0	/	0	/	0	/	4

One-minute interval-event recording

One-Minute Intervals																Percent of intervals in which disruptive behaviors were observed
Student	1	2	3	4	5	6	7	8	9	10	11	12	13	14	15	
Sheena	0	0	X	X	X	X	X	X	X	X	X	X	X	X	X	87%
Angela	0	0	0	0	0	0	X	0	0	0	X	0	X	0	X	27%

One-minute interval recording

FIGURE 5.6 ● A Comparison of the Sensitivity of Interval-Event and Interval-Only Recording

▶ How might the teacher use information from an interval-event recording?

sensitive to the difference between the two students. In minutes 7, 11, 13, and 15, both students participated in disruptive behavior, but by examining the interval-event scoring, one can see that the target student's disruptive behavior was more frequent during each of these time intervals than the typical student.

Establishing a Recording Interval

Sometimes it is difficult for the observer to continue to observe while recording. Proceeding from one interval to the next can be especially demanding when the observation interval is very brief, the behavior to be observed is complex, or the observer is recording the behaviors of a number of students. To help alleviate this problem, the observer can establish a recording interval. With this technique, the student is observed for a time interval, such as 30 seconds, and then the observer records the data during the next 30-second time interval. The observer then proceeds from one interval to the next, observing, recording, observing, and so on. This type of recording can be helpful in comparing the behavior of students like Maria, who displays hyperactive behavior, with two of her fellow students (see Figure 5.7; Snapshot: Maria).

▶ How would you interpret this data?

Category Recording

Category recording is a system of recording behavior in discrete groupings. Figure 5.8 on page 84 shows two different observation instruments that use category recording. Category recording can be as simple as two categories (e.g., on-task and off-task) or complex enough to contain many categories (e.g., uses words to express needs, raises hand to signal teacher for help, regards speaker, complies with requests). As with other types of observations, the behaviors must be discrete, be carefully defined, and have an observable beginning and end.

SNAPSHOT
Maria

Maria's teacher, Mr. Ramsdell, feels that she is hyperactive and is unable to attend in the classroom. He discusses his concerns with the special education teacher, who team teaches with him several mornings a week. They decide to plan and conduct several observations of Maria and two other students who were selected because Mr. Ramsdell identified them as typical students. The purpose of the observation is to provide a brief picture of Maria's behavior compared to other students in her classroom and to answer questions regarding her hyperactivity. The teachers decided that because the observation would focus on several students, a recording interval form (Figure 5.7) should be used to allow the observer time to record multiple data.

One-Minute Intervals										
	:00	:30	1:00	1:30	2:00	2:30	3:00	3:30	4:00	4:30
Student	O	R	O	R	O	R	O	R	O	R
Anna		×		×		×		×		
Maria				×		×				
Nan		×				×				×

O = Observe   R = record data

FIGURE 5.7 • Comparison of On-Task Behavior (First 5 Minutes of a 20-Minute Recording Interval Form)

Rating Scales

Rating scales can help to evaluate the quality of the behavior of one student or many students. In other words, **rating scales** measure the degree to which a student exhibits a prespecified behavior. Figure 5.9 on page 84 illustrates a teacher-developed rating scale to measure student behaviors. The teacher wished to increase reliability by using **descriptors.** Descriptors provide detailed information regarding each of the levels of the rating scale. These scales are useful when they are combined with other types of assessment, such as with data obtained from interval recording, event recording, and the results of other assessment approaches. While rating scales can be useful, they have been criticized as being impressionistic, lacking interrater reliability, and being affected by the subjectivity of the observer (Sattler, 2001).

Reducing Errors When Conducting Observations

Errors affect the accuracy of observations. Familiarity with the sources of error will help reduce the possibility of their occurrence. The following section examines typical errors when conducting observations.

▶ **CEC Common Core Knowledge and Skills.** The beginning teacher should understand the use and limitations of assessment instruments (CC8K4).

Student's name: Rebecca

	Two-Minute Intervals									
	0:00–2:00	2:00–4:00	4:00–6:00	6:00–8:00	8:00–10:00	10:00–12:00	12:00–14:00	14:00–16:00	16:00–18:00	18:00–20:00
On-task	X				X	X	X	X		
Off-task		X	X	X					X	X

Two-Category Instrument

	Two-Minute Intervals									
	0:00–2:00	2:00–4:00	4:00–6:00	6:00–8:00	8:00–10:00	10:00–12:00	12:00–14:00	14:00–16:00	16:00–18:00	18:00–20:00
Uses words to express needs	X		X				X	X		
Raises hand to signal teacher for help	X	X						X		
Regards speaker		X	X	X		X		X		
Complies with requests			X				X			

Four-Category Instrument

FIGURE 5.8 ● Category Reporting

Behavior	1	2	3	4
Student participates in small group activity.	Student regards others who are talking.	Student regards others who are talking and participates in group discussion.	Student uses materials to assist in group activity and all of #2.	Student evaluates own role in group activity and all of #3.
Student shows respect for personal boundaries.	At school, student keeps hands to self.	At school, student maintains personal space when speaking with others and keeps hands to self.	Student identifies behavior appropriate to the environmental setting (school, home, community) and all of #2.	Student displays behavior appropriate to the setting (school, home, community).

FIGURE 5.9 ● An Example of Descriptors in a Rating Scale

Planning and Conducting Student Observations

Let's visit with Rebecca's team as they plan several classroom observations. First, they discuss the purpose of the observation while one member records the information:

> Rebecca is a 17-year-old student who attends the Life Skills Program at Central High School. One of her IEP goals focuses on increasing prosocial behavior skills. The purpose of the observation is to collect information regarding the IEP goals in preparation for the annual review.

Team members begin by identifying some of the prosocial skills she has been learning. They note that one impediment has been Rebecca's angry outbursts. The team asks the special education teacher if she could observe Rebecca's angry outbursts. "What do you mean by 'angry outbursts'?", one member asked. The team works on the definition until they decide on: Angry behavior is defined by screeching and screaming as well as hitting other students.

"But let's not get sidetracked," interjected the special educator, "We want to focus on the prosocial skills that Rebecca is developing and look for ways that she can increase these skills. After some discussion, the team agrees. The member who was taking notes wrote:

> Rebecca's behavior to be observed includes prosocial skills such as using eye contact, greeting others, listening when other students are talking, and offering to help.

Next they discussed where the observations will occur. Observations of the student may take place in any number of settings. They decided that the observations of Rebecca will be conducted in the classroom and in the cafeteria. Some of the details that they hope to include are:

- The arrangement of tables
- The types of assistance from other students
- The types of assistance from teachers or cafeteria monitors
- The methods Rebecca uses to approach other students
- The initiations of other students talking to Rebecca

Next the team discussed the method of recording behavior. They knew that a direct observation such as this example may focus on the target student or on the target student interacting with other students. Several observations are necessary to ensure consistency or reliability of results. After completing each observation, they wanted to obtain feedback from the classroom teacher. "How typical was today's class?" "In what ways was it different?"

Finally, they discussed who would conduct the observations and write the report, integrating the results with other information about the student.

> ▶ What method of recording do you think the team chose? Provide a rationale for your answer. Use the information in Table 5.1 on page 74 to help you.

Errors of Omission

To leave out information that is helpful or important to understanding a student's behavior is an **error of omission.** Adding comments that provide a more complete picture of the observation is helpful in preventing errors of omission.

Consider the Snapshot of Jon. The teacher could record this observation in terms of the number of minutes that Jon was in the cafeteria before he began the self-abusive behavior (that is, latency recording), or the teacher could record the magnitude or degree of the behavior (intensity recording). However, these recordings would be incomplete. One important event has been omitted; namely, what happened when the student joined Jon. The question remains, "Did he affect Jon's behavior?"

SNAPSHOT
Observations of Jon

Jon is a 10-year-old student with autism. He has a number of self-abusive behaviors, including biting his wrists and banging his head. His teacher, concerned that the incidence of these behaviors is increasing, decided to conduct a series of classroom observations. The first observation was conducted during lunch in the cafeteria. Jon was observed as he entered the cafeteria and chose a seat at one of the tables. Another student sat down beside him at the table. Jon quickly opened his lunchbox and began eating while the observer was momentarily distracted when two students briefly obstructed the view. Jon began to slap his head with his hand, and the behavior escalated until the teacher assistant noticed the self-abuse and went over to speak to Jon.

Missing part of the sequence of events, even by a temporary distraction, jeopardizes the accuracy of an observation. In this case, the student who joined Jon may have sat too close or acted in a way that disturbed Jon. Perhaps Jon's abusive behavior was a communication attempt in response to the other student. Errors of omission can result from simply missing behaviors that occur.

Errors of Commission

Including information that did not actually occur is an **error of commission.** Errors of commission frequently occur when the observer is not able to take complete notes during the observation but must rely on memory to record the information at a later time.

Errors of Transmission

An **error of transmission** occurs when observers record behaviors in an improper sequence. Since many behaviors relate to each other and the order in which they occur is important, make precautions to guard against this type of error. Recording the time at which you observe a particular behavior or recording the number of times that a particular behavior begins or ends can reduce errors of transmission.

Observer Drift

Observer drift occurs when the observer shifts away from the original objectives of the observation. Usually, the observer is not aware of this alteration. To prevent this phenomenon from occurring, the observer needs to periodically check the established purposes and criteria for conducting the observation.

Predetermined Expectations

Bias can occur if the observer has a **predetermined expectation** about the observation. For example, if an observer knows that the target student has been referred for aggressive behavior, expectations of this behavior may influence the observation.

Student and Setting Characteristics

Certain characteristics of the student and the setting can influence the accuracy of an observation. The gender of the student, the complexity of the behaviors under observation, the predictability of the student's behaviors, and the observer's familiarity with the setting can all affect accuracy.

Thus, many different types of errors affect the accuracy of observations. To minimize these threats, Repp et al. (1988) recommend that:

1. Observers be well trained.
2. Observers use uncomplicated codes to record observations.
3. Both male and female observers conduct observations.
4. Observers avoid interaction with one another during the observation.
5. Observers check the accuracy of observations against a criterion.
6. Both observers and students have a period of time in which they can adapt to each other.
7. Observers conduct observations as unobtrusively as possible.
8. Teachers and other professionals conduct observations frequently and systematically.

Understanding More about Reliability

Reliability is an important concern when discussing direct observations. Reliability is the consistency or stability of the observations. We would hope that the behaviors observed are representative of the student.

Reliability of our observations can be compromised when conditions change because we are observing. **Reactivity** refers to the adjustments that individuals make in behaviors during an observation. Teachers may alter their instructions, give additional prompts, or increase the amount of feedback when someone is observing them. Students may improve behavior because of the "visitor," or they put on a good "show." These changes in behavior are threats to the accuracy of an observation. The use of videotapes and audiotapes also increases reactivity.

One type of reliability that is important in assuring accurate observations is interobserver reliability. Perhaps from our discussion in Chapter 3 you recall that interobserver reliability is the extent to which two or more observers agree on a student's score (in this case, student's behavior observed). Several factors can affect the accuracy of any one observer. These include observer drift, reliability checks, observer expectancy, the characteristics of the student, and the setting, discussed in the previous section.

Reliability Checks

The conduct of reliability checks can also affect the accuracy of observations. If an observer is aware that the accuracy of an observation is being monitored, the observer may change the usual methods of conducting the observation. Reliability of observations tends to increase when an observer is aware that someone is checking the observations.

Calculating Interobserver Reliability

There are several ways of determining reliability of observations (Alessi & Kaye, 1983; Frick & Semmel, 1978). To calculate reliability, it is important that (1) observers collect all data independently, (2) at least two observers conduct observations, and (3) the observers look at the same phenomenon.

Reliability of Event Recording

One way of determining interobserver reliability for event recording is to determine the percentage of agreements between the observers (Alessi & Kaye, 1983). The following formula can be used:

$$r = \frac{a}{a + d} \times 100$$

The number of times that the observers agreed with each other (a) is divided by the total number of times that the observers agreed (a) and disagreed (d) with each other. This number is then multiplied by 100 to give the percentage of agreements between the observers. For example, suppose two observers were using event recording to observe the number of times a student interrupted other students. The observers agreed 10 times and disagreed 4 times. Using the formula:

$$a = 10; d = 4$$

$$r = \frac{10}{10 + 4} \times 100$$

$$r = \frac{10}{14} \times 100$$

$$r = 71\%$$

▶ What would the percentage of agreement be if two observers agree 5 times and disagree 10 times?

Thus, the percentage of agreement between the observers in this example is 71 percent.

Understanding More about Validity

The validity of observational measures is a very important concern. Validity is the extent to which an instrument measures what it is intended to measure. Validity standards depend on the observability of behaviors, the objectivity of the instrument, observer variability, and the representativeness by instrument items of the behaviors that are observed (Herbert & Attridge, 1975). While there is some evidence of validity for some observational instruments, the validity of many instruments is either unsubstantiated or questionable. Hoge (1985), believes that instruments that broadly define behavior (e.g., on-task, off-task) are more likely to be valid than instruments that categorize behaviors into numerous subskills and categories.

Developing Informal Norms

Developing informal norms will help observers to evaluate the behavior they observe. The behavior of one or more students in the group can serve as the norm or comparison group for the student who is to be observed. In this instance, the other students in the group are known as the norm group, and the student who is to be observed is referred to as the target student. Without informal norms, it is difficult to determine if the target student's behavior is atypical or abnormal.

There are three ways to develop informal norms. The first is to take several students or a group of students as the norm sample and to use the scan-check method. The observer scans the sample group of students for several seconds over the observation period and counts the number of students who are exhibiting the behavior under observation. For example, every other minute an observer scans the target student and a group of ten students for 5 seconds and counts both the target student and the number of students in the group who are on-task. After this scan-check, the observer can watch the target student for the next 60-second period to see whether the student is on-task. Figure 5.10 is an example of the scan-method.

The second method of establishing an informal norm sample is to ask the teacher to identify a student whose behavior is typical or representative of the behavior of the students in the group. By watching the behavior of the typical student, the observer can use the scan-check method to compare the typical student's behavior with that of the target student.

A third way to develop an informal norm is to compare several observations of the behavior of the target student that were conducted during separate observation periods. In this way, the behavior of the target student is compared with previous observations of the same behavior (Alessi, 1980; Sattler, 2001).

▶ CEC Common Core Knowledge and Skills. The beginning special educator should know how to implement procedures for assessing and reporting both appropriate and problematic social behaviors of individuals with disabilities (GC8S1).

▶ CEC Common Core Knowledge and Skills. The beginning special educator should know how to monitor intragroup behavior changes across subjects and activities (GC8S5).

Observing the Classroom Environment

Teachers assess the needs of individual students within the context of the classroom environment. What can I do to help Timmy, a student with disabilities, feel a part of our classroom? How can we assist Boyanna in becoming more independent? The interaction of student learning and behavior is complex. The classroom environment can affect learning and behavior adversely, or the environment can be structured to promote positive behaviors, enhance positive conduct, and build self-esteem.

Well-structured environments provide the greatest access for students both with and without disabilities. Universal design in education is a concept that describes how students with a wide range of abilities can have meaningful access and participation in the

Student: Ben   **Observer:** D. Southard

Age: 10–8   **Date:** November 12

School: North   **Teacher:** Blesson

Reason for Observation: To determine the extent that Ben's behaviors differ from his peers

Activity Observed: Social studies class

Observation Technique Used: Interval recording, 1 min. intervals

Behavior Codes		Grouping Codes		Teacher and Peer Reaction Codes	
T	On-task	L	Large group	AA	Attention to all
O	Off-task	S	Small group	A+	Positive attention to target student
		O	One-to-one	A–	Negative attention to target student
				NA	No attention to target student

Time	Target Student Behavior	Percent of Students Engaged in On-Task Behavior during Group Scan	Anecdotal Notes	Group	Teacher	Peer
9:15	O			L	NA	NA
9:16	O	80%	making faces	L	A–	A+
9:17	O		making faces	L	A–	A+
9:18	T	70%		L	NA	NA
9:19	T		plays with pencil	L	NA	NA
9:20	T	80%		L	NA	NA
9:21	T		teacher praise	L	A+	NA
9:22	O	90%	pokes student in front	L	AA	NT
9:23	O		argues with student	L	A–	A+
9:24	O	80%	argues with teacher	L	A–	A+
TOTAL	4 /10					
Percent of time	40%	80%				

FIGURE 5.10 • Scan-Check Recording Sheet

general education curriculum. Universal design involves flexibility of materials, strategies, approaches, and technology. Educators in classrooms that embody universal design encourage students to use multiple ways of learning and demonstrating knowledge.

Three aspects of the classroom environment affect the student's learning and behavior: the physical environment, the learning or instructional environment, and the social environment. Checklists and classroom sketches are the most common ways of gathering information about the classroom environment. The following sections examine teacher-constructed tools for observing these three aspects of the classroom environment.

▶ **CEC Common Core Knowledge and Skills.** The beginning special educator should know how to gather relevant background information (CC8S1).

How It Works! Using Observation Skills

Timmy B. is an active 8-year-old boy who has been referred to the Student Assistance Team. His teacher is concerned about Timmy's lack of attention and engagement in the classroom. During the team meeting, members decided that they needed additional information about Timmy's functioning to determine how much he participates in classroom activities. Observing Timmy's performance during instructional time would provide information about his engagement during more focused activities and assist in planning intervention strategies.

Working together, the special educator and regular educator defined "engagement" as "looking at the speaker (teacher or other student), following directions, and using materials to complete assignments." Next they refined the observation question: "What percentage of time does Timmy spend appropriately engaged (e.g., listening, looking at the speaker, following directions, and using materials to complete assignments) in activities as compared to the typical student?"

The special educator completed two 20-minute classroom observations on October 3rd and October 10th. Using an interval recording, she recorded either the presence (X) or absence (0) of engaged behavior for both Timmy and the typical student at the beginning of each 2-minute interval. The data sheets are illustrated below.

OBSERVATION RESULTS: Timmy was observed for two 20-minute periods on two consecutive Mondays. During the first observation, he was observed during the introduction of new spelling words and an assignment that followed. The second observation included a writing activity that students were to complete independently in their writing notebooks. There were 18 students present during each of the observations, the classroom teacher, and classroom aide.

SUMMARY OF THE RESULTS: Timmy was engaged 40 percent of the time during the first observation and 40 percent of the time during the second observation. The comparison student was engaged 80 percent and 70 percent respectively. Both students were engaged at the beginning but Timmy quickly became disengaged. During both observations his complaining distracted the comparison student.

> ▶ What other information about Timmy and the teacher can you gather by studying the observation data sheets?

October 3 Interval Recording Data on Timmy Language Arts/Spelling

2-minute time intervals	Timmy	Comparison Student	Observer Comments
1:00	X	X	Teacher introduces spelling words.
1:02	X	X	
1:04	X	X	
1:06	0	X	Timmy crumples his paper and tears off small pieces, throwing them on the floor.
1:08	0	0	Timmy distracts other students by loud whispering while doodling on his desk with a pencil.
1:10	0	0	Timmy continues to distract other students with whispering and low-pitched noises. Teacher is helping other students.
1:12	X	X	Teacher hands Timmy new piece of paper and encourages him to write spelling words.
1:14	0	X	Timmy whispers loudly and makes faces.
1:16	0	X	Continues to complain.
1:18	0	X	Teacher assistant moves to Timmy.
Total	4 out of 10	8 out of 10	
Percent	40% engagement	80% engagement	

October 10   Interval Recording Data on Timmy   Language Arts/Spelling

2-minute time intervals	Timmy	Comparison Student	Observer Comments
1:00	X	X	Teacher asks students to get their writing notebooks.
1:02	0	X	All students but Timmy have retrieved their notebooks from the literacy shelf.
1:04	0	X	Timmy is still looking for his notebook and starts to speak to himself in an audible whisper.
1:06	X	X	Teacher tries to help find the notebook. Both Timmy and the teacher search the shelves.
1:08	0	X	Teacher locates notebook inside Timmy's desk.
1:10	0	0	Timmy distracts other students by scraping his chair on the floor then throws a small piece of paper at another student and says the student's name.
1:12	X	X	Teacher hands Timmy a pencil and encourages him by telling him she enjoyed his last entry in the journal. Timmy starts on the assignment.
1:14	0	X	Timmy breaks pencil (on purpose?) by snapping it over his knee. He plays with the broken pieces.
1:16	0	0	Distracts other students as he complains about the assignment. He avoids the teacher's looks.
1:18	X	X	Teacher helps Timmy write one idea in his notebook by helping him formulate his thoughts.
Total	4 out of 10	7 out of 10	
Percent	40% engagement	70% engagement	

INTERPRETATIONS AND RECOMMENDATIONS: These results reinforce the initial impression that Timmy is not engaging in activities at the level that might be considered typical in this classroom. The comparison student and Timmy both disengaged at similar points, but the comparison student reengaged more often and more quickly during these observations.

Timmy appears to be easily frustrated when completing written assignments. His lack of organization interferes with his work. Yet, he is able to refocus with adult support.

▶ Do you agree with special educator's interpretation of the data? Share your ideas.

This data suggest that the classroom teacher should:

1. Work with Timmy to find an appropriate place for his books and pencils and label them. Ensure that Timmy puts away materials in the same place every day.
2. Develop and review Timmy's daily schedule with him. Prepare him for transitions.
3. Assure that Timmy has little "down time" since he responds to structured, directed assignments.
4. Keep extra pencils and other consumable materials available for Timmy and other students.
5. Provide adult support before Timmy becomes frustrated. For example, the teacher could ask the classroom aide to monitor Timmy's behavior at the beginning of a new activity and provide support so that he can start and complete the activity successfully. During assignments, the teacher should monitor Timmy's independent work and provide direction at the first indication of frustration.
6. Seat Timmy near the teacher because he responds to prompts and praise.
7. Establish a system that reinforces positive behaviors, such as putting materials away, completing an assignment.
8. Assign tasks and activities that are at Timmy's academic level in order to reduce frustration.
9. Keep his assignments brief so that his attention can be kept focused on the assignments.

Physical Environment

▶ What other areas could you suggest that would be important in observing the physical environment?

The physical environment consists of seating arrangements, lighting, noise level, distractions, temperature, overall atmosphere, and general layout of the classroom. Some of the areas to consider in planning an observation of the physical environment are illustrated in Table 5.3.

The amount and arrangement of physical space affects student functioning. For example, grouping desks in sets of three or four encourages students to discuss and share ideas. The placement of furniture, equipment, and materials is critical for students with disabilities. Furniture and adaptive equipment need to maximize the student's potential

TABLE 5.3 ● Observing the Physical Environment	
Suggested Areas to Observe	**Assessment Questions**
1. Seating	• **positioning** Do the height and size of the chair give the student proper support? Are the student's feet supported (either resting flat on the floor or supported by a footrest)? Is the student seated in close proximity to other students?
2. Lighting	• **lighting intensity** Is the degree of lighting appropriate? Is the board or screen free from glare that might make reading difficult?
3. Noise	• **minimum noise level** Is the noise level of student work groups appropriate?
4. Distractions	• **sight** Does the room have displays that are visually distracting? • **sound** Is there noise distraction (such as a clock ticking or a radiator pinging)? • **events and activities** Are there activities in the room that are distracting to the student?
5. Climate	• **temperature** Is the temperature level of the classroom comfortable?
6. Classroom	• **atmosphere** Is the classroom atmosphere warm and accepting?
7. General layout	• **layout of the room; type and placement of furniture, equipment, and materials** Are all areas of the classroom accessible to the student? Are classroom materials accessible to the student? • **amount and type of space** Is there enough space to meet the student's needs? Is there an accessible place to store adapted materials and equipment? Can the student easily move between areas of the room?

for independent participation. The availability of accessible space allows a student with a physical disability full classroom access. Differences in texture or color of carpet between centers enable a student who is blind or has multiple disabilities to increase orientation and independent travel (mobility) skills. An organized environment helps all students learn appropriate storage of materials. Accessible storage of materials assists students with disabilities in locating and using materials independently.

Figure 5.11 illustrates a teacher-made classroom sketch that provided information about the physical layout of a kindergarten classroom. The drawing helped the teaching team to think about the classroom layout and how they might improve learning

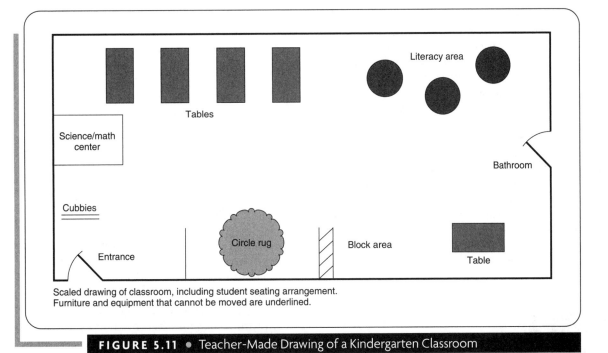

Scaled drawing of classroom, including student seating arrangement.
Furniture and equipment that cannot be moved are underlined.

FIGURE 5.11 • Teacher-Made Drawing of a Kindergarten Classroom

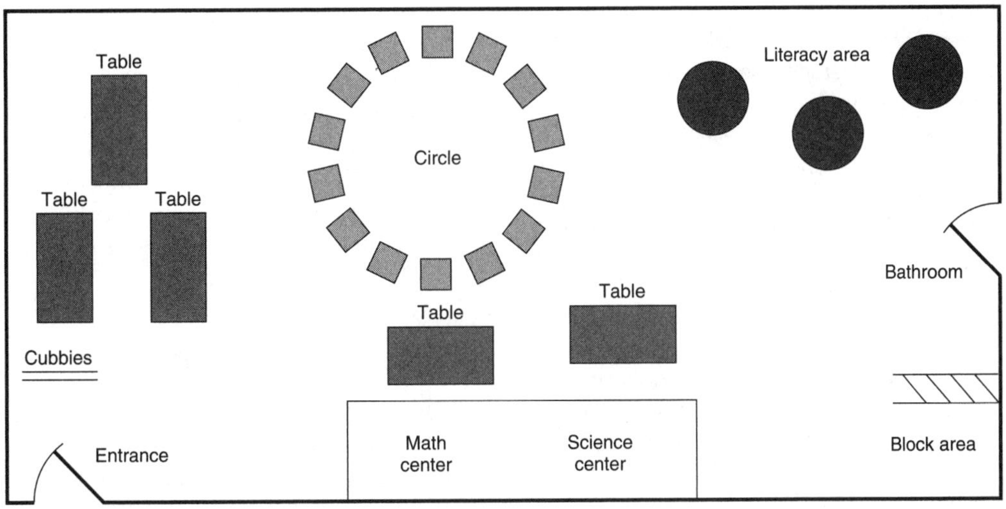

Scaled drawing of classroom, including student seating arrangement.
Furniture and equipment that cannot be moved are underlined.

FIGURE 5.12 • Rearranged Physical Environment

opportunities. The teachers decided to try moving the science and mathematics center closer to the block area to allow children to use the blocks in various mathematics and science activities. The teachers also discussed how the location of adjacent areas contributed to difficulties that they had experienced during circle time. They decided to move the circle area away from the block area, which was distracting to two students. They changed the center of the room to accommodate space for circle activities and added individual carpet squares to the area to help children understand individual space and reduce the likelihood of disruptive behavior. Figure 5.12 represents the rearranged environment.

SNAPSHOT

Stoney Brook Elementary Learning Environments

Stoney Brook Elementary School has three fourth-grade classrooms. The school district has adopted the state curriculum framework for English language arts and, among other areas, all fourth graders must demonstrate competency in researching and writing a paper about a topic of their interest. The fourth-grade teachers approach the teaching of skills in researching information in different ways. In one classroom, the teacher invites an author to come in and talk with students. The author shares resource materials and shows how his or her information was researched. The author's enthusiasm for writing sparks the children's interest. In a second classroom, the teacher makes arrangements to take the students to the library, where the school librarian gives them a tour of the library's resources and discusses ways to find information in the online catalogue. Later, the children will be divided into small work groups and return to the library to use the materials. In the third classroom, the children already use the computer daily to search and download information from the Internet. Their teacher will encourage them to use their skills independently in locating information for their individual papers.

SNAPSHOT

Lincoln High Learning Environments

The English teachers at Lincoln High use the state curriculum framework for secondary English language arts and approach student learning in different ways, use a variety of teaching strategies in the classroom, and hold different expectations for student achievement. Let's visit two classrooms to see what students experience.

In the first classroom, the teacher plans learning activities around projects that last from a few weeks to several months. Computers are available for student writing and editing, including word processing programs with word prediction features. The teacher encourages students to work together in small groups and plans conference meetings with individual students several times a week to monitor student progress.

Next door, the teacher relies primarily on the textbook to provide the curriculum content. Students complete daily assignments from textbook readings. Each class begins with a lecture that reviews the previous reading and provides some supplemental information. The teacher requires students to take notes. The teacher assesses student learning by short-answer tests that cover the textbook and classroom lectures.

> ▶ After reading about both of these schools, develop one or more assessment questions about these learning environments. Next, carefully review the teacher-made checklist (Table 5.4). Would this checklist help you gather information to answer your assessment question? What other area(s) could you suggest adding?

Learning Environment

What are the expectations of the classroom? How can the classroom be adapted to accommodate the student's learning needs? The learning or instructional environment consists of the teaching strategies that the teacher uses and the materials that are available for student use. Observing the learning environment involves examining the instructional materials as well as the methods of instruction. Table 5.4 illustrates some of the areas to consider in planning an observation of the learning environment.

Teacher expectations, teaching methods, and student requirements may be very different from one classroom to the next. These differences vary from the materials and equipment that are available to assist students in their work, to teaching methods that may require different skills from the students.

The classroom examples in the Snapshots of Stoney Brook Elementary and Lincoln High illustrate the variety of teaching methods, materials, and demands that students may encounter in the same grade. Students with disabilities at Stoney Brook or Lincoln High may experience difficulties in one or more of these classrooms.

Social Environment

The social environment consists of the general classroom atmosphere as well as the relationships among students and between students and teachers. Positive social environments assist students in managing frustrations, resolving conflicts, and developing respect and appreciation for individual differences. Teachers who foster positive social environments have

TABLE 5.4 • Observing the Learning Environment

Suggested Areas to Observe	Assessment Questions
1. Materials	• **variety** Do students have access to a variety of materials? • **format** Is the format of materials appropriate?
2. Manipulatives	• **availability and appropriateness** Are appropriate manipulatives available?
3. Learning Activities	• **instructional methods** Does the teacher use a variety of instructional methods? • **opportunities to make choices** Does the classroom teacher provide students opportunities to make choices during learning activities? • **opportunities to share ideas** Are student comments and questions respected and encouraged?
4. Instructional Demands	• **clear instructions for completing the assignments** Does the teacher provide clear instructions and check for student understanding before students begin learning activities and assignments? • **assignments that are appropriate in difficulty and in length** Are students assigned work that is appropriate in difficulty and length? • **learning activities and assignments that are relevant to the students** Do students perceive that the work is useful? Can students use a variety of materials?
5. Modifications	• **changes in furniture, equipment, or materials** Is there easy and convenient access to furniture and equipment? Can students use the materials or is there a need for accommodations or modifications?
6. Grouping	• **grouping of students** Do students complete some work independently? Can students work with a peer? Do students have opportunities to work cooperatively with others?
7. Instruction	• **adjustments** Are the instructional strategies appropriate or is there a need for revision? Is there a variety of instructional methods in use? • **pace of instruction** Is the pace of instructional delivery appropriate?

(continued)

Suggested Areas to Observe	Assessment Questions

TABLE 5.4 ● Continued

	• adequate levels of assistance Does the teacher (or teaching assistant) provide prompts and other types of assistance on an as-needed basis to students? Is assistance faded as soon as possible?
8. Expectations	• demands placed on students Are the teacher's expectations appropriate?
9. Student involvement	• teacher support Does the teacher encourage student involvement? Is the student actively involved in learning activities? Does the student participate in classroom discussions? • peer support Do other students interact with the student? Does the student interact with other students?
10. Assessment	• tools Does the teacher use a variety of assessment approaches in assessing student instructional needs and progress? • format If appropriate, does the teacher implement alternative formats? • feedback Does the teacher give students feedback and suggestions for improvement?
11. Curriculum	• curriculum reform and standards Does the curriculum reflect recent reform, standards, and contemporary views?
12. Schedule	• predictability of the daily schedule Does the classroom teacher follow a regular schedule? Is the schedule posted for students to see? Is there a minimum of interruptions?
13. Transitions	• preparation and follow-through Does the teacher prepare students for the transition from one activity to another? Does the teacher provide time for students to transition?

zero tolerance for bullying behaviors, which continue to plague many of our schools. According to a survey of over 2,000 eighth to eleventh graders (American Association of University Women, 2001), one student in five fears being hurt or bullied in school. Some of the areas to consider when assessing the social environment are illustrated in Table 5.5.

TABLE 5.5 ● Observing the Social Environment	
Suggested Areas to Observe	**Assessment Questions**
1. Teacher- student interactions	● **respect for oneself and others** Are all students valued for themselves? Does the teacher expect students to respect others? ● **supportive social environment** Does the teacher know how to communicate with students with disabilities? ● **interactions** Are interactions warm and friendly? Does the teacher encourage students to interact appropriately with the teacher? ● **behavior management** Are behavior management strategies effective? Are expectations of behavior posted?
2. Behavioral interventions	● **positive behavioral supports** Does the teacher use positive teaching strategies in helping students learn appropriate behavioral expectations? ● **behavior management** Are behavior management strategies effective? Are expectations of behavior posted in the classroom?
3. Peer interactions	● **student-to-student interactions** Do students know how to communicate with students with disabilities? Do students interact appropriately with each other? Are students courteous, respectful, and supportive of learning?
4. General atmosphere	● **positive classroom climate** Does the teacher have high expectations for all students? Is there an atmosphere of enthusiasm and support for students? Does the student appear to be comfortable in the social environment? ● **distractions** Are distractions kept to a minimum?

Other Informal Assessment Approaches

Checklists

A **checklist** consists of a number of characteristics or behaviors arranged in a consistent manner that allows the evaluator to check the presence or absence of the characteristic or behavior. While rating scales help to evaluate the degree or frequency of an item or a behavior, checklists usually require a simple yes or no response.

Some checklists provide space for comments or descriptions. Checklists are fairly easy to develop. The following guidelines are helpful when developing checklists (Beaty, 2002; Gronlund & Linn, 2000):

1. Checklist items should be brief, yet detailed and easily understood.
2. Word construction must be parallel. That is, the word order, subject, and verb tense should be the same for all items.
3. The items are nonjudgmental.
4. Provide a procedure for indicating the presence or absence of each item.

After carefully considering the areas to observe in the classroom environment, one special educator developed a checklist that included many of the areas that we have just discussed. In addition to each of the areas, she also included space for observer comments because sometimes observers find information that should be noted that is not on the form. Table 5.6 illustrates this checklist.

Interviews

Interviewing students, parents, colleagues, or other professionals is another approach that helps in answering assessment questions. The interview allows a face-to-face meeting in which participants discuss and share their individual perspectives.

Interviewing consists of asking the right questions and listening carefully to what the other person is saying. This skill demands that you know yourself and not let your own biases overshadow what is being told to you. If you use this technique, you must want to hear what the other person is saying. Being a good listener is a complex skill that calls for sensitivity and respect for others. Skillful interviewing requires training and practice.

The interview makes certain assumptions about the give and take of the communication process between individuals. Professionals need to be sensitive to assumptions that members of the dominant group hold about this communication process; these assumptions may not be the same for members of less dominant groups.

An interview usually follows a series of steps, beginning with planning the interview. The special educator contacts the individual and states the purpose of the meeting. The purpose may be to follow up on a student referral: "I'd like to sit down and talk further about your concerns about Sharda." The special educator suggests they find a convenient time and meeting place: "Do you have some time in the next few days that we could meet?" Since information shared during the interview may be confidential in nature, take care to arrange a meeting place that can ensure confidentiality. Locations that are public gathering spots, such as the cafeteria or teachers' lounge, are not appropriate.

Beginning the interview involves establishing rapport with the individual. Some interviewers spend a few minutes talking about a shared activity of mutual interest before sitting down to work. Acknowledge the fact that the individual has set aside time for the meeting. Begin the interview with broad questions and gradually ask more specific and focused questions (Nitko, 2001).

In conducting the interview, show a genuine interest in what the individual has to say. Create a positive tone by your respect, support, and warmth. Ask questions and rephrase statements to help clarify important points. Many professionals find it helpful to prepare a few questions in advance. As you think about the types of questions that would be helpful, consider the wording of the questions and the type of answers that may result. Open-ended questions are usually more helpful. For example, ask "What have you tried to address these behavior problems?" or "What are you thinking about doing?" Too often the teacher or other professional requesting assistance receives

▶ Consider the interviews in which you have participated. What skills can you identify that were helpful during the interview process?

TABLE 5.6 ● Teacher-Made Checklist for Observing the Classroom Environment

Student's Name __Joe_____   Date __10/19___   Time __9:15_____

Observer __Mr. T._____   Location __classroom_____

Physical environment	Always	Sometimes	Never
1. **Seating** Is the student seated properly?	X		

Suggestions for improvement:

2. **Lighting** Is the lighting appropriate?	X		

Suggestions for improvement:

3. **Noise** Is the noise level appropriate?		X	

Suggestions for improvement: When group activities are underway, the noise level of the classroom tends to rise. Teacher should monitor.

4. **Distractions** Is the student distracted by activities in the room?		X	

Suggestions for improvement: Joe should be seated in an area away from the door where distractions will be minimized.

5. **Temperature** Is the temperature of the room appropriate?	X		

Suggestions for improvement:

6. **General Atmosphere** Does the student appear to be comfortable in the environment?		X	

Suggestions for improvement:

(continued)

TABLE 5.6 • Continued

Learning environment	Always	Sometimes	Never
1. **Materials** Are a variety of reading materials available?	X		

Suggestions for improvement: All materials should be provided in both text and digital formats.

2. **Curriculum** Does the reading/writing curriculum reflect contemporary views of reading and writing?	X		

Suggestions for improvement:

3. **Activities** Is instruction oriented toward the use of various reading and writing materials?	X		

Suggestions for improvement:

4. **Instructional Demands** Are the instructional demands appropriate for the student?		X	

Suggestions for improvement: Although Joe has difficulty blending sounds together to form words, he is capable of keeping up with his peers. Instructional demands should be appropriate in keeping with his abilities.

5. **Modifications** Have modifications been made to instruction to accommodate the learning needs of the student?		X	

Suggestions for improvement:

6. **Assessment** Are a variety of assessment tools used to provide feedback to the student? Is information collected on the student's progress and performance?	X		

Suggestions for improvement:

TABLE 5.6 • Continued

Learning environment	Always	Sometimes	Never
7. **Materials**			
If grouping is used, is it appropriate?		X	

Suggestions for improvement: *Joe should be grouped with students who can actively engage Joe in group discussions during projects.*

	Always	Sometimes	Never
8. **Curriculum**			
Are teacher expectations appropriate?		X	

Suggestions for improvement: *Teacher expectations should be high. Although it may take Joe longer to complete assignments, he is able to achieve at a high level.*

	Always	Sometimes	Never
9. **Activities**			
Is the student actively involved in reading and writing activities?	X		

Suggestions for improvement:

	Always	Sometimes	Never
10. **Instruction**			
Is instruction matched to the assessed needs of the student? Are a variety of instructional methods used?	X		

Suggestions for improvement:

	Always	Sometimes	Never
11. **Pace of instruction**			
Is the pace of instruction appropriate?	X		

Suggestions for improvement:

	Always	Sometimes	Never
12. **Schedule**			
Is the student's schedule appropriate?		X	

Suggestions for improvement: *Joe may need a longer time than his peers to change classrooms.*

	Always	Sometimes	Never
13. **Transitions**			
Are transitions made smoothly?		X	

Suggestions for improvement: *Planning for transitions should occur. Joe may need extra time to take out and put away materials.*

(continued)

TABLE 5.6 • Continued

Social environment	Always	Sometimes	Never
1. **Teacher-Student Interactions** Are interactions warm and friendly?	X		

Suggestions for improvement:

Social environment	Always	Sometimes	Never
2. **Disruptions** Are disruptions kept to a minimum?	X		

Suggestions for improvement:

Social environment	Always	Sometimes	Never
3. **Behavioral interventions** Are behavioral interventions effective and appropriate?	X		

Suggestions for improvement:

Social environment	Always	Sometimes	Never
4. **Peer interactions** Are peer interactions appropriate?		X	

Suggestions for improvement: Due to Joe's reading difficulties, he is reluctant to initiate peer interactions. A circle of friends should be convened.

Social environment	Always	Sometimes	Never
5. **General Atmosphere** Does the student appear to be comfortable in the social environment?		X	

Suggestions for improvement: Some students seem to be uncomfortable with Joe. With his permission, the teacher could be asked to explain Joe's disabilities to the students. Joe can also be encouraged to share his feelings with the students.

questions in the form "Have you tried to address this problem by _____?" This line of questioning may produce single-word responses and a sense of frustration. Listen not only to hear but to understand what the individual is saying. Generally, interviews should not exceed an hour in length. Conclude the interview by summarizing the discussion.

Interviews with students are helpful both when students are having academic difficulties and when students are doing well. The interview provides information about a student's perspective in a wide variety of areas and is especially productive in giving insight into the student's overall patterns of behavior (Salvia & Ysseldyke, 2004) and self-concept. Student interviews are helpful in making adjustments to the class-room environment.

Interviews should be used with caution, however, as they can present difficulties for students with disabilities and for students who are English language learners. The interview technique requires skills in understanding and speaking the language of the interviewee. For example, an interviewer can inadvertently cut off students with processing difficulties, who may take longer to compose a response. Students who are not proficient in English can experience difficulty, even when a translator is present. The translator may or may not be proficient in the student's dialect, or the student may misinterpret the translation because the nuances in the language do not transfer.

Steps in Conducting Student Interviews

Merrell (2003) describes the steps in conducting a student interview:

1. Begin by asking generally for the student's reasons for having the interview. Allow time for discussion of the student's interests and attitudes.
2. Lead the discussion toward a specific probing of the problem. For example, the interviewer might ask the student to describe what happens just before the student gets involved in a fight.
3. Ask the student to describe any behavioral assets the student has.
4. Obtain the student's perspective on what positive and appropriate behaviors the student can marshal as well as a description of likes and dislikes.
5. Use this information along with other assessment information to develop a plan for addressing the problem behavior.

Questionnaires

Questionnaires consist of a set of questions designed to gather information. Educators and other professionals design questionnaires to collect various types of information and to assist in answering questions. Sometimes the use of a questionnaire is preferred over an interview or conference. For example, students who have difficulty with spoken English may be more comfortable answering a written question. Busy professionals may prefer completing information at a time that is convenient to them.

This section focuses on questionnaires developed for the purpose of gathering information about the student. For example, a special education teacher who is working with a student with problem behaviors might ask the general education teacher, parents, and others who know the student well to complete a questionnaire about the student's behavior at school, at home, and in the community.

Special educators can use questionnaires to ask students about their learning preferences. Using the information, a teacher can work towards improving the learning environment. Figure 5.13 illustrates a teacher-made questionnaire to be completed by the student. Do you think the questionnaire would provide helpful information to you, if you were the teacher?

Student Questionnaire

Name _____

Date _____

Teacher_____

Grade _____

1. What assignments have you enjoyed most so far this year? Why were they enjoyable?
2. Did you work alone or with others on these assignments?
3. How did you demonstrate what you learned?
4. If your parent or other relative were coming to school to see your work, what work would you show them?
5. What work would you probably not show them?

FIGURE 5.13 • Student Questionnaire

Research-Based Practices **Assessment Approaches**

Not only educators but professionals from other disciplines regularly use direct observations and interviews to gather information about students and their environments. For psychologists, the assessment of students with social, behavioral, and emotional disabilities has changed over the last few years. No longer do psychologists just administer intelligence tests, achievement tests, tests of perceptual-motor performance, or projective measures such as *Draw A Person*. According to a survey conducted by Shapiro and Heick (2004), over 1,000 members of the National Association of School Psychologists reported increased use of direct instruction, structured interviews, and rating scales. In fact, over 60 percent of the respondents indicated that they used these approaches frequently in addition to more traditional assessments.

Conferencing and Collaborating

Conferencing

Conferencing involves meeting with parents, teachers, therapists, or professionals in other agencies to share information, concerns, and ideas regarding common issues. Planning the conference takes some time and thought. Consider the concern and how you will describe it. Find a time and location that is convenient for each person.

During the conference, identify and clarify the situation. Describe the areas of concern: "I understand that Roberto has been having a difficult time. Could you describe what has been happening?" Ask questions or restate what has been said, if you are unsure of the issues. Determine the history and the frequency of the problem.

Generate ideas. Work together to brainstorm a list of interventions and write down each idea. Keep focused. Participants should feel that they are making progress identifying possible solutions. Make decisions by building consensus among those involved.

Develop a time line by writing down the activities and interventions that will be tried and when. Clarify the responsibilities of each member. Finally, schedule a follow-up meeting. In future meetings, share ideas of good experiences and solutions that have worked. (Adapted from Ferguson, 1994; Heward, 2001)

Collaborating

Collaborating is a more active process than simply meeting with others to discuss common issues. Collaboration involves a commitment on an individual's part to work cooperatively with others toward a common goal.

Building expertise in conferencing and collaborating begins with good interpersonal skills. Some individuals seem to have strong interpersonal skills; others need to develop and practice these faculties. Professionals improve interpersonal competence by working with others who demonstrate a strong commitment to teamwork and collaboration. Let's examine some of the characteristics of effective interpersonal skills.

- Individuals with strong interpersonal skills communicate in a positive, genuine manner.
- Interpersonal skills involve both verbal and nonverbal communication. Verbal communication refers not only to the spoken words but to the tone and pitch the speaker uses. Nonverbal communication consists of facial expression, body language, and gestures.
- Listen and hear the speaker out. Don't interrupt when a colleague is talking. Knowing all the answers is not important—or possible. Working together to create solutions is critical.

- Use everyday language and eliminate the use of jargon. The field of special education is filled with numbers and acronyms. Professionals from other disciplines may not be familiar with many of the terms that special educators use frequently.

Summary

- Through carefully planned observations, educators can gather a wealth of information about students and their environments and answer various types of assessment questions.

- Depending on the assessment question, observers use different recording methods including anecdotal records, running records, event recordings, duration recordings, intensity recordings, latency recordings, interval recordings, and category recordings.

- In conducting observations, the examiner needs to be aware of the sources of error that affect the accuracy of observations.

- Reliability refers to the consistency of observations. Observers can ensure reliability by taking steps to address factors such as observer drift, reliability checks, predetermined expectations, or student and setting characteristics.

- Validity, or the extent to which the observation measures what it is intended to measure, must be considered when planning the observation and defining the behavior.

- By using observation data, educators can develop informal norms.

- Interviewing, another assessment approach, involves the careful selection of questions and being a good listener.

- Conferencing consists of planned meetings with parents, teachers, therapists, or other professionals to share information, concerns, and ideas.

- Collaborating, a more active process than conferencing, involves commitments to work cooperatively with others toward a common goal.

Answer to Question: On p. 78 we asked if Stacy's behavior had improved after a two-month interval. The answer is:

$$\frac{15 \text{ occurrences}}{10 \text{ minutes}} = 1.5 \text{ occurrences per minute}$$

This represents an improvement.

REFERENCES

Alessi, G. J. (1980). Behavioral observation for the school psychologist: Responsive-discrepancy model. *School Psychology Review* 9: 31–45.

Alessi, G. J., & Kaye, J. H. (1983). *Behavior assessment for school psychologists.* Kent, OH: National Association of School Psychologists.

American Association of University Women (AAUW). (2001). *Hostile hallways: Bullying, teasing, and sexual harassment in school.* Washington, DC: AAUW Educational Foundation Research.

Beaty, J. J. (2002). *Observing development of the young child* (4th ed.). Upper Saddle River, NJ: Merrill.

Ferguson, D. L. (1994). Magic for teacher work groups. *Teaching Exceptional Children* 27(1): 42–47.

Frick, T., & Semmel, M. I. (1978). Observer agreement and reliabilities of classroom observational measures. *Review of Educational Research* 48: 157–184.

Gronlund, N. E., & Linn, R. L. (2000). *Measurement and assessment in teaching* (8th ed.). Upper Saddle River, NJ: Prentice-Hall.

Herbert, J., & Attridge, C. (1975). A guide for developers and users of observation systems and manuals. *American Educational Research Journal* 12: 1–20.

Heward, W. L. (2001). *Exceptional children: An introduction to special education* (6th ed.). Upper Saddle River, NJ: Prentice-Hall.

Hoge, R. D. (1985). The validity of direct observation. *Review of Educational Research* 55: 469–483.

Merrell, K. W. (2003). *Behavioral, social, and emotional assessment of children and adolescents.* Mahwah, NJ: Lawrence Erlbaum.

Nitko, A. J. (2001). *Educational assessment of students* (3rd ed.). Upper Saddle River, NJ: Prentice-Hall.

Repp, A. C., Nieminen, G. S., Olinger, E., & Brusca, R. (1988). Direct observation: Factors affecting the accuracy of observers. *Exceptional Children* 55: 29–36.

Salvia, J., & Ysseldyke, J. E. (2004). *Assessment* (9th ed.). Boston: Houghton Mifflin.

Sattler, J. (2001). *Assessment of children* (4th ed.). La Mesa, CA: Author.

Shapiro, E. S., & Heick, P. F. (2004). School psychologist assessment practices in the evaluation of students referred for social/behavioral/emotional problems. *Psychology in the Schools, 41*(5): 551–561.

Performance-Based, Authentic, and Portfolio Assessments

Chapter Objectives

After completing this chapter, you should be able to:

- Relate reasons for using alternative assessments.
- Describe performance-based assessment, authentic assessment, and portfolio assessment.
- Develop scoring rubrics.
- Develop and implement performance-based assessment approaches.

Key Terms

Performance-based assessment
Authentic assessment
Portfolio
Exhibition

Rubric
Analytic scoring
Holistic scoring

Benchmarks
Anchor papers
Consequential validity

Overview

This chapter examines alternatives to traditional assessment approaches. Each of these alternatives is evolving as we search for improved practices and tools for linking instruction with assessment. Portfolios, performance tasks, exhibitions, or other documentation of students' achievement represent students' accomplishments. While norm-referenced tests have their place in the assessment process, alternatives to norm-referenced tests provide a rich variety of methods to collect information about student progress, skills, and achievement.

Contemporary views of learning have influenced the development of alternative assessment approaches. From cognitive learning theory we know the following (Byrnes, 1996; Dixon-Krauss, 1996; Mayer, 1998):

1. Students can construct knowledge by connecting new information and prior learning. Implications for assessment:
   - Students learn divergent thinking, rather than searching for one right answer and multiple solutions.
   - Students develop multiple forms of expression.
   - Students develop critical thinking skills.
   - Students relate new information to prior knowledge.

2. Students of all ages and abilities can solve problems. Implications for assessment:
   - All students participate in problem-solving activities.
   - Problem solving and critical thinking do not have to be contingent on mastery of basic skills.
3. Students approach learning with a multiplicity of learning styles, attention spans, and developmental and cognitive differences. Implications for assessment:
   - Multiple choices in how to demonstrate what has been learned are available.
   - Teachers allot enough time to complete assessment tasks.
4. Students do better when they know the goals and understand how their performance will be evaluated. Implications for assessment:
   - Students participate in establishing goals.
   - Students can discuss and describe criteria for performance.
   - Students routinely receive examples of acceptable levels of performance.
5. Students should know when to use knowledge and how to direct their own learning. Implications for assessment:
   - Students have opportunities to monitor and evaluate their own learning.
   - Teachers utilize authentic (real-world) opportunities for assessment.
6. Students' learning is affected by motivation, effort, and self-esteem. Implications for assessment:
   - Teachers consider motivation, self-esteem, and the promotion of best efforts in designing assessments.

Performance-Based Assessment

Performance-based assessment describes one or more approaches for measuring student progress, skills, and achievements. Performance-based assessment consists of portfolios, performance tasks, exhibitions, or other documentation of student accomplishments. One way of looking at performance assessment is to think of it as the ultimate form of linking instruction with assessment. Wiggins (1993) has been a strong proponent of performance assessment. He has urged educators to use "clear, apt, published, and consistently applied teacher criteria in grading work and published models of excellent work that exemplifies standards" and create "ample opportunities [for students] to produce work that they can be proud of (thus, ample opportunity in the curriculum and instruction to monitor, self-assess, and self-correct their work)" (p. 28). Gardner (1991) has described performance-based assessments according to developmental levels.

Gardner views students as learners who are at various points in their learning. For example, some students might exhibit the performance of beginning learners, while others would demonstrate the performance of experts. Evaluations do not just have to focus on what students demonstrate about their academic or cognitive abilities but can determine the extent to which students work cooperatively, are sensitive to others, or contribute to the group.

Performance-based assessment is particularly useful when students are working on long-term projects. In this way, they are able to bring into play a variety of resources and to demonstrate mastery of various concepts and principles. Performance-based assessments relate most closely to the types of assessments that students will most likely engage in after they leave school.

For teachers of standards-based education, performance-based assessment serves several important functions (Arter & McTighe, 2001):

- Performance criteria help define the standards by specifying what one would look for as evidence of standards achievement.
- When made public, the performance criteria and scoring guides provide clear and consistent targets for students, parents, teachers, and others.

- Using performance-based assessment consistently across classrooms, schools, and districts makes the evaluation of student performance more reliable.
- Teaching criteria to students helps improve the very skills under assessment, thus integrating assessment and instruction. (pp. 15–16)

Developing Performance-Based Assessments

There are four questions that can guide us as we think about performance assessment (Diez & Moon, 1992):

1. What is important for students to know and to be able to do? This question requires us to rethink curricula, standards, and approaches to teaching.
2. What is acceptable performance? In establishing criteria for performance, we must think about mastery. What does mastery of a specific skill or behavior look like? The criteria must be general enough so that students can practice those skills on which they will be evaluated.
3. How can expert judgments be made? In developing the criteria for acceptable performance, we must be able to specify them in advance. For example, suppose we want to know how well a student can retell a story or demonstrate knowledge about the community in which the student lives. Criteria that could be specified in advance include the use of details, accuracy, vocabulary, and expression.
4. How can feedback be provided? Performance assessment always requires more than one solution or one type of performance. Is the student using the skills under consideration in school and at home? How can the family, educators, and peers provide feedback to the student? The criteria for making judgments become the goals for instruction and progress. Figure 6.1 is a checklist for use in developing performance-based assessments.

Performance Tasks "Worth Doing"

Criteria	Never	Sometimes	Definitely
1. *Essential*—The task is a "big idea" that fits the core of the curriculum.			
2. *Authentic*—The task relates to real-world problems.			
3. *Rich*—The task leads to new problems and raises questions.			
4. *Engaging*—The task is absorbing and thought-provoking.			
5. *Active*—The student is involved in developing solutions and creating new problems.			
6. *Feasible*—The task can be done within a reasonable time frame, is appropriate, and is safe.			
7. *Equitable*—The completion of the task requires a variety of learning styles.			
8. *Open*—The task has more than one solution.			

FIGURE 6.1 • Checklist for Developing Performance-Based Assessments

Source: Adapted from National Council of the Teachers of Mathematics. (1991). *Mathematics Assessments*. Alexandria, VA: National Council of the Teachers of Mathematics.

Using Performance-Based Measures with Students with Disabilities

Although performance-based assessments have been implemented widely, there has been some controversy about whether these assessments meet the technical standards of reliability and validity. Tindal, McDonald, Tedesco, and Glasgow (2003) conducted research on the implementation of performance tasks in reading and math assessments. Working with teachers, the researchers designed standardized performance tasks that were aligned with reading and mathematics standards and trained the teachers to administer the tasks and evaluate performance. The training addressed describing the test materials, modeling test administration and scoring procedures, and supervising practice administration for the teachers. The researchers emphasized that explicitness of the administration and scoring procedures contributed to the high reliability, or consistency, of the scoring. The researchers concluded that both the performance and progress of students with disabilities can be assessed using performance tasks when the tasks are aligned with standards, teachers are trained, and the tasks have documented reliability and validity.

Authentic Assessment

Authentic assessment is similar to performance assessment except that the student completes or demonstrates knowledge, skills, or behavior in a real-life context (Meyer, 1992), and real-world standards measure the student's knowledge, skills, or behavior. Authentic assessment is not a new concept for teachers working with students with moderate to severe disabilities (Alper, Ryndak, & Schloss, 2001). Learning and performing daily living and job-related skills has been a part of the functional life skills curriculum for some time.

The conditions for the authentic assessment are quite different from those of the performance assessment. In performance assessment, the circumstances are often contrived or artificial, while in authentic assessment the tasks are part of a real-world setting. For example, learning activities could focus on a student-run snack shop where students plan and order materials and make and sell items. Just as with performance-based assessment, evaluators must develop the criteria for authentic assessment.

Cushman (1990) discusses four characteristics of authentic performance:

Structure
- The activities are public.
- The activities involve an audience or panel.
- The activities require some collaboration.
- The activities are worth practicing.
- The activities involve the modification of school policies and schedules to support them.

Design
- The activities are essential.
- The activities are enabling.
- The activities are contextualized.
- The activities involve complex processes, not isolated tasks or outcomes.
- The activities assess habits, attitudes, behaviors, motivation, and creativity.
- The activities are representative.
- The activities are engaging.
- The activities are open-ended.

TABLE 6.1 ● Examples of Authentic Assessment

Literacy

audiotape of reading
videotape of peer conferencing
book review
book poster
article for school newspaper
job application
resumé

The Arts

scenery design for a play
play performance
musical performance
design for a public space
sculpture
dance performance

Science

experiment
original investigation
journal of observations
investigation of local pollution problems
designing and building a bridge
developing a solar car

Oral Expression

debate
book talk
play reading
phone call to obtain information
speech

Mathematics

solving real-life problems
using a checking account
designing and building a structure
development of a budget
teaching a lesson

Social Studies

map of a nature trail
development of a museum exhibit
development of a political campaign
design of a children's playground

Adapted from Poteet, J. A., J. S. Choate, and S. C. Stewart (1993). Performance Assessment and Special Education: Practices and Prospects. *Focus on Exceptional Children* 26: 1–20.

Scoring

- The activities involve criteria that are essential.
- The activities are graded according to performance standards.
- The activities involve self-assessment.
- The activities use multifaceted scoring, not one grade.

Equity

- The activities are fair.
- The activities involve multiple areas of learning.
- The activities are responsive to culture, gender, learning style, and language.

Table 6.1 presents a list of examples of authentic assessments.

Portfolio Assessment

A **portfolio** is a systematic collection of a student's work covering an extended period of time. Portfolios can include works in progress, a student's best work, or work of which the student is most proud. Materials in the portfolio are a direct link to a student's individualized education program and show growth toward the program's objectives (Swicegood, 1994; Wesson & King, 1996).

Special educators find portfolios helpful in answering questions regarding what a student knows and can do. First, portfolios demonstrate a student's growth and progress over time. Students can develop portfolios over the course of a school year and share them during parent-teacher conferences and during annual reviews of the student's individualized educational program. Portfolios may become part of the student's records, which move with the student from one grade or level to the next.

Second, portfolios present examples of the student's best work(s). Portfolios can reflect development over one or more years and be part of graduation requirements, be part of evaluations of individualized programs, or be part of the student's resume for potential employers to see the student's achievements.

How It Works!

Performance-Based Assessment in Science
How Is My Breathing Rate Related to My Pulse?

Melissa D. Williams describes the performance-based assessment in science for students in grades 6 through 8 that she developed.

MY STUDENTS My students had been studying the human body and its systems. We began with the circulatory system and investigated the heart and the purpose of blood. Students had also learned that blood carries certain things that are required by cells, tissue, and organs, such as nutrients, hormones, white blood cells, and oxygen. For this science investigation, I integrated a data collection activity from our Every Day Math curriculum. This allowed students to apply their mathematics knowledge of data collection and data display to our science unit on the human body.

WHAT THE TASK ACCOMPLISHES After studying the circulatory system, students have learned that the blood transfers oxygen to cells for necessary functions. This investigation shows how the circulatory system is related to the respiratory system. Students are able to apply their understanding of this relationship to actually investigating their own body systems. They are also asked to display their data in two different representations. The task addresses:

Big Ideas and Unifying Concepts
Cause-Effect
Systems
Form and Function
Change-Constancy

Life Science Concept
Structure and function

Science in Personal and Societal Perspectives Concept
Personal health

Mathematics Concepts
Measurement
Data representation—tables, line graphs

Time Required for the Task
Two or three 45-minute periods

THE PROBLEM Have you ever raced after someone, trying to catch up? When you finally caught up, you may have felt your heart pounding, and you were probably out of breath.

In this investigation, you'll use what you've learned about the circulatory and respiratory systems and the purpose of blood to understand the connection between your breathing rate and how fast your heart may be pounding. Your group will be assigned to a physical activity and work together to collect data on your heart and breathing rates. The task will have these roles: the "timer," the "runner/jumper," and the "pulse keeper." The "pulse keeper" should be the one who can find the pulse the easiest on the other person's wrist. You should practice taking these rates a few times before you begin investigating. Record your data at rest and after one minute of the activity. Then make a table to show your findings. Be sure to include titles for the columns and rows. Next, use your data table to create a double line graph that shows both rates and what you discovered about the relationship between breathing rate and pulse. Your conclusions should tell whether your prediction was supported by the data.

HOW THE STUDENTS INVESTIGATED THE PROBLEM Students work in groups of two to three. We had a brief discussion about the task to get them thinking about the topic. Recording sheets provided some directions on how they would investigate the question. Each group had a stopwatch and was assigned to either a jump rope or to the stairs. (Other possibilities might include running, doing jumping jacks, or engaging in any other physical activity.) Before beginning, students recorded their pulse rates while at rest. After they recorded their pulse rates, they recorded their breathing rate for one minute. (The "timer" keeps track during the same time as pulse is recorded.) Once students were in their groups, I asked the class to think about how well they were able to record their pulses. Could someone record his or her breathing rate without thinking much about it? If so, then that person might want to be the "runner." Another person, also good at recording, might want to be the recorder of the pulse. The third person could be the timer.

Then, students went to their designated activity. One student completes the activity, while another times it. Then the "timer" keeps the time for one minute, the "pulse keeper" records the pulse, and the runner/jumper counts breaths. While students are performing the experiment, I monitor the pulse and breathing rates that they are writing down. The students then switched, so that the first student's breathing rate returns to normal. The second and third students then complete the activity. Although the breathing rate and pulse may not be recorded at exactly the same time, the results are similar, and should not affect the graphing piece of the task.

(continued)

How It Works!
continued

After recording results in their tables, students should try this experiment at least one more time to ensure their results are accurate. They should then average their results. This might be a good place to break from the first class session. During the second class, students can create graphs (with titles and keys). The most difficult part of this that I found was the scale of "beats per minute." Have the students look at all of their information to determine the scale of the graph. By using a full piece of graph paper, divided by increments of 5, we found that our information would fit. You may prefer to have students do two separate graphs, although then the relationship between the two lines may not be as obvious.

EXTENSIONS OF THE ACTIVITY After completing this experiment, I found other examples of similar tasks. One variation was to use two separate graphs for pulse rate and breathing rate. Another was to time at more frequent intervals, from rest to 2 minutes at 30-second intervals. The experiments did not implicitly relate the two counts together, but instead were done to show how one could monitor both pulse and breathing rate.

Movement and Music
Students could select different types/tempos of music and predict how moving to each would affect heart and breathing rates. Most baroque music is very relaxing to listen to. It is often included in stress management programs because it can produce a heart rate of approximately 60 beats/minute in the listener. Students could explore the effects of listening to different music tempos and compare them to or rank them related to at-rest rates. Students could also collect heart rate and breathing rate data during a practice session for different sports or movement activities.

Mathematics
Students can construct line graphs of data for different physical activities for the purpose of comparing and ranking. Students could determine and discuss differences in the "average rates" for the class in terms of using the mean, median, or mode.

Health
Students can compare their investigation findings to research related to regular exercise, developing cardiovascular endurance, and physical fitness.

TEACHING TIPS AND GUIDING QUESTIONS Have all students measure their pulses at rest (in a classroom setting). Finding the pulse rate on the wrist is a bit harder, but safer than using the neck. (If students press on both sides of the neck at the same time, they could pass out.) Take some time to teach students how to find their pulses. Explain to them to press lightly with the fingertips on the outer side of the wrist (not with their thumbs). They can try counting for a full minute and then try a count for 15 seconds, multiplying it by 4, to verify.

Write the class results on the board. Notice that most resting pulse rates can range from 75 to 100 beats per minute. Athletes tend to have slightly lower rates, due to conditioning. Some students will have a difficult time finding and recording their pulses, but may see from the results of their peers that a pulse rate of 20, for example, is impossible! You may suggest that those students either try it again, or choose to be the timer in the experiment.

Calculate and write the average pulse rate of the class on the board so that students can refer to it when recording their own data (not to use that information as their data, but to check theirs for accuracy).

While students are working on their hypotheses, elicit information about what they know about both the circulatory and the respiratory systems. Ask:

What does each system do for your body?

How does that relate to exercise? To fitness training?

What causes you to have a pulse?

What connection does the blood have to breathing and the heart?

How can you determine who will be the "pulse keeper" and "time keeper"?

What titles should be on your table? (You may need to review with the class what a table should look like, or refer to a previous experiment in which they made a table with the class.)

Using your data, can you explain whether your hypothesis was correct?

Look at your graph. What specific information can you find to back up your conclusion?

What proof do you have that can help you to now answer the question "Is my breathing rate related to my pulse?"

What would happen if you stopped exercising? (This may help them think about a rule to connect breathing rate to pulse.) Encourage students again to think of the function of both the respiratory and circulatory systems.

SUGGESTED MATERIALS I had the following materials available for this activity: jump ropes, stopwatches, a space for physical activity, graph paper, and rulers. Students also had recording sheets (included at the end of this task).

I also suggest access to computers so that students can enter their data and create an electronic graphic representation for the data displays.

POSSIBLE SOLUTIONS The student should include a hypothesis, which states whether breathing rate is related to pulse. There should be some evidence of prior knowledge (of either the circulatory or respiratory system). The data table includes columns and rows, labels, and a title. Data for breathing rate and pulse rate are for at least three time frames. The data is accurately translated from the table and plotted on a graph (with title and accurate scale and labels for the axes of the graph). There should be a key on the graph to distinguish the two lines.

Conclusions accurately compare the breathing rate to the pulse rate and cite evidence from the data collected to support or refute the hypothesis.

The student gives a reasonable explanation of how he or she effectively used breathing rate, pulse, and a stopwatch to measure these.

NOTE: I usually score this type of assignment (one having many different parts to it) with points given for each section. This approach is called *analytic scoring*, rather than holistic scoring. I do this because many students can have, for example, a solid hypothesis and then a weak conclusions section, or an incomplete data table. Then I look to see where the strengths lie and try to weight the parts with the most important information a little more. This gives me the final holistic performance levels: Novice, Apprentice, Practitioner, and Expert.

Task Specific Rubric/Benchmark Descriptors

Novice
- The student's hypothesis is only a one-word answer, "yes." It does not state any prediction or reasoning about breathing rate or pulse rate rising or falling. There is no evidence of knowledge of the circulatory or respiratory systems.
- Data table and data collection are incomplete. Only two time frames are recorded. The rates appear to be inaccurate, being that the pulse rate at rest is recorded as = 80 and after one minute of exercise, it is only = 30.
- Some columns and rows have titles.
- Titles and labels are missing from the graph; however, a key is included. The scale and intervals on the graph are inconsistent. Data are plotted incorrectly on the graph.
- Conclusions do not show evidence of reasoning or conceptual understanding. Neither the circulatory system nor the respiratory system are explained in the conclusion. There is only limited evidence of understanding the relationship between breathing rate and pulse.

Apprentice
- The student's hypothesis states whether breathing rate is related to pulse.
- The data table includes a title and labels for the columns and rows, but does not have data in chronological order (from at rest to 3 minutes). The table includes data for breathing rate and pulse rate for a minimum of three time frames. Data appears to be accurate and complete.
- A title and axis labels are not included for the graph. No key is included.
- The intervals for each axis of the graph are consistent, but the data is not shown correctly on the graph.
- Conclusions accurately compare the breathing rate to the pulse rate.
- This student's solution is lacking in detail, in that no specific examples from the data are used to support the conclusions.
- The student's explanation attempts to show reasoning, but is not supported by data collected. The explanation does not show a cause-effect relationship and is not consistent with the available data.

Practitioner
- The student's hypothesis states whether breathing rate is related to pulse and includes some prior knowledge of the circulatory and the respiratory systems.
- The data table includes columns and rows, labels, and a title.
- The table includes data for breathing rate and pulse rate for at least three time frames, recorded chronologically.

(continued)

How It Works!
continued

Task Specific Rubric/Benchmark Descriptors *(continued)*

Practitioner
(cont.)
- Although a title is not included, labels for the axes of the graph are accurate (including measurement). The scale for each axis is appropriate for the data collected and is shown correctly on the graph.
- The data is accurately translated from the table and plotted on the graph.
- A key is included on the graph to distinguish the two lines.
- Conclusions accurately compare the breathing rate to the pulse rate.
- Conclusion clearly cites evidence from the data collected to support or refute the hypothesis. The student gives a reasonable explanation based on available data.

Expert
- The student's hypothesis (which states whether breathing rate is related to pulse) relates the respiratory system to the circulatory system. Examples show evidence of applying prior knowledge.
- The data table includes columns and rows, labels, and a title.
- The table includes data for breathing rate and pulse rate for three time frames, recorded chronologically. Data appears to be accurate.
- A title and labels for the axes of the graph are included and accurate (including measurement).
- The scale for each axis is appropriate for the data collected and is shown correctly on the graph.
- The data is accurately translated from the table and plotted on the graph.
- A key is included on the graph to distinguish the two lines.
- There is clear evidence of scientific reasoning in the conclusion.
- Conclusions are supported by data.
- There is evidence of extended thinking, such as what might happen when the person rests 3 to 5 minutes. The data trend is correctly identified from the graph and used to support reasoning.

> ▶ **CEC Common Core Knowledge and Skills.** A beginning special educator can interpret information from formal and informal assessments (CC8S5).

Portfolio assessment provides benefits to students, teachers, and family members (Airasian, 2005; Rogers & Graham, 2000; Stiggins, 1997; Wiggins & McTigue, 1998). These benefits include:

For students:
- Selecting items to include in the portfolios
- Engaging in a noncompetitive activity
- Experiencing a collaborative climate among students through peer collaboration activities
- Having ownership and tangible evidence of learning
- Building self-esteem
- Clarifying expectations
- Reflecting and judging their own works
- Having ongoing feedback regarding their works

For teachers:
- Connecting assessment and instruction
- Providing diagnostic information about a student's strengths and instructional needs

- Generating meaningful examples of student growth constructing knowledge of what constitutes high-quality work
- Having concrete examples of student performance to discuss with family members

For family members:
- Viewing student progress over time by having easy-to-understand examples

In one study (Shepard & Bliem, 1995) parents reported that talking about their child's progress and seeing samples of their child's work were very useful (77 percent and 60 percent, respectively), whereas only 43 percent of parents reported report cards useful and 14 percent reported standardized tests useful.

Contents of a Portfolio

The contents of a portfolio consist of product as well as process items. Product items are works such as papers, drawings, photographs, models, language samples, creative art, and other artifacts. Process items include successive drafts of a paper, works in progress, works in which students have cooperated with others, and self-reflections about a particular unit of study. Students' reflective statements are critical components of a portfolio (Cole, Ryan, & Kick, 1995). Finally, a portfolio may include teacher and parent comments, scores of standardized tests, school attendance records, and school activities.

Organizing the Portfolio

Materials in the portfolio can be organized according to curriculum areas, skill areas, or chronological order. In this section, we will examine ways to organize portfolios at various grade levels.

1. *Elementary Education.* The two models in Figure 6.2 apply to elementary-age students and illustrate ways that a teacher can conceptualize portfolios. Model A reflects curriculum areas, and Model B focuses on skill and knowledge areas. Model A shows some content modifications for a student with disabilities in the classroom, which relate to the student's IEP. Daryl, a fourth-grade student with a learning disability, is working on a portfolio linked to his IEP goals. You can read more about his work in the Snapshot on page 119.
2. *Middle School.* Portfolios can focus on documenting academic progress and on assisting students in understanding themselves. Figure 6.3 illustrates the portfolio components from one middle school.
3. *Secondary School.* Portfolios can help students synthesize information about career plans (Figure 6.4) or may be a graduation requirement.

Portfolios, because of their breadth and integrative format, are useful as part of graduation requirements. Central Park East Secondary School requires students to complete a portfolio across fourteen categories and to display their portfolios to a graduation committee (Darling-Hammond, Ancess, & Falk, 1995). The portfolio derives from the individual student's work; however, some portfolios have the group work requirements. Students present seven of the fourteen categories orally to a graduation committee comprising the student's faculty advisor, another faculty member, an adult chosen by the student, and another student. The student candidates may have to answer questions about the other seven categories during the Graduation Committee Hearing. Students also complete a final project that is in an area of particular interest to the student, such as exploring one of the portfolio items in greater depth.

▶ How are educators in your local school districts using performance-based assessments with students with disabilities? Make arrangements to interview a local special educator or administrator.

Model A: Curriculum Areas	

Language and Literacy

*1. Audiotapes of child retelling a story
2. Drawing of favorite part of the story
*3. Writing samples using word prediction software
4. List of favorite books written or dictated by child

Science and Mathematics

1. Paper and pencil drawings and written descriptions of mathematics problems
2. Written log/drawings of child's observations of science experiments
3. Chart with a series of predictions
4. Photographs of child engaged in measuring, sorting, classifying, or seriation activities
5. Child's graph of group data from the class

Art and Music

1. Paintings and drawings
2. Audiotape of song/music created by child
3. Photographs of art projects
4. Copies of projects drawn using software

Community and Culture

1. Student maps of the classroom, school, or community
2. Copies of student email sent to penpal in another city or state
3. Photographs and teacher-transcribed descriptions of field trips
4. Copies of student thank-you letters to community speakers

Physical Education

1. Photographs of child on climbing structure
*2. Checklist of child's skills completed by the teacher
*3. Videotapes of child participating in an activity
4. List of favorite activities written or dictated by child

Social Skills

*1. Child's evaluation of cooperative learning activities
2. Copies of peer evaluations of cooperative learning activities
*3. Videotapes of student working with others
*4. Checklists of skills or observations completed by the teacher

Model B: Knowledge and Skills	

Academic

1. Writing log and videotape of integrated unit activity
2. Student notes from learning a search process on the Internet

Self-Esteem

1. A series of drawings about feelings
2. Comments from teachers and peers on accomplishments

Cooperative Group

1. Teacher feedback notes regarding a cooperative learning activity
2. Student products, reflections on group activities

Citizenship

1. Summary of a community project and self-reflection
2. List of activities regarding "How I Helped My School"

---

*Some of the contents in this portfolio have been modified for a student with disabilities. The items that are asterisked (*) show how the teacher modified the contents for this portfolio.

FIGURE 6.2 • Portfolio Models in Elementary Schools

Helping Students Construct Portfolios

Students learn a great deal from making selections, assembling and reviewing their materials, and refining their portfolios. Teachers support students during each step in the construction process and in refining their portfolios. Teachers help students during each step in the construction process:

1. Deciding what they want to demonstrate in their portfolios. For portfolios to be valid, students must understand the performance they demonstrate. Teachers

I. Who I am
  A. Interests
  B. Friends
  C. Family
  D. Other

II. Skills that I am developing
  A. Working independently
  B. Working cooperatively with others
  C. Problem solving
  D. Conflict resolution
  E. Other

III. My academic progress
  A. Language Arts (reading, writing, listening, speaking)

  B. Mathematics
  C. Science
  D. Social Studies
  E. Music
  F. Art
  G. Other

IV. Service to my community
  A. Volunteer work
  B. Special projects
  C. Other

FIGURE 6.3 ● Portfolio Model for Middle School Students

Source: Adapted from portfolio models developed by Milton Union School faculty, June 1993, and Joan Schindler (Incarnation); Alvine Wilson, Mary Galdeen, Deborah Carey, Rae Ann Herman (West Carrollton Junior High School); and Cindy Hill (Weisenborn Institute), June 1993, as cited in Cole, D. J., C. W. Ryan, and F. Kick, 1995. *Portfolios across the curriculum and beyond.* Thousand Oaks, CA: Corwin Press, pp. 40–42.

I. Introduction
  A. Title page
  B. Table of contents
  C. Preface (student's reflection on the portfolio)

II. Student Profile
  A. Autobiography
  B. School service projects
  C. Community service

III. Educational Achievement
  A. My beliefs about my education (a personal philosophy)

  B. My education goals
  C. Copies of exceptional work
  D. Evaluations of education progress
  E. Other

IV. Preparing for the Future
  A. Interest surveys
  B. Career exploration
  C. Home and family
  D. Recreation
  E. Other

FIGURE 6.4 ● Portfolio Model for Students in an Alternative High School

Source: Adapted from portfolio models developed by LIMA OWE faculty, November 1991, as cited in Cole, D. J., C. W. Ryan, and F. Kick, 1995. *Portfolios across the curriculum and beyond.* Thousand Oaks, CA: Corwin Press, p. 44.

should discuss with students at the beginning of the year what to include in the portfolio and explain the evaluation process.

2. Incorporating self-reflections, which are important components of a portfolio. A self-reflection is a writing activity in which the student analyzes learning and accomplishments. In the written reflection, students describe their views of the learning process and the importance of the task. To help students become more familiar with the process of reflection, a teacher can use class discussions to encourage students to think about an activity or event. The teacher can model self-reflection or provide examples of student reflections. Students also should have opportunities to practice reflection with each other.

Cole, Ryan, and Kick (1995) suggest that the teacher develop several questions to assist:

a. Why is this your best work?

b. How did you go about accomplishing this task?

c. What would you do differently if you did a task like this again?

d. Where do you go from here? (p. 16)

3. Understanding portfolio evaluation. It is important that students understand how teachers will evaluate their portfolios. Teachers need to spend time discussing with the class the many ways of evaluating a work. Consider the following example of two elementary students who responded to an interviewer's question:

First Classroom:

Interviewer: "What kind of reader are you?"

Tara: "Pretty good."

Interviewer: "What makes you say that?"

Tara: "I'm in the Red Group."

Second Classroom:

Interviewer: "What kind of reader are you?"

Sheila: "I like funny stories and books about animals, but often I just kind of get stuck on the same author for months at a time." (Adapted from Johnston, as cited in Hewitt, 1995, p. 188)

4. Choosing the pieces to include. Students learn a great deal in choosing and selecting the materials to include in the portfolio. Teachers help students by choosing assignments that require a diversity of skills and with individual student ability and areas of interest in mind.

5. Determining how to present the pieces. Some content areas more readily lend themselves to one format than another. For example, a photograph may better represent the complexity or creativity of a model of a city or construction of a sailboat than a written text could. A videotape captures areas in which movements or interactions are important.

Using Technology

Teachers can organize and preserve student information, including text, sound (talking, singing, music, reading), scanned images (pictures, drawings, and photographs), and video (individual and group performances), on digital file and class home pages on the World Wide Web. Student- or teacher-developed websites can display the students' portfolios.

Incorporating the use of technology offers the capabilities of computer searching and combining information in meaningful ways. Preserving the contents of a portfolio on disk means the disk can follow students from one grade to the next. After graduation, students can provide a disk to prospective employers or to college or university admissions officers to illustrate what they know and are able to do.

Exhibitions

An **exhibition** is a display of a student's work that demonstrates knowledge, abilities, skills, and attitudes concerning one project or a unit of work. An exhibition provides students with the opportunity to summarize and to synthesize what they have accomplished. Exhibitions are useful in a variety of academic content areas and in interdisciplinary studies because students can realize by their own efforts that learning is more than just a series of worksheets or exercises and that it involves conceptual under-

Linking Daryl's IEP with Portfolio Assessment

Last year, when Daryl was in third grade, he was identified as having a learning disability. He had difficulties in reading, written language, and getting along with other students, and he was often argumentative. One of Daryl's IEP goals is that he will improve in reading.

His fourth-grade teacher is using portfolios to document student progress. His teacher believes that Daryl can demonstrate progress in language and literacy by documenting activities in the portfolio. Daryl will keep a reading log that lists the books that he has read and a brief summary of each. Periodically, Daryl will complete a more extensive book report. Daryl will use a word processing program with a word prediction feature that will allow him to record his thoughts more efficiently. Daryl will add copies of his writing drafts to the portfolio periodically. Daryl's teacher will share these materials with the IEP team during the annual review of Daryl's individualized education program.

Daryl's portfolio will also include a section on Working with Others. This area relates directly to another IEP goal for building social skills. Daryl and his teacher discussed ways in which Daryl can make and keep friends and decided how they should document his progress. One of the ideas that they discussed was for Daryl to complete a daily self-assessment checklist. The teacher talked about her observations of Daryl on the playground this week and some examples of cooperating with others. They agreed that she will continue to share her observations with Daryl at the end of the day and together they will record positive examples on a graph.

standing, problem solving, and reasoning. Exhibitions are useful for program planning and program evaluation.

Teachers and scientists sometimes create partnerships to develop performance tasks and opportunities for students to display their work. The Maine Mathematics and Science Alliance and six Maine high school teachers partnered with the Harvard Smithsonian Center for Astrophysics and Tufts University Wright Center for Science Education to create a set of embedded performance tasks and classroom activities that utilize the rich X-ray data being generated by the Chandra X-Ray Observatory (Keeley, 2001). One of the many learning tasks that the teachers and scientists developed was "Electromagnetic Pasta" (Figure 6.5).

The light that our eyes can see is called visible light. Different wavelengths of visible light are seen as different colors by our eyes. But the sun and stars send us more than just visible light; they send invisible light as well. Both visible and invisible light are referred to as electromagnetic radiation (EMR). Invisible light has either longer wavelengths or shorter wavelengths than the visible light we see with our eyes. When these different forms of light are placed side by side in order of increasing or decreasing wavelength, they make up the electromagnetic spectrum.

Your task: Using different types of pasta (spaghetti, linguini, cappellini, fettucini, lasagne, orzo, macaroni, rigatoni, manicotti, ziti, etc.), create a combined model/display. You will use these pasta analogies to explain the principal classification of the electromagnetic spectrum.

Your model/display must:

1. Clearly characterize each type of EMR.
2. Describe the human uses of each type of EMR.
3. Include an explanation for choosing each type of pasta to represent a portion of the electromagnetic spectrum by making an analogy between the pasta and the EMR it represents.
4. Include a critique of how the pasta analogy/model, providing at least one good explanation of how it does and does not represent the real thing.

You may choose to display your model using any medium you choose. Your display should be neat, well-organized, explanatory, and visually appealing!

FIGURE 6.5 • Electromagnetic Pasta

Source: Developed by Gary Glick (Falmouth [ME] High School) and Page Keeley (Maine Mathematics and Science Alliance) for the Chandra X-Ray Center with funding from NASA under Contract NAS 8-39073.

Responding to Diversity

Using performance-based, authentic, or portfolio assessment with students with disabilities requires teachers to be sensitive to the unique needs of these students. Gordon and Bonilla-Bowman (1996) report that portfolio assessment serves as a concrete reminder to students of their work and progress. Fuchs (1994) discusses challenges in using portfolio assessment with students with disabilities. Students who are experiencing difficulties in writing are at a disadvantage when constructing a writing portfolio, for example, because it may be difficult to determine whether an inadequate response results from poor writing skills, poor mastery of the content, poor problem-solving skills, lack of creativity, or a combination of these factors.

Portfolios may not be useful for students with chaotic lives or who have chronic health problems. Portfolios are not effective for students who come infrequently to school (Wolf, 1996). Understanding portfolio expectations requires regular school attendance and ongoing discussions with the teacher regarding one's work.

Gordon and Bonilla-Bowman (1996) discuss teachers' and parents' concerns regarding the use of portfolios with students from diverse cultural, ethnic, and linguistic groups. There are two potential difficulties with portfolio assessment for these students. First, students rely on their own use of language, more so than on standardized tests, and second, the teacher may introduce bias in assessing the portfolio. Portfolios have the potential of providing students with ways of demonstrating conceptual understandings beyond the ability to understand English. Yet, in a review of portfolios, Gordon and Bonilla-Bowman (1996) found little evidence or representation of students' home cultures and few portfolios that included students' home languages. Limited research is available on bias in portfolio assessment. Some research raises questions about bias in alternative assessment in general. For example, Nuttall and Goldstein (as cited in Madaus, Haney, & Kreitzer, 1992) found that the achievement gap between various groups of students was greater on alternative assessment instruments than on traditional tests. Identifying activities that are authentic, especially for students whose lives will be very different from the teacher's, is difficult (Fuchs, 1994).

Much research is needed on the use of portfolios and the effects of this method on student learning. Questions to keep in mind include: Does the use of portfolios in the classroom increase student achievement? Are portfolios effective measures for meeting the goals of the individualized education program for students with disabilities? What types of evidence show learning?

Developing Scoring Systems

Developing or selecting a scoring system is an important part of classroom-based assessment because effective systems provide valuable feedback to students, teachers, and parents regarding level of performance and progress in the curriculum. Teachers may use anecdotal notes, performance task checklists, or rubrics. Educators frequently use notes and checklists because they provide convenient ways of recording informal information. Yet, anecdotal notes do not provide the student (or teacher and parents) with information about the evaluation process. Furthermore, teachers who use anecdotal notes may find it difficult to be consistent (and reliable) from one student to the next without more objective criteria.

Checklists, on the other hand, can list the components of what is under evaluation during the performance. They are also easy to use but they do not provide any detailed information as to the quality of the achievement; they simply record whether one of the items in the performance was present or not. In the following section, we will discuss rubrics and how educators are using this scoring system in the classroom.

Rubrics

Rubrics are considered the most useful scoring system for performance-based, authentic, and portfolio assessments because they provide the greatest amount of detail regarding the performance. A **rubric** is an assessment scale that identifies the area(s) of performance and defines various levels of achievement. Within each level, the rubric should include descriptors, or detailed descriptions of each level of achievement. Descriptors provide specific information to students, teachers, and parents regarding what to expect at each achievement level. Descriptors also help teachers in scoring student performances consistently. Scoring systems generally fall into two main types: analytic and holistic.

▶ Develop a resource of websites that illustrate well-designed rubrics. Select a curriculum area and use a search engine to narrow your search to locate five to eight sites that you would recommend in English Language Arts, Science, Mathematics, Social Studies, or other curriculum areas. Share your findings with the class.

Analytic Scoring

An **analytic scoring** system reports an independent score for each of the criteria of the assessment scale. For a rubric developed for a writing portfolio there might be four criteria: organization, details, voice, and grammar. An analytic scoring system reports separate scores for each of these criteria. Within each of these criteria, the various levels of achievement can be described either numerically or categorically. In an example of a writing portfolio, we might identify the following achievement levels of organization:

> *Criterion: Organization*
>
> 4 = Extensive
>
> 3 = Moderate
>
> 2 = Slight
>
> 1 = Lacking

Notice that we have used both numerical and corresponding categorical descriptions of achievement in this rubric.

In our example, the rubric does not include descriptors of the levels of achievement. Thus, without further descriptions of the terms "moderate" and "slight," one teacher might rank the organization of a student's paper a "3" while another teacher would rank organization a "2." Detailed descriptors are helpful to teachers and others during evaluation procedures and serve to increase interrater reliability. One example of a rubric that provides detailed descriptors developed by the Vermont Strategic Reading Initiative is illustrated in Figure 6.6 (Boke & Hewitt, 2004).

Descriptors are helpful to students and parents. Detailed information regarding levels of achievement assists students in understanding not only how teachers will evaluate their work but how they can evaluate the work themselves. Descriptors are helpful to parents in understanding what their child can do. Depending on the richness and detail of the descriptors, analytic scoring can provide diagnostic information about the student's achievement. Teachers can examine scores on the individual criteria to identify areas of strengths and areas of improvement. Because this type of scoring system is an effective diagnostic tool, teachers should report student scores as categorical rather than numerical. By reporting analytic scores numerically, even if they show totals and averages, the result is a loss of rich analytic information (Hewitt, 1995).

The following rubric is often used to assess student writing:

	5	4	3	2	1
PURPOSE	Clear, consistent focus & intent	Clear focus and intent	Focus and intent are usually clear	Focus and intent are not very clear	No focus; intent difficult to discern
ORGANIZATION	Clear, predictable presentation	Clearly sequenced	Organization sometimes confusing	Confusing	No sense of organization
DETAILS	Details illuminate the information	Details explain the information	Details aid understanding	More, or better, details would help	No details
VOICE/TONE	Consistent, engaging voice or tone throughout	Voice or tone encourages reader to "stick with it"	Voice or tone fails to engage the reader	Voice or tone inconsistent	No sense of voice or tone

FIGURE 6.6 ● Vermont Strategic Reading Initiative Writing Rubric

Source: Boke and Hewitt (2004). Vermont Strategic Reading Initiative.

Let's return to the Electromagnetic Pasta activity (Figure 6.5). The activity asked students to describe the different types of wavelengths, to explain how the pasta types represented the information, and to critique their pasta model. The analytic scoring rubric (Figure 6.7) that the teachers and scientists developed provides detailed information for each level of achievement in content level, use of model or display, and critique of how their pasta model does and does not represent the real thing.

Holistic Scoring

Holistic scoring is a type of scoring in which the teacher assigns a single score to the student's work (Figure 6.8). For example, the writing portfolio receives a single overall score. The teacher does not analyze the writing by separate criteria such as organization, details, voice, and grammar. Like analytic scoring, holistic scoring should include descriptors of each of the achievement levels.

This type of scoring lacks the depth of information contained in analytic scoring; however, it tends to be easier to design and score than analytic scoring.

► Compare the various methods of scoring performance-based assessments. What are the advantages and disadvantages of each?

Benchmarks

Benchmarks are examples of student work that illustrate each scoring level on the rubric, either analytic or holistic. Teachers evaluate student work by using scoring standards and benchmarks. Benchmarks can be in the form of papers, such as example essays, or a small sample of student work, such as possible answers to a question. Student papers that represent writing at different levels of performance are sometimes called **anchor papers**. Figure 6.6 illustrates an example from a set of anchor papers developed by teachers in Vermont (2000–2001 5th Grade Writing Benchmarks).

Scoring Rubric: The Universe Rated R!				
Scoring Criteria	**1** **Attempted** **Demonstration**	**2** **Partial** **Demonstration**	**3** **Proficient** **Demonstration**	**4** **Distinguished** **Demonstration**
Content Knowledge Students' ability to describe the different types of electromagnetic radiation (EMR), including their uses by humans.	Student attempts to describe at least three types of EMR. Student attempts to arrange them by some criteria, and/or describes at least three human applications. There may be major errors.	Student describes at least five types of EMR, arranges them by increasing or decreasing wavelength, and describes at least five human applications. There may be slight omissions or minor errors.	Student correctly describes seven types of EMR, arranges them by increasing or decreasing wavelength, and describes a human application of each.	Student correctly describes, in supporting detail, seven types of EMR, arranges them by increasing or decreasing wavelength, and describes a human application of each. Student may offer sophisticated and/or insightful details.
Communicate with a Model/ Display Students' ability to represent the electromagnetic spectrum with a physical model/display that draws analogies between the model and the material used.	Student creates a physical model/display of at least three components of the electromagnetic spectrum, using pasta, and draws at least one analogy between the characteristics of the pasta and the EMR it represents. The model/display may contain major errors.	Student creates a physical model/display of at least five components of the electromagnetic spectrum, using pasta, and draws at least three effective analogies between the characteristics of the pasta and the EMR it represents. The model/display may contain minor errors.	Student creates an effective, neat, and organized physical model/display of the seven components of the electromagnetic spectrum, using pasta, and draws effective analogies between the characteristics of the pasta and the EMR it represents.	Student creates a highly effective, visually appealing, well-organized, self-explanatory physical model/display of the seven components of the electromagnetic spectrum, using pasta, and draws effective and logical analogies between the characteristics of the pasta and the EMR it represents. Student may offer sophisticated and/or insightful details.
Critique of a Model Students' ability to critique a model.	Student critiques the model, providing at least one reason why it is either like or unlike the real electromagnetic spectrum. Reason(s) may be irrelevant, overly obvious, or illogical.	Student critiques the model, providing at least one reason why it is either like or unlike the real electromagnetic spectrum.	Student critiques the model, providing at least one significant reason why it is both like and unlike the real electromagnetic spectrum.	Student effectively critiques the model, providing at least two significant reasons why it is both like and unlike the real electromagnetic spectrum. Reasons given may indicate higher level reasoning beyond the obvious features of the model.

FIGURE 6.7 • Analytic Scoring Rubric for Electromagnetic Pasta

Source: Developed by Gary Glick (Falmouth [ME] High School) and Page Keeley (Maine Mathematics and Science Alliance) for the Chandra X-Ray Center with funding from NASA under Contract NAS 8-39073.

Description	Numerical Score
The paper is will organized, provides a sufficient number of explicit details in supporting statements, and contains no major grammatical errors.	4
The paper shows organization but may lack coherence, details are appropriate, and/or it contains some grammatical errors.	3
The paper lacks consistency in organization, details are not elaborate, and/or it contains many grammatical errors.	2
The paper has serious problems in organization, lacks details, and/or it contains numerous grammatical errors.	1

FIGURE 6.8 • Holistic Rubric for Scoring Student Writing

Hewitt (1995) cautions teachers to select benchmark examples that demonstrate the midrange of each of the achievement levels. When a teacher scores a student's portfolio, benchmarks provide the teacher with a framework and serve to increase reliability.

Benchmarks can be helpful to students in understanding how teachers will assess their performance or portfolio. However, benchmarks should be shared carefully with students so that they will not think they must replicate the example, thus losing the individual nature of their work. Providing students with several different examples of benchmarks at various achievement levels can reduce this potential problem.

Ensuring Technical Adequacy

Reliability

The purpose of the assessment affects how crucial the issue of reliability is. Some assessments are low-stakes assessments; that is, the consequences of the assessment do not have a major impact on the student's future. For example, an assessment designed to answer questions regarding student progress is a low-stakes assessment.

Assessments that are part of graduation requirements have much higher stakes. High-stakes assessments refer to situations in which the collected information will have a direct and potentially adverse impact on the student. In high-stakes assessment, issues of reliability are critical.

Consistency and Stability

Reliability of performance-based assessments focuses on the consistency and the stability of the assessment. When using performance-based assessment, students frequently have multiple opportunities to perform individually. For example, a teacher is able to create a number of opportunities that require students to work together cooperatively; however, individual oral presentations on a unit of study occur infrequently because of the amount of class time these presentations require. In this case, consistency of student response is unknown due to low frequency of performance.

Multiple categories or points on the assessment scale affect the degree of interrater agreement. The more categories or points, the more difficult it may be to obtain interrater agreement, especially if the categories are vague. We have discussed one method of increasing consistency by including detailed descriptors in each of the achievement levels. We have examined how descriptors assist evaluators in making determinations regarding students' scores and help students evaluate their own work.

Another approach to addressing consistency actually adjusts for differences between evaluators by accepting adjacent scores (Hewitt, 1995). Two teachers reviewed a student's writing, illustrated in Figure 6.9, using the holistic scoring system in Figure 6.8. The first reader rated the paper a 1; the second reader rated the paper a 2. Since the evaluators have adjacent scores, they adjust the difference by averaging the two scores, and the student receives a score of 1.5.

Teachers also want assurance that the performance will be stable. Stability is a function of the scoring system and environmental factors. Errors in the scoring systems affect stability; for example, when the teacher assigns an incorrect score or makes a calculation error. Environmental factors also affect stability. The learning and social environments of the classroom impact the student's motivation, attitude, self-esteem, confidence, and anxiety, which in turn can alter the student's performance.

Trying to Convince Someone Not to Smoke

Topic is clearly stated in the title

I am trying to convince a friend not to smoke. My first reason is it's bad for you. My second reason is it's expensive. My third reason is it's social pressure. *Introduction is weak. States appropriate arguments.*

It's bad for you. You could get cancer. Smoking takes away your appetite and you don't eat as much. Smoking will make you have bad breath and teeth. Smoking is addicting. *Arranges ideas in a simple way, listing without relating to each other.*

Lacks transitions

It's expensive. Medical care for your health will cost alot because it's addicting. Dental care will cost alot of money for your teeth because the tar in cigarettes make your teeth black. The cost of the habit is over one thousand dollars a year. *Provides some supporting evidence for argument.*

Coherence is weak between and within paragraphs.

Social pressure. Cigarette advertisements make smoking look harmless and fun. Some advertisements help you stop. There are warning labels saying that if you're pregnant your baby could probably have birth weight. The labels are called Surgeon General Warnings. Just because someone you know or like smokes don't mean you have to smoke.

I never want to smoke and I hope you feel the same way. I hope you make the right chose and save money. *Conclusion is weak.*

The writer assumes the reader will find these ideas credible.

FIGURE 6.9 ● Example of a Fifth-Grade Writing Benchmark

Source: Reprinted from "2000–2001 5th Grade Writing Benchmarks" with permission of the Vermont Department of Education.

Consequential Validity

Consequential validity is the extent to which an assessment instrument promotes the intended consequences (Linn & Baker, 1996). This type of validity can describe performance-based assessments. One of the primary reasons for using this type of assessment is to improve student learning, and the extent to which performance-based assessment improves student learning defines consequential validity. Factors that can affect student learning, and thus impact consequential validity, include school reform activities, instructional improvements, staff development activities, levels of student achievement, and accountability systems (Linn & Baker, 1996).

Both student and teacher perspectives can affect consequential validity.

From the student's perspective: For the assessment to be valid, students must know what to expect. Students must know what skills and knowledge are in the assessment, what types of performance demonstrate these skills and knowledge, and what type of evaluation their performance will receive.

From the teacher's perspective: For the assessment to be valid, teachers must take care in designing tasks that accurately reflect achievement for students from nondominant cultures. For example, oral presentations may be difficult for students whose first language is not English. An oral presentation in science, for example, might be supplemented by information presented in another format, such as a detailed drawing to illustrate the concepts presented.

Fairness

Fairness of the assessment instrument is an important aspect of consequential validity. One of the driving forces behind the evolution of performance-based assessment has been the impetus to develop assessment instruments that are fair to students. Tests are opportunities for students to demonstrate learning regardless of culture, gender, race, socioeconomic status, or disability. Fairness means minimal bias, equitable assessment, and measures that are sensitive to diverse populations.

Improving Reliability and Validity

Airasian (2001) suggests several guidelines to improve reliability and validity of performance-based and portfolio assessments:

1. Know the purpose of the assessment.
2. Teach and give students practice on the assessment criteria.
3. State the criteria in observable behaviors.
4. Select criteria that are at an appropriate level of difficulty for the students.
5. Limit the number of criteria to a manageable number.
6. Maintain a written record.
7. Be sure the performance assessment is fair to all students. (pp. 254–255)

Cautions When Using Performance-Based, Authentic, and Portfolio Assessment

Careful design of performance, authentic, and portfolio assessments is important to ensure that educators, parents, and students draw appropriate conclusions. If we are unclear about our expectations, then we diminish the usefulness of the assessment. There are several questions that can guide us in using these assessment techniques.

Is the assessment representative of the student's work? For example, a performance task could demonstrate how a student develops a first draft of a book review, but not a finished one. Videotapes might contain images of play rehearsals, but not the opening-night production.

Are the criteria for assessment clear to all evaluators and students? Ambiguity, inconsistency in judging performance and authentic assessments, and subjectivity can be major problems. Both students and the educators must know what the assessment tasks are, what the performance conditions are, and what the criteria for evaluation are.

Have the criteria for evaluation changed over time? When designing an assessment, the educator may have specified the evaluation of all of the student's creative writings. Later, it may be unclear whether this meant all the finished writing or all the writing whether finished or not.

Who evaluates the contents? Depending on who evaluates the performance or authentic assessment tasks, interpretations can vary; and depending on the training of the educator, different conclusions can be reached (Arter & Spandel, 1991).

Are performance and authentic assessments fair? The use of performance and authentic assessments does not automatically mean that they show no bias toward students with disabilities, certain cultural groups, minorities, economic groups, and those to whom English is a second language.

▶ Why are concerns relating to reliability and validity so important when using performance-based assessments?

Considerations about Using Performance-Based Assessments

The development and implementation of performance-based assessments present challenges to educators. Although they are not without problems, these assessment procedures have the potential of helping us develop valid and fair approaches to assessing students. However, as this area continues to develop, we must proceed carefully. Table 6.2 on pages 128-132 summarizes the advantages and limitations of alternative assessment procedures.

Educators in professional organizations and state departments of education have developed sets of standards that specify what students should know and achieve. Assessment procedures should assist educators and policymakers in improving instruction and learning. If assessment is to be beneficial, the procedures must provide useful information about the capabilities of students. We believe that performance-based, authentic, and portfolio assessment will continue to be valuable assessment approaches. If the purposes of assessment are not beneficial, then neither the assessment nor the assessment procedures are valid.

All assessment procedures have to be fair to all students. Assessment procedures should contain no bias, and they should be attentive to differences in development and disabilities and to differences in culture, race, socioeconomic standing, and gender. Students must be given multiple opportunities to demonstrate what they know. A single test score cannot determine educational decisions.

The assessment tasks must be reliable and valid and represent the standards that children are to achieve. Multiple-choice tests give children inadequate opportunities to demonstrate what they know. Alternatives to traditional assessment, such as performance-based assessment, portfolios, and exhibitions, are rich sources of information (Hymes, Chafin, & Gonder, 1991).

Educators should be involved in the development and implementation of assessment procedures. Because assessment forms a close link with instruction, educators must participate in the development, administration, scoring, and interpretation of assessment procedures. We need to continue to develop and revise effective authentic and performance tasks.

Teachers and other evaluators should use caution when applying portfolios to high-stakes testing. High-stakes testing is the use of assessments to make classification, retention, or promotion decisions about students. The pressure of such a situation can compromise student work.

▶ Working with a small group of your peers, develop a set of questions for two or more chapters in this textbook. Your question sets should include multiple-choice, short-answer, and essay questions. Next, review the same chapters and identify how knowledge of the information could be demonstrated by either performance or portfolio assessment. What method of assessment do you prefer? Why?

TABLE 6.2 ● Advantages, Limitations, and Pitfalls of Alternative Types of Classroom Assessment Techniques			
Assessment Alternatives	**Advantages for Teachers**	**Disadvantages for Teachers**	**Suggestions for Improved Use**
Formative Assessment Techniques			
1. Conversations and comments from other teachers	(a) Fast way to obtain certain types of background information about a student. (b) Permit colleagues to share experiences with specific students in other learning contexts, thereby broadening the perspective about the learners. (c) Permit attainment of information about a student's family, siblings, or peer problems that may be affecting the student's learning.	(a) Tend to reinforce stereotype and biases toward a family or a social class. (b) Students' learning under another teacher or in another context may be quite unlike their learning in the current context. (c) Others' opinions are not objective, often based on incomplete information, personal life view, or personal theory of personality.	(a) Do not believe hearsay, rumors, biases of others. (b) Do not gossip or reveal private and confidential information about students. (c) Keep the conversation on a professional level, focused on facts rather than speculation and confidential so it is not overheard by others.
2. Casual conversations with students	(a) Provide relaxed, informal setting for obtaining information. (b) Students may reveal their attitudes and motivations toward learning that are not exhibited in class.	(a) A student's mind may not be focused on the learning target being assessed. (b) Inadequate sampling of students' knowledge; too few students assessed. (c) Inefficient: Students' conversation may be irrelevant to assessing their achievement.	(a) Do not appear as an inquisitor, always probing students. (b) Be careful so as not to misperceive a student's attitude or a student's degree of understanding.
3. Questioning students during instruction	(a) Permits judgments about students' thinking and learning progress during the course of teaching, gives teachers immediate feedback. (b) Permits teachers to ask questions requiring higher order thinking and elaborated responses. (c) Permits student-to-student interaction to be assessed. (d) Permits assessment of students' ability to discuss issues with others orally and in some depth.	(a) Some students cannot express themselves well in front of other students. (b) Requires education in how to ask proper questions and to plan for asking specific types of questions during the lesson. (c) Information obtained tends to be only a small sample of the learning outcomes and of the students in the class. (d) Some learning targets cannot be assessed by spontaneous and short oral responses; they require longer time frames in which students are free to think, create, and respond. (e) Records of students' responses are kept only in the teacher's mind, which may be unreliable.	(a) Be sure to ask questions of students who are reticent or slow to respond. Avoid focusing on verbally aggressive and pleasant "stars." (b) Wait 5 to 10 seconds for a student to respond before moving on to another. (c) Avoid limiting questions to those requiring facts or a definite correct answer, thereby narrowing the focus of the assessment inappropriately. (d) Do not punish students for failing to participate in class question sessions or inappropriately reward those verbally aggressive students who participate fully. (e) Remember the students' verbal and nonverbal behavior in class may not indicate their true attitudes/values.

TABLE 6.2 ● Continued			
Assessment Alternatives	**Advantages for Teachers**	**Disadvantages for Teachers**	**Suggestions for Improved Use**
4. Daily homework and seatwork	(a) Provide formative information about how learning is progressing. (b) Allow errors to be diagnosed and corrected. (c) Combine practice, reinforcements, and assessment.	(a) Tend to focus on narrow segments of learning rather than integrating large complexes of skills and knowledge. (b) Sample only a small variety of content and skills on any one assignment. (c) Assignment may not be complete or may be copied from others.	(a) Remember that this method assesses learning that is only in the formative stages. It may be inappropriate to assign summative letter grades from the results. (b) Failure to complete homework or completing it late is no reason to punish students by embarrassing them in front of others or by lowering their overall grade. Learning may be subsequently demonstrated through other assessments. (c) Do not inappropriately attribute poor test performance to the student's not doing the homework. (d) Do not overemphasize the homework grade and overuse homework as a teaching strategy (e.g., using it as a primary teaching method).
5. Teacher-made quizzes and tests	(a) Although primarily useful for summative evaluation, they may permit diagnosis or errors and faulty thinking. (b) Provide for students' written expression of knowledge.	(a) Require time to craft good tasks useful for diagnosis. (b) Focus exclusively on cognitive learning targets.	(a) Do not overemphasize lower level thinking skills. (b) Use open-ended or constructed response tasks to gain insight into a student's thinking processes and errors. (c) For better diagnosis of a student's thinking, use tasks that require students to apply and use their knowledge in "real-life" situations.
6. In-depth interviews of individual students	(a) Permit in-depth probing of students' understandings, thinking patterns, and problem-solving strategies. (b) Permit follow-up questions tailored to a student's responses and allow a student to elaborate answers. (c) Permit diagnosis of faulty thinking and errors in performances.	(a) Require a lot of time to complete. (b) Require keeping the rest of the class occupied while one student is being interviewed. (c) Require learning skills in effective educational achievement interviewing and diagnosis.	(a) If assessing students' thinking patterns, problem-solving strategies, etc., avoid prompting student toward a prescribed way of problem solving. (b) Some students need their self-confidence bolstered before they feel comfortable revealing their mistakes.

(continued)

TABLE 6.2 • Continued

Assessment Alternatives	Advantages for Teachers	Disadvantages for Teachers	Suggestions for Improved Use
7. Growth and learning progress portfolios	(a) Allow large segments of a student's learning experiences to be reviewed. (b) Allow monitoring of a student's growth and progress. (c) Communicate to students that growth and progress are more important than test results. (d) Allow student to participate in selecting and evaluating material to include in the portfolio. (e) Can become a focus of teaching and learning.	(a) Require a long time to accumulate evidence of growth and progress. (b) Require special effort to teach students how to use appropriate and realistic self-assessment techniques. (c) Require high-level knowledge of the subject matter to diagnose and guide students. (d) Require the ability to recognize complex and subtle patterns of growth and progress in the subject. (e) Results tend to be inconsistent from teacher to teacher.	(a) Be very clear about the learning targets toward which you are monitoring progress. (b) Use a conceptual framework or learning progress model to guide your diagnosis and monitoring. (c) Coordinate portfolio development and assessment with other teachers. (d) Develop scoring rubrics to define standards and maintain consistency.
8. Attitude and values questionnaires	(a) Assess effective characteristics of students. (b) Knowing student's attitudes and values in relation to a specific topic or subject matter may be useful in planning teaching. (c) May provide insights into students' motivations.	(a) The results are sensitive to the way questions are worded. Students may misinterpret, not understand, or react differently than the assessor intended. (b) Can be easily "faked" by older and testwise students.	(a) Remember that the way questions are worded significantly affects how students respond. (b) Remember that attitude questionnaire responses may change drastically from one occasion or context to another. (c) Remember that your personal theory of personality or personal value system may lead to incorrect interpretations of students' responses.

Summative Assessment Techniques

1. Teacher-made tests and quizzes	(a) Can assess a wide range of content and cognitive skills. (b) Can be aligned with what was actually taught. (c) Use a variety of task formats. (d) Allow for assessment or written expression.	(a) Difficult to assess complex skills or ability to use combinations of skills. (b) Require time to create, edit, and produce good items. (c) Craft task requiring students to apply knowledge to "real life." Class period is often too short for a complete assessment. (d) Focus exclusively on cognitive outcomes.	(a) Do not overemphasize lower level thinking skills. (b) Do not overuse short-answer and response-choice items. (c) Craft task requiring students to apply knowledge to "real life."

TABLE 6.2 • Continued

Assessment Alternatives	Advantages for Teachers	Disadvantages for Teachers	Suggestions for Improved Use
2. Tasks focusing on procedures and processes	(a) Allow assessments of nonverbal as well as verbal responses. (b) Allow students to integrate several simple skills and knowledge to perform a complex, realistic task. (c) Allow for group and cooperative performance and assessment. (d) Allow assessment of steps used to complete an assignment.	(a) Focus on a narrow range of content knowledge and cognitive skills. (b) Require great deal of time to properly formulate, administer, and rate. (c) May have low interrater reliability unless scoring rubrics are used. (d) Results are often specific to the combination of student and task. Students' performance quality is not easily generalized across different content and tasks. (e) Tasks that students perceive as uninteresting, boring, or irrelevant do not elicit the students' best efforts.	(a) Investigate carefully the reason for student's failure to complete the task successfully. (b) Use a scoring rubric to increase the reliability and validity of results. (c) Do not confuse the evaluation of the process a student uses with the need to evaluate the correctness of the answers. (d) Allow sufficient time for students to adequately demonstrate performance.
3. Tasks focusing on products and projects	(a) Same as 2(a), (b), and (c). (b) Permit several equally valid processes to be used to produce the product or complete the project. (c) Allow assessment of the quality of the product. (d) Allow longer time than class period to complete the tasks.	(a) Same as 2(a), (b), (c), (d), and (e). (b) Students may have unauthorized help outside of class to complete the product or project. (c) All students in the class must have the same opportunity to use all appropriate materials and tools in order for the assessment to be fair.	(a) Same as 2(a), (b), (c), and (d). (b) Give adequate instruction to students on the criteria that will be used to evaluate their work, the standards that will be applied, and how students can use these criteria and standards to monitor their own progress in completing the work. (c) Do not mistake the aesthetic appearance of the product for substance and thoughtfulness. (d) Do not punish tardiness in completing the project or product by lowering the student's grade.
4. Best work portfolios	(a) Allow large segments of a student's learning experience to be assessed. (b) May allow students to participate in the selection of the material to be included in the portfolio. (c) Allow either quantitative or qualitative assessment of the works in the portfolio. (d) Permit a much broader assessment of learning targets than tests.	(a) Require waiting a long time before reporting assessment results. (b) Students must be taught how to select work to include as well as how to present it effectively. (c) Teachers must learn to use a scoring rubric that assesses a wide variety of pieces of work. (d) Interrater reliability is low from teacher to teacher. (e) Require high levels of subject matter knowledge to evaluate students' work properly.	(a) Be very clear about the learning targets to be assessed to avoid confusion and invalid portfolio assessment results. (b) Teach a student to use appropriate criteria to choose the work to include. (c) Do not collect too much material to evaluate. (d) Coordinate portfolio development with other teachers. (e) Develop and use scoring rubrics to define standards and maintain consistency.

(continued)

TABLE 6.2 • Continued			
Assessment Alternatives	**Advantages for Teachers**	**Disadvantages for Teachers**	**Suggestions for Improved Use**
5. Textbook-supplied tests and quizzes	(a) Allow for assessment of written expression. (b) Already prepared, save teachers time. (c) Match the content and sequence of the textbook or curricular materials.	(a) Often do not assess complex skills or ability to use combinations of skills. (b) Often do not match the emphases and presentations in class. (c) Focus on cognitive skills. (d) Class period is often too short for a complete assessment.	(a) Be skeptical that the items were made by professionals and are of high quality. (b) Carefully edit or rewrite the item to match what you have taught. (c) Remember that you are personally responsible for using a poor quality test. You must not appeal to the authoriy of the textbook.
6. Standardized achievement tests	(a) Assess a wide range of cognitive abilities and skills that cover a year's learning. (b) Assess content and skills common to many schools across the country. (c) Items developed and screened by professionals, resulting in only the best items being included. (d) Corroborate what teachers know about pupils; sometimes indicate unexpected results for specific students. (e) Provide norm-referenced information that permits evaluation of students' progress in relation to students nationwide. (f) Provide legitimate comparisons of a student's achievement in two and more curricular areas. (g) Provide growth scales so students' long-term educational development can be monitored. (h) Useful for curriculum evaluation.	(a) Focus exclusively on cognitive outcomes. (b) Often the emphasis on a particular test is different from the emphasis of a particular teacher. (c) Do not provide diagnostic information. (d) Results usually take too long to get back to teachers, so are not directly useful for instructional planning.	(a) Avoid narrowing your instruction to prepare students for these tests when administrators put pressure on teachers. (b) Do not use these tests to evaluate teachers. (c) Do not confuse the quality of the learning that did occur in the classroom with the results on standardized tests when interpreting them. (d) Educate parents about the tests' limited validity for assessing a student's learning potentials.

Source: Nitko, Anthony, *Educational Assessment of Students*, 4th ed., © 2004. Reprinted by permission of Pearson Education, Inc., Upper Saddle River, NJ.

Summary

- Performance-based assessments consist of portfolios, performance tasks, exhibitions, and other documentation of student accomplishments.

- Authentic assessment occurs when the student completes or demonstrates knowledge, skills, or behavior in a real-life context.

- A portfolio is a systematic collection of a student's work covering an extended period of time.

- Although not without concerns, performance-based assessment procedures have the potential of helping us implement reliable, valid, and fair approaches to assessment.

REFERENCES

Airasian, P. W. (2001). *Assessment in the classroom* (4th ed.). New York: McGraw-Hill.

Airasian, P. W. (2005). *Classroom assessment* (5th ed.). New York: McGraw-Hill.

Alper, S., Ryndak, D. L., & Schloss, C. N. (2001). *Alternate assessment of students with disabilities in inclusive settings*. Boston: Allyn and Bacon.

Arter, J., & McTighe, J. (2001). Scoring rubrics in the classroom. In T. R. Guskey & R. J. Marzano (Eds.), *Experts in assessment*. Thousand Oaks, CA: Corwin Press.

Arter, J. A., & Spandel, V. (1991). *Using portfolios of student work in instruction and assessment*. Portland, OR: Northwest Regional Education Laboratory.

Boke, N., & Hewitt, G. (2004). *Vermont strategic reading initiative: Reading to learn*. Burlington: Vermont Department of Education.

Byrnes, J. P. (1996). *Cognitive development and learning in instructional contexts*. Boston: Allyn and Bacon.

Chandra X-Ray Observatory. *Electromagnetic pasta*. Retrieved June 26, 2001, from the World Wide Web: http://chandra.harvard.edu/edu/formal/pasta/task1.html.

Cole, D. J., Ryan, C. W., & Kick, F. (1995). *Portfolios across the curriculum and beyond*. Thousand Oaks, CA: Corwin Press.

Cushman, P. (1990). Performances and exhibitions: The demonstration of mastery. *Horace 6:* 17–24.

Darling-Hammond, L., Ancess, J., & Falk, B. (1995). *Authentic assessment in action*. New York: Teachers College Press.

Diez, M. E., & Moon, C. J. (1992). What do we want students to know? . . . and other important questions. *Educational Leadership 49:* 38–41.

Dixon-Krauss, L. (1996). *Vygotsky in the classroom*. White Plains, NY: Longman.

Exemplars.com. *How is breathing related to my pulse?* Retrieved April 20, 2005 from http://www.exemplars.com

Fuchs, L. (1994). *Connecting performance assessment to instruction*. Reston, VA: Council for Exceptional Children.

Gardner, H. (1991). *The unschooled mind*. New York: Basic Books.

Gordon, E. W., & Bonilla-Bowman, C. (1996). Can performance-based assessments contribute to the achievement of educational equity? In J. B. Baron & D. P. Wolf (Eds.), *Performance-based student assessment: Challenges and possibilities* (pp. 32–51). Chicago, IL: University of Chicago Press.

Hewitt, G. (1995). *A portfolio primer: Teaching, collecting, and assessing student writing*. Portsmouth, NH: Heinemann.

Hymes, D. L., Chafin, A. E., & Gonder, P. (1991). *The changing face of testing and assessment, problems and solutions*. Arlington, VA: American Association of School Administrators.

Keeley, P. (2001). *High school: Chandra performance tasks*. Maine Science Teachers Network Listserv [Online]. Available: maine_science@list.terc.edu.

Linn, R. L., & Baker, E. L. (1996). Can performance-based student assessments be psychometrically sound? In J. B. Baron & D. P. Wolf (Eds.), *Performance-based student assessment: Challenges and possibilities* (pp. 84–103). Chicago, IL: University of Chicago Press.

Madaus, G., Haney, W., & Kreitzer, A. (1992). *Testing and evaluation*. New York: Council for Aid to Education.

Mayer, R. E. (1998). *The promise of educational psychology*. Upper Saddle River, NJ: Merrill/Prentice-Hall.

Meyer, C. A. (1992). What's the difference between authentic and performance assessment? *Educational Leadership 49:* 39–40.

National Council of the Teachers of Mathematics. (1991). *Mathematics assessment*. Alexandria, VA: Author.

Nitko, A. J. (2001). *Educational assessment of students*. Upper Saddle River, NJ: Prentice-Hall.

Rogers, S., & Graham, S. (2000). *The high performance toolbox: Succeeding with performance tasks, projects, and assessments* (3rd ed.). Evergreen, CO: Peak Learning Systems.

Shepard, L., & Bliem, C. L. (1995). Parents' thinking about standardized tests and performance assessment. *Educational Researcher 24*(8): 25–32.

Stiggins, R. J. (1997). *Student-centered classroom assessment* (2nd ed.). Upper Saddle River, NJ: Merrill.

Swicegood, P. (1994). Portfolio-based assessment practices. *Intervention in School and Clinic 30*(1): 6–15.

Tindal, G., McDonald, M., Tedesco, M., & Glasgow, A. (2003). Alternate assessments in reading and math: Development and validation for students with significant disabilities. *Exceptional Children, 69:* 481–494.

Vermont Department of Education. (2001). *2000–2001 5th grade writing benchmarks*. Montpelier, VT: Author.

Wesson, C. L., & King, R. P. (1996). Portfolio assessment and special education students. *Teaching Exceptional Children 28*(2): 44–48.

Wiggins, G. P. (1993). *Assessing student performance*. San Francisco: Jossey-Bass.

Wiggins, G., & McTigue, J. (1998). *Understanding by design*. Alexandria, VA: Association for Supervision and Curriculum Development.

Wolf, D. (1996). *Performance-based student assessment: Challenges and possibilities*. Paper presented at the annual meeting of the American Educational Research Association, April. New York, New York.

7 Test Interpretation and Report Writing

Chapter Objectives

After completing this chapter,
you should be able to:

- Discuss the process of interpreting
  assessment.
- Explain the general principles that
  guide the development of assessment
  reports.
- Describe the components of an
  assessment report.
- Explain considerations in sharing
  reports with the student and with
  family members.
- Discuss the use of computer-generated
  test results and reports.

Key Terms

Hypothesis generation   Examiner bias

Overview

Interpreting and synthesizing assessment information takes skill and practice. This
chapter introduces the process that special educators use to analyze information obtained during testing. The interpretation of assessment results involves the practitioner in a series of analyses that lead to one or more explanations of the student's
performance and behavior. Next, the practitioner synthesizes this information into
a written report that becomes part of the student's record.

Interpreting Assessment Information

As soon as possible after completing an assessment, the practitioner scores each of the tests, double-checking any mathematical calculations. Then each test is analyzed separately. The practitioner begins by examining the student's overall performance by finding the test's composite score(s). The composite scores help build a picture of student performance. Next, the practitioner examines each of the subtests of behaviors, skills, and abilities. This process is followed for each test administered, then the results are synthesized.

General Guidelines

The following steps for test interpretation are adapted from the works of Flanagan and Kaufman (2004), Kamphaus (1993), Kaufman (1994), and McGrew (1994):

1. *Interpret overall test performance.* Examine the student's overall performance and consider an interpretation of the full-scale or total score performance.
2. *Interpret subtest performance.* Examine the student's performance in each area assessed. List the areas that indicate strong student performance as well as areas that indicate student weaknesses.
3. *Compare the subtest performance on all tests.* Consider each subtest and the skills, knowledge, or behaviors that it measures. Compare the shared abilities across assessments. Identify relative areas of student strengths and needs. If a student's score on one test looks different from a score on a different test, the practitioner will need to consider possible reasons for the discrepancy.
4. *Integrate the student's relative strengths and needs.* Compare all the test data, including the results of observations, interviews, and conferences, with more formal assessments such as norm-referenced, curriculum-based, or criterion-referenced assessments. Continue to build the picture of student performance by integrating the student's relative strengths and needs across assessment data.

Interpreting Results from Assessments with Accommodations or Modifications

Some students with disabilities need modified testing to participate in local and statewide assessments. For example, a student with a disability whose first language is not English may need extended time, or the test may be translated into the student's home language. Another student may need a modified test, with fewer items per page. Deborah Harris (2003) writes that these may improve the validity of the assessment scores. (The score of a student with a disability who takes the science test in his home language may be a more valid measure of science ability for this student.) However, Harris cautions that "tests scores that have been derived based on standard conditions must be interpreted with caution when those conditions have been altered" (p. 8). Deleting some items and modifying the time limits have been shown to have unanticipated effects (p. 8).

The more you use a test or conduct an observation or complete an interview, the more you will come to understand the information that can be gathered and how it can be interpreted. Beginning teachers who have opportunities to work with an experienced examiner or mentor can gain valuable skills. A mentorship must include time to discuss interpretation of various assessments. One method of interpreting results is a process called **hypothesis generation.**

Generating a Hypothesis

When interpreting the results of testing, we prefer the process described as hypothesis generation (Flanagan & Kaufman, 2004; Kaufman, 1994; McGrew, 1994) or integrative interpretation (Kamphaus, 1993). In test interpretation, a hypothesis is an explanation of a student's performance and behavior based on the collected assessment data.

As the examiner reviews the assessment information, several hypotheses will emerge. One hypothesis will relate to the referral questions; other hypotheses may relate to levels of achievement, behavior, cognitive ability, communication, development, functioning, motor development, or sensory functioning.

The examiner will use the test data (i.e., the results of the various assessment approaches, including standardized testing, curriculum-based assessment, performance-based assessment, observations, interviews, and so on) to support one or more hypotheses. For example, an examiner may integrate information obtained from interviews with teachers, therapists, support staff, the student, and family members with information obtained from behavioral observations of the student to support the determination of attention deficit hyperactivity disorder.

Kaufman, discussing his approach to test interpretation, cautions examiners to remember that hypotheses are not facts and that, later, they may prove to be artifacts. Hypotheses are informed assumptions; when evidence does not substantiate hypotheses, further investigation is necessary. The test data may need reanalysis, or the examiner may have to collect additional data to generate new or modified hypotheses.

▶ **CEC Common Core Knowledge and Skills.** A beginning special educator can interpret information from formal and informal assessments (CC8S5).

Examiner Bias

Examiner bias can arise in the interpretation of assessment results. Examiners need to be aware of the types of biases in order to identify and control them. Bias colors how the data will be viewed and interpreted. Bentzen (2005) describes two levels of potential bias. At one level is the personal bias and perspective of the examiner: The examiner brings individual experiences, abilities, attitudes, and knowledge to the interpretation process. Examiners need to take precautions to not let personal bias interfere with the careful, objective interpretation of information. The second level of bias is the result of formal training and includes bias shaped by theory, conceptual framework, or philosophy. These biases affect how you interpret a situation, event, or behavior.

Using Professional Knowledge

To interpret test results, the examiner must understand the purpose of the test itself, how it is administered, and what the test scores mean. In our discussion of norm-referenced tests and standardization samples in Chapter 4, you learned that a standardized test can be administered to students with characteristics that are similar to the norm group and that the examiner can compare the student's score with those of the norm group. In interpreting test results, the examiner must consider the norm sample of a test instrument; if the characteristics of the student tested are not similar to those of the norm group, the examiner will need to explain how this affects the test scores. The test scores of students who have characteristics different from the norm sample cannot be compared with the test scores of the students who participated in the standardization of the instrument.

Examiners need to understand the test scores and be able to explain them to others. For example, an examiner may be called upon to explain the difference between a percentile rank and a percentage-correct score or to clarify misperceptions about a grade equivalent score.

In interpreting assessment information, the examiner must be a keen observer of behavior and of environmental conditions that adversely affect student performance.

Research-Based Practices | **Interpreting Online Vocational Assessments**

Today, many vocational interest and basic skills tests can be administered and scored online. In an investigation of the feasibility of online delivery of a vocational interest inventory, Paul Jones and his colleagues at the University of Nevada (Jones, Harbach, Coker, & Staples, 2002) sought to answer whether there was a difference in individual satisfaction between those who received vocational test interpretation online and those who received the more traditional face-to-face delivery. A second question addressed the use of video cues and if they enhanced the perceived quality of an online interpretive session. Thirty-eight college students participated in the study. Although the sample was small and further studies are needed, the results were interesting and suggest that online interpretation of vocational scores could become a new tool for career development specialists. The authors note that "Online delivery of employment counseling services has obvious potential for increased access both by clients in rural or isolated locations and those in crowded urban settings where travel is difficult." (p. 134)

In previous chapters we examined the effects of the physical, learning, and social environments on performance. Observations of the environment and of the student will add valuable information. As the examiner synthesizes assessment results, the observations may corroborate information obtained during formal testing, or these observations may help to explain why a student's score was unexpectedly low.

Interpreting assessment information requires a wide range of knowledge concerning child and adolescent growth and development as well as disability. Examiners need professional knowledge of classroom curriculum and pedagogy, and a solid understanding of statistics is essential in interpreting test scores. Knowledge of special education, related services, state regulations, and federal law is essential in clarifying the information.

Responding to Diversity

Previous chapters discuss problems of test bias regarding students with diverse cultural, ethnic, racial and linguistic backgrounds, geographic regions of origin, and gender, disability, and economic groups. Examiners must be aware not only that standardized instruments but other assessment approaches can show bias. For example, Chapter 6 examines how portfolio assessments are, for the most part, biased against students who attend school infrequently.

You know that the purpose for one of the assessment steps, determining eligibility, is to identify students with disabilities who need special education services. Lyman (1986) describes these instruments:

Any test that is worthwhile must discriminate; after all, this is just another way of saying that it will "reveal individual differences." But the intended discrimination should be on the basis of the trait being measured, not on the basis of racial or ethnic background. (pp. 7–8)

General Principles for Report Writing

Once the examiner has interpreted the assessment information, results will by synthesized and organized into an assessment report. In writing the report, the examiner makes sure that general statements about the student's performance or recommendations can be supported by the assessment data. The following general principles guide the development of a well-written report.

Organize the Information

Organize the information systematically. Present information in sections with appropriate headings. Discuss recommendations at the end of the report; do not insert them in the body of the document.

Relate Only the Facts

Report only factual information. Do not include unsubstantiated information. When including information from other sources, such as other assessment reports, mention the date and name of the sources.

Include Only Essential Information

Write about the facts, but avoid extraneous information about the student or family. Although your report must be comprehensive, some information is not essential; you will need to make judgments about whether what you have learned is appropriate for inclusion. Use only information that contributes to the understanding of the student, the test results, and recommendations.

Be Aware of Bias

Avoid generalizations that can bias the report. Be careful about stereotyping groups. Critically review your report before submitting it.

Present Accurate Information

Make sure that the information is accurate. Review the information to check for accuracy. When calculating test scores on the test form, be sure to double-check your work. Some tests require scores of several different types, and it is easy to make errors converting from one type of test score to another. The examiner must always verify that the test scores were copied correctly from the test to the report. Be sure that there are no misinterpretations about performance due to inaccurate calculations or inaccurate copying.

Include Any Reservations

Incorporate, and discuss fully, any reservations about the assessment process and its effect on the results. Reservations may include observations of the student that indicate the results are not accurate or do not reflect the student's best abilities. Record any interruptions or other disturbances in the environment that may have affected the results, and note the limitations in technical adequacy of the instrument(s) for students with characteristics that the norming sample does not represent.

Avoid Technical Jargon

Use clear, understandable language. Avoid discussion of the formulas used to measure discrepancies or of the theoretical perspectives of various experts. Technical jargon can make the report confusing or ambiguous. How could the language in the following excerpt be simplified?

> Tony has dual diagnostic deficits that affect expressive and receptive language, articulation, internal regulation, and cognition. A coexisting diagnosis can be made of Attention-Deficit Hyperactive Disorder and mental retardation. This diagnosis is strongly suggested by biological maternal history of ethanol abuse, apparently during the gestational period, and Tony's striking physiognomy.

Write Clearly

Work to develop report-writing skills. Use the writing process to create a working draft. Reread and rewrite the working draft. Check the draft by using grammar and spell check. Avoid ambiguous language. Use a checklist like that found in Table 7.1 to ensure that you have included all the necessary information.

▶ Using these criteria, evaluate Gina's assessment. (see Snapshot on pp. 149–150)

TABLE 7.1 ● A Checklist for Evaluating an Assessment Report		
Report Section	**Yes**	**No**
A. Identifying Information		
1. Is the information complete?	_____	_____
2. Is the information accurate?	_____	_____
B. Reason for Referral		
1. Is the reason for referral clearly described?	_____	_____
2. Is the source of the referral included?	_____	_____
3. Does the reason for referral provide a reason for conducting the assessment?	_____	_____
C. Background Information		
1. Is this section complete?	_____	_____
2. Are any of the descriptions vague?	_____	_____
3. Can some information be omitted?	_____	_____
D. Behavioral Observations		
1. Are the observations clearly described?	_____	_____
2. Are any of the descriptions vague?	_____	_____
3. Does this section help the reader to visualize the student's behavior?	_____	_____
E. Assessment Approaches Used		
1. Are the sources of information identified?	_____	_____
F. Discussion of Results		
1. Does the discussion relate to the referral questions?	_____	_____
2. Is this section organized around themes?	_____	_____
3. Are the themes discussed separately, including references to appropriate tests and assessment procedures?	_____	_____
4. Are strengths and needs described?	_____	_____
G. Summary		
1. Does this section restate the major themes and how the testing addressed the reasons for referral?	_____	_____
2. Is this section too long?	_____	_____
H. Recommendations		
1. Do the recommendations logically follow from the rest of the report?	_____	_____
2. Can the recommendations be implemented?	_____	_____
3. Are recommendations for a variety of settings included?	_____	_____
4. Are the recommendations understandable?	_____	_____
I. General Evaluation		
1. Is the writing clear?	_____	_____
2. Has the report been proofread?	_____	_____
3. Have the spelling, grammar, and punctuation been checked?	_____	_____
4. Are the sections of the report identifiable?	_____	_____
5. Has technical language been minimized?	_____	_____
6. Is there any bias?	_____	_____

Synthesizing Information

Graphs allow us to illustrate assessment information in meaningful ways. They permit the viewer to think about the substance of the data and encourage the eye to compare different data (Tufte, 1990). Graphically displayed data enhance understanding and serve to highlight findings that may be embedded in an assessment report.

Two commonly used types of graphs are:

1. *Pie charts:* Pie charts display a circular graph cut into segments. This type of graph is most useful in displaying percentages of data when the examiner wants to illustrate parts of a whole.
2. *Bar graphs:* Bar graphs display rectangular sets of information with the length proportional to the amount of information represented. Bar graphs are most useful in displaying frequency counts or plotting trends over time.

How It Works !

Analyzing and Interpreting Assessment Information

Spencer Lanley, a special educator at Summit Middle School and a member of the school's student assistance team, has been asked by team members to conduct several classroom observations. The team has been working with a eighth-grade teacher who was concerned about Cindy, a student with a learning disability. Initially, the teacher had brought her concerns to the team because she was worried about Cindy's progress in mathematics. She had explained, "I'm really concerned about Cindy's participation in the classroom. All of the interventions we have tried just don't seem to be working. It doesn't seem that Cindy is paying attention or getting any work accomplished."

First, Spencer defined "math-related activities" as looking at the teacher during the class lesson, working with paper and pencil on math problems, and discussing solutions to the math problems with peers. Then he collected data over a period of three days. The data analysis indicated that Cindy engaged in several behaviors during the class period: She was out of her seat, out of the classroom, looking around the room, and engaged in math-related activities.

The three pie charts in Figure 7.1 allow comparison of Cindy's behavior on each day of observed. The pie graph depicts the percentage of time of time Cindy was engaged in each of the behaviors during math class.

The bar graph (Figure 7.2) compares each behavior over the three-day period. Which type of graph do you think best displays the data in answer to the observation question? Your answer should take into account the original assessment question!

▶ The pie chart is advantageous because it depicts the whole period of time available for mathematics and how Cindy spent this time during three different days.

▶ The bar graph is advantageous because it allows us to see the type of individual activities in which Cindy was engaged.

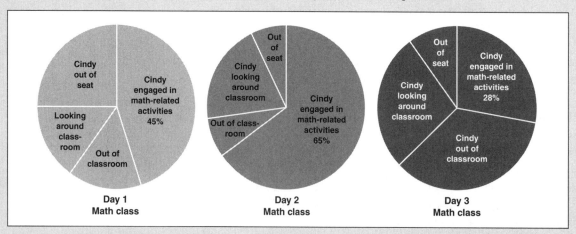

FIGURE 7.1 ● Data Presentation in Pie Charts

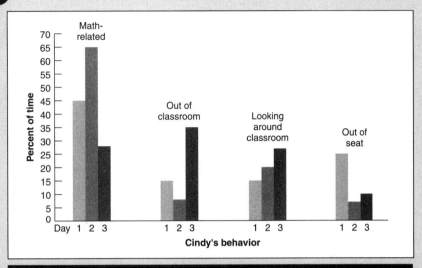

FIGURE 7.2 ● Data Presentation in a Bar Chart

The pie chart is the best way to display data in answer to the observation question because it allows the viewer to see how Cindy spends her time during the entire math class. If the observation question had been concerned with increasing or decreasing a behavior, then the bar graph would have been the best choice.

Spencer remembered an assessment class that he had taken in college and how the instructor had discussed the importance of comparing a target student to one or more students about whom the teacher has no concerns. He learned that a variation of the bar graph allows comparison of several students. He decided that this could provide additional information regarding whether the target student's behavior is atypical. Figure 7.3 compares Cindy's engagement in math-related activities with three other students across the different days. Spencer carefully analyzed this information. By looking at day 1 he saw that although Cindy wasn't engaged as long as Tanya and Maria, her level of engagement was similar to Susan. Day 2 provided evidence that not only Cindy but the other students were engaged for a high percent of the time, and Cindy's behavior on the third day didn't seem to be much different from the other students, except Maria.

Spencer planned to show the charts to Cindy's teacher and other team members. By working together, they will identify some teaching strategies and materials that will help the classroom teacher enhance learning opportunities for all the students.

▶ **CEC Common Core Knowledge and Skills.** A beginning special educator can monitor intragroup behavior changes across subjects and activities (GC8S3).

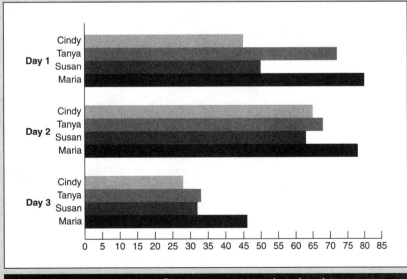

FIGURE 7.3 ● Percent of Engagement in Math-Related Activity for Four Students over Three Days

Types of Assessment Reports

Assessment reports are written for a variety of purposes, and the information they contain varies accordingly. Reports are written to (1) summarize a series of observations and synthesize the observational data, (2) report student progress over a period of time, (3) describe the results of administering an individual test, and (4) integrate and interpret the results of a comprehensive assessment.

Reports of Observations

A teacher customarily writes a report providing a synthesis of several observations conducted on a student. We have discussed the importance of conducting multiple observations to obtain an accurate sample of student behavior. The written report organizes the information the teacher collected from all the observations.

How to Write an Observation Report

Examiners should complete a written observation as soon as possible after the final observation. Observation reports include the following information:

1. *Student information:* Name, date of birth, age, grade, and teacher's name.
2. *Dates of observations.*
3. *Purpose(s) for conducting the observations:* The observations may focus on the environment or on the student. Clearly state the purpose of the observations and define the events or behaviors in observable terms.
4. *Setting(s) in which the observations took place.*
5. *Description of the environments:* The physical, learning, and social aspects.
6. *Behavioral observations:* Be sure to relate only observed information. Do not interpret or make judgments.
7. *Discussion:* Summarize your observations of the environment and the student's behavior. Include your interpretation of the assessment data.
8. *Recommendations:* State realistic suggestions for implementing progress or improvement.

The Snapshot about John Diamond illustrates an observation report written by the special education consultant.

Progress Reports

Progress reports are a summary of the advances a student makes during a specific time period and provide a link to the IEP, which requires periodic monitoring of student progress. Progress reports must relate information about the student with reference to these goals and intended outcomes of the IEP. Teachers can prepare these reports to accompany a report card at the end of the marking period or to provide an update of information to family and other team members. One example of a progress report is a checklist (Figure 7.6 on p. 145).

Individual Test Reports

Individual test reports describe the test results and the examiner's interpretation of student performance. Usually, these reports are shared at the team meeting and become part of the student's permanent record. Individual reports of tests present a limited

SNAPSHOT

Observation Report on John Diamond

The special education consultant, Marilyn Philbrick, was asked to observe an eighth-grade student, John, in his regular classroom. At the time, John was receiving speech therapy and had been referred to the school psychologist because the team was concerned with John's aggressive behavior. According to the eighth-grade teacher, "He is always in motion. He frequently hits and pushes other students, and he is verbally abusive."

Marilyn met with John's teacher to discuss John's problem behaviors more fully. The meeting helped to clarify the behaviors that were of concern and to plan the best time and place to conduct the observations. Marilyn decided to develop her own observation instrument based on an event-interval recording method described in Chapter 5.

After completing her observations, Marilyn wrote an observation report that summarized the findings. She also developed a graph to help explain the observation data. A copy of the graph (Figure 7.4) and one of her data sheets (Figure 7.5) that she developed to help explain her data follow her written report.

Observation Report

Name: John Diamond

Birth Date: 9/21/xx

Age: 13 years, 2 months

Grade: 8

Teacher: Dara Hall

Dates of Observations: 11/1/xx; 11/4/xx; 11/8/xx

Observer: Marilyn Philbrick

Purpose of Observations: The assessment team requested classroom observations because of concerns regarding John's behavior problems. Specific concerns include his out-of-seat behavior, hitting and pushing other students, and verbally abusing others. The purpose of the observations was to determine the degree to which John actually engages in the behaviors of concern.

Setting: Students change classes for each subject. Three observations were conducted over a two-week period; John was observed in mathematics and language arts classes and during the lunch period. Each observation consisted of 30 minutes and took place between 9:00 and 11:00 a.m.

Observations of the Environment: The classrooms are designed for small group work with student desks clustered in groups of four. Students are not assigned a particular desk but are free to choose where to work. The classrooms consisted of 20 to 23 students with one teacher and occasional other support staff.

Behavioral Observations: Results of the observations indicate that John did indeed display many aggressive behaviors. John pushed and poked other students 5 to 6 times during each of the observations; less frequently (3 to 4 times each observation), he hit and swore at other students and occasionally (2 times each observation) swore at the teacher. These behaviors usually occurred when students were changing classes.

At other times (5 to 6 times each observation), John joined the other students in laughter, volunteered answers, helped a student who was having difficulty with finding materials, and participated in activities willingly.

Discussion: John engages in pushing, hitting, and poking other students as well as swearing at others, including the teacher. These observations indicate that the teacher continually has to watch him closely and frequently has to intervene on behalf of the other students.

John's problem behaviors are most apparent when he is listening without being able to be active, when the general noise level in the classroom begins to escalate, and when he is anticipating transition.

Aggression was especially high during transition, with no instances occurring during a spelling activity in which the teacher directed the whole class and each student was actively engaged. Few aggressive behaviors occurred during small group math manipulative activities. Both spelling and math were structured and required him to be more involved.

John appears to be a happy youngster, laughing and participating in activities willingly, but shows little self-control or regard for his effects on others.

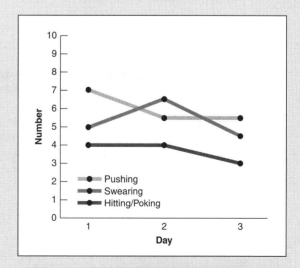

FIGURE 7.4 • Teacher-Developed Graphs

(continued)

Name: John					Date: November 1
Two-minute interval	Behavior: p = push, h = hit, s = swear	Total behaviors			Comments Math class
		p	h	s	
00–02					Teacher goes over assignment for following day. John asks questions to clarify.
02–04					
04–06		||		IIII	Class changes at 9:05 Behavior occurs during transition and in hallway.
06–08		||	||||		Hits and pokes the boy behind him.
08–10					Other occurrences? –unable to follow John closely during this period.
10–12				||	Language arts class begins at 9:12.
12–14		|			Helps student find materials.
14–16					Volunteers to assist teacher.
28–30					

FIGURE 7.5 • Teacher-Developed Data Sheet

Recommendations: John appears to benefit from structured learning activities that include active student participation. Classroom noise should be monitored, because this may have an adverse effect on his behavior. Positive behavior management strategies should be shared with his teacher and other support staff in the classroom.

account of a student's performance, thus they may be combined later into a comprehensive assessment report to provide more complete information on the student.

Each member of the team who conducts an assessment of the student must complete a written test report. At the team meeting, reports by several examiners, such as the special education teacher, the school psychologist, the physical or occupational therapist, or the speech and language pathologist, are considered.

Second Marking Period

	In Progress	Mastered
1. Uses correct punctuation to end a sentence.		×
2. Uses correct form of *you're* and *your.*	×	
3. Uses commas in a series correctly.		×
4. Correctly places apostrophe in contractions and possessives.	×	
5. Uses correct form of *their, there,* and *they're.*	×	
6. Uses correct form of adjectives.	×	

FIGURE 7.6 ● Progress Report

Comprehensive Assessment Reports

A comprehensive assessment report is usually extensive; it summarizes previously known information as well as information learned from the results of a thorough assessment. Typically, a comprehensive report relies on the many sources of assessment information described in this book.

▶ **CEC Common Core Knowledge and Skills.** A beginning special educator can create and maintain records (CC8S10).

Writing the Report

Examiners should organize individual test reports and comprehensive test reports according to the following areas:

1. Identifying data
2. Reason for referral/assessment
3. Background information
4. Observations of the environment
5. Behavioral observations
6. Tests, interviews, and performance-based assessment
7. Discussion of the results
8. Summary
9. Recommendations

Each area should be a separate section. Use appropriate subheadings to help organize the report, as suggested by the lists in the sections that follow.

Identifying Data

Information in the first section of the report identifies the student, the parents, the school, the test, and the examiner:

1. *About the student:* Include the student's name, address, phone number, chronological age in years and months, birthdate, and gender.
2. *About the family:* Include the names and addresses of family members.
3. *About the school:* Include the student's grade level, school's name, address, phone number, director or principal's name, and teacher's name.
4. *About the testing:* Include the name of the examiner, the date of testing, and the date the report was written.

School records, the referral form, interviews with family members or teachers, records of administered tests, and so forth, are standard sources for this information.

Reason for Referral/Assessment

The second section contains a summary of the reasons for referral and the name of the person who initiated the referral or the reasons for the current assessment. Throughout the report, be sure to directly address the reasons and make sure the conclusions and recommendations refer to them. As the report develops, one of its central themes will be the assessment questions and the extent to which the testing addressed these issues.

Background Information

Briefly summarize information about the student's background—the student's education, family history, medical care, and previous assessment results. Medical history can include a description of any unusual medical problems, diagnoses, extended hospital stays, continuing medical care, general health, and results of vision and hearing testing. Some students have experienced early and prolonged medical interventions; some of these students may have had extended hospital stays and received extensive care for genetic abnormalities or other conditions. Their medical folders can be quite lengthy, and the examiner will need to judge which information is pertinent. Extensive discussion of a student's medical history may bias the reader to think that the child has a severe disability or may be unusually difficult to manage.

Facts such as dates of attendance, regularity of attendance, type of placement or services in place, performance, interventions tried, and results of previous educational testing is available from school records, interviews, and home visits. A summary of child care experiences, depending on the age of the student, is also important.

Details of familial and/or cultural background can be useful, but use this type of information carefully and judiciously and only when it is relevant and helps to explain student behavior related to the results of testing. Knowledge about the family and cultural background is customarily obtained from interviews with the student, family members, teachers, and other professionals, and through a home visit.

Observations of the Environment

The description of the classroom environment includes the physical setting and the learning and social environments. Previous chapters discuss important environmental factors and suggest ways to gather information about these aspects of the classroom.

Behavioral Observations

The report includes a description of student behavior during testing. The examiner will want to observe whether the student was cooperative, distractible, attentive, tired, or shy, or exhibited other types of behavior. How did the student approach the testing situation? What was the student's behavior at the beginning of the testing? During the testing? At the end? This section reports any observations conducted in the classroom, playground, cafeteria, or other setting.

As Chapter 5 discusses, systematic observations can be an important source of data. Methodical observations help in understanding student behavior and learning strategies and can also inform us about intervention strategies. Nevertheless, observations about behavior in the testing situation may not be generalizable to other settings. Testing assesses a narrow sample of behavior. To a certain extent, the testing situation is artificial. Furthermore, a student's behavior can vary in different settings and with different examiners. These factors must be considered when interpreting results and drawing conclusions about a student's behavior.

In writing the report, use the following list of behaviors as a starting point for discussion (Sattler, 2001):

- Physical appearance
- Reactions to test session and to the examiner
- General behavior
- Typical mode of relating to the examiner
- Language style
- General response style
- Response to failures
- Response to successes
- Response to encouragement
- Activity level
- Attitude toward self
- Attitude toward the examiner and the testing process
- Visual-motor ability
- Unusual habits, mannerisms, or verbalizations
- Examiner's reaction to the student (p. 728)

Tests, Interviews, and Performance-Based Assessment

The report includes a list of the tests and other assessments, both formal and informal, that teachers and others conducted to collect the assessment data. All tests are briefly described in terms of the purpose of the test and the areas that the test assesses.

Discussion of Results

In listing the results of the assessments, begin by discussing the overall test performance. Discuss the student's total scores or composite scores and provide an interpretation of the meaning of the scores. This should provide a picture of the student's current level of functioning. Use the same types of scores throughout the section. Standard scores, percentiles, or stanines are preferable. Always include the confidence intervals when reporting standard scores. You may decide to report two or more types of scores, such as standard scores and percentiles. Some examiners like to report scores in a table format within the discussion of the results.

Next, consider each subtest and the skills, knowledge, and behaviors measured. Discuss the areas that indicate strong student performance as well as areas that indicate student weaknesses. Analyze each test separately, then synthesize the results.

Compare the shared abilities across all assessments given. Integrate the student's relative strengths and needs by discussing student performance across test data, including both formal and informal assessments.

Summary

This section should be brief. Summarize the major points that have been discussed and synthesize the results. Report the current level of functioning and indicate areas of relative strength and need. Answer the referral questions. Restate the themes that have emerged.

Recommendations

An assessment is conducted chiefly to answer questions about the student and to develop recommendations. The recommendations logically stem from the information in the assessment report. Suggest realistic, practical recommendations for implementation. Develop recommendations for the student in a variety of settings, including school, home, and community. Do not include specific goals and objectives in the assessment report; these are to be written in the IEP during the team meeting. The Snapshot about Gina on pages 149–150 illustrates an example of a comprehensive assessment report.

Evaluating the Report

Writing a report is an important way to communicate assessment findings. A report helps you to organize the results of testing systematically, to analyze a student's performance, and to make recommendations. You must write the reports clearly using correct grammar and spelling. Table 7.1 on page 139 illustrates a checklist for use when reviewing the adequacy of assessment reports.

Sharing Assessment Results with Others

Chapter 1 discusses the Family Educational Rights and Privacy Act (also known as the Buckley amendment). The Buckley amendment allows families access to their records held at any educational agency that accepts federal money, including a public school. Family members have a right to all assessment information, and you should provide a copy of the report to the family members that they can take with them, as is their choice.

The Buckley amendment also protects students and families from the illicit sharing of assessment information. Before the school can release assessment information to other agencies or individuals outside of the school system, the parent must sign a written consent form. The consent form specifies which records to release, to whom, and the reason for the release. A copy of the records to be released must be sent to the student's parents.

Family Members

Share assessment results and recommendations with family members as soon as possible after you have completed the report. Look over the test results and make sure that you can explain the test scores. You will want to be careful that your words are not misunderstood, because family members may be very anxious about the assessment outcome. It is good practice to plan the topics you will be covering and what you want to say. Using descriptive terms to interpret test scores is helpful for parents and other team members. Lyman (1986) suggests the following scale:

▶ **CEC Common Core Knowledge and Skills.** A beginning special educator can report assessment results to all stakeholders using effective communication skills (CC8S7).

Percentile ranks	*Descriptive terms*
96 or above	Very high; superior
85–95	High; excellent
75–85	Above average; good
25–75	About average; satisfactory or fair
15–25	Below average; fair or slightly weak
05–15	Low; weak
5 or below	Very low; very weak (p. 136)

The Student

Students usually are anxious to know, "How did I do?" When students pose this question during the test, the examiner should offer a neutral response. For example, "I can see that you are trying hard." Upon completion of the assessment the student may

SNAPSHOT

Gina's Comprehensive Assessment Report

Larry Kahn is one of the special education consultants for the Allen School District. He recently completed a comprehensive assessment of Gina A., a first-grade student. Gina was referred to the assessment team by her teacher, Maria Gordon, who was troubled about her high level of activity and her lack of skills, among other concerns. The assessment report follows:

Office of Special Services
14 Main Street
Allen,_____
Telephone: 200–299–2000

Name: Gina A.

Address: 1 Hill Road

Birthdate: March 4, xxxx

Age: 7 years, 2 months

Sex: female

Foster Parent: C. B.

Address: 1 Hill Road
Allen,_____
Telephone: xxx-xxx-xxxx

Date: May 10, xxxx

Date of testing: May 6, xxxx

Examiner: L. A. Kahn

School: Allen Elementary School

Principal: L. Lindly

Teacher: M. Gordon

Grade: 1

REASONS FOR REFERRAL: Gina was referred by her teacher because of problems of extreme activity within the classroom, developmental concerns, and a history of physical abuse.

BACKGROUND INFORMATION: Gina has been in foster care since the age of 4, when she was exposed to inappropriate sexual behaviors at home, neglect, and abuse. Her foster parents are very involved in her education and recreational activities in the community. Her biological mother, who has a history of physical and sexual abuse, is completing a prison sentence. Her brother, Paul, is living with a paternal grandmother. Her father has infrequent contact with Gina and her brother.

OBSERVATION OF THE ENVIRONMENT: Gina is currently in an inclusive first grade—that is, the classroom includes some children who have disabilities and some children who do not. There are 18 children in the classroom, with a teacher and an aide. The classroom is divided into four learning centers: math, science, reading, and community studies. There is much activity in the room as the children, teacher, and aide move about. Children's pictures and drawings cover the walls. The room appears to be stimulating and busy.

▶ Here's where the examiner will use information about the physical learning, and social environments to generate a hypothesis.

BEHAVIOR OBSERVATIONS: Informal testing and achievement testing were begun in a quiet corner of the classroom so that Gina could get used to the examiner before going to the examiner's office for further testing. The child was very reluctant to participate in the testing, and her behavior was consistently negative during the testing session. Gina repeatedly questioned why she was being asked to complete test items and several times she refused to try an item. Testing sessions were very brief because of her refusal to participate compounded by her short attention span. She could attend to a task for a few seconds but then was distracted by pictures on the wall, sounds from the radiator, and other background noise. She had to be coaxed to focus on the tasks. She was very distracted by all the test materials and touched everything throughout the session.

TESTS AND INTERVIEWS: The following tests were administered: The *Wechsler Intelligence Scale for Children®— Fourth Edition (WISC–IV®)* measures intellectual ability and the *Wechsler Individual Achievement Test—Second Edition (WIAT–II)* measures achievement skills and problem solving. Both of these assessments have a mean of 100 and a standard deviation of 15. The *Child Behavior Checklist,* which measures children's competencies and behavior/emotional problems, was completed by both Gina's teacher and her foster parents. Interviews also were

(continued)

conducted with Gina's foster parents and with her teacher. Gina was observed three different times in her classroom.

DISCUSSION OF RESULTS: Gina's performance on the *WISC–IV* indicates that she is functioning well within the average range of intellectual ability. Her full scale score of 101 ±5 places her within the average range (85–115). Her scores on each of the individual scales also fell within the average range, with a relative strength in verbal comprehension (112 ±6).

On the *Wechsler Individual Achievement Test-II,* Gina achieved a total composite score of 80 ±4. This places her in the low average range. Gina shows relative strengths in mathematics with a standard score of 96 ±7. Both written and oral language scores fell within the low average. Gina's reading score of 75 ±4 indicates an area of weakness.

WISC-IV Composite Scores Summary

Scale	Composite Score	95% Confidence Interval	Percentile Rank	Qualitative Description
Verbal Comprehension (VCI)	112	106–118	79	High Average
Perceptual Reasoning (PRI)	92	85–100	30	Average
Working Memory (WMI)	102	94–109	55	Average
Processing Speed (PSI)	91	83–101	27	Average
Full Scale (FSIQ)	101	96–106	53	Average

WIAT-II Composite Scores Summary

Composites	Composite Score	95% Confidence Interval	Percentile Rank
Reading	75	71–79	5
Mathematics	96	89–103	39
Written Language	82	74–90	12
Oral Language	81	70–92	10
Total	80	76–84	9

▶ Discuss how the hypothesis generation approach can be useful in interpreting Gina's test performance.

On the *Child Behavior Checklist,* Gina scored in the high range of externalizing behaviors: attention problems, 80th percentile; delinquent behavior, 70th percentile; and aggressive behavior, 77th percentile.

SUMMARY: Overall, it appears that Gina's short attention span and distractibility interfere with the formal testing. Her performance in verbal comprehension and oral language is not consistent. Observations confirmed that Gina performs somewhat better in the first-grade classroom than on the formal testing. However, when Gina's performance is compared with children of her age, she performs below her age peers. Classroom observations also indicate that Gina is reluctant to comply with requests made by her teacher and that she rarely cooperates with other children. She has a constant need for limit setting.

RECOMMENDATIONS: Gina needs intensive intervention services, including support in reading, consistent setting of limits, expectations for more age-appropriate behavior, and an environment with a great deal of structure.

Counseling and behavior management strategies should be offered to the foster family to help them deal with the negative behaviors, short attention span, and distractibility.

After completing the written report, Larry contacted Gina's foster parents to arrange for a convenient time to share the report with them. He wanted an opportunity to go over the report prior to the team meeting to allow the family an opportunity to ask questions and to discuss specific areas in more detail. During Gina's team meeting he will present the results and recommendations contained in the report, then file a copy of the report in the office of student records.

ask or expect you to explain some of the general results, depending on the age of the student, the student's interest in the testing situation, and your knowledge of the student. In some instances, your explanation may need to be a delicate balance between not discouraging the student on the one hand and helping the older student accept certain limitations and appreciate what can be accomplished on the other. Thus, you might say, "You may have to study harder and longer than some boys and girls do to get good grades" (Lyman, 1986, p. 135).

National and Statewide Assessments

Knowing how to interpret and use information from national and statewide assessments assists special educators in talking with other educators and parents. These tests usually feature common elements that describe individual and group scores. If the assessment is norm-referenced, the report allows comparison of the student to other groups of students who took the same test. If the assessment is criterion-referenced, then the report states how many questions the student attempted and many were answered correctly in each curriculum area. Table 7.2 illustrates typical scores from national and statewide assessments. Studying a specific student's score or the score of a group of students provides helpful information for linking assessment with instruction. By examining scores within each curriculum area, one can begin to target specific areas of instruction.

TABLE 7.2 ● Categories of Scores Reported in State and Local Assessment Reports

Type	Description	Interpretation
Standard score (SS)	This score allows comparison of the student to a group of other students. Standard scores have a mean of 100 and a standard deviation of 15. Scores falling between 85–115 are average.	A student received a score of 55, which is over 2 standard deviations below the mean, placing the student in the considerably below average range.
Grade equivalent (GE)	This score indicates the grade and month of the school year for which the score is average.	A student who is in the seventh grade and was tested in September scored 7.1. The score would be interpreted as average.
National percentile rank (NPR)	This score compares the student's score to the percentage of the norm group that performed at or below the student's score.	A student received a score of 39, which is interpreted as the student scored the same as or better than 39 percent of the students of the same age who took the same test.
Normal curve equivalent (NCE)	This score allows comparison of the student to a group of other students. This score has a mean of 50 and a range of 0–99.	A student received an NCE of 49, which means that the student scored about average for students of the same age who took this test.
National stanines (NS)	This score ranges from 1 to 9, with a score of 5 representing an average score.	A student received a score of 1, which means that the student scored significantly below average.

How It Works! Connecting Assessment and Instruction

Laura Chamberlain examined the results of the third-grade statewide assessment for Jamie, a student who receives math instruction in her resource room. Jamie had received a composite score of 25 (national percentile rank, NPR) and the following NPRs on the math subtests: computation 49, probability 15, data analysis 20, and geometry 8. Laura began thinking: How am I teaching the content of each of these areas? What materials am I using? Am I spending too much time on one area? How am I asking Jamie to demonstrate what he knows?

As Laura considered the instructional time with Jamie, she thought about other methods for teaching and learning activities that would help Jamie master concepts. Laura decided that she needed additional assessment information to pinpoint Jamie's difficulties. Planning ongoing assessment and instruction for Jamie would allow careful monitoring of his progress and provide Laura with information to adjust instruction such as reteaching or analyzing content to manageable units when needed.

▶ Curriculum-based measurement is a powerful assessment tool for linking assessment and instruction. Conduct a Web search to locate information about teachers who are using CBM in the classroom. You might start with www.interventioncentral.org

Using Local Assessments

Special educators use local assessment information to understand what students know and can do. As results are analyzed, they may consider one or more of the following questions:

- At which grade are these concepts/skills taught?
- How are students taught these concepts/skills?
- How are students required to demonstrate that they have mastered the concepts/skills? In other words, how are they assessed in the classroom? (Mertier, 2002, pg. 1)

Based on the answers to these questions, the special educator may plan a new method of instruction, use different instructional strategies or materials, or suggest that the IEP team consider the student's need for assistive technology.

Test Software

Test publishers frequently offer test software that not only computes test scores but also generates reports. Some publishers make available additional software for personal digital assistants (PDAs). Table 7.3 provides a software review checklist for evaluating test scoring and computer-generated reports. For most computer scoring programs, the examiner enters the identifying information and the raw scores. Raw scores are computed, and the results can be printed in a variety of formats (Figure 7.7). Test-scoring software and computer-generated reports help minimize scoring and computation errors and can be helpful in producing an individual test report.

▶ **CEC Common Core Knowledge and Skills.** A beginning special educator will use technology to conduct assessments (CC8S3).

▶ Review a computer program related to testing. Using the criteria in Table 7.3, evaluate the usefulness of this program.

However, educators must select and use these programs carefully. Since most of these programs yield a report based on a single test, they do not integrate information from other sources, such as additional assessments, observations, and interviews. Perhaps, more important, computer-generated reports do not provide the quality of interpretation that an experienced professional, using a variety of sources, can produce.

TABLE 7.3 ● Considerations for Evaluating Test-Scoring and Report Software

1. Name of software.
2. System requirements.
3. Ease of use: Is program easily installed and user friendly? Is there a telephone hotline? Is the documentation easy to use?
4. Does the program allow information to be entered by a scanner?
5. Does the program allow cross-referencing: To student's IEP?
6. What test scores does the program yield? Standard scores, Stanines, Percentiles, Other?
7. Does the program generate confidence intervals (with standard scores)?
8. Quality of the report: Does the report contain technical jargon? Does the report contain any generalizations that may bias the report?

Compuscore Version 1.1b	Summary and Score Report

Name: T1.1B, Chris

Date of Birth: 08/07/xxxx

Age: 11 years, 1 month

Sex: Male

Date of Testing: 09/14/xxxx

School: Stevenson

Teacher: Garrett

Grade: 5.0

Examiner: Ernest

Tests Administered: Chris was administered a set of tests from the *WJ®III Tests of Cognitive Abilities* and from the *WJ®III Tests of Achievement.* Because these two batteries are co-normed, direct comparisons can be made among Chris's cognitive and achievement scores. These comparisons help determine the presence and significance of any strengths and weaknesses among his abilities.

Test Report: Chris's overall intellectual ability is in the average range.

When compared to others at his grade level, Chris's performance is superior in comprehension-knowledge; high average in visual-spatial thinking; average in fluid reasoning and processing speed; low in long-term retrieval and auditory processing; and very low in short-term memory.

Chris's cognitive performance may be influenced by his phonemic awareness (limited), working memory capacity (limited), attentional resources (limited to average), cognitive fluency (average), and executive processes (average).

Chris's oral language skills are average when compared to the range of scores obtained by others at his grade level. His oral expression skills are high average; his listening comprehension skills are average.

When compared to others at his grade level, Chris's academic skills are within the low range. His fluency with academic tasks and his ability to apply academic skills are both within the average range. His level of knowledge is superior.

Chris's performance is high average in math reasoning; average in reading comprehension, math calculation skills, and written expression; and low in basic reading skills and basic writing skills. His knowledge of phoneme-grapheme relationships is low.

When compared to his overall intellectual abililty, Chris's achievement is significantly lower than predicted in the areas of reading, basic reading skills, written language, and basic writing skills. Chris's achievement is signigicantly higher than predicted in the areas of math reasoning and academic knowledge.

When all of his cognitive and achievement abilities are compared, Chris demonstrated significant strengths in comprehension-knowledge, visual-spatial thinking, math reasoning, and academic knowledge. He demonstrated significant weaknesses in long-term retrieval, auditory processing, short-term memory, phonemic awareness, working memory, basic reading skills, and basic writing skills.

Table of Scores: Woodcock-Johnson®III *Tests of Cognitive Abilities* and *Tests of Achievement.* Norms based on grade 5.0.

FIGURE 7.7 ● Example of a Computerized Scoring Program and Test Report

Source: Copyright © 2001. From the *Woodcock-Johnson®III.* Reprinted with permission of The Riverside Company. All rights reserved.

(continued)

Cluster/Test	Raw	GE	Easy to Diff		RPI	PR	SS (68% Band)	
GIA (Ext)	—	4.8	2.7	7.7	89/90	47	99	(97–101)
Verbal Ability (Ext)	—	8.8	6.4	12.1	98/90	93	122	(117–127)
Thinking Ability (Ext)	—	4.5	1.9	10.2	89/90	44	98	(95–100)
Cog Efficiency (Ext)	—	3.0	2.2	4.1	59/90	12	82	(78–86)
Comp-Knowledge (Gc)	—	8.8	6.4	12.1	98/90	93	122	(117–127)
L-T Retrieval (Glr)	—	2.0	K.3	8.1	80/90	7	77	(73–82)
Vis-Spatial Think (Gv)	—	14.9	5.5	>18.0	97/90	91	120	(114–125)
Auditory Process (Ga)	—	1.0	K.1	3.2	67/90	8	79	(74–84)
Fluid Reasoning (Gf)	—	6.3	3.9	9.9	94/90	63	105	(101–109)
Process Speed (Gs)	—	5.5	4.4	6.8	93/90	61	104	(100–108)
Short-Term Mem (Gsm)	—	K.8	K.1	1.5	13/90	2	68	(63–73)
Phonemic Aware	—	K.3	<K.0	1.8	54/90	3	71	(65–76)
Phonemic Aware III	—	K.9	K.1	2.1	49/90	2	69	(65–73)
Working Memory	—	1.8	1.0	2.7	35/90	6	76	(72–81)
Broad Attention	—	2.8	1.7	4.5	70/90	14	83	(80–87)
Cognitive Fluency	—	6.2	4.1	8.7	94/90	67	107	(104–109)
Exec Processes	—	5.8	3.4	9.5	92/90	62	105	(102–108)
Knowledge	—	9.4	7.1	12.9	99/90	96	126	(122–131)
- -								
Oral Language (Ext)	—	6.6	3.8	11.0	94/90	70	108	(104–112)
Oral Expression	—	7.8	4.4	12.9	96/90	78	112	(107–117)
Listening Comp	—	5.5	3.4	9.5	92/90	56	102	(98–107)
Total Achievement	—	3.6	2.8	4.6	67/90	22	88	(87–90)
Broad Reading	—	2.8	2.4	3.3	24/90	8	79	(77–81)
Broad Math	—	6.6	5.0	8.8	96/90	84	115	(111–118)
Broad Written Lang	—	2.7	1.9	3.7	51/90	8	79	(76–82)
Basic Reading Skills	—	2.2	1.9	2.5	5/90	4	74	(71–76)
Reading Comp	—	3.9	2.8	5.8	82/90	34	94	(91–97)
Math Calc Skills	—	5.7	4.2	7.8	93/90	68	107	(102–112)
Math Reasoning	—	7.2	5.7	9.7	98/90	87	117	(113–121)
Basic Writing Skills	—	2.2	1.7	2.8	17/90	4	74	(70–77)
Written Expression	—	4.0	2.7	5.8	82/90	30	92	(88–97)
Academic Skills	—	2.7	2.3	3.2	19/90	4	74	(71–76)
Academic Fluency	—	3.9	3.0	5.0	75/90	27	91	(89–93)
Academic Apps	—	5.5	3.9	8.2	94/90	61	104	(100–109)
Academic Knowledge	—	9.3	7.3	12.5	99/90	95	125	(120–131)

FIGURE 7.7 ● Continued

Summary

- Interpreting and writing assessment reports takes practice and a solid base of professional knowledge. Beginning teachers should have the opportunity to work with a mentor during the assessment process. A mentorship must include time to discuss interpretations of assessment information and to review and examine drafts of the assessment report.

- Care must be taken when interpreting low scores. Students often live up—or down—to our expectations. The report shared with family members and later filed in the student's records can have an impact on how the family and teachers perceive the student in years to come.

- The role of technology in assessment continues to evolve and will provide many exciting options in the future. We will need to keep abreast of these new developments and be prepared to learn new skills. The use of technology in interpreting and reporting assessment information may offer different promises tomorrow. Our challenge will be to use both our skills as professionals and our skills as thoughtful human beings to determine what is appropriate and what is not.

REFERENCES

Bentzen, W. R. (2005). *Seeing young children* (5th ed.). Albany, NY: Delmar.

Flanagan, D. P., & Kaufman, A. S. (2004). *Essentials of WISC–IV assessment.* Indianapolis: Wiley.

Harris, D. J. (2003). *Reporting and interpreting test results.* (ERIC Document Reproduction Service No. ED480039)

Jones, W. P., Harbach, R. L., Coker, J. K., & Staples, P. A. (2002). Web-assisted vocational test interpretation. *Journal of Employment Counseling 39*(3): 127–37.

Kamphaus, R. W. (1993). *Clinical assessment of children's intelligence.* Boston: Allyn and Bacon.

Kaufman, A. (1994). *Intelligent testing with the* WISC–III. New York: Wiley.

Lyman, H. B. (1986). *Test scores and what they mean* (4th ed.). Englewood Cliffs, NJ: Prentice-Hall.

McGrew, K. S. (1994). *Clinical interpretation of the Woodcock-Johnson tests of cognitive ability–revised.* Boston: Allyn and Bacon.

Mertier, C. A. (2002). *Using standardized test data to guide instruction and intervention.* (ERIC Document Reproduction Service No. ED470589)

Sattler, J. (2001). *Assessment of children* (4th ed.). La Mesa, CA: Author.

Tufte, E. R. (1990). *Envisioning information.* Cheshire, CT: Graphics Press.

8 Achievement: Overall Performance

Chapter Objectives

After completing this chapter, you should be able to:

- Describe assessment approaches relating to the assessment of achievement.

- Describe the influence of culture and language on assessment.

- Explain the integral link between instruction, assessment, self-assessment, and peer assessment.

- Compare approaches to the assessment of achievement, including norm-referenced standardized tests, curriculum-based assessment, criterion-referenced assessment, and alternative assessments such as performance-based assessment, self-assessment, and peer assessment.

- Describe how the assessment of the physical, learning, and social environments influences achievement, including norm-referenced achievement.

Key Terms

Achievement testing
Curriculum-based assessment (CBA)

Criterion-referenced test
Probe
Error analysis

Overview

Achievement testing is the assessment of past learning that is usually the result of formal and informal educational experiences. This chapter is concerned with approaches that assess the achievement of students. Several other chapters in this book also address aspects of the assessment of achievement. Chapter 6 discusses performance-based, authentic, and portfolio assessments; Chapters 9 and 10 examine the assessment of reading and written language; and Chapter 12 examines the assessment of mathematics.

The assessment of achievement occurs regularly throughout students' school careers. Achievement tests are designed for groups of students or for individual students in order to assess their formal and informal learning experiences.

156

Responding to Diversity

The assessment of achievement must be sensitive to an individual's culture, ethnicity, race, language, geographic region of origin, gender, disability, and economic status. Assessment approaches, including standardized tests, performance-based assessment, and the other approaches this chapter describes, must be free from bias. There are several ways in which achievement tests can show bias (Howell & Rueda, 1996):

- In the format of the test.
- If the test directions are too technical or do not translate easily into another language.
- If the content of achievement tests differs in importance across cultures.
- If the examinee test-taking behaviors vary from one culture to another.
- If the examiner's personality characteristics influence the examinee's responses.
- If the underlying psychological construct of the test is not universal.
- If the individual examinee does not represent the norm group.

There may be several flaws when assessing students who have limited English proficiency so that testing them with standardized instruments is improper (Salvia & Ysseldyke, 2004).

- Using nonverbal tests. There are several problems involved in using nonverbal tests with students who lack English language competency. Some tests, including the *Peabody Picture Vocabulary Test-III, Test of Nonverbal Intelligence-3, and the Leiter International Performance Scale-Revised,* are considered to be "nonverbal." However, just because test items do not require that students offer verbal responses, the tests may not be suitable because directions may be presented orally or through pantomime. When tests make assumptions about students' verbal comprehension and production, they may be invalid. Another problem with nonverbal tests is that many test items are not correlated with school success so that the results may not be pertinent to planning instruction.
- Testing as a cultural phenomenon. While testing in the United States is pervasive, it may be used rarely in other countries. Doing well on tests may not be emphasized or experienced by students in some cultures. Students from other cultures may be unfamiliar with the expectations of testing and the competitive nature of testing. Unfamiliarity with testing and lack of test-taking skills can lead to poor test performance.
- Using translations. Some tests are available or in other languages. Simply translating test items does not render the test appropriate. Vocabulary, cultural expectations, background knowledge, test demands, and norms may not be appropriate for students whose primary language is not English. Similar problems result in an interpreter is used when administering tests.
- Relating to others. Cultural conventions may confound testing. For example, relations between males and females may be strictly prescribed by certain cultures. Similarly, relating to strangers or adults may influence rapport between test examiners and students. Some cultures emphasize cooperation, modesty, and respect. These values may have an effect on the quantity, quality, and types of responses that students make.

Using a variety of approaches when assessing achievement reflects sensitivity to the student as well as a thorough attempt to understand what the student has learned.

The assessment of achievement includes standardized testing in addition to a variety of these other approaches:

- Curriculum-based assessment
- Criterion-referenced assessment
- Alternative forms of assessment, such as systematic observations, anecdotal records, interviews with family members and the students themselves, samples of students' work, videotapes, audiotapes, performances, portfolios, and exhibitions.

Standardized Instruments

Standardized tests of achievement are tests that follow strict procedures for administration, scoring, and interpretation. A standardized test is usually norm-referenced. As discussed in Chapter 3, a norm-referenced test (NRT) is a measure that compares a student's test performance with that of similar students who have taken the same test. In addition, scores from standardized tests can be used to make interpretations about an individual student's performance on several tests. The construction of a standardized test is often a lengthy and costly project that involves considerable research and development.

Steps in the Development of a Standardized Achievement Test

1. Test developers create specifications for the test.
2. Test items are written.
3. Test developers conduct an item tryout of initial draft items on a large group of individuals.
4. Test developers analyze the results of the item tryout, discard or modify some items, create new items, and develop methods of scoring and interpretation.
5. Test developers conduct a national standardization of the test. They select a national standardization sample representative of the United States, based on the results of the most recent census data. The sample participants represent balanced criteria for age, socioeconomic status, geographic region, urban/rural/suburban residence, race, ethnicity, and gender. The sample may include additional variables, depending on the purposes of the test.
6. Test developers analyze the data from the national tryout and develop norm tables. Norm tables help examiners compare the performance of individual students with the performance of the students' peers.
7. Final test materials, including test manuals, answer sheets, and scoring guides result from these steps.

Benefits

The benefits of using standardized tests are that the test materials describe the development of the tests in detail, including the test content, administration, norms, reliability, validity, scoring, and interpretation. Because standardized tests are usually norm-referenced, testers can make comparisons between the performance of an individual student, the student's peers, and the students in the standardized sample group. In addition, the tests allow for comparisons between a student's performance on several subtests or on several separate tests in order to identify relative strengths and weaknesses. Depending on the test, standardized achievement tests are helpful in screening, determining eligibility, program planning, monitoring progress, and program evaluation.

Disadvantages

Although standardized achievement tests have a number of advantages, they also have many disadvantages for students with special needs:

- The tests assume that all students have been exposed to the content tested.
- Many tests assume that students come from a homogeneous culture.
- Many tests show bias against students with disabilities, females, and certain cultures, ethnic groups, and economic groups.
- Many tests do not test what the curriculum has taught in schools.
- Many tests do not measure or consider creativity, interest, initiative, motivation, and values.
- Many tests result in labeling or mislabeling of students.
- The tests encourage teachers to teach toward the test.
- The tests result in competition among students, teachers, and schools.
- The tests generate fear (Nitko, 1996).
- Test standards usually require that students be able to read and write independently.

Steps and Purposes of Standardized Achievement Testing

Screening

One frequent use of standardized achievement tests is to identify students who perform below, at the same level, or above their peers. That is, the utility of achievement test results in the screening process is in identifying students who need further assessment. Examples of achievement tests to use for screening are the *Iowa Tests of Basic Skills* and the *Peabody Individual Achievement Test–Revised/Normative Update*.

Determining Eligibility

Using standardized achievement tests in conjunction with other types of tests can help determine eligibility for services. For example, using the *Wechsler Individual Achievement Test, Second Edition (WIAT–II)*, with a measure of cognitive ability can help determine eligibility for services.

Program Planning

Program planning and monitoring student progress connect instruction with assessment. Achievement tests can aid in instructional planning and can be helpful in identifying what the student knows and can do. Two useful tests for program planning are the *Peabody Individual Achievement Test–Revised/NU* and the *KeyMath–Revised/NU*. The teacher can also utilize other assessment approaches discussed in this chapter to assist with program planning.

Monitoring Progress

Regularly monitoring students' progress in literacy, mathematics, and other academic content areas is important. Norm-referenced tests may not be as useful in monitoring progress as are other assessment approaches because they are not sensitive to small changes in performance. Frequent monitoring assists the teacher in modifying instruction to meet the needs of the student. As with program planning, the teacher may also use other assessment approaches discussed in this chapter.

▶ **CEC Common Core Knowledge and Skills.** A beginning special educator can interpret information from formal and informal assessments a (CC9S5).

▶ The Buros Institute of Mental Measurements provides online reviews and information of thousands of tests. The website is http://www.unl.edu/buros.

Program Evaluation

Teachers and other professionals employ achievement tests to conduct two types of program evaluation: individual student programs as specified in an IEP and, more broadly, the progress that a class, grade, school, or the school district itself has made over a period of time. See Chapter 16 for further discussion of program evaluation.

Group Tests

Group tests of achievement are usually administered to groups of students in classrooms. Students with special needs who are in regular classrooms frequently participate in group achievement testing. The purposes of group achievement tests are to: (1) assist in screening students, (2) evaluate the relative performance of students when compared with their peers, (3) describe the relative effectiveness of methods of instruction, and (4) evaluate curricula. IDEA requires that general state- and districtwide assessments include students with disabilities, using appropriate accommodations where necessary.

Most group tests require using scripted directions that the test publisher provides. The tests usually have booklets that contain test items and separate answer sheets. Hand scoring is common, although some publishers either request or require that schools return the answer sheets for machine scoring. Group tests report a variety of types of scores, including standard scores, percentiles, stanines, and age and grade equivalents. These scores can generate profiles, thus facilitating the comparison of students, classrooms, individual schools, and school districts.

Benefits

Group testing with standardized tests permits the testing of large groups of students using the same administration, scoring, and interpretation procedures. While it is appropriate to administer group tests to individual students, it is not appropriate to administer individual tests to groups.

Disadvantages

Group testing has several disadvantages for students with special needs. The tests routinely require that students read and write independently. Further, many group achievement tests have separate test booklets that contain the test items and separate answer sheets. Some students may be able to correctly answer the questions but have difficulty transferring their answers to the answer sheet. Finally, many group achievement tests have multiple-choice answers. Students with disabilities as well as students from various culture or ethnic groups may have difficulty using this format.

Individual Achievement Tests

When testing individual students, achievement tests provide the examiner with the opportunity to get to know students. The student and the test examiner can establish a rapport, and the examiner can help the student feel at ease. Individual testing allows the examiner to observe the student's appearance, adjustment to the testing, cooperation, effort, motivation, attitudes, speech patterns, anxiety level, activity level, flexibility, impulse control, fine and gross motor abilities, distractibility, and mood (Sattler,

2001). The examiner can individualize the test administration according to the needs of the student. For example, if a student is tired or hungry, the examiner can stop the test so that the student can take a break.

▶ Compare the test items of a group achievement test with an individual achievement test. What are the similarities? Differences? When would it be appropriate to use each of these tests?

Kaufman Test of Educational Achievement/Normative Update

The *Kaufman Test of Educational Achievement/ Normative Update (K–TEA/NU;* Kaufman & Kaufman, 1998) is an individually administered test of achievement for students in grades 1 through 12. Collected data from 1995 to 1996 resulted in a complete renorming of the test. The age-based norms range from 6 years, 0 months to 18 years, 11 months. The *K–TEA/NU* has two forms, the Comprehensive Form and the Brief Form. Although the forms are not interchangeable, they do have overlapping uses. The applications listed for the Brief Form are contributing to a battery, screening, program planning, research, pretesting and posttesting, making placement decisions, student self-appraisal, use by government agencies, personnel selection, and measuring adaptive functioning. The Comprehensive Form has all of these uses except screening. In addition, the Comprehensive Form is recommended for analyzing strengths and weaknesses and for analyzing errors. There is some overlap of items between the *K–TEA/NU* and the *Kaufman Assessment Battery for Children (K–ABC)*.

DESCRIPTION OF THE SUBTESTS IN THE COMPREHENSIVE FORM The Comprehensive Form consists of five subtests: Mathematics Applications, Reading Decoding, Spelling, Reading Comprehension, and Mathematics Computation.

Mathematics Applications. The examiner presents the items orally while using pictures and graphs as visual stimuli. The items assess the application of mathematical principles and reasoning.

Reading Decoding. The items assess the ability to identify letters and to pronounce words that are phonetic and nonphonetic.

Spelling. The examiner pronounces a word and uses it in a sentence, then asks the student to write the word. If students cannot write, they may spell the word orally.

Reading Comprehension. The child reads a passage and responds either gesturally or orally to the items in the reading.

Mathematics Computation. The student uses a paper and pencil to solve written mathematical problems.

DESCRIPTION OF THE SUBTESTS IN THE BRIEF FORM The Brief Form consists of three subtests: Mathematics, Reading, and Spelling.

Mathematics. This subtest measures basic computational skills and the application of mathematical principles and reasoning.

Reading. The items assess both decoding, by asking the child to read words, and reading comprehension, by requiring the child to read statements.

Spelling. The items consist of words that the examiner reads and uses in a sentence. The student then writes the word or spells it orally, if the student is unable to write.

ADMINISTRATION Persons who have had training in educational and psychological testing as well as persons who have had limited training in these areas can administer the *K–TEA/NU*. For children in grades 1 through 3, the Comprehensive Form takes from 20 minutes to 1 hour to administer; the Brief Form requires from 10 to 35 minutes to administer.

SCORING Raw scores convert to standard scores, with a mean of 100 and a standard deviation of 15. These are available for both fall and spring testing by grade level or by age. In addition, percentile ranks, stanines, normal curve equivalents, age equivalents, and grade equivalents are available. The manual describes the following methods of interpreting *K–TEA/NU* scores: the size of the difference and the significance of the difference between subtests and between composite scores, analyzing strengths and weaknesses, and identifying errors.

STANDARDIZATION Test publishers renormed both the Comprehensive and the Brief Forms of the *K–TEA/NU* between October 1995 and November 1996. Stratification of the standardization sample followed age, gender, region, race, ethnicity, and economic status as estimated by parental education. The standardization sample of the *K–TEA/NU* was linked to the standardization samples for the *Peabody Individual Achievement Test–Revised (PIAT–R)*, *KeyMath–R*, and the *Woodcock Reading Mastery Tests–Revised (WRMT–R)*. For the *K–TEA/NU*, the renorming sample consisted of students from grade 1 through age 22. To obtain a linking sample, test examinees in the norm sample take one of the complete test batteries and one or more subtests from another battery. This linking approach permits the making of comparisons of test performance across batteries.

RELIABILITY The reliabilities of the Comprehensive Form's five subtests are in the mid to high .90s. Test-retest reliability coefficients for the Comprehensive Form are high. Reliabilities of the three subtests of the Brief Form are also high. The reliability of the Battery Composite is high.

VALIDITY The validity of the Comprehensive Form and the Brief Form were estimated using similar procedures. Content validity comes through consultation with curriculum experts in each subject area. Test developers conducted three national tryouts during the fall of 1981 and the spring of 1982. The final selection of the items emerged from these tryouts.

An estimate of construct validity resulted from showing that subtest and composite scores increased across age and grade levels. Correlating the results of the *K–TEA/NU* with the results of other tests given to the same students demonstrated criterion-related validity. These tests included the *Kaufman Assessment Battery for Children (K–ABC)*, *Wide Range Achievement Test–3 (WRAT–3)*, *Peabody Individual Achievement Test–R (PIAT–R)*, and other tests.

SUMMARY The *Kaufman Test of Educational Achievement/Normative Update* is an individually administered test of achievement for students in grades 1 through 12 whose ages range from 6 years, 0 months to 18 years, 11 months. The *K–TEA/NU* has two forms, the Comprehensive Form and the Brief Form. Although the forms overlap in content, they are not interchangeable. Evidence for the technical adequacy of the test is sufficient. The reliability is excellent, and validity of both forms is adequate. As with all achievement tests, educators must evaluate the content validity to determine how well it measures what has been taught.

TESTS-at-a-GLANCE

Kaufman Test of Educational Achievement/ Normative Update (K–TEA/NU)

- **Publication Date:** 1998
- **Purposes:** The Comprehensive Form measures Reading Decoding, Spelling, Reading Comprehension, Mathematics Applications, and Mathematics Computation. The Brief Form consists of three subtests: Reading, Mathematics, and Spelling.
- **Age/Grade Levels:** Grades 1 through 12; ages range from 6 years, 0 months to 18 years, 11 months.
- **Time to Administer:** 20 minutes to approximately 1 hour.
- **Technical Adequacy:** Renorming was based on data collected in 1995 to 1996. The reliability and validity of both forms is adequate. As with all achievement tests, educators must evaluate the content validity to determine how well it measures what has been taught.
- **Suggested Uses:** The Comprehensive Form can be used to measure overall achievement. The Brief Form should be used for screening.

Peabody Individual Achievement Test–Revised/Normative Update

The *Peabody Individual Achievement Test–Revised/Normative Update (PIAT–R/NU;* Markwardt, 1998) is an individually administered, norm-referenced test for students in grades kindergarten through 12 (5 years, 0 months to 18 years, 11 months). The manual states that the *PIAT–R/NU* has the following uses: individual evaluation, program planning, guidance and counseling, admissions and transfers, grouping students, follow-up evaluation, personnel selection, and research. The manual also describes the following limitations: (1) The *PIAT–R/NU* is not a diagnostic test; (2) it does not provide highly precise measurement of achievement; (3) it cannot sample the curriculum of individual schools—rather, it represents a representative curriculum of schools in the United States; and (4) the background and qualifications of the test administrator can have a varying influence on the interpretation of the test.

The test assesses achievement in six areas:

General Information. This subtest measures general knowledge. The examiner reads the open-ended questions aloud and the child answers orally.

Reading Recognition. The initial test items consist of ability to recognize the sounds associated with letters. Later test items consist of isolated words. The student reproduces the sounds and reads the words orally.

Reading Comprehension. The student reads a sentence silently and then is asked to identify the one picture out of four that best depicts the sentence.

Mathematics. Using a multiple-choice format, the test assesses knowledge of basic facts and applications. The examiner reads all of the test items to the student. For the first 50 items, the child sees only the responses and not the test items. For items 50 to 100, the student sees the printed questions and the response choices.

Spelling. The format for the responses is multiple choice. The items at the beginning of this subtest measure the student's ability to distinguish a printed letter from an object and to recognize letters after hearing their names or sounds. Later items assess the child's ability to identify the one correctly spelled word out of four that the examiner pronounces.

Written Expression. This subtest has two levels. Level I is effective for children in kindergarten or first grade and assesses copying and writing letters, words, and sentences that the examiner dictates. Children in grades 2 through 12 can test in Level II. The student writes a story in response to one of two picture prompts. Children have 20 minutes to complete Level II.

ADMINISTRATION The manual distinguishes between the qualifications of individuals who administer the *PIAT–R/NU* and those who interpret the results. According to the manual, almost anyone can learn to administer the test. Persons who provide an interpretation should have an understanding of psychometrics and curricula. Depending on the number of items, it takes approximately 30 minutes to an hour to administer the total test.

SCORING For all of the subtests except Written Expression, the test items are either correct or incorrect. Raw scores can convert to standard scores, percentile ranks, grade and age equivalents, stanines, and normal curve equivalents. A separate scoring guide is in the manual for the Written Expression subtest. Three composite scores are possible with this test. The Total Reading composite derives from the performance on the Reading Recognition and the Reading Comprehension subtests. The Total Test composite is a composite score from the performance on the first five subtests. There is an optional Written Language composite, which derives from the Written Expression and the Spelling subtests.

STANDARDIZATION Renorming of the *PIAT–R/NU* took place between October 1995 and November 1996. The standardization sample comprised groups according to age, gender, region, race, ethnicity, and economic status as estimated by parental education. The standardization sample of the *PIAT–R/NU* was linked to the standardization samples for the *K–TEA, KeyMath–R,* and the *Woodcock Reading Mastery Tests–Revised.* For the *PIAT–R/NU,* the renorming sample consisted of students who were in kindergarten through students age 22. For the linking sample, the test examinees in the norm sample took one of the complete test batteries and one or more subtests from another battery. This linking approach permits the making of comparisons of test performance across batteries.

RELIABILITY Split-half reliability coefficients are available by age and grade for all of the subtests, excluding Written Expression. The coefficients range from .84 (Mathematics) to .98 (Reading Recognition). The split-half reliability coefficients for the total test are in the high .90s. The test provides computed internal consistency reliability coefficients by grade and age for all of the subtests, except Written Expression. With few exceptions, the coefficients were in the mid to high 90s. Internal consistency reliability estimates for Written Expression resulted in reliability coefficients for Level I in the low .60s and .69 (grade 1). Calculations of internal consistency reliability coefficients for Level II of the Written Expression subtest were in the low 70s and high 80s. In order to estimate test-retest reliability, test developers randomly selected approximately 50 children from grades K, 2, 4, 6, 8, and 10 and retested them within a two- to four-week interval. Median test-retest reliability coefficients for the subtests, excluding Written Expression, ranged from .84 (Mathematics) to .96 (Reading Recognition).

VALIDITY The manual reports using the development process to establish content validity and consulting content area experts, tests reviewers, and others. As with any achievement test, however, the teacher should review the test to determine the extent to which the test has content validity. Subtest and composite scores increased across age and grade levels, demonstrating construct validity. Correlating the results of the *PIAT–R/NU* with the *PIAT* and the *Peabody Picture Vocabulary Test–Revised (PPVT–R)* demonstrated concurrent validity. Additional evidence is necessary to prove construct validity.

SUMMARY The *Peabody Individual Achievement Test–Revised/Normative Update* is an individually administered, norm-referenced test that is useful for children in grades kindergarten through 12. The test assesses achievement in six areas: General Information, Reading Recognition, Reading Comprehension, Mathematics, Spelling, and Written Expression. The standardization and the reliability are acceptable. As with all standardized achievement test, the teacher should evaluate the content validity of this test.

TESTS-at-a-GLANCE

Peabody Individual Achievement Test–Revised/ Normative Update (PIAT–R/NU)

- **Publication Date:** 1998

- **Purposes:** Measures overall achievement in the areas of General Information, Reading Recognition, Reading Comprehension, Mathematics, Spelling, and Written Expression.

- **Age/Grade Levels:** Grades K through 12; 5 years, 0 months to 18 years, 11 months.

- **Time to Administer:** Approximately 30 minutes to 1 hour.

- **Technical Adequacy:** The standardization sample and the reliability are acceptable. As with all standardized achievement tests, the teacher should evaluate the content validity of this test.

- **Suggested Uses:** Screening; measure of overall achievement in reading, mathematics, spelling, and written expression. The test assesses achievement in six areas: General Information, Reading Recognition, Reading Comprehension, Mathematics, Spelling, and Written Expression. The standardization and the reliability are acceptable. As with all standardized achievement tests, the teacher should evaluate the content validity of this test.

Wechsler Individual Achievement Test–II

The *Wechsler Individual Achievement Test–Second Edition (WIAT–II;* The Psychological Corporation, 2001) is an individually administered achievement test for students ages 4 years through adulthood. The *WIAT–II* contains nine subtests in four areas:

▶ Obtain a copy of a standardized achievement test. Review the test items in one curriculum area. What items represent the curriculum that is being taught in the local schools? What items differ? What conclusions and recommendations can you offer?

1. Oral Expression and Listening Comprehension
   - Oral Language
   - Listening Comprehension
2. Written Expression
   - Written Expression
   - Spelling
3. Basic Reading Skill and Reading Comprehension
   - Pseudoword Decoding
   - Word Reading
   - Reading Comprehension
4. Mathematics Calculation and Mathematics Reasoning
   - Numerical Operations
   - Mathematics Reasoning

ADMINISTRATION The *WIAT–II* is administered individually. It takes approximately 30 minutes to 2 hours to administer.

SCORING Raw scores convert to grade-based standard scores. Percentiles, age and grade equivalents, normal curve equivalents, and stanines are also available (Figure 8.1). It is possible to determine the discrepancy between *WIAT–II* standard scores and *Wechsler Preschool and Primary Scale of Intelligence–Revised (WIPPSI–R)* standard scores or *Wechsler Intelligence Scale for Children–III (WISC–III)* standard scores.

STANDARDIZATION Sample stratification occurred according to age, grade, gender, race/ethnicity (White, Black, Hispanic, Native American, Eskimo, Aleut, Asian, Pacific Islander, Other), geographic region, and the education of the parent(s) or guardian(s) based on 1998 data from the U.S. Census Bureau. The *WIAT–II* links with the *Wechsler Intelligence Scale for Children–Third Edition (WISC–III),* the *Wechsler Preschool and Primary Scale of Intelligence–Revised (WPPSI–R),* and the *Wechsler Adult Intelligence Scale–Third Edition (WAIS–III).*

RELIABILITY Three types of reliability coefficients are reported: split-half, test-retest, and interrater. Several coefficients for Listening Comprehension, for young children, and Written Expression are below .80. Overall, the reliability of the *WIAT–II* is adequate.

VALIDITY There is good evidence of construct validity. However, as with all tests, we recommend conducting independent validity studies in order to obtain additional information about the construct validity of the *WIAT–II.*

SUMMARY The *WIAT–II* is an individually administered test that assesses achievement in students ages 4 through adulthood. We encourage additional studies investigating the validity of the *WIAT–II* and the use of this test with students with disabilities. As with all

TESTS-at-a-GLANCE

Wechsler Individual Achievement Test, Second Edition (WIAT–II)

- **Publication Date:** 2001
- **Purposes:** Measures strengths and weaknesses in oral expression, listening comprehension, written expression, word reading skill, reading comprehension, spelling, mathematics calculation or mathematics reasoning.
- **Age/Grade Levels:** Ages 4 years through adulthood.
- **Time to Administer:** Approximately 30 minutes to 2 hours.
- **Technical Adequacy:** The standardization sample, reliability, and validity are very good.
- **Suggested Uses:** Measure of overall achievement.

FIGURE 8.1 • Summary Page of WIAT–II

Source: Copyright © 2001 by Harcourt Assessment, Inc. Reproduced with permission. All rights reserved.

How It Works! Achievement Tests

Ruth Firestone is 11 years old and attends Carmel School where she is in the fifth grade. She has been identified as a student with Attention-Deficit Hyperactivity Disorder and a specific learning disability with difficulties in phonemic awareness, reading comprehension, and reading fluency. Ruth's nonverbal problem solving is strong, and she requires time and repetition before she is able to process new information. She enjoys playing video games and soccer. Ruth receives direct services in the resource room with in-class support. She is on consultation status for occupational therapy and speech and language services.

The results of the most recent occupational therapy evaluation report indicate that Ruth has strong visual perceptual skills and a strong and intact sensory system. Producing written output and slow processing ability are challenges for Ruth.

The speech and language evaluation report indicates that Ruth is performing within the average range for receptive and expressive language skills, with the exception of written language, which falls below the average range.

The psychological evaluation report states that Ruth has high average verbal comprehension and perceptual reasoning, average working memory, and low average processing speed. Ruth has significant weakness in cognitive flexibility. Ruth is currently experiencing a considerable amount of anxiety.

The *Wechlser Individual Achievement Test, Second Edition (WIAT–II)* was administered to Ruth by the learning specialist. According to the learning specialist, Ruth is a highly engaging student. Her approach to the tasks was tentative and she was eager to know how she performed. The test produces standard scores that have an average score of 100 and a standard deviation of 15. Ruth's standard scores on *WIAT–II* subtests can be found in Figure 8.1.

Ruth's performance on the reading, spelling, and written expression subtests indicates that, when compared with her peers, she performs in the average range. Relative strengths are in Reading Expression, Math Reasoning, and Written Expresion. Ruth's performance on the Numeral Operations and Spelling subtests confirms that she continues to have difficulty in these areas.

Ruth's performance on the numerical operations subtest is a relative strength. However, her performance on the Math Reasoning subtest reveals that she has difficulty identifying essential from nonessential information and identifying correct mathematics processes. When doing mathematics problems, Ruth will benefit by making sure that she is able to read and understand mathematics word problems, paraphrasing problems, and underlining the important information in the problem.

achievement tests, use caution and carefully examine the test items to determine the degree to which they correspond with the curriculum that the student has been taught. In the Snapshot on page 168, a special education teacher talks about the administration of the *WIAT–II* to Patricia, a student with reading difficulties.

Wide Range Achievement Test–3

The *Wide Range Achievement Test–3 (WRAT–3;* Wilkinson, 1993) measures the "codes which are needed to learn the basic skills of reading, writing, spelling, and arithmetic" (p. 10). This purpose is the same as the purposes in the previous editions of this test. The meaning of the word "codes" is unclear, although professionals generally assume that it refers to basic academic skills that are essential in reading, spelling, and arithmetic. The *WRAT–3* has three subtests:

Reading. The examiner asks the students to recognize individual letters and words in isolation.

Spelling. The examiner asks the students to copy marks, write the student's name, and write single words that the examiner dictates.

Arithmetic. The student is asked to read numerals, solve problems that the examiner presents verbally, and compute arithmetic problems using pencil and paper.

TESTS-at-a-GLANCE

Wide Range Achievement Test–3 (WRAT–3)

- **Publication Date:** 1993
- **Purposes:** Measures reading recognition, spelling dictated words, and basic arithmetic skills.
- **Age/Grade Levels:** Ages 5 years through 75 years.
- **Time to Administer:** 15 minutes to 30 minutes.
- **Technical Adequacy:** Standardization and reliability are acceptable, validity is questionable.
- **Suggested Uses:** This instrument is best used as a screening instrument, if at all.

ADMINISTRATION The *WRAT–3* is individually administered and can be administered to individuals ages 5 to 75. There are two forms.

SCORING The *WRAT–3* is hand scored and six types of scores are available: raw, absolute, and standard scores, percentiles, normal curve equivalents, and grade equivalents.

STANDARDIZATION The standardization sample of the *WRAT–3* was based on the 1990 U.S. Census and consisted of 4,443 individuals. The sample stratifications include age, region of the country, gender, and ethnic group.

RELIABILITY Reliability appears to be adequate. Twenty-three age groups for each form of the test report internal consistency coefficients ranging from .85 to .91. Alternate form reliability is acceptable and median coefficients are: Reading, .92; Spelling, .93; and Mathematics, .89.

VALIDITY We strongly urge examiners to examine the content of the test items. Content validity is highly questionable because it is unclear how well the test items assess the content areas of reading, mathematics, and spelling. Additional research studies are necessary to substantiate the construct validity of this instrument.

SNAPSHOT

A Special Education Teacher's Comments

My name is J. J. Auburn, and I recently evaluated Patricia, who is in fourth grade. She has received special education services since kindergarten because of speech and language difficulties. When she was in third grade, Patricia's teacher raised concerns about Patricia's behavior in the classroom and asked Patricia's parent to seek a medical opinion about the possibility that Patricia had an attention-deficit hyperactivity disorder. The parent did not follow this advice, and the school did not follow up. Her current fourth-grade teacher has raised these concerns again and referred Patricia for further evaluation.

As part of the evaluation, I administered the *Wechsler Individual Achievement Test, Second Edition (WIAT–II)*. Patricia came willingly to the testing room. She seemed to listen carefully while I explained that some of the questions would be easy but would get harder since this was a test for older children as well. We proceeded through the subtests.

When we came to the Spelling subtest, I noticed an immediate change in her behavior and attitude. As soon as I gave her the spelling sheet and a pencil and asked her to write the words given to her, she became restless and silly. Her pencil grip seemed unsteady and she wiggled in her seat. She repeated every word slowly and talked to herself throughout this subtest.

After the Spelling subtest we took a short break, and then I proceeded to administer the remaining subtests in the *WIAT–II*. The restlessness was still present. When we were finished, I thanked Patricia and walked her back to her classroom.

I returned to my room and scored the test. An analysis of Patricia's performance showed that she had specific strengths and a number of weaknesses. I was very concerned about Patricia's behavioral changes when faced with tasks that involved writing.

Patricia's literacy instruction emphasizes phonemic awareness, vocabulary development, and fluency. I wondered if Patricia's behavior was an attempt to hide her perceived discomfort with reading and writing. In preparation for the IEP meeting, I summarized Patricia's performance and asked her teacher to bring samples of Patricia's classroom work and homework to the meeting. I also asked the teacher to bring samples of students who were performing "typically" so that the team would be able to compare Patricia's performance with the performance of students who were performing at this standard. Finally, I arranged for the consultant to conduct systematic observations of Patricia's behavior in her classroom.

SUMMARY The *Wide Range Achievement Test– 3* is an individually administered test of reading, spelling, and mathematics achievement. The format of the test has not significantly changed since it was first published. Although the standardization and reliability are acceptable, validity is questionable. We recommend using this instrument as a screening instrument, if at all.

Woodcock-Johnson Tests of Achievement III

The *Woodcock-Johnson III (WJ III;* Woodcock, McGrew, & Mather, 2001) is an individually administered battery that assesses cognitive and academic abilities in individuals ages 2 years through adulthood. The battery consists of two tests: *Woodcock-Johnson III Tests of Cognitive Ability (WJ III COG)* and the *Woodcock-Johnson III Tests of Achievement (WJ III ACH)*. Each part comprises a Standard Battery and a Supplemental Battery. Standard batteries can be administered alone or with the supplemental batteries. Chapter 13 describes the *WJ III COG*. The *WJ III* has the following purposes: (1) diagnosis, (2) determination of intra-ability and ability/achievement discrepancies, (3) program placement, (4) individual program planning, (5) guidance, (6) growth assessment, (7) program evaluation, and (8) research. The subtests combine to form five clusters in reading, mathematics, written language, oral language, and knowledge (science, social studies, and humanities). A description of the subtests can be found in Table 8.1. There are two parallel forms of the *WJ III ACH* Standard Battery.

ADMINISTRATION The time to administer the *WJ III ACH* varies from approximately 20 minutes to over an hour, depending on whether examiners use both the Standard Battery and the Supplemental Battery. Raw scores can convert to age and grade equivalents, percentile ranks, and standard scores. The scoring can be cumbersome, and it is advisable to use a computer scoring program.

STANDARDIZATION The *WJ III* was standardized on 8,818 individuals in over 100 communities. The preschool sample consisted of 1,143 children who were 2 years to 5 years of age and not enrolled in kindergarten. There were 4,783 individuals in the kindergarten through grade 12 sample. The rest of the standardization sample consisted of individuals who were in college or not in school. The sample was stratified according to region, community size, sex, race—Caucasian, African American, Native American, Asian Pacific, Hispanic (non-Hispanic, Hispanic), and other—funding of college/university, type of college/university, and occupation of adults. The norms are continuous-year norms, that is, the norms were collected throughout the year.

RELIABILITY The test manual provides extensive information on reliability for the *WJ III ACH* including: split-half reliabilities for all achievement subtests except the subtests that rely on speed of response (Reading Fluency, Math Fluency, and Writing Fluency); test-retest reliabilities for the speeded subtests; interrater reliabilities for the achievement subtests (Writing Samples, Writing Fluency, Handwriting) that require subjective judgment of responses; and alternative form reliabilities for equivalence of Forms A and B. The manual also provides information about standard errors of measurement for the subtests. Overall, the reliabilities of the subtests and the clusters are acceptable.

TESTS-at-a-GLANCE

Woodcock-Johnson III, Tests of Achievement (WJ III ACH)

- **Publication Date:** 2001
- **Purposes:** Measures overall achievement in reading, mathematics, written language, and general knowledge in science, social studies, and humanities.
- **Age/Grade Levels:** Ages 2 years through adulthood.
- **Time to Administer:** 20 minutes to over 1 hour.
- **Technical Adequacy:** Reliability information is acceptable. Validity is adequate; however, the teacher should determine content validity by comparing the test items with the curriculum that the student has been taught.
- **Suggested Uses:** Measure overall achievement; may be used to indicate general areas of strength and weakness.

TABLE 8.1 • Woodcock-Johnson III, Tests of Achievement

There are two parallel forms of the *WJ III ACH:* Standard Battery and Extended Battery.

The subtests can be combined to form five clusters in reading, mathematics, oral language, written language, and skills.

The *WJ III* Standard Battery consists of twelve subtests.

1. *Letter-Word Identification.* Assesses the ability to identify letters and words in isolation.
2. *Reading Fluency.* Measures the ability to read statements rapidly and answer "yes" or "no."
3. *Story Recall.* Assesses the ability to listen to and recall details of stories.
4. *Understanding Directions.* Measures the ability to comprehend and follow directions.
5. *Calculation.* Assesses the ability to solve mathematical calculations using a booklet in which the student can respond in writing.
6. *Math Fluency.* Assesses the ability to add, subtract, and multiply rapidly.
7. *Spelling.* Measures the ability to spell orally presented words.
8. *Writing Fluency.* Measures the ability to write fluently.
9. *Passage Comprehension.* Measures the ability to read a short passage and to identify the missing word.
10. *Applied Problems.* Measures the ability to solve practical mathematical problems.
11. *Writing Samples.* Measures the ability to respond in writing to various response demands.
12. *Story Recall–Delayed.* Measures the ability to recall previously presented story.

The *WJ III ACH* Extended Battery consists of ten subtests.

1. *Word Attack.* Assesses the ability to apply the rules of phonic and structural analysis to read unfamiliar and nonsense words.
2. *Picture Vocabulary.* Measures the ability to identify objects.
3. *Oral Comprehension.* Assesses the ability to identify missing words in a passage that is presented orally.
4. *Editing.* Measures the ability to correct errors in written passages.
5. *Reading Vocabulary.* Assesses the ability to supply one-word synonyms and antonyms after reading words.
6. *Quantitative Concepts.* Assesses the ability to identify mathematics terms, formulas, and number patterns.
7. *Academic Knowledge.* Measures the ability to answer questions about science, social studies, and humanities.
8. *Spelling of Sounds.* Assesses knowledge of letter combinations that form regular patterns in written English.
9. *Sound Awareness.* Measures the ability to rhyme words and to remove, substitute, and reverse parts of words in order to make new words.
10. *Punctuation and Capitalization.* Assesses knowledge of punctuation and capitalization rules.

VALIDITY The manual reports a number of validity studies for the achievement battery. In general, there is evidence to support content, concurrent, and construct validity. The extent to which various subtests reflect students' abilities depends on the instructional orientation of the teacher and the school curriculum.

SUMMARY The Tests of Achievements of the *Woodcock-Johnson III* assess academic abilities in individuals ages 24 months through adulthood. The battery is norm-referenced and individually administered. Reliability information is acceptable. A student's performance on the achievement subtests may be a reflection, in part, of the curriculum that has been taught.

Research-Based Practices   Testing Accommodations

To what extent do testing accommodations allow students with disabilities to be better able to demonstrate what they know and can do? Testing accommodations have been the subject of a great many research studies. The National Center for Educational Outcomes (NCEO) has examined research on this topic. According to NCEO, accommodations can be grouped into the following categories:

- Presentation, such as repeating directions, reading items aloud, signing directions, and using visual cues.
- Response, such as using a word processor, dictating responses, signing responses, and marking answers.
- Setting, such as individual, group, or specialized setting.
- Timing or scheduling, such as allowing extended time, providing frequent breaks, and allowing testing to occur over several days.

Allowing accommodations on tests can be controversial because there is uncertainty regarding the extent to which accommodations are beneficial to students with disabilities. Allowing extended time on tests is one of the most frequently allowed accommodations. Yet, some researchers have found that students with disabilities who have been allowed extended time do not perform at a higher level than students who have not been allowed extended time. Do your own research, beginning with the website of the NCEO at http://www.education.umn.edu/nceo. What do recent research studies say about the benefits of allowing extended time on tests? What about other accommodations, such as test administration in small and large groups, use of a word processor, use of text-to-speech software to read test questions in mathematics and science, and use of a person who acts as scribe?

Curriculum-Based Assessment

Curriculum-based assessment (CBA) is an approach to linking instruction with assessment. CBA has three purposes: (1) to determine eligibility, (2) to develop the goals for instruction, and (3) to evaluate the student's progress in the curriculum. Based on the performance on a CBA instrument, teachers and other professionals can specify instructional goals. Because there is such a close link between assessment and instruction, it is possible to conduct CBA frequently in order to determine whether to make any changes in instruction or the curriculum. Data collection, interpretation, and intervention are all integral parts of CBA. Other terms for CBA are curriculum-referenced measurement, curriculum-embedded measurement, frequent measurement, continuous curriculum measurement, and therapeutic measurement. CBA is useful because it:

- Links curriculum and instruction.
- Helps the teacher determine what to teach.
- Can be administered frequently.
- Is sensitive to short-term academic gains.
- Assists in the evaluation of student progress and program evaluation.
- Can be reliable and valid.
- Assists in improving student achievement. (Choate, Enright, Miller, Poteet, & Rakes, 1995; Wright, n.d., Retrieved March 1, 2005 from http://www.intervention central.org)

Developing a Curriculum-Based Assessment Instrument

While commercially published CBA instruments exist, there are advantages for teachers to develop their own. One important reason for this is that the curriculum may not correspond to the content of existing instruments. By constructing a CBA instrument using the steps listed below, teachers can specify goals, build into the instrument any special adaptations for test administration, and help to ensure that the CBA instrument is valid.

Step 1: Identify the Purpose(s)

Use the instrument to determine eligibility or entry into a curriculum, to develop the goals for intervention, or to evaluate the student's progress in the curriculum. Sometimes, one instrument can serve multiple purposes. For example, you can use the CBA instrument to develop goals and to evaluate the student's progress.

Step 2: Analyze the Curriculum

Determine what the curriculum teaches. Determine the specific tasks that the student should be learning.

Step 3: Develop Performance Objectives

Determine if a student has demonstrated progress in the curriculum. Specify behaviors that the student must demonstrate in order to indicate progress in the curriculum.

Step 4: Develop the Assessment Procedures

In this step, develop specific test items that correspond with the performance objectives. You can develop different types of items; for example, observing the student or requesting that the student perform specific actions or specific academic tasks, demonstrate particular behaviors, or answer particular questions. Make sure to delineate the scoring procedures. You will have to specify how you will determine how well the student performs. Considerations about reliability and validity are important. The CBA instrument must be valid. It must have a close correspondence with the curriculum.

Step 5: Implement the Assessment Procedures

Once the assessment procedures have been developed, you can collect information. How you decide to record and keep track of the information will be important. The way in which teachers assess students must be consistent each time. Recording sheets will be helpful in keeping track of the information you collect. Piloting, or trying out, the CBA items before actual implementation is a good idea. Although a great deal of thought has gone into the development and construction of the items, it is always good practice to try out the items before using them to assess students. You should administer CBA items according to the procedures that have been developed.

Step 6: Organize the Information

Summarize the information that you have collected. Tables, graphs, or charts can be useful.

Step 7: Interpret and Integrate the Results

Integrate the CBA information with information from standardized tests, observations, anecdotal records, and other forms of assessment. This is the point in the assessment process where instruction and assessment link. The decision-making process continues as educators, along with the team, decide where, when, and how instruction should proceed.

▶ Identify a curriculum area for instruction. Can you develop two assessment tasks that link instruction to assessment?

Criterion-Referenced Tests

A **criterion-referenced test (CRT)** measures a student's performance with respect to a well-defined domain (Anastasi, 1988; Berk, 1988). While norm-referenced tests discriminate between the performance of individual students on specific test items, criterion-referenced tests provide a description of a student's knowledge, skills, or behavior in a specific range of well-defined instructional objectives. This specific range is referred to as a domain. Criterion-referenced tests, instead of using norms, provide information on the performance of a student with respect to specific test items. The results of criterion-referenced testing are not dependent on the performance of other students, as with a norm-referenced test.

There are several characteristics that distinguish CRTs from norm-referenced tests. One of these is mastery. Performance on CRTs provides information on whether students have attained a predetermined level of competence or performance, called mastery. Performance can be interpreted as mastery, nonmastery, or intermediate mastery (Anastasi, 1988). While it is possible to construct a test that is both norm-referenced and criterion-referenced, teachers and other professionals must use caution when interpreting the results of these tests because it is difficult to combine both types of tests in one instrument.

Another distinction between criterion-referenced and norm-referenced tests is the breadth of the content domain that the test covers (Mehrens & Lehmann, 1991). Typical norm-referenced tests survey a broad domain, while CRTs usually have fewer domains but more items in each domain. CRTs typically sample the domain more thoroughly than norm-referenced tests (Mehrens & Lehmann, 1991).

CRTs can also be very useful in helping to make instructional planning decisions. Since they frequently cover a more restricted range of content than norm-referenced tests, they can provide more information about a student's levels of performance.

Teacher-Developed Criterion-Referenced Tests

Teachers can develop CRTs. The advantage to developing your own CRT is that you can directly link the test items to the curriculum. Use the following steps when developing a CRT (Rivera, Taylor, & Bryant, 1994–1995; Taylor, 2002).

Step 1: Identify the Knowledge, Processes, or Skills to Be Measured

Pinpoint the knowledge, processes, skills, and subskills that the student has been taught from the curriculum and from the student's individual educational program (IEP).

Step 2: Develop Instructional Objectives or Subobjectives for the Skills

Break down each of the skills and subskills into smaller steps; these become the instructional objectives and subobjectives.

Step 3: Develop Test Items for Each Objective or Subobjective

In order to measure each skill, develop test items for each one.

Step 4: Determine the Performance Standards or Criteria for Performance

Give each of the objectives and subobjectives at least one criterion that indicates acceptable levels of performance.

Step 5: Administer the Test Items

Once you have developed the CRT, you can administer the items. An advantage to using criterion-referenced tests is that, unlike norm-referenced tests, you can administer the items on a CRT frequently in order to document the student's progress.

Step 6: Score the Test Items and Present the Results in a Graph or Chart

Record the student's performance on the CRT. Graphing or charting the results can help both students and teachers in monitoring progress.

Step 7: Analyze and Interpret the Results

Knowledge about the student's level of performance facilitates the development of new instructional objectives and modifications.

▶ Choose a curriculum area with which you are familiar. Working with a partner, identify a unit of instruction. Using the steps suggested in this chapter, develop a criterion-referenced test. Share your CRT with other students.

Published Criterion-Referenced Tests

The *BRIGANCE® Diagnostic Inventories* are criterion-referenced tests that are similar in purpose, scoring, administration, and interpretation. They are useful in program planning and in monitoring programs. Table 8.2 summarizes the achievement sections of each of the inventories.

The administration and scoring for the *BRIGANCE inventories* is similar for all of the inventories. It is not necessary to administer all items or all subtests to a student. The examiner uses professional judgment to determine which items and subtests to administer. Each student has a record booklet that follows the student through several years of school.

Because these inventories are criterion-referenced, teachers can administer them frequently to monitor progress. Color-coding the student's responses to each item enables the teacher to see which skills the student has mastered. There are no summary scores. Instructional objectives accompany the items, facilitating program planning.

TABLE 8.2 ● BRIGANCE® Inventories

Name	Ages/Grades	Achievement Domains
BRIGANCE® Comprehensive Inventory of Basic Skills–Revised (Brigance, 1999)	pre-K through 9	1. Mathematics 2. Reading 3. Writing 4. Spelling 5. Reference Skills 6. Graphs and Maps 7. Measurement
BRIGANCE® Diagnostic Inventory of Early Development–Revised (Brigance, 1991)	ages birth to 7 years	1. Reading 2. Writing 3. Mathematics
BRIGANCE® Diagnostic Employability Skills Inventory (Brigance, 1995)	vocational secondary adult education job training	1. Reading 2. Writing 3. Mathematics

Connecting Instruction with Assessment: Alternative and Informal Assessment

The terms *alternative assessment* and *informal assessment* are sometimes used interchangeably to refer to these approaches. A fundamental principle of alternative approaches is that assessment of achievement should link to the curriculum. Linking instruction to the assessment of achievement means that:

- Assessment occurs as a normal part of the student's work. Assessment activities should emerge from the curriculum and the teaching situation. The student does not stop work to do an assessment; the work and the assessment are linked. Examples of this type of assessment include the use of journals, notebooks, essays, oral reports, homework, classroom discussions, group work, and interviews. These assessment activities can occur individually or in small groups and can take place during one session or over multiple sessions (Marolda & Davidson, 1994).
- The conditions for assessment need to be similar to the conditions for doing meaningful tasks. Students should have sufficient time, have access to peers, be able to use appropriate tools (books, calculators, manipulatives, etc.), and have the chance to revise their work.
- Assessment tasks should be meaningful and multidimensional. For example, they should provide students with the opportunity to demonstrate solving problems, drawing conclusions, understanding relationships, making inferences, and generating new questions.
- Feedback to students should be specific, meaningful, and prompt and should inform the students' thinking.
- Students participate in the assessment process. They help to generate and apply standards or rubrics. A rubric is an assessment scale that defines criterion for use in evaluating students. Self-assessment and peer assessment are part of the assessment process.

Assessment Approaches

Assessment activities and feedback from peers and teachers help promote student achievement. Ways in which the teacher can gather information and provide feedback to parents and students include:

- probes
- error analysis
- oral descriptions
- written descriptions
- checklists
- questionnaires
- interviews
- conferences
- student journals and notebooks
- performance-based assessment
- portfolios
- exhibitions (National Council of Teachers of Mathematics, 1991)

Probes

A **probe** is a diagnostic technique that modifies instruction in order to determine whether an instructional strategy is effective. Probes can help diagnose student problems and assist in planning instruction. For example, suppose a teacher wants to determine whether a fourth-grade student who is engaged in science investigations is ready to proceed to the next investigation.

The teacher can present a science problem to the student and observe the strategies that the student uses to solve it. The teacher probes with questions such as, "What will happen if the temperature is increased?" The student in this case is able to successfully solve the problem, but has difficulty understanding that an experiment may work under certain conditions but not under other conditions. The teacher then helps the student by further probing and guiding the student through the steps of the experiment.

The teacher can implement instructional probes during the process of instruction, using the following steps to design the probe:

1. The teacher identifies the targeted area of achievement and measures whether the student can perform the task. For example, in science the student is studying how pushing or pulling affects moving objects.
2. The teacher probes by modifying the task. For example, the teacher adds weight to one of the objects. (See the next section for examples of other instructional modifications.)
3. The teacher measures whether the student can perform the task.

When conducting a diagnostic probe, the teacher should document the student's performance during step 1 (baseline), step 2 (instruction), and step 3 (baseline).

Types of Accommodations for Use with Probes

Types of accommodations that can apply to instruction include:

Instructional accommodations

- change from written presentation to oral presentation
- combine verbal instruction with written explanation
- require fewer problems to be completed
- provide additional practice
- slow the pace of instruction
- provide additional time to complete problems

Materials accommodations

- use manipulatives
- place fewer questions, problems, or items on a page
- use color, word, or symbolic cues
- simplify the problem or the wording
- combine tactile mode with visual, oral, or kinesthetic modes

Environmental accommodations

- change location of instruction or probe
- change time of day for instruction or probe
- provide a work area that is quiet and free of distractions
- change lighting of work area
- change seating arrangements

Error Analysis

The purposes of **error analysis** are to: (1) identify the patterns of errors or mistakes that students make in their work, (2) understand why students make the errors, and (3) provide targeted instruction to correct the errors. When conducting an error analysis, the teacher checks the student's work and categorizes the errors.

After conducting an error analysis, the teacher summarizes the error patterns. However, many errors that students make may not fall into a pattern. Alternatively, if a pattern emerges, it does not mean that the problem is serious.

Teachers should view error analysis as a preliminary form of assessment and should always conduct further evaluation of the student's work. Teachers frequently use this approach to analyze student work when assessing students' reading abilities. Error analysis, when it is applied to reading, is commonly referred to as miscue analysis. When conducting a miscue analysis, teachers look for patterns of errors. According to Goodman (1984, 1989), these are "natural" errors rather than mistakes.

Oral Descriptions

Verbal descriptions of a student's work provide immediate feedback to a student by a teacher or peer. Oral descriptions are especially useful because they are quick, efficient, direct, and integrate easily into instruction. They are effective for program planning and program evaluation.

Oral descriptions do have several drawbacks, however. They can be subjective and, since the descriptions are verbal, there is no permanent record. In addition, specific disabilities may limit the ability of the student to understand, remember, or reply to what has been said.

Written Descriptions

A written description is a brief narrative that records feedback about the student's work. The teacher can share the narrative with students, teachers, or parents. A written description, like an oral description, conveys an impression of important aspects of the student's work. Teachers can use written descriptions for program planning and program evaluation.

Before writing the narrative, the teacher should carefully review the student's work. The teacher writes the description, noting areas of strength as well as problem areas. A written description provides feedback to the student about the quality of the work. Because it is recorded, it becomes a reference as the student continues to work. For example, a student who is engaged in environmental science has the following project: Investigate the migration patterns of killer bees. After developing graphs that depict migration patterns and studying the habitats of killer bees, the student develops conclusions and makes predictions about future migrations to new geographic areas.

After examining the student's work, a teacher can comment on labeling, graphing, spelling, and use of language. In addition, the teacher can discuss the use of graphing and knowledge of geography to solve real-world problems, completeness of the results, the student's disposition toward science, the ability to plan ahead, work habits, and attention to detail (Kulm, 1994). Two disadvantages of using written descriptions are that the parents may have difficulty reading or they may not have knowledge of written English.

▶ Identify one topic for instruction. Develop two assessment tasks that link the instruction directly to assessment.

Checklists and Questionnaires

Checklists and questionnaires are convenient ways to provide feedback about a student's work or attitudes. A checklist can be a quick and easy assessment approach. Figure 8.2 is an example of a checklist that provides feedback about student confidence,

My Beliefs about School

1. I like to go to school	most of the time	sometimes	never
2. My favorite subjects are	language arts social studies	mathematics health	science physical education
3. When I am at school I like to	read use the computer	write use the library	do projects use the playground
4. I like to work	by myself	with one other person	with several peers
5. I do homework	most of the time	sometimes	never
6. If I need help doing homework, I usually ask	my parent no one	my brother or sister	a friend
7. Some things I like about my teacher are:			

FIGURE 8.2 ● Assessing Attitudes, Interests, and Habits

willingness, perseverance, and interest. Checklists are helpful for screening, diagnosis, program planning, and program evaluation.

Questionnaires provide an opportunity for teachers and students to collect information in more detail than checklists. Questionnaires can be open-ended, allowing respondents to express their attitudes, opinions, and knowledge in depth, or they can have a more structured format so that the respondents just need to fill in one or two words, circle responses, or indicate the appropriate picture or icon.

Interviews

In Chapter 5 the topic of conducting interviews is discussed. Interviews help guide discussions, encourage students, determine motivation and enthusiasm, and identify work and study habits. One basic approach is to interview students individually about their likes and dislikes. Asking questions such as the following can be informative: "What do you like about social studies?" "What are your interests?" "What don't you like?" Interviews are useful for screening, diagnosis, program planning, and program evaluation.

Structured interviews provide a more systematic way to assess achievement. A structured interview offers the opportunity to observe, question, and discuss areas of achievement.

An example of using a structured interview in science is to ask students to observe the sky several times during one evening and the next day to answer the following questions:

1. What is the pattern of the stars as they move across the sky?
2. What is the pattern of the planets?
3. Do the planets follow the same pattern as the stars?
4. After showing students several pictures of the planets and stars, ask students to develop several hypotheses about their size, appearance, and motion.

Conferences

A conference is a conversation about the student's work that can include the student, educators, and parents. In a conference, participants share their views of the student's work with the goal of providing feedback and recommendations. Teacher–student conferences are helpful when assessing one piece of work or when summarizing the student's work over a period of time. The discussion in a conference can be strictly verbal, or it can be on audiotape, videotape, or written in summary form. Conferences can be useful for diagnosis, program planning, and program evaluation.

Student Journals

Students can keep a notebook or journal that allows them to record their work as well as their attitudes and feelings. A journal provides students the opportunity to record the steps to plan for an assignment, reflect on their own work, communicate about their learning, and document their progress (Kulm, 1994). In a journal, students can indicate what they like and don't like and areas in which they have difficulty. Journals are effective for program planning and program evaluation. The following is a sample journal outline (Kulm, 1994, p. 48):

Today's topic: Blue Mountains of Australia

Two important ideas: beautiful scenery, historic area

What I understood best: geography

What I need more work on: understanding aboriginal legends

How this topic can be used in real life: tourism, climate change, legends

Performance-Based Assessment

When used to assess achievement, performance-based assessment is the demonstration of knowledge, skills, or behavior. Performance assessment requires students to develop a product or to demonstrate an ability or skill based on an understanding of concepts and relationships. Chapter 6 describes performance-based assessment in detail.

Portfolios

A portfolio is a systematic collection of a student's work, assembled over a period of time. When documenting and assessing achievement, portfolios can provide information about conceptual understanding, problem solving, reasoning, communication abilities, habits, motivation, enthusiasm, creativity, work habits, and attitudes. Portfolios help students see that knowledge is interconnected. They are useful for program planning and program evaluation. A more extensive discussion of the use of portfolios can be found in Chapter 6.

Exhibitions

An exhibition is a display of a student's work that demonstrates knowledge, abilities, skills, and attitudes. Exhibitions are discussed in Chapter 6.

Self-Assessment

Self-assessment provides students with an opportunity to review concepts and identify processes. It is an occasion for students to reflect on their learning. Figure 8.3 is an example of a checklist that students use when assessing their own learning.

Student's Name				Date	
After completing my social studies assignment, I can	1 Great!	2	3	4	5
1. make comparisons among different points of view.					
2. distinguish between fact and opinion.					
3. apply new skills in using information.					
4. understand new vocabulary.					
5. make inferences about events.					
6. integrate new information.					
7. discuss new concepts and theories.					

FIGURE 8.3 ● Self-Assessment Checklist—Social Studies

Peer Assessment

Peer assessment allows students insight into the thinking and reasoning abilities of their peers. When conducting peer assessments, students have an opportunity to reflect on the learning processes of their peers as well as on their own. Figure 8.4 is an example of a checklist that students use when conducting a peer assessment.

Student's Name			Date
Peer's Name			
	Yes	No	Somewhat

1. My peer used new information to solve a problem.
2. My peer used new vocabulary.
3. My peer demonstrated the ability to think analytically.
4. My peer integrated and synthesized information.
5. My peer made several generalizations.

FIGURE 8.4 ● Peer Assessment—Science

Report Card Grades as Measures of Achievement

Report card grades can be helpful in understanding a student's achievement levels, strengths, and weaknesses. Report cards from the current and previous years can provide information about whether the student's problems are new or long-standing. They can indicate trends in student achievement. Is the problem recent? Did the student have difficulty during previous years? Is the problem in one area or in several areas? In what areas does the student do well?

There are two major viewpoints regarding the assignment of report card grades to students with disabilities (Gersten, Vaughn, & Brengelman, 1996). The first position considers grading standards to be absolute. Report card grades for all students should be based on the same standards—that is, an A, B, C, or failing grade means the same for a student with a disability or a student without a disability. The second perspective is that grading should be based on individual effort. However, this second option has several drawbacks: (1) It is difficult to measure effort; (2) basing grades on effort can prevent students from making progress because the grade creates the illusion that the student is making progress; (3) it is difficult to use just one grade to communicate multiple meanings such as progress, effort, and peer comparisons (Bursuck et al., 1996).

Grading Students with Disabilities

Alternatives to traditional report cards for students with disabilities are:

Supplementary Progress Reports

This is a written narrative that accompanies the traditional report card and that describes the student's academic and behavioral performance during a specific ranking period (Mehring, 1995).

Contracts

This is a written agreement between the student and the teacher that specifies the level of performance that the student must sustain to obtain a particular grade (Mehring, 1995).

Progress Checklist

This is a list of skills or competencies that are taught. Evaluation of the skills or competencies is made by checking a box under the column "mastered" or "needs improvement" (Mehring, 1995).

Modifications List

A list of options for the teacher when grading a student with a disability can be used. These modifications can be jointly developed by the teacher, student, and parents. Figure 8.5 presents suggested modifications.

Observing the Student in Various Environments

Chapter 5 discusses the importance of considering the student within the physical, learning, and social environments. The interactions between the student and the environment are important assessment considerations.

The following procedures could be jointly developed by the school, student, and parent when specifying grading options.

Tests

- Administer test orally, with questions and answers.
- Teacher, other student, or resource teacher reads regular test to student. (Please give resource teacher at least one day's notice.)
- Administer regular test using open book, class notes, or both.
- Modify modality of tests, written or oral, such as multiple choice instead of essay questions.
- Redo test if not passed.
- Lower criterion for passing.

In-Class Assignments

- Give regular assignments with lower criteria for passing.
- Shorten the regular assignment (e.g., half the questions).
- Grade assignments as "complete" rather than with a letter grade.
- Modify the set of questions students will answer.
- Pair the student with another student for help.

- Require the student to give oral answers to teacher.
- Redo assignments if incorrect.
- Give credit for appropriate behaviors not normally graded, such as taking notes.

Homework

- Same options as "In-Class Assignments."

Class Participation, Behavior, and Effort

- Same expectations as for other class members, but student may need extra encouragement and frequent feedback from teacher.
- Focus on a specific study skill or behavior deficit by giving a Pass/No Pass each day for that behavior. (Examples: coming prepared to class to class with correct materials or volunteering answers during class discussions.)

Other Considerations

- Give extra credit for projects that student or teacher suggests.
- Have student aide tape reading assignments or read aloud to student.
- Set expectations for attendance.

FIGURE 8.5 ● Sample Criteria for Grading a Student Who Receives Special Services

Source: "ASCD Yearbook 1996 Communicating Student Learning." Edited by Thomas R. Guskey, 1996, Alexandria, VA: Association for Supervision and Curriculum Development, Figure 5.1, pp. 52, and Figure 9.2, pp. 94.

The physical environment can influence the student's performance. The temperature, lighting, and seating arrangements of teaching and learning spaces can affect how well the student performs.

A comfortable learning environment facilitates the acquisition of a positive disposition and contributes to achievement. The curriculum, instructional methods, materials, and the assessment approaches are all areas of concern. A positive learning environment contributes to developing a positive disposition and contributes to achievement. The curriculum, instructional methods, materials, and assessment approaches are all areas of concern. A positive learning environment contributes to the development of a positive disposition.

Relationships with students and teachers can affect achievement. The social environment is important to the development of self-concept and self-esteem. These, in turn, contribute to a positive disposition toward achievement. By observing the social environment, teachers can study the relationships students have with peers and adults.

Summary

- Achievement tests, when carefully chosen, can be important sources of information.
- School records and past and current classroom performance are important sources of information.
- Other sources include criterion-referenced assessment, curriculum-based assessment, journals, notebooks, essays, oral reports, homework, discussions, group work, interviews, alternative assessment, performance testing, self-assessment, peer assessment, systematic observations, anecdotal records, interviews with teachers and students, and samples of student's work.
- The information that teachers gather through the assessment process should inform and support learning and instruction.

REFERENCES

Anastasi, A. (1988). *Psychological testing.* New York: Macmillan.

Balow, I. H., Farr, R. C., & Hogan, T. P. (2000). *Metropolitan achievement test 8.* San Antonio, TX: The Psychological Corporation.

Berk, R. A. (1988). Criterion-referenced tests. In J. P. Keeves (Ed.), *Educational research, methodology, and measurement: An international handbook,* (pp. 365–370). Oxford, UK: Pergamon Press.

Brigance, A. H. (1999). *BRIGANCE comprehensive inventory of basic skills–revised.* No. Billerica, MA: Curriculum Associates.

Brigance, A. H. (1991). *BRIGANCE inventory of early development–revised.* No. Billerica, MA: Curriculum Associates.

Brigance, A. H. (1995). *BRIGANCE employability skills inventory.* No. Billerica, MA: Curriculum Associates.

Bursuck, W., Polloway, E. A., Plante, L., Epstein, M. J., Jayanthi, J., & McConeghy, J. (1996). Report card grading and adaptations: A national survey of classroom practices. *Exceptional Children 62:* 301–318.

Choate, J. S., Enright, B. E., Miller, L. J., Poteet, J. A., & Rakes, T. A. (1995). *Curriculum-based assessment and programming.* Boston: Allyn and Bacon.

Gersten, R., Vaughn, S., & Brengelman, S. U. (1996). Grading and academic feedback for special education students and students with learning difficulties. In T. R. Guskey (Ed.), *ASCD yearbook* (pp. 47–57). Alexandria, VA: Association for Supervision and Curriculum Development.

Goodman, K. (1984). Unity in reading. In A. Purves & O. Niles (Ed.), *Becoming readers in a complex society: The 83rd yearbook of the National Society of the Study of Education, Part I* (pp. 79–114). Chicago, IL: University of Chicago Press.

Goodman, K. (1989). Roots of the whole-language movement. *Elementary School Journal 90:* 207–222.

Howell, K. W., & Rueda, R. (1996). Achievement testing with culturally and linguistically diverse students. In L. S. Suzuki, P. J. Meller, & J. G. Ponterotto (Eds.), *Handbook of multicultural assessment.* San Francisco: Jossey-Bass.

Kaufman, A. S., & Kaufman, N. L. (1998). *Kaufman test of educational achievement/Normative update (K-TEA/NU).* Circle Pines, MN: American Guidance Service.

Kulm, G. (1994). *Mathematics assessment.* San Francisco: Jossey-Bass.

Markwardt, Jr., F. C. (1998). *Peabody individual achievement test–revised/normative update.* Circle Pines, MN: American Guidance Service.

Marolda, M. R., & Davidson, P. S. (1994). Assessing mathematical abilities and learning approaches. In C. A. Thornton & N. S. Bley (Eds.), *Windows of opportunity* (pp. 83–113). Reston, VA: National Council of the Teachers of Mathematics.

Mehrens, W. A., & Lehmann, I. J. (1991). *Measurement and evaluation in education and psychology.* Fort Worth, TX: Holt, Rinehart & Winston.

National Council of the Teachers of Mathematics. (1991). *Mathematics assessment.* Reston, VA: Author.

Nitko, A. J. (1996). *Educational assessment of students.* Upper Saddle River, NJ: Prentice-Hall.

The Psychological Corporation. (2001). *Wechsler individual achievement test, second edition (WIAT–II).* San Antonio, TX: Author.

Rivera, D. P., Taylor, R. L., & Bryant, B. R. (1994–1995). Review of current trends in mathematics assessment for students with mild disabilities. *Diagnostique 20:* 143–174.

Salvia, J., & Ysseldyke, J. (2004). *Assessment.* Boston: Houghton-Mifflin.

Sattler, J. (2001). *Assessment of children.* La Mesa: CA: Author.

Taylor, R. L. (2002). *Assessment of exceptional students* (6th ed.). Boston: Allyn and Bacon.

Wilkinson, G. (1993). *Wide range achievement test–3.* Wilmington, DE: Wide Range.

Woodcock, R. W., McGrew, K. S., & Mather, N. (2001). *Woodcock-Johnson III.* Itasca, IL: Riverside.

Wright, J. (n.d.) *Curriculum-based measurement: A manual for teachers.* Retrieved March 1, 2005 from http://www.interventioncentral.org.

9 Reading

Chapter Objectives

After completing this chapter,
you should be able to:

- Contrast several perspectives regarding the development of literacy.

- Explain the appropriate use of and describe standardized achievement tests used in the assessment of literacy.

- Describe how literacy assessment is directly linked to instruction, program planning, and program evaluation.

- Describe how the physical, learning, and social environments influence literacy performance.

Key Terms

Literacy
Phonemic awareness

Phonics
Reading fluency

Syntax
Reading comprehension

Overview

Literacy involves being able to read, write, think, and communicate. Probably no other subject receives as much emphasis in the early grades. As students progress through the school, the ability to be literate is expected of all students. In school, literacy is linked to achievement. Once students leave school, being able to read and write is required in everyday life and is tied to success in many careers, economic level, and personal satisfaction.

Reading and writing are reciprocal processes. Reading is the process of constructing meaning through interactions that involve the reader's existing knowledge, text being read, and context of the reading situation. This chapter focuses on the teaching of reading. Chapter 10 is devoted to a discussion of the assessment of written language.

Contemporary instructional practices stress the integral link between reading and writing. A great deal is known about how individuals learn to read. Research (National Institute of Child Health and Human Development, 2000; Snow & Burns, 1998; Vaughn & Linan-Thompson, 2004) indicates that reading develops in social situations, involving the interaction of students, educators, and family. Reading requires the restructuring, application, and flexible use of knowledge in new situations. Skilled readers use a range of reading strategies independently and flexibly. Skilled readers integrate what they learn with prior knowledge and are knowledgeable and skilled in phonemic awareness, phonics and word study, reading fluency, syntax, vocabulary, and comprehension (National Reading Panel, 2000; Vaughn & Linan-Thompson, 2004).

Phonemic Awareness

A phoneme is the smallest unit of sound that has meaning in a language. The English language has approximately 44 phonemes that produce all spoken and written words. For example, the word *bat* consists of three phonemes: *ba, aah, tuh*. These sounds are represented as lbl, lael, and ltl.

Phonemic awareness involves the skills of recognizing separating, blending, and manipulating phonemes. The National Reading Panel (National Institute of Child Health and Human Development, 2000) indicated that teaching phonemic awareness as one part of a student's reading program can be very effective in improving reading performance. Activities that develop phonemic awareness involve practice with sounds and syllables.

Phonics

In contrast to phonemic awareness, **phonics** involves knowing how specific spoken sounds relate to particular written letters. For example, the letter *b* makes a "buh" sound. Phonics emphasizes knowledge of letter-sound correspondences. There has been considerable controversy over the place of phonics instruction in reading programs. However, many experts acknowledge that the teaching of phonics is important to beginning reading instruction (National Institute of Child Health and Human Development, 2000).

Word Study

Word study involves knowledge of phonemic awareness, phonics, decoding text, recognition of irregular and high-frequency words, and reading fluency. Automatically recognizing printed words that occur with high frequency allows students to fluently read a text. Sight vocabulary builds over time as students have multiple experiences with words in various contexts. Thus, students come to immediately recognize words that occur frequently "on sight." Examples of common sight words are *the, of, and, you*, and *from*.

Reading Fluency

Reading fluency involves reading letters, sounds, words, and text passages quickly, automatically, accurately, and smoothly. Being able to read fluently allows readers to understand and interpret what is read. Knowledge of phonemes, phonics, and sight words contribute to reading fluency. Students who have difficulty reading fluently frequently struggle with reading comprehension because they focus so much time and energy on decoding and recognizing words that they do not attend to the meaning of what is read (Vaughn & Linan-Thompson, 2004).

Syntax

Syntax relates to the flow of language and knowledge of rules for connecting words into meaningful sentences and simple sentences into complex ones. Syntactic tasks that are used to assess reading include:

- Request that students fill in the blank when reading sentences. For example, a student is asked to read the following sentence and provide the missing word: "When making predictions about the weather, it is helpful to check the weather _____ (forecast)."

- Invite students to combine the following two simple sentences into a longer, more complex sentence. For example, "Angelino likes to eat spaghetti " and "Angelino cooks spaghetti" can be combined in one sentence: "Angelino cooks spaghetti because he likes to eat it."
- Request that students change the verb tense in sentences. For example, students can be asked to change sentences from present to past tense such as, "Cooper plays videogames on the weekend" can be reworded in the past tense to read "Cooper played videogames on the weekend."

Vocabulary

▶ Standards for literacy and written language have been developed by the National Council of Teachers of English (NCTE). The vision behind these standards is that all students must be provided with opportunities to develop literacy skills in order to be productive, informed citizens. Review these standards at the website of the National Council of Teachers of English at http://www.ncte.org. Which ones apply to the teaching of reading?

Vocabulary is the knowledge that students have about the meanings of words. Knowledge of the meanings and use of spoken and written words significantly contributes to reading comprehension. Vocabulary instruction involves the explicit teaching of the meanings of words and assisting students to integrate word meanings into oral and written communications through instruction and practice.

Reading Comprehension

Reading comprehension involves being able to obtain meaning from a text, understand what is read, connect information within the context of a text, and relate what is being read to what is already known. Reading comprehension means that students are able to read for knowledge and information, obtain, interpret, retrieve, evaluate, and integrate information. Students are able to use the knowledge that is gained by reading to do further reading, thereby increasing interpretation skills (Mullis, Kennedy, Martin, & Sainsbury, 2004).

▶ **CEC Common Core Knowledge and Skills.** The beginning special education teachers should understand national, state or provincial, and local curricula standards (CC7K3).

Technological Literacy

▶ Can you suggest several technologies that you use frequently that provide access to electronic texts and media, communication, learning, and productivity?

With the ubiquitousness of technologies throughout our society, there has been a shift in the vision of what it means to be literate. New approaches to becoming literate go beyond text-based teaching that relies solely on skill-building activities. Technological literacy involves using technology for access to electronic texts and media, communication, learning, and productivity. For example, students should be able to search, identify, download, and read Web-based texts and information, access electronic books that are on disk or in various formats, such as MP3, read email messages and information, and use Web search engines and tools.

Research-Based Practices How Do U.S. Students Compare?

In the PIRLS (Progress in International Reading Literacy Study) 2006 Assessment Framework and Specifications (Mullis et al., 2004), researchers studied how well children in 35 countries can read. The results of this study indicate that there are concerns about the reading performance of U.S. students. This report provides important information on how reading is taught and assessed. For up-to-date information and sample test items, visit the website of the International Study Center at http://pirls.bc.edu

Assessing Reading

Attempts to improve literacy have focused on improving classroom practices and generating attitudes and skills that foster the development of lifelong readers. A priority is an emphasis on connecting and integrating assessment with improvements in classroom practices (Langer et al., 1995).

The assessment of reading abilities and skills should involve a variety of approaches in order to reflect an understanding of what students know and are able to do. Assessment of reading and writing should reflect integrated activities that evaluate students' ability to think, rethink, construct, and interpret knowledge. This means that as students read, they should know when to read, how to read, how to think about what they have read, and how to communicate their knowledge and understanding (Langer et al., 1995).

Assessment Principles

The International Reading Association (IRA) (Rhodes & Shanklin, 1993) issued "Resolutions on Literacy Assessment." These resolutions are comprehensive and state that the two major purposes of literacy assessment are (1) to inform learning and instruction and (2) to demonstrate that literacy programs are effective. Among the resolutions are several that are pertinent to the assessment of students with special needs:

- Assessments should include a variety of observations that consider the complexity of the processes involved in reading, in writing, and in using language. The assessment tasks must include high-quality texts, various genres, and authentic tasks.
- Assessment tasks should be age-appropriate.
- Assessment tools should not reflect bias.
- Assessment of reading, writing, and language must include a variety of approaches.
- Assessment approaches should consider the purposes of each assessment tool and the settings in which the assessment is conducted.
- Assessment activities should reflect instruction.

▶ The International Reading Association (IRA) has published resources on the assessment and teaching of reading. Visit IRA's website at http://www.reading.org and identify information on reading assessment.

According to Rhodes and Shanklin (1993), there are twelve principles of literacy assessment:

1. *Assess authentic reading and writing.* When students read and write, they must know the letters and their associated sounds (graphophonics), understand the meaning of language (semantics), and grasp the flow of the language (syntax).
2. *Assess reading and writing in various contexts.* An understanding of students' reading and writing abilities must consider the contexts in which reading and writing occur. Contexts relate to the types of reading materials, the purpose of the reading, and strategies in use.
3. *Assess the literacy environment, instruction, and students.* Reading and writing assessment must consider the environments in which reading occurs, the types of instruction in use, and the characteristics of students.
4. *Assess processes and products of reading.* The assessment of reading processes and students' products can provide a comprehensive understanding of students' abilities.
5. *Analyze error patterns.* The understanding of patterns of errors in reading and writing can help improve student performance. Errors in reading include miscues, omissions, substitutions, additions, repetitions, self-corrections, and pauses.
6. *Include the assessment of background knowledge.* Experience, prior learning, and background knowledge influence reading and writing performance.

Research-Based Practices | Screening Students Who Are at Risk for Reading Problems

In a review of more than 450 studies, Hammill (2004) explored the variables that appear to predict future reading problems in preschool and kindergarten children. Because of parental attention and television, he stresses that young children today know quite a bit about what it means to read and write. These skills include handling books, reproducing letters and numbers, writing their own names, selecting print and nonprint items, writing letters and numbers, identifying abbreviations, and reading a few words.

Skills that have only a moderate relationship to future reading include phonemic awareness, rapid naming, spoken language, and memory. Hammill concludes by stating that when screening young children who are at risk for developing reading problems, the emphasis should be "on actual reading (e.g., decoding and comprehension) and other print activities because they correlate the highest with reading performance" (Hammill, 2004, p. 466).

7. *Consider developmental patterns in reading and writing.* Knowledge of typical developmental patterns in reading and writing can contribute to our understanding of reading and writing abilities.

8. *Use sound principles of assessment.* Use sound principles or standards when assessing students. These standards apply to reliability, validity, observation, and scoring. Chapters 3 and 4 discuss many of these principles.

9. *Use triangulation.* Triangulation means that conclusions about student performance derive from multiple (here, at least three) sources of information. Rhodes and Shanklin (1993) advise caution when drawing conclusions about students when using only one source of information.

10. *Include students, parents, teachers, and other school personnel in the assessment process.* The involvement of students, parents, and other educators in the assessment process provides for the inclusion of multiple perspectives.

11. *Assessment activities should be ongoing.* Assessment activities should occur frequently and routinely. In this way, assessment activities integrate into and inform instruction.

12. *Record, analyze, and use assessment information.* Assessment information is effective only when it is in use. Record assessment data frequently, analyze it, and use it on a routine basis to guide instruction.

Standardized Instruments

Gray Oral Reading Tests–4

The *Gray Oral Reading Tests–4 (GORT–4;* Wiederholt & Bryant, 2001) is an individually administered norm-referenced test of reading comprehension and oral reading for students ages 6 years through 18 years. Each of the two forms of the *GORT–4* contains 13 reading passages arranged in order of difficulty. Although the title of the test indicates that the *GORT–4* is a revision of the previous edition, this test is almost identical to its predecessor, *Gray Oral Reading Tests–3 (GORT–3).*

ADMINISTRATION For each passage, the examiner reads one or two sentences that provide motivation. After reading each passage orally, the student responds to five multiple-choice questions that the examiner reads aloud. The examiner records the student's responses.

SCORING The test reports scores as age and grade equivalents; percentiles; standard scores for the total scores for rate, accuracy, and comprehension; and Oral Reading Comprehension Score.

STANDARDIZATION The *GORT–4* was standardized on more than 1,600 students, ages 6 years through 18 years. The sample selection came from U.S. Census reports and was stratified according to geographic region, race, grade, gender, and ethnicity.

RELIABILITY Average internal consistency reliability coefficients are .90. In general, the reliability coefficients are adequate.

VALIDITY For the most part, the *GORT–4* bases concurrent validity on the *GORT–3*. The major criticism of the validity of this test is that the manual does not report whether the *GORT–4* actually measures the authors' stated purposes.

SUMMARY The *Gray Oral Reading Tests–4* is an individually administered norm-referenced test of reading comprehension and oral reading. The standardization is adequate. However, information is lacking as to the socioeconomic status of the sample and whether test developers systemically included students with disabilities and students whose first language is not English. While the reliability is acceptable, additional evidence of validity is needed.

TESTS-at-a-GLANCE

Gray Oral Reading Tests–4 (GORT–4)

- **Publication Date:** 2001
- **Purpose:** Measures reading comprehension and oral reading.
- **Age/Grade Levels:** Ages 6 years through 18 years.
- **Time to Administer:** 15 to 45 minutes.
- **Technical Adequacy:** Evidence of reliability and validity is adequate. Test items should be examined by the evaluator in order to determine congruence with reading instruction.
- **Suggested Use:** Measures oral reading skills. Caution should be used because many students attain higher reading comprehension scores when reading silently rather than aloud.

Stanford Diagnostic Reading Test 4

The *Stanford Diagnostic Reading Test 4* (*SDRT4*; Harcourt Brace Educational Measurement, 1995) is a norm-referenced test for students in grades 1.5 through 13. The test has six overlapping levels:

Grade Level

1.5 through 2.5	red
2.5 through 3.5	orange
3.5 through 4.5	green
4.5 through 6.5	purple
6.5 through 8.9	brown
9.0 through 13.0	blue

The purposes of the *SDRT4* are to assist in making eligibility decisions, diagnose difficulties in reading, evaluate programs, and provide information about program effectiveness. The test assesses phonetic ability, vocabulary, reading comprehension, and the ability to scan for information.

ADMINISTRATION The *SDRT4* is a group-administered test. Examiners need not administer all subtests, but can decide to administer only one or two of the subtests. The items are a combination of multiple choice and free response. Examiners can administer this test individually following standardized procedures for test administration.

Stanford Diagnostic Reading Test 4

- **Publication Date:** 1995

- **Purposes:** Assesses phonetic ability, vocabulary, reading comprehension, and the ability to scan for information.

- **Age/Grade Levels:** Grades 1.5 through 13.

- **Time to Administer:** 15 minutes to 45 minutes

- **Technical Adequacy:** Reliability and validity are acceptable. The evaluator should examine the congruence between how reading is taught to students with disabilities and test items.

- **Suggested Use:** Measures phonetic ability, vocabulary, reading comprehension, and the ability to scan for information. Although this test has been designed to be administered to groups of students, it can be administered individually.

▶ **CEC Common Core Knowledge and Skills.** The beginning special educator will understand national, state, or provincial, and local curricula standards (CC8K4).

SCORING Raw scores convert to percentiles, stanines, normal curve equivalents, grade equivalents, and scaled scores. Teachers can score the *SDRT4* by hand (using a stencil provided by the publisher) or send it away for machine scoring.

STANDARDIZATION The standardization sample is representative of socioeconomic status, size of school district, and geographic region.

RELIABILITY The test reports both alternate form and internal consistency reliabilities. The reliability coefficients are adequate.

VALIDITY The test reports content and criterion-related validity. Teachers should examine the test items to determine the extent to which the SDRT4 matches reading as they have taught it.

SUMMARY The *Stanford Diagnostic Reading Test 4* is a norm-referenced test for students in grades 1.5 through 13. The test has six overlapping levels and is applicable to groups of students. However, it can be useful for assessing individual students. The items consist of both multiple-choice and free-response items.

Test of Reading Comprehension–3

The *Test of Reading Comprehension–3 (TORC–3;* Brown, Hammill, & Wiederholt, 1995) is an individually administered norm-referenced test of vocabulary and silent reading comprehension for students ages 7 years through 17 years, 11 months. The TORC–3 contains eight subtests:

General Vocabulary. The student reads three words and then selects two other words that relate to the three words.

Syntactic Similarities. The student reads five sentences and then chooses the two sentences that are most closely related.

Paragraph Reading. After reading brief paragraphs, the student answers multiple-choice questions for each paragraph.

Sentence Sequencing. After reading five sentences, the student must arrange them in a logical sequence.

Mathematics Vocabulary. This subtest is similar to the General Vocabulary subtest, except that the vocabulary consists of words related to mathematics.

Social Studies Vocabulary. This subtest is similar to the General Vocabulary subtest except that the vocabulary consists of words related to social studies.

Science Vocabulary. This subtest is similar to the General Vocabulary subtest except that the vocabulary consists of words related to science.

Reading the Directions of Schoolwork. The student reads directions and responds on the answer sheet.

ADMINISTRATION The *TORC–3* is individually administered. However, teachers can administer it to small groups of students.

SCORING Raw scores convert to age and grade equivalents, percentiles, and standard scores.

STANDARDIZATION *TORC–3* is the third edition of the *TORC,* originally published in 1968 and revised in 1986. This third edition was renormed. The test reports information about the proportion of students by age, geographic region, gender, residence, race, ethnicity, and disabilities in the standardization sample.

RELIABILITY The test reports test-retest and internal consistency reliability coefficients. Reliability for the *TORC–3* is adequate.

VALIDITY The test reports content and criterion-related validity. Teachers should examine the test items in order to determine alignment with instruction.

Woodcock Reading Mastery Test–Revised/Normative Update

The *Woodcock Reading Mastery Test–Revised/Normative Update (WRMT–R/NU;* Woodcock, 1998) is an individually administered test of reading skills and reading comprehension for individuals from kindergarten through age 75. The *WRMT–R/NU* consists of six tests arranged in clusters. The Visual-Auditory Learning and Letter Identification tests compose the Readiness Cluster. The Word Identification and Word Attack tests form the Basic Skills Cluster, and the Word Comprehension and Passage Comprehension tests constitute the Reading Comprehension Cluster. Form G of the test includes a Supplementary Letter Checklist. The following section describes each of the tests.

> *Visual-Auditory Learning.* The student looks at rebuses representing words and must "read" the rebuses.
>
> *Letter Identification.* The student looks at upper- and lowercase letters of the alphabet and must name each of the letters.
>
> *Supplementary Letter Checklist* (Form G only). The student must recognize and name letters in sans serif type.
>
> *Word Identification.* The student must read single words that are in the test.
>
> *Word Attack.* The student must demonstrate a knowledge of phonics and word attack skills by pronouncing nonsense syllables.
>
> *Word Comprehension.* This subtest is composed of three parts: Antonyms, Synonyms, and Analogies. The student must connect words according to these categories.
>
> *Passage Comprehension.* The student reads a brief passage and supplies the missing words.

ADMINISTRATION The *WRMT–R/NU* is administered individually.

SCORING Raw scores are converted to standard scores, percentiles, and age and grade equivalents. In addition, there is a relative performance index (RPI) that provides an estimate of expected performance. The *WRMT–R/NU* scoring forms include visual profiles for describing performance.

TESTS-at-a-GLANCE

Test of Reading Comprehension–3 (TORC–3)

- **Publication Date:** 1995
- **Purpose:** Measures vocabulary and reading comprehension.
- **Age/Grade Levels:** Ages 7 years through 17 years, 11 months.
- **Time to Administer:** One to 3 hours, depending on the age of the student.
- **Technical Adequacy:** Evidence of reliability and validity is adequate. Test items should be examined by the evaluator in order to determine congruence with reading instruction.
- **Suggested Use:** Measure of vocabulary; indicates strengths and weaknesses in silent reading comprehension.
- **Summary.** The *Test of Reading Comprehension–3* is a norm-referenced test of vocabulary and reading comprehension. Evidence of reliability and validity is adequate. However, the teacher should examine the test items in order to determine congruence with the school curriculum.

TESTS-at-a-GLANCE

Woodcock Reading Mastery Test–Revised/NU (WRMT–R/NU)

- **Publication Date:** 1998
- **Purposes:** Measures reading readiness, reading skills, and reading comprehension.
- **Age/Grade Levels:** Kindergarten through adulthood.
- **Time to Administer:** 30 to 50 minutes.
- **Technical Adequacy:** For the 1998 edition, new norms were not collected. Existing standardization data were reanalyzed. Reliability is adequate. Validity is acceptable; however, teachers should examine the test items to determine the extent to which the items assess the curriculum taught. Many of the test items reflect a skills approach to learning to read.
- **Suggested Use:** As a limited measure of overall reading achievement. Examiners should evaluate the test items because the test does not reflect contemporary approaches to the teaching of literacy. The NU edition does not update the norms. There is some question about validity of the test in view of current approaches to teaching literacy.

STANDARDIZATION For the 1998 edition, test publishers did not collect new norms, but rather, reanalyzed existing standardization data. The school-age sample data are from 1983 to 1985. The college and university sample data are from 1984 through 1985. Adult data are from 1984 through 1985. The standardization sample represents age, gender, region, race, ethnicity, and economic status as estimated by parental education. The standardization sample of the *WRMT–R/NU* forms a link with the standardization samples for the *Kaufman Test of Achievement (K–TEA/NU)*, the *Peabody Individual Achievement Test–Revised/NU (PIAT–R/NU)*, and the *KeyMath–R*. The renorming sample for the *WRMT–R/NU* consisted of students in kindergarten through age 22. There is no update for the sample of individuals over the age of 22. For the linking sample, the test examinees in the norm sample took one of the complete test batteries and one or more subtests from another battery. This linking approach permits the making of comparisons of test performance across batteries.

RELIABILITY Test publishers report internal consistency reliability coefficients only for grades 1, 3, 5, 8, and 11, and for adults. The coefficients are in the .80s and .90s. Test-retest reliability coefficients are not available.

VALIDITY The manual provides evidence of content validity. The test reports concurrent validity with the *Woodcock-Johnson Psychoeducational Battery–Revised*. The *WRMT–R/NU*

SNAPSHOT

Joseph

Joseph is in the ninth grade at the Creative Arts Charter School. Although he is a very capable student and a talented artist, his school achievement is considerably below expectations. Joseph and his family have moved several times and this is the third school in which he has been enrolled in the past two years. At a recent parent-teacher meeting with Mr. Holmes, Joseph's teacher, and Kayla Smith, Joseph's mother, Mr. Holmes expressed concerns about Joseph's school performance.

Joseph's school attendance is a concern, and homework is rarely completed. Joseph appears to be reluctant to complete reading assignments for language arts, social studies, and science. A recent report by the school psychologist indicated that Joseph is experiencing difficulties in organization, concentration, attention, and self-esteem.

Mr. Holmes reviewed Joseph's performance on the *Woodcock Reading Mastery Tests-NU*, which the school's learning strategist had recently administered to Joseph.

Joseph had difficulty with the Word Identification and Word Attack subtests. He often lost his place, added, or omitted syllables. He was unable to apply common phonics rules. For some words, he pronounced them one syllable at a time.

On the Passage Comprehension subtest, Joseph responded acceptably when he was able to read the words in the passages, but errors were made when he was unable to decode words or determine the correct syntax for missing words.

Mr. Holmes commented that because Joseph struggles with reading, he is discouraged. Assignments in the content areas are frustrating, and Joseph's motivation has decreased. Mr. Holmes related that Joseph's team had met to identify interventions that would lead to school success. The interventions will concentrate on phonics, vocabulary building, fluency, and strategies for comprehending expository and narrative texts. Can you suggest other steps that should be explored?

uses a traditional, somewhat outdated approach to reading. Evidence to support the validity of the clusters is lacking. Examiners should carefully review the test in order to determine the correspondence between test items and the literacy curriculum.

SUMMARY The *WRMT–R/NU* is an individually administered test of reading skills and reading comprehension for individuals from kindergarten through adulthood, consisting of six tests in three clusters. The NU edition does not update the norms. There is some question about the validity of the test in view of current approaches to teaching literacy.

▶ Examine a norm-referenced standardized reading test. Explain how this test provides information about reading skills and abilities.

Concerns about Standardized Reading Tests

Norm-referenced tests of reading can be useful in identifying students with reading difficulties, pinpointing strengths and weaknesses, and evaluating programs. However, many experts have voiced concerns about those tests. In 1991 the International Reading Association directly addressed concerns about the use of standardized reading tests when it "resolved that literacy assessments must be based in current research and theory, not limited by traditional psychometric concepts, and must reflect the complex and dynamic interrelationship of reading, writing, and language abilities" (Rhodes & Shanklin, 1993, p. 47). Most experts in reading believe that standardized norm-referenced tests of reading have a number of shortcomings (see Table 9.1).

Connecting Assessment with Instruction

Curriculum-based assessment (CBA), introduced in Chapter 8, is a broad approach to linking assessment with instruction. CBA has three purposes: (1) to determine eligibility, (2) to develop the goals for instruction, and (3) to evaluate the student's progress in the curriculum.

TABLE 9.1 ● Shortcomings of Norm-Referenced Tests When Compared to Contemporary Approaches	
Norm-Referenced Tests of Reading	**Contemporary Approaches to Reading Assessment**
Contain brief, incomplete passages	Have longer, complete passages
Fail to tap background knowledge	Encourage the reader to use background and prior knowledge while reading
Pose literal questions	Encourage the use of higher order thinking, which involves the restructuring, application, and flexible use of knowledge in new situations
Can contain biased questions	Offer equitable assessment strategies
Pose multiple-choice questions	Pose open-ended questions
Have only one correct answer to each question	Encourage more than one answer
Fail to assess the use of a variety of reading strategies	Assess a variety of reading strategies
Do not assess reading attitudes and habits	Assess reading attitudes and habits
Offer few or no direct links to instruction	Directly link instruction assessment tools to instruction

Assessment of Reading

Ravi is in fifth grade. He is a motivated student who wants to be engaged in learning. Ravi reads on the primer level. He cannot recall letter sound associations. He has received support in the regular classroom and resource room since first grade. Despite this support, his reading and written language skills continue to lag considerably behind his peers.

At times, he may lose focus on school work. Although Ravi is able to understand information that is given verbally and recall key concepts, he has so much difficulty reading that he is unable to keep up with other students. Ravi is embarrassed about not being able to read and write, and he is reluctant to ask for help.

The *Gray Oral Reading Test-4* was administered to Ravi in two separate sessions to determine specific strengths and weaknesses. During the session, Ravi tried hard but it was evident that he experiences frustration when asked to read.

Ravi has considerable difficulty in accuracy, fluency, and reading comprehension. Decoding is delayed, and he is unable to use context clues to figure out new words. He frequently confuses letters such as *b/d* and *m/w*. His reading comprehension has declined because he does not have the appropriate decoding skills. He guesses at words based on the context but the guesses are not accurate.

Gray Oral Reading Test-4

Subtest	April 10, 2XXX		
	Standard Score	*Percentile Rank*	*Grade Equivalent*
Rate	4	2	3.4
Accuracy	2	<1	2.0
Fluency Score	1	<1	2.7
Comprehension Score	4	2	

Ravi's teachers determined that careful and close instruction and monitoring are required in order to build reading skills and abilities. Attention should be focused on a balanced approach that includes phonological awareness, phonics, reading and decoding strategies, sight word development, practice with controlled reading materials, and integration of reading instruction into content areas including mathematics, science, and social studies. Ravi's teachers should consider the integration of technology to support reading development and comprehension.

Principles

A fundamental principle of reading instruction is that instruction should be linked directly with assessment. Connecting instruction to assessment in reading means that:

▶ **CEC Common Core Knowledge and Skills.** The beginning special educator should understand national, state or provincial, and local curricula standards (CC8S5).

- Assessment occurs as a normal part of the student's work. Assessment activities emerge from the teaching situation. The student does not stop work to do an assessment; the work connects with the assessment. Examples of this type of assessment include the use of journals, notebooks, essays, oral reports, homework, classroom discussions, group work, and interviews. These assessment activities can occur individually or in small groups and can take place during one session or over multiple sessions.
- The conditions for assessment should be similar to the conditions for doing meaningful tasks. Students must have sufficient time, have access to peers, be able to use appropriate literacy materials, and have the chance to revise their work.
- Assessment tasks need to be meaningful and multidimensional. They should provide students with the opportunity to demonstrate a variety of reading abilities and skills.
- Feedback to students is frequent, specific, meaningful, and prompt, and assists students' acquisition of reading.
- Students participate in the assessment process. They help to generate and apply standards or rubrics. Self-assessment and peer assessment are part of the assessment process.

There are several approaches to developing and using curriculum-based assessment instruments in the assessment of literacy. We will examine two approaches: curriculum-based assessment and curriculum-based measurement.

Curriculum-Based Assessment: Idol, Nevin, Paolucci-Whitcomb Model

Curriculum-based assessment can measure the rate of reading, reading errors, accuracy, and reading comprehension. Although the developers (Idol, Nevin, & Paolucci-Whitcomb, 1996) presume a basal reading series as part of the curriculum, this model can adapt to a literature-based reading program. Teachers can use instruction materials to construct the CBA and to establish levels of mastery. The following steps describe how to develop and administer the CBA:

1. The teacher photocopies three 100-word passages from the first quarter of each of the basal readers for grades 1 through 6. For preprimers and primers, teachers select passages of 25 or 50 words, then label and arrange them in order of difficulty.
2. On three successive days, beginning with the easiest passage and proceeding to the more difficult ones, the student reads one of the passages orally. The teacher records the total number of seconds it took for the student to read the passage. From this, the teacher can determine the number of correct words the student reads per minute.
3. The teacher records errors made while the student is reading. Types of errors include omissions, substitutions, additions, repetitions, self-corrections, and pauses. To determine the percentage of reading accuracy, the number of words read correctly is divided by the total number of words in the passage. For example, Peter read a 100-word passage and made 5 errors. To calculate reading accuracy, his teacher followed these steps:
   - Subtract total number of errors from number of words in the passage

     100 – 5 = 95 words read correctly

   - Divide the number of words read correctly by the total number of words in the passage

     95/100 = 95% level of accuracy

4. After each passage is read, the teacher asks the student six comprehension questions that the teacher has constructed. The acceptable level of performance is answering 5 of the 6 questions correctly. Teachers should construct the questions as follows:
   - Two text-explicit (TE) questions. These are questions with answers that the student can find precisely in the passage.

     Example: What is the name of the main character?

   - Two text-implicit (TI) questions. These are questions with answers that the passage implies.

     Example: What is a solar system?

   - Two script-implicit (SI) questions. These are questions that require the reader to combine prior knowledge with details from the passage.

     Example: What is the moral of the story?

▶ There are many Web-based resources on curriculum-based measurement. Using a Web browser, search for these resources using one or more of the following search terms: "curriculum-based assessment" and "curriculum-based measurement."

Curriculum-Based Measurement

Curriculum-based measurement (CBM; Marston, 1989) is a type of curriculum-based assessment that emphasizes repeated direct measurement of student performance. CBM is based on the belief that reading fluency depends on speed and accuracy of reading. Like the previous model, CBM emphasizes: (1) the direct link between the assessment and the student's curriculum; (2) brief, frequent assessments; (3) multiple forms of the assessment instrument; (4) the low cost of developing assessment materials; and (5) a sensitivity to measuring the improvement of student performance.

To construct a CBM, the teacher selects a brief passage or word list and asks the student to read it orally. When the student finishes reading, the teacher counts the number of correctly and incorrectly read words. The teacher and the student use a graph to plot the number of correctly read words. Teachers can repeat this process many times in order to document the progress that the student makes.

Criterion-Referenced Assessment

Instead of comparing a student's performance to a norm group, criterion-referenced assessments measure a student's performance with respect to a well-defined content domain (Anastasi, 1988), as Chapter 8 discusses. While norm-referenced tests in reading discriminate between the performance of individual students on specific test items, criterion-referenced tests provide a description of a student's curriculum-referenced knowledge, skills, or processes.

The *BRIGANCE® Inventories* are criterion-referenced tests that are similar in purpose, scoring, administration, and interpretation. Chapter 8 describes the tests in detail, and Table 9.2 summarizes the reading sections of several inventories.

Informal Assessment Approaches

Formal assessment and feedback from peers and teachers encourage the development of reading abilities. Ways in which the teacher can gather information and provide feedback to parents and students include:

- Probes
- Miscue (or error) analysis
- Cloze procedure
- Think-alouds
- Retelling
- Oral descriptions

TABLE 9.2 • BRIGANCE® Inventories That Assess Reading

Name	Ages/Grades	Achievement Domains
BRIGANCE Comprehensive Inventory of Basic Skills– Revised (Brigance, 1999)	Pre-K through grade 9	1. Word Recognition 2. Oral Reading 3. Reading Comprehension 4. Word Analysis 5. Functional Word Recognition
BRIGANCE Life Skills Inventory (Brigance, 1994)	Vocational Secondary Adult education	1. Words on Common Signs 2. Words on Common Labels
BRIGANCE Employability Skills Inventory (Brigance, 1995)	Vocational Secondary Adult education Job training	1. Reading Grade-Placement 2. Direction Words 3. Words Related to Employment 4. Abbreviations

- Written descriptions
- Checklists and questionnaires
- Interviews
- Conferences
- Student journals and notebooks

- Performance-based assessments
- Sharing portfolios
- Exhibitions
- Self-assessment
- Peer assessment

Probes

A probe is a diagnostic technique in which instruction is varied in order to examine whether an instructional schema is working. As Chapter 8 indicates, probes are valuable for diagnosing student problems and assisting in planning instruction. For example, suppose a teacher wants to determine whether a student is ready to proceed to a more difficult reading book. The teacher can present the student with a selection from the book and observe the strategies that the student uses when reading. The student may be able to read the words on the page but needs some help learning new vocabulary. The teacher can then help the student by introducing the new vocabulary and providing background knowledge.

Teachers implement instructional probes during the process of instruction. When designing an instructional probe, we suggest the following steps:

1. The teacher identifies the area of reading that is to be the target and determines whether the student is able to do the tasks or use certain reading strategies. Examples include locating the title page, retelling a story, and recognizing common warning signs such as "Danger" and "Keep Out."
2. The teacher modifies the assignment. For example, to facilitate the recognition of warning signs, the teacher can have the student say "trace," "recognize," and "write the words." To assist in retelling, a teacher can ask: "What happened after? Tell me more about where the story takes place."
3. The teacher determines whether the student can read the words or retell the passage.

When conducting a diagnostic probe, the teacher should document the student's performance during step 1 (baseline), step 2 (instruction), and step 3 (baseline).

Miscue (or Error) Analysis

As defined in Chapter 8, the purposes of error analysis are to: (1) identify the patterns of errors or miscues that students make in their work, (2) understand why students make the errors, and (3) provide instruction to help correct the errors. In a miscue or error analysis of reading skills, the student reads aloud and the teacher categorizes the errors. Figure 9.1 shows common symbols and how teachers use them when marking miscues.

After conducting a miscue analysis, the teacher should summarize the error patterns. However, many errors will not have a pattern, and a pattern of errors does not mean that there is a serious problem. Miscue analysis is always a preliminary form of assessment; teachers should always conduct further evaluation of the student's work.

Students will frequently correct their own miscues. Calling attention to the student's miscues can interrupt the student's understanding of the passage. Teachers should allow students to proceed to the end of the sentence or paragraph before providing feedback. Teachers can gather useful assessment information when observing whether the student makes self-corrections when rereading a passage.

The *Classroom Reading Miscue Assessment (CRMA;* Rhodes & Shanklin, 1993) (Figure 9.2) was developed to assist teachers in using miscue analysis. As the student reads a passage, the teacher uses the *CRMA* to determine the types of miscues that the student makes. To begin, the teacher selects a complete passage or story, from 300 to 500 words in length, with which the student is unfamiliar. The passage should be at an acceptable

brothers bothers	Longhand superscriptions denote substitutions miscues—oral observed responses that differ from expected responses to printed text.
^	Insertion miscue (word not printed in text, added by oral reader).
	Example: Gwen ^ poured him a big glass. *(proudly above ^)*
(word)	Circled word or words; circled period or other punctuation indicates omission miscue—word in printed text, omitted in oral reading.
st-	In substitution miscues, partial word plus hyphen stands for partial word substituted in oral reading for text word.
(Billy\cried)	Reversal miscue of words in text by oral reader.
ⓡ Then he	In passages recording miscues, underlines denote repetitions—portions the reader repeats in oral reading.
ⓒ	Miscue corrected through regression.
	Example: ⓒ *the* Then he …
ⓤⓒ	Miscue with unsuccessful attempt at correction through regression.
	Example: ⓤⓒ *All* Tell me what you see …
ⓐⓒ	Reader abandons correct form. Reader replaces an initially correct response with an incorrect one.
ⓓwith	Circled letter d preceding a miscue superscription denotes a variation in sound, vocabulary, or grammar resulting from a dialect difference between the author and the reader.
$	Nonword miscue. The reader either produces a nonword orally in place of text word or supplies a phonemic dialect variation.
	Examples: *$ larther* I sat in a large leather chair. *$ cawed* What his mother called him depended on what he did last.
+	Oral reader sounds out the word in segments.
	Example: *$ sooth + thing* I guess they do have a soothing sound.

FIGURE 9.1 ● Miscue Symbols

Source: Reprinted by permission from *Windows into Literacy: Assessing Learners K–8* by Lynn K. Rhodes and Nancy L. Shanklin © 1993 by Lynn K. Rhodes and Nancy Shanklin. Published by Heinemann, a division of Reed Elsevier, Inc., Portsmouth, NH. All rights reserved.

level of difficulty, which is estimated at between 1 and 9 semantically unacceptable miscues in the first 100 words that the student reads. As the student reads the passage, the teacher marks the miscues.

Once the teacher identifies the miscues, the teacher asks the student to retell the story. The teacher can use open-ended probes to assist in the retelling (Figure 9.3).

Reader's Name ___Richard_____   Date _____

Grade level ___Gr 4-Chapter 1_____   Teacher _____

Selection read ___Wolf_____

Classroom Reading Miscue Assessment

I. What percent of the sentences read make sense?

	Sentence by sentence tally	Total
Number of semantically acceptable sentences	̶H̶H̶ ̶H̶H̶ ̶H̶H̶ ̶H̶H̶ ̶H̶H̶ ̶H̶H̶ ̶H̶H̶ ̶H̶H̶ ̶H̶H̶ ̶H̶H̶ I	51
Number of semantically unacceptable sentences	̶H̶H̶ III	8

Number of semantically acceptable sentences
──────────────────────────────────── × 100 = ___86___ %
Total number of sentences read

	Seldom	Sometimes	Often	Usually	Never
II. In what ways is the reader constructing meaning?					
A. Recognizes when miscues have disrupted meaning	①	2	3	4	5
B. Logically substitutes	①	2	3	4	5
C. Self-corrected errors that disrupt meaning	①	2	3	4	5
D. Uses picture and/or other visual cues	1	2	3	④	5
In what ways is the reader disrupting meaning?					
A. Substitutes words that don't make sense	1	②	3	4	5
B. Makes omissios that disrupt meaning	①	2	3	4	5
C. Relies too heavily on graphophonic cues	1	②	3	4	5

III. If narrative text is used:	No	Partial			Yes
A. Character recall	1	2	3	4	⑤
B. Character development	1	2	3	4	⑤
C. Setting	1	2	3	4	⑤
D. Relationship of events	1	2	3	4	⑤
E. Plot	1	2	3	④	⑤
F. Theme	1	2	3	4	5
G. Overall retelling	1	2	3	4	⑤

If expository text is used:	No	Partial			Yes
A. Major concepts	1	2	3	4	5
B. Generalizations	1	2	3	4	5
C. Specific information	1	2	3	4	5
D. Logical structuring	1	2	3	4	5
E. Overall retelling	1	2	3	4	5

FIGURE 9.2 ● Classroom Reading Miscue Assessment

Source: Reprinted by permission from *Windows into Literacy: Assessing Learners K–8* by Lynn K. Rhodes and Nancy L. Shanklin © 1993 by Lynn K. Rhodes and Nancy Shanklin. Published by Heinemann, a division of Reed Elsevier, Inc., Portsmouth, NH. All rights reserved.

Character Recall:	Who else was in the story?
Character Development:	What else can you tell me about _____?
Setting:	Where did _____ happen?
	When did _____ happen?
	Tell me more about _____ place.
Events:	What else happened in the story?
	How did _____ happen?
Event Sequence:	What happened before _____?
	What happened after _____?
Plot:	What was _____'s main problem?
Theme:	What did you think (the major character) learned in the story?
	What do you think the author might have been trying to tell us in this story?

Good probes to use with expository text are:

Major Concept(s):	What was the main thing the author wanted you to learn?
Generalizations:	What other important information about _____ did the author tell you?
Specific Information:	Is there any other information you remember the author told about?
	What specific facts do you remember?
Logical Structuring:	How did the author go about presenting the information? (comparison, examples, steps in a process, etc.)

FIGURE 9.3 • Probes

Source: Reprinted by permission from *Windows into Literacy: Assessing Learners K–8* by Lynn K. Rhodes and Nancy L. Shanklin © 1993 by Lynn K. Rhodes and Nancy Shanklin. Published by Heinemann, a division of Reed Elsevier, Inc., Portsmouth, NH. All rights reserved.

Cloze Procedure

The cloze procedure is generally used to determine whether reading material is within a student's ability. The teacher selects a passage to be read and reproduces it, leaving out every fifth word. The assumption of the technique is that if the student can fill in the blanks, the reading is within the student's ability. Some alternatives to using the fifth-word rule are:

• The teacher decides which words to omit.
• The teacher can read orally and ask the student to fill in the missing word.
• Blanks can be left so that various parts of speech are omitted. (Rhodes & Shanklin, 1993)

Think-Alouds

A think-aloud is the verbalization of a student's thoughts about a text before, during, or after reading. Think-alouds provide insight into the student's comprehension abilities and thinking processes. For example, before beginning to read a story about immigrants in the United States, the teacher could ask, "What do you think that this story will be about?" or "What do you already know about immigrants?" During the reading, the student might verbalize, "I don't know that word" or "My mother told me about that." After reading, the student might say "I didn't understand that" or "That was hard."

When eliciting think-alouds, teachers can use the following procedures:

1. Ask students to think aloud while they are reading. Explain that thinking aloud will help students to understand the text.
2. Indicate where the student should stop reading in order to think aloud.
3. Model how a think-aloud is done.
4. While the student is thinking aloud, record the student's comments.
5. Analyze the think-aloud for patterns, such as the use of context clues, substitutions, misunderstandings, inferences, use of information, and the addition of information to the text. (Rhodes & Shanklin, 1993)

Retelling

Retelling is a comprehension exercise in which the student retells as much of a text as can be remembered after reading it. Retelling provides considerable information about comprehension. The following procedures are useful in retelling:

1. Tell the student that you will request a retelling at the end of the reading.
2. Once the student has finished reading, request the retelling.
3. Audiotape the retelling.
4. Once the student has finished the retelling, ask if there is anything else that the student would like to add.
5. At this point, you can choose to ask questions or use prompts to elicit additional information.
6. Use a checklist or record form to analyze the retelling for patterns and trends in knowledge of story structure, story elements, use of details, and use of language. (Rhodes & Shanklin, 1993)

Oral Descriptions

Verbal descriptions of a student's work can provide immediate feedback to a student by a teacher or peer. Oral descriptions are useful because they are quick, efficient, direct, and integrate easily into instruction. They are adaptable for program planning and program evaluation. An example of providing oral feedback to a student who has just completed reading a passage is: "You did a nice job recognizing when words didn't make sense. You understood the events that occurred in the passage and retold the story with only two prompts." Oral descriptions do have several drawbacks, however. They are subjective and, since the descriptions are given verbally, there is no permanent record. In addition, specific disabilities may limit the ability of the student to understand, remember, or reply to what has been said.

Written Descriptions

A written description is a brief narrative that records feedback about the student's work and teachers can share with the student, other teachers, or parents. A written description, like an oral description, conveys an impression of important aspects of the student's work. Written descriptions are also useful for program planning and program evaluation.

Before writing the narrative, the teacher should carefully review what the student has accomplished. The teacher then writes the description, noting areas of strength as well as problem areas. Such written description provides feedback to the student about the quality of the student's reading. Because it is recorded, the student can refer to it and can also share it with other teachers or family. The disadvantage of using written descriptions arises when parents have difficulty reading or do not have knowledge of written English.

Checklists and Questionnaires

Checklists and questionnaires are convenient ways to provide information about a student's work. A checklist is a procedure that a teacher can complete quickly. Figure 9.4 is an example of a checklist for students that provides feedback to parents and teachers about students' reading habits and attitudes, and Figure 9.5 is a checklist for gathering information about students' knowledge of books. Checklists are useful for screening, diagnosis, program planning, and program evaluation.

My Beliefs about Reading

1. I like to go to school	most of the time	sometimes	never
2. I like to read	books	magazines	newspapers
3. I like to read the following types of stories	fiction	science	history/politics
	adventure	science fiction	biography/autobiography
4. I like to read at home	most of the time	sometimes	never
5. I talk with my friends about what I read	most of the time	sometimes	never
6. I think I am a good reader	most of the time	sometimes	never
7. Some books that I like to read are:			

FIGURE 9.4 • Checklist for Assessing Attitudes, Interests, and Habits

Student's Name _____ Date _____

Teacher's Name _____

Directions: Show a book that is unfamiliar to the student. Ask the student to tell you about the book.

Concept	Demonstrates	Does Not Demonstrate	Observations
1. front			
2. back			
3. title			
4. author			
5. letters			
6. words			
7. pictures			
8. page numbers			
9. punctuation			

FIGURE 9.5 • Checklist for Assessing Knowledge of Books

Questionnaires provide an opportunity for teachers and students to collect information in more detail than checklists permit. Open-ended questionnaires allow respondents to express their attitudes, opinions, and knowledge in depth. Structured questionnaires ask only that the student fill in one or two words or circle a response.

Interviews

There are special considerations when using interviews in reading assessment. Interviews are helpful when guiding discussions, encouraging students, and determining reading attitudes and habits. One basic approach is to interview students individually about their likes and dislikes. Asking questions such as "What do you like about reading?" "What are your interests?" or "What don't you like?" can be informative. Interviews are also useful for screening, diagnosis, program planning, and program evaluation. Figure 9.6 is an example of a parent interview that gathers information about how parents view their child's development as a reader.

Conferences

A conference is a conversation about the student's work that can include the student, educators, and parents. In a conference, participants share their views of the student's work with the goal of providing feedback and recommendations. Teacher-student conferences are helpful when assessing the student's reading ability. The discussion in a conference can be strictly verbal, or it can be audiotaped, videotaped, or summarized in written form. Conferences are useful for diagnosis, program planning, and program evaluation. Figure 9.7 is an example of a progress report that a teacher can use as a guide when having a conference with a parent.

Student Journals and Notebooks

Students can keep a notebook or journal that allows them to record their work as well as their attitudes and feelings about reading and what they have read. In a journal, students can indicate what they like and don't like about reading and list areas in which they have difficulty. A journal provides students the opportunity to reflect on their reading, to communicate about their learning, and to document their progress. Journals can be used for program planning and program evaluation. The following is a sample reading journal outline:

What I read today:

Two important ideas:

What I liked best about the passage or story:

What I didn't like about the passage or story:

What the author was telling us:

Performance-Based Assessment

When measuring reading ability, performance-based assessment refers to the demonstration of reading and writing abilities, skills, and behavior. Performance-based assessment requires students to demonstrate that they can read a passage or story for a purpose, use one or more cognitive skills as they construct meaning from the text, and write about what they read, usually in response to a prompt or task (Farr & Tone, 1994). This assessment approach is useful in program planning and program evaluation.

Name _____ Date _____

Child's Name_____ Grade _____

Parent Interview

1. How do you think your child is doing as a reader/writer? Why? (If a young child: What signs have you seen that your child is ready to learn to read/write?)

   _____

   _____

   _____

   _____

2. What would you like your child to do as a reader/writer that he or she isn't doing now?

   _____

   _____

   _____

   _____

3. Do you ever notice your child reading/writing at home? Tell me about it.

   _____

   _____

   _____

   _____

4. What do you think your child's attitude is toward reading/writing? What do you think has helped to create this attitude?

   _____

   _____

   _____

   _____

5. What sorts of questions about your role in helping your child become a better reader/writer might you like to ask me?

   _____

   _____

   _____

   _____

6. Since I like to help the children read and write about things they are interested in, it helps me to know each individual child's interests. What kinds of things does your child like to do in his or her free time?

   _____

   _____

   _____

   _____

7. Is there anything about the child's medical history that might affect his or her reading/writing? Is there anything else that might affect his or her reading/writing?

   _____

   _____

   _____

   _____

8. Is there anything else that you think would be helpful for me to know in teaching your child?

   _____

   _____

   _____

   _____

FIGURE 9.6 ● Parent Interview

Source: "Parent Interview" by Lynn K. Rhodes. Reprinted by permission from *Literary Assessment: A Handbook of Instruments,* edited by Lynn K. Rhodes. Copyright© 1993 by Heinemann. Published by Heinemann, a division of Reed Elsevier, Inc., Portsmouth, NH. All rights reserved.

	Marking Period			
	1st	2nd	3rd	4th
READING				
Level at which child is working				
Phonics and word attack skills				
Word recognition				
Comprehension				
Reference skills				
Oral reading				
Independent reading				
Completes assignments				
Demonstrates effort				
SPELLING				
Mastery of spelling words				
Application of spelling skills in written work				
Completes assignments				
Demonstrates effort				
LANGUAGE				
Correctly uses language mechanics (punctuation, capitalization, etc.)				
Grammar (word usage/sentence structure)				
Demonstrates creative written expression				
Oral expression				
Completes assignments				
Demonstrates effort				
HANDWRITING				
Conforms to letter form, size, spacing, and slant				
Writes legibly and neatly in daily work				
Demonstrates effort				

FIGURE 9.7 • Progress Report

Source: Reprinted by permission from *Windows into Literacy: Assessing Learners K–8.* by Lynn K. Rhodes and Nancy L. Shanklin © 1993 by Lynn K. Rhodes and Nancy L. Shanklin. Published by Heinemann, a division of Reed Elsevier, Inc., Portsmouth, NH.

The following are examples of performance tasks teachers might ask students to undertake after reading a book or story:

▶ Develop two assessment tasks that link instruction in reading directly to assessment of reading.

- Write a poem.
- Draw pictures with captions.
- Build a model.
- Develop a story map.
- Write a review for the newspaper.
- Interview the author or a character in the story.
- Engage in a discussion with a peer, teacher, or other adult.
- Write a letter to the author.
- Write a letter to the editor of a newspaper or magazine.
- Write a report about a subject related to the story.
- Adapt a nonfiction article or book to fiction.
- Write lyrics to a song.
- Write a play.

Portfolios

A portfolio is a deliberate collection of a student's work that demonstrates the student's efforts, progress, and achievement. When documenting and assessing reading ability, portfolios provide information about reading, skills, comprehension, attitudes toward reading, work habits, and written communication abilities. Portfolios in literacy assessment are useful for program planning and program evaluation. Chapter 6 provides a more extensive discussion of the applications of portfolios.

▶ As part of mandated statewide testing programs, many states allow school districts to submit alternative assessment portfolios for students with disabilities. Research the assessment guidelines that individual states require.

A portfolio is not just a folder of worksheets or of all the work that the student has completed. Selecting the pieces to include in the portfolio requires careful consideration. The following are suggestions for inclusion in student portfolios:

- Writing samples collected over time
- Photographs of student projects
- Student logs
- Projects that involve students in portraying characters or plot
- Journals in which students record their thoughts about what they have read
- Written dialogues between student and teacher
- Audiotapes of students reading
- Videotapes of students conferencing with each other
- Teacher-developed tests
- Anecdotal records
- Student think-alouds

▶ Develop guidelines for assembling portfolios that are used to assess student progress and communicate progress to parents. What should be included? Who should make the decision about contents? Teachers? Parents? Students?

Exhibitions

An exhibition is a display of a student's work that demonstrates knowledge, abilities, skills, and attitudes concerning one project or a unit of work. An exhibition offers an opportunity to summarize and to synthesize the student's accomplishments. In reading and writing assessment, exhibitions are valuable because students can realize that reading and writing involves integration, understanding, problem solving, and reasoning. This tool is useful for program planning and program evaluation. Examples of exhibitions in reading and writing include:

- Storyboards
- Series of letters to editors
- Diary of one of the characters in the story
- Reviews of related books
- Dialogues among the characters
- Maps depicting the travels of the characters

Self-Assessment

Self-assessment provides students with an opportunity to analyze their own reading and writing. It is an occasion for students to reflect on their learning. Figure 9.8 is an example of a checklist that students use when assessing their own learning.

Peer Assessment

Peer assessment allows students insight into reading and writing abilities of their peers. Students have an opportunity to reflect on the learning processes and strategies of others as well as on their own. Figure 9.9 is an example of a checklist that students use when conducting a peer assessment.

Student's Name			Date		
After reading the story, I:	**1** **Great!**	**2**	**3**	**4**	**5** **Darn!**
1. understand the assignment.					
2. believe that I can restate assignment.					
3. feel that I can complete the assignment in a timely manner.					
4. feel that I am a usually successful reader.					

FIGURE 9.8 • Self-Assessment Checklist

Student's Name _____   Date _____

Peer's Name _____

	☹	😐	☺
1. My peer understood the story.			
2. My peer understood the assignment.			
3. My peer completed the assignment.			
4. My peer conferenced with me.			
5. My peer's work is neat.			

FIGURE 9.9 • Peer Assessment Checklist

Summary

- The assessment of literacy must reflect the integral link between reading and written language and produce results useful in planning instruction.

- Evaluators should use individual standardized tests of reading cautiously. Because reading and writing instruction varies considerably throughout the United States, it is important to screen assessment instruments carefully in order to select the instrument that best matches the curriculum.

- Teachers should conduct assessments routinely. The slogan for the assessment of literacy is "multiple, multiple, and frequent"—use multiple approaches, multiple instruments, and assess frequently!

> ► Consider developing several guides that gather information about students. You can choose to develop a checklist or rating scale that assesses students' attitudes and habits in reading. A second choice is to develop an interview guide for use with parents to assess students' reading attitudes and habits at home.

REFERENCES

Anastasi, A. (1988). *Psychological testing*. New York: Macmillan.

Brigance, A. H. (1999). *BRIGANCE® comprehensive inventory of basic skills–revised*. No. Billerica, MA: Curriculum Associates.

Brigance, A. H. (1995). *BRIGANCE® employability skills inventory*. No. Billerica, MA: Curriculum Associates.

Brigance, A. H. (1994). *BRIGANCE® life skills inventory*. No. Billerica, MA: Curriculum Associates.

Brown, V. L., Hammill, D. D., & Wiederholt, J. L. (1995). *Test of reading comprehension–3*. Austin, TX: Pro-Ed.

Farr, R., & Tone, B. (1994). *Portfolio and performance assessment*. Fort Worth, TX: Harcourt Brace College.

Hammill, D. D. (2004). What we know about the correlates of reading. *Exceptional Children* 70 (4): 453–468.

Harcourt Brace Educational Measurement. (1995). *Stanford diagnostic reading test 4* (4th ed.). San Antonio, TX: Harcourt Brace Educational Assessment.

Idol, L., Nevin, A., & Paolucci-Whitcomb, P. (1996). *Models of curriculum-based assessment*. Austin, TX: Pro-Ed.

Langer, J. A., Campbell, J. R., Neumann, S. B., Mullis, I. V. S., Persky, H. R., & Donahue P. L. (1995). *Reading assessment redesigned*. Washington, DC: U.S. Department of Education.

Marston, D. (1989). A curriculum-based measurement approach to assessing academic performance: What it is and why do it. In M. R. Shinn (Ed.), *Curriculum-based measurement* (pp. 18–78). New York: The Guilford Press.

Mullis, I., Kennedy, A., Martin, M., & Sainsbury, M. (2004). *PIRLS (Progress in International Reading and Literacy Study) 2006*. Chestnut Hill, MA: TIMSS & PIRLS International Study Center.

National Institute of Child Health and Human Development. (2000). *Report of the National Reading Panel*. Retrieved December, 26, 2005 from http://www.nichd.nih.gov

Rhodes, L. K., & Shanklin, N. (1993). *Windows into literacy: Assessing learners K–8*. Portsmouth, NH: Heinemann.

Snow, C. E., & Burns, S. M. (Eds.). (1998). *Preventing reading difficulties in young children*. Washington, DC: National Academy Press.

Vaughn, S., & Linan-Thompson, S. (2004). *Research-based methods of reading instruction*. Alexandria, VA: Association for Supervision and Curriculum Development.

Wiederholt, L., & Bryant, B., (2001). *Gray oral reading test–4*. Austin, TX: Pro-Ed.

Woodcock, R. (1998). *Woodcock reading mastery tests–revised/ normative update*. Circle Pines, MN: American Guidance Service.

10 Written Language

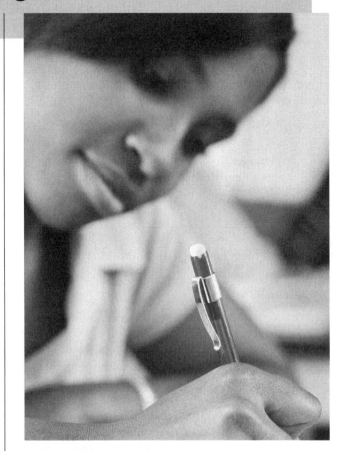

Chapter Objectives

After completing this chapter, you should be able to:

- Understand contemporary views of written language instruction and assessment.

- Describe approaches to written language assessment, including norm-referenced standardized tests, curriculum-based assessment, writing samples, journals, notebooks, essays, homework, discussions, group work, interviews, alternative assessment, performance testing, self-assessment, and peer assessment.

- Describe how physical, learning, and social environments influence written language performance.

Overview

▶ Standards for literacy and written language have been developed by the National Council of Teachers of English (NCTE). The vision behind these standards is that all students must be provided with opportunities to develop literacy skills in order to be productive, informed citizens. Review these standards at the website of the National Council of Teachers of English at http://www.ncte.org. Which standards apply to the teaching of written language?

▶ **CEC Common Core Knowledge and Skills.** The beginning special educator should understand national, state or provincial, and local curricula standards (CCS73).

Contemporary instructional practices stress the integral link between reading and writing for both instruction and assessment. In the previous chapter we discussed approaches to the assessment of literacy, emphasizing the assessment of reading. This chapter continues this discussion and highlights the assessment of written language.

Communication is critical to human growth and development and is a prerequisite to academic learning. Communication involves the exchange of information between individuals and may involve written language, spoken language, gestures, signs, signals, or other behaviors.

Some teachers stress close association between the development of reading and writing and view the development of written language as a process. Other teachers may focus on topic development, organization, use of details, and language and writing style. Still other teachers may emphasize the development of specific skills such as correct spelling, punctuation, capitalization, and grammar. Assessment of written language can inform instruction by providing information on students' skills and abilities. Depending on their background and orientation, teachers may use one or more of the assessment approaches in Table 10.1.

TABLE 10.1 ● Instructional Approaches in the Development of Written Language				
Instructor Variables	**Direct Instruction**	**Explicit Instruction**	**Cognitive Approach**	**Whole Language**
Orientation to reading and writing	Emphasis is on the teaching of subskills (e.g., punctuation, capitalization, grammar, spelling, etc.)	Skills are explicitly taught	Meaning is constructed from the text	Immersion in a print environment; close link between reading and writing activities
Instruction	Directed by teacher	Directed by teacher	Teacher and student collaborate	Student, with teacher guidance
Instructional materials	Workbooks, worksheets, spelling lists	Worksheets, literature-based program	Literature-based program, small discussion groups, writing projects	Literature-based program, integrated writing, individual and small discussion groups

Adapted from Stahl, S. A., & Kuhn, M. R. (1995). Does Whole Language or Instruction Matched to Learning Styles Help Children Learn to Read? *School Psychology Review 24:* 393–404.

Assessing written language usually means making a direct connection between reading and writing and following these principles:

1. Assess reading and writing in various contexts. Reading and writing vary with the context. Contexts relate to the types of reading materials, the purpose of the writing, and strategies students use. An understanding of students' reading and writing abilities must consider the contexts in which reading and writing occur.
2. Assess the literacy environment, instruction, and students. Reading and writing assessment must consider environments in which reading and writing occur, types of instruction, and student factors.
3. Assess processes and products of writing. The assessment of writing processes as well as the products can provide a comprehensive understanding of students' abilities.
4. Analyze error patterns. Understanding the patterns of errors in writing improves student performance.
5. Include the assessment of background knowledge. Experience, prior learning, and background knowledge influence reading and writing performance.
6. Consider developmental patterns in reading and writing. Knowledge of typical developmental patterns in reading and writing contributes to our understanding of reading and writing abilities.
7. Use sound principles of assessment. Employ sound principles or standards when assessing students. These standards apply to reliability, validity, observation, and scoring, discussed in previous chapters.
8. Use triangulation. Triangulation signifies that conclusions about student performance are the result of multiple (here, at least three) sources of information. In turn, teachers should corroborate information about students by using several sources of data. Teachers must proceed with considerable caution when drawing conclusions about students and using only one source of information.
9. Include students, parents, teachers, and other school personnel in the assessment process. The involvement of students, parents, and other educators in the assessment process ensures the inclusion of multiple perspectives.
10. Assessment activities should be ongoing. Assessment activities can inform instruction best when they occur frequently and routinely.

11. Record, analyze, and use assessment information. Record assessment data frequently, analyze it, and use it on a routine basis to guide instruction.

Linking instruction with assessment means that:

- Assessments include a variety of observations that consider the complexity of the processes involved in reading, writing, and language.
- Assessment tasks are age-appropriate.
- Assessment tools are unbiased.
- Assessment of reading, writing, and language must incorporate a variety of approaches.
- Assessment approaches should consider the purposes of each assessment tool and the settings in which the assessment is conducted.
- Assessment should reflect classroom instruction. (Rhodes and Shanklin, 1993)

Content Validity

Content validity is a primary concern of any achievement test, including tests of written language. This type of validity measure relates the extent to which the test items reflect the instructional objectives of a test. An estimate of the content validity of a test results from thoroughly and systematically examining the test items to determine the extent to which they reflect the intended instructional objectives and content.

While the test developer must describe the process that established the content validity of a test, the test examiner must make an independent determination. This is especially important when deciding on the content validity of written language tests. The test examiner has to compare the test objectives, format, number of responses or prompts, and types of responses or prompts with the taught curriculum.

Scoring Written Language Tests

Scoring tests of written language can be problematic for the test examiner. Students vary in their writing abilities, and many test manuals contain general directions, which are sometimes ambiguous, for scoring writing samples. Because test examiners must use judgment in scoring, there may be variations and inconsistencies between test scores.

Standardized Instruments

This section describes some of the commonly used individual, standardized tests of written language. All of these tests use standardized procedures for norm-referencing, administering, and scoring. The results of standardized tests of written language can be used to make interpretations and comparisons about an individual student's performance on several tests.

Test of Written Expression

The *Test of Written Expression (TOWE;* McGhee, Bryant, Larsen, & Rivera, 1995) is intended for students ages 6 years, 6 months through 14 years, 11 months. This test can be administered to individuals or groups. The *TOWE* assesses written language skills, such as ideation, grammar, vocabulary, capitalization, punctuation, spelling, and general ability to produce written language.

TESTS-at-a-GLANCE

Test of Written Language–3 (TOWL–3)

- **Publication Date:** 1996

- **Purposes:** Assesses writing conventions, grammar, syntax, vocabulary, spelling, sentence construction, and story construction.

- **Age/Grade Levels:** Ages 7 years, 6 months through 17 years, 11 months.

- **Time to Administer:** 1.5 hours.

- **Technical Adequacy:** The standardization sample is adequate. Reliability is good; requires further evidence of validity.

- **Suggested Use:** Provides evidence of strengths and weaknesses in written language, spelling, and vocabulary. Examiners should evaluate the test items to determine the extent to which they reflect writing as it has been taught to the student.

- **Summary.** The *Test of Written Language–3* is a third-edition norm-referenced test of skills and abilities associated with written language and the writing process. Evidence of reliability and validity is adequate. However, the teacher should examine the test items in order to determine congruence with the school curriculum.

▶ **CEC Common Core Knowledge and Skills.** A beginning special educator can interpret information from formal and informal assessments (CC8S5).

▶ Examine a norm-referenced, standardized writing test. Compare the development of this test with the contemporary views of assessment discussed in this chapter.

Test of Written Language–3

The *Test of Written Language–3* (TOWL–3; Hammill & Larsen, 1996) is the third edition of this test. The TOWL–3 is intended for use with students ages 7 years, 6 months through 17 years, 11 months. It contains eight subtests organized into two formats: spontaneous and contrived. The spontaneous format assesses students' written essays, and the contrived format directly assesses specific skills associated with writing. Table 10.2 shows the subtests and abilities/skills measured.

ADMINISTRATION The TOWL–3 is individually administered. However, it can be administered to small groups of students.

SCORING Raw scores convert to percentiles and standard scores.

STANDARDIZATION The TOWL–3 is the third edition of the TOWL, originally published in 1978. It was revised in 1988. This renormed third edition, published in 1994, reports information about the age, geographic region, gender, residence, race, ethnicity, income of parents, education of parents, and disabilities factors that the standardization sample represents.

RELIABILITY The test reports test-retest and internal consistency reliability coefficients. The reliability for the TOWL–3 is adequate.

VALIDITY The test reports content, criterion-related, and construct validity. Teachers should examine the test items to determine the extent to which the TOWL–3 matches writing in the taught curriculum.

TABLE 10.2 • Test of Written Language–3 Subtests

Subtest	Abilities/Skills Assessed
Spontaneous Format	
• Contextual Conventions	• Capitalization, punctuation, spelling
• Contextual Language	• Vocabulary, syntax, grammar
• Story Construction	• Plot, character development, general composition
Contrived Format	
• Vocabulary	• Word usage
• Spelling	• Correct spelling
• Style	• Capitalization, punctuation
• Logical Sentences	• Rewriting of sentences so that they make sense
• Sentence Combining	• Rewriting of one sentence from two sentences

How It Works! Assessment of Written Expression

Sheri is 11 years old and is in the fourth grade. She has cerebral palsy that affects her gait and causes limited use of her left hand. She is very verbal and friendly. She loves playing outside with her dog.

Sheri's strengths include her ability to communicate and her hearing. Her weaknesses include visual fluency during reading, math, composing written material, fine motor ability, and organization.

The *Test of Written Language–3* was administered to Sheri to identify specific strengths and weaknesses. During the session, Sheri became fatigued, and a brief break was taken.

Sheri has difficulty with capitalization, punctuation, forming words, word usage, writing conceptually sound sentences, and story construction. The gap between her performance and that of her peers continues to increase. The spelling errors indicate that Sheri has difficulty associating the sounds of letters with printed letters. Sheri is unable to correctly spell basic sight words, such as "the," "she," and "over."

Sheri was observed after being asked to write about a picture of a child playing with several puppies. In the fifteen minutes that she was allotted, she wrote:

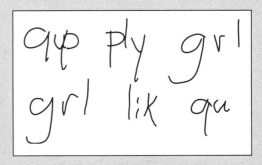

When asked to read what she had written, Sheri stated, "Puppies play with the girl. The girl likes the puppy."

Sheri had difficulty generating initial, middle, and final sounds of words and demonstrated lack of phonological conventions. When writing sentences, she omits words and reverses letters, such as *p/q*.

After reviewing the results of standardized tests, observations, and work sample, Sheri's special education teacher recommended that written language instruction should address sounds in words, letter and symbol associations, spelling strategies, sentence development, and conventions of written language.

Subtest	April 2, XXXX		
	Standard Score	Percentile Rank	Grade Equivalent
Contextual Conventions	4	2	<2.0
Contextual Language	5	5	2.2
Story Construction	8	25	3.4

Test of Written Spelling–4

The *Test of Written Spelling–4* (TWS–4; Larsen, Hammill, & Moats, 1999) is the fourth edition of this test and is for use with students in grades 1 through 12. The *TWS–4* assesses predictable words (words with spellings that are predictable using letter-sound patterns) and unpredictable words (words with spellings that are unpredictable, or are "word demons"). In administering the test, examiner says a word, says a sentence that contains the word, and says the word again. The student writes the word only; words are not written in sentences.

▶ **CEC Common Core Knowledge and Skills.** The beginning special educator should understand national, state or provincial, and local curricula standards (CC8S5).

Concerns about Standardized Tests of Written Language

► **CEC Common Core Knowledge and Skills.** The beginning special educator will understand the use and limitations of assessment instruments (CC8S4).

The International Reading Association directly addressed concerns about the use of standardized reading tests in 1991. Most experts in literacy believe that standardized, norm-referenced tests of writing have a number of shortcomings, which are summarized in Table 10.3.

Connecting Assessment with Instruction

It is a fundamental principle that assessment of written language abilities and skills must form a direct link to reading instruction. Linking instruction to assessment in reading and written language means that:

- Assessment occurs as a normal part of the student's work. Assessment activities should emerge from the teaching and learning situation. Examples of this type of assessment include the use of journals, notebooks, essays, oral reports, homework, classroom discussions, group work, and interviews. These assessment activities can occur individually or in small groups and can take place during one session or over multiple sessions.
- The conditions for assessment are similar to the conditions for doing meaningful tasks. Students should have sufficient time, have access to peers, be able to use appropriate literacy materials, and have the chance to revise their work.
- Assessment tasks are meaningful and multidimensional. They should provide students with the opportunity to demonstrate a variety of writing abilities and skills.
- Feedback to students is specific, meaningful, prompt, and informs the students' work.

TABLE 10.3 • Shortcomings of Standardized, Norm-Referenced Tests

Norm-Referenced Tests of Written Language	Theories of Written Contemporary Language Assessment
Assess writing abilities separately from reading abilities	Link the assessment of writing with the reading abilities assessment of reading
Fail to tap background knowledge	Encourage the writer to use background knowledge while writing
Emphasize skills (spelling, punctuation, writing processes capitalization, grammar, etc.)	Assess a variety of writing processes
May show bias in the questions	Demonstrate equitable assessment strategies
Present multiple-choice questions	Present open-ended questions
Do not assess writing attitudes and habits	Assess writing attitudes and habits
Show few or no direct links to instruction	Link assessment tools links directly to instruction

Research-Based Practices | Revision Strategies during Written Language Assessments

Researchers Crawford, Helwig, and Tindal (2004) explored the strategies and behaviors that students with disabilities employ during written language assessments. In an analysis of research on written language, these researchers concluded that extended time alone may not be sufficient to improve performance of students with disabilities on written language assessments. There are several explanations for this finding, including that students with disabilities:

- May make low-quality revisions that do not influence the quality of their writing.
- Infrequently make corrections to compositions that have been handwritten.

- May only make superficial revisions, such as basic punctuation or capitalization changes.
- Lack the skills required to make qualitative changes in successive drafts.

Can you think of additional reasons why the written language performance of students with disabilities does not seem to improve when revisions are made? What suggestions do you have for assessing the compositions of students with disabilities?

- Students participate in the assessment process. They help to generate and apply standards or rubrics. Self-assessment and peer assessment are part of the assessment process.

Ways in which the teacher can gather information and provide feedback to parents and students include:

- Curriculum-based measurement
- Criterion-referenced assessment
- Probes
- Error analysis
- Oral descriptions
- Written descriptions
- Checklists and questionnaires
- Interviews
- Conferences
- Student work samples and products
- Student journals and notebooks
- Performance-based assessment
- Portfolios
- Exhibitions
- Self-assessment
- Peer assessment

Curriculum-Based Measurement

Chapter 6 introduced curriculum-based measurement (CBM). To construct a CBM in writing, the teacher selects a brief story starter or topic sentence and asks the student to complete the exercise in three minutes. When the student finishes writing, the teacher has four choices for scoring:

1. Count the number of words written correctly.
2. Count the number of words spelled correctly.

▶ Develop two assessment tasks that link the instruction in writing directly to assessment of writing.

3. Count the number of letters written correctly.
4. Count the number of correct word sequences. Word sequences are two words together that are both correctly spelled and grammatically correct. The teacher and the student can then use a graph to plot the results. By repeating this process over time, the teacher can document the progress that the student

Criterion-Referenced Assessment

Teachers can create criterion-referenced tests in written language. Such teacher-developed criterion-referenced tests are useful for screening, determining eligibility, diagnosis of strengths and needs, program planning, progress monitoring, and program evaluation. For example, a teacher can enumerate spelling words that the student must spell correctly, can identify punctuation that the student must use accurately, or can list words that require correct capitalization in order to develop a criterion-referenced test.

BRIGANCE® Inventories

The *BRIGANCE® Inventories* are criterion-referenced tests that contain subtests in written language. The inventories are similar in purpose, scoring, administration, and interpretation. Chapter 6 describes the tests in detail.

Informal Approaches

Probes

A probe is a diagnostic technique that can be especially useful in diagnosing student problems and in planning instruction in written language. For example, suppose a teacher wants to determine whether a student has considered feedback from peers when revising a writing sample. The teacher can review the student's written draft, inquire about the use of peer feedback, and assist the student in incorporating peer feedback into a revision of the draft.

Error Analysis

The purposes of error analysis are to (1) identify the patterns of errors or mistakes that students make in their work, (2) understand why students make the errors, and (3) provide instruction to correct the errors. A systematic approach to error analysis helps both the student and the teacher identify errors and correct them.

A checklist, developed by the teacher, the student, or through collaboration, can be helpful in identifying errors. Figure 10.1 is an example of a checklist that Toni, a sixth grader, developed with her teacher to help Toni with editing.

Spelling

Error analysis is important in the development of spelling. Spelling evaluation should be a part of the process of developing written language rather than a

Checking and Correcting Work				
Editing	**Checked**		**Corrected**	
	yes	*no*	*yes*	*no*
1. Grammar				
2. Periods				
3. Question marks				
4. Exclamation points				
5. Quotation marks				
6. Paragraphing				
7. Spelling				

FIGURE 10.1 ● Toni's Editing Checklist

finished product. Teachers should consider four principles in evaluating spelling (Wilde, 1989a):

1. Evaluate spelling on the basis of natural writing rather than by tests of words in isolation.
2. Evaluate spelling analytically rather than as correct or incorrect.
3. Analyze spelling by discovering the strategies the student used in the context of writing.
4. As a matter of good professional practice in this area, learn about language development and about language disabilities and how they can affect the development of written language.

Questions to ask about a student's spelling include:

1. Is the word spelled as it sounds?
2. Is the spelling unusual?
3. Is the word a sight word?
4. Is the word a real word?
5. Is the word a "placeholder"?
6. Is a homophone used?
7. What strategies does a student use when the spelling is unknown?
   a. writes down what it sounds like?
   b. writes down what student thinks the word looks like?
   c. looks around the classroom to find the word?
   d. thinks about parts of the word?
   e. uses spelling rules?
   f. uses a dictionary or spell checker?
   g. asks someone for the correct spelling?
   h. uses a personal spelling list? (Rhodes & Shanklin, 1993; Wilde, 1989a, 1989b)

▶ Develop a checklist or rating scale that assesses students' attitudes and habits in writing.

Oral Descriptions

Verbal descriptions of a student's work provide immediate feedback to the student by a teacher or peer. Oral descriptions are quick, efficient, and direct, and they integrate easily into instruction. However, they should not be off-the-cuff expressions, but rather as well thought out as written descriptions. Oral descriptions are useful for program planning and program evaluation. An example of providing oral feedback to a student who has just completed writing a first draft is, "You did a nice job getting your ideas down. While developing your ideas, you consulted several sources and asked a peer for help with spelling."

Notwithstanding, oral descriptions do have several drawbacks. They can be subjective, and there is no permanent record. In addition, specific disabilities may limit the ability of the student to understand, remember, or reply to them.

Written Descriptions

A written description is a brief narrative that records feedback about the student's work and that the student, other teachers, or parents can review. A written description, like an oral description, conveys an impression of important aspects of the student's work. Written descriptions are effective for program planning and program evaluation.

Before writing the narrative, the teacher carefully reviews what the student has accomplished. The teacher should write the description noting areas of strength as well as problem areas. A written description provides feedback to the student about the quality of the student's writing, and because it provides a record, the student can refer to it and share it with his or her family.

Two potential problems of written descriptions are that parents who have difficulty reading or who do not have knowledge of written English are at a disadvantage.

Checklists and Questionnaires

Checklists and questionnaires are convenient ways to provide feedback about a student's work. A checklist is fast and easy to complete. Questionnaires enable teachers and students to collect information in more detail than checklists. Questionnaires can be open-ended, allowing respondents to express their attitudes, opinions, and knowledge in depth, or they can be structured so that the student just needs to fill in one or two words or to circle a response. Figure 10.3 is an example of an open-ended questionnaire.

Interviews

In Chapter 5 we discussed the topic of conducting interviews. There are special considerations when using this technique in the assessment of written language. Interviews are useful in developing ideas for writing, encouraging students, learning more about a student's written piece, and determining writing attitudes and habits. Asking questions such as the following can be informative: "What do you like about writing?" "Describe the process you use in developing a new piece of writing." "What are your interests?" "What don't you like?" Interviews are helpful for screening, diagnosis, program planning, and program evaluation.

Conferences

▶ Identify three assessment approaches this chapter discusses. Compare the purposes, advantages, and disadvantages of each approach.

A conference is a conversation about the student's work that can include the student, educators, and/or parents. In a conference participants share their views of the student's work with the goal of offering feedback and recommendations. Teacher–student conferences can be helpful when assessing the student's written language. The discussion can be strictly verbal, or it can be recorded electronically or summarized in written form. Conferences are useful for diagnosis, program planning, and program evaluation.

Student Journals and Notebooks

Keeping a notebook or journal allows students to record their work as well as their attitudes and feelings about reading and writing. A journal can contain sample pieces the student has written as well as spontaneous types of entries. Journals are useful in program planning and program evaluation. The following samples of written language can be part of a journal:

- Poems
- Short stories
- Writing fragments
- Student's comments about writing
- Log entries on specific topics
- Interdisciplinary writing
- Quotations from the student's readings
- Comments by peers or teachers

Student Work Samples and Products

Examining students' written work provides an opportunity to identify the skills, abilities, and processes that the student uses while developing the written piece.

Figure 10.2 contains a checklist for use when providing feedback to students. The writing process breaks down into overlapping steps (Rhodes & Shanklin, 1993):

1. **Writing authentic work.** Students should have opportunities to engage in authentic writing. This means that when students write in school they must write for the same reasons they write outside of school. Students need to have control over their writing. They should have the necessary materials available, know how to use

---

Writing Process			
Student's Name _____	Date _____		
Authentic writing	Always	Sometimes	Never

   1. Does the writer have an authentic, meaningful reason to write?
   2. If the written piece is to be shared, does the writer know the audience?
   3. Is the writer able to take risks in order to express ideas?
   4. Is the writer able to critique the written text?

☐ Suggestion for improvement:

Rehearsal of writing	Always	Sometimes	Never

   5. To what extent does the writer think or plan before writing?
   6. To what extent does the writer consult with others before writing?
   7. To what extent does the writer use readings as a source of ideas?
   8. To what extent does the writer help others develop ideas?

☐ Suggestion for improvement:

Developing the draft	Always	Sometimes	Never

   9. To what extent is the writer able to put thoughts on paper?
  10. Do the ideas flow?
  11. Is the writer able to physically write? Is an alternative input device or communication device used?
  12. Is the writer hindered due to spelling difficulties?
  13. Does the writer's attitude support writing?
  14. Does the writer read and reread the written text?
  15. Does the writer need to be prompted to read and reread the written text?
  16. Does the writer make changes based on the reading and rereading of the written text?

(continued)

FIGURE 10.2 • Assessing the Writing Process

Source: Adapted from Rhodes, L. K., & N. Shanklin (1993). *Windows into Literacy: Assessing Learners K–8.* Portsmouth, NH: Heinemann.

Revising	Always	Sometimes	Never
17. Does the writer elaborate or add information?			
18. To what extent does the writer incorporate feedback?			
19. Does the writer use transitions?			
20. Does the writer develop one or more introductions or endings to determine which is suitable?			

☐ Suggestion for improvement:

Developing the Draft	Always	Sometimes	Never
21. To what extent is the writer able to edit:			
a. spelling			
b. capitalization			
c. punctuation			
d. grammar			
e. paragraphing			
22. Is the writer willing to edit the draft?			

☐ Suggestion for improvement:

FIGURE 10.2 • Continued

them, know the purposes for writing, and know how much time is available to them.

2. Rehearsing writing. Rehearsing means that students know what to expect and are able to choose the type of writing that is appropriate for the purpose. Rehearsing can involve drawing pictures, developing semantic webs, taking notes, and brainstorming.

3. Developing the first draft. Writing the first draft entails fluency, spelling, and rereading. Fluency is being able to put ideas into writing and having the thoughts flow. Spelling is a consideration in this step as well, because like writing, spelling is a process. Reading and rereading the draft are important because this allows the student to identify and correct errors and to elaborate ideas.

4. Conferencing with peers and/or teachers. Feedback from peers or teachers can yield important suggestions and ideas as the student develops the written piece.

5. Revising the written piece. Revising a piece of writing gives the student an opportunity to reflect on his or her own reading of it and on the feedback from peers and teachers. The student can choose to elaborate, clarify, take away information, make corrections, and change the sentence or paragraph structure.

6. Editing. Editing allows the student to make surface corrections to the written piece. This means making the

piece conform to writing conventions and it also involves organization and ideas (Rhodes & Shanklin, 1993).

7. Producing and sharing the finished piece. The final piece can take various forms, depending on the purpose for writing. For example, the written piece may be a newspaper article, review of a story, poem, play, story, or report.

Figure 10.3 is a checklist for use with students.

What Kind of Writer I Am

1. Things I like to write at home (examples: notes, letters, poems, stories, etc.):
2. What other people think of my writing:
3. What I think of myself as a writer:
4. Things I like to write at school:
5. What I like about my writing:
6. What I don't like about my writing:

FIGURE 10.3 • Open-Ended Writing Questionnaire

Performance-Based Assessment

Performance-based assessment of reading and writing abilities measures the integration of reading and writing and evaluates demonstrations of reading and writing abilities. Performance-based assessment requires students to read a passage or story for a purpose, use one or more cognitive skills as they construct meaning from the text, and write about what they read, usually in response to a prompt or task (Farr & Tone, 1994). Performance-based assessment can be used in program planning and program evaluation.

Portfolios

A portfolio, as we have discussed, is a deliberate collection of a student's work that demonstrates the student's efforts, progress, and achievement. When documenting and assessing written language ability, portfolios provide valuable information about reading, writing, spelling skills, comprehension, attitudes, and work habits. Portfolios in literacy assessment are useful for program planning and program evaluation. See Chapter 7 for a more extensive discussion of portfolio use.

The following are suggestions for materials that students could include in student writing portfolios:

- Newsletter articles
- Student logs
- Plays
- Poems
- Lyrics to a song
- Creative writing
- Nonfiction writing
- Projects that involve students in portraying characters or plot
- Journals in which students record their thoughts about what they have read
- Written dialogues between student and teacher
- Videotapes of students conferencing with each other
- Photographs of student writing projects

Exhibitions

An exhibition displays a student's work and demonstrates how the student combines knowledge, abilities, skills, and attitudes. This tool gives students the opportunity to summarize and synthesize their accomplishments. In reading and writing assessment, exhibitions are useful because students realize that reading and writing involves integration, understanding, problem solving, and reasoning. In this way, teachers have concrete information for program planning and program evaluation.

SNAPSHOT

Pangea

Joy Kamena, a fifth-grade teacher, reviewed a writing sample developed by Yizhong, one of her students, Develop a checklist that she can use to analyze Yizhong's writing.

PANGEA

Pangea was the supercontenient that was made up of the seven other continents linked together. This explains how I think the continents dissembled themselves and how they got where they are today. South America which was nestled in the curve of Africa rotated 90° to the right and moved westward. North America above South America was connected to Europe with the middle part of Canada. This medium size continent made another 90° right turn and again moved to the west. After these continents unhooked themselves Africa followed by moving south west detaching itself from Saudi Arabia and Europe. Now it was Australia's turn to slide out the Bengal bay and float south east. Aisa and Europe which was the main link for Pangea stayed where they were. This explains how continents moved with the continental drift.

The elements of an exhibition that involve writing do not necessarily occur in a sequential order, but they are useful when thinking about the development of exhibitions (Willis, 1996):

- *Prompt:* A prompt is what teachers ask students to do. This can be as basic as "write a research report about the city in which you live," "write a description of a new tool that would make a task easier," or as comprehensive as "develop an exhibition of your vision for the city of the future."
- *Vision:* A vision is what the exhibition will be like. For example, the exhibition on cities will include oral, written, and multimedia components that demonstrate students' skills and abilities to reflect on their learning, to analyze, to conduct research, and to synthesize. Teachers may ask students to integrate one or more disciplines, to write reports, create multimedia presentations, and incorporate the arts.
- *Agreement on Standards:* Educators and students must agree on what makes an exhibition good. Various scoring systems or rubrics can assist in the evaluation of exhibitions.
- *Audience:* Students' work is exhibited to other students, educators, parents, or community members.
- *Coaching:* Peers and teachers should coach students toward the development of their exhibitions. Coaching, rather than evaluating, is important in the development phase of the exhibition.
- *Reflection:* All participants should reflect on their exhibitions. This allows all of the participants to develop an appreciation for what they have learned and accomplished. Reflection also provides an opportunity to think about how to do it better the next time.

Examples of exhibitions in reading and writing include:

- Storyboards
- Series of letters to editors
- Diary of one of the characters in the story
- Reviews of related books
- Dialogues among the characters
- Maps depicting the travels of the characters

Self-Assessment

Self-assessment provides students with an opportunity to analyze their own writing and to reflect on their own learning. Figure 10.4 is an example of a questionnaire that students can use when assessing their own writing.

Peer Assessment

When conducting peer assessments, students have an opportunity to reflect on the writing processes, skills, and strategies of their peers as well as on their own writing processes, skills, and strategies. Figure 10.5 on page 224 is an example of a checklist that students use when conducting a peer assessment.

Scoring

Teachers use two types of scoring, holistic and analytic, when evaluating writing samples, written products, portfolios, performance assessments, and exhibitions.

Student's Name _____   Date _____

Authentic Writing   **My Comments**

1. I know my audience.

2. I take risks when I write.

Rehearsal of Writing

3. I think or plan ahead when I write.

4. I consult with my peers.

5. I use print and nonprint media as sources.

6. I help others to write.

Developing the Draft

7. I feel that I can put my thoughts down on paper.

8. I have a good attitude toward writing.

9. I am able to spell most words.

10. I know which words to capitalize.

11. I know how to use punctuation.

12. I make changes to my text based on rereading.

Revising

13. I incorporate feedback.

14. I make changes, such as beginnings, transitions, and endings.

Editing

15. I am willing to edit my draft.

16. I am able to edit and correct spelling.

17. I am able to edit and correct punctuation.

18. I am able to edit and correct capitalization.

19. I am able to edit and correct grammar.

20. I am able to edit and correct paragraphing.

FIGURE 10.4 ● Self-Assessment Checklist

Holistic Scoring

Holistic scoring (Figure 10.6) is a quick and efficient type of scoring. Holistic scoring produces one score that provides an impression of writing ability. Holistic scoring rests on the assumption that all of the elements of writing, such as organization, mechanics, and fluency, work together in the whole text. This type of scoring can be useful when the teacher is looking for one or two previously identified characteristics in a student's work. One important disadvantage of holistic scoring is that it does not provide detailed information about the success of the student in specific areas of writing (Spandel & Stiggins, 1990).

Student's Name_____   Date _____

Peer's Name_____

	🙁	😐	🙂
1. My peer writes for a purpose.			
2. My peer consulted me before writing.			
3. My peer made changes based on my feedback.			
4. My peer conferenced with me.			
5. My peer uses transitions.			
6. My peer is able to edit the written text.			

FIGURE 10.5 ● Peer Assessment Checklist

Holistic Scoring Guide—Writing

Score	Criteria
5	The paper is superb. The ideas are very well developed. If there are any errors in mechanics, grammar, or spelling, they are very minor. Sentence structure is very clear and varied. There is a clear sense of purpose and audience. Ideas are explained and very well supported.
4	The paper is very good. The ideas are very well developed. There are few errors in mechanics, grammar, or spelling. Sentence structure is clear and varied. There is a clear sense of purpose and audience. Ideas are explained and supported.
3	The paper is good. The ideas are well developed. There are some errors in mechanics, grammar, or spelling. Sentences follow a similar pattern. There is some sense of purpose or audience. Ideas are not always explained or supported.
2	The paper is moderate. Some ideas are developed. There are frequent errors in mechanics, grammar, or spelling. Sentences follow a similar pattern. There may be sentence fragments. There is little sense of purpose or audience. Ideas are infrequently explained or supported.
1	The paper is poor. Ideas are rarely developed. There are many errors in mechanics, grammar, or spelling. Sentences follow a similar pattern. There are sentence fragments. There is no sense of purpose or audience. Ideas are rarely explained or supported.

FIGURE 10.6 ● Holistic Scoring

Analytic Scoring

Analytic scoring (Figure 10.7) is a type of scoring that produces a detailed analysis of the written text. The teacher uses a scale or rubric to assign points to different levels of performance in each of the assessed areas. For example, a teacher wants to describe the writing performance of students in organizing, using mechanics, and using paragraphing. The teacher rates the students' writing samples on a scale, from 1 to 5 or 1 to 6, in each of these three areas, and the student receives three separate scores. Teachers should take care when scoring each of these areas not to let their impressions in one area—for example, organization—influence the impression in another area—such as mechanics in this example (Spandel & Stiggins, 1990).

Analytic scoring is frequently done by two or more raters, working independently, who rate the same written text. When they have finished, comparisons are made between their ratings to determine their similarity. If the ratings are dissimilar, the two teachers can discuss why they gave certain ratings, or a third teacher can rate the text.

Analytic Scoring—Writing					
	1	**2**	**3**	**4**	**5**
Development of Ideas	Little understanding of audience; little elaboration of ideas	Some understanding of audience; some elaboration of ideas	Good understanding of audience; good elaboration of ideas	Very good understanding of audience; very good elaboration of ideas	Excellent understanding of audience; superb elaboration of ideas
Organization	No evidence of an organized plan for writing; ideas and paragraphs run together	Some evidence of an organized plan for writing; ideas and paragraphs are loosely organized	Good evidence of an organized plan for writing; ideas and paragraphs are organized	Very good evidence of an organized plan for writing; ideas and paragraphs are well organized	Excellent evidence of an organized plan for writing; ideas are original and paragraphs are well organized
Fluency	Language is very limited and repetitive; written text is very brief	Language is somewhat limited and repetitive; written text is brief	Language is good and there are few repetitions; written text has adequate elaboration	Language is very good and varied; there are no repetitions; written text has very good elaboration	Language is excellent and varied; there are no repetitions; written text has excellent elaboration
Spelling	Few words are spelled correctly	Most words are spelled phonetically; most sight words are spelled correctly	Most words are spelled correctly; some errors with homophones and endings	Words are spelled correctly; there are few errors	Words are spelled correctly; errors are minor
Capitalization and Punctuation	No capitalization or punctuation	Some evidence of correct capitalization and punctuation	Good evidence of capitalization and punctuation	Very good evidence of capitalization and punctuation; few errors	Excellent evidence of capitalization and punctuation; errors are rare

FIGURE 10.7 • Analytic Scoring

Anchor Papers

Anchor papers are students' papers that represent different writing levels of performance. They can be useful in the development of rubrics. For example, after a group of students completes a writing assignment, the teacher reviews all of the papers to determine which three represent, by degrees, high-quality performance, typical or average performance, and low performance. These are the anchor papers. Next, the teacher evaluates all of the student papers, using the anchor papers as guides to determine high, typical, or low performance.

Summary

- The assessment of literacy must reflect the close link between the development of reading and written language.

- Best practice requires that teachers conduct literacy assessments frequently and use the results to guide instruction.

- Scoring tests can be problematic. Students vary in their abilities, and most test manuals contain general directions for scoring. The test examiner must use judgment in scoring. This can be a problem because the test examiners' judgment differs, which can lead to inconsistencies in scoring and interpretation.

- Assessment of literacy requires the use of multiple approaches, including standardized tests, curriculum-based assessment, criterion-referenced assessment, and alternative forms of assessment.

REFERENCES

Crawford, L., Helwig, R., & Tindal, G. (2004). Writing performance assessments: How important is extended time? *Journal of Learning Disabilities 37* (2): 132–142.

Farr, R., & Tone, B. (1994). *Portfolio and performance assessment.* Fort Worth, TX: Harcourt Brace College.

Hammill, D. D., & Laren, S. C. (1996). *Test of written language, 3rd ed.* Austin, TX: Pro-Ed.

Larsen, S. C., Hammill, D. D., & Moats, D. (1990). *Test of written spelling, 4th ed.* Austin, TX: Pro-Ed.

McGhee, R., Bryant, B. R., Larsen, S. C., & Rivera, D. M. (1995). *Test of written expression.* Austin, TX: Pro-Ed.

Rhodes, L. K., & Shanklin, N. (1993). *Windows into literacy: Assessing learners K–8.* Portsmouth, NH: Heinemann.

Spandel, V., & Stiggins, R. J. (1990). *Creating writers.* New York: Longman.

Stahl, S. A., & Kuhn, M. R. (1995). Does whole language or instruction matched to learning styles help children learn to read? *School Psychology Review 24:* 393–404.

Wilde, S. (1989a). Looking at invented spelling: A kidwatcher's guide to spelling, Part I. In K. S. Goodman, Y. M. Goodman, & W. J. Hood (Eds.), *The whole language evaluation book* (pp. 213–226). Portsmouth, NH: Heinemann.

Wilde, S. (1989b). Understanding spelling strategies: A kidwatcher's guide to spelling, Part II. In K. S. Goodman, Y. M. Goodman, & W. J. Hood (Eds.), *The whole language evaluation book* (pp. 227–236). Portsmouth, NH: Heinemann.

Willis, S. (1996). Student exhibitions put higher-order skills to the test. *Education Update 38* (March): 1, 3.

Woodcock, R. W., McGrew, K. S., & Mather, N. (2001). *Woodcock-Johnson psychoeducational battery–III.* Itasca, IL: Riverside Publishing.

11 Oral Language

Chapter Objectives

After completing this chapter,
you should be able to:

- Contrast several theoretical perspectives regarding the development of language.
- Discuss examples of best practice when assessing English language learners.
- Describe the use of standardized tests for assessing oral language.
- Compare assessment approaches that form a link with instruction, program planning, and program evaluation.
- Describe how the physical, learning, and social environments influence oral language.

Key Terms

Language
Communicate
Speech
Shaping
Expansion
Speech disorder
Language disorder
Curriculum-based measurement
Expressive language

Receptive language
Inner language
Phonology
Phonemes
Graphemes
Morphology
Morpheme
Mean length of utterance (MLU)
Semantics

Syntax
Pragmatics
Language probe
Language samples
Modeling
Augmentative or alternative
    communication system
    (AAC)

Overview

Language involves the use of symbols to communicate thoughts, feelings, ideas, and information. To **communicate** meaning, humans speak these symbols or produce them through synthesized speech, write them by using the visual symbols of the language, or express them manually through signing or gestures. Each of us uses these symbols of language every day.

This chapter focuses on one aspect of language: speaking and understanding oral language. We'll also look briefly at the actual production of oral language, **speech.** Contemporary perspectives on the development of speech and language skills and abilities provide a basis for the various approaches to assessment. We examine three different perspectives: the behavioral approach, the social learning theory approach, and the psycholinguistic approach.

Behavioral Approach

This approach emphasizes the importance of external factors (outside of the individual) in influencing and promoting language development. Antecedent conditions, or events that occur just before the behavior, influence language as does the consequence, or the events that follow the student's behavior.

According to this approach, verbal ability develops as a result of the relationships among the antecedent, the behavior, and the consequence. For example, a teacher asks a student a thought-provoking question (antecedent), the student vocalizes an answer (verbal response behavior), and the teacher responds with a smile and praise (the consequence of vocalization).

Language abilities become refined through the process of reinforcing, or shaping, the sounds or word as the vocalization more closely approximates the sound or word in the language. For example, a teacher says to a young child, "Give the card to your friend." The child makes the response "car? fren?" As time goes on, the child's responses approximate the actual word, "Give card to friend." The teacher smiles and responds, "Yes!!! Give the card to your friend!" Gradually, the child's responses duplicate the actual words.

Shaping is a behavioral term that refers to reinforcing the behavior (each progressive step) as it becomes more and more like the target behavior. Thus, as children become older, gradual reinforcement for making sounds common to the language occurs. Eventually, children shape strings of sounds to approximate words.

What is the influence on assessment practices? Assessment practices that follow this theoretical perspective focus on the stimulus or antecedent (A), the verbal response or behavior (B), and the reinforcements or consequences (C) offered in the environment. This type of assessment is often referred to as the ABC approach. The behavior (B) may be divided into smaller steps, depending on the needs and abilities of the individual. Breaking the behavior into small, discrete, sequential steps is called task analysis. Chapter 15 contains a detailed explanation of the ABC approach and task analysis procedures in assessment practices.

Social Learning Theory

According to this perspective, individuals learn a set of rules concerning the order of words in sentences or phrases, or syntax, through the modeling of language by others (Bandura, 1977). Syntax is the system of rules that dictates how people combine words into meaningful phrases and sentences; syntax governs the arrangement of word sequences. This set of rules allows people to produce new and novel combinations of words, such as phrases or sentences, that they have never heard or produced before. When a child develops competence in syntax, the child can speak and understand an infinite number of sentences.

Adults frequently use a technique called **expansion** to increase language development. Expansion involves restating the child's language and adding words and more complex phrases.

Child: "Wan dawg."

Adult: "You want to pat the dog?"

Child: "Wan pa dawg."

What is the influence on assessment practices? Assessment practices that follow this theoretical perspective emphasize the importance of adults and peers in the student's environment and their effect on the development of language. The modeling of language, the use of syntax, and the expansion of language are areas of assessment focus.

Psycholinguistic Approach

The psycholinguistic approach, developed by Noam Chomsky (1967), rests on the belief that children are born ready to develop language skills and that they have an inborn language-developing ability that helps them understand and learn language. This is called the "language acquisition device," and it enables the child to interpret language, construct grammatical rules, and generate an infinite variety of phrases and sentences.

What is the influence on assessment practices? This perspective presents difficulties to educators who work with students with language disabilities. The view that children and youth are innately predisposed and have an inborn ability implies that individuals with language impairments are not born with this ability and will never have this ability. This approach provides little encouragement for intervention and instruction for students who are experiencing delays in language development.

Understanding Speech and Language Disorders

Teachers are often the first to notice student difficulties in understanding speech or expressing thoughts and ideas because they have considered questions such as: Does the student have a history of earaches, colds, or allergies? Does the student follow directions? Does the student ask to have directions repeated? Does the student speak clearly or demonstrate language difficulties?

Students with suspected speech and language disorders are screened first for possible hearing loss. The hearing screening consists of listening to several tones within the speech range. If a student has difficulty hearing one or more of these tones, the examiner refers the student for a complete hearing assessment.

Speech Disorders

A **speech disorde**r refers to a difficulty in articulation, such as the way words are pronounced; the fluency of speech, including rate and rhythm; and the pitch, volume, and quality of the voice. Ricardo, a student in the Snapshot on page 230, has a speech disorder. You can follow his teacher's questions and the steps that she took to help Ricardo.

Assessment questions arise when a parent or teacher has difficulty in understanding a student's speech. A speech and language pathologist (SLP) usually conducts the assessment. In fact, the speech and language pathologist is the primary practitioner to plan assessment in this area.

Students who have difficulty producing the correct sounds of speech generally have problems in one or more of four areas of speech production.

Respiration: To produce sounds, an individual must be able to control the inhaling and exhaling of breath. This must occur while forcing air through the larynx.

Phonation: An individual must contract specific muscles to allow the vocal folds of the larynx to be drawn together. Forcing air through the larynx causes the air to vibrate and produce sound.

Resonation: The vibrating air passes through the throat, mouth, and sometimes the nasal cavities, shaping the quality of the sound.

Articulation: The position of the tongue, lips, teeth, and mouth form the specific sounds of speech that an individual produces.

SNAPSHOT

Ricardo

"C-c-can I sh-sh-sharpen my pencil?"

Ms. Wong looked up to see Ricardo waving his hand in the air. She nodded and motioned toward the pencil sharpener. As Ricardo left his work group of three other students, Ms. Wong thought again about Ricardo's stuttering problem.

He was a new student in her class this year. When she had first observed his stuttering problem, she had checked the records that were forwarded by Ricardo's former school. They contained no mention of a stuttering problem. She thought that Ricardo might overcome the stuttering with time; but it did not seem to disappear. In fact, today marked the beginning of the third week of school and he seemed to be having more difficulty getting his ideas across as time went on.

Will the stuttering become worse or will he outgrow it in time? Should she try to correct him? She wrote herself a reminder to fill out a referral form concerning Ricardo's speech problems before the end of the week. The referral form would be sent to the school's coordinator of the assessment team.

By the end of the school year, Ricardo was very grateful to his teacher for recognizing his speech problem and referring him for assessment. Through the IEP process, Ricardo received services from the speech and language pathologist, who taught him specific strategies to counter his stuttering. By learning ways to control his breathing and planning what he wanted to say in class, Ricardo was able to learn skills to decrease his stuttering problem.

Questions and concerns about a student's oral language always need to be referred as soon as possible to the assessment team. In Ricardo's case, after filling out the referral form, his teacher should consult with members of the team, such as the speech and language pathologist, about ways to work with Ricardo in the classroom. She needs to address her questions regarding how to handle classroom stuttering as soon as she notices the difficulty.

Language Disorders

A **language disorder** refers to a difficulty or inability in decoding or encoding the set of symbols used in language or an inability to effectively use inner language. The Snapshot of Bethany describes some of the difficulties experienced by one student with a language disorder. Assessment questions focus on the student's expressive language, receptive language, or inner language. While some standardized instruments, such as the *Oral and Written Language Scales* (Carrow-Woolfolk, 1996), assist in identifying these language areas, educators frequently use classroom-based approaches, such as **curriculum-based measurement**, to assess, plan, and monitor instruction.

Expressive language refers to the student's ability to use language to communicate information, thoughts, feelings, and ideas with others. Assessing expressive language involves examining the actual production of sound, speech, and language.

Receptive language refers to the student's understanding of the language of others. Assessment of receptive language usually involves having the student listen to words or phrases and then demonstrate understanding. For example, a student might be asked to put the book on top of or under the table or to point to the picture that shows the boy putting on a jacket. **Inner language** involves the use of language during thinking, planning, and other mental processes. The assessment of inner language skills and abilities is a complex process.

Responding to Diversity

Today, many children are English language learners; that is, English is not their first language. They come from homes in which the family's native language is spoken exclusively or nearly exclusively. School personnel consider the home language to be the students' first language and regard them as culturally and linguistically diverse students. As the United States continues to become an increasingly diverse society,

SNAPSHOT
Bethany

The teacher's words fell on Bethany's ears at an overwhelming rate. Bethany knew that the teacher was explaining the assignment for tomorrow. Although Bethany has average intelligence, she is not able to comprehend all that the teacher says. Before dismissing the class, Bethany's teacher handed her a written copy of the assignment, and Bethany smiled quickly as she gathered her books.

Bethany's teacher returned the smile as she remembered the problems that Bethany had experienced earlier in the year. Through the referral and assessment process, the teacher was able to discover Bethany's difficulty in comprehending oral directions and in following class discussions.

It all began early in the year, after the school nurse had conducted a hearing screening on all the students in her classroom. Bethany passed the screening with no problems. However, as the first month of school passed, Bethany's teacher observed that even though Bethany seemed to be attentive, she had difficulty in following daily class discussions. Bethany frequently submitted incomplete homework assignments and, when questioned, would apologetically add that she didn't " . . . know we had to do that." As the difficulty seemed to persist, the teacher decided to confer with Bethany's former teachers. Both teachers vaguely remembered that Bethany was not consistent in her work. Some of the assignments were done well, they remembered. One teacher felt that she did not seem to be motivated.

The following week, the teacher called Bethany's parents and asked them to come in for a conference. Both parents were surprised to hear about the teacher's concerns. When asked if Bethany needed to have the volume high on the television, her mother replied that Bethany seldom seemed to be interested in watching television or in going to the movies. Bethany's parents were concerned about her missing assignments. They tried to pinpoint some of their concerns: Why doesn't Bethany turn in complete assignments? Why doesn't she participate in class discussions? Is there a reason why Bethany does not like to watch television or go to the movies? They agreed that the teacher should make a referral to the assessment team. Perhaps the team might be able to provide some answers to these puzzling questions.

Through the assessment process, the team identified Bethany's problem. She had difficulty processing oral language. Today she regularly works with the speech and language pathologist. In the classroom, her teacher uses several accommodations, such as written assignment slips and outlines of lecture material, to help Bethany be more successful.

children from culturally and linguistically diverse backgrounds make up a greater percentage of the school population. In some large-city school districts, these students comprise up to 80 percent of the student body (Improving Results for Culturally and Linguistically Diverse Students, 2000).

In order to benefit from their education program, many children who are culturally and linguistically diverse need second-language instruction. Some children need additional tutoring due to limited linguistic experiences, but most children who are culturally and linguistically diverse do not have a special need that requires a referral to special services.

Yet, some students are not linguistically competent in their first language. This compounds the difficulties in assessing children. How can teachers distinguish language differences from speech and language disorders in linguistically and culturally diverse students? First, a teacher can observe speech production and refer the student if the student's speech contains mispronunciations, dysfluencies, unusual pitch, rate, hoarseness, omitted words or word endings, words used in unusual ways, or atypical sequences when compared to dialect peers (Moran, 1996).

Second, a teacher should refer a linguistically and culturally diverse student to the assessment team when the teacher observes some of the following behaviors in comparison to similar peers:

- Nonverbal aspects of language are culturally inappropriate.
- The student does not express basic needs adequately.
- The student rarely initiates verbal interaction with peers.
- When peers initiate interaction, the student responds sporadically/inappropriately.

- The student replaces speech with gestures and communicates nonverbally when talking would be appropriate and expected.
- Peers give indications that they have difficulty understanding the student.
- The student often gives inappropriate responses.
- The student has difficulty conveying thoughts in an organized, sequential manner that is understandable to listeners.
- The student shows poor topic maintenance ("skips around").
- The student has word-finding difficulties that go beyond normal second-language acquisition patterns.
- The student fails to provide significant information to the listener, leaving the listener confused.
- The student has difficulty with conversational turn-taking skills (may be too passive or may interrupt inappropriately).
- The student perseverates (remains too long) on a topic even after the topic has changed.
- The student fails to ask and answer questions appropriately.
- The student needs to hear things repeated, even when they are stated simply and comprehensibly.
- The student often echoes what others say. (Roseberry-McKibbin, 1995)

The focus of the assessment question "How does the student communicate within the first-language setting?" and the standard that teachers can apply is whether the student's language reflects characteristics that are different from the student's first-language community (Moran, 1996). Teachers should not identify students as having a speech and language disability simply by comparing the student's language with the dominant language—such as European American English—of the school community.

There is a shortage of teachers and other professionals qualified to assess culturally and linguistically diverse students, and many standardized instruments are woefully

---

What should IEP team members do when assessing to determine eligibility for special education services for a student who shows linguistically and culturally diverse traits?

- Gather information to determine whether the difficulties stem from language or cultural differences, from a lack of opportunity to learn, or from a disability as part of a preferral and intervention process.
- Include interpreters, bilingual educators, and an individual who is familiar with the student's culture and language as members of the IEP team.
- Assess the student's language dominance and proficiency to determine which language to use in the assessment process for special education services, if the student's home language is other than English.
- Select nonbiased, appropriate instruments along with other sources of information (observation, interviews) from a variety of environments (school, home, community) to produce a multidimensional assessment.

FIGURE 11.1 • Best Practice for IEP Team Members Working with Students Who Are Linguistically and Culturally Diverse

Source: Adapted from Burnette, 2000.

inadequate (Burnette, 2000). To help IEP team members who are struggling with insufficient training and materials, a number of solutions and best practice have been identified (Figure 11.1).

Speech and Language Assessment

An assessment of speech and language reflects, to some degree, the perspectives of the examiner who is gathering the information as well as the choice of the assessment approach. Many standardized instruments focus only on expressive and receptive language, whereas authorities in the field (Bloom & Lahey, cited in Kaiser, Alpert, & Warren, 1988; Semel, Wiig, & Secord, 2003) describe oral language as consisting of three main areas or components: form, content, and use.

Form

Form relates to the structural properties of language, including the sounds and written symbols of language and the letters that form a unit of meaning. The term **phonology** refers to the system of speech sounds of a language. The smallest units of sound are **phonemes.** For example, the English language makes use of only about 44 different phonemes. The word *truck* consists of four phonemes (/t/r/u/k/). Students with articulation disorders often have difficulty in producing sounds. Substituting one phoneme for another and omitting phonemes are common mistakes that students make. Speech and language pathologists may describe this as a problem in articulation; for example, substituting letter(s) (*wabbit* for *rabbit*) or omitting letter(s): (*car* for *cars*).

Some students have difficulty in associating phonemes with their written equivalents, called **graphemes.** One of the reasons that English is such a difficult language is that (1) a single grapheme can represent more than one phoneme (for example, c—*cake* c—*circus*) and (2) different graphemes can represent the same phoneme (for example, c—*cake* k—*kite*) (Polloway & Smith, 2000). In teaching that a single grapheme can represent more than one phoneme, we say that a letter has different sounds. For example, how many sounds does the letter *a* have?

Morphology is the study of the units of letters that form a single unit of meaning. The basic unit of meaning is a **morpheme.** A morpheme can be a word such as *house,* or *car,* or a meaningful part of a word such as *re* in *renew.* Prefixes and suffixes, such as *re-, in-, -s,* and *-er* are morphemes. Because morphemes are units of meaning, examiners frequently use them to measure expressive language development by obtaining a sample of the student's language and counting the individual morphemes per speech utterance. A speech utterance is the single phrase or sentence that the student expresses. The number of morphemes is totaled and divided by the number of speech utterances to obtain the average **mean length of utterance (MLU).**

The following conversation was part of a five-minute observation of Andre during free play in the kindergarten classroom.

> *Other Child:* My block . . . [2 morphemes]
>
> *Andre:* No, I want this. [4 morphemes]
>
> *Andre:* You can be the driver. [6 morphemes]

Adding up Andre's use of morphemes, the total comes to 10 and is divided by the number of Andre's speech utterances (2). Although the MLU may be an oversimplification of the concept of spoken language, the MLU is useful in comparing levels of linguistic development and increases in individual mastery of expressive language (Polloway &

Smith, 2000). Other considerations that will affect the MLU are (1) the length of the recording needed to obtain an adequate language sample of speech utterances and (2) the environment(s) that will be observed.

Content

Content relates to the meaning of language and includes semantics and syntax.

Semantics

Semantics is the study of word meanings. Development of semantics begins with association of single concrete morphemes, for example, the association of *Mama* with a particular person. Development typically progresses to understanding complex utterances; for example, "Please get me the book" and more complex language such as, "It's raining cats and dogs."

Syntax

Syntax refers to the rules for arranging words into a sentence or phrase. In English, for example, adjectives are commonly placed before nouns. The combination of syntax and morphology is known as grammar.

Use

▶ Interview a speech-language pathologist regarding assessment of speech and language skills. What assessment approaches does this individual use in gathering information about content, form, and use?

Use of language is important in social situations! **Pragmatics** refers to the ability to use language in functional ways: for example, the ability to use language in taking turns, to enter into a conversation or discussion with other children (or adults), to continue the conversation, to interpret the meaning of the speaker, or to "read" the listener's non-verbal cues. Figure 11.2 illustrates the relationship between the aspects of speech and language we have discussed.

Standardized Tests of Oral Language

▶ **CEC Common Core Knowledge and Skills.** A beginning special educator can administer nonbiased formal and informal assessments (CC8S2).

This section highlights some of the commonly used individual, standardized tests of oral language. All the tests in this section are norm-referenced and use standardized procedures for administering and scoring. The tests yield a variety of scores, including standard scores, percentiles, stanines, age equivalents, and normal curve equivalents (NCEs).

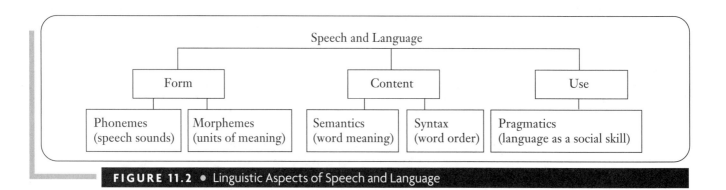

FIGURE 11.2 • Linguistic Aspects of Speech and Language

How It Works! Connecting Assessment and Instruction

Rosalinda is 15 years old and a sophomore at Valley High. Her first language is Spanish. She loves horses and hopes to be a veterinary assistant when she finishes school. Rose has mild mental retardation and delays in receptive and expressive language skills in both English and Spanish as noted in her IEP. Rosalinda's IEP goals include using English to communicate in social settings and using appropriate style and tone for audience and occasion in conversation. Her teacher, Bri Wescott, is helping Rosalinda work on initiating conversations, making friends, recognizing positive and negative peer pressure, and recognizing her own feelings and emotions.

Bri developed a series of four structured lessons to help Rosalinda and the other students use expressive and receptive English language skills to participate in group discussions. These included starting a conversation, how to make friends, positive and negative peer pressure, and feelings and emotions. Bri used direct instruction along with pre- and posttests for each lesson to document each student's progress. During the lessons she used sensitive error correction (accepting all answers in English) and also used the data projector to post possible answers for all the students to see. Bri asked all the students to read and respond to questions. She made sure that each student had enough time to compose his or her answers, and she carefully checked for understanding.

The pre- and posttests consisted of short realistic scenarios, such as the following example:

> You have stopped by the convenience store to pick up a half gallon of milk when Joey, a popular boy at school, asks you to loan him $10. You know you only have about $10 left after you buy the milk and payday isn't for another two days. Would you let Joey borrow the money? Why or why not? What would you say to him?

Rosalinda and the other students were each asked to videotape their responses to each scenario. Later Bri viewed the tapes, informally noting appropriate style and tone. She also counted MLUs. The pre- and posttest results showed that the lessons had assisted Rosalinda and the other students in both receptive and expressive language skills. An unexpected outcome was that later Bri observed Rosalinda volunteering to participate in role-play scenarios. (Adapted from Beckett, Nevin, Comella, Kane, Romero, & Bergquist, 2002)

Research-Based Practices — Understanding the Link between Oral Language, Reading, and Writing

Language is not only important in communicating thoughts and ideas; language is important to school success. Research findings indicate a complex relationship between oral language and developing skills in literacy. The National Institute of Child Health and Human Development (2005) conducted a longitudinal study following children from age 3 through third grade to examine the role of oral language in developing reading competence. The results suggest that oral language (language including grammar, vocabulary, and semantics) plays both an indirect and a direct role in word recognition and serves as a better foundation for reading than vocabulary alone.

In addition to reading, a child's difficulties in oral language also may affect written language, although the research is more limited in this area. Mackie and Dockrell (2004) examined the nature and extent of children's written language using two groups of 11-year-old children, one group of children with specific language impairments and a second group of children without disabilities. Their research found that children with specific language impairments wrote fewer words and produced more errors in syntax than children without disabilities.

▶ For more information about research on oral language, reading, and writing, you might examine one or more of the following journals: *Learning Disability Quarterly, Journal of Child Psychology and Child Psychiatry, Mind and Language,* or *Journal of Speech, Language, and Hearing Research.*

TESTS-at-a-GLANCE

**Clinical Evaluation of Language Fundamentals®
Fourth Edition (CELF®–4)**

- **Publication Date:** 2003
- **Purposes:** Measures selected receptive and expressive skills in morphology, syntax, semantics, and memory.
- **Age/Grade Levels:** Ages 5 through 21.
- **Time to Administer:** 30 to 60 minutes.
- **Technical Adequacy:** The standardization sample, reliability, and validity are adequate.
- **Suggested Use:** Identify, diagnose, and follow up the evaluation of language skills deficits. For Spanish-speaking individuals, the *CELF–4 Spanish Edition* is a parallel, not translated, version of the instrument.

Clinical Evaluation of Language Fundamentals® Fourth Edition (CELF®–4)

The *Clinical Evaluation of Language Fundamentals® Fourth Edition (CELF®–4;* Semel, Wiig, & Secord, 2003) uses a four-step process to assess a child's language and pinpoint areas of difficulty. By administering the core subtests, an examiner can obtain a Total Language Score to determine if a problem exists and whether the student qualifies for services. Additional assessment helps to determine the nature of the language disorder and the student's language strengths and weaknesses. Subtests include: Receptive Language Score, Expressive Language Scores, Language Structure, Language Content, and Language Content and Memory.

ADMINISTRATION The *CELF®–4 is* administered individually and takes between 30 and 60 minutes.

SCORING Raw scores are converted to standard scores, percentile ranks, and age equivalents.

STANDARDIZATION Norms have been updated to reflect the 2000 U.S. census. While additional research is necessary to contribute to our understanding of it, this instrument is useful in the assessment of students.

RELIABILITY AND VALIDITY The examiner's manual reports reliability and validity studies, although additional research will add to our knowledge of these technical considerations.

SUMMARY The *Clinical Evaluation of Language Fundamentals ® Fourth Edition (CELF®–4)* provides information regarding a student's language disorder and eligibility for services. This instrument is also available in Spanish. Scoring software is available and allows the examiner to generate various reports, including, for example, a summary report, an item analysis, or a pragmatics profile.

Expressive Vocabulary Test

The *Expressive Vocabulary Test (EVT;* Williams, 1997) measures expressive vocabulary and word retrieval for Standard American English in individuals ages 2 years, 5 months through 90+ years. The *EVT* is administered using a stimulus book with pictures that contain a good balance of gender and ethnic representations. The examinee must respond to two types of items, labeling and synonyms. For labeling items, the examiner points to a picture or a part of the body and asks a question. For the synonyms, the examiner presents a picture and a stimulus word.

ADMINISTRATION The *EVT* is administered individually and takes 10 to 25 minutes.

SCORING Raw scores convert to standard scores, percentile ranks, stanines, NCEs, or age equivalents, with calculable confidence intervals at the 90 and 95 percent level. The *EVT* standard score has a mean of 100 and a standard deviation of 15.

STANDARDIZATION The *EVT* was standardized on 2,725 individuals, the same population used in the *Peabody Picture Vocabulary Test–III* standardization. Based on the 1990 census data, test developers controlled the sample for age, gender, race/ethnicity, region, and SES (based on parent or self-education level).

RELIABILITY Test-retest reliability ranged from .77 to .90; split-half reliability ranged from .83 to .97. Internal reliability was high.

TESTS-at-a-GLANCE

Expressive Vocabulary Test (EVT)

- **Publication Date:** 1997
- **Purposes:** Measures expressive vocabulary and word retrieval.
- **Age/Grade Levels:** Ages 2 years, 5 months through 90+ years.
- **Time to Administer:** 10 to 25 minutes.
- **Technical Adequacy:** The standardization sample, reliability, and validity studies are adequate.
- **Suggested Use:** Identify, diagnose, and follow up the evaluation of expressive language and word retrieval skill.

VALIDITY The test presents evidence for content and construct validity. Criterion-related validity studies for the *EVT* and the *Oral and Written Language Scales (OWLS)* showed correlations in the moderate to high range. The reason for this range is that the *EVT* only measures one area of language, expressive vocabulary, while the *OWLS* measures language in a broad context. Additional criterion-related validity studies would be helpful.

Several small studies examined the performance of different clinical groups matched to control groups. Children in clinical groups represented specific diagnostic or special education categories, including speech impairment, language delay, language impairment, mental retardation, learning disability (reading), and hearing impairment. Clinical groups also included gifted students and adults with mild mental retardation. Individuals from these studies were not in the standardization sample.

SUMMARY The *Expressive Vocabulary Test* measures expressive vocabulary and word retrieval for Standard American English in individuals representing a wide age range (ages 2 years, 5 months through 90+ years). The test has adequate technical characteristics, although additional criterion-related validity studies would be helpful.

▶ Evaluate the technical aspects of one of the standardized instruments for assessing language. Share your results with classmates.

Oral and Written Language Scales

The *Oral and Written Language Scales (OWLS*; Carrow-Woolfolk, 1996) is an individualized test of oral and written language. The *OWLS* has three scales: Listening Comprehension, Oral Expression, and Written Expression. In this section we will examine the Listening Comprehension and Oral Expression Scales, which are intended for use with children and young adults ages 3 through 21. The *OWLS* measures vocabulary, syntax, pragmatics, and higher order thinking, including interpretation of figurative language, inference, synthesizing information, and so on.

ADMINISTRATION The Listening Comprehension and Oral Expression Scales are individually administered.

SCORING Raw scores convert to standard scores, including percentile ranks, normal curve equivalents, and stanines with possible confidence intervals of 68 percent, 90 percent, or 95 percent.

Oral and Written Language Scales (OWLS)

● **Publication Date:** 1996

● **Purposes:** Measures written and oral language including vocabulary, syntax, pragmatics, and higher order thinking, including interpretations of figurative language, inference, and so on.

● **Age/Grade Levels:** Ages 3 through 21.

● **Time to Administer:** 15 to 25 minutes.

● **Technical Adequacy:** Standardization sample is adequate, reliability is weak for some age groups. Validity is adequate.

● **Suggested Use:** Assesses listening comprehension, oral expression, and written expression.

STANDARDIZATION Standardization of the *OWLS* occurred between April 1992 and August 1993. The standardization sample was based on 1991 U.S. Census Bureau data and included 1,985 individuals who represented strata of age, gender, race, ethnic group, geographic region, and economic status, based on the mother's level of education. The three scales of the *OWLS* were co-normed.

RELIABILITY The test presents reliability information for split-half reliability, test-retest reliability, and interrater reliability. For the Listening Comprehension Scale, the split-half reliability coefficients range from .75 (age 8) to .89 (age 4); for the Oral Expression Scale, the coefficients range from .76 (ages 19 through 21) to .91 (age 4). For test-retest reliability, the coefficients for the Listening Comprehension Scale range from .73 to .80; for the Oral Expression Scale the coefficients range from .77 to .86. Interrater reliability for the Oral Expression Scale ranged from .90 to .93.

VALIDITY The test presents adequate evidence of content, criterion-related, and construct validity. The *OWLS* was administered concurrently with the *Test for Auditory Comprehension of Language–Revised, Peabody Picture Vocabulary Test–Revised, Clinical Evaluation of Language Fundamentals–Revised, Kaufman Assessment Battery for Children, Wechsler Intelligence Scale for Children–Third Edition, Kaufman Brief Intelligence Test, Kaufman Test of Educational Achievement, Comprehensive Form,* and the *Woodcock Reading Mastery Tests–Revised.*

While test developers conducted small studies with students who were identified as having a speech impairment, language delay, language impairment, mental disability, learning disability, hearing impairment, or as receiving Chapter One assistance in reading, these studies were not part of the standardization sample. These studies produced limited results because each group participated in only one study and because the samples were so small.

SUMMARY The *OWLS* is an individualized test of oral and written language. The instrument provides in-depth information regarding the use of oral language, including vocabulary, syntax, pragmatics, and higher order thinking, as well as the use of written language. Internal and test-retest reliability is weak for some age groups. Interrater reliability is good for the Oral Expression Scale. The test presents adequate evidence of validity.

Peabody Picture Vocabulary Test–Third Edition

The *Peabody Picture Vocabulary Test–Third Edition (PPVT-III;* Dunn & Dunn, 1997) measures receptive language (vocabulary) for individuals 2 years, 5 months through 90+ years of age. In the development of this revised instrument, a bias review panel reviewed test items and completed an analysis for item bias by race/ethnicity, gender, and region.

The test consists of a series of pictures or test plates that include depictions of individuals from various ethnic backgrounds and individuals with disabilities. Each plate has four pictures and the examinee must point to the one that best tells the meaning of the word (Figure 11.3). This instrument has two parallel forms, Form IIIA and Form

IIIB. This test is also available in Spanish (*TVIP: Test de Vocabulario en Imágenes Peabody*). The *TVIP* (Dunn, Lugo, Padilla, & Dunn, 1986) measures the receptive vocabulary of Spanish-speaking students, ages 2 years, 5 months through 18 years.

ADMINISTRATION The *PPVT–III* is an individually administered test.

SCORING Examiners record the individual's response to each test item and mark the item pass/fail. Raw scores are converted to standard scores, percentiles, stanines, NCEs, or age equivalents and evaluators can calculate confidence intervals at the 68, 90, and 95 percent level. *The PPVT–III* standard score has a mean of 100 and a standard deviation of 15.

STANDARDIZATION The norming sample consisted of 2,725 individuals ages 2 years, 5 months through 90 years. Based on the 1994 population survey, the sample reflects controls for age, gender, race/ethnicity, region, and SES (based on parent or self-education level). In the Spanish version, norms are available for both combined and separate Mexican and Puerto Rican standardization samples.

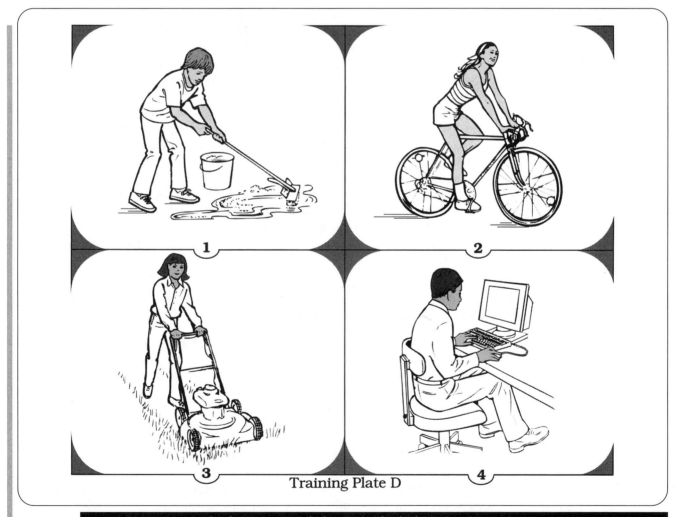

Training Plate D

FIGURE 11.3 • Peabody Picture Vocabulary Test–Third Edition

Source: From the Peabody Picture Vocabulary Test–Third Edition © 1997 by Lloyd M. Dunn and Leota M. Dunn. American Guidance Service, Inc., 4201 Woodland Road, Circle Pines, MN 55014. Reprinted with permission of the Authors/ Publisher. All rights reserved.

RELIABILITY Internal consistency reliabilities indicated a high degree of item uniformity within each of the forms: Correlations ranged from .83 to .97 with a median reliability of .94 for Form IIIA and .91 for Form IIIB. Test-retest and alternate form reliabilities were high.

VALIDITY The test manual reports rationale to support content and construct validity. The results of criterion-related validity studies with instruments of intelligence and oral language and two small studies with the *PPVT–III* and the *OWLS* show correlations in the moderate to high range (.63 to .83). The reason for this range is that the *PPVT–III* only measures one area of language, receptive vocabulary, while the *OWLS* measures language in a broad context. Additional criterion-related validity studies would be helpful.

Several small studies examined the performance of different clinical groups matched to control groups. The clinical groups represented specific diagnostic or special education categories including speech impairment, language delay, language impairment, mental retardation, learning disability (reading), and hearing impairment, and included gifted students as well as adults with mild mental retardation.

SUMMARY The *Peabody Picture Vocabulary Test–III* is a standardized instrument for assessing receptive language skills in children, youth, and adults from 2 years, 5 months through 90+ years of age. The drawings that illustrate the stimulus words consist of gender and ethnic balance. The instrument is well normed and technically adequate, although additional criterion-related validity studies would be helpful.

This instrument is available in Spanish, *TVIP: Test de Vocabulario en Imágenes Peabody,* and assesses receptive vocabulary of Spanish-speaking students. The *TVIP* is a direct translation of an earlier version of the *PPVT–III*, the *Peabody Picture Vocabulary Test–R* (Dunn & Dunn, 1981).

Preschool Language Scale–4

The *Preschool Language Scale–4 (PLS–4*; Zimmerman, Steiner, & Pond, 2002) measures language acquisition and prelanguage skills in children ages birth through 6 years, 11 months. The test has two subscales: auditory comprehension and expressive communication, which includes preverbal communication skills. The test also has a Spanish-language version, the *Preschool Language Scale–4, Spanish Edition,* designed to test receptive and expressive language in Spanish. According to the manual, common dialectal variations are listed for testing children who live in different Spanish-speaking regions, including Cuba, Mexico, Guatemala, and Puerto Rico.

ADMINISTRATION This instrument takes approximately 20 to 30 minutes to administer. Both English and Spanish versions use the same materials.

SCORING The test reports scores as standard scores and percentile ranks by age. Language age equivalents are also available.

STANDARDIZATION Approximately 1,500 children from ages 2 weeks through 6 years, 11 months participated in the standardization sample. The sample was stratified by race, parent education level, and geographic region. The sample approximated the 2000 U.S. Census. Spanish-speaking children from various regions in the United States participated in the standardization sample for the Spanish version.

RELIABILITY The test reports three types of reliability: internal consistency, test-retest, and interrater reliability. Reliability coefficients for each type were within the acceptable range.

VALIDITY The test reports three types of validity: content, construct, and concurrent, all within the acceptable range.

SUMMARY The *Preschool Language Scale–4* is a standardized instrument for measuring preverbal and language skills in young children ages birth through 6 years, 11 months. The norming sample is representative of the 2000 U.S. Census according to race, parent education level, and geographic region of the country. Reliability studies report good internal consistency and high test-retest and interrater reliability coefficients. Construct validity studies found the instrument to be somewhat successful in identifying children who had previously been identified as having a language disorder. The *Preschool Language Scale–4, Spanish Edition,* assesses Spanish expressive and receptive language skills. The instrument addresses the common Spanish dialects and is useful for children who come from different geographic regions.

> ## TESTS-at-a-GLANCE
>
> ### Preschool Language Scale–4 (PLS–4)
>
> - **Publication Date:** 2002
> - **Purposes:** Measures auditory comprehension and expressive communication that includes preverbal communication skills.
> - **Age/Grade Levels:** Ages 2 weeks through 6 years, 11 months.
> - **Time to Administer:** 20 to 30 minutes.
> - **Technical Adequacy:** Norming sample is based on 2000 U.S. Census.
> - **Suggested Use:** Assesses language acquisition and prelanguage skills in children. A Spanish edition is designed to test receptive and expressive language in Spanish.

Test of Adolescent and Adult Language–3

The *Test of Adolescent and Adult Language–3 (TOAL–3*; Hammill, Brown, Larsen, & Wiederholt, 1994) assesses language skills in individuals ages 12 years through 24 years, 11 months. The test consists of ten areas, including listening, speaking, reading, writing, spoken language, written language, vocabulary, grammar, receptive language, and expressive language.

ADMINISTRATION The *TOAL–3* can be administered individually or to a small group. Administration time is 1 to 3 hours.

SCORING Raw scores transform to composite quotients, with a mean of 100 and a standard deviation of 15 for each of the ten areas assessed. Additionally, obtaining an Overall Language Ability quotient is possible.

STANDARDIZATION The standardization sample derives from the 1990 U.S. Census. The *TOAL– 3* was standardized on approximately 3,000 individuals who reflect controls for region, gender, age, and race.

RELIABILITY The test presents reliability information for internal consistency and test-retest reliability, and all coefficients exceed .80.

TESTS-at-a-GLANCE

Test of Adolescent and Adult Language–3 (TOAL–3)

- **Publication Date:** 1994

- **Purposes:** Assesses listening, speaking, reading, writing, spoken language, written language, vocabulary, grammar, receptive language, and expressive language.

- **Age/Grade Levels:** Ages 12 years through 24 years, 11 months.

- **Time to Administer:** One to 3 hours.

- **Technical Adequacy:** The standardization sample, reliability, and validity are adequate.

- **Suggested Use:** Assesses language skills in youth and young adults.

> Obtain two or more standardized tests for assessing oral language. Compare and contrast the content of the two instruments. Would one of these instruments be helpful in answering assessment questions identified in one of the Snapshots in this chapter?

TESTS-at-a-GLANCE

Test of Language Development–Primary: 3 (TOLD–P:3)

- **Publication Date:** 1997

- **Purposes:** Assesses language skills.

- **Age/Grade Levels:** Ages 4 through 8.

- **Time to Administer:** 30 minutes to 1 hour.

- **Technical Adequacy:** The standardization sample, reliability, and validity are adequate.

- **Suggested Use:** As part of a comprehensive assessment in determining eligibility or in evaluating a child's progress.

VALIDITY The test gives adequate evidence of content, criterion-related, and construct validity. The *TOAL–3* was administered concurrently with the *Test of Language Development–I:2, Peabody Picture Vocabulary Test, Detroit Test of Learning Abilities–3,* and *Test of Written Language–2.*

SUMMARY The *TOAL–3* assesses language skills in individuals ages 12 years through 24 years, 11 months. The test consists of ten areas: listening, speaking, reading, writing, spoken language, written language, vocabulary, grammar, receptive language, and expressive language. Evidence of reliability and validity appears to be adequate.

Test of Language Development–Primary: Third Edition

The *Test of Language Development–Primary: Third Edition (TOLD–P:3;* Newcomer & Hammill, 1997) is for children ages 4 through 8. According to the manual, the purposes of the *TOLD–P:3* are (1) to identify children who are significantly below their peers in language proficiency, (2) to determine specific strengths and weaknesses in language skills, (3) to document progress in language as a result of an intervention program, and (4) to measure language in research studies. The test consists of the following nine subtests: Picture Vocabulary, Relational Vocabulary, Oral Vocabulary, Grammatic Understanding, Sentence Imitation, Grammatic Completion, Word Discrimination, Phonemic Analysis, and Word Articulation.

ADMINISTRATION There are no time limits on the *TOLD–P:3,* and the time to administer the test may vary from 30 minutes to 1 hour.

SCORING Test examiners may transform raw scores into standard scores, percentiles, and age equivalent quotients for the composites. The manual explains the calculation of composite scores well.

STANDARDIZATION One thousand children from 28 states, selected to represent 1990 U.S. census data, participated in the *TOLD–P:3* standardization.

RELIABILITY The examiner's manual reports three types of reliability: internal consistency, test-retest, and interscorer. The *TOLD–P:3* meets acceptable criteria (r =.80) for subtests as well as composites.

VALIDITY The examiner's manual provides evidence for content, construct, and criterion validity.

SUMMARY The *Test of Language Development–Primary: Third Edition (TOLD–P:3)* is a norm-referenced instrument. The test is for use with children ages 4 through 8 and is individually administered. Reliability and validity are adequate. The test may be useful in identifying children with speech and language impairments.

Concerns about Standardized Tests of Oral Language

Receptive Language

The assessment of receptive language requires determining the student's understanding of language. Many standardized tests use symbols in test items to represent word meanings, then take symbol recognition as a key measure of receptive language; therefore, teachers must examine these symbols for appropriateness and clarity. We know that during an individual's cognitive development, understanding of symbols moves from concrete to abstract levels. A test item that measures the student's understanding of common objects in the environment might include the task, "Point to the ball." Test developers vary in how they represent the object "ball," that is, some pictures provide a more abstract representation than others. In the following list of test materials, how could the items be ordered from most concrete to most abstract?

> black and white line drawing of a ball
>
> cartoon of a ball
>
> photograph of a ball

The test should represent items in an appropriate way for the student. For example, items presented in abstract terms or items that are culture-bound may not be a true measure of the student's receptive language. The type of symbols used, the inclusion of regional or cultural items familiar to the individual, and the response method that the student receives to indicate a choice are all particularly salient factors in the assessment of receptive language skills.

Expressive Language

An individual must have a reason for using language as well as one for wanting to respond. Young children may not care to perform, or a student may not want to comply with the examiner's request. The student's need or desire to communicate will directly affect the assessment results from standardized instruments.

Connecting Assessment with Instruction

Alternative assessment approaches can be more effective in connecting assessment with instruction than the use of standardized instruments. These approaches assist educators in determining where to start instruction and to monitor progress. In the following section, we examine some of these assessment approaches.

Curriculum-Based Measurement

Curriculum-based measurement links instruction with assessment by emphasizing repeated, direct measurement of student performance. This method is an effective way to assess and monitor student progress. A teacher begins by identifying the academic behavior to be improved. This usually relates directly to the student's IEP. Next, the teacher selects the assessment approach that will be used to determine where to begin instruction and how to monitor progress. Finally, the teacher determines the type of error correction procedure to use.

How It Works! Using Curriculum-Based Measurement

Maria Gomaz, a special educator, recently received a new student in the resource room. Juan is a 6-year-old native Spanish speaker who has auditory processing deficits. His current IEP has goals relating to auditory memory and phonemic awareness, specifically to the ability to name letters and sounds. Maria observed that Juan tends to give up easily or takes a long time to recall information. For example, on the *Brigance® Assessment of Basic Skills,* Juan was asked his address . . . fifteen minutes later he blurted out the answer. Maria wonders if this makes it difficult to focus on what the teacher is saying during the time it takes him to recall an answer.

Maria began keeping detailed records of Juan's progress so that she could measure the level of understanding and the rate of acquisition. By keeping a daily notebook on Juan's progress, she was able to determine if the activities were actually impacting his learning. Below is an excerpt from the notebook.

Last week we did a letter-sorting activity with the three letters that Juan knows. We practiced identifying capital and lowercase as well as letter sounds. I found that on Monday Juan was able to recall the letter names and sounds for all three letters. This let me know that the kinesthetic action as well as the verbalization of the names and sounds worked well for him. This is a strategy we will repeat. Then, we did an activity in which Juan used an alphabet chart to help him put together an alphabet puzzle. After adding each piece of the puzzle we would review each letter name and sound. By the end of the puzzle Juan had added three letters to his repertoire. I thought hooray!! However, the next day Juan could not remember the letter names of the new letters. The repetition worked in the short term but he did not retain the information. Because I check for retention each day, I was able to determine that this particular activity was not effective for increasing Juan's retention of letter names and sounds.

[The error correction procedure that Maria uses is immediate correction. If he incorrectly identifies a letter sound, she immediately corrects him, pointing out similar sounds.] According to the daily data, Maria decides if Juan is ready to add a new letter. Once Juan has recalled the letter name, sound, and symbol three days is a row, she introduces a new letter (Figure 11.4.) Once they get further along, she will introduce a new letter when Juan is able to recall 90 percent of the information. (Adapted from Nevin & Hood, 2002).

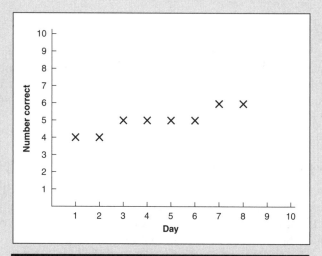

FIGURE 11.4 ● Juan's Daily Progress in Phonemic Awareness

Language Probes

▶ **CEC Common Core Knowledge and Skills.** A beginning special educator can evaluate instruction and monitor progress of individuals with exceptional learning needs (CC8S8).

A **language probe** is a sampling of words or sounds that elicit specific information on a receptive or expressive skill (Polloway & Smith, 2000). For example, the high school special education teacher in a life skills class selects six objects from a job setting. The teacher presents each object to the student twice and the teacher asks, "What is this? What is this used for?" The teacher sets the criteria for correct responses for each item. Probes are helpful diagnostic techniques and assist in planning instruction because they take advantage of the natural environment.

Language Samples

Language samples are examples of a student's use of language, such as explaining a topic of interest, telling a story, or stating and supporting an opinion. Language samples yield information about the student's vocabulary, use of syntax, understanding of semantics, proficiency in articulation, and the ability to use language in functional ways. Samples should also include examples of conversations with peers.

Samples of the student's language can be tape-recorded or written on a chart. Teachers and parents collect samples of the student's language during various daily routines, activities, and assignments.

Mean Length of Utterance (MLU)

Earlier in this chapter we described the term mean length of utterance (MLU) and the way teachers calculate MLUs by using a child's language sample. Sometimes teachers who want a quick sample of a child's language will gather several MLUs over the course of the day. MLUs are useful in monitoring a young child's progress in language development or an older student's progress in the increasing use of language for communication in functional life skills.

▶ **CEC Common Core Knowledge and Skills.** A beginning special educator can develop or modify individualized assessment strategies (CC8S4).

Other Approaches

In previous chapters, we describe and examine other helpful approaches in linking assessment questions to instruction. In assessing oral language, these approaches aid the teacher in gathering information and providing feedback to students and parents regarding skill-level and progress. These approaches include:

- Oral descriptions
- Written descriptions
- Checklists and questionnaires
- Interviews
- Conferences
- Audio- and videotapes
- Discussions with students, parents, and teachers

▶ The assessment of oral language skills is important when assessing achievement, development, ability, and behavior. How might the assessment of language skills relate to assessment in another area?

Observing the Student within the Environment

In previous chapters we discuss the importance of considering the student within the physical, learning, and social environments. The interactions between the student and the environment are important assessment considerations when assessing oral language.

Physical Environment

The physical setting can influence the student's development and use of language. Cooperative classroom activities, such as gathering information on the Web, provide opportunities to use language in less formal ways and possibly to enhance language acquisition. However, observations outside the regular classroom, such as in the hallways, in the cafeteria, and on the playground, may provide a better understanding of the student's language than in the more structured classroom (Moran, 1996).

▶ *Handbook for K–12 Teachers: The Internet: An Inclusive Magnet for Teaching All Students* is a rich resource detailing how to reach ALL students through technology. This handbook, published by the World Institute on Disability, includes information on using the Internet to enhance language acquisition. http://www.wid.org/archives/handbook.pdf

Learning Environment

The learning environment influences and promotes the development of a student's language. For example, the types of questions a teacher asks directly influence the level of response that a student gives. Which of the following questions would encourage you to continue the conversation about the movie?

> "What was the name of the movie you saw?"
>
> "What was the movie about?"

Some questions require a yes or no; these are minimal-response (or closed-ended) questions. Some questions require students to think about the materials that they are using; these are thought-provoking questions and may require a phrase or a few sentences to answer. Other questions require students to think and weigh possible responses; they are open-ended questions.

In addition to questioning techniques, there are other teaching strategies to promote the development of oral language. Expansion and modeling are two such strategies that are effective in the classroom.

▶ Ask a friend to tape a conversation of you working with a student. Conduct an analysis of the tape. How did you support the student's use of language? What types of questions did you pose (minimal response, thought-provoking, or open-ended)? Did you use expansion or modeling strategies? What might you do differently next time?

▶ **CEC Common Core Knowledge and Skills.** A beginning special educator can teach individuals with disabilities to monitor for errors in oral and written language (GC6S3).

● Expansion.

Expansion is a strategy that helps students learn syntax by supplying omitted structures. Billy, who is in kindergarten, told his teacher, "I want to use that thing." His teacher answered, "You want to use the scale at the science table?" The Snapshot of Nina describes how her teacher is helping Nina develop oral language skills.

● Modeling.

In addition to expansion, teachers can assist students in learning semantic features by **modeling** or by combining the two. Peers also can be instrumental in modeling language. Let's listen in on some teacher conversations.

> *Conversation one:*
>
> *Agata:* My brother got shot at the doctor's yesterday.
>
> *Teacher:* Don't say "got;" say "had a shot."

> *Conversation two:*
>
> *Agata:* My brother got shot at the doctor's yesterday.
>
> *Teacher:* Your brother had a shot at the doctor's yesterday? And did you get a shot at the doctor's, too?

If you were Agata, which conversation would encourage you to continue telling about your experience? Teachers are more effective when they use expansion and modeling frequently and use correction sparingly. A checklist of strategies for supporting language can be found in Figure 11.5.

SNAPSHOT

Nina

Nina is in the eleventh grade and enjoys all her classes in school. Nina also has mental retardation and receives special education and related services. Her IEP states that the speech-language pathologist will work with Nina and will consult with her special education teacher. Her special education teacher has been working with the speech-language pathologist to provide a rich language environment not only for Nina but for all the students in her classroom. Her teacher encourages Nina to expand her vocabulary and to articulate clearly so that others can understand her. Assessment focuses on planning for instruction and evaluating progress.

Each week the teacher invites the students to share a story or discuss current community and national events. Each student has an individual audiotape and is encouraged to make a recording of his or her individual participation. The following segment reflects Nina's latest recording.

The School Boar (Board) is going to meet tonight. My father is going. They are going to vo (vote). Many people want low (lower) tax (taxes). I don't want them to cut the swim (swimming program). Everyone should vo (vote).

Nina's teacher will replay the sample for Nina, and they will discuss whether to add it to Nina's portfolio.

Observation Setting

Physical Environment

1. How does the physical setting encourage conversations among students?

Learning Environment

2. Does the teacher provide materials and activities that encourage discussion?

3. Does the teacher create student groups during some learning activities?

4. Does the teacher use appropriate modeling of language?

5. Does the teacher provide opportunities for students to use language for different purposes?

   For example:

   _____ recalling a story or event

   _____ dictating directions

   _____ presenting facts or an opinion

   _____ other

6. Does the teacher provide opportunities for using language with different audiences?

   For example:

   _____ telling a fable to younger children

   _____ making a presentation to the PTA

   _____ describing an exhibit to community members

   _____ taking a position on an issue and defending it to peers

   _____ other

7. Does the teacher employ techniques to enhance language opportunities?

   For example:

   _____ using expansion techniques

   _____ asking questions that are thought-provoking or open-ended

   _____ other

Social Environment

8. Does the school day provide for "free time" socialization among students?

   For example:

   _____ informal time before classes begin

   _____ informal time before departure at end of day

   _____ other

9. Is lunchtime scheduled in such a way as to support socialization?

   _____ sufficient time to eat and socialize

   _____ students have choices where they may sit

   _____ students are allowed to talk

   _____ other

FIGURE 11.5 • Checklist for Observing a Language-Rich Environment

► Create a checklist for observing the physical, learning, or social environment. Visit two different classrooms and use your checklist to identify aspects in the environment that support the students' oral language.

Social Environment

The social environment is important to the development of self-concept and self-esteem. These, in turn, contribute to skills in communicating effectively with others, in communicating with a variety of audiences, and in listening to others. By observing the social environment, teachers can study the relationships students have with peers and adults. Positive and supportive relationships influence language usage.

Students with Severe Communication Disorders

Some students have severe communication disorders as a result of or in combination with other disabilities, such as physical and developmental disabilities. These disabilities affect the ability to communicate.

Augmentative or Alternative Communication Systems (AAC)

Students with severe communication disorders are not able to use oral language efficiently. For example, 10-year-old Felix is an honor-roll student who loves basketball games. He has cerebral palsy and uses a motorized wheelchair. The cerebral palsy has affected Felix's ability to use oral language. Although he can produce some sounds, his oral speech is not an effective way to communicate.

Felix, like many other students with severe physical disabilities, uses an **augmentative or alternative communication (AAC)** system for oral language assistance. AAC, which IDEA considers to be assistive technology, is any method or device that assists communication. IDEA provides for the functional evaluation of a child with a disability and assistance in selecting, acquiring, and using an assistive technology (AT) device. An AAC device could be a picture book or a communication board comprising symbols. These materials require the student to point to a picture, symbol, or letter.

Many AAC systems program synthesized speech (produced electronically) or digitized speech (human speech recorded using a microphone) into the device. This type of AAC enables students with severe communication disabilities to participate more fully among peers without disabilities. Students may access the device in any number of ways: by pointing to pictures, by using a single switch, or by activating the device through eye gaze. These access methods provide a wider range of input options than traditional communication books and boards. The communication device can store frequently used messages and allows the user to access a prestored message with only one keystroke. Some systems have a word prediction feature for older children who are using written language. However, it is important to remember that AAC is only a part of a student's communication system. AAC users, as well as other people, employ a variety of communication forms, including gestures or eye gaze, eye blinks, and winks!

► **CEC Common Core Knowledge and Skills.** A beginning special educator knows communication and social interaction alternatives for individuals who are nonspeaking (GC6K2).

Assessment for AAC

The assessment and selection of a specific communication device should be a team decision, including the individual (when possible), family members, a speech-language pathologist, an occupational therapist, and an educator, as well as other interested team members. The assessment of an individual for an augmentative/alternative communication device depends on a number of factors, including chronological age, imitative ability, motor control, cognitive ability, and visual needs. As members of the team, educators contribute information on classroom and academic performance. Educators assist other team members by defining the communications skills the student needs to

► **CEC Common Core Knowledge and Skills.** A beginning special educator knows augmentative and assistive communication strategies (CC6K4).

1. What are the environments where the student spends a portion of the day?

   _____ home

   _____ school

   _____ afterschool care

   _____ other (please specify)

2. What types of communication does the
   student presently use?   How well do others understand?

   _____ points   poor   good   excellent

   _____ gestures   poor   good   excellent

   _____ eye gazes   poor   good   excellent

   _____ other (please specify)   poor   good   excellent

3. During a typical day:

   a. with whom might the student interact?

   _____   _____   _____

   _____   _____   _____

   _____   _____   _____

   b. what are some messages that the student might use?

   To state a feeling:

   To make a request:

   To ask a question:

   To greet someone or say goodbye:

4. How could additional opportunities to communicate be provided:

   a. by modifying the present system?

   b. by using another device?

FIGURE 11.6 • Questionnaire for Assessment of an Augmentative/Alternative Communication Device for a Student

complete academic and vocational courses and to interact with classmates. Some of the key questions for teachers, students, and family members to consider during an assessment are listed in Figure 11.6.

Summary

- Educators must identify young students who are experiencing difficulties as soon as possible or early problems in oral language will develop into difficulties with written language and reading.

- Educators work closely with speech-language pathologists in assessing and planning instruction for students with speech and language impairments.

- Once students are identified, best practice recommends ongoing assessment activities for the purpose of planning and monitoring instruction.

REFERENCES

Bandura, A. (1977). *Social learning theory*. Englewood Cliffs, NJ: Prentice-Hall.

Beckett, C., Nevin, A., Comella, S., Kane, N., Romero, P., & Bergquist, G. (2002). *Meeting the special needs of dual language learners with disabilities: Integrating data based instruction and the standards for teaching English for speakers of other languages.* (ERIC Document Reproduction Service No. ED 464429) [online]. Retrieved May 16, 2005. from http://www.eric.ed .gov/ERICDocs/data/ericdocs2/content_storage_01/ 0000000b/80/0d/e5/f0.pdf

Burnette, J. (2000). *Assessment of culturally and linguistically diverse students for special education eligibility* (ERIC EC Digest N. E604) [online]. Retrieved April 26, 2001 from: http://www.ericec. org/digests/e604.html.

Carrow-Woolfolk, E. (1996). *Oral and written language scales*. Minneapolis, MN: American Guidance Service.

Chomsky, N. (1967). The formal nature of language. In E. Lenneberg (Ed.), *Biological foundations of language*. New York: John Wiley.

Dunn, L. M., & Dunn, L. M. (1981). *Peabody picture vocabulary test–revised*. Circle Pines, MN: American Guidance Service.

Dunn, L. M., & Dunn, L. M. (1997). *Peabody picture vocabulary test–third edition*. Circle Pines, MN: American Guidance Service.

Dunn, L. M., Lugo, D. E., Padilla, E. R., & Dunn, L. M. (1986). *Test de vocabulario en imágenes Peabody*. Circle Pines, MN: American Guidance Service.

Hammill, D. D., Brown, V. L., Larsen, S. C., & Wiederholt, J. L. (1994). *Test of adolescent and adult language: Third edition.* Austin, TX: Pro-Ed.

Improving results for culturally and linguistically diverse students. (2000). *Research Connections 7* (Fall): 1.

Kaiser, A. P., Alpert, C. L., & Warren, S. F. (1988). Language and communication disorders. In V. B. VanHasselt, P. S. Strain, & M. Hersen (Eds.), *Handbook of developmental and physical disabilities*. New York: Pergamon Press.

Mackie, C., & Dockrell, J. E. (2004). The nature of written language deficits in children with specific language impairment. *Journal of Speech, Language, and Hearing Research 47*(6): 1469– 1483.

Moran, M. R. (1996). Educating children with communication disorders. In E. L. Meyer (Ed.), *Exceptional children in today's schools* (3rd ed.; pp. 281–314). Denver, CO: Love.

National Institute of Child Health and Human Development. (2005). *Pathways to reading: The role of oral language in the transition to reading. Developmental Psychology 41*(2): 428– 442.

Nevin, A., & Hood. A. (2002). *Improving the learning outcomes of pre-school-grade 12 students with disabilities through collaborative action research and data based instruction.* (ERIC Document Reproduction Service No. ED 467726) [online]. Retrieved May 16, 2005 from: http://www.eric.ed.gov/ERICDocs/data/ ericdocs2/content_storage_01/0000000b/80/27/a7/8e.pdf

Newcomer, P. L., & Hammill, D. D. (1997). *Test of language development primary: Third edition*. Austin, TX: Pro-Ed.

Polloway, E. A., & Smith, T. E. C. (2000). *Language instruction for students with disabilities* (2nd ed.). Denver, CO: Love.

Roseberry-McKibbin, C. (1995). Distinguishing language differences from language disorders in linguistically and culturally diverse students. *Multicultural Education* (Summer): 12–16.

Semel, E., Wiig, E. H., & W. Secord, (2003). *Clinical evaluation of language fundamentals ® Fourth Edition (CELF®–4)*. San Antonio TX: The Psychological Corporation, Harcourt Brace Jovanovich.

Williams, K. T. (1997). *Expressive vocabulary test*. Circle Pines, MN: American Guidance Service.

Zimmerman, I. L., Steiner, V. G., & Pond, R. E. (2002). *Preschool language scale–4*. San Antonio, TX: The Psychological Corporation.

12 Mathematics

Chapter Objectives

After completing this chapter, you should be able to:

- Describe contemporary thinking about mathematics.
- Describe approaches to mathematics assessment.

Overview

Mathematics assessment questions can focus on screening, identification of specific mathematics difficulties, program planning, program monitoring, and program evaluation. The assessment questions determine the assessment approaches and tests that will be used. For example, teachers may ask questions such as:

- Does the student have a disability in mathematics?
- What types of accommodations should be made?
- Where should mathematics instruction begin?
- Is the student making progress in the current mathematics curriculum?

Mathematics is an organized subject area that has comprehensive learning standards published by the National Council of Teachers of Mathematics (NCTM) (NCTM, 2000). These standards provide detailed descriptions of what students should be able to do in nine areas:

- Numbers and Operations
- Algebra
- Geometry
- Measurement
- Data Analysis and Probability
- Problem Solving
- Reasoning and Proof
- Communication
- Connections
- Representation

▶ For information on mathematics learning standards, visit the website of the National Council of Teachers of Mathematics (http://www.nctm.org).

251

The vision of NCTM is that all students, regardless of their ability, culture, ethnicity, race, language, geographic region of origin, gender, disability, or economic status, will receive high-quality mathematics instruction and assessment. This vision, coupled with the importance most schools place on learning standards, means that students with special needs should be doers of mathematics and special educators must be knowledgeable about how to assess students' mathematical knowledge and skills.

The contemporary view of mathematics instruction is based on certain beliefs. These beliefs stress that all students need to learn mathematics in order to function successfully in the world today, must develop skills and confidence that will enable them to be capable problem solvers, should be able to communicate and reason mathematically, and need to value mathematics as important and useful (Trafton & Claus, 1994).

Today's mathematics programs emphasize mathematics problems that build on students' knowledge and prior experiences and actively engage students in accomplishing mathematics. According to the NCTM, knowing mathematics means doing mathematics. The doing of mathematics necessarily involves students in problems and tasks that

- Are mathematically meaningful.
- Require students to think rather than to memorize.
- Require students to hypothesize and to generalize.
- Generate further mathematics questions or problems.
- Require that students learn while solving a task.
- Allow for more than one acceptable answer. (Speer & Brahier, 1994)

> ▶ **CEC Common Core Knowledge and Skills.** The beginning special educator should understand national, state or provincial, and local curricula standards (CC7K3).

Evaluating Mathematical Abilities

According to the *Statement of Principles on Assessment in Mathematics and Science Education* (U.S. Department of Education and the National Science Foundation [NSF], n.d.), all assessment programs have as their foundation the equity principle. This means that "Assessment should support every student's opportunity to learn important mathematics and science" (p. 9). In designing the *Statement of Principles,* the U.S. Department of Education and the NSF emphasize that *all* students are to participate in instruction and assessment activities and that assessment instruments by design and intent are to be equitable. While not specifically mentioning students with disabilities, these major government organizations indicate that all assessment tools must consider or be applicable to *all* students and that they must yield information that will improve student learning. Accordingly, all assessment programs should

- Assess knowledge and understanding in complex ways and include the assessment of higher order thinking and problem solving.
- Be fair, valid, and reliable.
- Demonstrate knowledge of how students develop and learn.
- Demonstrate administration procedures that can be interpreted only for the program's designed purposes.
- Work to improve instruction and develop curriculum.
- Promote equity by providing optimal opportunities for students to demonstrate their knowledge.

Equitable evaluation of mathematical abilities and skills presupposes a variety of approaches in order to reflect an understanding of students' abilities, culture, ethnicity, race, language, geographic region of origin, gender, disability, and economic status in assessments. Educators must place an emphasis on students' solving real-world prob-

Research-Based Practices   Two Important Research Studies

In the report "Women, Minorities, and Persons with Disabilities in Science and Engineering," the National Science Foundation (NSF) (National Science Foundation, 2004) identified an alarming trend that shows the low enrollment of persons with disabilities in advanced mathematics and science education courses and their low representation in careers that require mathematics and science. Although persons with disabilities represent approximately 20 percent of the U.S. population, they are underrepresented in mathematics and science careers. This trend is alarming because low levels of education, in general, lead to underemployment and because persons with disabilities can make unique, valuable contributions to advancing mathematics and science. For up-to-date information, visit the website of the National Science Foundation (http://www.nsf.gov).

In the "International Mathematics Report," researchers at the International Association for the Evaluation of Educational Achievement assessed the mathematics achievement of fourth and eighth graders in 49 countries. The results of this study indicate that there are concerns about mathematics achievement of U.S. students. This report provides important information on how mathematics is taught and assessed. For up-to-date information and sample test items, visit the websites of the National Center for Education Statistics at http://nces.ed.gov/timss and the International Study Center at http://www.timss.bc.edu.

lems that involve making conclusions, understanding relationships, and generating new questions (Marolda & Davidson, 1994). Assessment methods include standardized testing as well as other kinds of approaches.

Responding to Diversity

Multicultural mathematics is the study of the way persons all over the world use mathematics in a variety of activities, including counting, measuring, performing calculations, using calendars, building homes, and playing games. Attention to the ways persons of various cultures use mathematics is important to our understanding of equity in the teaching and the assessment of mathematics (Zaslavsky, 1996). Consider the following:

- The Mende people of Sierra Leone and the Yup'ik (Inuit) count by twenties. They count fingers, and toes are counted symbolically.
- The Chinese, Islamic, and Hebrew calendars are lunar. For the Islamic calendar time is reckoned from 622 C.E.
- People often base measures of length on body parts. In fact, the "foot" is still part of our system. Other cultures use the palm, hand span, and the cubit. (The cubit is an old measure based on the length of a person's forearm.) The Yup'ik people use the width of the fingers to measure the openings for fish traps.

These few examples point out the importance of using assessments that are sensitive to specific customs and practices. A student's culture, ethnicity, race, language, geographic region of origin, gender, disability, and economic status have to be considered when assessing mathematics performance.

Standardized Instruments

This section describes the use of standardized, norm-referenced tests of mathematical abilities. Standardized, norm-referenced tests are effective for screening, determining eligibility, and conducting program evaluations. Evaluators may be able to compare scores from these tests with the performance of students of similar age or grade who are part of a standardization sample. Scores from standardized mathematics tests can be used to make interpretations about an individual student's performance on several tests.

▶ **Common Core Knowledge and Skills.**
A beginning special educator can interpret information from formal and informal assessments (CC8S5).

KeyMath–Revised/Normative Update: A Diagnostic Inventory of Essential Mathematics

KeyMath–Revised/Normative Update: A Diagnostic Inventory of Essential Mathematics (Key-Math–R/NU; Connolly, 1998) is an individually administered test of mathematics skills, concepts, and operations. It is intended for use with children in kindergarten through grade 9. There are two forms, and, according to the author, the *KeyMath–R/NU* has the following five uses:

1. To guide general instructional planning.
2. To develop remedial instruction.
3. To assist in global assessment by making comparisons with the results of other instruments.
4. To use as a pretest and posttest instrument when conducting research and program evaluation.
5. To assist in assessing the usefulness of mathematics curriculum.

When developing the scope and sequence of the test content, the author surveyed the basal mathematics textbooks of many publishers as well as materials published by the National Council of the Teachers of Mathematics, then organized the resulting scope and sequence into three areas: Basic Concepts, Operations, and Applications. These comprise thirteen strands, which in turn comprise four domains (Table 12.1).

ADMINISTRATION The *KeyMath–R/NU* can be administered by regular and special education teachers, aides, paraprofessionals, counselors, and school psychologists. Depending on the age of the student, it takes approximately 35 to 50 minutes to administer this test. The Snapshot of Kara on page 257 describes how her teacher evaluated her performance on this test.

SCORING Raw scores are converted to standard scores, percentile ranks, grade and age equivalents, stanines, and normal curve equivalents. Using an optional scoring procedure for domain scores, evaluators can rate a student's scores as weak, average, or strong. Figure 12.1 shows the front cover of the test record form.

STANDARDIZATION The *KeyMath–R/NU* was renormed between October 1995 and November 1996. Stratification of the standardization sample reflects categories of age, gender, region, race, ethnicity, and economic status as estimated by parental education. The standardization sample of the *KeyMath–R/NU* was linked to the standardization samples for the *Kaufman Test of Educational Achievement (K–TEA), Peabody Individual Achievement Test–Revised (PIAT–R),* and the *Woodcock Reading Mastery Tests–Revised (WRMT–R).* For the *Key-Math–R/NU* the renorming sample comprised students who were in kindergarten through age 22. Test examinees in the norm sample took one of the complete test batteries and one or more subtests from another battery to create the linking sample. This linking approach permits the making of comparisons of test performance across batteries.

TESTS-at-a-GLANCE

KeyMath–Revised/Normative Update: A Diagnostic Inventory of Essential Mathematics (KeyMath–R/NU)

- **Publication Date:** 1998

- **Purposes:** Measures mathematics concepts, skills, operations, and applications.

- **Age/Grade Levels:** Kindergarten through grade 9.

- **Time to Administer:** 35 to 50 minutes.

- **Technical Adequacy:** Standardization sample is acceptable. The reliabilities for the subtests and the areas are too low to make instructional decisions. Examiners should determine content validity by comparing the test items with the curriculum for congruence.

- **Suggested Use:** Provides evidence of strengths and weaknesses in mathematics knowledge and skills.

TABLE 12.1 ● Content Specification of KeyMath-R/NU: Areas, Strands, and Domains

AREAS:	Basic Concepts	Operations	Applications
Strands and Domains	**Numeration** 1. Numbers 0–9 2. Numbers 0–99 3. Numbers 0–999 4. Multidigit numbers and advanced numeration topics **Rational Numbers** 1. Fractions 2. Decimals 3. Percents **Geometry** 1. Spatial and attribute relations 2. Two-dimensional shapes and their relations 3. Coordinate and transformational geometry 4. Three-dimensional shapes and their relations	**Addition** 1. Models and basic facts 2. Algorithms to add whole numbers 3. Adding rational numbers **Subtraction** 1. Models and basic facts 2. Algorithms to subtract whole numbers 3. Subtracting rational numbers **Multiplication** 1. Models and basic facts 2. Algorithms to multiply whole numbers 3. Multiplying rational numbers **Division** 1. Models and basic facts 2. Algorithms to divide whole numbers 3. Dividing rational numbers **Mental Computation** 1. Computation chains 2. Whole numbers 3. Rational numbers	**Measurement** 1. Comparisons 2. Using nonstandard units 3. Using standard units—length, area 4. Using standard units— weight, capacity **Time and Money** 1. Identifying passage of time 2. Using clocks and clock units 3. Monetary amounts to one dollar 4. Monetary amounts to one hundred dollars and business transactions **Estimation** 1. Whole and rational numbers 2. Measurement 3. Computation **Interpreting Data** 1. Charts and tables 2. Graphs 3. Probability and statistics **Problem Solving** 1. Solving routine problems 2. Understanding nonroutine problems 3. Solving nonroutine problems

Source: Connolly, A. J. (1998). *KeyMath–Revised/NU.* Circle Pines, MN: American Guidance Service, p. 6. Reprinted with permission of the publisher.

RELIABILITY The author determined alternate-form reliability by retesting approximately 70 percent of the children in grades kindergarten, 2, 4, 6, and 8 who took part in the fall standardization. The tests took between two and four weeks to administer. The reported reliability coefficients are for the subtests, areas, and the total test score. Alternate-form reliability is not available for each grade. For the subtests, the reliability coefficients ranged from the .50s to .70s; for the areas, the correlations were in the low .80s. The average alternate-form correlation for the total test was .90. The test reports split-half reliabilities by grade and calculates them by correlating the odd and even test items. For the subtests, most of the correlations were in the .70s and .80s; for the areas, the split-half reliability coefficients were in the .90s. The total test reliability coefficients were in the middle to high .90s.

VALIDITY When developing the *KeyMath–R/ NU,* the author developed a test blueprint that detailed the content of the test for the areas, strands, and domains. Next, the author developed items intended to assess mathematics achievement according to the

A — INDIVIDUAL TEST RECORD

KeyMath REVISED/NU

a diagnostic inventory of essential mathematics

AUSTIN J. CONNOLLY

Student's Name: S.C. Sex: M/F
School: _____ Grade: _____
Mathematics Teacher: _____
Examiner: L. G. Allen Date: 05-05-XX

	YEAR	MONTH	DAY
Test date	XX	7	8
Birth date	XX	3	17
Chronological age			

DATA FROM OTHER TESTS

Test	Date	Results

SCORE SUMMARY

Derived-score tables are in Appendix E of the *Manual*. For standard scores and scaled scores, indicate your selection of grade or age and fall or spring norms by circling the number of the appropriate table:

Standard Scores and Scaled Scores	Grade	Age
Fall norms (August–January)	Table 1	Table 2
Spring norms (February–July)	Table 3	Table 4

See Table 9 for percentile ranks, stanines, and normal curve equivalents. Obtain grade equivalents and age equivalents from Tables 10 and 11, respectively.

Norms used: ☐ Updated ☐ Original

BASIC CONCEPTS

Subtest	Raw Score	Scaled Score	%ile Rank
Numeration	(19)	15	95
Rational Numbers	(5)	—	—
Geometry	(16)	16	98

BASIC CONCEPTS AREA

	Raw Score	Standard Score	%ile Rank
	40 (1.)	131	98

Grade/Age Equivalent: 4.3

OPERATIONS

Subtest	Raw Score	Scaled Score	%ile Rank
Addition	(13)	18	99
Subtraction	(11)	19	99
Multiplication	(7)	16	98
Division	(3)	12	75
Mental Computation	(8)	17	99

OPERATIONS AREA

	Raw Score	Standard Score	%ile Rank
	42 (2.)	126	96

Grade/Age Equivalent: 4.2

APPLICATIONS

Subtest	Raw Score	Scaled Score	%ile Rank
Measurement	(18)	19	99
Time and Money	(22)	19	99
Estimation	(12)	19	99
Interpreting Data	(11)	16	98
Problem Solving	(12)	16	98

APPLICATIONS AREA

	Raw Score	Standard Score	%ile Rank
	75 (3.)	145	99

Grade/Age Equivalent: 7.0

TOTAL TEST

	1.	2.	3.	Total Test Raw Score	Standard Score	%ile Rank	NCE (optional)	Stanine	Grade Equivalent (optional)	Age Equivalent
	40	42	75	= 157	136	99	99	9	5.5	11-3

FIGURE 12.1 ● KeyMath–Revised/NU Individual Test Record

Source: KeyMath: A Diagnostic Inventory of Essential Mathematics Revised Normative Update (KeyMath-R/NU) Individual Test Record Summary by Austin J. Connolly © 1998 American Guidance Service, Inc., 4201 Woodland Road, Circle Pines, Minnesota 55014–1796. Reproduced with permission of publisher. All rights reserved. www.agsnet.com

blueprint. When using these achievement tests, educators must determine the content validity themselves. Test examiners should review the taught curriculum and determine the extent to which the test items measure the curriculum.

According to the manual, test developers determined construct validity in several ways. The manual presents evidence demonstrating that knowledge about mathematics increases with age, that the subtests intercorrelate with the areas and the total test score, and that scores on the *KeyMath–R/NU* correlate with scores on other tests of mathematical achievement.

SUMMARY The *KeyMath–Revised/Normative Update: A Diagnostic Inventory of Essential Mathematics* is an individually administered test of mathematics achievement. The reliabilities for the subtests and the areas are too low to make instructional decisions. The educator should determine content validity by comparing the test items with the curriculum for congruence.

Research-Based Practices | **What Are the Effects and Perceived Consequences of an Extended Time Accommodation on Mathematics Tests?**

A frequently used test accommodation for students with disabilities is the use of extended or extra time on standardized mathematics tests. Two researchers (Elliott & Marquart, 2004) investigated the effects and consequences of extended time on mathematics tests in three groups of students. The students were identified as either having a disability, not having a disability, or educationally at risk in mathematics. Surprisingly, the only group that appeared to benefit from extended time was the at-risk students. There was little difference in the performance between the groups who were identified as having or not having disabilities.

The most frequently used test-taking strategies that all students employed were answering every question, reviewing pictures or graphs, rereading questions, and reviewing difficult test items. However, the students with disabilities reported that they felt more motivated and relaxed with extended time. The students at risk in mathematics disclosed that the extended time accommodation enabled them to perform better and that the test seemed easier.

Elliott and Marquart speculated about why the group with disabilities did not appear to benefit from extended time. They wondered whether students with disabilities can maintain attention, effort, and motivation during extended time. The researchers suggested that unless specific test-taking strategies or other accommodations are coupled with extended time, this accommodation may have little benefit for students with disabilities. What do you think? Should students with disabilities be provided with extended time on tests? Why or why not?

SNAPSHOT

Kara

Kara is a 12-year-old in sixth grade. Her interests include drawing and soccer. Kara has an exuberant sense of humor and loves to play jokes on her friends and family. She has just finished making a book of her drawings that she intends to give to her grandmother who lives with Kara, her 5-year-old brother John, and her mother and father. Kara was diagnosed as having a learning disability in mathematics when she was in third grade.

OBSERVATION: Kara was observed in her sixth-grade classroom. The 25 other students in the classroom were working in small groups solving problems that the teacher had assigned. The class was lively and the students were engaging in their work—all except Kara. Kara sat with a small group of three other students. Kara appeared to be unsure of how she could contribute to the problem-solving activity. She was quiet, had a puzzled look on her face, and was listening to the students in the group.

TEACHER'S COMMENTS: Kara has lagged considerably behind her peers in mathematics. The rest of the class has been working on graphing, geometry, and probability. An examination of Kara's recent homework showed that she has trouble with basic number facts and that she reverses numbers when writing them.

SUMMARY OF TEST PERFORMANCE: At the end of the last school year, the IEP team met to review Kara's program. The special education consultant reported that Kara's full scale intelligence as measured by the *Wechsler Intelligence Scale–III (WISC–III)* was 128, above average. On the *Kaufman Test of Educational Achievement (K–TEA/NU)*, Kara scored above average on the reading and spelling subtests but considerably below average on the Mathematical Applications and Mathematical Computation subtests. On the *KeyMath–Revised/NU* her scores in the areas of Basic Concepts, Operations, and Applications were all well below average.

PLANNING INSTRUCTION: Kara's teacher and the school's learning specialist met to discuss the assessment results. It was apparent that Kara was struggling with basic mathematics processes but that she grasps mathematics concepts. Kara's teacher felt that instruction should emphasize basic mathematics processes, such as addition, subtraction, multiplication, and division and that it was critically important to continue instruction on mathematics concepts. Curriculum materials were selected and a guide was identified to track Kara' progress.

How It Works! Assessing Mathematics

Tiffany is a 14-year-old who lives in the northwestern United States. Because her parents are in the military, she moved several times during her early years of schooling. Although there were repeated referrals to special education, school teams determined that Tiffany did not meet eligibility criteria for services. Two years ago, her family moved again, and she started a new school. Upon her arrival, a referral was made and Tiffany was identified as a student with a learning disability, with specific difficulties in reading, written language, and mathematics.

Mr. Wu, Tiffany's special education teacher, reported that Tiffany experiences difficulties with math facts, basic mathematics operations, such as addition, subtraction, multiplication, and division. Basic mathematics facts are not automatic. She seems to work best when using concrete manipulative aids, such as blocks, when learning mathematics. The meanings of mathematics vocabulary terms, such as "together," "sum," and "in all" are frequently confused. She frequently transposes numbers such as 6 and 9.

The *KeyMath/NU* was administered to Tiffany in order to determine specific strengths and weaknesses. During the session, Tiffany was pleasant and cooperative. Rapport was established easily and she was appropriately interactive. During the testing session, Tiffany tended to become discouraged as the items became more difficult. It was sometimes necessary to slow the pace of the verbal questions and directions. The average of mean score is 100 and the *Key-Math Revised/NU* has a standard deviation of 15.

Tiffany's performance on the *KeyMath* showed below average performance on both the age and grade norms. When the subtests were compared, she had relatively stronger performance on the Geometry, Multiplication, and Measurement subtests. She experienced considerable difficulties on Mental Computation, which requires memory, and demonstrated frustration when completing the items on this subtest. She had difficulties reading dates such as 10/21/07. Her performance suggests that attention is needed in rational numbers, addition, subtraction, long division, mental computation, time and money, estimation, interpreting data, and problem solving.

Area/Subtest	Scaled Score Age Norms	Scaled Score Grade Norms	Percentile Rank Age Norms	Percentile Rank Grade Norms
Basic Concepts (area)	80	81	9	10
Numeration	5	5	5	5
Rational Numbers	6	6	9	9
Geometry	8	8	25	25
Operations	79	80	8	9
Addition	5	5	5	5
Subtraction	6	6	9	9
Multiplication	9	10	37	50
Division	5	5	5	5
Applications	82	84	12	14
Measurement	8	8	25	25
Time and Money	7	7	16	16
Estimation	6	6	9	9
Interpreting Data	7	7	16	16
Problem Solving	5	5	5	9
Total Test	81	82	10	12

Test of Mathematical Abilities–2

The *Test of Mathematical Abilities–2* (TOMA–2; Brown, Cronin, & McEntire, 1994) is a norm-referenced test of attitudes toward mathematics, mathematics vocabulary, computation, general information relating to mathematics, and mathematical story problems. The *TOMA–2* can be individually administered or group administered to students in grades 3 through 12 and contains five subtests:

Attitude Toward Math. Students respond to questions on a 3-point scale on their opinions about mathematics. This scale is an adaptation of the *Estes Attitude Scales* (Estes, Estes, Richards, & Roettger, 1981).

Vocabulary. Students read 20 mathematical terms and define them in writing in English. This subtest is administered to students who are at least 11 years old.

Computation. Students solve 25 arithmetic problems in writing in an answer booklet.

General Information. Students respond orally to 30 problems relating to general applications about mathematics.

Story Problems. After reading a word problem, students respond in writing in an answer booklet. This subtest is not administered to students who are nonreaders.

ADMINISTRATION The *TOMA–2* can be individually administered or group administered.

SCORING Raw scores convert to standard scores and percentile ranks. Subtest scores have a mean of 10 and a standard deviation of 3. The total test scores are called Math Quotients; they have a mean of 100 and a standard deviation of 15. The test examiner can perform an error analysis on individual responses to items that students have written in the student answer booklet.

STANDARDIZATION The standardization sample for *TOMA–2* includes approximately 1,500 students residing in five states. The sample approximated U.S. census information according to gender, residence, geographic region, and race.

RELIABILITY Reliability coefficients are in the .80s and .90s. Reliability is acceptable.

VALIDITY While there is some evidence of validity, much of it is from the previous edition. Examiners should carefully compare the mathematics curriculum with the test items in order to determine content validity.

SUMMARY The *Test of Mathematical Abilities–2 (TOMA–2)* is an individually administered or group administered test of various aspects of mathematical abilities. Information of reliability and validity is sketchy. Test examiners should evaluate the content validity of the test. The *TOMA–2* is most useful as a screening test.

TESTS-at-a-GLANCE

Test of Mathematical Abilities–2 (TOMA–2)

- **Publication Date:** 1994
- **Purposes:** Measures attitudes toward mathematics, mathematics vocabulary, computation, general information relating to mathematics, and mathematical story problems.
- **Age/Grade Levels:** Grades 3 through 12.
- **Time to Administer:** 45 to 90 minutes.
- **Technical Adequacy:** Information on reliability and validity is sparse. Test examiners are encouraged to evaluate the content validity of the test. The *TOMA–2* is best used as a screening measure.
- **Suggested Use:** Provides some evidence of strengths and limitations in mathematics knowledge and skills. Should be used in combination with other instruments.

Connecting Assessment with Instruction

A fundamental principle is that assessment of mathematical abilities and skills forms a link with mathematics instruction. Linking instruction with assessment in mathematics means that assessment occurs as a normal part of the student's work. Assessment activities should emerge from the teaching situation. The student does not stop work to do an assessment; the work and the assessment are linked. Examples of this type of assessment include the use of journals, notebooks, essays, oral reports, homework, classroom discussions, group work, and interviews. These assessment activities can occur individually or in small groups and can take place during one session or over multiple sessions (Marolda & Davidson, 1994).

The conditions for assessment are similar to the conditions for doing meaningful tasks. Students should have sufficient time, have access to peers, be able to use appropriate tools (books, calculators, manipulatives, etc.), and have the chance to revise their work. Assessment tasks are meaningful and multidimensional. They should provide students with the opportunity to demonstrate mathematical abilities, including problem solving, drawing conclusions, understanding relationships, and generating new questions. Feedback to students is specific, meaningful, prompt, and informs the students' thinking about mathematics. Students participate in the assessment process. They help to generate and apply standards or rubrics. Self-assessment and peer assessment become part of the assessment process.

One of the most important aspects of assessment is feedback. Standardized, norm-referenced assessment coupled with feedback from peers and teachers encourages the development of mathematical and scientific thinking. Ways in which the teacher can gather information and provide feedback to parents and students, in addition to standardized norm-referenced tests, include:

- Criterion-referenced assessment
- Probes
- Error analysis
- Oral descriptions
- Written descriptions
- Checklists and questionnaires
- Curriculum-based assessment
- Interviews
- Conferences
- Student journals and notebooks
- Performance-based assessment
- Portfolios
- Exhibitions (NCTM, 2006)

Criterion-Referenced Assessment

Instead of comparing a student's performance to a norm group, criterion-referenced tests measure a student's performance with respect to a well-defined content domain. While norm-referenced tests in mathematics allow for discrimination between the performance of individual students on specific test items, criterion-referenced tests provide a description of knowledge, skills, or behaviors in a specific range, or domain, of test items.

BRIGANCE® Diagnostic Inventories

The *BRIGANCE® Diagnostic Inventories* are criterion-referenced tests that are similar in purpose, scoring, administration, and interpretation. These inventories assess mastery of mathematics skills and concepts, and they are useful in program planning and in monitoring programs.

Curriculum-Based Assessment

Curriculum-based assessment (CBA) is an approach that uses direct assessment to determine what students know and can do. When using CBAs in mathematics, students respond to questions, vocabulary, or carefully selected mathematics problems chosen from the students' mathematics curriculum. These carefully selected problems or questions are used with CBA to sample mathematics knowledge and skills and are helpful in diagnosing and assisting with students' difficulties and assist in planning and evaluating instruction. For example, suppose a teacher wants to determine why a student seems to confuse basic mathematics operations. The student seems to be able to successfully solve problems, but there seems to be confusion.

▶ Search the ERIC database at http://www.eric.ed.gov to find additional resources on curriculum-based assessment. Share your results with other learners.

The teacher presents the problems, but this time they are grouped according to the algorithm as in Figure 12.2. The teacher then can help by showing the student how organize the problems. Eventually, using another probe, the teacher is able to use fading to gradually lighten the lines that separate the problems until the student does not need them to successfully complete the problem.

Teachers can implement CBA during the process of instruction. When administering a CBA, the teacher should document the student's performance during each of the following steps: step 1 (baseline), step 2 (instruction), and step 3 (new baseline):

Step 1 (Baseline). The teacher identifies the area of mathematical performance that needs observation and measures whether the student can perform the task. Examples include number recognition, counting, addition, subtraction, and so on.

Step 2 (Instruction). The teacher probes the task. For example, to facilitate number recognition the teacher asks the student to say, trace, recognize, and write a numeral.

Step 3 (New Baseline). The teacher measures whether the student can perform the task.

Suggestions for Accommodations When Using CBAs in Mathematics

Teachers may find that accommodations are useful when constructing and administering CBAs in mathematics. The following list contains three types of accommodations when considering CBA in mathematics instruction:

1. *Instructional accommodations*
   - Change from written presentation to oral presentation.
   - Combine verbal instruction with written explanation.

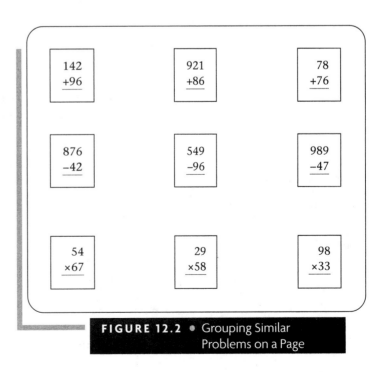

FIGURE 12.2 • Grouping Similar Problems on a Page

Research-Based Practices Using Curriculum-Based Assessment to Identify Early Mathematics Skills

In a research study of first-grade students, Clarke and Shinn (2004) determined that curriculum-based assessment measures of early mathematics skills are reliable, valid, and sensitive. Four CBAs were administered to students:

1. The *Oral Counting Measure* required students to count aloud. If students stopped or hesitated for 3 seconds to say the next number, they were told to say the next number. Scores were based on the total number of numbers that were correctly counted in 1 minute.

2. The *Number Identification Measure* required students to say aloud the numbers between 0 and 20 when presented in written form. When students stopped or hesitated for 3 seconds to recognize the number, the number was identified as incorrect. Scores were based on the total number of printed numerals recognized in 1 minute.

3. The *Quantity Discrimination Measure* involved students identifying the larger of two written numerals. When students stopped or hesitated for 3 seconds, students were directed to attempt the next item. Scores were based on the total number of printed numerals recognized as larger in 1 minute.

4. The *Missing Number Measure* required that students identify the missing number from a list of numbers between 0 and 20. When students stopped or hesitated for 3 seconds to identify the number, the researcher told students the correct answers and asked to proceed to the next Item. Students' scores were calculated based on the total number of missing numbers that were accurately identified in 1 minute.

- Require fewer problems to be completed.
- Provide additional practice.
- Slow the pace of instruction.
- Provide additional time to complete problems.
- Take tests orally.
2. *Materials accommodations*
- Use manipulatives.
- Place fewer problems on a page.
- Use color cues or other cues for mathematical operations.
- Simplify the problems.
- Combine tactile mode with visual, oral, or kinesthetic modes.
3. *Environmental accommodations*
- Change location of instruction or test.
- Change time of day for instruction or test.
- Provide a work area that is quiet and free of distractions.
- Change lighting of work area.
- Change seating arrangement.

▶ **CEC Common Core Knowledge and Skills.** A beginning special educator selects, adapts, and modifies assessments to accommodate the unique abilities and needs of individuals with disabilities (GC8S3).

Error Analysis

The purposes of error analysis are to (1) identify the patterns of errors or mistakes that students make in their work, (2) understand why students make the errors, and (3) provide targeted instruction to correct the errors. When conducting an error analysis, the teacher checks the student's mathematics problems and categorizes the errors. The following is a list of errors that students commonly make in various mathematical areas (Ashlock, 1986; Tindal & Marston, 1990).

Addition and Subtraction

- Lack of understanding of regrouping.
- Confusion of 1s and 10s in carrying and writing.
- Forgetting to carry 10s and 100s.
- Forgetting to regroup when subtracting 10s and 100s.
- Regrouping when it is not required.
- Incorrect operation (the student subtracts instead of adding or vice versa).
- Lack of knowledge of basic number facts.

Multiplication and Division

- Forgetting to carry in multiplication.
- Carrying before multiplying.
- Ignoring place value in division.
- Recording the answer from left to right in multiplication.
- Lack of alignment of work in columns.
- Lack of knowledge of basic number facts.

Fractions

- Incorrect cancellation.
- Failure to reduce to lowest common denominator.
- Ignoring the remainder.
- Incorrect conversion of mixed numbers to fractions.

Word Problems

- Difficulty in reading.
- Inability to relate to context of problem.
- Inability to understand the language and vocabulary of the problem.
- Difficulty in identifying the relevant and the irrelevant information.
- Difficulty in identifying the number of steps required to solve the problem.
- Trouble in doing mathematical operations (addition, subtraction, multiplication, division).

After conducting an error analysis, summarize the error patterns. Notice, however, that many errors that students make do not fall into a pattern, and some patterns that emerge do not indicate a serious problem. Teachers must view error analysis as a preliminary form of assessment and should conduct further evaluation of the student's work.

Oral Descriptions

Verbal descriptions of a student's work provide immediate feedback to a student by a teacher or peer. Oral descriptions are quick, efficient, and direct, and blend easily into instruction. They must not be off the cuff; oral descriptions should be as well thought out as written descriptions. Oral descriptions are helpful for program planning and program evaluation. Oral descriptions do have several drawbacks, however. They can be subjective and, since the descriptions are given verbally, there is no permanent record. In addition, specific disabilities limit the ability of the student to understand, remember, or reply to the description.

Written Descriptions

A written description is a brief narrative that records feedback about the student's work that the student, teachers, or parents can share. A written description, like an oral description, conveys an impression of important aspects of the student's work. Written descriptions are useful for program planning and program evaluation.

Before writing the narrative, the teacher carefully reviews the student's work. The teacher then writes the description, noting areas of strength as well as any problems. A written description provides information to the student about the quality of the work. Because it is a record, the student can refer to it as he or she continues to work.

For example, a student is asked to solve the following problem:

> Luke wants to paint one wall of his room. The wall is 20 feet wide and 8 feet high. It takes one can of paint to cover 80 square feet, and the paint is sold at $10.99 a can. What else does Luke need to think of? Make a plan for Luke's trip to the store for supplies for this painting job. (Kulm, 1994, p. 12)

After examining the student's solution, a teacher can comment on the organization, labeling, problem-solving processes, computations, spelling, and language use. Moreover, the teacher can discuss the use of mathematics to solve real-world problems, completeness of the solution, the student's disposition toward mathematics, the ability to plan ahead, work habits, and attention to detail (Kulm, 1994). Two disadvantages to using written descriptions are that the parents may have difficulty reading or they may not have knowledge of written English.

Checklists and Questionnaires

Checklists and questionnaires are convenient ways to provide feedback about a student's work. Teachers can quickly complete a checklist. Figure 12.3 is an example of a checklist for teachers to provide feedback about the mathematical disposition or student confidence, willingness, perseverance, and interest in doing mathematics. Checklists are useful for screening, diagnosis, program planning, and program evaluation.

Questionnaires allow teachers and students to collect information in more detail than checklists. Open-ended questionnaires allow respondents to express their attitudes, opinions, and knowledge in depth; structured questionnaires allow respondents simply to fill in one or two words or circle a response.

Interviews

Chapter 5 discusses the topic of conducting interviews. There are special considerations when using this technique in mathematics assessment. Interviews can guide discussions, encourage students, and determine disposition toward mathematics. One basic approach is to interview students individually about their likes and dislikes, asking questions such as "What do you like about mathematics?" "What are your interests?" "What don't you like?" Interviews can help in screening, diagnosis, program planning, and program evaluation.

Structured interviews are a more systematic way to assess mathematics performance. A structured interview is an opportunity to observe, question, and discuss mathematics and to elicit unexpected information about the student. Kulm (1994) wrote that teachers can question students about a physical activity, usch as measuring the length of a table. Students who lack reading or communication skills can use pantomime or objects to demonstrate what they know.

What students have experienced:	Date and Activity	
1. Confidence in using mathematics	*10/29* Correctly solved all problems assigned.	*1/19* Actively worked as part of small group that solved a problem.
2. Flexibility in doing mathematics	*11/2* Generated several ways of solving an addition problem.	*4/8* Students challenged each other on solution methods.
3. Persevering at mathematical tasks	*9/29* Worked all day on collecting and displaying data – favorite ice cream.	*2/5* Kept working on different ways of making change for 50¢ – all ways found.
4. Curiosity in doing mathematics	*11/10* Solved a "what if" question, expressing answer in own words.	*4/7* In small group generated own units for measuring room.
5. Reflecting on their own thinking	Every day students explain working on a problem.	their thinking after
6. Valuing applications of mathematics	*2/23* All students brought in pictures for math applications bulletin board.	*5/24* field trip to science museum to see how mathematics is used.
7. Appreciating role of mathematics	*10/15* Brought in newspaper articles that used mathematical terms.	*1/29* Appreciated place-value system by finding sums using Roman numerals.

FIGURE 12.3 • Mathematics Disposition

Source: Reprinted with permission from *Curriculum and Evaluation Standards for School Mathematics,* copyright © 1989 by the National Council of Teachers of Mathematics. All rights reserved.

One example of using a structured interview is to give students a piece of rectangular-shaped paper. The teacher records the students' answers to the following questions (Kulm, 1994):

1. What is a perimeter of a rectangle?
2. What is a perimeter used for?
3. Show me the perimeter of the rectangle.
4. How could you measure the perimeter?
5. How would you estimate the perimeter?
6. What do you estimate the perimeter to be?
7. Here is a ruler. Can you use this to check your estimate by measuring the perimeter?
8. How could we use this information?
9. Are there other ways to find the perimeter without measuring all four sides?

Conferences

A conference is a conversation about the student's work that can include the student, educators, and/or parents. Participants in a conference share their views of the student's work with the goal of providing feedback and recommendations. Teacher-student conferences can be helpful when assessing one piece of work or when summarizing the student's work over a period of time. The discussion in a conference can be strictly verbal, or the teacher or evaluator may choose to audiotape it, videotape it, or summarize it in written form. Conferences are effective for diagnosis, program planning, and program evaluation.

Student Journals

Journals induce students to reflect on their own work, communicate about their learning, and document their progress (Kulm, 1994). Students can keep a notebook or journal that allows them to record their work, attitudes, and feelings about mathematics. In a journal students can indicate what they like and don't like about doing mathematics and which areas are giving them difficulty. Journals are effective for program planning and program evaluation. The following is a sample mathematics journal outline (Kulm, 1994):

Mathematics topic:

Two examples of problems that I solved:

Two important ideas:

What I understand best:

What I need more work on:

How I can use this topic in real life:

Performance-Based Assessment

As a measure of mathematics instruction, performance-based assessment requires students to demonstrate mathematical abilities, skills, and dispositions, such as developing a product or demonstrating an understanding of concepts and relationships. This type of assessment is useful in program planning and program evaluation. The following are examples of performance tasks:

- Pretend we own an electronics store. We need to know whether to have more CD players or more MP3 players for sale in our store. What could we decide to do?
- Here is a rectangle. About how many centimeters long would you estimate its perimeter to be? Use the ruler to measure the perimeter. How close was your estimate? (Kulm, 1994, p. 44).
- Use a spreadsheet program to make a table of multiples of the first five whole numbers (Kulm, 1994, p. 45).

Figure 12.4 provides descriptors for mathematics performance.

Portfolios

As described in Chapter 6, a portfolio is a deliberate collection of a student's work over time that demonstrates the student's efforts, progress, and achievement. When documenting and assessing mathematical abilities, portfolios provide information about conceptual understanding, problem solving, reasoning, communication abilities, disposition toward mathematics, creativity, work habits, and attitudes. Mathematics portfolios help students see that the study of mathematics is more than discrete rules and procedures (Kulm, 1994). Portfolios in mathematics assessment aid in program planning and program evaluation.

Descriptors for Grades K–2

Exploration: Becomes aware of math concepts; interacts with materials.

Emergent: Begins to understand math concepts: needs assistance to produce work.

Beginning: Solves problems with assistance: begins to learn and apply math facts.

Developing: Solves problems with some assistance.

Capable: Solves problems independently; demonstrates accuracy on math tasks.

Experienced: Uses varied strategies to solve problems independently.

Descriptors for Grades 3–5

Emergent: Some understanding of math concepts; needs considerable assistance to complete work.

Beginning: Solves problems and complete assignments with support; has some understanding of math concepts.

Developing: Solves problems with assistance; needs support to complete assignments.

Capable: Completes assignments in a timely fashion; requires occasional assistance.

Strong: Completes some enrichment/extra credit math work; almost always solves problems independently.

Exceptional: Applies previously learned math concepts; independently completes math assignments.

FIGURE 12.4 ● Math Descriptors

Source: Adapted from "ASCD Yearbook 1996 Communicating Student Learning," edited by Thomas R. Guiskey, 1996. Alexandria, VA: Association for Supervision and Curriculum Development, Figure 5.1, p. 52, and Figure 9.2, p. 94.

A portfolio is not just a folder of practice worksheets or of all the work that the student has completed. The selection of the contents of a portfolio is always a carefully considered process. The following are suggestions for inclusion in student mathematics portfolios:

- Photographs of students' bridge-building projects, using rods of different lengths
- Worksheets that involve students' creating new shapes
- Projects that involve students' using software to design quilts from squares
- Performance tasks that require students to demonstrate knowledge of geometry
- Journals in which students record problem-solving processes
- Experiments with probability
- Audiotapes of students collaborating on projects
- Videotapes of students constructing designed structures or demonstrating what they have learned after analyzing data on rainfall (Kulm, 1994; National Research Council, 1993)

Exhibitions

An exhibition is a display of a student's work that summarizes and synthesizes what the student has accomplished. Customarily, it demonstrates knowledge, abilities, skills, and attitudes concerning one project or a unit of work. In mathematics assessment, exhibitions are useful because students realize that doing mathematics is more than just a series of worksheets or exercises, that it involves conceptual understanding, problem solving, and reasoning, and teachers find them effective in program planning and program evaluation.

Self-Assessment

Self-assessment provides students with an opportunity to review concepts and identify mathematical processes. It is an occasion for students to reflect on their learning. Figure 12.5 is an example of a checklist that students use when assessing their own learning.

Student's Name _____		Date _____			
After reading the mathematical word problem I can:	1 Great!	2	3	4	5 Darn!
1. draw a picture to help solve the problem.					
2. identify the operations to solve the problem.					
3. list the steps to solve the problem and explain why each step is necessary.					
4. use correct labeling.					
5. use numbers and symbols to write equation(s) to solve the problem.					
6. verify the results.					
7. interpret the results.					

FIGURE 12.5 ● Self-Assessment Checklist

Peer Assessment

Peer assessment allows students insight into the thinking and reasoning abilities of their peers. By engaging in collaborative learning and problem solving, students have an opportunity to reflect on the learning processes of their peers as well as on their own. Figure 12.6 is an example of a checklist that students use when conducting a peer assessment.

Observing the Student within the Classroom Environment

In Chapter 5 you learned about the importance of considering the student within the physical, learning, and social environments. The interactions between the student and the environment are crucial assessment considerations.

Physical Environment

The physical environment can influence the student's mathematics performance. The temperature, lighting, and seating arrangements of the teaching and learning spaces affect how well the student performs.

Learning Environment

A comfortable learning environment mathematics and can contribute to mathematics achievement. The curriculum, instructional methods, materials, and the assessment procedures are all areas of concern. The learning environment can promote a positive disposition toward mathematics. Students will be willing to do mathematics when

	😞	😐	🙂
Student's Name_____ Date _____ Peer's Name_____			
1. My peer used the data in the tables to solve the mathematical story problem.			
2. My peer used correct mathematical notation.			
3. My peer used pictures to illustrate the story problem.			
4. My peer used labeling.			
5. My peer's work is neat.			

FIGURE 12.6 ● Peer Assessment

(1) mathematics problems are challenging, (2) students realize that mathematics problems are worth doing, (3) mathematics problems are accessible to a wide range of students, (4) a variety of instructional approaches are available, and (5) multiple assessment procedures check learning.

Social Environment

Relationships with students and teachers affect mathematics and achievement. The social environment is pivotal in the development of self-concept and self-esteem. These, in turn, contribute to a positive disposition toward mathematics. By observing the social environment, teachers can study the relationships students have with peers and adults.

Summary

- Contemporary views of mathematics stress that all children need to learn mathematics in order to function successfully in the world today.
- Equitable assessment of mathematical abilities and skills presupposes a variety of approaches in order to reflect an understanding of students' abilities, culture, ethnicity, race, language, geographic region or origin, gender, disability, and economic level.
- Standardized norm-referenced tests of mathematics are effective for screening, determining eligibility, and conducting program evaluations.

- Mathematics assessment should be linked with instruction.
- Curriculum-based assessment uses direct assessment to determine what students know and can do.
- Mathematics assessment strategies include error analysis, oral descriptions, written descriptions, checklists and questionnaires, interviews, conferences, student journals, performance-based assessment, portfolios, exhibitions, self-assessment, and peer assessment.

REFERENCES

Ashlock, R. B. (1996). *Error patterns in computation: A semi-programmed approach* (5th ed.). Columbus, OH: Merrill.

Brown, V. L., Cronin, M. E., & McEntire, E. (1994). *Test of mathematical abilities, 2nd ed.* Austin, TX: Pro-Ed.

Clarke, B., & Shinn, M. R. (2004). A preliminary investigation into the investigation and development of early mathematics curriculum-based measurement. *School Psychology Review 33*(2): 234–248.

Connolly, A. J. (1998). *KeyMath–revised/NU*. Circle Pines, MN: American Guidance Service.

Elliott, S. N., & Marquart, A. M. (2004). Extended time as a testing accommodation: Its effects and perceived consequences. *Exceptional Children 70*(3): 349–367.

Estes, T. H., Estes, J. J., Richards, H. C., & Roettger, D. (1991). *Estes attitude scale.* Austin, TX: Pro-Ed.

Kulm, G. (1994). *Mathematics assessment.* San Francisco: Jossey-Bass.

Marolda, M. R., & Davidson, P. S. (1994). Assessing mathematical abilities and learning approaches. In C. A. Thornton & N. S. Bley (Eds.), *Windows of opportunity* (pp. 83–113). Reston, VA: National Council of Teachers for Mathematics.

National Center for Education Statistics. (2003). *Third international mathematics report.* Washington, DC: Author.

National Council for Teachers of Mathematics. (2006). *NCTM standards.* Retrieved January 20, 2006 from http://www.nctm.org/standards/

National Research Council. (1993). *Measuring up.* Washington, DC: National Academy Press.

National Science Foundation. (2004). *Women, minorities, and persons with disabilities in science and engineering.* NSF 04–317. Retrieved December 26, 2005 from http://www.asp.gov

Speer, W. R., & Brahier, D. J. (1994). Rethinking the teaching and learning of mathematics. In C. A. Thornton & N. S. Bley (Eds.), *Windows of opportunity* (pp. 41–59). Reston, VA: National Council of the Teachers of Mathematics.

Tindal, G. A., & Marston, D. B. (1990). *Classroom-based assessment.* Columbus, OH: Merrill.

Trafton, P. R., & Claus, A. S. (1994). A changing curriculum for a changing age. In C. A. Thornton & N. S. Bley (Eds.), *Windows of opportunity* (pp. 19–39). Reston, VA: National Council of the Teachers of Mathematics.

U.S. Department of Education, and National Science Foundation. (n.d.). *Statement of principles on assessment in mathematics and science education.* Washington, DC: U.S. Department of Education and National Science Foundation.

Zaslavsky, C. (1996). *The multicultural classroom.* Portsmouth, NH: Heinemann.

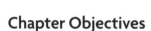

13 Cognitive Development

Chapter Objectives

After completing this chapter,
you should be able to:

- Explain the concept of intelligence tests
  as samples of behavior.
- Discuss the stability of test performance.
- Describe specific tests of intelligence.

Overview

What is intelligence? What makes us intelligent? The nature of intelligence has received a great deal of attention over the years. One view of intelligence is that it is an arbitrary concept, impossible to define or quantify. Other views are that intelligence consists of multifaceted, complex, highly organized abilities that are identifiable and measurable. One common conception is that intelligence is the ability to apply prior knowledge to new situations. The specific intelligence tests we describe in this chapter reflect the many views of the construct of intelligence.

Although there is still a great deal that we do not know about intelligence, Sternberg (1996) has described nine "truths" about intelligence:

- Intelligence is multidimensional. There is still a great deal that we have to learn about the dimensions of intelligence.
- The social order of our society is in part the creation of tests, which sort and categorize people according to the abilities they measure.
- Intelligence is teachable to some extent, but extreme changes are unlikely at this time.
- Intelligence tests measure skills that are of considerable importance in school and of moderate importance in success on the job.
- Intelligence tests can be helpful when measuring abilities, but only under proper use and with proper interpretation.

- Intelligence test scores have been rising since the 1930s in the United States and in other countries.
- Intelligence is the result of the influences of heredity and environment.
- We still have much to learn about the relationships between race, intelligence, and environment.
- While tests of intelligence provide an indication of cognitive skills, they are not measures of the worth of individuals.

Intelligence Tests as Samples of Behavior

If intelligence could be measured directly, we would be able to monitor the electrical activities, neurochemical changes, and neurobiological changes that occur during cognition. As educators, we rely, instead, on indirect measures or tests to estimate intelligence. Intelligence tests don't sample intelligence, but rather the behaviors that we associate with intelligence. We use intelligence tests to sample intelligent behavior. While intelligence tests sample behaviors, our assumption is that the sample provides information about the intellectual abilities of individuals.

In addition to standardized tests, there are other sources of information about students' abilities (McLouglin & Lewis, 2005). These information resources can be useful in confirming the results of standardized instruments; for students who have minority group heritage, educators may need to rely on sources other than standardized tests for clues about cognitive abilities. Sources of information that can be gathered when determining cognitive abilities include school records; standardized results on achievement, behavior, and other tests; developmental histories; report card grades; observations of students; and parental reports.

Although there are many intelligence tests, an analysis of them shows that they sample similar behaviors. Salvia and Ysseldyke (2004) have described these behaviors:

Discrimination. Intelligence tests sample skills that relate to figural, symbolic, or semantic discrimination usually by asking the student to find the item that is different from the other items.

Generalization. Intelligence tests sample skills relating to figural, symbolic, or semantic understanding by asking students to recognize the response that goes with the stimulus item.

Motor Behavior. Intelligence tests ask young children to demonstrate a motor response, such as throwing objects, constructing block towers, or placing objects in certain places on a board. The tests ask older students to draw geometric forms, solve mazes, or reproduce designs from memory. In addition to these items, many other test items evaluate motor abilities by asking students to point out, imitate, or perform other motor activities in order to complete certain test items.

General Information. These items evaluate what the individual has learned. Examples of these items include, "What is the opposite of uncle?" and "How many eggs are in a dozen?"

Vocabulary. Intelligence tests assess knowledge of vocabulary in different ways—by asking individuals to point to a picture the test has named, to define words the examiner presents orally, or to identify a word that matches a definition.

Induction. Intelligence tests present students with several stimuli and ask them to induce or to infer a general principle. For example, after seeing a rock, block of wood, metal object, and a toothpick, the individual must describe the general rule about why certain objects float.

Comprehension. Intelligence tests ask students to demonstrate understanding of or the nature of meaning of certain stimuli. Students have to show that they understand directions, certain materials, or societal customs. Some tests ask the student to respond to certain situations such as, "What should you do if you see a young child playing with an electrical cord?"

Sequencing. Intelligence tests require students to identify the correct sequences for a series of items. The items can, for example, consist of numbers, geometric figures, or abstract geometric designs.

Detail Recognition. A few tests evaluate detail recognition by asking individuals to identify details that are missing from a picture or to draw a picture and evaluate the drawing on the basis of how many details individuals include.

Analogies. Intelligence tests present items consisting of a statement to which the student must give the appropriate response. The stimuli may consist of a series of words, geometric designs, or numbers. An example of an item is: parent: child:: goose:.

Abstract Reasoning. Intelligence tests present various types of items that assess abstract reasoning by asking students to identify the absurdity in a statement or picture, to state the meaning of a proverb, or to solve problems of arithmetical reasoning.

Memory. Intelligence tests present a variety of test items that evaluate both long-term and short-term memory by asking students to repeat sentences or a series of digits, to retell what they have read, or to reproduce a design from memory.

Pattern Completion. Intelligence tests ask students to complete a pattern or matrix that has a missing piece.

There are many behaviors that intelligence tests do not sample or sample inadequately. These behaviors include mechanical, musical, artistic, motivational, and emotional behaviors (Anastasi, 1988). Recent research on the nature of intelligence has begun to explore the contribution of these behaviors to our understanding of intelligence.

▶ Can you add to this list of behaviors that intelligence tests do *not* sample?

▶ How are intelligence and adaptive tests alike? different?

▶ **CEC Common Core Knowledge and Skills.** The beginning special educator should understand basic terminology used in assessment (CC8K1).

Responding to Diversity

There has been much debate over the years about the value of intelligence testing. Arguments against the use of intelligence testing claim that testing limits opportunities, can be harmful to individuals from various cultural and ethnic groups, and facilitates the placement of students into categories. Advocates of intelligence testing have argued that intelligence testing assists in diagnosis, helps to identify individuals who need specialized instruction or therapy, and promotes educational opportunities (Sattler, 1988). Membership in a cultural or ethnic group, socioeconomic status, educational attainment, language, and acculturation can affect intelligence test scores. Educators can reduce or prevent bias in the assessment of intelligence by being: (1) aware of individual characteristics; (2) knowledgeable in test use and test selection; and (3) sensitive when administering, scoring, and interpreting performance (Suzuki, Vraniak, & Kugler, 1996).

Intelligence tests provide us with only a part of what we want to know about an individual. The assessment of individuals should never depend on the results of one test; rather, good practice requires that we use the results of additional standardized tests, as well as observations, interviews, checklists, rating scales, samples of work, and other types of assessment, in appropriate combination, to gather information.

▶ When measuring intelligence, what special considerations do we need to make when testing a student from another culture?

▶ What does the following statement mean? The results of intelligence tests should describe rather than explain behavior.

Standardized Instruments

As stated previously, there are a great many standardized tests of intelligence on the market. This chapter highlights several frequently used tests.

Batería–R Tests of Cognitive Ability and Achievement

The *Batería–R COG* and the *Batería–R ACH* (Woodcock & Muñoz-Sandoval, 1996) form a parallel Spanish version of the *Woodcock-Johnson Psychoeducational Battery–Revised*. The *Batería–R COG* and *ACH* is an individually administered battery that assesses cognitive, academic, and language abilities in Spanish-speaking individuals ages 2 years through adulthood. The battery consists of two parts, *Tests of Cognitive Ability (Batería–R COG)* and the *Tests of Achievement (Batería–R ACH)*.

Like the *Woodcock-Johnson Psychoeducational Battery–Revised,* the *Batería–R COG* derives from the Horn-Cattell theory of cognitive processing, which we discuss later in this chapter in the description of the *Woodcock-Johnson Psychoeducational Battery–Revised.* Although the *Woodcock-Johnson Psychoeducational Battery–Revised* has been replaced by the *Woodcock-Johnson-III,* the *Batería-R* has not been updated.

ADMINISTRATION The *Batería–R* takes from 20 minutes to more than 2 hours to administer, depending on whether you are using both parts. Raw scores convert to age and grade equivalents, percentile ranks, and standard scores. The scoring can be cumbersome, and it is advisable to use a computer scoring program.

▶ **CEC Common Core Knowledge and Skills.** A beginning special educator can interpret information from formal and informal assessments (CC8S5).

TECHNICAL ADEQUACY Technical adequacy of the *Batería–R* derives from the *Woodcock-Johnson Psychoeducational Battery–Revised (WJ–R).* The authors used the standardization sample of the *WJ–R* to develop the scoring procedures and other technical information for the *Batería–R* and calibrated it on 3,911 native Spanish-speaking individuals from Costa Rica, Mexico, Peru, Puerto Rico, Spain, Arizona, California, Florida, New York, and Texas. The purpose of this calibration was to develop a parallel form of the *WJ–R.*

The authors argue that because of this calibration with the *WJ–R,* reliability and validity information from the *Woodcock-Johnson Psychoeducational Battery–R* is applicable to this test.

SUMMARY The *Batería–R COG* and the *Batería–R ACH* form a parallel Spanish version of the *Woodcock-Johnson Psychoeducational Battery–Revised.* This norm-referenced, individually administered battery assesses cognitive, academic, and language abilities in Spanish-speaking individuals ages 2 years through adulthood. Reliability information is lacking. The tests warrant additional investigation of validity.

TESTS-at-a-GLANCE

Batería–R Tests of Cognitive Ability

● **Publication Date:** 1996

● **Purposes:** The *Batería–R* is a parallel Spanish version of the *Woodcock-Johnson Psychoeducational Battery–Revised.* The *Batería–R* assesses cognitive, academic, and language abilities in Spanish-speaking individuals.

● **Age/Grade Levels:** 2 years through adulthood; grades kindergarten through college.

● **Time to Administer:** 20 minutes to more than 2 hours, depending on whether both the Tests of Cognitive Ability and the Tests of Achievement are administered.

● **Technical Adequacy:** Reliability information is lacking. Additional investigation of validity is warranted.

● **Suggested Use:** Measures general cognitive abilities, aptitude, and achievement in Spanish-speaking students. Results should be cautiously used. Although the *Woodcock-Johnson Psychoeducational Battery–Revised* has been replaced by the *Woodcock-Johnson-III,* the *Batería–R* has not been updated.

Cognitive Abilities Test, Form 6

The *Cognitive Abilities Test, Form 6 (CogAT6;* Lohman & Hagen, 2001) developed out of the Lorge-Thorndike intelligence tests and consists of a series of group-administered cognitive ability tests for students in grades kindergarten through 12. The *CogAT6* assesses general reasoning abilities to learn new tasks and solve problems and verbal, quantitive, and non-verbal abilities. According to the manual, the three primary uses of *CogAT* scores are to (1) provide information that can be useful in adapting instruction, (2) provide a measure of cognitive abilities, and (3) to assist in the identification of students whose predicted levels of achievement are considerably different from their current levels of achievement.

ADMINISTRATION The teacher reads aloud all of the directions for Levels 1 and 2. Students do not have to read but must be able to follow the directions of the teacher. The student responds by identifying the one correct response and filling in an oval. Levels A–H are administered to groups of students, rather than to individual students.

SCORING Each battery has a separate score, and there is a Composite score. Individual subtests do not report scores. Reported scores include percentiles, stanines, and standard scores.

TESTS-at-a-GLANCE

The Cognitive Abilities Test, Form 6

- **Publication Date:** 2001

- **Purposes:** Measures verbal, quantitative, and nonverbal abilities.

- **Age/Grade Levels:** Grades kindergarten through 12.

- **Time to Administer:** 45 minutes to 2 hours.

- **Technical Adequacy:** Information about the standardization sample is adequate. Evidence of reliability and validity is lacking.

- **Suggested Use:** *CogAT6* may be useful as a screening instrument and an instrument that provides general information about patterns of development. It should be used cautiously until additional information relating to validity can be gathered. It should not be used to make entitlement decisions about students with disabilities.

STANDARDIZATION Age and grade norms are provided. The *CogAT6* was co-normed with the *Iowa Tests of Basic Skills* and the *Iowa Tests of Educational Development.*

RELIABILITY Internal consistency reliability is acceptable. Other types of reliability are lacking.

VALIDITY There is little evidence of validity in the manual.

SUMMARY The *Cognitive Abilities Test, Form 6* is a group test of cognitive ability for students in kindergarten through grade 12. While the standardization of this test is commendable, evidence of reliability and validity is lacking.

Comprehensive Test of Nonverbal Intelligence

The *Comprehensive Test of Nonverbal Intelligence* (*CTONI;* Hammill, Pearson, & Wiederholt, 1996) is a nonverbal measure of abstract/figural problem solving and reasoning for use with individuals ages 6 years through 18 years, 11 months. It is useful for assessing the performance of individuals who have language or motor problems that in some cases make it difficult for them to respond to more traditional tests. The test is made up of six subtests: Pictorial Analogies, Geometric Analogies, Pictorial Categories, Geometric Categories, Pictorial Sequences, and Geometric Sequences. For each of these subtests, the examinee must solve a visual problem that consists of either pictures (e.g., shoe, ball, cube) or geometric shapes (e.g., triangle, circle, diamond).

ADMINISTRATION The test items are contained in a stiff book that is set up like an easel. The examiner can pantomime the instructions or give them orally. If the examiner chooses to pantomime the instructions, the examiner uses facial gestures, hand

TESTS-at-a-GLANCE

Comprehensive Test of Nonverbal Intelligence (CTONI)

- **Publication Date:** 1996

- **Purposes:** Measures nonverbal abstract/figural problem solving and reasoning in individuals who have language or motor problems that may make it difficult for them to respond to more traditional tests.

- **Age/Grade Levels:** Ages 6 years through 18 years, 11 months.

- **Time to Administer:** 20 to 45 minutes.

- **Technical Adequacy:** Information about the standardization sample is sparse. Reliability is adequate but additional information concerning validity is needed.

- **Suggested Use:** The *CTONI* may be useful as a screening instrument. It should be used cautiously until additional information relating to validity can be gathered.

movements, and head movements. The student shows the correct response by pointing or by some other motor response. This nonverbal method of test administration does have several advantages. The examinee does not have to listen to directions, speak, read, or write. There is no time limit for the test. *CTONI* software is available that allows an examinee to respond to computer-administered items that are automatically scored.

SCORING Examiners score items as either correct or incorrect. Raw scores convert to standard scores, percentile ranks, and age equivalents.

STANDARDIZATION The *CTONI* standardization sample consisted of 2,129 individuals, ranging in age from 6 years to 18 years, 11 months. It is unclear whether the sample was stratified according to major demographic variables. Characteristics of the sample include age, gender, race (white, black, other), ethnic group (Native American, Hispanic, Asian, African American, other) geographic region, residence (rural, urban), family income, disability status, and educational background of the parents.

RELIABILITY The test reports internal consistency reliability and test-retest reliability. The average coefficient for internal consistency was .97. The test reports test-retest reliability coefficients only for students enrolled in third grade, eleventh grade, and the total sample. These coefficients ranged from .79 to .94.

VALIDITY Validity determines whether a test measures what it purports to measure. While the manual reports the results of several validity studies, more extensive research is necessary in order to determine whether this instrument measures the construct of intelligence and to determine its usefulness in measuring intellectual abilities of persons with disabilities.

SUMMARY The *CTONI* is a nonverbal measure that assesses visual problem solving and reasoning. Reliability is adequate. Teachers should use it cautiously until additional information relating to validity is available.

Detroit Tests of Learning Aptitude–Primary: Second Edition

The *Detroit Tests of Learning Aptitude–Primary: Second Edition* (DTLA–P:2; Hammill & Bryant, 1991) measures the intellectual aptitudes or abilities of individuals ages 3 years to 9 years, 11 months. This is the second edition of the *DTLA–P*. According to the authors, the *DTLA–P:2* has four uses: (1) to discover strengths and weaknesses among mental abilities; (2) to identify children who perform significantly below their peers; (3) to predict future performance; and (4) to aid as a research tool when investigating children's aptitude, intelligence, and cognitive ability. Depending on the child's age and abilities, the *DTLA–P* takes between 15 and 45 minutes to administer.

The *DTLA–P:2* consists of 100 items arranged in order from the easiest to the most difficult. The items yield six subtest scores and a general, overall mental ability score. The six subtests and the domains in which they are grouped are as follows:

Linguistic Domain
- *Verbal Quotient:* Assesses the understanding, integration, and use of spoken language.
- *Nonverbal Quotient:* Assesses spatial relationship and nonverbal symbolic reasoning abilities.

Attentional Domain
- *Attention-Enhanced Quotient:* Evaluates immediate recall, memory, and ability to concentrate.
- *Attention-Reduced Quotient:* Measures long-term memory, understanding, reasoning ability, and comprehension of abstract relationships.

Motoric Domain
- *Motor-Enhanced Quotient:* Assesses complex motor abilities, especially fine-motor abilities.
- *Motor-Reduced Quotient:* Evaluates aptitude with reduced demands for motor activities. The child indicates the correct response by either pointing or speaking.

ADMINISTRATION Examiners must have some background in assessment. Directions for administration are on the test protocol. For some items, directions for administration are in the examiner's manual. The test is administered individually. Since the items are in order from least to most difficult, the examiner begins testing at certain entry points. The student's chronological age determines these entry points. When testing reaches a predetermined ceiling, it stops.

SCORING The examiner scores the responses as either correct or incorrect and uses the scores for each item to compute the total score and the subtest scores. Raw scores can convert to age equivalents, percentiles, and quotients, which are standard scores that have a mean of 100 and a standard deviation of 15.

STANDARDIZATION The standardization sample of the *DTLA–P:2* consisted of 2,095 children in 36 states. In developing this instrument, the authors used data from the standardization sample (March–June 1985) of the *DTLA–P* and tested an additional 619 children between September 1989 and June 1990. These two samples then combined to form the standardization sample for the *DTLA–P:2*. The test reports information on the percentage of children for each of the following variables: gender, residence (urban, rural), race, geographic area (Northeast, North Central, South, West), ethnicity (American Indian, Hispanic, Asian, other), and age.

RELIABILITY Test authors used a random sample of 350 protocols from the standardization sample to estimate internal consistency. The average reliabilities for the total score and the six subtests ranged from

TESTS-at-a-GLANCE

Detroit Tests of Learning Aptitude–Primary: Second Edition (DTLA–P:2)

- **Publication Date:** 1991
- **Purposes:** Measures general intellectual aptitudes or abilities.
- **Age/Grade Levels:** Ages 3 years to 9 years, 11 months.
- **Time to Administer:** 15 to 45 minutes.
- **Technical Adequacy:** Questions remain as to the appropriateness of the standardization sample, reliability, and validity.
- **Suggested Use:** The *DTLA–P:2* can be used as a screening instrument. Caution should be exercised when using test scores to make decisions regarding the identification of students and eligibility for special services.

.88 to .94. The test also reports test-retest reliability, but provides little information about the characteristics of the sample, qualifications of the examiners, or the test-retest interval.

VALIDITY The authors maintain that the *DTLA–P:2* has content validity because it measures behaviors that Salvia and Ysseldyke (2004) have developed. To demonstrate concurrent validity, the authors used evidence from four concurrent validity studies that were conducted with the *DTLA–P.* The size of the samples in each of these correlations ranged from 28 to 68 children. The reported reliability coefficients ranged from .31 to .87.

The *DTLA–P:2* manual contains no evidence of predictive validity. While the authors present evidence of construct validity, additional validity studies are necessary.

SUMMARY The *Detroit Tests of Learning Aptitude–Primary: Second Edition* is an individually administered test for children ages 3 years to 9 years, 11 months. It measures intellectual ability using six subtests and a general, overall score. Questions remain as to the appropriateness of the standardization sample, reliability, and validity. Until the authors present additional evidence, teachers should use the test cautiously.

Detroit Tests of Learning Aptitude: Fourth Edition

The *Detroit Tests of Learning Aptitude–Fourth Edition* (*DTLA–4;* Hammill, 1998) measures the intellectual aptitudes or abilities of students ages 6 through 17. According to the author the *DTLA–4* measures intelligence, aptitude, and achievement. The *DTLA–4* consists of ten subtests:

Word Opposites: The student must verbalize the opposite of a word that the examiner says.

Design Sequences: The student must arrange cubes in a pattern from memory after being shown a picture of the pattern for 5 seconds.

Sentence Imitation: The student repeats a sentence after listening to the examiner say the sentence.

Reversed Letters: The examiner recites a series of letters. The student must record the letters, reversing their order of presentation.

Story Construction: After viewing three pictures, the student makes up three stories.

Design Reproduction: The student must draw a design from memory after being shown a design for 5 seconds.

Basic Information: The student responds to factual questions.

Symbolic Relations: The student views a design and must choose from among six designs the one that completes the pattern.

Word Sequences: The student repeats a series of unrelated words after listening to the examiner recite the words.

Story Sequences: The student arranges a series of cartoonlike pictures to make a story.

ADMINISTRATION Examiners should have some background in assessment. Directions for administration are on the test protocol. For some items, directions for administration are in the examiner's manual. Administration takes between 50 minutes and 2 hours.

SCORING Examiners score the responses as either correct or incorrect. The scores for each item make up the computation of the total score and the subtest scores. Raw scores can convert to age equivalents, percentiles, and quotients, which are standard scores that have a mean of 100 and a standard deviation of 15.

STANDARDIZATION The standardization sample of the *DTLA–4* consisted of 1,350 students in 37 states. In developing this instrument, the author used data from the standardization sample of the *DTLA–3* and selected additional samples. The standardization of the *DTLA–4* is confusing and ambiguous.

RELIABILITY Estimations of internal consistency reliability came from the standardization sample. The average reliabilities for the total score and the six subtests ranged from .82 to .93. Test-retest reliability derived from a sample of 98 students living in Austin, Texas. The coefficients ranged from .71 to .96.

VALIDITY The authors maintain that the *DTLA–4* has content validity because it measures behaviors that Salvia and Ysseldyke (2004) have developed and because it relates the subtests to the theories of intelligence. While the authors present evidence of construct validity, additional validity studies are necessary.

TESTS-at-a-GLANCE

Detroit Tests of Learning Aptitude–4 (Fourth Edition) (DTLA–4)

- **Publication Date:** 1998

- **Purposes:** Measures general intellectual aptitudes or abilities and achievement.

- **Age/Grade Levels:** Ages 6 years through 17 years.

- **Time to Administer:** 50 minutes to 2 hours.

- **Technical Adequacy:** Questions remain as to the appropriateness of the standardization sample, reliability, and validity.

- **Suggested Use:** May be helpful in determining areas of strength and weakness. Exercise caution when using test scores to make decisions regarding the identification of students and eligibility for special services.

- **Summary:** The *Detroit Tests of Learning Aptitude–4* is an individually administered test for students ages 6 through 17. Questions remain as to the appropriateness of the standardization sample, reliability, and validity.

Differential Ability Scales

The *Differential Ability Scales* (*DAS;* Elliott, 1990a) is a revision of the *British Ability Scales*. The *DAS* measures cognitive ability and achievement in individuals ages 2 years, 6 months to 17 years, 11 months. The test does not base itself on any one theory of mental ability. According to the manual, the test is built on a collection of subtests that sample a range of human abilities thought to be useful in assessing individuals, particularly students with learning difficulties. The selection of the abilities sampled was influenced by a variety of theoretical approaches (Elliott, 1990b, p. 14).

The structure of the *DAS* is hierarchical. The first level consists of the subtest scores, at the next level are the cluster scores, and at the general level the *DAS* yields a general cognitive ability score (GCA). The test contains 17 cognitive subtests and 3 school achievement subtests. Not all of the subtests are given to every individual. Teachers administer selected subtests depending on the age of the student. Table 13.1 describes the subtests and clusters.

ADMINISTRATION The administration of the *DAS* calls for an examiner who has a background in the principles of assessment. The total time to administer the *DAS* is approximately 35 minutes for children ages 2 years, 6 months to 3 years, 5 months; administration to children ages 3 years, 6 months to 5 years, 11 months takes approximately 65 minutes; and it takes between 65 and 85 minutes for students older than 6 years of age. The manual provides separate directions for administering each of the subtests.

TABLE 13.1 ● Differential Ability Scales: Subtests and Clusters		
Tests	**Age Range**	**Applications**
Preschool Core Subtests		
Block Building	2 years, 6 months to 4 years, 11 months	Measures motor and perceptual abilities. The individual copies wooden block designs.
Verbal Comprehension	2 years, 6 months to 6 years, 11 months	Measures receptive language ability. The child points to named pictures or places objects and chips according to the examiner's instructions (e.g., under the bridge).
Picture Similarities	2 years, 6 months to 7 years, 11 months	Measures nonverbal reasoning ability. After observing a row of four pictures or designs, the child must choose the best picture or design that goes with the ones that are shown.
Naming Vocabulary	2 years, 6 months to 8 years, 11 months	Measures expressive vocabulary. The child names several objects and pictures that are shown.
Pattern Construction	3 years to 17 years, 11 months	Measures visual-spatial problem solving. The individual constructs patterns using foam squares and plastic blocks.
Early Number Concepts	2 years, 6 months to 7 years, 11 months	Measures prenumerical and number concepts and skills. The child counts chips and answers questions about pictures. Many, but not all of the subtests, are nonverbal.
Copying	3 years, 6 months to 7 years, 11 months	Measures ability to copy, motor ability, and the ability to perceive similarities. After observing a line drawing, the child reproduces it.
School-Age Core Subtests		
Recall of Designs	5 years through 17 years, 11 months	Assesses short-term recall, motor ability, and visual-spatial ability. After observing a nonpictorial line drawing for five seconds, the individual must draw it from memory.
Word Definitions	5 years through 17 years, 11 months	Measures verbal knowledge. The examiner says a word and the individual must provide the meaning.
Pattern Construction	3 years through 17 years, 11 months	This subtest description is in the *Preschool Core Subtests* section.
Matrices	5 years through 17 years, 11 months	Measures nonverbal reasoning ability. The student observes a series of matrices. For each one, the student chooses the design that best completes the matrix.
Similarities	5 years through 17 years, 11 months	Measures verbal reasoning. The individual must respond orally to a series of questions.
Sequential and Quantitative Reasoning	5 years through 17 years, 11 months	Assesses the ability to perceives sequential patterns or rules in numerical relationships. The items consist of abstract figures or numbers to which the student must respond.
Diagnostic Subtests		
Matching Letterlike Forms	4 years through 7 years, 11 months	Measures the ability to visually discriminate among similar letterlike figures. The student matches similar figures that look like letters and are rotated on a page.
Recall of Digits	2 years, 6 months through 17 years, 11 months	Assesses short-term auditory-sequential recall of digits. The individual must repeat a series of 2 to 9 digits.
Recall of Objects– Immediate and Delayed	4 years through 17 years, 11 months	Assesses short-term and delayed verbal memory. The individual recalls as many objects as possible after being shown a card with a number of objects on it.

TABLE 13.1 • Continued

Tests	Age Range	Applications
Diagnostic Subtests (continued)		
Recognition of Pictures	2 years, 6 months through 17 years, 11 months	Assesses short-term visual memory. After observing a card with one or more pictures for a few seconds, the individual observes another set of pictures and must point to the pictures that were in the first set.
Speed of Information Processing	5 years through 17 years, 11 months	Assesses speed of simple mental operations. After observing a page consisting of figures or numbers, the individual must mark, as quickly as possible, the circle containing the largest number of boxes or the highest number.
School Achievement Tests		
Basic Number Skills	6 years through 17 years, 11 months	Assesses basic computational skills. The individual solves problems on a worksheet.
Spelling	6 years through 17 years, 11 months	Assesses ability to spell based on phonetically regular and irregular words. Children ages 6 years, 0 months to 8 years, 11 months are also asked to write their names. The examiner says the word, uses the word in a sentence, and repeats the word, and the individual writes the words.
Word Reading	5 years through 17 years, 11 months	Assesses ability to decode words in isolation. The student reads a series of words that are shown on a card.
Clusters of the Preschool Level of the Cognitive Battery	3 years, 6 months through 5 years, 11 months	Verbal Ability. Assesses learned verbal concepts and knowledge. The subtests that form this cluster are Verbal Comprehension and Naming Vocabulary.
Nonverbal Ability		Assesses complex, nonverbal mental processing. The subtests that form this cluster include Picture Similarities, Pattern Construction, and Copying.
Clusters of the School-Age Level of the Cognitive Battery	6 years through 17 years, 11 months	Verbal Ability. Assesses verbal mental processing and acquired knowledge. The subtests that form this cluster are Word Definitions and Similarities.
Nonverbal Reasoning Ability		Assesses nonverbal inductive reasoning and mental processing. The subtests that form this cluster include Matrices, Sequential, and Quantitative Reasoning.
Spatial Ability		Assesses complex visual-spatial processing. The subtests that form this cluster are Recall of Designs and Pattern Construction.

The administration of the *DAS* does have several unique features. These include decision points, alternative stopping points, teaching a failed item, extended selection of subtests, and out-of-level testing. While the starting points for each subtest depend on the individual's age, the administration of items continues until the individual reaches a *decision point*. At that decision point, the examiner decides whether to stop, to continue to administer the difficult items, or to drop back and administer easier items. Alternative stopping points are available so that the examiner can halt the test administration if the items are too difficult or if the examiner and the student have not developed a rapport. In addition to these features, some subtests allow the examiner to teach the individual the failed item. *Extended selection* of subtests refers to the option of allowing the examiner to administer additional subtests that measure similar abilities. This may occur with young children when further assessment is considered necessary. *Out-of-level testing* refers to the administration of additional subtests to individuals who have unusually low or high abilities. These subtests may not be appropriate for individuals who have average ability.

For individuals with hearing impairments or speech or language problems, non-verbal subtests are available. These include Block Building and Picture Similarities. The scores from these subtests form a Special Nonverbal Composite, which, according to the manual, can replace the GCA. However, the test does not include separate norms for special populations.

SCORING Raw scores compare to Ability Scores. These are scores that are unique to the *DAS* and provide an estimate of the individual's performance on specific subtests. However, ability scores of different subtests have an important limitation: They are not comparable. Converting Ability Scores to T-scores (T-scores have a mean of 50 and a standard deviation of 10), percentiles, and standard scores (mean of 100, standard deviation of 15) requires another transformation. The test provide age and grade equivalents for the achievement tests and separate guidelines for scoring each of the subtests.

STANDARDIZATION The standardization sample consisted of 3,475 individuals distributed by gender, with 175 individuals for each six-month interval for ages 2 years, 6 months to 4 years, 11 months and 200 individuals at one-year intervals for ages 5 years, 0 months to 17 years, 11 months. Other stratification variables were race/ethnicity (black, Hispanic, white, other including Asian, Pacific Islander, American Indian, Eskimo, Aleut), parent education, geographic region, and educational preschool enrollment.

The standardization sample included individuals with learning disabilities, speech impairments, emotional disturbances, physical impairments, and mental retardation, as well as gifted individuals in approximate proportion to U.S. population data, excluding individuals with severe disabilities. The test does not provide separate norms. According to the manual,

> The mere inclusion of individuals with exceptional needs in a norm sample does not make the instrument appropriate for use with such children, nor does their exclusion make the test inappropriate. During item and subtest development, the *DAS* team sought to create tasks that would be suitable in content, format, and difficulty for many exceptional children. Research that focuses on how the test works with such children will determine the success of these efforts, like those of any other test development project. (Elliott, 1990b, p. 116)

RELIABILITY The test reports internal reliabilities for each of the subtests and for out-of-level testing. For the most part, the reliabilities were within the moderate range. To estimate test-retest reliability, studies selected 100 individuals from the standardization sample for each of the following age ranges: 3 years, 6 months to 4 years, 5 months; 5 years, 0 months to 6 years, 11 months; and 12 years, 0 months to 13 years,

---

TESTS-at-a-GLANCE

Differential Ability Scales (DAS)

- **Publication Date:** 1990

- **Purposes:** Measures cognitive ability and achievement.

- **Age/Grade Levels:** 2 years, 6 months through 17 years, 11 months.

- **Time to Administer:** 35 to 85 minutes.

- **Technical Adequacy:** The standardization sample is acceptable. Reliability is adequate. Additional evidence of validity is needed.

- **Suggested Use:** Can be helpful in determining areas of strength and weakness. Exercise caution when using test scores in making decisions regarding identification of students with special needs and determining eligibility for special services.

- **Summary:** The *DAS* is an individually administered ability test for use with individuals ages 2 years, 6 months to 17 years, 11 months. The subtests are designed to measure cognitive ability and selected areas of achievement. Reliability is adequate. However, additional evidence of validity is necessary before educators can use it with confidence for individuals with exceptional needs.

11 months. The testing interval ranged from two to seven weeks. While the reliabilities were in the moderate range for the subtests, the reliabilities of the clusters and the general cognitive ability score were higher than the reliabilities for the subtests.

VALIDITY The manual does provide evidence of the separate factor structure for the subtests and the clusters and reports concurrent validity with other ability tests and achievement tests. In addition, studies describe small samples of students labeled educably mentally disabled, learning disabled, reading disabled, and gifted. However, since this is a relatively new test, independent researchers will need to conduct additional studies in order to confirm and extend our understanding of the validity of this instrument. Evaluators should use caution when interpreting the performance of individuals with special needs.

Kaufman Adolescent and Adult Intelligence Test

The *Kaufman Adolescent and Adult Intelligence Test* (*KAIT;* Kaufman & Kaufman, 1993) is a test of general intelligence for individuals ages 11 to over 85 years. Three theories of intellectual functioning—Golden's modification of the Luria-Nebraska system of neuropsychological assessment, Piaget's formal operations stage, and the Horn-Cattell theories of fluid and crystallized intelligence—form the basis of the test.

The *KAIT* comprises two scales: crystallized intelligence and fluid intelligence. Crystallized intelligence "measures acquired concepts and depends on schooling and acculturation for success" (p. 1) while fluid intelligence measures "the ability to solve new problems" (p. 1). The test has a Core Battery and an Expanded Battery. In addition, a supplementary subtest assesses the respondent's attention and orientation. Table 13.2 shows a description of the subtests and the abilities they measure.

ADMINISTRATION The *KAIT* is an individually administered test that requires supervision by persons who have had graduate training in individual assessment of intelligence. The average time to administer the Core Battery is 65 minutes; the Expanded Battery takes approximately 90 minutes.

SCORING Each of the three intelligence scales, Crystallized, Fluid, and Composite, yields an IQ score with a mean of 100 and a standard deviation of 15. In addition, percentile ranks are obtainable. Each of the ten subtests yields standard scores with a mean of 10 and a standard deviation of 3. Figure 13.1 shows the front page from the *KAIT* Individual Test Record Form.

STANDARDIZATION The *KAIT* was standardized between 1988 and 1991. Over 2,600 individuals, ages 11 to 94 years, at 60 sites participated in the sample, using census information from 1988. The final standardization sample from the initial group comprised 2,000 individuals composed of 14 age groups.

The proportion of males and females closely approximated census data. The northeastern geographic region was somewhat underrepresented, and the western region was slightly overrepresented. The north central and central regions approximated census data. Socioeconomic status, race, and ethnic groups closely matched census information.

RELIABILITY For split-half reliability of the subtests, average coefficients ranged from .79 (Memory for Block Designs) to .93 (Rebus Learning); for the scales, the average split-half reliability coefficients were .95 (Crystallized, Fluid) and .97 (Composite Intelligence). Test-retest reliability calculations applied to two test administrations of the

TABLE 13.2 • Kaufman Adolescent and Adult Intelligence Test	

Core Battery Subtests

Definitions	Respondents identify a word after observing the word with several letters missing and after receiving a definition of the word. *(crystallized intelligence)*
Rebus Learning	Respondents associate a word or concept with a rebus and then "read" phrases and sentences that comprise several rebuses. *(fluid intelligence)*
Logical Steps	Respondents are presented with logical premises in both visual and aural form. They answer a question that relates to these premises. *(fluid intelligence)*
Auditory Comprehension	After listening to a recording of a news story, respondents answer literal and inferential questions. *(crystallized intelligence)*
Mystery Codes	After looking at the codes associated with several pictures, the respondents solve the code for a pictorial stimulus. *(fluid intelligence)*
Double Meanings	After examining two groups of words, respondents recall a word that is associated with the two groups of words. *(crystallized intelligence)*

Expanded Battery

Rebus Delayed Recall	Respondents "read" phrases and concepts that are formed from rebuses that they learned earlier in the test. *(delayed recall)*
Auditory Delayed Recall	Respondents answer questions about news stories that they listened to earlier in the test. *(delayed recall)*
Memory for Block Designs	Respondents construct a block design from memory after briefly looking at a printed copy. *(fluid intelligence)*
Famous Faces	After looking at a picture of a famous person and hearing a clue about the person, respondents name the person. *(crystallized intelligence)*

Supplementary Subtest

Mental Status	Respondents answer ten questions relating to their attention and orientation to the world.

KAIT to 153 individuals. The interval between the administrations ranged from 6 to 99 days with an average interval of 31 days. Average test-retest coefficients for the scales are .94 (Crystallized), .87 (Fluid), and .94 (Composite). One study reports a sample of 60 individuals who took the test again after an interval of one year. Average test-retest coefficients for the scales are .85 (Crystallized), .79 (Fluid), and .92 (Composite).

VALIDITY Construct validity is based on studies of age changes on the subtests and the IQ scales, correlations between the subtests and the IQ scales, factor analyses of the *KAIT*, and correlations between the *KAIT* and other tests.

The studies of age changes on the *KAIT* demonstrate that as individuals grow older, *KAIT* scores change. According to the test manual, this pattern of age changes is consistent with the Horn-Cattell theory of fluid and crystallized intelligence.

The test shows correlations between the *KAIT* subtests and the Composite IQ score. For the six Core subtests, coefficients ranged from .64 (Mystery Codes) to .75 (Definition), with an average coefficient of .70. These coefficients indicate some support that the *KAIT* subtests measure a unifying ability.

KAIT

*Kaufman
Adolescent & Adult
Intelligence Test*

by Alan S. Kaufman and Nadeen L. Kaufman

**Individual
Test Record**

Name _____ ☐ Male ☐ Female

Home address _____ Phone _____

Parent or Guardian _____
(if applicable)

School _____ Grade _____
(if applicable)

Current or previous occupation _____
(if applicable)

Highest school grade completed _____

Examiner _____

	Year	Month	Day
Test date	___	___	___
Birth date	___	___	___
Chronological age	___	___	___

Mental Status

Raw Score | Descriptive Category

SUBTESTS	Raw Score	Subtest Scaled Score (Table D.1) M = 10, SD= 3 Crystallized Scale	Fluid Scale	Delayed Recall	Percentile Rank	Other Data Specify:
CORE BATTERY						
1. Definitions						
2. Rebus Learning						
3. Logical Steps						
4. Auditory Comprehension						
5. Mystery Codes						
6. Double Meanings						
EXPANDED BATTERY						
7. Rebus Delayed Recall						
8. Auditory Delayed Recall		*Add only if substituting for Subtest 1, 4, or 6.	**Add only if substituting for Subtest 2, 3, or 5.			
9. Memory for Block Designs			** ( )	DO NOT ADD		
10. Famous Faces		* ( )				

	Crystallized Scale	Fluid Scale	Composite Intelligence Scale
Sum of Three Core Subtest Scaled Scores		+	=
IQ	(Table D.2)	(Table D.3)	(Table D.4)
Confidence Interval ☐ 90% ☐ 95%	—	—	—
Percentile Rank			
Mean Scaled Score			
Descriptive Category			

Crystallized and Fluid IQ Comparison

Crystallized IQ ◯
Fluid IQ ◯
IQ Difference ◯

Statistical Significance (check one)
☐ NS
☐ .05
☐ .01

Difference Required for Significance at .05 and .01 Levels		
Age	.05	.01
14 or younger	11	14
15 - 34	9	12
35 or older	8	11

FIGURE 13.1 • Kaufman Adolescent and Adult Intelligence Test

Source: Kaufman Adolescent & Adult Intelligence Test (KAIT) Individual Test Record summary page by Alan S. Kaufman and Nadeen L. Kaufman © 1993 American Guidance Service, Inc., 4201 Woodland Road, Circle Pines, Minnesota 55014–1796. Reproduced with permission of publisher. All rights reserved. www.agsnet.com

Factor analyses computations support the authors' assertion that the *KAIT* measures theory-based intelligence. Results of the factor analyses demonstrated that the *KAIT*'s two factors are consistent with the crystallized and fluid scales. The authors conducted additional factor analyses between the *KAIT* and the *Wechsler Intelligence Scale for Children–Revised (WISC–R)* and the *Wechsler Adult Intelligence Scale–Revised (WAIS–R)*. These studies indicate that the *KAIT* Fluid Scale and the Wechsler Performance Scales measure different constructs. However, the *KAIT* Crystallized Scale and the Wechsler Verbal Scales are almost the same.

The test reports concurrent validity calculations by computing correlations between the *KAIT* and the *Kaufman Brief Intelligence Test (K–BIT)* and the *Peabody Picture Vocabulary Test–Revised (PPVT–R)*. The correlations between the *KAIT* Composite IQ and the *K–BIT* Composite IQ were .81 at ages 11 to 19 years and .87 at ages 20 to 88 years. The correlations between the *KAIT* Composite IQ and the *PPVT–R* standard scores were .83 for ages 15 to 40 years and .66 for ages 41 to 92 years. Note that the norm tables for the *PPVT–R* only reach 40 years, so concurrent validity calculations used to norm tables for ages 35 to 40. Additional concurrent validity studies are necessary using additional instruments.

The manual reports several studies regarding the diagnostic validity of the *KAIT* using various samples such as Alzheimer's patients and persons with neurological impairments, clinical depression, or reading disabilities. The studies support the diagnostic utility of the *KAIT* in these areas. We commend the authors for their initial investigations of the diagnostic validity of this test and recommend further studies in this area.

SUMMARY   The *Kaufman Adolescent and Adult Intelligence Test* is an individually administered test of general intelligence for persons ages 11 to over 85 years that combines three theoretical models of intelligence. The test is well standardized. There is good evidence for reliability and validity.

Kaufman Assessment Battery for Children, Second Edition

The *Kaufman Assessment Battery for Children, Second Edition (KABC-II;* Kaufman & Kaufman, 2004) is revision of the 1983 edition. This test assesses the intelligence and achievement of individuals ages 3 through 18 years. The test consists of 18 subtests that take from 30 minutes for young children to more than one hour for elementary and high school-age students. According to the manual, the *KABC-II* "measures a range of abilities including sequential and simultaneous processing, learning reasoning, and crystallized ability that are relevant to understanding children and adolescents from a variety of backgrounds" (Kaufman & Kaufman, 2004, p. 1).

The *KABC-II* is based on two theoretical models of mental processing. The first model was developed by Luria and others and holds that mental processing occurs in three blocks, which are the individual's ability to maintain arousal, code and store information, and plan and organize behavior. The Cattell-Horn-Carroll Theory, the second model, conceptualizes intelligence as fluid and crystallized. Fluid intelligence is the ability to solve problems using logical reasoning; crystallized intelligence is the ability that is closely related to the accumulation of knowledge, language development, information about one's culture, achievement, and communication abilities. Interpretation of test performance can be based on both models.

A unique feature of the *KABC-II* is that items on many subtests can be explained, demonstrated, administered a second time, and taught to students. Although a Spanish translation is included in the test kit, the manual cautions that the KABC-II "is not intended to be administered in Spanish" (Kaufman & Kaufman, 2004, p. 1). Depending on the age of the individual, examiners can combine various subtests to form the Nonverbal Scale. The Nonverbal Scale provides an estimate of intelligence for individuals who demonstrate communication problems and is useful with children who are deaf, hearing-impaired, speech or language disabled, autistic, or who do not speak English. The examiner responds through movement.

ADMINISTRATION The manual provides comprehensive directions for administering the *KABC-II*. The student's chronological age determines the starting point for each subtest, and each subtest has a designated stopping point in order to avoid administering too many items to any student. In addition, the test contains a discontinue rule if a student misses a number of items in a row.

STANDARDIZATION The standardization sample of the *KABC-II* consisted of 3,025 individuals between the ages of 3 and 18 years. The standardization was conducted from September 2001 through January 2003 based on the March 2001 Current Population Survey. Students within each age group were included according to education level of the student's mother or female guardians, geographic region, and ethnic group. Students were only included in the sample if they spoke English, were noninstitutionalized, and did not have physical or perceptual difficulties that would prevent them from participation.

Subtest scores are reported as scaled scores with a mean of 10, standard deviation of 3. These subtest scores can combined to yield standard scores (mean of 100, standard deviation of 15) for the indexes. Index scores can be derived for sequential processing, planning, learning, simultaneous processing, knowledge, and nonverbal abilities.

RELIABILITY The manual reports internal consistency and test-retest reliabilities. For the most part, the reliability coefficients are acceptable. Many coefficients exceed .90 and, in general, the Index scores are more reliable than the individual subtest scores.

VALIDITY The manual reports the results of studies examining the validity of the *KABC-II*. Concurrent validity of the *KABC-II* was investigated through correlations with other tests, including the *WISC-IV*. The *KABC-II* is a significant revision of the earlier version. The manual does provide evidence for the separate factor structure. However, additional research studies are necessary in order to add to our knowledge about the validity of the *KABC-II*.

Although not systematically included in the standardization sample, the manual reports "clinical validity" (Kaufman & Kaufman, 2004, p. 126) studies of students who have disabilities in reading, mathematics, and writing. Separate studies were conducted with students who have learning disabilities, emotional disturbance, and hearing loss, as well as students are gifted.

SUMMARY The *Kaufman Assessment Battery for Children, Second Edition (KABC-II)* assesses the abilities of individuals ages 3 through 18 years. According to the manual, the test measures sequential processing, planning, learning, simultaneous processing, knowledge, and nonverbal abilities. The manual presents evidence for the reliability and validity of the test. Additional research is advisable to confirm validity.

TESTS-at-a-GLANCE

Kaufman Assessment Battery for Children, Second Edition (KABC-II)

- **Publication Date:** 2004

- **Purposes:** Assesses sequential processing, planning, learning, simultaneous processing, knowledge, and nonverbal abilities.

- **Age/Grade Levels:** 3 years through 18 years.

- **Time to Administer:** 30 to 75 minutes.

- **Technical Adequacy:** The standardization sample is dated. Reliability is very good; validity is acceptable. However, additional evidence of validity is needed to support the theoretical bases of this test and its use with special populations.

- **Suggested Use:** Although the manual does report several "clinical validity" studies with special populations, the *KABC-II* should be used cautiously with students who have disabilities because students with disabilities were not systematically included in the standardization sample.

Stanford-Binet Intelligence Scale: Fifth Edition

The *Stanford-Binet Intelligence Scale: Fifth Edition* (Roid, 2003) is a revised edition of the *Stanford-Binet Intelligence Scale* (Thorndike, Hagen, & Sattler, 1986). The test was originally developed by Alfred Binet and Theodore Simon in France in 1905. Lewis M. Terman, a professor at Stanford University, revised the Binet-Simon test and introduced it to the United States in 1916. In 1937, Terman, along with Maud A. Merrill, standardized it again and created two revised forms, *Form L* and *Form M*. In 1960, the authors created *Form L-M* from the two forms but did not restandardize the test until 1972. The long-awaited *Fourth Edition* was published in 1986. The *Fifth Edition* has some similarities to previous editions: (1) It spans the same age range; (2) many of the item types are the same or adapted; and (3) it uses basal and ceiling levels.

The *Fifth Edition* of the Stanford-Binet assesses cognitive abilities in individuals ages 2 through 85 years and older. Like the *Fourth Edition,* the *Fifth Edition* uses a hierarchical model of intelligence with a global *g* (general intellectual ability) factor and several broad factors At the top level, there is *g*, general reasoning ability. The second level consists of broad factors titled Fluid Reasoning, Knowledge, Quantitative Processing, Visual-Spatial Processing, and Working Memory. The manual states that there are extensive high-end items for those who are gifted and low-end items for improved assessment of young children and individuals who are low functioning. The *Fifth Edition* contains ten subtests that assess verbal and nonverbal abilities:

Verbal	*Nonverbal*
Verbal Fluid Reasoning	Nonverbal Fluid Reasoning
Verbal Knowledge	Nonverbal Knowledge
Verbal Quantitative Reasoning	Nonverbal Quantitative Reasoning
Verbal Visual-Spatial Processing	Nonverbal Visual-Spatial Processing
Verbal Working Memory	Nonverbal Working Memory

ADMINISTRATION Administration of specific subtests depends on the age of the individual under assessment. The test provides specific instructions for each subtest.

TESTS-at-a-GLANCE

Stanford-Binet Intelligence Scale: Fifth Edition

- **Publication Date:** 2003
- **Purposes:** Assesses general intellectual abilities (g) and cognitive abilities in five broad areas: Fluid Reasoning, Knowledge, Quantitative Processing, Visual-Spatial Processing, and Working Memory.
- **Age/Grade Levels:** 2 through 85+ years.
- **Time to Administer:** One to 2 hours.
- **Technical Adequacy:** Well-normed, reliable instrument. Evidence of validity is adequate.
- **Suggested Use:** Assesses intellectual ability, strengths and weaknesses. Can be used, in combination with other tests and forms of assessment, to identify students with special needs and determine eligibility for services; can be used when conducting a psychoeducational assessment and for clinical and neuropsychological assessment.

SCORING The manual provides clearly written directions for scoring. The scoring of the subtests varies from one subtest to another. Scores are calculated for Full Scale IQ, Verbal and Nonverbal IQ, and Composite Indices spanning 5 factors with a standard score mean of 100, standard deviation of 15. The subtest scores have a mean of 10, standard deviation of 3.

STANDARDIZATION Five variables—geographic region, community size, ethnic group (white, African American, Hispanic, Asian/Pacific Islander), age, and gender—and data matches to the 2000 Census formed the basis for the standardization sample. A total of 4,800 individuals between the ages of 2 and 85+ years participated in the standardization.

RELIABILITY Reliabilities for the Full Scale IQ, Nonverbal IQ, and Verbal IQ, range from .95 to .98. Reliabilities for the Factor Indexes range from .90 to .92. For the ten subtests, reliabilities range from .84 to .89.

VALIDITY The manual reports factor analyses of the subtest scores across all ages in the standardization sample to measure construct validity. While the authors present evidence of validity, we recommend additional research over time with varied populations.

SUMMARY The *Stanford-Binet Intelligence Scale: Fifth Edition* is a well-normed, reliable instrument. Evidence of validity is adequate. However, additional studies must be undertaken that investigate construct validity. While one important strength of the instrument is that a broad age range of individuals can take the test, but all examinees do not take all subtests. Thus, comparisons between the performance of examinees over time is difficult. Another disadvantage is that the administering of the *Fifth Edition* can be more time-consuming compared with other intelligence tests.

Test of Nonverbal Intelligence–Third Edition

The *Test of Nonverbal Intelligence–Third Edition* (*TONI–3*; Brown, Sherbenou, & Johnsen, 1997) is a nonverbal measure of abstract/figural problem solving for use with individuals ages 6 years to 89 years, 11 months. It can assess the performance of individuals who have language or motor problems that make it difficult for them to respond to more traditional tests. The authors state that it can be useful when assessing persons who have aphasia, hearing impairments, lack of proficiency with spoken or written English, cerebral palsy, stroke, or head trauma. The test has two forms, each containing 45 items. The items consist of a series of abstract figures that require individuals to select the correct response by problem solving.

ADMINISTRATION The test items sit on an easel and the examiner pantomimes the instructions. The examiner begins the testing by pointing to a blank square in a pattern of figures, making a broad gesture to indicate the possible responses, pointing to the blank square again, and then looking questioningly at the individual. The student shows the correct response by pointing, using an eyeblink, head stick, light beam, or by some other meaningful response. Throughout the administration of this instrument, neither the examiner nor the examinee speaks. This test is untimed and encourages the examiner to allow examinees sufficient time to respond to each test item. The total time to administer the *TONI–3* is approximately 15 minutes. The advantages of this nonverbal method of test administration are that the examinee does not have to listen to directions, speak, read, or write.

According to the authors, teachers, psychologists, psychological associates, educational diagnosticians, and speech and language therapists can administer the *TONI–3*. Examiners should have sufficient training and knowledge in the area of assessment.

TESTS-at-a-GLANCE

Test of Nonverbal Intelligence–Third Edition (TONI–3)

- **Publication Date:** 1997

- **Purposes:** Nonverbal measure of abstract/figural problem solving that can be used when assessing the performance of individuals who have language or motor problems that may make it difficult for them to respond to more traditional tests.

- **Age/Grade Levels:** 6 years to 89 years, 11 months.

- **Time to Administer:** 15 to 20 minutes.

- **Technical Adequacy:** The standardization sample is just acceptable. Reliability and validity coefficients are low to moderate.

- **Suggested Use:** The *TONI–3* assesses one aspect of intelligence—problem solving. It is to be used with caution.

- **Technical Adequacy:** Reliability coefficients are satisfactory. Validity is concerned with determining whether a test measures what it purports to measure. The manual reports the results of studies conducted by the authors of the *TONI–3* and by independent researchers. Validity coefficients from a number of validity studies range from low to moderate for correlations of the *TONI–3* and measures of achievement and measures of intelligence.

- **Summary:** The *TONI–3* is a nonverbal measure that assesses one aspect of intelligence, namely, problem solving. Reliability and validity coefficients are low to moderate. Caution is advisable when assessing young children.

SCORING Examiners score items as either correct or incorrect. Raw scores convert to deviation quotients (standard scores with a mean of 100 and a standard deviation of 15) and percentile ranks. Since there are no subtests, the *TONI–3* reports only the total score.

STANDARDIZATION The *TONI–3* standardization sample consisted of 3,451 individuals, ranging in age from 6 years to 89 years, 11 months stratified by age. The sample groups characteristics according to gender, race, ethnic group, geographic region, residence (rural, urban, suburban), disability status, and income. These demographic characteristics approximated the U.S. population.

RELIABILITY Test authors calculated reliability for the *TONI–3* in several ways. Internal consistency reliability has a mean reliability coefficient of .93 for both Form A and Form B.

The authors calculated alternate-form reliability for the various age groups in the sample by correlating the scores from Forms A and B after administering them to the same individuals back-to-back. The mean reliability coefficient was .84; reliability coefficients by age were: age 6 (.85), age 7 (.79), and age 8 (.79).

The authors also administered the alternate forms in a delayed retest design. Examiners administered both forms of the *TONI–3* seven days apart to individuals ranging in age from 13 years to 40 years. The estimated reliability coefficient was .91. The manual also reports reliability coefficients for special populations, such as individuals who were learning disabled, deaf, gifted, and Spanish-speaking. The reported coefficients were in the moderate range. However, for the most part, the number of persons included in the special population samples is small and additional research is advisable in this area.

Wechsler Intelligence Scale for Children–Fourth Edition Integrated

The *Wechsler Intelligence Scale for Children–Fourth Edition Integrated* (*WISC–IV Integrated*; Wechsler, 2004) is a major revision of the third edition of the *Wechsler Intelligence Scale for Children,* which was originally published in 1949. The *WISC–IV Integrated* incorporates the *WISC-IV* (2003) and is an individually administered test that assesses the intellectual ability of children ages 6 years through 16 years, 11 months. The test measures cognitive abilities and problem-solving processes. According to the manual, the *WISC–IV* is useful for a number of purposes, including psychoeducational assessment, diagnosis of exceptional needs, and clinical and neuropsychological assessment.

Previous versions of this instrument have classified subtests into Verbal and Performance Scales. However, the *WISC–IV* subtests are classified into four composites: Verbal Comprehension Index, Perceptual Reasoning Index, Working Memory Index, and the Processing Speed Index. Figure 13.2 on page 293 shows a completed *WISC–IV* Record Form. A description of the indexes and subtests can be found in Table 13.3.

ADMINISTRATION The *WISC–IV* is administered individually by a skilled professional who is credentialed in school psychology. The Snapshot of Andres on page 294 describes his performance on this test. The manual clearly explains the directions for administration and scoring for each of the subtests. Each subtest has separate starting points, and the rules for stopping vary among the subtests. Administration time is approximately 60 to 90 minutes.

TABLE 13.3 • WISC–IV Indexes and Subtests

Index	Subtest	Description
Verbal Comprehension Index	Similarities	The student explains the correspondence between pairs of words.
	Vocabulary	The examiner presents words orally and the examinee defines them orally.
	Comprehension	The examiner presents oral questions that assess understanding of familiar problems and social concepts.
	Information (supplementary)	The student responds orally to general information questions.
	Word Reasoning (supplementary)	The student responds to one or more clues that are presented by the examiner.
Perceptual Reasoning Index	Block Design	The examinee reproduces a pattern using blocks.
	Picture Concepts	The student selects the correct drawing from several rows of drawings.
	Matrix Reasoning	The student selects the correct design from five choices.
	Picture Completion (supplementary)	The student observes a picture with a missing part and identifies the missing piece.
Working Memory Index	Digit Span	The student repeats a series of numbers forward in the Digits Forward section and a series of numbers in reverse order in the Digits Backward section.
	Letter-Number Sequencing	The student repeats a series of numbers and letters. The numbers are repeated, lowest to highest, and the letters are repeated in alphabetical order.
	Arithmetic (supplementary)	The student solves mathematical problems mentally and responds to them verbally.
Processing Speed Index	Coding	The student copies geometric symbols that are paired with either numbers or shapes.
	Symbol Search	The student searches two or three groups of paired shapes to locate the target shape.
	Cancellation (supplementary)	The student identifies target pictures that are presented.

SCORING The manual provides clearly written directions for scoring. The scoring of the subtests varies from one subtest to another. Raw scores convert to scaled scores, which are a form of standard score with a mean of 100 and a standard deviation of 15. Five composite scores are calculated: Full Scale IQ, Verbal Comprehension Index, Perceptual Processing Speed Index, Working Memory Index, and Processing Speed Index.

STANDARDIZATION The *WISC–IV* based its standardization sample on 2000 data from the U.S. Bureau of the Census. The standardization sample consisted of 2,200 children extending from 6 to 16 years and stratified according to age, gender, race/ethnicity, geographic region, and parental education. Students who were not fluent in English were excluded from the sample.

TESTS-at-a-GLANCE

Wechsler Intelligence Scale for Children–Fourth Edition (WISC–IV)

- **Publication Date:** 2004
- **Purposes:** Cognitive abilities and problem-solving.
- **Age/Grade Levels:** 6 years through 16 years, 11 months.
- **Time to Administer:** 60 to 90 minutes.
- **Technical Adequacy:** The standardization sample is excellent. Reliability is very good. Validity is excellent.
- **Suggested Use:** Can be used when conducting a psycho-educational assessment, diagnosis of exceptional needs, determining eligibility for services, and clinical and neuropsychological assessment.

The *WISC–IV* standardization sample did not include students with exceptional needs nor does it provide separate norms for these children. However, the manual provides summaries of several studies conducted with special populations, including those with mental retardation, learning disabilities, autism, and attention-deficit hyperactivity disorder, behavior disorder. The manual states that approximately 5.7 percent of students from these studies of special populations was added to the standardization sample. For the most part, these studies are few in number and contain small samples. However, they are encouraging. Additional research is needed in this area.

RELIABILITY   Reliability refers to the consistency or stability of test performance. The manual reports split-half reliability coefficients for each of the subtests, for the three IQ scales, and for the four factor-based scales. Because the length of a test affects reliability, the highest reliability coefficient was for Full Scale IQ (.97). For the subtests, reliability coefficients ranged from .79 to .90. Reliability coefficients for the Index scores range from .88 to .94.

Test-retest reliability is an estimate of the stability of test scores over time. The test-retest reliabilities for the Full Scale IQ and Index scores is satisfactory. Interscorer reliability coefficients are .95 or higher.

How It Works! Cognitive Assessment

Hayley, who is 11 years old, was referred for special education services because her teachers observed that she has specific difficulties in reading, written language, and mathematics.

Emily Lauren Martinez, the school psychologist, is a member of the special services team. While the school's learning specialist focuses on Hayley's academic achievement, Emily concentrates on the assessment of cognitive abilities and problem-solving processes. She observed Hayley in several classes, examined work samples, and interviewed her.

Hayley told Emily that she feels that she has difficulty completing assignments that require reading and writing. She enjoys participating in class discussions, especially when class discussions involve topics such as human rights and social justice. Hayley told Emily that she would like to be a social worker or lawyer when she grows up so that she can help people. Emily decided to administer an intelligence test to Hayley so that teachers have additional information about Hayley's potential.

After administering the *WISC-IV* to Hayley, Emily met with Hayley's teachers and explained the test's results

to them. The Record Form summarizing Hayley's performance can be found in Figure 13.2. She said that Hayley demonstrated overall average intelligence with a Full Scale score of 101. When compared with other areas, Hayley has relative strengths in Verbal Comprehension, with highest scaled scores in Vocabulary and Comprehension. Hayley seemed to have average Working Memory and relatively weak performance in Processing Speed and Perceptual Reasoning. Emily concluded that Hayley has relative difficulty with visual-perceptual and visual-motor activities, resulting in problems with planning and organization. Relative weaknesses in these areas may indicate that Hayley has difficulty figuring out how to begin activities and organize her work. She has difficulty keeping track of homework and long-term assignments. Hayley exhibits difficulty with impulse control, which affects her ability to reflect on school assignments and integrate new learning with prior learning. Emily wrote that there are a number of interventions that teachers can implement and strategies that Hayley can use to ameliorate these difficulties. These will be discussed at the upcoming planning meeting and incorporated into Hayley's IEP.

How It Works!
continued

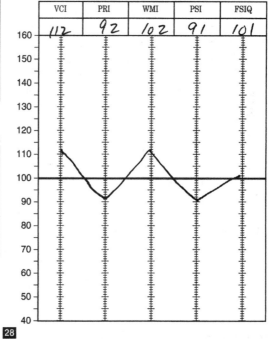

WECHSLER INTELLIGENCE SCALE FOR CHILDREN®
FOURTH EDITION – INTEGRATED

Child's Name _Hayley Keller_

Examiner's Name _Emily Lauren Martinez_

Calculation of Child's Age

	Year	Month	Day	Year	Month	Day
Date of Testing	xxxx	5 6	42 xx	xxxx	6 7	40 10
Date of Birth	xxxx	2	18	xxxx	2	18
Age at Testing	11	3	24	11	4	22

Total Raw Score to Scaled Score Conversions

Subtest	Raw Score	Scaled Scores			
Block Design	32	9	9		9
Similarities	26	12	12		12
Digit Span	16	10		10	10
Picture Concepts	16	8	8		8
Coding	45	9		9	9
Vocabulary	44	13	13		13
Letter–Number Seq.	18	11		11	11
Matrix Reasoning	20	9	9		9
Comprehension	28	12	12		12
Symbol Search	21	8		8	8
(Picture Completion)			( )		( )
(Cancellation)	73	9		(9)	(9)
(Information)	20	12	(12)		(12)
(Arithmetic)	23	10		(10)	(10)
(Word Reasoning)			( )		
Sums of Scaled Scores		37	26	21	17 101

Verbal Comp.   Perc. Rsng.   Work. Mem.   Proc. Speed   Full Scale

Sum of Scaled Scores to Composite Score Conversions

Scale	Sum of Scaled Scores	Composite Score	Percentile Rank	__% Confidence Interval
Verbal Comprehension	37	VCI 112	79	105–118
Perceptual Reasoning	26	PRI 92	30	85–100
Working Memory	21	WMI 102	55	94–109
Processing Speed	17	PSI 91	27	83–101
Full Scale	101	FSIQ 101	53	96–106

PsychCorp™

To reorder WISC–IV Integrated
Record Forms, call 1-800-211-8378

Summary Page

Subtest Scaled Score Profile

Verbal Comprehension					Perceptual Reasoning				Working Memory			Processing Speed		
SI	VC	CO	(IN)	(WR)	BD	PCn	MR	(PCm)	DS	LN	(AR)	CD	SS	(CA)
12	13	12	12		9	8	9		10	11	10	9	8	9

Composite Score Profile

VCI	PRI	WMI	PSI	FSIQ
112	92	102	91	101

28

FIGURE 13.2 • Example of Completed Summary Page

VALIDITY Concurrent validity of the *WISC-IV* was investigated with other tests including the *WISC–II* and the *Wechsler Individual Achievement Test–Second Edition*. According to the manual, because the *WISC–III* is valid, the *WISC–IV* is also valid. While it is true that there is considerable evidence for the validity of the *WISC–III*, the *WISC–IV* is a substantial revision of the earlier version. The manual does provide evidence for the separate factor structure with exceptional students. This evidence supports the validity of the *WISC–IV*. However, additional research studies are necessary in order to add to our knowledge about the validity of the *WISC-IV*.

SUMMARY The *WISC–IV* is an individually administered test of intelligence. Validity appears to be adequate. While additional research is necessary to contribute to our understanding of it, this instrument is useful in the assessment of students.

SNAPSHOT

Andres

Andres is 11 years old and is in the fifth grade. He grew up in his neighborhood, and he has many friends there. Routinely, when Andres arrives home after school, he has a snack and then races outdoors. Andres has disliked school ever since he can remember. He always had a hard time with reading, writing, and spelling, but he achieved somewhat better grades in mathematics.

Last week, there was a meeting at the school to discuss Andres's continuing academic difficulties. Andres attended the meeting along with his parents. His teachers, while praising him for working hard, reported that Andres lags considerably behind his peers in academic areas. His teachers agreed that Andres is a delight to have in class. The participants in the meeting agreed that an assessment of Andres's cognitive abilities should be conducted in order to gain a better understanding of his learning needs.

After permission was obtained from Andres's family, the psychologist administered the *WISC–IV* to Andres. Keeping in mind that a standard score of 10 ± 3 falls within the average range, the following is a summary of the results:

Verbal Scale	Standard Score
Information	6
Similarities	11
Arithmetic	8
Vocabulary	9
Comprehension	7
Digit Span	7
Verbal Scale Intelligence Quotient (VSIQ)	90

Peformance Scale	Standard Score
Picture Completion	10
Coding	8
Picture Arrangement	15
Block Design	15
Object Assembly	8
Symbol Search	14
Performance Scale Intelligence Quotient (PSIQ)	108

Scale	Index
Verbal Comprehension Index	91
Perceptual Organization Index	113
Freedom from Distractibility Index	87
Processing Speed Index	106

The psychologist summarized Andres's performance on the *WISC–IV*. She wrote that Andres had significant strengths in both verbal and nonverbal concept formation, abstract reasoning, and visual sequencing, and relative weaknesses, although still within the average range, in using short-term memory and in visualizing the whole from the sum of its parts.

The psychologist recommended presenting new concepts globally first and then breaking them down into their components, taking into consideration the weaknesses in short-term memory when instructing in academic areas. Andres will need repetition in content areas when learning new concepts and help in organizing his thoughts to make connections with prior knowledge in order to retrieve information at a later time.

Wechsler Intelligence Scale for Children–Fourth Edition (WISC–IV Spanish)

A Spanish edition of the *WISC–IV* (PsychCorp, 2005) is available. This edition can be administered to children ages 6 through 16 years, 11 months. According to the publisher, the Spanish edition represents the U.S. Spanish-speaking population, including those whose origins are Mexico, Cuba, Puerto Rico, Dominican Republic, Central America, and South America. The norms allow comparison to English language-speaking children who have similar educational experiences and parental educational levels.

In many instances, test items were directly translated from the Spanish. For items in which no direct translation was possible, new items were generated. The Spanish edition includes the same ten core subtests that can be found in the *WISC–IV* and four of the five supplemental subtests. The subtests are grouped into four indices: Verbal Comprehension, Perceptual Reasoning, Working Memory, and Processing Speed.

Woodcock-Johnson III Tests of Cognitive Ability

The *Woodcock-Johnson III* (*WJ III*; Woodcock, McGrew, & Mather, 2001) is an individually administered battery that assesses cognitive and academic abilities in individuals ages 2 years through adulthood. The battery consists of two tests, *Woodcock-Johnson III*

Research-Based Practices   **To What Extent Do Intelligence Test Scores Predict Reading Ability?**

A misleading belief in the assessment field is that intelligence scores predict reading ability. In a review of more than 450 studies, Hammill (2004) explored the variables that are related to reading achievement. The variables that were analyzed included:

Variables Related to Reading Achievement	Description
Writing conventions	Spelling, punctuation, capitalization
Letters	Recognition of individual letters
Written language	Vocabulary, sentence combining, story construction, logical sentences, contextual language
Rapid naming	Rapid digit and letter naming
Phonological awareness	Contrasting speech sounds, segmenting and blending phonemes
Intelligence	Abilities related to verbal, nonverbal, and quantitative reasoning
Spoken language	Speaking and understanding verbal speech
Perceptual and motor	Perceptual abilities that involve auditory and visual stimuli; motor abilities

Hammill found that the largest predictors of reading are writing conventions and letters. Moderate predictors, listed in order from highest to lowest, are written language, rapid naming, phonological awareness, intelligence, and memory. What are the implications of these results for interpretation of scores on tests of cognition and intelligence?

Tests of Cognitive Ability (WJ III COG) and the *Woodcock-Johnson III Tests of Achievement (WJ III ACH)*. The *WJ III* measures general intellectual ability, specific cognitive abilities, scholastic aptitude, oral language, and academic achievement.

The *WJ III COG* is an application of the Cattell-Horn-Carroll (CHC) theory of cognitive processing. According to the authors, the *WJ III COG* measures: General Intellectual Ability, Predicted Achievement, Intra-cognitive Discrepancies, Cognitive Categories (Verbal Ability, Thinking Ability, and Cognitive Efficiency), CHC Factors (Comprehension-Knowledge, Long-Term Retrieval, Visual-Spatial Thinking, Auditory Processing, Fluid Reasoning, Processing Speed, Short-Term Memory), and Clinical Clusters (Phonemic Awareness, Working Memory, Broad Attention, Cognitive Fluency, and Executive Processes). The *WJ III COG* comprises two batteries, a Standard Battery and an Extended Battery. Teachers and other professionals can administer the Standard Battery alone or with the Extended Battery. Subtests 1 through 10 make up the Standard

---

TABLE 13.4 ● Woodcock-Johnson III Cognitive Battery Subtests

The Standard Battery of the *WJ III COG* consists of subtests 1 through 10. The Extended Battery comprises subtests 11 through 20.

Subtest		Narrow Ability	Broad Cognitive Factor
1	Verbal Comprehension	Lexical Knowledge	Comprehension
		Language Development	Knowledge
11	General Information	General Information	
2	Visual-Auditory Learning	Associate Memory	Visual Spatial Thinking
12	Retrieval Fluency	Ideational Fluency	
10	Visual-Auditory Learning—Delayed	Associate Memory	
3	Spatial Relations	Visualization Spatial Relations	Auditory Processing
13	Picture Recognition	Visual Memory	
19	Planning	Spatial Scanning	
4	Sound Blending	Phonetic Coding Analysis	Auditory Processing
14	Auditory Attention	Speech Sound Discrimination	
8	Incomplete Words	Phonetic Coding Synthesis	
5	Concept Formation	Induction	Fluid Reasoning
15	Analysis-Synthesis	Sequential Reasoning	
6	Visual Matching	Perceptual Speed	Processing Speed
16	Decision Speed	Semantic Processing	
18	Rapid Picture Naming	Naming Facility	
20	Pair Cancellation	Attention Concentration	
7	Numbers Reversed	Working Memory	Short-Term Memory
		Memory Span	
17	Memory for Words	Memory Span	
9	Auditory Working Memory	Working Memory	
		Memory Span	

Battery and subtests 11 through 20 make up the Extended Battery. Subtests combine to form clusters. Table 13.4 lists the subtests and the Broad Cognitive Abilities that they measure.

ADMINISTRATION The time to administer the *WJ III* varies from 20 minutes to several hours depending on whether administering both the *WJ III COG* and the *WJ III ACH* and whether including the Extended Battery. The test provides age (ages 2 years through adulthood) and grade norms (kindergarten through first year graduate school). A computer scoring program is necessary to assure accurate scoring. Raw scores are converted to age and grade equivalents, percentile ranks, and standard scores. The manual reports confidence bands for standard scores for the 68 percent, 90 percent, and 95 percent confidence bands. It is possible to interpret intra-individual, intra-cognitive, and intra-achievement discrepancies, as well as predicted achievement.

> **TESTS-at-a-GLANCE**
>
> ## Woodcock-Johnson III Tests of Cognitive Ability (WJ III COG)
>
> - **Publication Date:** 2001
> - **Purposes:** Assesses cognitive abilities, general intellectual ability.
> - **Age/Grade Levels:** 2 years through adulthood.
> - **Time to Administer:** Approximately 1 hour.
> - **Technical Adequacy:** The standardization sample is appropriate. Reliability and validity are strong.
> - **Suggested Use:** Diagnosis, determining intra-individual, intra-cognitive, and intra-achievement discrepancies, determining predicted achievement, determining eligibility for services, program placement, individual program planning, program evaluation.

NORMS The standardization sample for the *WJ III* comprised 8,818 individuals in over 100 communities. The preschool sample consisted of over 1,000 children who were 2 to 5 years of age and not enrolled in kindergarten. There were 4,784 individuals in the kindergarten through grade 12 sample. More than 1,000 individuals made up the college/university sample. The rest of the standardization sample consisted of adults. The stratification sample was selected according to census region, community size, sex, race (Caucasian, African American, Native American, Asian Pacific, Hispanic), type of school (elementary, secondary, public, private, home), type of college/university (two-year college, four-year college or university, public, private), education of adults (less than ninth grade, less than high school diploma, high school diploma, one to three years of college, bachelor's degree, master's degree or higher), occupational status of adults (employed, unemployed, not in labor force), and occupation of adults in labor force (professional/managerial, technical/sales/ administrative, Armed Forces/police, farming/ forestry/fishing, precision product/craft/repair, operative/fabricator/laborer).

RELIABILITY The reliability of the *WJ III* has greatly improved from the previous version of this test. The authors provide extensive information on reliability of the subtest scores, clusters, and the discrepancy scores. Reliabilities for the broad cognitive and achievement clusters are in the .90s.

VALIDITY The manual reports a number of validity studies for both the cognitive and achievement batteries. In general, there is evidence to support content, concurrent, and construct validity. Evaluators should remember that the cognitive portion represents a single perspective, the Cattell-Horn-Carroll (CHC) theory. The extent to which various subtests and interpretations reflect students' abilities depends on the orientation of the team to assessment.

SUMMARY The *WJ III COG* is a substantially improved version of its predecessor, the *Woodcock-Johnson Psychoeducational Battery–Revised (WJ–R*; (Woodcock & Johnson, 1989). It is a norm-referenced, individually administered battery that assesses cognitive and academic abilities in individuals ages 2 years through adulthood. The cognitive battery consists of two parts, Standard Battery and the Extended Battery. Documentation of reliability and validity are extensive.

▶ Examine several different intelligence tests. How do they differ in form and content?

Summary

- Our understanding of intelligence has developed and changed over the years.

- Variables that can affect performance on intelligence tests include student's background, culture, primary language, environment, motivation, health, and emotional state, as well as examiner's skills and bias.

- Intelligence tests sample behaviors. Performance on a test helps us in our understanding of the student's approach to the demands of the tasks that are presented.

- Scores on an IQ test represent the examinee's performance at a given moment in time.

> ▶ What do you think intelligence tests will be like twenty years from now?

REFERENCES

Anastasi, A. (1988). *Psychological testing.* New York: Macmillan.

Brown, L., Sherbenou, R. J., & Johnsen, S. K. (1997). *Test of nonverbal intelligence–3.* Itasca, IL: Riverside.

Elliott, C. D. (1990a). *Differential ability scales—Administration and scoring manual.* San Antonio, TX: The Psychological Corporation.

Elliott, C. D. (1990b). *Differential ability scales—Introduction and technical handbook.* San Antonio, TX: Psychological Corporation.

Hammill, D. D. (1998). *Detroit tests of learning aptitude–4.* Itasca, IL: Riverside.

Hammill, D. D. (2004). What we know about the correlates of reading. *Exceptional Children 70* (4): 453–468.

Hammill, D. D., & Bryant, B. R. (1991). *Detroit tests of learning aptitude–primary: Second edition.* Itasca, IL: Riverside.

Hammill, D. D., Pearson, N. A., & Wiederholt, J. L. (1996). *Comprehensive test of nonverbal intelligence.* Austin, TX: Pro-Ed.

Kaufman, A. S., & Kaufman, N. L. (1993). *Kaufman adolescent and adult intelligence test.* Circle Pines, MN: American Guidance Service.

Kaufman, A. S., & Kaufman, N. L. (2004). *Kaufman assessment battery for children, second edition.* Circle Pines, MN: American Guidance Service.

Lohman, D., & E. Hagen (2001). *Cognitive abilities test.* Itasca, IL: Riverside Publishing Company.

McLoughlin, J. A., & Lewis, R. B. (2005). *Assessing students with special needs* (6th ed.). Upper Saddle River, NJ: Pearson.

PsychCorp. (2005). *Wechsler intelligence scale for children–IV, Spanish Edition.* San Antonio, TX: Author.

Roid, G. (2003). *The Stanford-Binet intelligence scale: Fifth edition, Examiner's handbook.* Itasca, IL: Riverside.

Salvia, J., & Ysseldyke, J. (2004). *Assessment.* Boston: Houghton-Mifflin.

Sattler, J. (1988). *Assessment of children.* La Mesa, CA: Author.

Sternberg, R. (1996). Myths, countermyths, and truths about intelligence. *Educational Researcher, 25:* 11–16.

Suzuki, L. A., Vraniak, D. A., & Kugler, J. F. (1996). Intellectual assessment across cultures. In L. A. Suzuki, P. J. Meller, & J. G. Ponterotto (Eds.), *Handbook of multicultural assessment,* (pp. 141–177). San Francisco: Jossey-Bass.

Thorndike, R. L., Hagen, E. P., & Sattler, J. M. (1986). *Stanford-Binet intelligence scale: Fourth edition.* Itasca, IL: Riverside.

Wechsler, D. (2004). *Wechsler intelligence scale for children–IV Integrated.* San Antonio, TX: PsychCorp.

Woodcock, R. W., McGrew, K. S., & Mather, N. (2001). *Woodcock-Johnson III tests of cognitive ability.* Itasca, IL: Riverside.

Woodcock, R. W., & Johnson, H. B. (1989). *Woodcock-Johnson psychoeducational battery–revised.* Itasca, IL: Riverside.

Woodcock, R. W., & Muñoz-Sandoval, A. F. (1996). *Batería–R tests of cognitive ability.* Itasca, IL: Riverside.

14 Adaptive Behavior

Chapter Objectives

After completing this chapter, you should be able to:

- Define and describe the concept of adaptive behavior.
- Describe maladaptive or problem behavior.
- Describe specific tests of adaptive behavior, adaptive skills, and maladaptive behavior.

Key Terms

Adaptive behavior
Supports

Maladaptive behaviors

Informant

▶ **CEC Common Core Knowledge and Skills.** The beginning special educator will understand specialized terminology used in the assessment of individuals with disabilities (GC8K1).

Overview

This chapter focuses on adaptive behavior and the skills that individuals need to function day-to-day. Assessments of adaptive behavior assess functioning of individuals who have disabilities such as behavior challenges or mental retardation. Because our views of adaptive behavior have changed and will continue to change over time, there is considerable disagreement over how current assessment instruments measure these skills. No one instrument measures the entire adaptive behavior domain. In fact, adaptive behavior instruments reflect different views of adaptive behavior and the skills involved.

Adaptive Behavior

Adaptive behavior is the collection of conceptual, social, and practical skills that individuals learn in order to function in their everyday lives (American Association on Mental Retardation [AAMR], 2002, p. 73). The concept of adaptive behavior is most closely associated with mental retardation. For students who are in school, the assessment of adaptive behavior plays a part in determining whether a student is labeled as having mental retardation. According to the American Association on Mental Retardation,

> mental retardation is a disability characterized by significant limitations both in intellectual functioning and in adaptive behavior as expressed in conceptual, social, and practical adaptive skills. This disability originates before age 18. (AAMR, 2002, p. 13)

For the purpose of diagnosing mental retardation, a student must demonstrate significant limitations in adaptive behavior on standardized measures that are normed on people with and without disabilities. Scores must fall at least two standard deviations below the mean. That is, standard scores of less than 70 on each assessment where the mean equals 100 and the standard deviation equals 15 are considered to be significant. Significant scores must represent either one or more of the types of adaptive behavior including conceptual, social, or practical or an overall score of conceptual, social, and practical skills (AAMR, 2002, p. 76). Table 14.1 illustrates the skills associated with the three areas of adaptive behavior.

Supports

Assessment of adaptive behavior must include the assessment of supports needed for the individual to participate in the environment. **Supports** are

resources and strategies that aim to promote the development, education, interests and personal well-being of a person and that enhance individual function. Services are one type of support provide by professional and agencies. (AAMR, 2002, p. 15)

Figure 14.1 illustrates the interrelationships between a person's capabilities, support areas, support function, and personal outcomes.

Maladaptive Behaviors

Maladaptive behaviors are those behaviors that are considered to be problem behaviors. Examples of maladaptive behaviors include bed wetting, unusual physical aggressiveness, poor attention, impulsivity, self-injurious behaviors, rocking back and forth repetitively, and poor eye contact. In general, we consider a student's actions a problem when they adversely affect the student, another student, or the environment (Bruininks, Thurlow, & Gilman, 1987). Problem behaviors affect the extent to which individuals will integrate into social and community settings. With older students, the presence of problem behaviors can have a negative impact on vocational and community placements (Bruininks et al., 1987).

The concept of maladaptive behavior, like the concept of adaptive behavior, is not without controversy. The assessment of

TABLE 14.1 • Adaptive Behavior Skills	
Adaptive Skill Area	**Representative Skills**
Conceptual	Language
	Reading and writing
	Money concepts
	Self-direction
Social	Interpersonal
	Responsibility
	Self-esteem
	Gullibility
	Naïveté
	Follows rules
	Obeys laws
	Avoids victimization
Practical	Activities of daily living
	Instrumental activities of daily living
	Occupational skills
	Maintains safe environments

Source: Adapted from AAMR, 2002, p. 82.

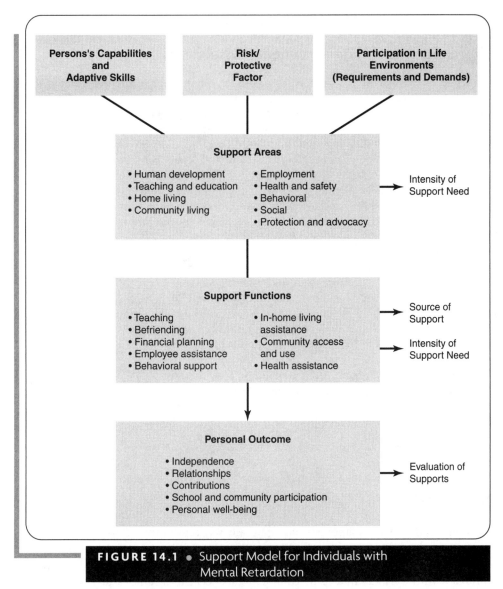

FIGURE 14.1 ● Support Model for Individuals with Mental Retardation

Source: American Association on Mental Retardation, *Mental Retardation: Definition, Classification and Systems of Support* (10th ed.). Washington, DC: Author. © 2002 American Association on Mental Retardation. Reprinted with permission.

maladaptive behavior relates to expectations tied to the student's age, family, culture, gender, and community. For example, thumb sucking is not a maladaptive behavior for a 2-year-old, but may be so for an 8-year-old.

Responding to Diversity

Gender, race, ethnicity, culture, community expectations, and the life cycle all influence adaptive behavior. The quality of adaptive behavior that an individual demonstrates changes at various ages. In addition, the presence of a disability can compound the identification of adaptive behavior. Limitations in motor ability, in expressive and receptive abilities, or in other areas can make assessing adaptive behavior a difficult task.

Research-Based Practices | Adaptive Behavior and Achievement of Students with Developmental Disabilities

Research studies show that when teachers teach students how to use learning strategies, such as self-monitoring, or use teaching strategies, such as peer tutoring, students with disabilities can improve adaptive behaviors. For students with developmental disabilities, self-management strategies and decreasing maladaptive behaviors are important for success in the general education classroom. King-Sears (1999) found that self-monitoring can be used successfully by second-grade students with multiple disabilities. At the high school level, Michael Wehmeyer and colleagues (2003) conducted a small study involving three students with developmental disabilities. The researchers designed an intervention program that involved teaching self-regulation procedures to the students. Their findings indicated that all three students improved adaptive behaviors related to class participation or decreased maladaptive behaviors such as inappropriate verbalizations and other disruptive behaviors.

In another study, researchers at the University of Utah (McDonnell, Thorson, Disher, Mathot-Buckner, Mendel, & Ray, 2003) explored the use of teaching strategies in inclusive classroom settings with both students with developmental disabilities and students without disabilities. Eleven students with developmental disabilities participated in the study, all with a wide range of needs and functioning

levels. In the classroom, the students with developmental disabilities received a number of different supports such as curriculum and instructional adaptations, embedded instruction, parallel instruction, circles of friends, peer tutoring, and direct instruction. Teachers used both large and small group instruction, cooperative learning, and co-teaching between general and special educators. At the end of the school year, the results indicated that students with developmental disabilities made significant gains in adaptive behavior, as measured by the *Scales of Independent Behavior-Revised (SIB-R)*.

Using mandated state-level criterion referenced tests in reading/language arts and mathematics, the researchers also compared the 324 students without disabilities who were in inclusive classrooms with 221 students without disabilities who were in classrooms where there were no students with developmental disabilities. They found no significant differences in academic achievement between the two groups of students.

▶ How would you explain the gain in adaptive behaviors for students with developmental disabilities? How would you explain that there were no significant differences in academic achievement between the two groups of students without disabilities?

Informants

Instruments that assess adaptive behavior usually rely on informants. An **informant** is an individual who knows the student well and provides information about the student. The informant responds to questions about the individual either through an interview with the examiner or by completing a checklist or rating scale. Because the assessment of skills and behavior relies on ratings that informants provide, it is possible and advantageous to administer them frequently.

The informant can be a parent, teacher, counselor, aide, nurse, or social worker. Informants provide different information about students, although there may be considerable overlap. For instance, the teacher, social worker, or counselor provides information about peer relationships while the parent offers information about sibling relationships and activities around the home.

The information that the informants provide is necessarily judgmental and can vary from one informant to the next. Informants bring their own perspectives, experiences, attitudes, response styles, and biases. Because of these variables, it is important to evaluate the reliability and validity of the information that the informant supplies, and to ask more than one informant to complete an instrument or scale (Sattler, 2001).

▶ **CEC Common Core Knowledge and Skills.** The beginning special educator will implement procedures for assessing and reporting both appropriate and problematic social behaviors of individuals with disabilities (GC8S1).

▶ **CEC Common Core Knowledge and Skills.** The beginning special educator will use exceptionality-specific assessment instruments with individuals with disabilities (GC8S2).

Standardized Instruments

The instruments in this chapter have the specific purpose of evaluating adaptive behavior. There are many other tests besides these that assess adaptive skills and behavior. In the following section, we will examine the most common.

Adaptive Behavior Assessment System® Second Edition

The *Adaptive Behavior Assessment System® Second Edition (ABAS®II;* Harrison & Oakland, 2003) is a norm-referenced assessment of adaptive behavior for children through adults, ages birth to 89 years. This assessment measures the same ten adaptive skill areas specified in the *Diagnostic and Statistical Manual of Mental Disorders (DSM–IV–TR)* (American Psychiatric Association, 2000): communication, community use, functional academics, school living/home living, health and safety, leisure, self-care, self-direction, social, and work. According to the authors, these skill areas comprise the three general areas of adaptive behavior—conceptual, social, and practical—identified by AAMR. The *ABAS® II* includes Spanish-language Parent and Teacher Forms. An example of a parent rating summary, generated by the ABAS-II Scoring Assistant Software, is illustrated in Figure 14.2. On this report, scaled scores have a mean of 10 and a standard deviation of 3.

Child Information

Child's Name:	Emily R Sample	Completion Date:	10/15/XX
Sex:	Female	Date of Birth:	5/4/xx
Race/Ethnicity:	White not Hispanic Origin	Age at Testing:	9 year(s)
School:	Larkspur Elementary		5 month(s)
Disabling Condition:	No	Grade:	4th
Job Status:	N/A	City:	San Antonio
		State:	TX

Parent Information

Parent's Name:	Lauren Sample
Occupation:	Accountant
Number of Child's Siblings at Home:	None
Relationship to Child:	Parent

Raw Score to Scaled Score Conversions

Skill Areas	Raw Score	Scaled Scores
Communication (Com)	61	9
Community Use (CU)	50	12
Functional Academics (FA)	63	13
Home Living (HL)	47	8
Health and Safety (HS)	57	11
Leisure (LS)	60	13
Self-Care (SC)	64	8
Self-Direction (SD)	56	10
Social (SC)	63	11

FIGURE 14.2 ● Parent Rating Summary Report from the Adaptive Behavior Assessment System (ABAS-II)

Source: From the *Adaptive Behavior Assessment System–Second Edition.* Copyright © 2003, 2000 by Harcourt Assessment, Inc. Reproduced with permission. All rights reserved.

TESTS-at-a-GLANCE

Adaptive Behavior Assessment System® Second Edition (ABAS II)

- **Publication Date:** 2003
- **Purpose:** To assess adaptive behavior skills and to identify strengths and limitations as well as monitor progress.
- **Age/Grade Levels:** Birth through 89 years.
- **Time to Administer:** 15 to 20 minutes.
- **Technical Adequacy:** Standardization sample reflects the 2000 U.S. Census. Good reliability and clinical validity.
- **Suggested Use:** This instrument provides forms that may be used by the individual, parents, teachers, and others to assess the daily functional skills of an individual.

ADMINISTRATION Multiple forms allow parents, teachers, family members, and the individual to provide information. Skill items are scored on a rating scale with 0 (is not able), 1 (never when needed), 2 (sometimes when needed), and 3 (always when needed). A separate column allows the informant to indicate if the item required a guess. Approximate time to complete is 15 to 20 minutes.

SCORING Norm-referenced scaled scores are available for each on the skill areas (mean = 10, standard deviation = 3) and standard scores for the composite areas (mean =100, standard deviation = 15). Confidence intervals of 90 percent and 95 percent may be calculated.

STANDARDIZATION For children birth to 5 years, the standardization sample consisted of 2,100 individuals. For children 5 years through adult, the sample consisted of 5,270 individuals who were representative of the 2000 U.S. census in terms of sex, race/ethnicity, geographic regions, and parent education level.

RELIABILITY Internal consistency reliability coefficients for the overall general adaptive composite are in the high .90s for all age groups. Reliability coefficients for the skills areas range from .91 to .98. Test-retest reliability coefficients for the general adaptive composites are in the .90s. Interrater reliability coefficients on the general adaptive composites (teacher form) are .91 for students between ages 5 and 9 and .87 for students between ages 10 and 21. On the parent form, the interrater reliability coefficients for the general adaptive composites are .83 to .85 for both age groups.

VALIDITY The manual reports clinical validity studies to support the use of the *ABAS® II* to assist in identifying mental retardation. Mean scores of almost 300 individuals with mental retardation ranged from 55 to 73 points, which was significantly lower than the matched control groups, where individuals' scores ranged from 95 to 101. Additionally, there were significant differences between the mean general adaptive composite scores of individuals with mild and moderate mental retardation.

SUMMARY The *Adaptive Behavior Assessment System® Second Edition* is a well-designed norm-referenced rating scale that is aligned with DSM-IV adaptive skill areas and incorporates the American Association of Mental Retardation (AAMR) guidelines for evaluating the three composite areas of adaptive behavior: conceptual, social, and practical. This assessment has been renormed according to the 2000 U.S. census. Scoring software may be purchased separately.

SNAPSHOT

Trina

Six-year-old Trina and her family recently moved to a new city where her mother enrolled Trina and shared the following information about her daughter. Several months after Trina was born, the pediatrician noticed a delay in her motor development and referred Trina to a pediatric neurologist who diagnosed Trina as having mild cerebral palsy. The family was referred to a regional program of early intervention services. Later, follow-up visits to the neurologist indicated that Trina was also experiencing developmental delays in other areas. Trina's mother provided consent to have the previous school's records forwarded.

Shortly after Trina was enrolled in her new school, the IEP team convened to discuss Trina's records, including past assessments and her current education program. They recommended additional assessments. Team members felt that Trina should have both cognitive and adaptive behavior assessments to better understand her needs and to plan an appropriate program.

▶ What do you think was the rationale behind this decision? Under what eligibility criteria might Trina continue to receive services?

Adaptive Behavior Scales–School, Second Edition (ABS–S:2)

Originally developed by the American Association on Mental Retardation, the *Adaptive Behavior Scales–School, Second Edition (ABS–S:2;* Lambert, Leland, & Nihira, 1993), is intended for use with individuals who are from 3 through 18 years, 11 months and who will be attending school or are in school. A Profile/Summary Form is illustrated in Figure 14.3. This form shows the two parts of this assessment and the areas assessed. Part One comprises the nine domains listed below:

Independent Functioning. Assesses eating, toileting, maintaining a clean and neat appearance, dressing, and using transportation and other public facilities.

Physical Development. Evaluates physical and motor abilities.

Economic Activity. Assesses ability to manage money and to be a consumer.

Language Development. Evaluates receptive and expressive language and behavior in social situations.

Numbers and Time. Examines basic mathematical skills.

Prevocational/Vocational Activity. Assesses skills related to school and job performance.

Responsibility. Assesses the extent that an individual can be held accountable for his or her actions, belongings, and duties.

Self-Direction. Examines whether individuals choose to maintain an active or passive lifestyle.

Socialization. Assesses the ability to interact with others.

Part Two focuses on social maladaptation. These behaviors are divided into the seven domains listed below.

Violent and Antisocial Behavior. Examines behaviors that are physically or emotionally abusive.

Rebellious Behavior. Assesses aspects of rebelliousness.

Untrustworthy Behaviors. Examines behaviors that are related to stealing, lying, cheating, and showing disrespect for public and private property.

Stereotyped and Hyperactive Behavior. Assesses behaviors such as making inappropriate physical contact, behaving in stereotypical ways, and being overactive.

Eccentric Behavior. Examines behaviors considered to be very unusual.

Withdrawal. Assesses the degree to which an individual withdraws or fails to respond to others.

Disturbed Behavior. Examines bothersome types of behaviors.

ADMINISTRATION An interviewer administers the *ABS–S:2.*

SCORING Raw scores convert to standard scores and percentiles. Scores also convert to quotients that have a mean of 100 and a standard deviation of 15.

TESTS-at-a-GLANCE

Adaptive Behavior Scales–School, Second Edition (ABS–S:2)

- **Publication Date:** 1993
- **Purposes:** To assess personal independence, coping skills, daily living skills, and maladaptive or problem behaviors.
- **Age/Grade Levels:** Ages 3 through 21.
- **Time to Administer:** Approximately 30 minutes in an interview format.
- **Technical Adequacy:** The standardization sample is representative. Reliability and validity are very good.
- **Suggested Use:** Can be used to determine adaptive and maladaptive (problem) behaviors in individuals who have mental retardation, who are developmentally delayed, or who exhibit problem behaviors. This test needs to be renormed and updated.

ABS-S:2

AAMR Adaptive Behavior Scale–School
Second Edition
PROFILE/SUMMARY FORM

Section I. Identifying Information

Name: Jenna Brown Male ___ Female ✓

	Year	Month	Day
Date of Rating	XX	07	28
Date of Birth	XX	11	11
Age	8	8	17

School: WPS
Examiner's Name: L. Spencer
Examiner's Title: Sp Ed Director
Respondent's Name: parent
Relationship to Subject: ___
Normative Tables Used: ____ MR ✓ Non-MR

Section II. Record of ABS-S:2 Domain Scores

Part One Domain Scores	Raw Score	Percentile	Standard Score	Age Equiv.	Rating
I. Independent Functioning	80	16	7		below average
II. Physical Development	23	63	11		average
III. Economic Activity	0	1	3		very poor
IV. Language Development	29	9	6		below average
V. Numbers and Time	6	16	7		below average
VI. Prevocational/Vocational Activity	6	16	7		below average
VII. Self-Direction	18	37	9		average
VIII. Responsibility	4	16	7		below average
IX. Socialization	20	9	6		below average
Part Two Domain Scores					
X. Social Behavior	8	63	11		average
XI. Conformity	5	50	10		average
XII. Trustworthiness	1	63	11		average
XIII. Stereotyped and Hyperactive Behavior	8	16	7		below average
XIV. Self-Abusive Behavior	1	50	11		average
XV. Social Engagement	0	63	11		average
XVI. Disturbing Interpersonal Behavior	1	84	13		above average

FIGURE 14.3 • AAMR Adaptive Behavior Scale Profile Summary

Source: From *Adaptive Behavior Scale–School* (Second Edition). Washington, DC: American Association for Mental Retardation: Copyright © 1993. Reprinted with permission.

STANDARDIZATION Standardization of the *ABS–S:2* consisted of a norming sample from 31 states, including individuals with and without disabilities.

RELIABILITY AND VALIDITY According to the authors, the *ABS–S:2* is a reliable and valid instrument, and there is considerable research that documents the usefulness of this instrument.

SUMMARY The *Adaptive Behavior Scales–School, Second Edition* is an instrument that assesses the adaptive and maladaptive behavior of school-age children. The test is administered by interview and scores are reported as a quotient with a mean of 100 and a standard deviation of 15. This test needs to be renormed and updated.

Checklist of Adaptive Living Skills

The *Checklist of Adaptive Living Skills (CALS;* Moreau & Bruininks, 1991) is a criterion-referenced checklist of approximately 800 items in the areas of self-care, personal independence, and adaptive functioning. It measures the adaptive behaviors of infants through adults and is individually administered, using an interview format, to a respondent who knows the individual well. The *CALS* relates, conceptually and statistically, to the *Scales of Independent Behavior (SIB;* Bruininks, Woodcock, Weatherman, & Hill, 1984). The reason for this, according to the manual, was to allow users to predict scores on the *SIB.* The *Adaptive Living Skills Curriculum (ALSC;* Bruininks, Moreau, Gilman, & Anderson, 1991), which is linked to the *CALS,* contains training objectives, strategies, and activities to facilitate program planning and intervention. The *CALS* comprises four domains: Personal Living Skills, Home Living Skills, Community Living Skills, and Employment Skills. Each of these domains breaks down into 24 specific skills modules. Each item covers a range of behaviors and proceed in order of difficulty.

ADMINISTRATION The respondent must know the student well. Persons with varied backgrounds, including parents, rehabilitation counselors, teachers, aides, and others can serve as respondents. The student need not test on all items. Because the *CALS* is a criterion-referenced checklist, teachers or other professionals can readminister the items periodically. It takes approximately 60 minutes to complete.

SCORING The examiner checks items if the student performs the skill independently.

STANDARDIZATION This measure is criterion-referenced and was not standardized. The manual states that 627 individuals who ranged in age from infancy to over 40 years old took the *CALS.* The respondents were from 8 states. Approximately one-half of the sample were individuals with disabilities, and the sample had an approximately equal number of females and males. The manual provides little demographic information about the sample.

RELIABILITY Calculations of internal consistency and split-half reliabilities are available. The information on reliability is limited.

VALIDITY Evidence of criterion-related validity is based on two studies and is very limited.

SUMMARY The *CALS* is a criterion-referenced instrument that shows limited evidence of reliability and content and construct validity. Additional information about the sample is necessary. We recommend using this instrument with caution. It may be most appropriate for program planning.

Responsibility and Independence Scale for Adolescents

The *Responsibility and Independence Scale for Adolescents (RISA;* Salvia, Neisworth, & Schmidt, 1990) is a measure of adaptive behavior of individuals who are between the ages of 12 years and 19 years, 11 months. The scale measures responsibility and independence in adolescents. Responsibility is defined as "a broad class of adaptive behaviors that meet social expectations and standards of reciprocity, accountability, and fairness and that enable personal development through self- and social management, age appropriate behavior and social communication" (p. 2). Individuals who are responsible are "dependable, trustworthy, and able to shape, as well as comply with, social rules" (p. 2). Independence is defined as "a broad class of adaptive behaviors that allow individuals to live separately and free from the control or determination of others and to conduct themselves effectively in matters such as domestic and financial management, citizenship, personal organization, transportation, and career development" (p. 2). Independence means that an individual can make good decisions, makes plans, and deals effectively with situations that might affect self-reliance.

The 136 items are arranged in two subtests: Responsibility and Independence. The Responsibility subtest has 52 items that cluster in three areas: Self-Management, Social Maturity, and Social Communication.

ADMINISTRATION An interviewer administers the *RISA* to an individual who is familiar with the student. Informants can be a parent, guardian, surrogate parent, or spouse. The 136 questions take between 30 to 45 minutes to administer.

SCORING The scoring is dichotomous with a score of 1 given when the informant responds yes, or a variation such as the phrase "I'm pretty sure" (p. 3). A score of 0 given when the informant answers no, or a variation such as the phrase "I don't think so" (p. 3). Scores can convert to percentiles and standard scores. Standard score differences can be available but the manual urges caution when using these differences.

STANDARDIZATION The sample consisted of ratings of 1,900 adolescents who were from nine age groups. Gender, community size, educational level of the parents or guardians, and geographical region were weighted so that the sample approximated the 1980 census. Race and ethnic group were not weighted because the sample closely represented the proportions in the U.S. population.

RELIABILITY The manual reports split-half and test-retest reliability. The coefficients are at least .90 or higher.

VALIDITY The manual reports three types of validity: content, criterion-related (concurrent), and construct. Content validity appears to be adequate. To demonstrate concurrent validity, the authors correlated the *RISA* with the *Vineland Adaptive Behavior Scales* and the *Scales of Independent Behavior*. The sample consisted of only 93 individuals, thus evidence of concurrent validity is weak. The coefficient for the *Vineland Adaptive Behavior Scales* total scale is .55, and the coefficient for the *Scales of Independent Behavior* total .55. Several studies that the manual reports discuss construct validity. Additional research is necessary to confirm construct validity.

SUMMARY The *Responsibility and Independence Scale for Adolescents (RISA)* is an individually administered measure of adaptive behavior of adolescents. The scale should measure responsibility and independence. Evidence of reliability is adequate. Additional studies are necessary to confirm construct validity. This test needs to be renormed and updated.

Scales of Independent Behavior–Revised

The *Scales of Independent Behavior–Revised (SIB–R;* Bruininks, Woodcock, Weatherman, & Hill, 1996) is an individually administered, norm-referenced measure of adaptive behavior that measures the adaptive and problem behavior of individuals ages infant through adult. According to the authors, the *SIB–R* is useful for identification, placement, program planning, and monitoring progress. The instrument consists of 14 subscales that form four adaptive behavior clusters: Motor Skills, Social Interaction and Communication Skills, Personal Living Skills, and Community Living Skills. There are four clusters of maladaptive or problem behavior also: General Maladaptive Behavior,

Internalized Maladaptive Behavior, Asocial Maladaptive Behavior, and Externalized Maladaptive Behavior. In addition, there are two short forms: *SIB–R Short Form* and the *Early Development Form*.

ADMINISTRATION The Full Scale takes from 30 to 45 minutes to administer, and the *Short Form* or the *Early Development Form* takes 15 to 20 minutes.

STANDARDIZATION The *SIB–R* standardization sample consisted of 2,182 individuals representing the 1990 U.S. Census. It is linked to the *Woodcock-Johnson Psychoeducational Battery–Revised*. The sample included persons with and without disabilities.

SCORING The test shows various types of scores, including age scores, percentile ranks, standard scores, stanines, normal curve equivalents, and expected scores.

RELIABILITY Median reliability coefficients for the clusters are in the .80s and .90s.

VALIDITY Content validity for the *SIB–R* is adequate. Criterion-related validity was established by correlating the *SIB–R* with other adaptive behavior scales and with the *Woodcock-Johnson Psychoeducational Battery–Revised*. Information relating to content validity and criterion-related validity also support the claims of construct validity.

SUMMARY The *Scales of Independent Behavior–Revised* is an individually administered, norm-referenced measure of adaptive behavior intended to measure the adaptive and problem behavior of individuals ages infant through adult. Evidence of reliability and validity is acceptable. This test needs to be renormed and updated.

> ► In what ways are instruments that assess functional skills similar to adaptive behavior scales?

TESTS-at-a-GLANCE

Scales of Independent Behavior–Revised (SIB–R)

- **Publication Date:** 1996
- **Purposes:** Measures adaptive and problem behaviors.
- **Age/Grade Levels:** Ages infant through adult.
- **Time to Administer:** Approximately 30 to 45 minutes in an interview format.
- **Technical Adequacy:** Reliability and validity are acceptable.
- **Suggested Use:** Can be used for identification, placement, program planning, and monitoring progress of individuals who have mental retardation, who are developmentally delayed, or who exhibit problem behaviors. This test needs to be renormed and updated.

Vineland Adaptive Behavior Scales, Second Edition

The *Vineland Adaptive Behavior Scales, Second Edition (Vineland–II*; Sparrow, Cicchetti, & Balls, 2005) measures personal and social skills from birth to adulthood. This instrument assists in identifying and classifying mental retardation, and other disorders such as autism, Asperger syndrome, and other developmental delays. The *Vineland–II* includes four forms:

1. Survey Interview. This consists of open-ended questions that the examiner uses in talking with the parent or caregiver.
2. Parent/Caregiver Rating Form. A parent or caregiver completes a rating scale on the content covered in the Survey Interview. This provides an alternative format to the interview.
3. Expanded Interview. This includes more comprehensive information helpful for planning a student's specialized education program and may be used as a following up to the Survey Interview.
4. Teacher Rating Form. This questionnaire, appropriate for children ages 3 through 21, is completed by the student's teacher. The first three forms are also available in Spanish.

The *Vineland–II* measures the following domains and subdomains:

Communication
Receptive
Expressive
Written

Daily Living Skills
Personal
Domestic
Community

Socialization
Interpersonal Relationships
Play and Leisure Time
Coping Skills

Motor Skills
Fine
Gross

Maladaptive Behavior (optional)
Internalizing
Externalizing
Other

According to the examiner's manual, the first three broad domains (Communication, Daily Living Skills, and Socialization) correspond to the three broad domains of adaptive functioning recognized by the American Association of Mental Retardation (AAMR, 2002).

ADMINISTRATION Survey Interview and Parent/Caregiver Rating Forms take 20 to 60 minutes.

TESTS-at-a-GLANCE

Vineland Adaptive Behavior Scales, Second Edition (Vineland–II)

- **Publication Date:** 2005
- **Purposes:** Identifies adaptive and maladaptive behaviors.
- **Age/Grade Levels:** Birth to age 90.
- **Time to Administer:** 20 to 60 minutes.
- **Technical Adequacy:** The test has been renormed to reflect the 2000 U.S. census. Reliability and validity are good.
- **Suggested Use:** Can be used to identify adaptive and problem behaviors in students. Useful for determining eligibility, program planning, and program monitoring.

SCORING Domain and adaptive behavior composite scores are reported as standard scores (mean = 100; standard deviation = 15). Percentile ranks, adaptive levels, and age equivalents may also be reported. Subdomain scores are reported as scaled scores (mean = 15; standard deviation = 3), percentile ranks, adaptive levels, and age equivalents.

STANDARDIZATION Norms are representative of the 2000 U.S. census.

RELIABILITY AND VALIDITY According to the authors, the *Vineland–II* is a reliable and valid instrument; there is considerable research that documents the usefulness of this instrument.

Jean's Assessment Results

"I'm concerned about Jean," remarked Mr. Chen, referring to Jean, a 14-year-old student who is in Mr. Chen's homeroom. She is currently identified as having a language disability, mental retardation, and a behavior disorder. According to her school records, Jean was administered the *Wechsler Individual Intelligence Scale–IV (WISC–IV)* last year and obtained a Full Scale IQ of 66 (1st percentile). The *Vineland Adaptive Behavior Scales II* were administered in order to evaluate Jean's adaptive behavior and to review areas of behavioral concern. Jean's mother and her classroom teacher were the respondents. Jean's scores on the *Vineland–II* revealed her to be functioning well below the average range when compared to other 14-year-old students. The scores are reported in standard scores where the mean equals 100 and the standard deviation equal 15. The *Adaptive Behavior Composite* was 23 (±6), which constitutes functioning at less than the first percentile. Her skill domain scores were:

Domain	Standard Score	95% Confidence Interval
Communication	23	
Daily Living Skills	20	
Socialization	34	
Motor	44	
Adaptive Behavior Composite	23	±6

Jean's score in the Maladaptive Behavior Domain was judged to be significant with a score of 19. Areas of noted concern were the student's tendency to be withdrawn and having poor concentration and attention.

In a conference with Jean's teachers, Jean's mother expressed great concern regarding Jean's future. She noted that Jean has "no friends in the neighborhood" and prefers to play with her 6-year-old sister. In thinking about Jean's future, her mother believes that Jean would be able to get a job at a local motel as a chambermaid. She does admit, however, that Jean has generally low levels of skill in this area. The special education teacher commented that Jean had not expressed any interest in a particular vocational activity.

In her conversation with Jean's mother, Jean's special education teacher described Jean as generally withdrawn. She noted that Jean had no friends in the school and that she tended to gravitate toward the youngest and smallest students during recess.

Jean stated that she liked being around young children. This led the team to discuss possibilities of her enrolling in a child care course with work experience as a teacher's aide in the community child care program. Members of Jean's IEP team began to brainstorm a list of supports that would help to promote Jean's interests.

▶ Obtain a copy of the *Vineland–II* examiner's manual. Use the appropriate table to complete the information on confidence intervals for Jean's report.

▶ **CEC Common Core Knowledge and Skills.** The beginning special educator will interpret information from formal and informal assessments (CC8S5).

▶ If you were a member of Jean's IEP team, what supports would you suggest for Jean? What additional questions might you ask Jean about her interests?

SUMMARY The *Vineland Adaptive Behavior Scales, Second Edition* consists of four forms, also available in Spanish, that aid in diagnosing mental retardation and other disorders. The instrument measures the following domains: communication, daily living skills, socialization, motor skills and maladaptive behavior (optional). Norms have been updated to reflect the 2000 U.S. census.

▶ Examine two or more of the instruments described in this chapter. Compare the test items. Which instrument would you recommend? Why?

Summary

- Limitations in adaptive behavior along with significantly below-average intellectual functioning determines whether a student will be identified as having mental retardation.

- The assessment of skills and adaptive behavior relates to age, gender, race, cultural and ethnic norms, and disability. As individuals develop, cultural expectations change.

- The concept of adaptive behavior is dynamic and our views of this construct change over time.

- Assessment of adaptive behavior will continue to be important for identification, determining eligibility, program planning, and program evaluation.

REFERENCES

American Association on Mental Retardation (AAMR). (2002). *Mental retardation* (10th ed.). Washington, DC: Author.

American Psychiatric Association. (2000). *Diagnostic and statistical manual of mental disorders* (4th ed., text revision). Washington, DC: Author.

Brandt, J. E. (1994). *Assessment and transition planning: A curriculum for school psychologists and special educators.* Biddeford, ME: University of New England.

Bruininks, R. H., Thurlow, M., & Gilman, C. J. (1987). Adaptive behavior and mental retardation. *Journal of Special Education 21*(1): 69–88.

Bruininks, R. H., Moreau, L. E., Gilman, C. J., & Anderson, J. L. (1991). *Manual for the adaptive living skills curriculum.* Allen, TX: DLM.

Bruininks, R. H., Woodcock, R. W., Weatherman, R. F., & Hill, B. K. (1984). *Scales of independent living.* Itasca, IL: Riverside.

Bruininks, R. H., Woodcock, R. W., Weatherman, R. F., & Hill B. K. (1996). *Scales of independent behavior–revised.* Itasca, IL: Riverside.

Harrison, P. L., & Oakland, T. (2003). *Adaptive behavior assessment system® Second Edition (ABAS® Second Edition).* San Antonio, TX: Psychological Corporation.

King-Sears, M. E. (1999). Teacher and research co-design self-management content for an inclusive setting: Research training, intervention, and generalization effects on student performance. *Education and Training in Mental Retardation and Developmental Disabilities, 34,* 134–156.

Lambert, N., Leland, H., & Nihira K. (1993). *Adaptive behavior scales–school edition: 2.* Austin, TX: Pro-Ed.

McDonnell, J., Thorson, N., Disher, S., Mathot-Buckner, C., Mendel, J., & Ray, L. (2003). The achievement of students with developmental disabilities and their peers without disabilities in inclusive settings: An exploratory study. *Education and Treatment of Children 26*(3): 224–236.

Moreau, L. E., & Bruininks, R. H. (1991). *Checklist of adaptive living skills.* Itasca, IL: Riverside.

Salvia, J., Neisworth, J., & Schmidt, M. W. (1990). *Responsibility and independence scale for adolescents.* Itasca, IL: Riverside.

Sattler, J. (2001). *Assessment of children: Behavior and clinical applications* (4th ed.). La Mesa, CA: Author.

Sparrow, S., Cicchetti, D., & Balla, D. (2005). *Vineland adaptive behavior scales, second edition.* Circle Pines, MN: American Guidance Service.

Wehmeyer, M. L., Yeager, D., Bolding, N., Agran, M., & Hughes, C. (2003). The effects of self-regulation strategies on goal attainment for students with developmental disabilities in general education classrooms. *Journal of Developmental and Physical Disabilities 15*(1): 79–91.

Behavior in the Classroom

Chapter Objectives

After completing this chapter,
you should be able to:

- Differentiate among various perspectives
  on emotional and problem behaviors and
  their influences on assessment practices.
- Discuss the process for conducting a
  functional behavioral assessment.
- Describe considerations in assessing
  the physical, learning, and social
  environments.
- Compare standardized assessment
  instruments.

Key Terms

Externalizing behaviors
Internalizing behaviors
Stimulus
Positive reinforcer
Negative reinforcer

Antecedents
Consequences
Task analysis
Target behavior
Critical periods

Functional behavioral
  assessment
Scatter plot
Triangulation

Overview

This chapter views student behaviors as occurring within the context of various environments. This conceptual framework influences the way we gather assessment information. Assessing behavior in the classroom involves examining classroom management strategies and other aspects of the learning environment as well as observing strategies that classroom teachers employ to help students build skills in working with others. The assessment process also examines the behavior to determine the function that it serves for the student. By organizing and interpreting this information, teachers and other team members are able to develop one or more recommendations.

Types of Problem Behaviors Observed in the Classroom

Problem behaviors in the classroom include antisocial behavior, aggression, withdrawal behavior, delayed social skills, and difficulties with interpersonal relationships. The term **externalizing behaviors** refers to a broad array of disruptive and antisocial behavior, whereas the term **internalizing behaviors** includes social withdrawal, anxious or inhibited behaviors, or somatic problems. Educators, school counselors, and school psychologists can measure and change behaviors in the classroom on a number of dimensions (White & Haring, as cited in Alberto & Troutman, 2002). A behavior can occur many times or only occasionally (frequency); a behavior can last a long or a short time (duration); upon the request of the adult or another student, a behavior can occur immediately or after a period of time (latency); a behavior can be described (topography); a behavior can be performed strongly or weakly (intensity); and a behavior can occur in one or more locations (locus).

Along each of these dimensions, cultural expectations dictate a range of behavior. "Typical" behaviors differ, depending on the expectations of the group members. Observers can identify atypical behavior by comparing the individual's behavior with that of members of the comparison group.

In the classroom, students exhibit a range of behavioral dimensions. Students with problem behaviors of high frequency or behaviors that have a strong intensity are easily identifiable. Students who exhibit low frequency or low levels of intensity of behavior are often equally needy; however, observers may not identify these students as easily because problem behaviors in students who are quiet, withdrawn, or depressed may go unnoticed. You can read more about one teacher's observation of his students in the Snapshot about Mr. Norford's seventh-grade class.

▶ Visit two or more classrooms and observe one student in each. Compare their classroom behaviors.

Perspectives for Assessing Problem Behaviors

Examiners hold different perspectives about problem behaviors, depending on their backgrounds and theoretical approaches. Table 15.1 describes some of these. In the following section, we examine these perspectives in more detail.

SNAPSHOT

Mr. Norford's Seventh-Grade Class

Andy has difficulty sitting still; he plays with his pencil, shuffles his feet, and jingles the coins in his pocket. Mr. Norford describes his activity level, or frequency of behavior, as high. When Andy becomes upset, he reacts strongly. He becomes angry, shouts, and quickly resorts to pushing and shoving. The intensity of his behavior is also high.

Shelly is an average student. When she becomes upset, she becomes sullen and uncooperative. She refuses to talk with the teacher or to other students. Mr. Norford describes Shelly's level of activity as low, but her intensity is high. Her behavior may be overlooked more readily than Andy's behavior. Shelly's problem behavior may not be as disruptive to the classroom as Andy's problem behavior, but it is disruptive to her learning.

Kenichi enrolled in the middle school last spring, soon after his family moved to this country from Japan. Kenichi had no difficulty understanding English, as he had studied the language for several years. Over the past few months, Mr. Norford has observed that he has become very quiet and rarely speaks in class. Walking between classes and in the cafeteria, Kenichi is usually seen alone. His teacher believes that he is experiencing periods of sadness and depression for many days at a time. The frequency of Kenichi's behavior often is low and the intensity of his behavior is weak. Mr. Norford has observed these behaviors in several locations.

TABLE 15.1 ● Current Perspectives on Assessing Behavior

Perspective	Associated Keywords	Focus
Behavioral	Applied behavior analysis Antecedents (A) Behavior (B) Consequences (C) Learning theory Task analysis Chaining	Behavior is learned and can be modified. Learning a complex behavior can be accomplished by identifying the components of the behavior.
Biological	Neuroanatomical and/or neurochemical components Biochemical inhibitors	Behaviors are the result of neuroanatomical features or chemical imbalances in the brain. Biologically based brain disorders affect individuals' behavior.
Developmental	Critical periods Bonding	A student's early experiences and nurturing are critical in social-emotional development.
Ecological	Environment	Behaviors can be improved by altering the environment.
Emotional	Emotional intelligence	The individual's emotional intelligence is important for success.
Humanistic	Self-direction Self-motivation	The social environment is critical in supporting student behavior.
Psychoanalytical	Id Ego Superego Life crises	Assessment is conducted by a licensed psychologist or psychiatrist for the purpose of uncovering the illness or pathology.
Psychoeducational	Motivation	The interaction of pathology and the individual's motivation or underlying conflicts result in problem behaviors.
Temperament	Rhythmicity Mood Activity Adaptability Distractibility Persistence Threshold Intensity Approach	The relationship between an individual's disposition, behavior, and the environment is critical.

Behavioral Perspective

The behavioral perspective emphasizes the importance of factors external to or outside of the student as catalysts for the development of problem behaviors. Events in the environment provide stimuli for the behaviors to occur and reinforcement for the behaviors to occur more frequently.

A basic principle of the behavioral perspective holds that behaviors are learned as a result of the individual's interactions with the environment. Behaviors may be manipulated by a **stimulus,** such as environmental conditions, or by events, teachers, or other individuals. A stimulus that is presented, contingent upon a response, and that increases the future probability of the response, is called a **positive reinforcer.** A positive reinforcer may or may not be pleasant; however, it has the effect of increasing the probability of the behavior if it is satisfying to the individual. For example, a teacher's angry look can operate as a positive reinforcer if behavior increases in the future after the teacher's look is delivered, contingent upon behavior. To whatever degree, the teacher's attention itself is satisfying to the student.

A **negative reinforcer** involves the removal of a stimulus, contingent upon a response, which increases the future probability of the response. The stimulus could be, for example, a loud noise, a bright light, or extreme cold or heat. Behaviors that are followed by consequences that are satisfying to the individual tend to be repeated, whereas behaviors that result in consequences that are not satisfying tend not to be repeated. Repeated behaviors are learned behaviors.

The events that happen before the behavior occurs are called **antecedents.** The antecedents are the stimuli for the behavior and act as cues for the behavior to reoccur. When the antecedent changes or is no longer there, the behavior may decrease or stop. The events that follow the behavior are called **consequences.** Negative consequences can be effective in discouraging unwanted behaviors, while positive consequences can promote positive behaviors.

Thus, the two basic principles in this approach are (1) behaviors can be learned, taught, and modified; and (2) behaviors (B) can be controlled by antecedents (A) and consequences (C).

What Is the Influence on Assessment Practices?

An examiner using a behavioral perspective conducts observations within a specified time period, defines the behavior in observable terms, and carefully records the consequence(s) that follow the behavior and the antecedent event(s). The assessment focus is on the events that cause and sustain specific problem behaviors. When problem behaviors are serious and reoccurring, teachers work with other team members to conduct a functional behavioral assessment. Later in this chapter, we study this type of assessment in more detail.

Task Analysis

Task analysis is a procedure for identifying the subskills that comprise a specific skill or behavior in order to assist a student in acquiring that skill or behavior. The behavior that will be acquired or eliminated is referred to as the **target behavior.** Target behaviors are acquired (or eliminated) by manipulating the antecedents and consequences. During a task analysis, the examiner follows a series of steps in assessing the target behavior and in planning for instruction (Figure 15.1).

WHAT IS THE INFLUENCE ON ASSESSMENT PRACTICES? Assessment includes a task analysis, data collection, and monitoring procedures. Using task analysis, the observer identifies the target behavior's subskills, assesses the student attempting the skills, and records data on a checklist or rating scale. Assessment occurs while the student actively engages in or carries out an activity.

Biological Perspective

The biological perspective focuses on the effects of the biological, chemical, neurological, and physical status of the individual and the individual's behavior. A biological approach often is helpful in assessing students with severe emotional behaviors.

Neurobiological Disorders

An individual's behavior is affected by changes in the neuroanatomical and/or imbalances in neurochemical components. Assessment involves the use of medical biochemical tests and diagnosis. This type of analysis is helpful in assessing students who have emotional problems related to an organic disorder.

The examiner

1. Describes the target behavior in observable terms so that the behaviors can be measured and the student's progress can be evaluated.
2. Examines the behavior and divides it into small, discrete, sequential steps.
3. Assesses the student's skill levels in one or more of these sequential steps.
4. Plans instruction that focuses on the sequential steps of the target behavior.
5. Links the sequential steps, or subskills, from the task analysis to achieve the more complex target behavior.
6. Carefully determines the reinforcement by observing the student's behavior.
7. Carefully arranges antecedent events to elicit behaviors and plan consequences to reinforce behavior. This step serves to increase the frequency and/or intensity of behavior.
8. Examines the student's everyday routines to determine the behaviors that need to be taught.

FIGURE 15.1 • Steps in Conducting a Task Analysis

Temperament

An individual's disposition or tendencies affect the individual's behavior. Temperament includes a number of general features such as the student's overall demeanor, the ability to adapt to new situations, and the ability to attend to or persist in an activity. A visit to a school classroom reveals individual differences in temperment. Some students work quietly by themselves; others talk with others or signal frequently for the teacher's attention. There is a reciprocal nature between an individual's temperament and the physical, learning, and social environments. Figure 15.2 illustrates the general features of temperament.

The general features of temperament (Thomas & Chess, 1977; Thomas, Chess, & Birch, 1970) include:

- *Rhythmicity:* The regularity of the student's activity patterns, such as eating, playing, studying, bladder, and bowel functions.
- *Mood:* The student's overall demeanor, such as happy or sad, friendly or unfriendly.
- *Activity:* The frequency of movement.
- *Adaptability:* The ability of the student to adapt to new situations.
- *Distractibility:* The ease with which the student is interrupted from an activity.
- *Persistence:* The student's ability to attend to or persist in an activity.
- *Threshold:* The student's sensitivity to stimuli and changes in the environment, such as noise or temperature.
- *Intensity:* The student's magnitude of response to a specific stimulus, such as the tendency to smile or laugh when amused or to scream or whimper when hurt.
- *Approach:* The student's attraction or withdrawal to novel stimuli and situations.

FIGURE 15.2 • General Features of Temperament

What Is the Influence on Assessment Practices?

Standardized instruments, including behavior rating scales, interviews, and checklists, assess various aspects of temperament. For example, the *Child Behavior Checklist/6–18* (Achenbach, 2001a), the *Conners' Rating Scales–Revised* (Conners, 1997), and the *Temperament and Atypical Behavior Scale (TABS*; Neisworth, Bagnato, Salvia, & Hunt, 1999) contain items that assess aspects of temperament.

Developmental Approach

The developmental perspective focuses on the social-emotional development of the student. Theories that focus on a developmental approach to understanding social-emotional development (Brazelton, 1992; Erikson, 1950; Greenspan, 1992; Kopp, 1994; White, 1975; Zero to Three National Center for Clinical Infant Programs, 1995) emphasize that all children progress through regular stages or periods. Individual variations affect the amount of time a given individual remains at a certain stage. Thus, qualitative differences within stages are common, depending on individual differences.

The foundation for social and emotional skills begins during a child's early years. These early years are critical in providing the basis for social-emotional development in later childhood, adolescence, and adulthood. These times are often referred to as **critical periods.** Critical periods refer to "having a certain kind of experience at one point of development that has a profoundly different impact on future behavior than having the same experience at any other point in development" (Bailey, Bruer, Symons, & Lichtman, 2001, p. 4).

Critical Periods of Development

The theory of critical periods states that there is an interval of time in which the child is most responsive. If the individual has little or no opportunity to develop the skill or behavior during this period, the individual may have difficulty in doing so later on. Skills and behaviors that are fundamental to success in school begin to develop during the first three years of life (Zero to Three, 1992, p. 3). Children who do not have opportunities to develop these skills (Figure 15.3) can exhibit problem behaviors in the classroom. These behaviors continue to escalate as they become older, unless observers identify the problem behaviors and implement intervention.

What Is the Influence on Assessment Practices?

Interviews with parents, caregivers, and teachers provide information about the student during critical periods of development.

---

1. *Confidence:* The child has a sense of being successful and that adults will be helpful.
2. *Curiosity:* The child has a sense that learning is positive and pleasurable.
3. *Intentionality:* The child has a desire to and the capacity to have an impact and to act upon that with persistence.
4. *Self-control:* The child can control personal actions in age-appropriate ways.
5. *Relatedness:* The child can engage with others, can understand, and can be understood.
6. *Capacity to communicate:* The child wants to and has the ability to communicate.
7. *Cooperativeness:* The child has the ability to balance own needs with those of others in a group activity.

FIGURE 15.3 • Skills and Behaviors Important to School Success

Adapted from Zero to Three, 1992.

Humanistic Perspective

The humanistic perspective is built on the belief that teaching and learning should be meaningful to the student (Rogers, 1983). Humanists believe that students learn best and most efficiently when the learning is personally significant and that choosing the direction of one's learning is highly motivating. Equally important in this view is designing the learning environment so that students may have responsibility for their learning, thereby decreasing problem behaviors. A social environment that is thus responsive to the student's feelings and that is free from threat enhances learning.

What Is the Influence on Assessment Practices?

Assessment practices focus on understanding problem behavior from the perspective of the student. During assessment activities, student interviews provide information about the problem behaviors from the student's perspective. Observers examine aspects of the learning and social environments and record ways in which the learning environment is responsive to the student.

Responding to Diversity

Expectations of society, schools, and teachers contribute to or compound problem behaviors in the classroom. Some behaviors may be tolerable or acceptable as the norm in the community, yet these behaviors may not be tolerable to the school or acceptable to the classroom teacher. Additionally, teacher expectations differ widely. The teacher's tolerance for activity level and intensity level affects whether the teacher refers the student for special education services or whether the teacher handles behavior concerns in the classroom.

A student's disability can hasten the development of problem behaviors. For example, a student with Tourette's syndrome develops multiple motor and one or more vocal tics over time. These symptoms occur many times throughout the day, although not necessarily simultaneously. Sometimes the student develops patterns of verbal outbursts, such as words and phrases that are inappropriate. The student is not able to repress these outbursts, and medication may not control the problem satisfactorily. The problem behaviors contribute to decreases in the student's self-concept and self-esteem and affect the development of social skills and interpersonal relationships.

Disabilities in communication can foster problem behaviors. Students with disabilities who have difficulty communicating quickly learn to use behaviors that attract another's attention. Some attention behaviors are appropriate while others are antisocial, aggressive, or inappropriate.

Precribed medication for students who have inattention or hyperactivity can affect student behavior. Methylphenidate, sold under the trade name Ritalin, is one of the most frequently prescribed medications. Methylphenidate temporarily controls overactivity, inattention, and impulsivity; however, its side effects (insomnia, irritability, and reduced emotional affect) can influence problem behaviors.

Observing the Student within the Environment

Physical Environment

A teacher can positively affect the physical environment by creating a structure and a set of expectations for student behavior. The structure consists of predictable classroom routines, schedules, and behavioral expectations that the teacher clearly displays on a list for all to see.

Learning Environment

Frequent interruptions, unclear directions, activities that are too difficult, and a variety of other circumstances are apt to foster problem behaviors. Teacher movement throughout the classroom and the position of the teacher in relation to the student can help in preventing behavior problems. One study (Gunter, Shores, Jack, Rasmussen, & Flowers, 1995) found that paraprofessionals responsible for monitoring the student area remained seated 91.7 percent of the time. When the time that they were seated decreased, the time that students remained on task increased.

▶ To learn more research-based prevention strategies in K-8 classrooms, download an electronic guide at http://www.cecp.air.org/preventionstrategies/Default.htm

Social Environment

Classroom teachers employ strategies that affect students' behavior and help them build skills in working with others. These strategies allow students to build relationships with their peers by creating an environment that promotes skills in communication, conflict resolution, and respect for others. During a visit to the classroom, the observer may note teachers using one or more of these strategies. Classroom strategies that are effective in promoting social relations among students with and without disabilities include the following:

1. Teachers actively facilitate social interactions. Teachers plan and work to facilitate social exchanges between students. They place students in cooperative groupings and encourage collaborative problem solving. Teachers create opportunities for peer tutoring and assign students to various classroom roles of assisting and helping others. Teachers structure the classroom schedule so that students have opportunities to develop social relationships.
2. Teachers involve students in the responsibility for social inclusion of all students.
3. Teachers build a feeling of community in the classroom. Teachers work to create a climate of concern for others among students.
4. Teachers model acceptance.

Research-Based Practices   Using Auditory Processing Strategies to Address Problem Behaviors

Researchers Kathy Rowe, Ken Rowe, and Jan Pollard wondered what role auditory processing plays in behavior problems and low achievement. They had observed that children with learning disabilities and attention difficulties frequently exhibited problems with auditory processing. The children had trouble following directions as well as difficulties in reaching developmental and literacy milestones.

The researchers found that many of the students responded to simple interventions that changed the way verbal information was presented. This made a significant difference in reducing special education referrals in addition to strengthening literacy skills. The interventions implemented by the teachers included:

1. Attracting the child's attention.
2. Speaking slowly, using short sentences, eye contact, and visual cues (waiting for students to comply with instructions).
3. Pausing between sentences and repeating when necessary.
4. Using visual cues (such as a blank look or shrug of the shoulders) and repeating instructions as needed.
5. Creating hearing, listening, and compliance routines for students. (Rowe, Rowe, & Pollard, 2004)

How It Works ! Classroom Behaviors within an Intervention Context

Assessing behavior problems in the classroom occurs within the context of interventions. When a behavior problem first occurs, the classroom teacher assesses the use of classroom management strategies. The teacher customarily confers with the school assistance team, behavioral specialist, or special education consultant in order to develop and implement successful management strategies to address problem behaviors. This process can involve implementing one or more different strategies over a period of weeks. Figure 15.4 illustrates a behavior management observation form that a special education teacher developed when conferring with classroom teachers.

Let's visit Mr. Wing's classroom where we will learn more about some of the classroom management difficulties that a first-year teacher is experiencing. Mr. Wing is be-

ginning his first year of teaching. His class consists of 23 students; three students have been identified as having disabilities. Mr. Wing is concerned about one of these students, Mark D., and how to help him. Mr. Wing worries if he is meeting Mark's needs and decides to ask the special education consultant, Mr. Sanford, for help.

Mr. Wing describes his concerns: "During class time, Mark never seems to pay attention. When I call on him, he is usually on the wrong page of our book. He rarely knows the answer to my questions. I don't think he has ever participated in class discussions, and he is very disruptive when others are talking. Academically, his grades are very low this first quarter."

Mr. Sanford listened carefully as Mr. Wing talked about Mark. He thought about how he could lead the conversation away from focusing on the student to a more

---

◀ POINT STREET SCHOOL ▶
Behavior Management

Student's Name _____   Date _____ Time _____

Observer _____

Teacher _____

Location _____

Characteristic

1. Classroom Guidelines
Are behavior guidelines posted in the classroom?
Are guidelines written in positive terms describing the behavior expected of students?
✔ Suggestions for improvement:

2. Student Understanding
Does the student understand the classroom guidelines for behavior?
✔ Suggestions for improvement:

3. Teacher Reinforcement
How does the teacher react when the student behaves appropriately?

Does the teacher use:
_____ social reinforcers
_____ activity reinforcers
_____ tangible reinforcers
_____ edible reinforcers
✔ Suggestions for improvement:

FIGURE 15.4 ● Point Street School Classroom Observation Form

(continued)

How It Works!
continued

4. **Teacher Interventions**
   How does the teacher react when the student behaves inappropriately?

   Does the teacher:

   _____ ignore some behaviors
   Explain:

   _____ use directives
   Explain:

   _____ use contingency contracts

   _____ teach pro-social skills
   Explain:

   ✔ Suggestions for improvement:

5. **Classroom Consequences**
   What consequences does the teacher use when the student behaves
   inappropriately?

   ✔ Suggestions for improvement:

6. **Classroom Consistency**
   Is the teacher consistent in managing the student's behavior?
   Is the management of the student's behavior consistent with that of all students
   in the classroom?
   ✔ Suggestions for improvement:

FIGURE 15.4 • Continued

general discussion of classroom management strategies. When there was a pause in the conversation, he asked, "When Mark or some other student disrupts class, what strategies have you found that work well in dealing with this behavior?" The two teachers spent some time talking about strategies and Mr. Wing's apparent frustrations. As the discussion proceeded, Mr. Wing expressed an interest in reviewing his classroom management plan and translating his expectations into procedures and rules. Together the educators made some changes based on the following principles for behavior management:

▶ As you reflect on this first-year teacher's experience, consider the key principles in managing student behaviors. What might you suggest to Mr. Wing?

1. Establish clear guidelines for the expected classroom behavior for students. Ideally, these guidelines are clearly visible in the classroom as a reminder to students.

2. State rules, or guidelines, in terms of what the student should do so that the behavioral expectations are clear. ("We listen when another student is talking.")
3. Provide positive reinforcement to students engaged in appropriate classroom behavior.
4. Use directive statements to tell students how to act correctly and responsibly. ("Holly, if you don't want Mark to push the back of your chair, you need to use words to tell him to stop.")
5. Teach pro-social skills such as:
   a. How to ask for help
   b. How to join a group of students engaged in an activity
   c. How to join a group discussion
   d. How to make friends
6. Provide consequences for students who disregard behavior guidelines.
7. Be consistent with all students in their management of classroom behavior.

Assessment Questions, Purposes, and Approaches

If the student's problem behavior continues after a series of teaching and classroom interventions, the teacher notifies the student's parents and completes a referral to the IEP team. For serious and recurring behavior problems, the IEP team recommends a functional behavioral assessment.

Functional Behavioral Assessment (FBA)

When a student's behavior continues to significantly interfere with participation, performance, or achievement, teachers, school psychologists, counselors, and other team members work together to complete a functional behavioral assessment. A **functional behavioral assessment** is a systematic process of gathering information that identifies the causes of and interventions for addressing problem behaviors.

To comply with IDEA requirements, teachers need to know how to conduct functional behavioral assessments. If a student with behavior problems receives disciplinary action—for example, for carrying a weapon to school or possessing illegal drugs—IDEA requires the IEP team to meet within ten days to begin a functional behavioral assessment plan. If a behavior plan is already in place, the team must review the plan and revise it, if necessary, to address the behavior.

Typically, a functional behavioral assessment examines the physical environment, the learning environment, and the social environment in which the student's problem behaviors occur. The assessment includes both indirect and direct assessment approaches such as a review of the student's records, interviews with the teachers (and other significant adults), a student interview, and direct observations of the student on several different occasions. These multiple approaches allow teachers and other professionals to gather information from a variety of perspectives concerning the problem behaviors.

Problem behaviors usually serve a function for the student, such as gaining attention from adults or peers. The function, itself, is usually appropriate (most of us like attention), but the behavior itself is not appropriate (such as acting out in class). A functional behavioral assessment involves identifying (1) the behavior and the function that it serves; (2) specific triggers, or antecedents, such as events or actions that preceded the behavior (for example, a teacher-directed lesson); (3) the events or actions that occur after the behavior, or consequences (such as other students laughing), that help maintain the behavior; and (4) developing an intervention plan.

▶ **CEC Common Core Knowledge and Skills.** The beginning special educator will understand legal provisions and ethical principles regarding assessment of individuals (CC8K2).

▶ **CEC Common Core Knowledge and Skills.** The beginning special educator will understand specialized terminology used in the assessment of individuals with disabilities (GC8K1).

Conducting a Functional Behavioral Assessment

Team members work together by following a sequence of steps for conducting a functional behavioral assessment (Figure 15.5). In the following sections, we describe these individual steps.

1. *Verifying the Seriousness of the Problem Behavior.*

    Because a functional behavioral assessment is time-consuming, the IEP team begins by verifying the seriousness of the problem. Team members address questions such as:

    - Does the student's behavior significantly differ from that of other classmates?
    - Does the student's behavior lessen the possibility of successful learning for the student and others?
    - Have past efforts to address the student's behavior using classroom management strategies been unsuccessful?
    - Does the student's behavior represent a behavioral problem, rather than a cultural difference?

1. Verify the seriousness of the problem behavior.
2. Define the problem behavior in observable terms.
3. Collect assessment information using multiple approaches, including review of student's records; teacher, parent, and student interviews; and direct observations.
4. Analyze assessment information and examine possible functions of the problem behavior.
5. Establish a hypothesis to determine possible functions of the behavior.
6. Develop and implement behavior intervention plan.
7. Monitor and evaluate the behavior intervention plan.

FIGURE 15.5 ● Steps in Performing a Functional Behavioral Assessment

- Is the student's behavior serious, persistent, chronic, or a threat to the safety of the student or others?
- If the behavior persists, is some disciplinary action likely to result? (Center for Effective Collaboration and Practice, 1998b)

If the answer to these questions is yes, then the team proceeds with a functional behavioral assessment.

2. *Defining the Problem Behavior in Observable Terms.*

Defining the problem behavior allows teachers and other members to pinpoint the concerns and to plan assessment approaches. Team members will develop a definition of the problem behavior in terms that are observable. Describing the behavior in this way helps to ensure accurate, reliable observations. For example, if the teacher has concerns about a student's "aggressive" behavior, the team needs to agree on how they will know if a student is "aggressive." By developing a definition of aggression that is observable, such as "physically hitting or verbally abusing another person" observers will be able to see and record the behavior whenever it occurs. Many times a teacher refers a student because of vague concerns. In these cases, the teacher or other team member will need to observe the student's behavior across several different settings to help in defining the behavior. These initial observations often involve watching and recording two or three students at the same time, including typical peers as well as the student who has been referred to the IEP team. As we discuss in Chapter 5, conducting observations on several students simultaneously allows the observer to determine how different the behavior of the student in question is from the behavior of others. Sometimes initial observations indicate that several students have similar problems and the greater difficulty is one of classroom management, rather than individual student behavior.

When the referred student is an English language learner, team members will need to take into account possible differences in behavioral expectations that are an integral part of cultural beliefs. In these instances, parents can be a valuable source of information to assist team members in their understandings of cultural expectations. Moreover, team members may identify a school or community member who is knowledgeable about the student's cultural background to serve on the IEP team as an additional resource person.

3. *Collecting Assessment Information Using Multiple Approaches.*

a. *Reviewing the Student's Records.* The student's cumulative records provide a starting place to gather information about medical history, school attendance, achievement, assessments, IEPs and behavior management plans, and past disciplinary actions. By reviewing the student's records, a team gleans additional information about medications, patterns of truancy, prolonged difficulties with achievement, positive behavioral intervention, strategies, and supports described in previous behavior management plans, or trends in disciplinary referrals. One or more of these areas can contribute to the current behavior problem.

▶ **CEC Common Core Knowledge and Skills.** The beginning special educator will gather relevant background information (CC8S1).

b. *Interviewing.* Structured interviews provide information about the student from others who know the student well and the contextual variables that surround problem behaviors (Repp & Horner, 1999). Sometimes the IEP team will select a commercial interview tool, or they may decide to construct a structured interview with questions that they have identified. A team member experienced in interviewing techniques, such as the school social worker or school psychologist, usually conducts the structured interviews.

(i) *Teachers.* Teachers and teacher assistants can provide information about how the student interacts with materials and with other students and adults in the classroom. The structured interview might include:
- In what settings and under what conditions do you observe the behavior?
- Are there any settings/situations in which the behavior does not occur?
- Who is present when the behavior occurs?
- What activities or interactions take place just prior to the behavior?
- Are there other events that may trigger the behavior?
- What activities or interactions take place immediately following the behavior?
- Are there other behaviors that occur along with the problem behavior?
- Can you think of any reasons why the student might behave this way?
- What would be a more acceptable way for the student to achieve the same outcome? (Center for Effective Collaboration and Practice, 1998b)

(ii) *Parents.* Parents provide yet a different perspective. Parents can share their own expectations regarding their child's behavior. They can provide information about their child's behavior difficulties in the past and the types of interventions that were attempted and successful. They can describe complications or changes in the family structure that the child is currently experiencing at home, including parents' unemployment, death, birth, and divorce, all of which create additional stressors on family members. The structured interview might include:
- Have there been any changes at home or new events in your child's life recently?
- Does your child experience any problems that you are aware of?
- Do you think your child is interested in school this year? Why or why not?
- Do you think that the academic work is too easy or too hard? Could you explain?

(iii) *The Student.* The student can provide valuable information in identifying the motivational factors supporting inappropriate behavior (Figure 15.6).

Although functional interviews often yield valuable information, team members are aware, too, that the information may be biased. The teacher may have preconceived ideas about the student and the reasons for the problem behaviors. Although these ideas are recorded as part of the teacher interview, they may not

> *School Social Worker:* Is there anything that is happening at home that is bothering you?
>
> *Student:* No.
>
> *School Social Worker:* Is there something new at school that is bothering you?
>
> *Student:* Not really . . . Well, we're getting a lot of homework this year.
>
> *School Social Worker:* Does it bother you?
>
> *Student:* No, I mean, well . . . it takes a lot of time and I have a part-time job now.
>
> *School Social Worker:* Let's talk a little about what happened in class today. What was the teacher doing right before you made the comments that made the other students laugh?
>
> *Student:* I don't know, I think he was giving some directions.
>
> *School Social Worker:* Do you remember what he was asking everyone to do?
>
> *Student:* Well, when he talks so much it's very hard to follow everything. Like he tells us five things and I'm still back on the first.
>
> *School Social Worker:* Do you remember what were you thinking right before you made the comments?
>
> *Student:* I was just so mad and frustrated!
>
> *School Social Worker:* When you make noises and comments in class, what usually happens afterward?
>
> *Student:* Everyone laughs and gives me high fives.
>
> *School Social Worker:* How does that make you feel?
>
> *Student:* Pretty cool, I guess. . . .

FIGURE 15.6 ● Functional Interview with a Student

be representative of the actual situation. Or, the parent may deny that a problem exists by not responding in full to the interview questions. Or, the student may misrepresent thoughts and feelings during the structured interview because of embarrassment or shame.

c. *Conducting Observations.* Chapter 5 discusses the various methods of recording observation data. These same methods—event recording, duration recording, intensity recording, latency recording, interval recording and category recording—are useful when conducting direct observations, as part of a functional behavioral analysis. You'll recall that each method has particular strengths, depending on the assessment question. For example, event recording is useful when our question involves "how often" or "how frequently" (Figure 15.7). In conducting observations, team members will gather information not only about occasions when the student displays problem behaviors but also occasions when the student maintains appropriate behavior. Since one observation represents only a snapshot of the student, the team will collect multiple observations to produce more accurate and reliable information. Observations may include one or more comparison students as well.

Observers may use specific forms to record observation data, such as a scatter plot. A **scatter plot** is a type of interval recording form that the observer uses to record single behaviors or a series of behaviors during the observation period. Scat-

▶ **CEC Common Core Knowledge and Skills.** The beginning special educator will monitor intragroup behavior changes across subjects and activities (GC8S5).

Event recording helps answer questions such as:

- How many times does (student) . . . ?
- How frequently does (student) . . . ?
- How often does (student) . . . ?
- At what rate does (student) . . . ?

Duration recording helps answer questions such as:

- How long does (student) . . . ?

Intensity recording helps answer questions such as:

- To what degree does (student) . . . ?
- To what level does (student) . . . ?

Latency recording helps answer questions such as:

- Given a request, how long does it take (student) to begin . . . ?

Interval recording helps answer questions such as:

- What amount of time does (student) . . . ?
- What percent of time does (student) . . . ?

FIGURE 15.7 ● How to Select an Appropriate Observation Recording Method

ter plots are useful for initial and follow-up observations to identify patterns of behavior that relate to specific contextual conditions (Center for Effective Collaboration and Practice, 1998b, p. 9). Figure 15.8 is a scatter plot conducted on one student, Trish, during recess. The observer collected information about her appropriate and inappropriate behavior on the playground and the consequences of each during 20-second time intervals. Best practice dictates that two or more additional observations will enhance the reliability of this information.

An Antecedent-Behavior-Consequence (ABC) recording form provides a way to record the problem behavior within a contextual condition. These forms are used when an observer wants to organize descriptive information in such a way that classroom conditions that trigger and maintain behavior can be identified. Three columns on the form allow the observer to record the antecedent events, the behavior, and the consequences that followed the behavior. ABC recording sheets can come in various formats and can record various aspects of the behavior, such as the frequency, duration, intensity, or latency of the behavior. Figure 15.9 illustrates an example of an ABC recording form.

d. *Rubrics.* In Chapter 6, we examine rubrics as types of assessment scales used to measure performance. We discussed how a rubric consists of descriptors that provide detail about each level of achievement. Rubrics are useful tools in functional behavioral assessment, too, when the assessment question concerns the degree of intensity or severity of a behavior, such as disruptive outbursts. To identify the severity of a behavior, the team develops descriptions of the different levels of intensity, assigning a numeric score or categorical label to each level. Figure 15.10 illustrates a rubric that measures the severity of disruptive behavior. When the team uses detailed descriptions and examples for each of the different levels, they increase the reliability of the rubric.

▶ **CEC Common Core Knowledge and Skills.** The beginning special educator will interpret information from formal and informal assessments (CC8S5).

▶ Make arrangements to visit a classroom and observe student behavior. Create an ABC form and fill in the information that you observe. What classroom behaviors did you witness? What were the consequences that followed each behavior that occurred? Could you identify the antecedent conditions?

Student __Trish__   Setting __playground__   Observer(s) _____

Activity __free play__   Date __9/26__

No. of Students __50__   Start Time __9:00__   End Time __9:15__   Total _____

Observation Interval   Time Sampling Procedure

10 sec ___ 15 sec ___ 20 sec _X_   1. Continuous Recording _____   2. Non-Continuous _X_   3. Other _____

(every 3 min.)

APPENDIX A SCATTERPLOTS

Phase / ACTIVITY	Appropriate Responses							Total	Consequences of Appropriate Responses	Inappropriate Responses							Total	Consequences of Inappropriate Responses
	Peer interaction	Alone	Adult interaction	Organized games	Parallel play					Peer interaction	Alone	Adult interaction	Organized games	Parallel play				
		X																
		X																
					X													
					X													
										X								Gets football from Marsha
	X								Plays catch with Rae ↓									
	X																	
	X									X		X						
										X		X						
										X		X	X					
Other												X	X					
Total																		
Comments:																		

FIGURE 15.8 • Functional Assessment Scatter Plot

Source: Center for Effective Collaboration and Practice. (1998). Addressing Student Problem Behavior-Part II: Conducting a Functional Behavioral Assessment. Retrieved June 4, 2001, from http://www.cecp.air.org/fba/problembehavior2/main2.htm. © 2002, Sopris West, Inc., Longmont, CO.

4. *Analyzing Assessment Information and Examining Possible Functions of the Problem.*

Analyzing data involves studying and synthesizing the results of all the information collected, while looking for patterns of behavior. The team considers key questions such as:

• What student behaviors occurred under different antecedent conditions?
• Did the behavior in question occur under one or more than one antecedent condition?
• What consequences occurred after the behavior in question?

As the team examines the collected information, they look for recurring instances of the problem behaviors. They work to synthesize information across the multiple assessment approaches by asking:

• How does the information from the interviews corroborate or confirm the ABC observations?
• Based on the review of student records, what other factors may be contributing to the behavior?

To help in synthesizing all the information, they use a process called triangulation.

Interval Time (5-minute intervals)	Activity	Antecedent	Behavior	Consequence	Comments
0:00–0:05					
0:05–0:10					
0:10–0:15					
0:15–0:20					
0:20–0:25					
0:25–0:30					
0:30–0:35					
0:35–0:40					
0:40–0:45					
0:45–0:50					
0:50–0:55					
0:55–1:00					

Student: ___ Observer: ___
Grade: ___ Teacher ___
Behavior Observed: ___

FIGURE 15.9 • Sample ABC Recording Form

Severity of Disruptive Behavior Rating Rubric

1. Behavior is confined only to the observed student. May include such behaviors as: refusal to follow directions, scowling, crossing arms, shouting, muttering under student's breath.
2. Behavior disrupts others in the student's immediate area. May include: slamming textbook closed, dropping book on the floor, name-calling, or using inappropriate language.
3. Behavior disrupts everyone in the class. May include: throwing objects, yelling, open defiance of teacher directions, or leaving the classroom.
4. Behavior disrupts other classrooms or common areas of the school. May include: throwing objects, yelling, open defiance of school personnel's directions, or leaving the school campus.
5. Behavior causes or threatens to cause physical injury to student or to others. May include: display of weapons, assault on others.

FIGURE 15.10 • Rubric for Measuring Intensity of a Behavior

Source: Center for Collective Collaboration and Practice. (1998). Addressing Student Problem Behavior–Part II: Conducting a Functional Behavioral Assessment. Retrieved June 4, 2001, from http://cecp.air.org/fba.problembehavior2/main2.htm. © 2002, Sopris West, Inc., Longmont, CO.

Triangulation is the process of drawing conclusion based on an analysis of multiple sources of data. A data triangulation chart (Figure 15.11) allows team members to record the multiple sources of data that they have collected and to visually compare the information. Using the data triangulation chart, team members can develop deeper understandings of the behavior and the function that it serves.

5. *Establishing a Hypothesis: Possible Function of the Behavior Problem.*

After analyzing the data, team members develop one or more possible explanations for the student's behavior. Let's return to the IEP team that is working with Trish. Using information from the direct observations, including the scatter plots of her playground behavior, discipline records, and teacher interviews, the team developed the following hypothesis:

> Trish knows how to respond appropriately, based on the four playground observations. In fact, much of the time she engages in appropriate behavior. She is more verbally aggressive than physically aggressive. When she calls other children names, pushes and shoves others, grabs the ball, and hits other children, she usually gets her way. In addition, she receives individual attention from her teachers and the playground supervisors when she engages in appropriate behavior. In Trish's case, the team feels that Trish's behavior serves as an attempt to join her classmates and also to receive attention from adults.

▶ **CEC Common Core Knowledge and Skills.** The beginning special educator will implement procedures for assessing and reporting both appropriate and problematic behaviors of individuals with disabilities (GC8S1).

Data Triangulation Chart

Student ____Trish____   Date(s) __9/26–10/8__

Source 1	Source 2	Source 3
ABC chart:	Interview with playground supervisor:	Scatter plot:
Trish yells at students when they don't do what she says. She hits students when she does not get her way.	Trish yells at and hits other girls when she doesn't get her way. This usually happens when there are no adults nearby.	Trish engages in appropriate behavior on the playground about 73 percent of the time; verbally aggressive behavior about 19 percent of the time; and physical aggression 8 percent of the time.

Interpretation:

1. Precipitating events: *Playground, undersupervised games involving girls.*
2. Maintaining consequences: *Trish usually gets her way when she becomes verbally or physically aggressive. She also gets to spend time with the playground supervisor.*
3. Function(s): *Trish's behavior allows her to get her way (albeit for a short time) and play with other girls. She thinks this is an effective way to join groups.*

FIGURE 15.11 ● Data Triangulation Chart

Source: Center for Effective Collaboration and Practice (1998b). Addressing Student Problem Behavior—Part II: Conducting a Functional Behavioral Assessment. Retrieved June 4, 2001, from http://www.cecp.air.org/fba/problembehavior2/main2.htm. © 2002, Sopris West, Inc., Longmont, CO.

6. *Developing the Behavior Intervention Plan.*

After establishing the hypothesis, team members develop the student's behavior intervention plan. The plan may include manipulating the antecedents and/or consequences, teaching more acceptable behaviors, making accommodations and/or modifications, or acquiring supplementary aids and supports to address the problem behaviors. Let's return once more to Trish's team.

> As part of her behavior intervention plan, the special education teacher will help Trish learn more appropriate replacement behaviors. The teacher will provide instruction in social skills training, helping Trish to learn different strategies for joining a group of peers. In addition, the team will ask the playground supervisors and her teachers to begin a conscious effort to recognize Trish for appropriate behavior.

7. *Monitoring and Evaluating the Behavior Intervention Plan.*

A student's behavior intervention plan needs reviewing on a regular basis, at least annually. Problem behaviors can appear and quickly escalate if left unattended. When problem behaviors resurface, team members recognize that the original plan may not be working and reconvene to discuss the student's current needs.

Standardized Instruments for Assessing Problem Behaviors

Standardized instruments usually are in the form of rating scales or checklists designed to be completed by school psychologists, teachers, parents, or the students themselves. Instruments that assess problem behaviors focus on one or more specific areas. The choice of an instrument depends on the presenting questions and concerns. The following section describes several of these instruments in more detail.

▶ **CEC Common Core Knowledge and Skills.** The beginning special educator will use exceptionality-specific assessment instruments with individuals with disabilities (GC8S2).

Behavior Assessment System for Children, Second Edition

The *Behavior Assessment System for Children, Second Edition (BASC-2*; Reynolds & Kamphaus, 2005) is a set of rating scales and forms to understand behaviors and emotions of children and adolescents, 2 years through 21 years, 11 months. The materials allow for multiple collections of data from the perspectives of the individual, home, and school and include: Teacher Rating Scales (TRS), Parent Rating Scales (PRS), Self-Report of Personality (SRP), Student Observation System (SOS), and Structured Developmental History (SDH). Parent and student forms also are available in Spanish. The rating scales describe positive and negative behaviors. The teacher or parent indicates how often the student displays each of these behaviors by answering *Never, Sometimes, Often,* or *Almost always.* The phrases are grouped into different scales, with each scale relating to a specific areas of behavior:

activities of daily living	functional communication
adaptability	hyperactivity
aggression	leadership
anxiety	learning problems
attention problems	social skills
atypicality	somatization
conduct problems	study skills
depression	withdrawal

ADMINISTRATION Administration takes approximately 10 to 20 minutes (teacher and parent forms) and 30 minutes for the Self-Report of Personality. For students and parents who have difficulty reading, the items are available on CD.

STANDARDIZATION Norms are based on the 2000 U.S. census.

SCORING This instrument reports assessment results in T scores (mean equals 50, standard deviation equals 10) and percentiles for both the general population and clinical population. Scoring may be completed by hand or with the BASC-2 ASSIST ™ Plus software purchased separately. An example of the Teacher Rating Scale (TRS) Report produced by the software is illustrated in Figure 15.12. This figure shows the rating scores

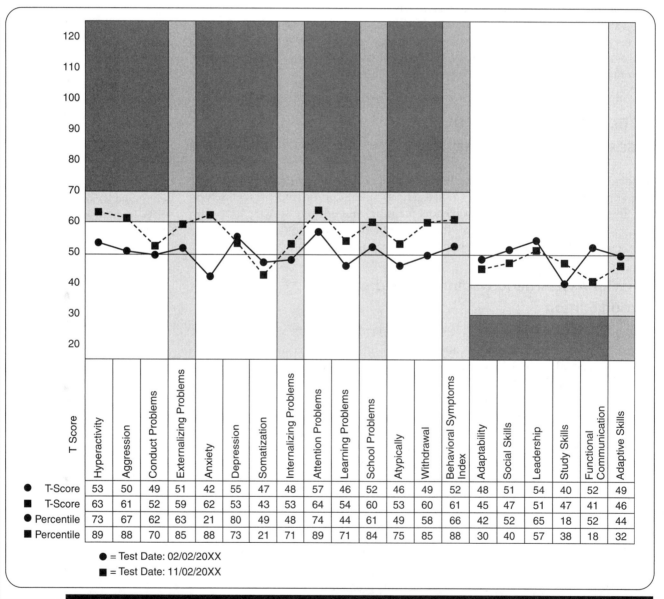

	Hyperactivity	Aggression	Conduct Problems	Externalizing Problems	Anxiety	Depression	Somatization	Internalizing Problems	Attention Problems	Learning Problems	School Problems	Atypically	Withdrawal	Behavioral Symptoms Index	Adaptability	Social Skills	Leadership	Study Skills	Functional Communication	Adaptive Skills
● T-Score	53	50	49	51	42	55	47	48	57	46	52	46	49	52	48	51	54	40	52	49
■ T-Score	63	61	52	59	62	53	43	53	64	54	60	53	60	61	45	47	51	47	41	46
● Percentile	73	67	62	63	21	80	49	48	74	44	61	49	58	66	42	52	65	18	52	44
■ Percentile	89	88	70	85	88	73	21	71	89	71	84	75	85	88	30	40	57	38	18	32

● = Test Date: 02/02/20XX
■ = Test Date: 11/02/20XX

FIGURE 15.12 ● Sample Progress Report from Teacher Rating Scale (TRS), *Behavior Assessment System for Children Second Edition* (BASC-2)

completed by the math teacher concerning a sample child, Timmy, age 8, and his progress from the first test date to the second. The *BASC-2* also offers software for conducting observations on a laptop or PDA.

RELIABILITY AND VALIDITY Both reliability and validity are adequate.

SUMMARY The *BASC-2* is a comprehensive assessment system designed for use with children and youth from 2 years through 21 years, 11 months. The system consists of various rating scales and other forms that are completed by the examiner, parent, teacher, and student. These multiple sources of information provide a variety of perspectives on behaviors and emotions. This second edition has been renormed to reflect the 2000 U.S. census.

TESTS-at-a-GLANCE

Behavior Assessment System for Children, Second Edition (BASC-2)

- **Publication Date:** 2005

- **Purpose:** The *Behavior Assessment System for Children, Second Edition (BASC-2)* provides multiple forms to gather information about behavior and emotions of children and adolescents.

- **Age/Grade Levels:** 2 years through 21 years, 11 months.

- **Time to Administer:** 20 to 30 minutes.

- **Technical Adequacy:** The *BASC-2* has been renormed to reflect the 2000 U.S. census. Reliability and validity are adequate.

- **Suggested Use:** The *BASC-2* provides information from various perspectives (student, teacher, parent) on a range of behaviors typically seen in the classroom. Rating scales are available in both English and Spanish and on an audio CD.

Child Behavior Checklist System

The *Child Behavior Checklist System (CBCL*; Achenbach & Rescorla, 2000b, 2001; McConaughy & Achenbach, 2001b) consists of various behavior checklists and report forms for gathering information about children and youth from 1 year, 6 months to 18 years and about young adults from 18 years through 30 years. The *CBCL System* conceptualizes emotional or behavioral problems as external and internal behavioral clusters. The *System* includes several *Diagnostic and Statistical Manual* (2000) *(DSM)*-oriented scales that are consistent with *DSM* diagnostic categories. Although the *CBCL* is entitled a "checklist," the instruments are really rating scales in that they require the observer to rate items on a numerical scale. These forms have been translated in over sixty languages and are available from the publisher. Published reports describe the use of the *Child Behavior Checklist System* from fifty cultures. The *CBCL* consists of three age levels, each with its own technical manual and scoring system. These include:

Ages 1½ through 5

1. *Child Behavior Checklist for Ages 1½ –5 (CBCL/1½ –5*; Achenbach and Rescorla, 2001). This checklist consists of 99 items and is designed for the parent or other caregiver to complete. The *CBCL/1½ –5* includes the *Language Development Survey (LDS)* for identifying language delays. Similar to the checklist for older children, scores on this instrument can convert to percentile ranks and T-scores. A Spanish version is available.
2. *Caregiver-Teacher Report Form/1½–5 (C–TRF*; Achenbach, 2000). This form obtains ratings by child care providers and early childhood teachers on 99 items and descriptions of problems or concerns. Similar in layout to the *Child Behavior Checklist for Ages 1½–5*, the forms allow the examiner to compare responses.

Ages 6 through 18

3. *Child Behavior Checklist for Ages 6–18 (CBCL/6–18*; Achenbach, 2001a). This scale is designed for the parent to complete and consists of two sections: competence items and problem items. A student's score converts to percentile ranks and T-scores. This checklist has adequate technical characteristics. A Spanish version is available.

4. *Teacher's Report Form for Ages 6–18 (TRF*; Achenbach, 2001b). This scale is similar to the *CBCL/6–18* and is designed for completion by the teacher. The *Teacher's Report Form* consists of three main areas: academic performance, adaptive functioning, and behavioral/ emotional problems. Percentiles and T-scores can be calculated.

5. *Youth Self-Report for Ages 11–18* (Achenbach, 2001c). This rating scale is for youth ages 11 through 18 years of age. Students must have at least fifth-grade reading ability, or the teacher can administer the items orally. Test items are similar to those in the *CBCL/6–18*. Scores can convert to percentile ranks and T-scores. A Spanish version is available.

6. *Direct Observation Form for Ages 5–14* (Achenbach, 1986). This form is used to collect observation data on the student during a 10-minute observation period. A list of problem behaviors is provided to assist in organizing observation of the student. Many of the items correspond to the *CBCL/6–18* and the *TRF/6–18*. Percentile and T-scores can be calculated to determine whether the student's behavior falls within clinical or normal range. The *Direct Observation Form* was normed on 287 children (non-referred) who were observed as classroom controls for problem children.

7. *Semistructured Clinical Interview for Children and Adolescents (SCICA*; McConaughy & Achenbach, 2001a). The *SCICA* uses a protocol of questions and probes for interviewing students ages 8 through 18 years. The examiner also completes an observation of the student and the student completes a self-report form. Administration time is 60 to 90 minutes, and this instrument should be completed by an experienced interviewer.

Ages 18 through 30

8. *Young Adult Behavior Checklist for Ages 18–30 (YABCL*; Achenbach, 1997a). The *YABCL* is an upward extension of the *Child Behavior Checklist for Ages 6–18*. Parents and others who know the young adult well complete this form, which has 107 items that describe specific behavioral and emotional problems. Like the other checklists, scores can be converted to T-scores and percentiles. The *YABCL* was normed on 1,074 non-referred young adults.

9. *Young Adult Self-Report Form for Ages 18–30 (YASR*; Achenbach, 1997b). The *YASR* is an upward extension of the *Youth Self-Report*. In addition, there are three other areas concerning adaptive functioning as youth move to adulthood: education, job, and spouse (or partner). These sections are answered only by individuals who have attended secondary or postsecondary institutions, been employed, or who have lived with a spouse or partner within the past six months. An additional section provides open-ended questions regarding physical problems, disabilities, concerns, and strengths. Scores can be converted to T-scores and percentiles. This instrument was normed on 1,058 young adults aged 18 to 30. One-week test-retest reliability of the total problems scores is r =.89.

ADMINISTRATION The various forms take 10 to 45 minutes to complete, depending on the amount of information to be recorded.

STANDARDIZATION For the *CBCL/6–18*, the norming sample consisted of 1,753 children, ages 6 through 18 years. The sample was stratified by age, gender, geographic region, urban/suburban/rural, socioeconomic status, and ethnicity. For the *CBCL/1½ –5*, 700 children participated in the normative sample.

SCORING Scoring may be completed by hand or by the Assessment Data Manager (ADM) software that can be purchased separately.

RELIABILITY For the *CBCL/6–18,* adequate reliability coefficients are reported for interrater, test-retest, and internal consistency. For the *CBCL/ 1½–5,* small studies were completed that suggest moderate to adequate reliability. Additional studies are needed.

VALIDITY Reported evidence supports construct validity for the *CBCL/6–18.* Reported criterion-related validity between the *CBCL* and the *Conners' Rating Scales* and the *Revised Behavior Problem Checklist* is .82 and .81, respectively. Evidence of content validity, criterion-related validity, and construct validity is presented for the *CBCL/1½–5.*

SUMMARY The *CBCL* is a comprehensive assessment system designed for use with children and youth from 1 year, 6 months through 30 years of age. The system consists of various instruments that are completed by the examiner, parent, teacher, and student. These multiple sources of information provide a variety of perspectives on the problem behaviors.

Conners' Rating Scales–Revised

The *Conners' Rating Scales–Revised (CRS–R;* Conners, 1997) are designed to assess behaviors in children and youth ages 3 to 17 years. The *CRS–R* consist of a set of main scales and a set of auxiliary scales. The main scales include: two parent, two teacher, and two adolescent self-report scales for assessing problem behaviors, each consisting of two versions, a long form and a shorter form.

TESTS-at-a-GLANCE

Child Behavior Checklist System (CBCL)

- **Publication Date:** 2000, 2001
- **Purposes:** Assesses behavior in terms of internal and external behavior clusters. School-related areas include academic functioning, adaptive characteristics, and behavioral/emotional problems.
- **Age/Grade Levels:** The *Child Behavior Checklist System* consists of two different rating scales, the *CBCL/1½ –5,* designed for children ages 1 year, 6 months through 5 years, and the *CBCL/6–18* designed for students ages 6 years through 18 years. The *System* also includes various teacher and self-report forms, a direct observation form, and a semi-structured clinical interview. For young adults, ages 18 through 30 years, there is the *Young Adult Behavior Checklist (YABCL).*
- **Time to Administer:** 10 to 45 minutes, depending on the amount of information to be recorded.
- **Technical Adequacy:** The manuals present evidence of adequate reliability and validity.
- **Suggested Use:** Measures behaviors from multiple perspectives, including the student, parent, and teacher. Rating scales are available in Spanish. Many of the forms have been translated into other languages and are available from the publisher.

MAIN SCALES

1. *Long Forms.* The long form is typically used for comprehensive information or for a diagnosis according to the *Diagnostic and Statistical Manual of Mental Disorders–Fourth Edition, Text Revision (DSM–IV–TR)* (American Psychiatric Association, 2000). The *Conners' Parent Rating Scale–Revised: Long Form (CPRS–R:L)* consists of 80 statements to which parents (or guardians) indicate agreement or disagreement regarding their child's behavior over the past month. The statements include a broad range of behaviors, for example, "Does not get invited to friends' houses" and "Clings to parents and other adults." The statements of the *Conners' Parent Rating Scale–Revised: Long Form* are divided among the following twelve subscales:

   - Oppositional-Defiant*
   - Cognitive Problems*
   - Hyperactivity-Impulsivity*
   - Anxious-Shy
   - Perfectionism
   - Social Problems
   - Psychosomatic
   - Conners' Global Index
   - ADHD Index*
   - *DSM–IV* Symptom Scale
   - *DSM–IV* Inattention
   - *DSM–IV* Impulsivity

   The "*" indicates the subscales that are also on the short form.

   The *Conners' Teacher Rating Scale–Revised: Long Form (CTRS–R:L)* contains the same subscales as the parent long form with the exception of the Psychosomatic subscale. Teachers are asked to consider the student's behavior and actions during the past month. The scales contain 59 items such as "Appears to be unaccepted by group" or "Poor in spelling."

2. *Short Forms.* The short version is typically used considering when multiple administrations over time. The parent version, *Conners' Parent Rating Scale–Revised: Short Form (CPRS–R:S)*, contains 27 items divided among the four subscales indicated above by the "*." For teachers, the *Conners' Teacher Rating Scale–Revised: Short Form (CTRS–R:S)* contains 29 items and the same subscales as in the short form for parents. The similarities between the forms help facilitate comparisons between parent and teacher responses. Test scores are plotted to create a profile of the problem behaviors.

3. *Adolescent Self-Report Scales.* The *Conners-Wells' Adolescent Self-Report Scales: Long Form (CASS:L)* and the *Conners-Wells' Adolescent Self-Report Scales: Short Form (CASS:S)* are useful with adolescents who have at least a fifth-grade reading level. The scales are designed to obtain information that is available from no one else but the individual student. Use the long form when the assessment requires extensive information and *DSM–IV–TR* compliance. Sample items include "My parents' discipline is too harsh" and "My parents do not reward or notice my good behavior."

AUXILIARY SCALES The auxiliary scales include a global index (the hyperactivity index in the original *Conners' Rating Scales*) for parents and teachers and a set of ADHD/DSM–IV scales for the parent, teacher, and student.

1. *Conners' Global Index.* Both the parent and teacher scales, *Conners' Global Index–Parent (CGI–P)* and *Conners' Global Index–Teacher (CGI–T)* consist of 10 items each. The items on this scale, formerly known as the hyperactivity index, are divided between two separate factors: emotional lability and hyperactivity.

2. *Conners' ADHD/DSM–IV Scales.* These scales include a scale for parents, *Conners' ADHD/DSM–IV Scales–Parent (CADS–P)*, for teachers, *Conners' ADHD/DSM–IV Scales–Teacher (CADS–T)*, and for the student, *Conners' ADHD/DSM–IV Scales–Self Report (CADS–S)*.
   Each scale contains 30 items that are divided between the following areas:
   • ADHD Index
   • DSM–IV Symptom Scale
   • Inattention
   • Hyperactivity
   For screening purposes, the examiner can choose to administer just the ADHD Index; to confirm *DSM–IV* diagnoses, the examiner can use the *DSM–IV* Symptom Scale.

ADMINISTRATION All of the short scales take 5 to 10 minutes to administer; the long scales take between 15 and 20 minutes.

SCORING T-scores may be calculated for each of the scales.

STANDARDIZATION The rating scales were originally developed on a clinical population at Johns Hopkins University Hospital in Baltimore. The manual states that 8,000 individuals participated in the norms for the new scales. The manual states that the norm sample included individuals from over 95 percent of the states and provinces in North America and that there were large samples obtained for all of the age groups and for both genders. The manual further states that samples represented minority groups.

RELIABILITY Internal reliability is adequate for both the short and long forms of the parent and teacher rating scales and the adolescent self-report scales. Test-retest reliability was examined following a six to eight week interval. In general, test-retest reliabilities for the *CRS–R* were adequate across the various forms.

VALIDITY Reported construct validity for the teacher, parent, and self-report forms is adequate. Small studies report the correlation between the *CRS–R* and the *Children's Depression Inventory* and performance measures. Continued research will be helpful.

SUMMARY The *Conners' Rating Scales–Revised (CRS–R)* consist of a set of scales for parents, teachers, and students to assist in gathering information about problem behaviors. The revised scales add several important dimensions to the original *Conners' Rating Scales*. The self-report forms provide information from the student's perspective. The auxiliary ADHD forms provide information from parent, teacher, and student perspectives and link the information to *DSM–IV*. Usefulness of the instrument would be enhanced if more information were provided about the sample of individuals who participated in the development of this revised edition. The *CRS–R* is available in English, Spanish (U.S.), and French (Canadian) and can be administered by computer or scored using computer software.

TESTS-at-a-GLANCE

Conners' Rating Scales– Revised (CRS–R)

- **Publication Date:** 1997

- **Purposes:** Assesses behavior in terms of oppositional-defiant, cognitive problems, hyperactivity-impulsivity, anxious-shy, perfectionism, social problems, psychosomatic (parent scale), a global index (emotional lability and hyper-activity), and ADHD.

- **Age/Grade Levels:** The *CRS–R* are designed for children and youth ages 3 to 17 years and are available in English, Spanish (U.S.), and French (Canadian).

- **Time to Administer:** Short scales take 5 to 10 minutes to administer; the long scales take between 15 and 20 minutes.

- **Technical Adequacy:** Adequate reliability and validity. Additional information regarding the standardization sample would be helpful.

- **Suggested Use:** Measures student behavior from the perspectives of the parents, teachers, and the individual.

Summary

- Answering assessment questions and planning, implementing, monitoring, and evaluating an individualized education program for a student with emotional or problem behaviors involves working closely with the school psychologist, social workers, and mental health practitioners.

- This team of professionals, along with the parents and the student, gather and examine information regarding problem behaviors and the functions that they serve.

- Together they develop behavioral intervention plans that involve teaching new skills that students lack or replacement behaviors that are more appropriate, while providing positive behavior supports.

> ▶ Reread the Snapshot about the students in Mr. Norford's class on page 314. If you were the teacher, how would you gather information about these problem behaviors? What additional information would you gather about Kenichi? What resources would be available in your community? Work with a small group of other students to develop your ideas. Present your findings to the class.

REFERENCES

Achenbach, T. M. (1986). *Direct observation form for ages 5–14*. Burlington, VT: ASEBA.

Achenbach, T. M. (1997a). *Young adult behavior checklist for ages 18–30 (YABCL)*. Burlington, VT: ASEBA.

Achenbach, T. M. (1997b). *Young adult self-report for ages 18–30 (YASR)*. Burlington, VT: ASEBA.

Achenbach, T. M. (2000). Caregiver-teacher report *form for ages 1½–5 (C–TRF/1½ –5)*. Burlington, VT: ASEBA.

Achenbach, T. M. (2001a). *Child behavior checklist for ages 6–18 (CBC/6–18)*. Burlington, VT: ASEBA.

Achenbach, T. M. (2001b). *Teacher's report form for ages 6–18 (TRF)*. Burlington, VT: ASEBA.

Achenbach, T. M. (2001c). *Youth self-report for ages 11–18 (YSR)*. Burlington, VT: ASEBA.

Achenbach, T. M., & Rescorla, L. A. (2000). *Manual for the ASEBA preschool forms and profiles*. Burlington, VT: ASEBA.

Achenbach, T. M., & Rescorla, L. A. (2001). *Manual for the ASEBA school-age forms and profiles.* Burlington, VT: ASEBA.

Alberto, P. A., & Troutman, A. C. (2002). *Applied behavior analysis for teachers* (6th ed.). Upper Saddle River, NJ: Merrill, Prentice-Hall.

American Psychiatric Association. (2000). *Diagnostic and statistical manual of mental disorders* (4th ed., text revision). Washington, DC: Author.

Bailey, D. B., Bruer, J. T., Symons, F. J., Lichtman, J. W. (Eds.). (2001). *Critical thinking about critical periods.* Baltimore, MD: Paul H. Brookes.

Brazelton, T. B. (1992). *Touchpoints: Your child's emotional and behavioral development.* Reading, MA: Addison Wesley.

Center for Effective Collaboration and Practice. (1998). *Addressing student problem behavior—Part II: Conducting a functional behavioral assessment.* Retrieved June 4, 2001. Available: http://www.cecp.air.org/fba/problembehavior2/main2/htm

Conners, C. K. (1997). *Conners' rating scales–revised.* North Tonawanda, NY: Multi-Health Systems.

Erikson, E. (1950). *Childhood and society.* New York: Norton.

Greenspan, S. I. (1992). *Infancy and early childhood: The practice of clinical assessment and intervention with emotional and developmental challenges.* Madison, CT: International Universities Press.

Gunter, P. L., Shores, R. E., Jack, S. L., Rasmussen, S. K., & Flowers, J. (1995). On the move. *Teaching Exceptional Children 28*(1): 12–14.

Kopp, C. (1994). *Baby steps: The "whys" of your child's behavior in the first two years.* New York: W. H. Freeman.

McConaughy, S. H., & Achenbach, T. M. (2001a). *Semistructured clinical interview for children and adolescents (SCICA).* Burlington, VT: ASEBA.

McConaughy, S. H., & Achenbach, T. M. (2001b). *Manual for the semistructured clinical interview for children and adolescents, 2nd ed. (SCICA).* Burlington, VT: ASEBA.

Neisworth, J. T., Bagnato, S. J., Salvia, J., & Hunt, F. H. (1999). *Temperament and atypical behavior scale (TABS).* Baltimore: Paul H. Brookes.

Repp, A. C., & Horner, R. H. (1999). *Functional analysis of problem behavior.* Belmont, CA: Wadsworth.

Reynolds, C. R., & Kamphaus, R. W. (2005). *Behavior assessment system for children, second edition (BASC-2).* Circle Pines, MN: American Guidance Service.

Rogers, C. R. (1983). *Freedom to learn for the 80's.* Columbus, OH: Merrill.

Rowe, K., Rowe, K., & Pollard, J. (2004). *Literacy, behaviour and auditory processing: Building "fences" at the top of the "cliff" in preference to "ambulance services" at the bottom.* Background paper to invited address presented at the ACER Research Conference, Adelaide SA, 24–26 October 2004. Retrieved January 2, 2006 from http://www.acer.edu.au/research/programs/documents/Rowe-ACERResearchConf_2004 Paper.pdf

Thomas, A., & Chess, S. (1977). *Temperament and development.* New York: Bruner/Mazel.

Thomas, A., Chess, S., & Birch, H. G. (1970). The origin of personality. *Scientific American 223*: 102–109.

White, B. (1975). *The first three years of life.* Englewood Cliffs, NJ: Prentice-Hall.

Zero to Three. (1992). *Heart start: The emotional foundations of school readiness.* Arlington, VA: Zero to Three.

Zero to Three/National Center for Clinical Infant Programs. (1995). *Diagnostic classification: 0–3: Diagnostic classification of mental health and developmental disorders of infancy and early childhood.* Arlington, VA: Zero to Three/National Center for Clinical Infant Programs.

16 Implementing Program Evaluation

Chapter Objectives

After completing this chapter, you should be able to:

- Define the term *evaluation* and describe a rationale for conducting evaluations.
- Compare and contrast different models of evaluation.
- Describe the process of review and evaluation of the IEP.
- Identify important areas to address in conducting program evaluation.

Key Terms

Evaluation
Stakeholders
Internal evaluator

External evaluator
Formative evaluation
Summative evaluation

Quantitative data
Qualitative data
Focus groups

Overview

Evaluation is a critical aspect of our work with students and their families. This chapter uses the definition developed by Smith and Glass (1987), which states that evaluation is the process of establishing a value judgment based on the collection of actual data.

There are many different ways of "evaluating." In fact, evaluation can focus on one of three different programmatic levels. First, one can examine ways of gathering information about the student on an ongoing basis. This, you will recall, is the monitoring step. Special educators need to evaluate and document advancement toward the goals developed in the IEP. As a result of monitoring a student's progress, an educator often decides to make changes in instruction and in the services. Some professionals believe that the process of monitoring IEPs is largely neglected. This is disturbing, given the critical need to carefully review services as they are being provided and the lost opportunity to make necessary changes during the program year.

At another level, a special educator evaluates the student's overall program annually to determine the student's progress as a result of the specialized instruction and other special education and related services. This level is the evaluation step in the assessment process and is conducted for students with IEPs. Does the student continue to need special education services?

Third, special educators should evaluate the services that the school or agency offers to ensure the program is effective. One can gather information from several different sources for this kind of inquiry. A special educator will want to gather information from parents or other family members. Are they satisfied with their child's education program? Do they feel that the teachers are responsive to their questions and concerns? Are they involved in the process of making educational decisions? Educators can also aggregate information about the progress of groups of students in order to examine a program's success and benefits. If the program is funded by public monies, such as IDEA or Title 1, then periodic evaluations are necessary to demonstrate accountability for funds expended. In addition, teachers can provide administrators with information regarding work conditions, equipment needs, or training priorities. Many programs that have a high staff turnover can gain valuable feedback through regular program evaluation.

Introduction to Program Evaluation

Evaluation is a process that we all undertake frequently, especially as college and university students. We compare instructors, "Dr. DiMatina is so much more interesting than Dr. Doyle." We rate the exams, "That exam was terrible—it didn't cover what I had studied." Or we measure classroom learning activities: "That small-group exercise in class really helped me understand the different group dynamics involved in teamwork."

In terms of an overall course evaluation, we could provide our instructor with several different types of information. We could provide feedback on lectures: Are they interesting? Are they delivered too quickly? Or on the classroom climate, both physical and social: Is it too cold? Is the seating comfortable? Is there a feeling of support and encouragement? Or on the assignments: Are there too many? Do they relate to the course objectives stated in the syllabus? The results of our evaluation will be helpful to the instructor. Perhaps some changes will be made before the next term!

The Joint Committee on Standards for Education Evaluation, which includes individuals representing the major educational organizations, has published a list of standards for designing and implementing evaluations of educational programs. According to the Joint Committee (1994), a good evaluation must satisfy four important criteria.

- *Utility:* An evaluation should be informative and useful as well as timely.
- *Feasibility:* An evaluation should be appropriate to the setting and cost-effective.
- *Propriety:* An evaluation should protect the rights of individuals affected by the evaluation.
- *Accuracy:* The evaluation instrument should be valid and reliable.

The field of evaluation has its own terms for the individuals who participate in the evaluation process. **Stakeholders** are individuals who are interested in the results of the evaluation. An evaluation of the effectiveness of the program at a local school will have several different groups, or stakeholders, who are interested in the findings. The teachers, therapists, and other staff at the school will want to know the results of the evaluation, as will the parents and administrators. On the other hand, an evaluation of the cost-effectiveness of the same program may be of primary interest to the school board members and administrators.

An individual with a background in research design, measurement, and evaluation should conduct the evaluation. The person may be an **internal evaluator**, such as a teacher or administrator who is trained in these skills, or from the outside, an **external evaluator** who is hired specifically for the purpose of completing the evaluation.

There are advantages as well as disadvantages in using an inside or outside evaluator. Which of the following aspects do you consider to be an advantage in hiring an inside evaluator? an outside evaluator?

- No bias
- Knowledge of special education programs
- Time to complete evaluation
- Cost savings
- Knowledge of questions to ask
- Knowledge of effective strategies for evaluation

The client who has requested the evaluation hires the evaluator. The client may be one person, such as the administrator of the program, or the client may be a group of people, such as an advisory board, parent group, or state education department.

When Does Program Evaluation Happen?

Formative Evaluation

An evaluation that is ongoing during the period of program implementation is called a **formative evaluation.** Formative evaluation is very useful to teachers and therapists who are providing direct services because, by examining the data, they can make adjustments and changes before the end of the program cycle.

In this example, practitioners conduct an evaluation to monitor the student's progress throughout the program year. If the data indicate a need to adjust the program substantially from what the education program describes, they must call an IEP team meeting, and parents must approve these changes.

Summative Evaluation

An evaluation that is completed at the end of the cycle is called a **summative evaluation.** Summative evaluations can be completed on an individual student's program plan. For example, the IEP team completes a summative evaluation during the annual review of the IEP.

Educators and others can conduct summative evaluations on entire programs, too. Depending on the focus, these evaluations provide administrators with a variety of information, including accountability and cost-effective data, parent or staff satisfaction data, or program effectiveness data.

Program Evaluation and Special Education Services

One of the most well-known models for evaluating special education services was developed by Ralph Tyler, one of the founders of educational evaluation. This model—called objectives-based evaluation—has long been in use by teachers and administrators in special education in several different ways:

1. To evaluate a student's ongoing progress toward the goals described in the IEP.
2. To evaluate the student's program at the end of a time period or unit of study.
3. To evaluate the overall program of the school.

The first step in conducting an *objectives-based evaluation* begins with identifying the set of objectives for measurement. The next step is to identify or develop the procedures or instruments to assess these objectives. Teachers and therapists who are monitoring IEP progress collect products of the student's work, use portfolios, make periodic videotapes of the student, administer tests, or develop their own instruments for measuring progress. They then collect and analyze products and test data to ascertain whether the objectives have been met. This approach is a recurring sequence that needs repeating on a regular, ongoing basis.

Dick, Carey, and Carey (2000) have described a similar model, which stresses the identification of student skills and the collection of data in order to revise instruction. The various steps in using an objectives-based model are seen in Figure 16.1.

Planning an Evaluation of a Specific Student's Program

Teachers and other professionals who provide special education and related services must evaluate the education program periodically. This review is important because services that the IEP team originally identified during the team meeting may need alterations or adjustments. (A note about terminology: This chapter uses the term *review* to address the process of examining the IEP and the term *monitor* to address the ongoing process undertaken by teachers and therapists for evaluating a student's daily or weekly progress.)

Steps to Monitoring and Evaluating the IEP

Step 1: Identifying Annual Goals and Evaluation Criteria

The team writes measurable annual goals, including academic and functional goals, that meet the child's needs and enable the child to be involved in and make progress in the general education curriculum. Goals should also address each of the child's other

▶ Research other models of evaluation. For example, you might look at consumer-oriented or naturalistic models.

▶ **CEC Common Core Knowledge and Skills.** The beginning special educator will understand legal and ethical principles regarding assessment of individuals (CC8K2).

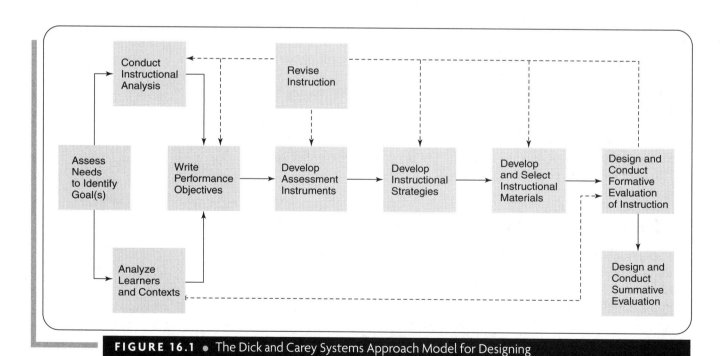

FIGURE 16.1 ● The Dick and Carey Systems Approach Model for Designing and Evaluating Instruction

Source: From Walter Dick, Lou Carey, and James O. Carey, *The Systematic Design of Instruction,* 5th ed. Copyright © 2001 by Allyn and Bacon. Reprinted by permission.

educational needs that result from the child's disability (20 USC Sec. 417 (d)(1)(A)). Goals should describe gains that are reasonably achievable during the program year. The team should also explain evaluation procedures for these goals. Examples of an annual goal might be:

Written language: By June, Raymond will demonstrate improvement in written language by his ability to write a three-paragraph story with 90 percent accuracy in grammar.

or

Adaptive: Alexandra will eat lunch independently in the school cafeteria by the end of the program year.

Step 2: Identifying Short-Term Objectives and Evaluation Criteria

IDEA requires that a student's IEP contain short term objectives, if the student will take alternate assessments that are aligned with alternate achievement standards (20 USC Sec. 614 (d)(1)(A)). Written statements of specific objectives, or benchmarks, help the student meet the annual goal and assist the educator by providing a "road map" for instruction. These statements must be written so that a teacher can readily identify whether the student is meeting objectives. Objectives that are written in this manner are called *behavioral objectives* because they describe a student's behavior and are not left to a chance interpretation.

Objectives include criteria for determining whether the student has achieved the objective, what the evaluation procedures are, and when the team will review the objective. Thus, objectives have the following components:

1. They describe the behavior in observable terms.
2. They state the criteria for successful performance.
3. They describe the method of evaluating the behavior.
4. They indicate the time period for review.

There are many different styles used in writing objectives. The following examples illustrate two different styles of writing objectives with criteria for evaluation.

Given ten computational problems in mathematics (sums to 10) and a set of manipulatives (e.g., blocks or sticks), Robin will calculate the correct answer with 100 percent accuracy as measured by teacher observation. To be reviewed: June 20xx.

By June, Robin will compute correctly ten mathematical problems (sums to 10) using a calculator as measured by the *BRIGANCE®Comprehensive Inventory of Basic Skills.*

Step 3: Monitoring Progress

Teachers and others should monitor a student's progress on an ongoing basis. Teachers and therapists will want to review objectives each marking period, or sooner, in order to monitor progress. Some of the questions to ask include: Is the student making progress toward this objective? Is this objective still appropriate, or have conditions changed? This provides an opportunity to make adjustments, if necessary. IDEA requires that the IEP include information regarding when periodic progress reports will be issued (such as through the use of quarterly or other periodic reports, concurrent with the issuance of report cards) (20 USC Sec. 614 (d)(1)(A)).

Graphing is an excellent way of monitoring progress, and there are many different types and formats. Figure 16.2 illustrates a graph of a student's progress in decreasing undesirable behaviors. The teacher observed the frequency of a student's verbal

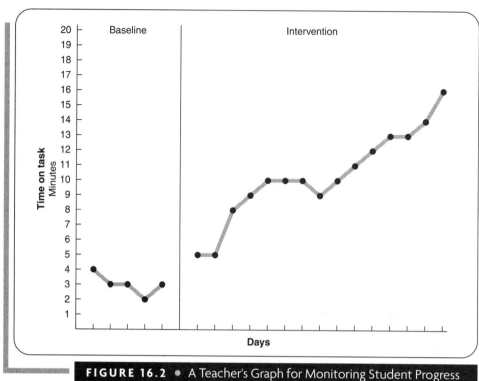

FIGURE 16.2 ● A Teacher's Graph for Monitoring Student Progress

▶ **CEC Common Core Knowledge and Skills.** The beginning special educator will evaluate instruction and monitor progress of individuals with exceptional learning needs (CC8S8).

Staying Out of Fights

1. Stop and count to 10.
2. Decide what your problem is.
3. Think about your choices:

   Walk away.

   Talk to the person.

   Ask someone for help.
4. Act out your best choice.

How did I do?

FIGURE 16.3 ● Student Cue Card

Source: From *Skillstreaming the Elementary School Child: New Strategies and Perspectives for Teaching Prosocial Skills* (rev. ed., p. 216) by E. McGinnis and A. P. Goldstein, 1997, Champaign, IL: Research Press. Copyright 1997 by the authors. Reprinted by permission.

outbursts during homeroom period for one week and recorded them as baseline data. The following week, the teacher began an intervention program and observed and recorded the number of undesirable behaviors for each day over the next three weeks. The procedure provides information to the teacher regarding the effectiveness of the intervention and allows continuous monitoring of the student's behaviors, presenting a profile of progress over a time. One of the disadvantages to graphing is that the adult must find time to record the information.

Students may take responsibility for graphing their progress. In fact, students can increase their independence by being able to record their own behavior through self-monitoring. Even preschool children with disabilities have increased appropriate behaviors through self-monitoring (Sainato, Strain, Lefebvre, & Rapp, 1990). McGinnis and Goldstein (1997) describe another method as an alternative to graphing. Students use a self-scoring cue card (Figure 16.3) to record and monitor their progress in making good choices and demonstrating appropriate behaviors.

Self-monitoring techniques help students with disabilities increase opportunities for success in regular classroom settings. Dunlap, Dunlap, Koegel, and Koegel (1991) describe several examples of using self-monitoring for increasing on-task time, increasing responsivity to questions for a child with autism, and increasing accuracy on subtraction problems.

Step 4: Evaluation

IDEA states that the IEP team must review existing evaluation data. On the basis of the review and input from the student's parents, the team identifies what additional data is needed. During this reevaluation, the team will consider whether the student continues to need services, what the present level of performance and educational needs of the student are, and whether the student needs changes in the type of services or in the amount of service time.

▶ **CEC Common Core Knowledge and Skills.** The beginning special educator will gather relevant background information (CC8S1).

Responding to Diversity

Evaluations that include family members must be responsive to family diversity. To encourage family participation, you will need to consider the following questions: What family members should I contact? What are the preferences for communication? Should I send written materials? If so, are there alternative formats (such as Braille) or translations that will be necessary?

Design evaluation procedures and the evaluation questions so as to encourage family members to contribute information. The Snapshot about Iliana Hernandez illustrates a case in point.

▶ Consider the families with whom you have worked. What procedures would work best in encouraging families to contribute information?

Planning an Evaluation of a Program

Identifying the Focus

An evaluation of an overall program, such as a specialized reading program, generates much useful information to advisory boards, administrators, staff, and parents. A program evaluation focuses on four general categories (Gall, Borg, & Gall, 1996). These include:

1. *Program goals:* What are the goals of the program? Does the program achieve the goals through the various services and activities? A goal is the purpose that the program attempts to achieve. Some programs may have goals that are very specific; other programs may have more general goals. However, goals are critical to the worth of the program.
2. *Program resources:* What are the program resources? Are they sufficient to meet the program goal(s)? Program resources may include a variety of areas, such as personnel, volunteers, transportation, materials, equipment, and space.
3. *Program procedures:* What procedures does the program use to achieve its goal(s)? Procedures may include teaching techniques and strategies or arrangements of the environment.

SNAPSHOT

Iliana Hernandez

Iliana Hernandez (1996) talks about her work with parents.

I don't look Hispanic, but I am 100 percent, born in Cuba of Spanish descent.... I helped found Parent to Parent of Miami. My first attempt inviting parents to a Spanish-speaking meeting was a translated flyer. Guess what happened? Nobody showed up. That's when I said, "Well, if I want to start helping my people, I have to know my people.... We needed more than language. We needed cultural understanding."

For instance, something I realized is the impact of the grandmother. There is nothing more powerful in a Hispanic family than the grandmothers. That old lady is the one who sets the rules of the house.

Another thing that works well with Hispanic families is one-to-one support. We work more effectively on a personal basis. We hate papers. Parents tell me, "I don't want to read it. I want you to tell me what you have for me...." (p. 6)

4. *Program management:* How does the program monitor resources and procedure? Is the management as efficient as it can be?

The school administration team usually determines the focus of the evaluation, although a school board could set an evaluation agenda. More often than not, several different areas of concern or global questions regarding the program may have arisen and the team must decide which area needs evaluating. These individuals, in consultation with the evaluator, will determine the evaluation procedures.

Developing a Needs Assessment Questionnaire

Sometimes administrators need assistance in specifying an area for evaluation. A survey or needs assessment questionnaire is an excellent way of identifying the area(s) of greatest need. There are several considerations in developing a questionnaire.

- Keep questionnaires fairly short and state questions simply.
- Incorporate items that can be checked and are easy to complete.
- Include some open-ended questions that allow individuals to respond to areas that you may have overlooked.
- People are much more likely to fill in and return questionnaires that are brief and easy to complete. Remember, a key issue in evaluation is obtaining as many responses as possible from all the relevant parties.

The design and development of questionnaires is beyond the scope of this book. We encourage the interested reader to refer to resources specific to the development of questionnaires and surveys.

Identifying the Informants

There are a number of individuals, or informants, who may provide information, including students, parents and other family members, teachers and support staff, administrators, and community members. When deciding whom to include in completing the evaluation, consider the questions that the program evaluation will need to answer. Generally speaking, program evaluations should include information from the consumers of services.

How It Works! **An Informal Method for Identifying Needs at the Waverly School District**

Laurel Fuller, the special education director at Waverly School District, was working on a schedule of in-service training. Because she wanted to identify the content areas that would be most beneficial to the teachers, she decided to conduct a needs assessment that would solicit input from all the teachers and prioritize training needs. At the weekly teachers' meeting, she distributed sheets of paper and asked the educators to identify four areas that they felt needed attention, numbering them in order of priority. The papers were collected and priorities were assigned points from 4 to 1. (The highest number was assigned to the first priority listed.) The total number of points was then calculated for each of the items listed, and the top-priority item was identified. Through this informal needs assessment, Dr. Fuller was able to utilize information solicited from each member of the staff.

Collecting Information

You can collect evaluation data in a variety of ways, depending on the evaluation model you adopt. For example, using a rating scale format, teachers, administrators, and other school staff assess a variety of areas including assessment, curriculum, instruction, and indicators of student learning. The instrument may collect both quantitative and qualitative data.

Quantitative Data

Quantitative data are information that can be assigned a number or score. Program evaluations often include pretest and posttest scores. Data collection includes the use of surveys or questionnaires on which individuals rate different statements. Family members as well as teachers and students can complete surveys and rating scales. The rating forms the basis of quantitative data. Quantitative data provides statistical information and analyses.

Qualitative Data

Qualitative data are descriptive rather than numeric. Interviews, discussions, observations, written answers, or students' work are the sources for qualitative data. Products that students have produced from work and play activities and video- and audiotape recordings are all examples of qualitative data. Products of the program such as newsletters or monthly calendars of activities are also good sources. Anecdotal and running records as well as specimen records are other excellent sources. Although qualitative data are more difficult to synthesize, this type of data often provides helpful and, sometimes, unexpected findings.

Focus Groups

Focus groups also provide an informal way of collecting information. Focus groups can be small gatherings of individuals from similar constituencies or from different backgrounds, and the group may respond to specific questions or simply offer informal feedback to the group facilitator regarding the program.

A parent focus group can involve several family units; individual members may include mothers, fathers, grandparents, aunts, and other important individuals. Some groups include a deliberate mix of family members to encourage dialogue. Usually, families prefer focus groups because of their informal nature. Group interaction can often determine preferences and satisfaction with programs and services.

Teacher-Developed Program Evaluation Instruments

Teachers and administrators often develop their own forms, tailored to meet the needs of the evaluation. Figure 16.4 illustrates a teacher-developed form that focuses on the school's IEP team process. The IEP team developed this form as the result of a schoolwide effort to increase home-school partnerships. During the schoolwide meeting of all teachers, the special education staff decided to look at the IEP process. Some of the questions that they wanted to answer included: Do parents feel welcome at the IEP team meetings? Do parents feel that their contributions are valued? Are there areas that could be improved?

▶ The Annenberg Institute maintains a website of tools for school-improvement planning. What types of evaluation forms can you find there? http://www.annenberginstitute.org/tools/tools/index.html

Costs Involved

The final step in planning an evaluation is examining the costs involved. Typical cost items are consultant fees, including mileage, lodging, and meals; telephone; postage; computer time, including graphics production and supplies; copying; and so on.

Question	Please circle the appropriate number: 1 = always, 2 = usually, 3 = sometimes, 4 = rarely.				Additional Comments
1. Were you given adequate notice of the team meeting?	1	2	3	4	
2. Did you feel welcome at the team meeting?	1	2	3	4	
3. Did you feel that other team members were interested in your comments during the meeting?	1	2	3	4	
4. Did you feel that your questions or concerns were addressed adequately during the meeting?	1	2	3	4	
5. Did you feel satisfied with the outcome of the team meeting?	1	2	3	4	

FIGURE 16.4 ● A Teacher-Developed Form: Parent Satisfaction with the IEP Team Process

▶ Make an appointment to talk to the special education administrator at your local school. How are special services evaluated?

▶ To learn more about using data for instructional decision making and school improvement, go to the North Central Regional Educational Laboratory at http://www.ncrel.org/datause/dataprimer/

▶ **CEC Common Core Knowledge and Skills.** The beginning special educator will understand the use and limitations of assessment instruments (CC8K4).

Of course, costs do not only have to do with money. Other cost considerations include: How much time is involved? How much staff time should be allocated? What will be the additional costs of staffing substitutes? What are the potential "costs" in terms of psychosocial issues to the staff? to the students? to the parents and other family members?

Designing and Conducting Evaluations

In planning locally developed program evaluations, teachers and administrators must carefully consider the best methods for collecting evaluation information. In Figure 16.4 the teachers and administrators were interested in gathering information about parents' feelings regarding the team process. Notice that items in the questionnaire are worded so as to gather information from the individual's perception.

Research-Based Practices   **Evaluating School Voucher Programs**

Florida's McKay Scholarship Program for Students with Disabilities makes a voucher available to any student receiving special education services in public school to attend a private McKay school. This is the second largest school voucher program in the United States. To evaluate this program, Jay Greene and Greg Forster (2003), two researchers at the Manhattan Institute for Policy Research, conducted two telephone surveys of parents: one of parents currently using a McKay voucher and the other of parents who previously used a voucher but no longer do.

The results showed that parents were more satisfied with their experiences in private McKay schools than in public schools, for both surveys of parents. One of the key findings was that students were victimized far less by other students because of their disabilities in McKay schools. Parents reported that 46.8 percent were bothered often and 24.7 percent were physically assaulted in public school; while in McKay schools 5.3 percent were bothered often and 6.0 percent were assaulted. More parents (86 percent) reported that they received all services required under federal law from the McKay schools, while only 30 percent said they received all services from their public school. McKay schools generally provided the same or slightly more money per pupil than is spent by public schools.

▶ What do you know about vouchers and school choice? What might be some reasons to explain these results?

Section I. (Organization)

1. I write down the due date of my assignments

   _____ always _____ usually _____ sometimes _____ never

2. I use the Study Skills Outline to plan my week

   _____ always _____ usually _____ sometimes _____ never

3. I remember to bring home the materials needed to finish my homework.

   _____ always _____ usually _____ sometimes _____ never

Section II. (Survival Skills)

4. I can locate information in an appliance manual (for example, a manual for a DVD player).

   _____ always _____ usually _____ sometimes _____ never

5. I can use my calculator to compute the correct amount of money at the shopping center.

   _____ always _____ usually _____ sometimes _____ never

6. I can use a computer to search for information

   _____ always _____ usually _____ sometimes _____ never

Section III. (School/Work)

7. I feel that this job allows me to practice my skills

   _____ always _____ usually _____ sometimes _____ never

FIGURE 16.5 • First Draft of an Evaluation Form

In another school the special education administrator and teachers needed to know if the transition program at the high school was successful. The evaluation plan was to examine student test scores and to survey parents and students. Several school faculty members volunteered to work with the administrator in developing a draft student questionnaire (Figure 16.5).

After reading the draft, one of the teachers made the observation that there is only one question in this survey worded appropriately to gather information from the students' perspective. Which question is this?

▶ Instead of a survey, what are alternative ways to gather information regarding some of the other questions? Would these ways be advantageous? Why?

Participating in an Evaluation of Your Program by Others

IDEA provides for the regular evaluation of local educational agencies, such as public schools, that serve students with disabilities. In fact, each state department of education in the United States must submit a plan to the national department of education in Washington that includes, in part, a description of their plan for evaluation. This plan must assess the effectiveness of a sample of programs in the state that are serving individuals with disabilities. The state evaluation must also address the effectiveness of the IEPs for individual students as well as the overall effectiveness of their program. The Snapshot of Sandy Brook Public School illustrates one way staff in a state department of education can choose to conduct their evaluation.

SNAPSHOT

Evaluating Special Education Services at Sandy Brook Public School

Three months ago, Josh Liebermann, the Director of Special Education Services at Sandy Brook Public School, received a form letter from the State Department of Education. The letter described the federal requirement that each local education agency that receives federal monies for the education of students with disabilities must be evaluated periodically by members of the State Education Department Program Review Team. Josh scanned the names of the individuals who were on the Department of Education team. There were four people who would be arriving: two consultants from the state education department, a special education director from a nearby school district, and an administrator from a school district in the southern part of the state. The letter described a tentative schedule for the visit and the items that the team would like to review.

The letter contained a clear description of what the team would need. They wanted to review several different IEPs, and they wanted to talk with several of the parents as well as teachers in the building. Later, the team would send a report summarizing their findings and recommendations for improvement, if necessary.

▶ How does your state department of education conduct evaluations of special education services in the local schools?

Summary

- Program evaluation must be a routine aspect of all programs.
- The most useful program evaluations include both quantitative and qualitative data from a variety of sources.
- As funding continues to be an issue in the types of services that are offered, programs will be under more and more pressure to demonstrate effectiveness and accountability. Implementing program evaluation is an important component in the assessment process and should not be left to chance or excess funding at the end of a program cycle.
- As our field continues to grow and develop, we will need to continue the search for adequate methods and approaches with which to measure our work with students and their families.

REFERENCES

Dick, W., Carey, L., & Carey, J. O. (2000). *The systematic design of instruction*. Boston: Allyn and Bacon.

Dunlap, L. K., Dunlap, G., Koegel, L. K., & Koegel, R. L. (1991). Using self-monitoring to increase independence. *Teaching Exceptional Children 23*(3): 17–22.

Gall, M. D., Borg, W. R., & Gall, J. P. (1996). *Educational research an introduction* (6th ed.). New York: Longman.

Greene, J. P., & Forster, G. (2003). *Vouchers for special education students: An evaluation of Florida's McKay Scholarship Program*. (Report No. CCI-R-38). New York: Manhattan Institute Center for Civic Innovation. (ERIC Document Reproduction Service No. ED481851)

Hernandez, I. (1996). Reaching underserved populations. *Families and Disabilities Newsletter 7*(1): 6.

Joint Committee on Standards for Educational Evaluation. (1994). *The program evaluation standards* (2nd ed.). Thousand Oaks, CA: Sage.

McGinnis, E., & Goldstein, A. P. (1997). *Skillstreaming the elementary school child: New strategies and perspectives for teaching prosocial skills* (rev. ed.). Champaign, IL: Research Press.

Sainato, D. M., Strain, P. S., Lefebvre, D., & Rapp, N. (1990). Effects of self-evaluation on the independent work skills of preschool children with disabilities. *Exceptional Children 56*(4): 540–549.

Smith, M. L., & Glass, G. V. (1987). *Research and evaluation in education and the social sciences*. Englewood Cliffs, NJ: Prentice-Hall.

17 Involving Families

Chapter Objectives

After completing this chapter,
you should be able to:

- Define the term *family* and describe
  areas that are important to consider in
  working with families.
- Identify the important issues in being
  responsive to family diversity.
- Identify areas important for working
  with families of children and youth
  ages 3 through 21.
- Describe the role of families in the
  assessment process as outlined by
  federal law.
- Compare assessment tools designed
  for parent use.
- Use techniques for listening to and
  understanding parents.
- Discuss important components of
  conferencing with parents.

Key Terms

Family   Family-centered philosophy   Early childhood team

Overview

Educators work closely with family members in identifying student strengths and
needs, in planning the education program, and in assessing progress. Within each
family, adult members may have similar or very different priorities for their children.
They may wish to be involved in their child's program in a variety of ways. Family
members are often at different points in their understanding and acceptance of their
child's disability. For example, one parent wants to assist the team by sharing medical
reports and discussing the child's diagnosis; another parent looks to team members for
help and explanations. In working with families, you will need to identify the extent
to which families wish to be involved in their child's assessment process and in the
development of the individualized program as well as the preferred methods of home
and school communication.

Working with diverse family groups involves many skills: listening carefully,
understanding and being responsive to various perspectives, sharing meaningful information, and planning together to develop an appropriate education program. Each

family unit is unique. The uniqueness of families includes such diverse aspects as culture, disability, economic status, ethnicity, gender, geographic region of origin, language, and race. Professionals who work with families must be sensitive to and responsive to all elements of diversity. This chapter will give you a foundation in these skills.

Understanding More about Families

Our definition of the term **family** continues to undergo changes. Today, the term reflects our understanding of the increasing diversity of family patterns and structures. Although there continues to be much debate regarding the definition, many agree that a family consists of two or more individuals who may or may not be related but who have extended commitments to each other.

Although families can include many or only a few members, each family unit is affected by four major factors. Turnbull and Turnbull (1997) developed a family systems model, consisting of four components, to assist in organizing concepts about these important factors:

1. A family's interaction system
2. Family functions
3. Family characteristics
4. A family's life cycle

The first component, a family's interaction system, is the center of the model and involves the interactions of individual family members on a daily and weekly basis. There are four major subsystems of interaction: adult and adult; parent and child; child and child; and extended family, friends, neighbors, and professionals.

The second component, family functions, or the needs of the family, is met by tasks that fall into seven broad categories:

1. Economic considerations
2. Daily care
3. Recreation
4. Socialization
5. Affection
6. Self-definition
7. Educational/vocational considerations

Certain functions or needs are more important to some families than to other families because of personal desires or cultural traditions.

The third component, family characteristics, includes not only the individual characteristics of family members but the characteristics of the family unit as well. For example, the number of family members, their cultural background(s), and their socioeconomic status all affect family characteristics. A child's disability, including any special challenges the child's disability presents, affects family characteristics as well.

Finally, families, like individuals, have life cycles. Progressing through a lifetime, an individual experiences a series of transitions during stages of growth. These stages of the life cycle may be characterized by changing interests and needs. Similarly, all families go through periods of transition during growth stages as the family unit's needs and interests change. For example, a young family's immediate needs may be finding a job and a place to live. The family may be coping with any number of related problems, including poverty, illiteracy, and lack of job skills. Young children make many demands, both physical and emotional, just when parents would rather spend time finding friends for themselves or perhaps someone to assist with child care.

As children grow older, the role of parents shifts from one of meeting children's needs to one of assisting them to become independent. Families in this stage become more involved in their children's schooling and in planning for their future. Families of various backgrounds approach these roles differently. Family traditions can become an issue as parents develop an understanding of their own roles and adjust their dreams for their children. As children move into adulthood, families will experience other challenges and needs, such as accepting decisions of adult children and encouraging them in their chosen vocations.

▶ Think about your own family based on the concepts identified by a family systems model. How does this help you in understanding the complexity of the family unit?

For families that include a child with a disability, there will be additional considerations at each of these stages. Young families with an infant with special needs frequently must adjust a dream about their child's future. The child they envisioned running and skipping may never walk, hear, or speak. Grandparents who had looked forward to the birth of a grandchild may also need help in their acceptance of the infant with special needs. Later on, families with a pre-teenager find that they have to arrange for continued supervised child care. They will need to find time to attend team meetings at school and to meet with their child's teacher. Eventually, families with a young adult must make decisions regarding independent housing and moving from the familiar education system to a new service system. Rehabilitative services, which often have different criteria for eligibility, will replace educational services. Families eventually need information about guardianship, estate planning, and wills.

Thus, while in many ways, the basic life-cycle experience is common, whether the family unit includes a child with special needs, the challenges that the disability presents create additional demands. Furthermore, different expectations for the child and

Research-Based Practices — Parent Involvement in and Perception of Special Education Services

Because parents are considered equal team members in providing information about their children, participating in educational decision making, and in designing their children's individualized education programs, some researchers have wondered about parents' perception of their involvement. Sammy Spann and colleagues (Spann, Kohler, & Soenken, 2003) conducted telephone surveys with 45 families of children with autism who were part of a parent support group. Among other areas, the researchers were interested in (1) the frequency and nature of parents' communication with school personnel, (2) parents' knowledge about and involvement in their children's IEP, and (3) parents' priorities for their children and overall satisfaction with school services.

They found that 100 percent of the parents reported that they communicated with "someone pivotal to their child's education." Over 80 percent of parents of younger students reported that they interacted with school person-

nel at least once a week, whereas only 50 percent of the parents of students ages 15–18 interacted on a weekly basis. A majority of the parents indicated that they shared information related to their children's progress or behavior and also brainstormed with school personnel to solve problems that arose at school or home.

Parents indicated a high to moderate involvement in the IEP process, with parents of young children reporting greater involvement and parents of students ages 10 to 14 indicating less input. Similarly, parents of young children felt that the school was doing more to address their children's needs than parents of older children. Sadly, over 80 percent of the parents of children 15 to 18 years believed that schools were doing little or nothing to address their children's needs. Parents felt that teachers needed more information on autism and that their children needed to have more opportunities to interact with children without disabilities.

different concerns during the family life-cycle frame different perspectives for families who have recently moved to this country, who come from poverty, who speak a home language different from the majority group, or who represent a nondominant group.

Responding to Diversity

Educators, therapists, and other service providers who work with families and children with disabilities begin their work by developing an understanding of the family's culture, economic status, ethnicity, geographic region of origin, language, and race. These professionals know that assumptions by members of the dominant group may not be appropriate or relevant to members of less dominant groups. For example, the birth of a child with an hereditary disorder does not deter an Amish couple from having more children. A child with a disability is accepted as "God's will," and genetic counseling is inappropriate for an Amish family (Waltman, 1996). Individuals working with this family will need to accept and respect the family's decisions and to reassure them that professionals can work cooperatively with the family and not in opposition.

Often, professionals assume that because a family has lived in this country for many years, family members have become acculturated. Some families deliberately avoid adopting the "American way" in an effort to retain their cultural uniqueness. Thus, several generations may grow up not holding the values of the dominant culture.

Cultural heritages, values, and beliefs may dramatically affect the family's perception of and participation in the assessment process (Haney & Knox, 1995; Hanson, Lynch, & Wayman, 1990), development of the intervention, and plans for the future. Other aspects of diversity may affect a family's cooperation. Table 17.1 summarizes the important considerations in working with families and developing a sensitivity to diversity.

▶ Begin a list of resources to help you become responsive to diversity. What books would you include? What journals regularly publish helpful articles? What websites would you recommend? What families in your area would be willing to be a resource?

Aspirations

A family's hopes for its child may range from appropriate to elevated or depressed expectations. Family aspirations have an impact on the levels of involvement that families choose: from making the referral for assessment, to participating in the assessment process, to helping develop a plan for services. Certain cultural or regional expectations can also influence family aspirations. For example, residents in some regions place a high value on family and community. A family from this region may hope that after completing school their child will join the family business.

Assistance

The family may actively seek help from others, or the family may view its needs and problems as private matters to be addressed only within the family. For example, residents in some rural areas place a high value on personal independence and self-sufficiency. They may be reluctant to ask for additional assistance.

Authority of the School

Cultural beliefs, such as feelings about school authority in decision making (Turnbull & Turnbull, 1997) or respect of authority (Alper, Schloss, & Schloss, 1994), often affect the level and type of involvement family members choose. Some families have difficulty with the joint decision-making process of parents and professionals working together. They consider professionals authority figures to be respected and obeyed. Such family members may try to avoid confrontation in discussions, or they may reject school authority altogether.

Area of Consideration	Issues in Being Responsive to Diversity
TABLE 17.1 ● Considerations in Responding to Family Diversity	
Aspirations	A family's hopes for its child may range from appropriate aspirations to elevated or depressed expectations.
	Family aspirations affect the level of involvement families choose in making the referral, in participating in the assessment process, and in helping to develop a plan of services. Family aspirations are influenced by culture, economic status, gender, or geographic regional expectations.
Assistance	Family members may actively seek help or they may view needs and concerns as private matters. Family views are influenced by one or more aspects of diversity.
Authority of the school	Some families wish to participate in parent professional partnerships. Families from some cultural communities naturally defer to authority.
Child rearing	Families approach child rearing from various perspectives, including independence, communication, and physical contact.
Communication	Some families use an assertive style in their verbal communication that assists them in referring their child and in entering the service system. Other families naturally defer to authority figures and do not pursue issues.
	Some families use nonverbal communication, including eye gaze and gestures to communicate important wants or needs.
	Communicating takes on a special significance to some groups. Finishing a conversation is more important than being on time.
	Communication that involves technology may be a barrier for some families.
Disability	A disability may be viewed as shameful, or the person with a disability may be viewed as having a second-class status.
	A disability can present social or physical barriers. These barriers may be perceived, or they may be actual barriers of access.
	Issues of acceptance involve one or more of the following groups: parents, extended family, community.
Legal status	Families may lack knowledge of their rights.
	Families with illegal status often fear government authorities or school officials.
Literacy and language	Family members may not have literacy skills in their own language or in English.
	Information and materials are seldom available in the family's native language.
	Translators may not be available.
	Standardized instruments often lack a representative norming sample.
	Examiners may not be familiar with aspects of diversity.
Medical practices	Medical practices differ and can cause misinterpretation between families and school personnel.
Meetings and support groups	The format of group discussions can cause difficulty for families of some communities.
Parental roles	In many cultures, the person who makes the decisions is the principal male family member.
Transient status	Families that are homeless or move frequently have difficulty entering the service system.

Child Rearing

Families approach child rearing from various perspectives too. In some families there is much close physical contact between mother and child, and communication is characterized more by touch than by vocal stimulation. Other families spend much time talking and singing to their children. Some families do not encourage their childen to participate in gross motor activities for safety concerns. Other families of young children promote independent exploration and travel.

Communication

Communication involves active listening and responding to both verbal and nonverbal communication. Being sensitive and responsive to family diversity includes appreciating that family groups may have unique communication patterns. For example, some regional and cultural groups support and value assertiveness in making needs and wishes known to others; some groups view assertiveness as rude and avoidable.

Communication styles can help or hinder family members' efforts to seek services. For example, to receive services, family members have to make an initial referral, make follow-up phone calls, complete paperwork, and deal with a service system with various requirements and eligibility procedures. The variety of communication and interpersonal skills needed to negotiate the service system can create barriers for some families in obtaining services.

Some family groups have unique nonverbal communication patterns—for example, avoiding eye contact with elders to signify respect. The art of communication may take on a special significance to some groups. For instance, a focus on relationships rather than on tasks can mean it is more important to continue a conversation with a friend than it is to be on time for an appointment to discuss a child's assessment.

For families newly arrived in this country, communication that involves technologies can create additional barriers. For example, families may not be acquainted with the procedure of operating a phone to negotiate a computer-assisted telephone call or using voice mail.

Disability

Perceptions of disability encompass a range of emotions for family members: embarrassment and shame, guilt and blame, grief and acceptance. Some groups may view a person with a disability as having second-class status. Family members may believe that there are social or physical barriers because their child has a visible disability. Parents may lack knowledge about their child's disability and have difficulty in locating information to develop realistic expectations. Various issues relating to the acceptance of the disability involve the parents, the extended family, and the community. The extended family's perceptions and the cultural community's acceptance of the disability often play a critical role for the immediate family.

Legal Status

Families may lack knowledge of their rights regarding services for their children. Parents who have an illegal status commonly fear government and school officials and are reluctant to have their children assessed.

Literacy and Language

Some family members may not have the ability to speak, read, or write English. Other family members may have poor literacy skills in their native language. Even families who have strong literacy skills may be limited by the availability of materials in their native languages or dialects. Identifying translators and their availability is critical for families so that they can participate in the assessment process. The challenge of translating exact meanings between two languages is often difficult. For families who speak a dialect different from the translator's, this challenge sometimes becomes a barrier.

When family members participate in the assessment process, they find that few standardized assessment instruments are written in languages other than English. This may be true of a parent questionnaire as part of a screening or a parent form of a behavior rating scale. Additionally, many standardized instruments do not include representative samples from cultural, racial, ethnic, and linguistic groups. To compound the problem, examiners can lack familiarity with family diversity.

Medical Practices

Medical practices differ across cultures and can cause misinterpretation by school personnel. One example of a traditional practice that has led to misunderstandings in the U.S. culture is the use of coin rubbing. This massage treatment is utilized by the Vietnamese community to treat disorders such as headaches and colds. Coin treatment, or *Cao Gio*, literally translates to "scratching the (bad) wind out of the body." The treatment involves the massaging of chest and back with a medicated substance, like Ben-Gay®, and the striking or scratching of the skin with a coin or spoon. This process leaves superficial bruises and, when spotted by professionals who are unaware of the technique, has often resulted in a referral for child abuse. This practice provides a clear example of differences and also dramatically underscores the issues in diagnosis and interpretation when the various cultures meet (Hanson et al., 1990, p. 122).

Meetings and Support Groups

Support groups are often helpful for family members who would like assistance yet the group discussion format is more difficult for some individuals than others. Shapiro (1994) describes how problems can be overcome in support groups among Latino families. Approaches that are beneficial include the development of ethnically competent group facilitators (who have a familiarity with Latino ethnic history and culture), the involvement of community leaders, outreach using the Latino media, repeated personal contact, attention to making the group culturally relevant, and meeting in a neutral location.

Parental Roles

In many cultures, the person who makes the decisions is the principal male family member. This could be the father, grandfather, uncle, or brother-in-law. Although the mother or other female family representative might attend all meetings regarding the child, she may refuse to make any decisions or sign any papers. The male figure may never attend any of the meetings, yet the decisions are his to make. This decision-making process can be frustrating to the team; however, if the team has knowledge of the parental roles beforehand, additional attempts can be made to accommodate the male family member's schedule.

Transient Status

Understanding and being responsive to diversity is a complex process that involves working with various perspectives that family members hold, including families who are transient. The skills involved require you to be thoughtful and reflective in practice. You must exercise care not to promote stereotypes by making generalities about cultural groups. A key point to remember in working with families is to *ask*. Asking families to determine preferences and needs avoids stereotypical assumptions as well as careless regard for family heritage. Some families move frequently from one residence to another and some can be homeless for periods of time. Locating children and providing services is challenging when families move from one service area to another.

Federal Legislation and the Role of Parents

Federal legislation that regulates the provision of services to children and youth with disabilities has long recognized the role of the parents. One of the most important aspects of this legislation is the defining of parent and guardian rights. IDEA describes these rights under the broad term *due process*. Due process refers to the legal safeguards professionals must follow during the assessment process and the delivery of services. These safeguards protect the rights of families and their children.

Guaranteed Rights

School personnel must notify the child's parent(s) or guardian of any assessment procedure (*right of notice*) and provide consent (*right of consent*) for the assessment of their child. Before the assessment process begins, school personnel must send the parents a written form that describes the types of assessments to be conducted. The parent provides consent by signing and returning the form. However, the parent can revoke consent at any time during the assessment process by notifying the school. The parent can request that a full assessment of all areas associated with the disability be completed. This assessment must include multiple measures, must be conducted by a multidisciplinary team, and, for children ages 3 through 21, must be completed within 60 days of referral. Sixty days is the maximum number of days; some states have passed legislation that specifies a 45-day maximum. Teachers and examiners should check with state department of education personnel to determine the laws in a specific state.

Infants and toddlers ages birth through 2 and preschoolers who will have an individualized family service plan must have assessment procedures completed 45 days after the initial referral (*right of evaluation*). Parents may request a reevaluation or obtain an independent evaluation if there are any questions or concerns regarding the evaluation (*right to an independent evaluation*). Table 17.2 describes these and other important rights.

The Assessment Process for Families of Young Children

In this section we will examine some of the questions and decisions that parents make concerning the assessment of young children. Early childhood teachers and other professionals who work with families of young children provide services within the context of a **family-centered philosophy**. A family-centered philosophy requires that teachers and therapists attempt to create opportunities for families to acquire the knowledge and skills necessary to strengthen the functioning of the family. Thus, families are not merely recipients of services but rather active participants in the assessment, implementation, and evaluation of special services. Parents of young children frequently have questions about their children's development and the ability to do well in school. Some parents have questions about their children's behavior.

TABLE 17.2 • The Rights of Parents and Guardians According to IDEA	
Right of Parents and Guardians	**Definition**
Beginning the Assessment Process	
Right of notice	The parent must receive a notification of the proposed assessment in the family's native language or principal mode of communication.
Right of consent	The parent must give consent before the child is assessed to determine eligibility for special education services.
Right of evaluation	The assessment must include multiple measures, be conducted by a multidisciplinary team, and be completed within 60 days of referral for special services. For young children who will have an IFSP, the assessment must be completed within 45 days of the initial referral.
Right to an independent evaluation	The parent has a right to request an evaluation by an independent evaluator if there are questions or concerns regarding the child's evaluation conducted by school personnel.
Using the Assessment Information	
Right of participation	The parent must be invited to participate in the writing of the child's educational plan (an individualized family service plan or an individualized educational program).
Right of notice	The parent must receive a notification of the proposed changes in the education program, which must be in the family's native language or principal mode of communication.
Right of access	The parent must be allowed access to all educational records.
Right to confidentiality	The educational records are confidential. The parent must give consent to have the child's records released to other institutions or agencies. The parent has the right to refuse disclosure of information contained in the records to other professionals or agencies.
Right to hearing	The parent has the right to a hearing with an impartial hearing officer. The parent has a right to present evidence and to cross-examine school staff.
Right to mediation	The parent has the right to a process, called mediation, which attempts to resolve differences with school personnel before going to a hearing.
Right to resolve differences	If the parent is not satisfied with the decision of the hearing officer, a second step, the right to appeal to the state court system, can be implemented.

Initial Questions and Decisions

During the early years of a child's growth, parents and other family members may develop concerns about their child's development. In fact, parents are often the first to question or to observe areas of difficulty for their child, such as happened in the Snapshot of Juan and his family (see page 360). Parents sometimes share their concerns with someone close to their child, such as a teacher or child care provider.

SNAPSHOT

Questions Concerning Juan's Physical Development

Juan was born 3½ months premature and is now 4 years old. He lives at home with his mother, father, maternal grandmother, and two younger brothers. Every day his grandmother takes him for a ride in his red wagon when she goes down to the corner store. He enjoys watching the activities at a construction site along the way. His grandmother and his father have some concerns about Juan's development. He was slow to walk and talk, and his speech is still difficult to understand. He prefers to play alone or to watch cartoons on television.

His grandmother shared her concerns with a neighbor who works at the community child care center. The staff at the center had recently completed an in-service workshop on child development. The neighbor listened sympathetically and then suggested that the grandmother could take Juan to the child center for a free community screening on the first Monday of the month.

Teachers and child care personnel should listen to parents and encourage discussions about their children. They should inform parents about neighborhood screening activities and encourage them to have their children screened periodically. Assisting parents and other adults to become aware of screenings, programs, and services for children with special needs is called *Child Find*.

Preschool teachers, public health nurses, social workers, and doctors are some of the professionals involved with Child Find. Personnel from state agencies who work with children and families conduct a variety of Child Find activities throughout the year. For example, radio and television announcements or newspaper articles describe community screenings and dates screenings will be held. Brochures distributed in public places explain ways to observe a young child's development and list common questions that arise for parents. These printed materials also contain information about community screenings. Families with questions about their children may decide to take advantage of these free screenings, or families may decide to discuss their concerns with their primary medical provider.

TESTS-at-a-GLANCE

Ages and Stages Questionnaires (ASQ) Second Edition

- **Publication Date:** 1999

- **Purposes:** A parent-completed first-level screening test that measures the following areas of development: communication, gross motor, fine motor, problem solving, and personal-social. The *Ages & Stages Questionnaires* are also available in Spanish, French, and Korean. A set of intervention activities is included in the ASQ User's Guide, and these may be photocopied for parents.

- **Age/Grade Level:** Ages 4 months through 60 months.

- **Time to Complete:** 5 minutes.

- **Technical Adequacy:** The instrument has undergone extensive development and reliability and validity are adequate.

- **Suggested Use:** May be used as part of an overall screening procedure.

Screening Questions and Decisions for Families

Parents can share their observations and concerns during screening. A social worker, nurse practitioner, or educator usually meets with the parent(s) to discuss their questions and concerns and to record information about their child's development. The assessment question is: Does this child have a problem that requires further assessment? Parents usually complete a checklist or parent report form concerning various milestones in their child's development. Many standardized screening tools provide a parent report form as an integral part of the screening profile.

One example of a standardized screening tool, the *Ages & Stages Questionnaires (ASQ) Second Edition* (Bricker & Squires, 1999) consists of comprehensive parent questionnaires (Figure 17.1). These questionnaires are designed to provide information in five developmental areas: communication, gross motor,

Problem Solving *Be sure to try each activity with your child*

	Yes	Sometimes	Not Yet
1. While your child watches, line up four objects like blocks or cars in a row. Does your child copy or imitate you and line up *four* objects in a row? (You can also use spools of thread, small boxes, or other toys.)	☐	☒	☐
2. If your child wants something he cannot reach, does he find a chair or box to stand on to reach it?	☐	☐	☒
3. When you point to the figure and ask your child, "What is this?" does your child say a word that means a person? Responses like "snowman," "boy," "man," "girl," and "Daddy" are correct.	☒	☐	☐

Please write your child's response here: "A Mommy"

FIGURE 17.1 ● Selected Items from the Ages and Stages Questionnaire (ASQ) Second Edition

Source: Bricker, D., & Squires, J. (1999). *Ages and stages questionnaires: A parent-completed, child-monitoring system* (2nd ed.; p. 5). Baltimore: Paul H. Brookes..

fine motor, problem solving, and personal-social skills. The parent rates whether the child performs different activities within each of these five areas by indicating "yes," "sometimes," and "not yet." Parent questionnaires are available in English, Spanish, French, and Korean.

If there are concerns after collecting all the information about the child, the screening team forwards the results to a team of professionals known as the early childhood team or the IEP team. The **early childhood team** consists of the parents, the family service coordinator, and representatives of various disciplines who assess, design, implement, monitor, and evaluate early intervention services. The team makes decisions regarding eligibility and services for children birth through age 2 and, in some states, for children ages 3 to 5. This team will invite the child's parent(s) to participate and, together, they decide what additional assessment information is necessary. Once the assessment information is complete, the team meets to determine if the child is eligible for special education services.

▶ **CEC Common Core Knowledge and Skills.** The beginning special educator will use procedures for early identification of young children who may be at risk for disabilities (GC8K4).

How Parents of Children and Youth Are Involved in the Assessment Process

Addressing Parent Questions and Concerns

In Chapter 1 we discuss a prereferral system for special education services. In this model an assistance team consisting of regular classroom teachers and special educators in the school building meets to discuss parent or teacher concerns about a student's behavior or academic work and, following a problem-solving approach, plans one or more interventions.

Questions about Alexandra's General Academic Work

Mrs. Balinsky is worried about her daughter's grades. She remembers with pride how Alexandra put a puzzle together when she was only 2 years old. Later, in elementary school, she always brought home report cards with As. But now, in ninth grade, Alexandra seems to have lost interest in schoolwork and good grades. She barely passed English and math last year. Why could there be such a change in Alexandra? Mrs. Balinsky decides to contact the school with her questions and concerns.

▶ **CEC Common Core Knowledge and Skills.** The beginning special educator will understand the types and importance of information concerning individuals with disabilities available from families and public agencies (GC8K3).

Questions about Elaina's Behavior

Elaina's mother is discouraged. Some days, Elaina seems to argue constantly with her sisters and neighborhood friends. She comes running into the house, slams the screen door, and screams that she hates everyone. Her mother has tried to talk with her, but Elaina usually ends up crying and locking herself in the bedroom. Her mother feels that the other children are becoming resentful and don't want to include Elaina in their plans.

Elaina's mother contacts the school and arranges to meet with Elaina's teacher and guidance counselor. During the meetings, the guidance counselor suggests several strategies to try at home. Elaina's teacher agrees to follow up in the classroom. However, as the months go by, the mother becomes more concerned with the lack of progress. She again contacts the school and fills out the referral form.

During the implementation of the intervention, the teacher or, when appropriate, the parent, carefully records its effectiveness. If the first intervention is not successful, the team will identify and implement additional interventions and record the results.

Screening Questions and Decisions

The law mandates screening for all students enrolling in school for the first time and for students who move into a new school district. During the child's school career, teachers will contact parents regarding their concerns or parents can contact school personnel with their questions as the Snapshot of Alexandra illustrates. Physicians, too, refer a student for evaluation.

Teachers should encourage parents to discuss any questions or concerns that they have throughout the school year. Teachers can assist parents by asking informal questions such as, "What would be helpful for me to know about Alexandra?" or leading questions such as, "Tell me what Alexandra likes to do at home."

Referral and Decisions for the Team

When questions about a student persist, the student assistance team completes a written referral form and forwards the referral to the coordinator of the special services team. This team consists of the student's parents, school personnel, and the student, when possible. The team may be known as the IEP team or child study team.

The special services team receives the formal referral delineating questions about the student, which comes directly from the child's parents, teachers, student assistance team, or the student, who may self-refer. The special services team makes decisions regarding assessment procedures and develops an assessment plan. This plan describes questions the team is trying to answer about the student's special needs, the tests and procedures the team will use, and the individuals who will complete the assessments. The parent or guardian must sign a written permission before the assessment process begins. As team members, parents contribute information to this process. They may provide copies of medical records and/or educational reports. Parents frequently add observations of the student at home and in the community. They also assist the team in gathering information by using informal tools such as checklists, rating scales, or video recordings.

Eligibility Questions and Decisions

In this step of the assessment process the team addresses the following question: Does the student meet the criteria for a disability? Does the

Jimmy's Parent and the Prereferral Model

Using the prereferral model, Jimmy's mother contacted his teacher at Bennington Middle School to discuss her concerns about her son. Fourteen-year-old Jimmy seems to struggle with completing his homework, she explained. After supper, he looks forward to watching his favorite television program before beginning his algebra and English assignments. After the program finishes, Jimmy sits down to work on the couch; yet, his mother has noticed that he gets up frequently and wanders around the house to find an assignment, a pencil, or a book. He becomes distracted easily and often forgets what he has set out to find. He rarely finishes his work before bedtime. After listening to these concerns, Jimmy's teacher, Jon Parker, explained that he, too, had become increasingly concerned about his work in class.

After listening to the parent's concerns, Jon discussed the school's Student Assistance Team (the SAT) and explained that the team met on a regular basis to provide assistance to students and teachers. Jimmy's mother expressed an interest in attending a SAT meeting.

Within a couple of weeks, arrangements were made for Jimmy's mother to attend. At the meeting, Jimmy's mother and teacher shared their concerns. The team worked to de-

vise an intervention plan for Jimmy. Some examples of strategies that they discussed included teaching Jimmy a self-monitoring strategy when doing his homework and creating a list of incentives. Figure 17.2 shows an example of one of the materials, a parent-student monitoring sheet that Jimmy, his teacher, and his mother developed.

As a result of their discussions, Jimmy's mother agreed to let him work at the kitchen table because other family members usually watch television in the living room each evening. She agreed to remind him of the time they have set for evening homework. Jimmy's teacher suggested she can assist Jimmy in organizing his materials. The SAT agreed that she will help him decide where to keep school supplies such as pencils, dictionary, and paper. During the homework hour, Jimmy agreed to record his progress on the monitoring sheet. If he receives six checks out of a possible seven areas, he can choose a previously agreed-upon reward.

Perhaps for Jimmy these interventions will address the problem, and the assessment process will end. However, when assistance team members think that a student requires more extensive remediation, they provide a formal referral to the special services team.

Jimmy's Daily Homework Check

September 13

Six checks for extra hour of TV

	Parent checks	Comments
Quiet area for homework	_____	
Study hour starts at 7:30 P. M.	_____	
School supplies available	_____	

	Jimmy checks	Comments
Working on homework 1 to 15 minutes	_____	
Working on homework 16 to 30 minutes	_____	
Working on homework 31 to 45 minutes	_____	
Working on homework 46 to 60 minutes	_____	

FIGURE 17.2 • Parent-Student Monitoring Sheet

student need special education to learn and to develop? Parents and other team members must decide if the student's special needs meet the eligibility requirements as described in IDEA and discussed in Chapter 1.

The IEP team plans an individual assessment to determine if the child has a disability and to determine what the educational needs of the child are. The child is assessed in all areas related to the suspected disability including, if appropriate,

- Health
- Vision
- Hearing
- Social and emotional status
- General intelligence
- Academic performance
- Communication
- Motor abilities

The information collected during the assessment process determines the decisions regarding eligibility. Parents provide helpful information and a unique perspective—for example, in the Snapshot about Elaina on page 362, her mother shares information regarding her behavior at home and in the community. Furthermore, she is the only team member who can provide a historical perspective. In Alexandra's case, this information is necessary to develop a more comprehensive picture of the assessment questions.

Parents can provide information informally through discussions or contribute information on a standardized instrument. There are numerous instruments that solicit parent information as part of the profile. An example of one of these instruments, the *Child Behavior Checklist* (Achenbach, 2001), is provided in Figure 17.3.

► **CEC Common Core Knowledge and Skills.** The beginning special educator will understand screening, prereferral, referral, and classification procedures (CC8K3).

Questions and Decisions in Planning Services

If the team decides that the student is eligible for special services, the next step involves questions and decisions regarding the student's program and writing the IEP. One of the rights of parents is to participate with other team members in planning the special education services that their child will receive. During the IEP meeting, the team addresses several questions: What types of special education does the student need? Where should the student receive the services? How should planners coordinate and evaluate the services?

Team members may decide to place the student in the regular classroom with the special education teacher providing consulting services. On the other hand, some parents may question whether their child will receive as much support in the regular classroom as in the resource room. Parents and other team members will need to discuss these difficult questions and make decisions based on the assessment process. The IEP team has 30 days to complete the writing of the IEP after the student qualifies for special education. In planning services the team will make decisions about the types of services that will be provided, including related services as illustrated in Table 17.3.

TABLE 17.3 ● Related Services for Children and Youth under IDEA 2004

- Transportation.
- Speech-language pathology.
- Audiology services.
- Interpreting services.
- Psychological services.
- Physical therapy.
- Occupational therapy.
- Recreation, including therapeutic recreation.
- Social work services.
- School nurse services designed to enable a child with a disabilities to receive a free appropriate public education as described in the individualized education program of the child.
- Counseling services, including rehabilitation counseling.
- Orientation and mobility services.
- Medical services (except that such medical services shall be for diagnostic and evaluation purposes only), as may be required to assist a child with a disability to benefit from special education, and including the early identification and assessment of disabling conditions in children.
- Exception: Related services do not include a medical device that is surgically implanted, or the replacement of such device.

Source: 20 USC Sec. 602 (26)

Questions and Decisions in Monitoring Services

Once the plan is in place, communication between home and school is very important in monitoring services. The assessment questions during this step include: Is the student making progress? Does the

---

Please print. Be sure to answer all items

Below is a list of items that describe children and youths. For each item that describes your child **now or within the past 6 months** please circle the **2** if the item is **very true or often true** of your child. Circle the **1** if the item is **somewhat or sometimes true** of your child. If the item is **not true** of your child, circle the **0**. Please answer all items as well as you can, even if some do not seem to apply to your child.

---

0 = Not True (as far as you know)   1 = Somewhat or Sometimes True   2 = Very True or Often True

---

0 1 2   1. Acts too young for his/her age

0 1 2   2. Drinks alcohol without parents' approval (describe): _____

_____

0 1 2   3. Argues a lot

0 1 2   4. Fails to finish things he/she starts

0 1 2   5. There is very little he/she enjoys

0 1 2   6. Bowel movements outside toilet

0 1 2   7. Bragging, boasting

0 1 2   8. Can't concentrate, can't pay attention for long

0 1 2   9. Can't get his/her mind off certain thoughts; obsessions (describe): _____

_____

0 1 2   10. Can't sit still, restless, or hyperactive

0 1 2   11. Clings to adults or too dependent

0 1 2   12. Complains of loneliness

0 1 2   13. Confused or seems to be in a fog

0 1 2   14. Cries a lot

0 1 2   15. Cruel to animals

0 1 2   16. Cruelty, bullying, or meanness to others

0 1 2   17. Daydreams or gets lost in his/her thoughts

0 1 2   18. Deliberately harms self or attempts suicide

0 1 2   19. Demands a lot of attention

0 1 2   20. Destroys his/her own things

0 1 2   21. Destroys things belonging to his/her family or others

0 1 2   22. Disobedient at home

0 1 2   23. Disobedient at school

0 1 2   24. Doesn't eat well

0 1 2   25. Doesn't get along with other kids

0 1 2   26. Doesn't seem to feel guilty after misbehaving

0 1 2   27. Easily jealous

0 1 2   28. Breaks rules at home, school, or elsewhere

0 1 2   29. Fears certain animals, situations, or places, other than school (describe): _____

_____

0 1 2   30. Fears going to school

0 1 2   31. Fears he/she might think or do something bad

0 1 2   32. Feels he/she has to be perfect

0 1 2   33. Feels or complains that no one loves him/her

0 1 2   34. Feels others are out to get him/her

0 1 2   35. Feels worthless or inferior

0 1 2   36. Gets hurt a lot, accident-prone

0 1 2   37. Gets in many fights

0 1 2   38. Gets teased a lot

0 1 2   39. Hangs around with others who get in trouble

0 1 2   40. Hears sound or voices that aren't there (describe): _____

_____

0 1 2   41. Impulsive or acts without thinking

0 1 2   42. Would rather be alone than with others

0 1 2   43. Lying or cheating

0 1 2   44. Bites fingernails

0 1 2   45. Nervous, highstrung, or tense

0 1 2   46. Nervous movements or twitching (describe):

_____

0 1 2   47. Nightmares

0 1 2   48. Not liked by other kids

0 1 2   49. Constipated, doesn't move bowels

0 1 2   50. Too fearful or anxious

0 1 2   51. Feels dizzy or lighthearted

0 1 2   52. Feels too guilty

0 1 2   53. Overeating

0 1 2   54. Overtired without good reason

0 1 2   55. Overweight

0 1 2   56. Physical problems **without known medical cause:**

0 1 2   a. Aches or pains (**not** stomach or headaches)

0 1 2   b. Headaches

0 1 2   c. Nausea, feels sick

0 1 2   d. Problems with eyes (**not** if corrected by glasses) (describe): _____

_____

0 1 2   e. Rashes or other skin problems.

0 1 2   f. Stomachaches

0 1 2   g. Vomiting, throwing up

0 1 2   h. Other (describe): _____

_____

FIGURE 17.3 • Sample Items from the Child Behavior Checklist (Ages 6–18)

Source: From *Child Behavior Checklist for Ages 6–18,* T. M. Achenbach (2001). Burlington, VT: ASEBA.™ © 2001 by ASEBA. Reprinted with permission.

> *October 5   Jenny had an appointment with the doctor this afternoon. The doctor told us that she wants to change the dosage of her medication. This morning Jenny began the increased amount. The doctor said it may take her a few days to adjust.*
>
> *Mrs. Williams*

FIGURE 17.4 ● Entry from a Traveling Log Book

program need to be modified? Teachers and parents will monitor student progress by observing the student's work and behavior or by completing informal assessments. For example, parents, as well as the student's teachers, can use a log book to enter comments about daily or weekly progress. Figure 17.4 illustrates information provided by the parent. These informal tools that parents utilize are helpful to the team in monitoring the student's individualized program.

Questions and Decisions in Evaluating Services

Evaluating the special education services that students with disabilities receive involves two types of decision making: First, the team addresses questions regarding the student; and second, school personnel focus on questions regarding the overall program. Parents should have the opportunity to assist in both types of evaluations.

Evaluating Student Gains

Parents must receive written notification of each IEP meeting concerning their child. The team will address questions regarding whether the student is making gains or if the program needs changing. They will review the part of the IEP form that lists the annual goals and objectives, if appropriate, and discuss the student's progress. Teams will need to consider whether the student still requires special service(s) to benefit from the education program. Parents may actively participate in the evaluation of student gains by completing checklists, videotapes, parent reports, or other recording sheets. Let's examine some specific examples of information that parents share during team meetings:

- A father shares information with the team regarding his son's behavior after school and on the weekend, while the teacher shares information regarding her observations of the student in the lunch room and on the playground.
- A grandmother records by audiotape information about homework habits and other behaviors at home.
- A mother and special education teacher report information that they have compiled together, using observations of the student.

The Three-Year Review

The IEP team must reevaluate students every three years, or more often if the parent(s) or school personnel believes it is necessary. The IEP team meets to review existing evaluation data and identifies what additional data is needed. Once team members gather additional assessment information, they reconvene to discuss the results. Based on the reevaluation assessment information, team members make a decision about the student's eligibility for special education. If the team makes the decision that the student is no longer eligible, then the student exits the special services system. If the team makes the decision that the student continues to be eligible for special services, then the next step is to write the new IEP.

Evaluating the Education Program

As consumers, parents can contribute valuable information in this assessment step because they are most familiar with the day-to-day operation of the program. Parents commonly provide feedback to school personnel through the use of informal instruments, such as the teacher-made questionnaire illustrated in Figure 17.5.

To improve education programs, state departments of education and local school districts develop Web-based program evaluation questionnaires that parents complete. Figure 17.6 on page 368 illustrates a form that is designed for parents to provide feedback regarding their children's education program.

May 15

Dear Parent,

We are evaluating your child's reading program this spring, and we would appreciate your help. Please take a few minutes to answer the following questions. If possible, could you please return this letter in the enclosed stamped envelope by Friday.

Thank you,
Sandy Files
W.G. Willard School

	Yes	Sometimes	No
1. My child brings home books from the school library.	_____	_____	_____
2. My child likes to read out loud to other family members.	_____	_____	_____
3. My child enjoys reading activities at school.	_____	_____	_____
4. I feel that my child is making progress in reading.	_____	_____	_____
5. My child completes homework assignments in a reasonable amount of time.	_____	_____	_____
6. Please add additional comments or suggestions.			

Thank you for your help.

FIGURE 17.5 • A Teacher-Developed Program Evaluation Form

Parent Questionnaire

Use a pencil to completely fill in the circle next to your choice.

Indicate how much you agree or disagree with each statement by filling in one of the circles.

Strongly Disagree	Disagree	Neutral	Agree	Strongly Agree	
○	○	○	○	○	23. The way they teach at this school works well with my child.
○	○	○	○	○	24. My child is given a fair chance to succeed at school.
○	○	○	○	○	25. There are good learning materials at my child's school.
○	○	○	○	○	26. My child likes attending this school.
○	○	○	○	○	27. I can talk with my child's teachers or principal whenever I need.
○	○	○	○	○	28. My child's school is a good place to learn.
○	○	○	○	○	29. My child uses computers effectively at school.
○	○	○	○	○	30. I know how well my child is doing in class.
○	○	○	○	○	31. I feel my child is safe at school.
○	○	○	○	○	32. I am welcome to discuss my child's education needs with the school.
○	○	○	○	○	33. My child's school building is in good condition.
○	○	○	○	○	34. The community provides enough money to the schools to do a good job.
○	○	○	○	○	35. Discipline in my child's school is handled fairly.
○	○	○	○	○	36. If I could, I would send my child to a different school.
○	○	○	○	○	37. In our community people tend to trust each other.
○	○	○	○	○	38. The school encourages parents to be involved.
○	○	○	○	○	39. The school board listens to parents' concerns.
○	○	○	○	○	40. It is important for students to have access to computers at school.
○	○	○	○	○	41. My child has been taught in school about respect for other cultures.

FIGURE 17.6 • School Program Evaluation Questionnaire for Parents—Selected Items

Source: Data Analysis for Comprehensive Schoolwide Improvement by Victoria Bernhardt, published by Eye On Education, 6 Depot Way West, Larchmont, NY, 10538, (914) 833–0551, www.eyeoneducation.com. Reprinted with permission.

Techniques for Listening to and Understanding Parent Perspectives

Parents and other family members have a wealth of knowledge about their children. Some people are more comfortable in sharing this information by filling out a form or checklist. Others prefer a more personal approach. Interviews and family stories allow families who are comfortable in talking to others to share descriptive information.

In using these techniques, the first step is to acknowledge that you want to hear what parents are saying (Cohen & Spenciner, 1994). Careful listening ensures that your own biases do not overshadow what parents are relating to you. Listening to families requires complex skills, including sensitivity and respect.

▶ **CEC Common Core Knowledge and Skills.** The beginning special educator will gather relevant background information (CC8S1).

Interviews

The interview format allows different family members to talk and to share their individual perspectives. An interview that is a face-to-face meeting may be easier for some family members, while an interview conducted over the telephone may better fit other family members' needs. Like other forms of assessment, the interview should be responsive to diversity. Create a positive tone by your respect, acceptance, support, and warmth. Set aside your own beliefs and judgments. You will need to focus on listening carefully and not let personal bias be a source of error.

Be sensitive in your probing. Respect parents' right to share only the information that they wish. Some parents are not ready to discuss some areas initially, or they do not want to confront a topic at certain periods of time. Conducting an interview with the family (Dunst, Trivette, & Deal, 1988) includes several steps: planning the interview, meeting the family, and completing the interview.

Planning the Interview

When you contact the family, be sure to state the purpose of your visit. For example, "I'd like to visit with you and Alexandra's father to talk further about your concerns." Decide on a mutually convenient place and time. Some families prefer a meeting in their home where they feel more comfortable in talking about their concerns in familiar surroundings. Other families prefer meeting in the home due to a strong sense of duty or cultural tradition to entertain a guest in their home. Some families are more comfortable meeting in a community setting, perhaps a quiet coffee shop or at the school.

Many professionals find it helpful to prepare a few questions in advance. Prepared questions can help family members in "getting started." As you think about the types of questions that would be helpful, consider the wording of the questions and the type of answer that might result.

For example, a question such as, "Could you tell me about some of the difficult times during the day for Alexandra?" encourages an extended response. Leading questions such as, "Tell me more about . . ." are helpful too. Asking "What time of day is most difficult for Alexandra?" will likely lead to a word or phrase response, whereas "Is getting ready for school in the morning a difficult time for Alexandra?" will probably result in a minimal response (yes or no). These latter types of questions serve to stop or limit discussion.

Meeting the Family

Four important aspects help ensure that the interview will go well. The first is to acknowledge each family member who is present and to thank each person for taking the time to be there. Next, establish rapport with family members by showing a genuine interest in what they have to say. Repeat the purpose of the visit. "I know that you have some concerns about Alexandra and I hope that from our visit I can better understand them." Finally, help family members clarify important points by asking questions and rephrasing statements.

Completing the Interview

Remember that family members have many obligations and that they have probably made special arrangements to be present. Generally, interviews should not exceed an hour in length. Conclude the interview by summarizing the discussion and by thanking each of the family members present.

▶ Make arrangements to interview a parent. In thinking about your conversation, did the parent identify family needs and priorities for the child? Did the parent mention resources important to the functioning of the family? Which interview questions were most helpful? What questions might you include in another interview?

Family Stories

Sharing a family story can be the easiest and the least intimidating assessment technique for family members. Family stories represent events and people that are important to the family. Family stories often include valuable information regarding how others in the household relate to the child with special needs. By listening to family stories, you learn about the family's cultural values and practices, attitudes, habits, and behaviors. Family stories provide a good idea of how families see themselves and how they want others to see them.

In preparing to conduct a family story, the following guidelines have been developed based on work by Robert Atkinson (1992).

1. Choose an appropriate setting: The setting should be quiet and comfortable.
2. Explain the purpose of the family story: Family members should understand that the information to be shared is valuable and will help you in understanding the child and in developing the education program. Photographs, drawings, and other materials are helpful in assisting the storyteller.
3. Use open-ended interview techniques. Questions that encourage extended responses will assist the storyteller. Encourage family members to remember stories and events. Try to focus your questions around certain areas:
   a. The child
      1. How would you describe your child's growth and development?
      2. What do you think your child inherited from you?
      3. Who are the important family members or people in the community?
   b. Family traditions
      1. What beliefs or ideals do you want to pass on to your child?
      2. What holidays or celebrations are important to your family?
   c. Social factors
      1. How does your family like to spend free time together?
      2. What does your child like to do during these times?
   d. Education
      1. What do you hope your child will learn in school?
      2. How would you like me to contact you . . . by telephone . . . by mail . . . by email?
4. Be a good listener: Build trust and show that you care about what is being shared. At times you will want to ask follow-up questions, probe for details, and be responsive.
5. Look for connections: Family stories frequently provide useful information about the child's early years and present skills and competencies. Family stories are especially helpful in learning about family diversity in your classroom. Storytellers may become classroom resources to assist you in planning special events or celebrations.

The Snapshot of La Donna Harris illustrates the importance of "family" to the Comanche people as told by this family story. After reading this snapshot, consider the following questions: What are some important themes in this family story? How might these themes affect the assessment process?

Planning Parent Conferences

Parent-teacher conferences can be effective ways to share information with parents and to learn more about the student from the parent's perspective. In addition to sharing and receiving information, parents and professionals can develop a rapport and a better ability to cooperate in preventing and solving problems (Turnbull & Turnbull, 1997). However, the key to successful conferences is planning. During parent–teacher conferences, the teacher typically has a limited amount of time scheduled for meetings. Parents, too, often have made several special arrangements to come to the school at the scheduled conference time.

▶ **CEC Common Core Knowledge and Skills.** The beginning special educator will know the types and importance of information concerning individuals with disabilities available from families and public agencies (GC8K3).

▶ **CEC Common Core Knowledge and Skills.** The beginning special educator will report assessment results to all stakeholders using effective communication skills (CC8S7).

SNAPSHOT

La Donna Harris, a Comanche Woman

(This snapshot includes excerpts from her speech, given a few years ago at the first Comanche training session [Harris, n. d.].)

I am the daughter of Lily Tabbytite, the granddaughter of Wakeah, and the great-granddaughter of Kotsepeah, who was the daughter of Maria, a Spanish captive. My grandfather was Tabbytite, son of Hohwah and Tsa-ee.

I do this so that you will know how we are related; if not by blood, then by extended family, the "Indian Way." It not only shows our relationship, but it shows me how I should behave toward you. Tribal governments and tribal societies were built on relationships and kinships; how you were related showed you the etiquette of how you should behave to one another. In a tribal society, one would never openly criticize a relative. There were other ways of doing it. There were only certain people that could do the criticism or the correcting—not necessarily criticism—but they could show you the way to behave properly. When we try to make tribal societies work like Western societies, sometimes it doesn't fit and creates a lot of stress in our community.

The first time that I went to tribal council, I remember Edgar Monetachi. Because he was such an eloquent speaker, people would ask him to speak for them, even if they disagreed with his position. He had a responsibility to those relatives and talked for them because he had the power and medicine to be able to be a good speaker.

It was always amazing to me when kaku and papa would go downtown to Walters and we would run into an old Comanche lady. The old lady would call me sister or daughter and they would chat for a while. Afterward, I'd say, "I didn't know that we were related to her" and kaku would trace it back to some wonderful thing that happened between families that made us kin—not between her and that other old lady, but between families. Those relationships made me feel strong and gave me a feeling of belonging to everybody. . . .

Planning the Conference

Planning the conference consists of notifying the parent(s) and preparing the conference agenda. Notify the parents of the date and purpose of the conference. Many schools routinely schedule conference days at the beginning of the year and send written notices. If the meeting is to be an IEP conference, a written notice must be sent prior to the meeting.

Families generally appreciate a follow-up telephone call. However, be sure to ask the parent whether you have called at a convenient time. If not, ask when a better time would be for you to call back. The telephone conversation allows the parent to ask questions about the conference and to decide on which family members should attend. Families may want to decide whether the student with a disability should be present at the conference.

Planning the conference also includes identifying the agenda items. Notify other professionals who are working with the student and who may not be aware of the scheduled conference. For example, the speech therapist, occupational therapist, or physical therapist may want to be present.

Review the student's folder and gather samples of the student's work. Plan a tentative agenda of areas or items to be covered. Consider where you will be meeting. Several chairs placed at a small round table look inviting and less threatening than chairs placed around your desk.

Conference Time

To establish rapport, talk informally with parents and other family members before beginning the conference. Express your gratitude to family members for making arrangements to attend the conference. Have an interpreter or translator present for family members, if needed.

Begin with the student's accomplishments. Provide examples of student work or share classroom anecdotes. Discuss areas of growth and areas of concern. Encourage parents to ask questions or to make comments. Ask for clarification when you are unsure of the information that family members have shared. Use good communication skills, including jargon-free language. Remember, body posture and head nods, as well as the words you speak, are important ways of showing your interest in what family members have to say.

At the close of the conference, summarize the important points. End the meeting on a positive note and thank family members again for coming.

Completing Postconference Activities

After the conference is over, there are two activities that need attention. First, teachers should record a brief summary of the conference as soon as possible after the meeting. These notes should include the date, the participants, highlights of the meeting, and any decisions made. These notes are particularly important if there is a due process hearing at some future time. If the conference were an IEP or IFSP meeting, teachers must mail a copy of the minutes of the meeting to the parents.

Next, regardless of whether the student attended the conference, set aside time to talk about the meeting with the student. Briefly summarize the meeting and any decisions that were made. Answer any questions the student may have about the conference.

Summary

- Parents have an important role in the assessment process.
- Family priorities will probably change over time. Always check to see if family members feel that the information they have provided in the past is current.
- Involve families to the extent that they wish to be involved in the assessment process and accept the wishes of family members as to their levels of participation. Individual family members can differ in their preferences: One member will be more comfortable in just talking;

- another family member will prefer to provide information by completing a questionnaire or a rating scale.
- Be open to issues in working with families different from your own. Family diversity can include issues of culture, disability, economic status, gender, geographic region or origin, and race. Avoid stereotypical assumptions.
- Work to become familiar with families in your community. When in doubt, ask families to determine preferences and needs.

REFERENCES

Achenbach, T. M. (2001). *Child behavior checklist for ages 6–18.* Burlington, VT: ASEBA.

Alper, S. K., Schloss, P. J., & Schloss, C. N. (1994). *Families of students with disabilities.* Boston: Allyn and Bacon.

Atkinson, R. (1992). *The life story book from autobiography to personal myth.* Gorham, ME: University of Southern Maine, Center for the Study of Lives.

Bricker, D., & Squires, J. (1999). *Ages & stages questionnaires: A parent-completed child monitoring system* (2nd ed., p. 5). Baltimore, MD: Paul H. Brookes.

Cohen, L. G., & Spenciner, L. J. (1994). *Assessment of young children.* White Plains, NY: Longman.

Dunst, C., Trivette, C., & Deal, A. (1988). *Enabling and empowering families.* Cambridge, MA: Brookline.

Haney, M., & Knox, V. (1995). *Project unidos para el bienestar de los ninos y de su famila* (Project UBNF). Paper presented at the Zero to Three Conference, December, Atlanta, Georgia.

Hanson, M. J., Lynch, E., & Wayman, K. I. (1990). Honoring the cultural diversity of families when gathering data. *Topics in Early Childhood Special Education 10*(1): 112–131.

Harris, L. (n.d.). Summarized version of the speech given by La Donna Harris at the first Comanche training session. Unpublished manuscript.

Shapiro, J. (1994). Educational/support group for Latino families of children with Down syndrome. *Mental Retardation, 32*(6): 403–415.

Spann, S. J., Kohler, F. W., & Soenken, D. (2003). Examining parents' involvement in and perceptions of special education services: An interview with families in a parent support group. *Focus on Autism and Other Developmental Disabilities, 18*(4), 1088–3576.

Turnbull, A. P., & Turnbull, III, H. R. (1997). *Families, professionals, and exceptionality: A special partnership* (3rd ed.). Columbus, OH: Merrill.

Waltman, G. H. (1996). Amish health care beliefs and practices. In M. C. Julia (Ed.), *Multicultural awareness in the health care professions.* Boston: Allyn and Bacon.

Assessment of Young Children

Chapter Objectives

After completing this chapter,
you should be able to:

- Explain the considerations involved in assessing young children.
- Identify and describe how to select appropriate screening and developmental assessment approaches.
- Discuss transition assessment of young children.
- Discuss universal pre-K initiatives and school readiness.

Key Terms

Developmental domains
Young children

False negative

False positive

Overview

Gathering information about the development of young children before they are enrolled in school is very different from the assessment of school-age children. Working with young children and their families can involve locating a mother and her preschool child in a homeless shelter, receiving a referral form from a community clinic, or working with a family recently arrived from another country where services for young children and families are not available. Assessment questions focus on the young child's general development in one or more areas. These areas, or **developmental domains**, concern physical, cognitive, communication, social-emotional, and adaptive development. The focus on development differs in significant ways from the focus on academic and achievement difficulties of school-age children and youth we have been discussing.

Teachers and administrators in public school programs usually define young children as students in grades kindergarten through 3; early childhood educators use the term to identify children between the ages of birth through 5 years or birth through

8 years. Thus, the definition of the term "young children" may imply different age ranges, depending on the professional's frame of reference. Two national organizations of professionals, the Division of Early Childhood (DEC) of the Council for Exceptional Children (CEC) and the National Association for the Education of Young Children (NAEYC), define **young children** as children ages birth through age 8. We will use this latter definition in our discussion of young children.

Professionals feel that development, which is influenced by the child's interests, abilities, and opportunities in the natural environment, proceeds at individual variations during the early years. For example, 4-year-old Arron is interested in dinosaurs and can identify which are carnivores and which are herbivores. Will, who is also 4 years old, spends much of his time playing with his dump trucks. He speaks in two- to three-word phrases. The variations between Arron and Will may be due to genetic or biological factors such as the child's temperament or to prenatal factors such as consumption of alcohol or use of tobacco during pregnancy. Moreover, social expectations and ways of caring for Arron and Will or opportunity or its absence can influence their development. Most probably, according to many developmental theorists, two or more factors interact.

Today, tests can provide screening early in life for young children with special needs who can benefit from special services. Medical professionals identify many newborns with or at risk for a disability before leaving the hospital; visiting nurses and early intervention specialists screen infants in their homes; and early childhood special educators work with toddlers and preschoolers in their homes, child care centers, or early education programs. Professionals working with young children and their families represent a variety of disciplines, including audiology, family counseling, medicine, occupational therapy, physical therapy, psychology, social work, speech and language pathology, as well as education.

▶ Research the position statements of two or more professional organizations such as Division of Early Childhood (DEC), a subdivision of the Council for Exceptional Children (CEC) or the National Association for the Education of Young Children (NAEYC). What are their positions regarding the assessment of young children? How do these positions compare? Develop your own position statement.

Screening

Screening is a process that identifies children who may have a disability and who need a comprehensive assessment. Some of the common questions raised by parents, caregivers, and early childhood teachers include: Is my child developing typically? Does the child have any problems that I need to know about?

Screening typically involves testing large numbers of young children, usually in a short amount of time. Screening does not identify children for services but rather pinpoints children who need further assessment. Using a comprehensive assessment, evaluators may identify some children as needing early intervention or special education and related services.

In many cases, families are unaware of early childhood screenings and need to learn about the benefits of early intervention and purposes of screening. These awareness activities are known as Child Find. Through Child Find, parents and caregivers become aware of screening activities, the first step in the process of identifying young children who fit the eligibility criteria for special services.

The community can sponsor screenings through the public school, through the state early intervention agency, or through community agencies. Customarily, a screening has several components, such as a physical examination by a doctor or nurse, a developmental history obtained by interviewing the parent, vision and hearing tests, and an assessment of the child's general development, including the physical, cognitive, communication, social-emotional, and adaptive domains. Professionals typically use a screening instrument to assist in making decisions regarding the screening outcome. Figure 18.1 illustrates the setup of a typical community screening program. You can read about one family's experience at a community screening in the Snapshot about Luiz and his mother on page 376.

▶ **CEC Common Core Knowledge and Skills.** The beginning special educator will understand procedures for early identification of young children who may be at risk for disabilities (GC8K4).

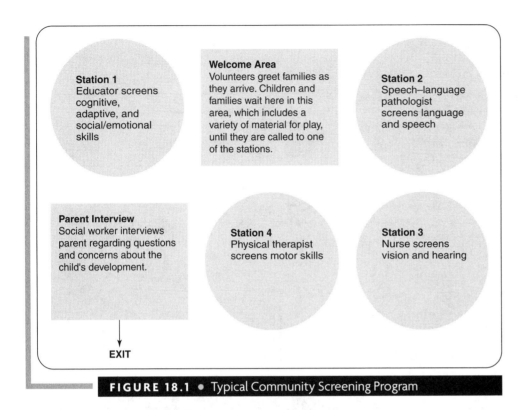

FIGURE 18.1 • Typical Community Screening Program

Choosing Appropriate Screening Instruments

According to Meisels and Wasik (1990) developmental screening tests "should be brief, norm-referenced, inexpensive, standardized in administration, objectively scored, broadly focused across all areas of development, reliable, and valid" (p. 613). Generally, the purpose of screening tests is to evaluate large numbers of children to determine if further assessment is necessary; accordingly, they paint a broad picture and provide general information. Too narrow a focus can result in missing important aspects about the child. Communities can then devote valuable time and money to conducting comprehensive assessments on those children who need further help.

Screening calls for norm-referenced tests, which compare a child's performance with the performance of other children who have taken the test. The norm sample must include children who have similar backgrounds and characteristics to the target child or children. For example, if the children under evaluation come from an inner-city area, then the screening instrument must have included children from urban areas for the norming sample.

Many different professionals and paraprofessionals administer and score screening tests. The administration of screening tests is standardized, as is their scoring. This means that the directions, calculation of scores, and determination of outcomes must contain clear explanations and must be the same for

TESTS-at-a-GLANCE

Developmental Indicators for the Assessment of Learning–Third Edition (DIAL–3)

- **Publication Date:** 1998
- **Purposes:** Screening test that addresses the following areas: Motor, Language, and Concepts. Parent questionnaire provides information about self-help and social skills.
- **Ages/Grade Levels:** Ages 3 years through 6 years, 11 months.
- **Time to Administer:** 30 minutes.
- **Technical Adequacy:** Reliability and validity are adequate.
- **Suggested Use:** For use as part of an overall screening procedure. The Spanish edition was normed on a sample of 605 Spanish-speaking children. The *DIAL–3* Spanish edition is not a direct translation but, rather, test developers made efforts to adjust and validate the test for use in a different linguistic or cultural context.

SNAPSHOT

Luiz and His Mother Visit the Community Screening Clinic

Recently Luiz's mother, Maria Hermetz, heard about a community screening clinic from a friend at the local convenience store. The clinic is held on the first Tuesday of each month at the community center and is free for all children in the community. Health and education professionals are available to answer questions about children's development.

Although Ms. Hermetz does not have any specific questions about 4-year-old Luiz, she decided that she would like to know if he is doing "what he should be doing" at this age. The following month she brought Luiz to the screening.

When Ms. Hermetz arrived at the community center, she observed that the large room had been separated into various areas (Figure 18.1 on p. 375).

The central area had a variety of toys and books for the children and chairs for the parents. "¡Buenos días!" Ms. Hermetz was greeted by one of the clinic volunteers and asked to complete a brief form with questions regarding her son's development. Ms. Hermetz was relieved to learn that she could choose either an English or Spanish version of the form. Although she speaks English, she prefers to use her native Spanish. An early childhood special education teacher invited Luiz to join two other children who were playing with blocks nearby.

As part of the screening process, the teacher will complete observations of the children as they play alone or together with other children in the waiting area. Earlier, during the planning of the screening program, the screening team identified the questions and the method that the teacher will use for recording the observation data, as Chapter 5 discusses. Observing children, the teacher watched and noted important information in order to answer the following questions: How does the child approach the toys and other children? How does the child interact with the materials? How does the child communicate with adults? With other children?

An early childhood special educator gave Luiz a colorful name tag (Figure 18.2) and invited him to come with her to one of the four screening stations. This teacher, along with other members of the screening team, was using *Developmental Indicators for the Assessment of Learning–Third Edition (DIAL–3)* (Mardell-Czudnowski & Goldenberg, 1998). They presented Luiz with a number of activities in the areas of motor skills, conceptual abilities, and language skills.

FIGURE 18.2 • Name Tag

Luiz liked pointing to various pictures in the examiner's book. After completing this station, Luiz moved to the next station to work with the speech and language pathologist. Later, he worked with the physical therapist at the motor development station. At the last station, a volunteer checked his hearing and vision. At each station he received another colored sticker on his name tag. This procedure allowed the examiners to quickly determine which stations the child had completed.

After the screening, the nurse met with Ms. Hermetz to talk about the results of the screening and to answer any questions. Depending on the family's needs, the nurse may discuss various community resources. Today, she and Ms. Hermetz chatted about Luiz's development. About a week later, Ms. Hermetz received a letter in the mail that stated that the screening results had been completed and that no further assessment was indicated.

> ► Make arrangements to visit a kindergarten or community screening program. What are the components of the screening program?

> ► Conduct a comprehensive review of several screening instruments. Compare their administration, standardization, and scoring procedures. What do the manuals state about reliability and validity?

all children who come for screening. The outcomes of screening should not be subject to the judgment and biases of the many individual test examiners who administer and score the tests.

Planning the Screening Procedure

In planning the screening procedure, the screening team must address several key areas.

Environment

The screening should always take place in a setting that is quiet and free from distractions. The child should be in the company of a familiar caregiver during the assessment. It is important never to challenge young children during assessment activities by separating them from their parent or caregiver (Greenspan & Meisels, 1993, p. 14).

Rapport

Each examiner must allow time for the child to become familiar with the situation. Many children take time to "warm up" to strangers. If the child does not feel comfortable, the responses the child gives may not reflect the child's ability.

Physical Status

As routine practice, an examiner observes the child's current health status. Young children frequently have colds, leading to middle ear infections (a result of which is a temporary decrease in hearing). Can the child hear the directions? Does the child appear to be tired? If so, consider screening at another time. Don't forget that young children have a limited attention span. A child's attention will wander or be lost if the screening test has too many test items.

Development

Although educators define separate areas of development (physical, cognitive, communication, social-emotional, and adaptive), these areas are not independent, but interact in complex ways. Screening procedures must be comprehensive in coverage and not focus on one or two developmental areas.

Parent Concerns

Some parents are very anxious about their children's screening tests. "When will my child start talking?" or "Will this person find something wrong with my child?" parents may ask—or may not ask, although it is a matter of primary concern. Be sure that parents fully understand the reason for screening their children. An important component of any screening procedure is a period for answering parents' questions, either before or after the testing.

Limitations of Screening

The screening process has several significant limitations. Members of assessment teams must be knowledgeable about these limits because screening results determine whether the child receives a referral for a comprehensive assessment.

A screening instrument's results, like some other assessment approaches, show a snapshot of a child's development at one point in time. There are many variables that can affect screening results. These include the child's physical, emotional, or motivational states; the examiner's familiarity with the screening tools; the examiner's understanding of child development and ability to establish rapport; the examiner's familiarity with children who are linguistically and culturally diverse; and the screening environment.

Since the results of screening present only a brief picture, best practices in screening suggest that a child receive periodic screening tests. The advantages of giving the child the same standardized instrument for each screening are the ease and usefulness of comparing the child's development on subsequent administrations. However, the cumulative effect of repeating items on periodic screenings and the tendency of some caregivers to "practice" the items with the child reduces the instrument's effectiveness.

Screening Tasks

Most standardized screening instruments include toys and ask the child to use or to play with the toys in specific ways. For example, a common test item on several screening instruments requires the examiner to tell the child to build a tower with a small pile of 1-inch cubes. Using toys in very specific ways is a new experience for many young children. Most early education programs encourage children to choose a toy, to explore its properties, and to use it in a way that they choose. Thus, when given several small cubes, a child may decide to make a train rather than a tower. To pass this item on a screening test, the child must make a tower; however, a young child may have no motivation or interest to comply with the examiner's request because the child has a more interesting idea (the train or a road).

False Negatives

A child who, in fact, does have a disability may pass through the screening without being identified for further assessment. The causes of **false negative** results are a lack of sensitivity of the screening instrument, a lack of training or limited clinical knowledge of the examiner(s), or other factors.

False Positives

A child who does not have a disability may be identified for further assessment. These **false positive** results increase parental anxiety and place an extra burden on the family until a comprehensive assessment is completed. The causes of false positives are a lack of specificity of the screening instrument, a lack of training or lack of clinical knowledge of the examiner(s), or other factors.

▶ **CEC Common Core Knowledge and Skills.** The beginning special educator will understand the use and limitations of assessment instruments (CC8K4).

Special Challenges

Family situations, too, can present special challenges to the screening process. Families who are homeless or who have illegal immigrant status may be difficult to locate. You can read more about these special challenges in the Snapshot entitled "Special Challenges."

SNAPSHOT
Special Challenges

Some families face special challenges that impact on Child Find activities and the screening and referral processes. We meet several families in the following snapshots:

- Fourteen-year-old Cheryl and her baby, Samantha, live on the streets of a large urban city. They occasionally sleep at a downtown shelter or in one of the vacant buildings on the waterfront.
- Sandy and her husband Brad commute long distances daily to their respective jobs. Baby James goes to his grandmother's home while his parents are at work. With their busy work schedules, Sandy and Brad don't have time to learn about James's development.
- Mindy and her 3-year-old son are immigrants living with her cousin in a small apartment house. Mindy worries

that city officials will relocate her and return her and her child to their native country.
- Andreas graduated from college a few years ago and finds himself torn between the responsibilities of his job and his toddler. He often resents the demands that his child makes.
- Rita and Alexander and their three preschoolers live in a trailer at the end of a dirt road several miles from town. They have exhausted their meager savings since the mill closed and both parents lost their jobs. This rural family cannot readily access community resources and services.

▶ Choose one family from this Snapshot and discuss how its situation will affect the assessment process.

How It Works! Addressing Concerns about Bennie

Bennie Laurent is a shy, 3-year-old child who has frequent colds, earaches, and fevers. When he isn't sick, he likes to ride on the family tractor. At the urging of Grandmother, Bennie's father brought him to a well-baby and screening clinic in their rural community. Grandmother was concerned about Bennie's health and his slow development. Just recently he had begun to talk in complete sentences.

As part of the screening process, Bennie took the *Battelle Developmental Inventory (BDI-2) Screening* (Newborg, 2004), as did each child who came to the screening clinic. Based on observations conducted during the screening, the parent's report, and the *BDI-2* scores, Bennie was referred to the Developmental Evaluation Clinic for a comprehensive assessment.

At the Developmental Evaluation Clinic, the assessment team included a physician, a physical therapist, a speech and language pathologist, a psychologist, a special educator, and a social worker. Bennie's appointment lasted all morning and part of the afternoon. During this time, each member of the team observed or assessed Bennie and spoke with his dad.

For Bennie and his family, the developmental assessment will be helpful In answering questions about his development: Is there a developmental delay? Does he qualify for special services? What skills are developing? What are the child's needs?

Comprehensive Developmental Assessment

As a result of screening procedures, a young child may be referred to a multidisciplinary assessment team. The team addresses concerns about the child's development, and individual team members participate in planning and conducting a comprehensive assessment. Most states require that standardized instruments be part of the developmental assessment to determine eligibility for early intervention or special education and related services. Team members include the child's parents and professionals representing various disciplines, encompassing education, medicine, occupational therapy or physical therapy, psychology, speech and language pathology, and social work.

Team members must complete the assessment of each child (including the needs identified by the family) within 45 calendar days from the time the child is referred to them. The law also provides that the team, with the consent of the parents, can begin early intervention services before completion of the assessment if the team writes an interim Individualized Family Service Plan (IFSP). The IFSP includes information about the child's level of functioning, the goals or outcomes for the child, and the services they will receive. The services described in the plan can include some for the family as well as for the child. Figure 18.3 lists the required components of the IFSP related to assessment.

Early childhood special educators play a major role on the multidisciplinary team. They often conduct observations of the child in an early education setting, or they complete a developmental assessment on the child. Typically, developmental assessments cover a variety of developmental areas, including physical (gross and fine motor), cognitive, communication, social or emotional, and adaptive development.

▶ A young child received a referral for a comprehensive assessment as a result of the screening test. After examining the results of the comprehensive assessment, team members decided that the child was developing typically and there was no indication of delay. Explain several possible reasons why the child was referred as a result of the screening test.

TESTS-at-a-GLANCE

Battelle Developmental Inventory 2nd Edition (BDI-2)

- **Publication Date:** 2004
- **Purpose:** Screening and assessment for determining eligibility.
- **Age/Grade Levels:** Birth to 7 years 11 months.
- **Time to Administer:** The Screening Test takes 10 to 30 minutes; the complete *BDI-2* takes 1 to 2 hours.
- **Technical Adequacy:** Normative sample closely matches the 2000 U.S. census. Reliability and validity are adequate.
- **Suggested Use:** This instrument can be used during the screening and assessment process. The *BDI-2 Spanish* is an adaptation/translation of the *BDI-2* English materials. Additional materials include scoring software and software for Palm PDAs to collect data.

(1) A statement of the infant's or toddler's present levels of physical development, cognitive development, communication development, social or emotional development, and adaptive development, based on objective criteria.

(2) A statement of the family's resources, priorities, and concerns relating to enhancing the development of the family's infant or toddler with a disability.

(3) A statement of the measurable results or outcomes expected to be achieved for the infant or toddler and the family, including preliteracy and language skills, as developmentally appropriate for the child, and the criteria, procedures, and timelines used to determine the degree to which progress toward achieving the results or outcomes is being made and whether modifications or revisions of the results or outcomes or services are necessary.

(4) A statement of specific early intervention services based on peer-reviewed research, to the extent practicable, necessary to meet the unique needs of the infant or toddler and the family, including the frequency, intensity, and method of delivering services.

(5) A statement of the natural environments in which early intervention services will appropriately be provided, including a justification of the extent, if any, to which the services will not be provided in a natural environment.

(6) The projected dates for initiation of services and the anticipated length, duration, and frequency of the services.

(7) The identification of the service coordinator from the profession most immediately relevant to the infant's or toddler's or family's needs (or who is otherwise qualified to carry out all applicable responsibilities under this part) who will be responsible for the implementation of the plan and coordination with other agencies and persons, including transition services.

(8) The steps to be taken to support the transition of the toddler with a disability to preschool or other appropriate services.

FIGURE 18.3 ● Assessment Information Required in the IFSP

Source: 20 USC Sec. 636 (d).

Developmental Assessment and Theories of Child Development

Many of the instruments that assess development derive from various theories of child growth and development.

Piaget

Jean Piaget developed a theory of cognitive development that emphasizes the interaction of early motor abilities with developing cognitive abilities. During cognitive development, according to Piaget, a child passes through specific developmental stages; however, one child may pass through a stage at a different time than another. Assessment instruments and practices that are built on Piagetian theory include test items that address these cognitive stages: sensorimotor intelligence, preoperational thought, concrete operations, and formal operations. Preoperational thought typically develops between the ages of 2 years and 7 years and is the stage when the child becomes capable of symbolic representations.

WHAT IS THE INFLUENCE ON ASSESSMENT PRACTICES? An examiner who comes from a Piagetian perspective may choose to gather information about the child's development by observing the child at play. Let's sit in on the observation of two children, both of whom have been referred for a developmental assessment. Jamie, who is 3 years old, walks over to the table, picks up the crayons, and randomly drops them to the floor. Occasionally, he puts one in his mouth. Sarah, who is also 3 years old, sits down at the table, picks up a crayon, and deliberating begins to draw lines and circles, selecting different colors to complete her picture. She explains to the observer that she is drawing a picture "with pretty flowers."

Functional Approach

In contrast, the functional (behavioral) approach emphasizes the importance of factors external to the child in skill development. The functional approach emphasizes the skills a child will need to live and play in their natural environment. Many of the instruments are criterion-referenced.

WHAT IS THE INFLUENCE ON ASSESSMENT PRACTICES?

Let's join another examiner who is conducting an assessment of the two 3-year-old children whom we met earlier, Jamie and Sarah. The examiner is using a criterion-referenced instrument, *The Carolina Curriculum for Preschoolers with Special Needs* (Johnson-Martin, Attermeier, & Hacker, 2004). According to this instrument, at 3 years of age, children should be able to copy a circle. How will this examiner's orientation to gathering information differ in the use of the crayons with Jamie and Sarah?

Biological Approach

A third approach to developmental assessment focuses on the physical state of the child and originates within the fields of neurology and pediatrics. The biological approach emphasizes the importance of the reciprocity between the child's temperament and behavior and the caregiver's response. There appears to be some evidence that assessment within this framework can be used across cultures with infants (Barr, 1989).

Choosing Appropriate Developmental Assessment Instruments

One of the purposes of a developmental assessment is to answer questions about the child's development using the referral and screening information. The developmental assessment results may indicate that the child's development is significantly behind and that the child has a developmental delay. Perhaps you'll remember from Chapter 1 that the term *developmental delay* is a term that describes eligibility for services. Additionally, the developmental assessment is helpful in answering questions about program planning. For children who are already receiving services, a developmental assessment provides a method of monitoring progress. Good practice dictates that assessment teams combine developmental assessment instruments with observations of the child and a parent report. The Snapshot about the Hodgkin family on page 383 describes how all this information helps the team in monitoring Danny's progress.

A number of commonly used instruments, both norm-referenced and criterion-referenced, are for use with a broad age range of young children, ages birth through 2 years

---

TESTS-at-a-GLANCE

The Carolina Curriculum for Preschoolers with Special Needs, second edition

- **Publication Date:** 2004

- **Purposes:** A criterion-referenced test that includes the following development areas: cognitive, communication, gross motor, fine motor, and personal-social.

- **Age/Grade Levels:** 2 through 5 years.

- **Time to Administer:** Varies since only areas of interest need to be assessed.

- **Technical Adequacy:** Criterion-referenced instrument; reliability and validity are adequate.

- **Suggested Use:** Assesses a wide area of development in young children and provides suggestions for intervention activities.

▶ Research procedures at your state department of education regarding its eligibility system for young children. How does the system determine eligibility? What criteria does it use?

TESTS-at-a-GLANCE

Bayley Scales of Infant and Toddler Development, Third Edition (Bayley III)

- **Publication Date:** 2005

- **Purposes:** This comprehensive assessment is designed to identify delays or disabilities in the five developmental domains.

- **Ages/Grade Levels:** 1 to 42 months.

- **Time to Administer:** 30 minutes to 1 hour (depending upon age of child).

- **Technical Adequacy:** Normative sample closely matches the 2000 U.S. census. Reliability and validity are adequate.

- **Suggested Use:** A useful assessment for infants and toddlers to assist in determining eligibility for early intervention services. Additional PDA scoring software available.

TESTS-at-a-GLANCE

Assessment, Evaluation, and Programming System (AEPS®) for Infants and Children, Second Edition

- **Publication Date:** 2002

- **Purposes:** Criterion-referenced instrument for program planning, monitoring, and evaluating a child's progress. The AEPS® addresses the following areas: fine motor, gross motor, adaptive, cognitive, social-communication, and social.

- **Ages/Grade Levels:** Birth to 3 years (volumes 1–2); ages 3 years through 6 years (volumes 3–4).

- **Time to Administer:** Variable, depending on the number of areas assessed.

- **Technical Adequacy:** Criterion-referenced instrument; reliability and validity are adequate.

- **Suggested Use:** Useful to assist in planning and monitoring child's development across the five developmental domains addressed by IDEA. Volumes 2 and 4 provide excellent curriculum ideas for enhancing the child's development. The AEPS® comes with a Parent Report, which allows parents to observe and record their child's progress, too.

▶ Review two or three developmental assessment instruments. Compare the test items for a particular age group. What are the similarities? How are the items different? If you are assessing for the purpose of planning the child's program, which test items would provide the most helpful information?

and older. For example, the *Bayley Scales of Infant and Toddler Development, Third Edition* (*Bayley III*; Bayley, 2005) is a norm-referenced instrument that assesses the five developmental domains. The parent/caregiver participates in aspects of the administration. Another norm-referenced assessment, the *Battelle Developmental Inventory* (*BDI-2*; Newborg, 2004), is designed to be used with children ages birth to 7 years 11 months (see TESTS-at-a-Glance box on page 378). This instrument may be used by a team of professionals or by an individual examiner. The *Assessment, Evaluation, and Programming System* (*AEPS®*) *for Infants and Children, Second Edition* (Bricker, 2002) provides both examiner and parent forms to gather information and to monitor a child's progress. Criterion-referenced assessments, such as the *AEPS®* and the *The Carolina Curriculum for Preschoolers with Special Needs, second edition* provide additional materials for program planning.

Concerns Regarding the Assessment of Young Children

Practitioners should be aware of a number of concerns regarding developmental assessment. First, instruments that focus on assessment of infants, toddlers, and preschoolers typically include the following developmental domains: cognitive, expressive and receptive language, fine and gross motor, and adaptive. Notice that these are not exactly the same as the domains included under the term *developmental delay*. In Chapter 1 we discussed that developmental delay refers to a delay in one or more of the following areas: physical development including fine and gross motor, cognitive, communication, social or emotional, or adaptive development. Many commonly used instruments do not include the social-emotional domain. Yet this area is perhaps one of the most critical in increasing opportunities for young children of differing abilities to play and work together.

Another concern is the fact that criterion-referenced tests group items by the age at which children who are developing typically acquire that skill. However, development may not occur this way, particularly for children with special needs. For example, children who are blind can lag behind their peers in gross-motor development. In addition, acquisition of certain other skills for these children may not follow the same sequence as for children with normal vision. In planning and monitoring children's progress, team members will want to supplement criterion-referenced assessment information with observations, videos and audiotapes, and other assessment approaches.

SNAPSHOT

The Hodgkin Family

The Hodgkin family consists of Danny, age 4, Joe, age 7, and their parents. Shortly after birth, Danny was identified as having Trisomy 21 (Down syndrome). Danny and his family have been involved in early intervention services since he was a baby. For the past two years, an early intervention specialist has conducted weekly home visits, helping Danny in his development. Recently, his parents have become increasingly concerned with Danny's lack of progress in talking. An evaluation completed by a speech and language pathologist includes a suggestion that the family begin to explore teaching Danny sign language. Both of Danny's parents hope that he will be able to go to a neighborhood preschool in the fall. Figure 18.4 illustrates a portion of Danny's IFSP, which provides an opportunity for parents to indicate the areas that are important to them.

Based on family concerns, priorities, and resources as they relate to Danny's development, the team will identify one or more outcome statements that describe what they would like to work on in the next six months. The outcome statements will guide the choice of services Danny will receive. In Danny's IFSP, the outcome statements reflect both child and family outcomes:

Major Outcomes: Child
Danny will learn to communicate in order to make his needs known.

Major Outcomes: Family
Mr. and Mrs. Hodgkin will receive information about parent groups in the community in order to meet other parents and receive peer parent support regarding issues of mutual interest including learning more about using sign language.

Individualized Family Service Plan: Family Considerations

Child's name: Danny Hodgkin   Person providing information: Mrs. Hodgkin

1. Please describe your child (likes, dislikes, and strengths)

   Danny is a happy, outgoing child. He has not been sick over the last 6 months. He seems to understand a lot that is said to him.

2. What are your concerns or how would you describe your child's needs?

   We are worried about his lack of talking—and his slow progress in speech therapy.

3. What do you believe the strengths of your family are in meeting the child's needs?

   My husband spends time playing with Danny and takes him shopping.

4. What would be helpful for your child and family?

   To understand how to help Danny more. We want to understand what he wants and what he is trying to tell us.

5. Which of the following are concerns or areas about which you would like more information?

   About the child
   ____ feeding
   _X_ communicating
   _X_ learning
   ____ vision or hearing
   ____ problem behaviors
   ____ equipment or supplies

   About the family
   _X_ meeting other families whose child has similar needs
   _X_ finding out more about different services
   ____ child care
   _X_ transportation
   ____ information about my child's disability
   ____ information about SSI or Medicaid

6. Are there other concerns that you would like to discuss at the IFSP meeting?

   We would like to meet families who use sign language with their children.

FIGURE 18.4 ● From Danny's IFSP

Teachers and therapists must guard against planning the child's program by looking solely at test performance. It is inappropriate for a planning team to identify items that the child fails as discrete items that the child needs to learn. For example, from the test item "Child stacks 3 blocks," an inappropriate objective would be, "Randy will stack 3 blocks." A more appropriate programming activity would provide the child opportunities to manipulate a variety of materials in different ways, one of which might involve stacking.

In discussing appropriate practices for primary grades serving 6- through 8-year-olds, Bredekamp and Copple (1997), writing for the National Association for the Education of Young Children (NAEYC), describe best practices in assessing children's learning, in connecting assessment with instruction, and in avoiding grade retention.

> Because they advance through sequential curriculum at different paces, children can progress in all areas as they acquire competence. Children who fall behind receive individualized support, such as tutoring, personal instruction, focused time on areas of difficulty, and other strategies to accelerate learning progress. Efforts are made to avoid grade retention of children who fail to make expected progress, because retention generally does not improve achievement and harmfully alters children's attitude toward school. (p. 176)

Linking Assessment with Early Childhood Activities

To monitor children's progress, many early childhood educators prefer to use portfolios, exhibits, performances and other performance-based assessments such as those Chapter 7 discusses. Unlike more traditional assessments, these approaches encourage assessment results to be public and visible. Reggio Emilia, originally developed in Italy, is an approach to curriculum planning, implementing, and assessing children's progress that places emphasis on public assessments. Using this approach, teachers set up documentation panels to record children's experiences and progress. Teachers display materials on the documentation panel that include some of the many ways children express their skills and knowledge: photographs, drawings, explanatory notes, and children's comments. Because the panels display documentation prominently in the classroom, children and teachers can refer to it during the day and share the children's work and progress with parents and other classroom visitors. Sometimes teachers use documentation panels in the classroom even though they are not following a Reggio Emilia approach to curriculum. Cooney and Buchanan (2001) describe five guidelines for implementing documentation in the classroom:

1. Decide on the focus/purpose for the documentation panel. Is it to demonstrate one child's progress toward IEP goals? Is it to assess and inform the impact of the curriculum activities on the group of children? If the purpose is to show progress toward IEP goals, decide which IEP goals lend themselves to authentic assessment and how the documentation panel will supplement traditional forms of assessment.
2. When planning curriculum and intervention activities, plan how to record the child's learning process from the beginning to end. Photographing, videotaping, audiotaping, observing and recording, and artifact collecting are useful strategies.
3. During the activities, collect as much information as possible that shows the children's thinking about the concepts related to the lesson. Record children's quotations, collect children's drawings with their explanations, and record children's expression of ideas during other curriculum activities.

4. Carefully choose some of the collected data and neatly organize it on a large panel.
5. Display the panel in the classroom or hallway at the children's eye level. Share it with the children and parents as a way of revisiting the activity to remember it or connect it to future learning activities. (p. 15)

Working with Families

For some parents, learning that their child has a disability comes as a surprise, but for other parents, the finding comes as a relief. These parents may have had questions and concerns for some time regarding their child's development. Figure 18.5 presents a number of general tips for sharing assessment information with family members.

In sharing knowledge and information, respect the point where the family is at any one period of time. One strategy is to offer choices. For example, in discussing the inconclusive results of a diagnostic assessment, the practitioner might ask, "Do you want to know the range of options or just the more likely?"

Be honest. Say, "I don't know" when you don't, but also always follow up with "I'll find out" or "The field just doesn't know at this point."

Transition and Assessment

Children with special needs and their families usually become involved in transitions during three time periods: first, when the child turns 3 years old and moves from infant and toddler early intervention to preschool services; second, when the child turns 5 years old and moves from preschool to school-age services; and, third, when the young adult leaves the education system and moves to the community, to work, or to further education. Transition is often a difficult time for children and families, perhaps because of a new school program, new teachers and therapists, or new procedures. Rosenkoetter, Hains, and Fowler (1994) describe *transition* as times during which children and families begin working with a new set of professionals, start attending new programs,

---

- Provide family members with an opportunity to receive the assessment report in a one-to-one setting rather than during a large IFSP or IEP team meeting. This meeting allows the family time to ask questions with an empathetic practitioner and to reflect on the information prior to the larger, full-staff meeting.

- Share information with both parents (or major caregivers) at the same time.

- Be honest and straightforward regarding the disability.

- Be willing to say when you don't know.

- Allow time for families to express their feelings.

- Be sensitive to families if they are not ready to hear details.

- Offer to provide additional information.

- Suggest additional resources.

- Be available to the family for further discussions.

- Arrange to have a native-language interpreter available if families need assistance.

FIGURE 18.5 • Tips for Sharing Eligibility Information with Families

adjust to new schedules and customs, accept altered expectations, and meet new challenges and opportunities.

Transitions involve careful planning by the early childhood team so that the movement between programs can be successful. Assessment questions that the team addresses involve aspects of the new program and needs of the child. Let's examine some of the transition questions regarding the new program.

- What is the physical layout of the room, and what types of adaptations to the environment will the child need?
- What materials are available, and are they accessible to children?
- What are the classroom routines and expectations of children? For example: Do children have a designated place for their clothing and materials? Are the children permitted to carry materials from one center to other centers?
- What are the classroom procedures? For example: Do children clean up after themselves? Do children obtain and return materials independently? Do some centers have a limit in the number of children who can be at them at any one time?

A teacher can collect information about the new program by means of a checklist or rating scale. By identifying this information early, teachers can complete adapta-

---

Research-Based Practices   School Readiness and the Move to Universal Pre-K

Teachers and other educators working with young children often hear questions about a child's "readiness" for school. The concept that children must obtain certain skills before entering school is troublesome for many educators. In spite of what we know about child development, some schools persist in using school readiness tests to exclude children from regular class placement, testing children before they enter school.

Readiness tests are a form of high-stakes testing because they affect decisions about children's entrance into school. High-stakes testing, as we have discussed before, is the use of readiness or achievement tests to make classification, retention, or promotion decisions about children (Meisels, 1989). A child's performance on a school readiness test can determine whether the child will (1) have to wait to enter school, (2) enter school with the child's age-mates, (3) receive a coding of "at-risk" and participate in additional testing, or (4) participate in a special class before entering kindergarten. Many experts regard the latter decision as a form of retention. Thus, a child can be retained before actually entering school.

Shepard (1990) believes that the research on readiness, especially on reading readiness, is "outmoded and seriously flawed" (p. 169) and inadequate. The tests rely on outdated theories in which learning becomes fragmented into skills and subskills. The child is supposed to somehow integrate these skills at a later time. Another criticism of school readiness tests is that they lack predictive validity. That is, for the most part, there are limited data on how accurately school readiness tests predict performance in school. In addition, these tests are inadequate as technical bases for such decisions about school placements as those involving special education placements, two-year kindergarten placements, and delays in school entry (Shepard, 1990).

In contrast to the notion that "children must be ready for school" is the idea that "schools must be ready for children." The Division for Early Childhood of the Council for Exceptional Children (1992) published a position paper stating that schools should be ready to accept and effectively educate all children. Schools must not screen children into or out of early education programs; rather, all children must have an opportunity to learn. Teachers must receive training in a wide variety of developmentally appropriate curricula, materials, and procedures to maximize each child's growth and development. Schooling will succeed or fail, not children.

To this end, the field of early childhood has been examining the possibility of universal prekindergarten in the United States and the challenges to implementation. In a report commissioned by the Foundation for Child Development, Gene Maeroff (2003) writes that pre-K should be part of an education experience that begins at age 3 and follows through to age 8, a P-3 continuum. This continuum would build a firm foundation and help children retain their learning at each level. Historically, changes in education have happened slowly. What do you think of the future of a universal pre-K?

▶ **CEC Common Core Knowledge and Skills.** The beginning special educator will understand legal provisions and ethical principles regarding assessment of individuals (CC8K2).

tions to the environment and teach the child some of the routines or expose the child to new procedures before the child enters the new program.

Transition assessment also includes identifying the skills that will be helpful to the child in the new program. Transition activities provide opportunities for parents and teachers to work together, to exchange information, and to build common understandings before a child enters a new program. During transition activities, parents and early childhood teachers and caregivers have increased opportunities to facilitate skills before the child enters kindergarten.

Transition assessment should never aim at excluding children from programs. Transition assessment does not mean assessing school readiness. Rather, it means identifying the needs and supports that will make entry into the new program as successful as possible.

Summary

- Teachers and other professionals need to become familiar with the characteristics of good screening and developmental assessments. The use of observations and the careful recording of data must be integral aspects of assessing young children.

- Sensitivity to parent concerns and involvement of parents and caregivers throughout the assessment process are key components in working with young children.

- Assessment should not determine if children are "ready" for school or whether to delay children's entrance into school until they reach a certain level. Rather, children who are entering school for the first time benefit from a transition assessment that identifies needs and supports to make entry into the new program successful.

REFERENCES

Barr, R. G. (1989). Recasting a clinical enigma: The case of infant crying. In P. R. Zelazo & R. G. Barr (Eds.), *Challenges to developmental paradigms: Implications for theory, assessment, and treatment* (pp. 43–64). Hillsdale, NJ: Lawrence Erlbaum Associates.

Bayley, N. (2005). *Bayley scales of infant and toddler development, third edition (Bayley-III).* San Antonio, TX: The Psychological Corporation.

Bredekamp, S., & Copple, C. (Eds.). (1997). *Developmentally appropriate practice in early childhood programs.* Washington, DC: National Association for the Education of Young Children.

Bricker, D. (Ed.). (2002). *Assessment, evaluation, and programming system (AEPS ®) for infants and children, second edition.* Baltimore: Paul H. Brookes.

Cooney, M. H., & Buchanan, M. (2001). Documentation: Making assessment visible. *Young Exceptional Children 4*(3): 10–16.

Division for Early Childhood of the Council for Exceptional Children. (1992). DEC position statement on goal one of America 2000: All children should begin school ready to learn. *DEC Communicator 19*(3): 4.

Greenspan, S. I., & Meisels, S. (1993). *Toward a new vision for the developmental assessment of infants and young children.* Paper presented at the Zero to Three/National Center for Clinical Infant Programs' Eighth Biennial National Training Institute, December, Washington, DC.

Johnson-Martin, N. M., Attermeier, S. M., & Hacker, B. J. (2004). *The Carolina curriculum for preschoolers with special needs, second edition.* Baltimore: Paul H. Brookes.

Mardell-Czudnowski, C., & Goldenberg, D. S. (1998). *Developmental indicators for the assessment of learning–3, third edition (DIAL–3).* Circle Pines, MN: American Guidance Service.

Maeroff, G. I. (2003). *Universal pre-kindergarten.* New York: Foundation for Child Development. (ERIC Document Reproduction Services No. ED 482856)

Meisels, S. J. (1989). High-stakes testing in kindergarten. *Educational Leadership 46*(7): 16–22.

Meisels, S. J., & Wasik, B. A. (1990). Who should be served? Identifying children in need of early intervention. In S. J. Meisels & J. P. Shonkoff (Eds.), *Handbook of early childhood intervention* (pp. 605–632). Cambridge, UK: Cambridge University Press.

Newborg, J. (2004). *Battelle developmental inventory, second edition.* Itasca, IL: Riverside Publishing.

Rosenkoetter, S. E., Hains, A. H., & Fowler, S. A. (1994). *Bridging early services for children with special needs and their families.* Baltimore: Paul H. Brookes.

Shepard, L. (1990). Readiness testing in local school districts: An analysis of backdoor policies. *Journal of Education Policy 5*(5): 159–179.

19 Youth in Transition

Chapter Objectives

After completing this chapter, you should be able to:

- Define the concept of transition.
- Compare several approaches to transition assessment.
- Explain the purposes of transition assessment.
- Describe the ways in which students' transition needs and preferences are assessed.

Key Terms

Transition
Transition services

Person-centered planning
Self-determination

Curriculum-based vocational assessment

Overview

The provision of transition services is critical in preparing students with disabilities for adult life. Although students with disabilities continue to fall behind their typical peers in postschool employment, wages, postsecondary education, and residential independence, they are making gains. The federal commitment to supporting transition activities once students leave school has contributed to these improvements (Blackorby & Wagner, 1996). The federal government mandates that students with disabilities be provided with services that will facilitate their transition from school to postschool activities, including postsecondary education, vocational training, integrated employment (including supported employment), continuing and adult education, adult services, independent living, and community participation.

Cooperation between experts and interagency collaboration are essential to the assessment process. Professionals who come from a variety of disciplines and incorporate input from parents, caregivers, and the student should conduct the assessment of transition needs and preferences. Collaboration is important to the success of a student's transition.

A variety of assessment tools is available to conduct transition assessment. These include standardized instruments, curriculum-based assessment, performance-based assessment, direct observation, checklists, and informal approaches. Much more experimentation with various assessment methods, especially in how and when to use them, is necessary in order to continue to develop approaches that educators can apply with confidence.

While transitions occur across an individual's life span, the transition from the school setting to adult life is one that requires careful assessment and planning. The effects of this transition have great impact on the individual with a disability. The Division of Career Development and Transition (DCDT) of the Council for Exceptional Children has adopted the following definition when referring to youth who are in transition:

> **Transition** refers to a change in status from behaving primarily as a student to assuming emergent adult roles in the community, participating in postsecondary education, maintaining a home, becoming appropriately involved in the community, and experiencing satisfactory personal and social relationships. The process of enhancing transition involves the participation and coordination of school programs, adult agency services, and natural supports within the community. The foundations for transition should be made during the elementary and middle school years, guided by the broad concept of career development. Transition planning should begin no later than age 14, and students should be encouraged to the full extent of their capabilities, to assume a maximum of responsibility for such planning. (Halpern, 1994)

Legal Requirements

The Individuals with Disabilities Education Improvement Act (IDEA) is the federal legislation that mandates transition services. The focus is on assisting the individual with a disability to make a smooth transfer from the school to independent adult life. IDEA requires the IEP team to begin school transition planning early, update transition plans annually, and include a statement of individual needs for transition services as a component of the IEP. IDEA requires that secondary transition services be implemented by age 16.

IDEA requires that schools base individual transition planning on present levels of performance. Transition planning is an outcome-oriented process in which the focus is on the attainment of prespecified performance objectives. Assessment of students' transition needs and preferences is an important part of the transition process and should include assessment of vocational, career, academic, personal, social, and living needs. This requires a variety of approaches and because transition planning is a process that occurs over a long period of time, periodic transition assessments and monitoring of transition plans is vital.

According to IDEA, **transition services** means a coordinated set of activities for a student, designed with an outcome-oriented process, that promotes movement from school to post-school activities, including postsecondary education, vocational training, integrated employment (including supported employment), and continuing and adult education.

A coordinated set of activities means that all transition activities must meet the student's needs and complement, not duplicate, each other. The transition process involves many individuals and agencies. The coordinated set of activities that IDEA outlines must be based upon the individual student's needs, taking into account the student's preferences and interests and include

- Instruction.
- Community experiences.
- The development of employment and other postschool adult living objectives.
- If appropriate, acquisition of daily living skills and functional vocational evaluation. (20 USC Sec. 1401 [a] [19])

Although progress has been made, there are several challenges that remain. The National Transition Longitudinal Study and the National Council on Disability have defined these challenges as (1) increasing secondary-aged students' access to relevant and rigorous curricula and information technology, while at the same time increasing the numbers of students who successfully complete high school; (2) expanding the range of options for students who enter employment after graduation from high school; (3) improving access to higher education opportunities; (4) ensuring that there is wide range of opportunities for vocational and educational opportunities for individuals with disabilities who do not complete a high school program; and (5) increasing the level of accountability in government-funded programs that provide postsecondary education, vocational training, and employment (National Council on Disability and the Social Security Administration, 2000; Wagner, Newman, Carneto, & Levine, 2005).

▶ Read more about the challenges to transition on the website of the National Transition Longitudinal Study http://www.ntls2.org. Identify one or more challenges and suggest strategies for addressing them.

Transition Assessment

▶ Interview a school guidance counselor or a rehabilitation counselor regarding transition services and assessment approaches that the school offers to students. Share your findings with the class.

Beginning at age 16 (or sooner if determined by the Pupil Evaluation Team) and updated annually, the IEP team must develop a statement of transition services needs of the student that focuses on the student's courses of study. When the student is 16, the IEP team must discuss and document transition services at every IEP meeting until the student leaves school. Figure 19.1 includes questions that the IEP team should address and methods of collecting data when assessing transition needs.

As individuals with disabilities transition from school to adult life, assessment is crucial in career and vocational education and in life-skill development. Transition assessment can be defined as: The ongoing process of collecting data on the individual's

---

Research-Based Practices **Education and Employment**

Research on U.S. youth has yielded disturbing findings relating to education and employment. Greene and Kochbar-Bryant (2003) summarized the research and found that when compared with all Americans, almost twice as many students with disabilities do not complete high school. Students with disabilities are much less likely to complete postsecondary education. Of those students who do participate in postsecondary education, many have poor self-concept and socialization skills and experience stress and anxiety. These students are reluctant to let

instructors know that they need accommodations because they fear that they will be stigmatized. One of the most disturbing findings is that students with disabilities are much less likely to be employed than students without disabilities. A growing number of students apply for Supplemental Security Income (SSI), a federal program that assists persons with disabilities by providing funds to meet basic needs for food, clothing, and shelter each year. Thus, there is an ever widening gap between persons with and without disabilities relating to education and income.

Assessment Questions to Ask	Methods of Collecting Information
Employment	
1. What does the student like to do? 2. What types of employment options (e.g., supported employment, competitive employment) are feasible for the student? 3. What types of accommodations, modifications, and supports will the student need on employment sites? 4. What types of skills does the student need to acquire/learn to meet the career goal? 5. What types of job benefits does the student need to become an independent member of society? 6. Does the student have job-seeking skills? 7. Does the student need assistance from an adult service provider to find and maintain a job?	Interviews • student • family • school personnel • work study teachers • employers Situational assessment • in-school jobs • community-based jobs • vocational courses Work samples Learning style Inventories Aptitude testing Assistive technology assessment
Postsecondary Education	
1. Does the student want or need postsecondary education or training programs? 2. What subject(s)/major is the student interested in studying to prepare for employment? 3. Can the student express a desire for support services, accommodations, and modifications if needed? 4. What types of accommodations will the student need in a postsecondary setting? 5. Does the student need assistance from an adult agency to attend a postsecondary institution?	Situational assessment Interviews • student • family • school personnel Background review • medical records • psychological • financial status Interest inventories Functional academics Simulated application package
Community Involvement	
1. What public transportation is the student able to use in the community? 2. Does or will the student have a driver's license? 3. Does the student need special travel arrangements made on an ongoing basis? 4. What leisure/community activities does the student enjoy? 5. Does the student need accommodations, modifications, or supports in order to participate in leisure activities? 6. Can the student locate/use community services, such as stores, banks, and medical facilities? 7. Does the student participate in the political process (e.g., voting)? 8. Is the student knowledgeable about the law?	Situational assessment • physical education teacher • community recreation services • extracurricular activities Interviews • student • family • teachers • peers Community survey Record review

FIGURE 19.1 • Strengths, Needs, Opportunities, and Worries

Source: Adapted from Sitlington et al., 1996.

(continued)

Assessment Questions to Ask	Methods of Collecting Information
Personal/Social	
1. Does the student interact with and have support from family members? 2. Does the student have age-appropriate friends? 3. Does the student know how to act in social situations? 4. Is the student able to self-advocate in employment, leisure, and community situations? 5. Does the student demonstrate an understanding of rights as a person with a disability? 6. Does the student participate in the IEP process? 7. Is the student able to understand and express strengths, needs, and accommodations? 8. Does the student need advocacy support?	Interviews • student • family • teachers • peers Background review Observation • IEP meetings • classrooms • lunchtime • employment sites • community sites Situational assessment • community • employment • role plays
Independent Living	
1. What kinds of accommodations/supports will the student need to function in an independent living situation? 2. Is the student aware of how to find independent living quarters? 3. Can the student purchase and prepare food? 4. Does the student know how to arrange for utility services? 5. Can the student follow daily routines (e.g., get up in the morning, do dishes, clean)? 6. Is the student able to maintain personal and hygiene skills? 7. Can the student manage money appropriately?	Interviews • student • family • teachers • employers Functional academics Background review Observations • grocery store • food service class • home • banks • shopping Situational assessments • home • community • school Simulated class activities

FIGURE 19.1 • Continued

strengths, needs, preferences, and interests as they relate to the demands of current and future working, educational, living, and personal and social environments. Assessment data serve as the common thread in the transition process and form the basis for defining goals and services that will make up the Individualized Education Program.

Transition assessment relates to the life roles of individuals with disabilities and the supports they need before, during, and after the transition to adult life. Figure 19.2

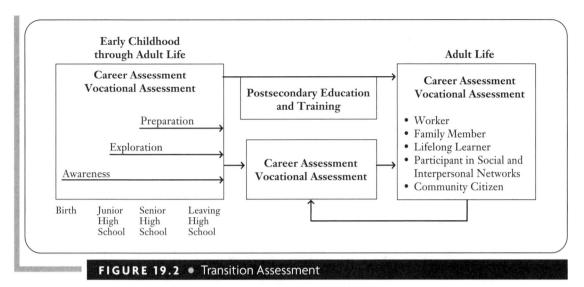

FIGURE 19.2 ● Transition Assessment

Source: Adapted from Transition assessment—Where have we been and where should we be going? by P. L. Sitlington, *Career Development for Exceptional Individuals 19,* 1996, page 163. Copyright 1996 by The Council for Exceptional Children. Reprinted with permission.

illustrates the transition assessment process. The data collected in transition assessment is vital in assisting individuals with disabilities and their families to make choices that take into account the individual's strengths, needs, and preferences about postsecondary education, career development, vocational training, community living, and personal and social goals.

Purposes of Transition Assessment

Transition focuses on facilitating improved postsecondary outcomes for persons with disabilities. Transition assessment assists individuals with disabilities, their families, educators, specialists, employers, and community members to develop, implement, and evaluate the transition process. Transition assessment is integral to instruction and program planning. Because transition planning can begin as early as the elementary years, transition assessment is an ongoing process. While the purposes of transition change as the student gets older, the major purposes are to

- Identify the person's level of career development.
- Determine the individual's strengths, abilities, interests, and preferences regarding postsecondary education, employment, independent living, community involvement, and personal and social goals.
- Identify the individuals who exhibit interests and skills.
- Identify the accommodations, modifications, supports, and services that the individual will need in order to be a responsible and contributing community member (Sitlington, Neubert, Begun, Lombard, & Leconte, 1996).

▶ After reviewing the purposes of transition assessment, identify specific assessment tools and approaches that fit these purposes.

▶ **CEC Common Core Knowledge and Skills.** The beginning special educator can interpret information from formal and informal assessments (CC8S5).

Involving Families

Parental and family involvement and support are integral to the transition process. Beginning in the early elementary years, parental involvement throughout the process is important. Educators should periodically interview parents about their aspirations for their children. As children progress through school, parents' views of their children's abilities will change. Educators should welcome parents as partners throughout the transition process (Wehman, 2001). Questions that can be discussed with parents include:

Expectations

- What are your expectations for your child?
- What work experiences has your child had?
- What are your child's daily responsibilities at home?
- To what extent did your child enjoy the work?
- In what types of jobs do you think that your child will be successful?
- What are your goals for your child's future?
- In what types of jobs do you think that your child will be successful? Unsuccessful?

Transportation

- Does your child drive a car?
- Does your child use public transportation? If so, are there any problems?
- What are your expectations for transportation to take your child to and from work?

Education

- Do you feel that your child will need further education and/or training after completing high school? If so, what types of education or training would be beneficial?
- What steps have you taken to obtain further information on this education and/or training? (Hutchins and Renzaglia, 1998)

Person-Centered Planning

Person-centered planning means that the student with the disability engages in an active meaningful way with parents, educators, community members, and others during the assessment, planning, and service delivery processes. Person-centered planning is focused on self-determination and on the students' hopes, dreams, and desires. Natural supports—the individuals and supports that the general population uses, rather than specialized services—are emphasized. Examples of natural supports include neighbors, employers, clergy, and other community members.

Person-centered planning encourages students with disabilities to take a leadership role during the transition activities. Person-centered planning should result in a comprehensive plan that addresses educational opportunities, employment opportunities, financial and income needs, friendship and socialization needs, transportation needs, health and medical needs, and legal and advocacy needs (Wehman, Everson, & Reid, 2001). Person-centered planning has several characteristics:

- Person-centered planning focuses on abilities, rather than disabilities.
- Person-centered planning encourages planning that is oriented toward the future.
- Involvement of community members and organizations is integral to person-centered planning.
- Person-centered planning emphasizes supports, connections, and commitment rather than programs and services.
- Person-centered approaches are individualized according to each student's needs and desires. The student with the disability and family members provide strong direction for transition planning and implementation activities. (Wehman et al., 2001)

When developing IEPs that are person-centered, individuals who are part of the student's personal network should be identified. Along with the student and the family, this personal network develops a vision or dream of the student's future. These individuals can include the student, family members, special educators, general educators, vocational educators, vocational rehabilitation counselors, providers of adult services, and other community members. Each major transition should connect to a part of the student's dream.

The IEP team should identify the experiences, supports, and services that need to be in place in order to achieve the dream. Achieving the IEP goals and objectives should move the student closer to the dream and to inclusion in the community. A variety of instruments can be useful in person-centered planning:

- Learning styles inventories
- Classroom observation instruments
- Curriculum-based assessments
- Learning environment assessments
- Physical environment assessments
- Social environment assessments
- Future planning questionnaires
- Interviews with students
- Interviews with parents and family members
- Adaptive behavior instruments
- Behavioral and functional assessments
- Technology evaluations
- Self-determination checklists (Clark, 1996)

▶ The American Association on Mental Retardation has made available resources on person-centered planning. Visit its website at http://www.aamr.org. Can you explain the importance of this approach?

Self-Determination Skills

Student self-determination is at the center of transition planning. All activities in the transition process, including assessment, planning, implementation, and evaluation, must include the individual with the disability as an active participant to the maximum extent possible. **Self-determination** means that the individual's hopes, dreams, and desires influence the types of assessments that the transition team implements. Figure 19.3 contains an example of a worksheet that may help a student express hopes and dreams. Transition assessment should include and document self-determination skills. Various instruments assist in this process, including one or more interviews with

Strengths	Needs
What skills have I learned that will help me reach my dreams? Things I can do well are . . .	What do I still need to learn to do to reach my dreams? What skills do I have trouble with? What do I need help with?
Opportunities	**Worries**
What is helping me now to reach my dreams? Who can assist me concerning my dreams? How can they help?	What worries me when I think about reaching my dreams?

FIGURE 19.3 • Sample Worksheet for Students' S. N. O. W.

Source: Adapted from the Maine Transition Network/Maine Committee on Transition and Southern Maine Advisory Council on Transition, 1997.

the individual, interviews with parents and family members, checklists, and observations (Sitlington et al., 1996). Suggested questions to ask include:

▶ The American Association on Mental Retardation has made available resources on self-determination. Visit its website at http://www.aamr.org. Can you explain the importance of this approach and its relationship to person centered-planning?

- Does the individual understand the transition planning process? Does the individual understand her rights under the law? Does the person demonstrate self-advocacy skills?
- Can the individual explain his role in the transition planning process? Can the person identify interests and preferences?
- Can the individuals describe their own transition goals?

Research-Based Practices   Views of Latina Mothers

Cultural beliefs and understandings are essential when considering the transition needs of individuals. The assumptions that transition activities should be focused on independent functioning and productivity are challenged in a study of Latina mothers conducted by researchers Rueda, Monzo, Gomez, and Blacher (2005). The mothers, who were interviewed, believed that the focus of education should be on life skills, such as personal self-help, living, and care arrangements, rather than on employment and career development. Although viewed as adults under the law, the mothers expressed that their children should not make be able to make independent decisions until marriage, not when they left home. One mother commented, "When your own daughters are grown, never tell them to leave, because that is very Anglicized" (Rueda,

Monzo, Gomez, & Blacher, 2005, p. 406). The mothers viewed the outside world as dangerous, expressing that their children may be targets of discrimination and may not be cared for as well outside family settings. The researchers write that the mothers' views may suggest that there has been alienation, marginalization, confusion, and misunderstanding.

These findings may not be representative of the views of all Latina mothers and should not be generalized. However, they do point out that views of transition are not homogeneous. While current laws reflect the beliefs of a dominant society that values productivity, independence, and assimilation, they do not necessarily reflect the views of all families.

SNAPSHOT

Miguel

Miguel is 14 years old and in the sixth grade. He has been identified as having mild mental retardation and an emotional disability. Miguel's language abilities are well below the range of an average 14-year-old. Miguel often gets frustrated when he is unable to communicate effectively and sometimes responds inappropriately by striking out at others.

In a conversation with his special education teacher, Shauna Moore, Miguel talked about feeling different from his classmates. He stated that this made him angry and sad. When asked what he likes to do, he responded, "I like to play video games and play with my dog." Shauna asked Miguel what he would like to do for a career when he was older. Miguel indicated that he would like to be a "vet" (veterinarian). When asked why he wanted to be a veterinarian he said, "animals can understand me."

In an interview, Miguel's mother expressed concern about his future. She worries that he will not be able to do the things that other students are going to be doing "like drive a car" or "have a girlfriend." She stated that he prefers to

play alone or with his dog, but has "no friends." She does not have many problems understanding her son, but knows that he does get easily frustrated when he is unable to communicate well with others. When asked about Miguel's future after high school, she thought that he might be able to work as a building custodian as long as he was supervised.

Shauna suggested that the team should begin to plan for Miguel's transition by first assessing Miguel's vocational interests and aptitudes. Once these are shared with the team, the team will set goals with Miguel for his life after school and develop a plan of action that will enable him to reach his goals.

▶ Visit a local school and interview a special education teacher who provides transition services. Consider the types of assessment instruments and approaches that are used.

▶ Youthhood.org is an interactive website that has been developed for individuals who are preparing for the transition after high school. The site contains resources for planning future educational activities, entering the work force, and independent living.

Transition Assessment

Brita, who is almost 16 years old, has been thinking about her future. When she has time in her busy schedule, she thinks about what she would like to do when she leaves high school. Ever since she can remember, Brita has enjoyed cooking. She loves to bake breads and cook soups and stews. Her recent successful placement as an apprentice chef has reinforced her desire to enter the cooking field. Her dream is to become a restaurant chef.

Brita's transition team is meeting in a few weeks to plan transition activities that support her as she leaves high school and enters the next phase of her life. Brita's team includes her mom, special education teacher, vocational rehabilitation counselor, work-site coordinator, and transition specialist.

In preparation for the meeting with her team, Brita has completed the Strengths, Needs, Opportunities, and Worries worksheet with her special education teacher. Here is Brita's form.

Strengths

What skills have I learned that will help me reach my dreams? Things I can do well are . . .

measure ingredients
read recipes
follow directions

Needs

What do I still need to learn to do to reach my dreams? What skills do I have trouble with? What do I need help with?

finding new recipes
doing math
completing community-college applications

Opportunities

What is helping me now to reach my dreams? Who can assist me concerning my dreams? How can they help?

my mentor-Ms. Cara.
applying for cooking school

Worries

What worries me when I think about reaching my dreams?

How can I pay for school?
Need help finishing high school classes

Mr. Kane, Brita's special education teacher, will be discussing Brita's performance on recent tests, including achievement and cognitive ability assessments. Mr. Kane will report that Brita is very motivated and has experienced success in her apprenticeship. She continues to experience difficulty in reading and mathematics, but the introduction of assistive software has enabled Brita to keep up with her academic classes.

Brita's work-site coordinator, Ms. Kerem, will share her impressions of Brita's performance in the cooking apprenticeship. Brita has been working in a natural foods restaurant during the past two months. When she started the apprenticeship, Brita helped to set up the ingredients for making breakfast muffins. Now, she is able to set up the ingredients, mix them in the commercial mixer, and put the trays in the ovens. Ms. Kerem believes that Brita has been very successful and is enthusiastic about her progress.

The transition specialist, Ms. Barker, will be assessing Brita's skills for leaving high school. Ms. Barker knows that Brita and her family would like Brita to continue her education at the community college where she can earn a certificate as a chef. Transition skills that should be considered include completing school applications, living independently, self-advocacy, organizational abilities, study skills, and interpersonal skills. In preparation for the transition assessment, Ms. Barker and Brita met to discuss the supports that are already in place to help Brita fulfill her dream. Here is the circle of supports that Brita and Ms. Barker developed.

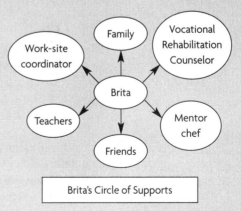

Brita's Circle of Supports

What are the next steps that Brita and her team can take in planning for Brita's transition?

Assessment Instruments

This chapter describes published instruments that provide information on transition assessment. However, many instruments are outdated or have other limitations. As with all assessment instruments, users should carefully review technical aspects and administration procedures and consider how to apply the results of the assessment. Some of these instruments have little relevance in supporting students' preparation for transition; consequently, educators need to think about how to collect more pertinent information.

Vocational Interests

The team that is helping to plan for a student's transition may need to gather information about the student's vocational interests. These interest inventories can assist individuals in investigating educational and occupational alternatives, learning about careers, and setting goals for the future.

Reading-Free Vocational Interest Inventory–2

The *Reading-Free Vocational Interest Inventory–2 (R–FVII*; Becker, 2000) is a vocational interest inventory for students who have mental retardation or learning disabilities. The test consists of 55 sets of three pictures. The pictures are black-and-white drawings that depict women and men in work activities.

ADMINISTRATION The *R–FVII* can be administered to individuals or to groups of students. The examiner reads the directions to students, and they circle the drawings that depict the work that they prefer to do. The test requires no reading by students.

SCORING The consumable student booklets are hand scored. Raw scores transform to T-scores, percentiles, and stanines. Scores that fall above the 75th percentile indicate areas of high interest; scores falling below the 25th percentile indicate areas of low interest.

STANDARDIZATION The *R–FVII* was standardized on over 8,000 students with mild mental retardation or learning disabilities in grades 7 through 12. In addition, adult norms derived from the test performance of over 3,000 adults with mental retardation and economic or environmental disadvantages. Although the test manual describes a study of students in grades 7 through 12 who showed moderate mental retardation, the norm tables do not incorporate this information. However, the manual suggests that the norms are appropriate for students who show moderate mental retardation.

RELIABILITY Test-retest and internal consistency reliability is adequate, with coefficients generally in the .70s and .80s.

VALIDITY Although the manual states that experts reviewed the items, the description of content validity is sketchy. Concurrent validity was determined by comparing the *R–FVII* with the 1964 revision of the *Geist Picture Interest Inventory* (Geist, 1964). The description of construct validity is limited.

SUMMARY The *Reading-Free Vocational Interest Inventory–2* measures the vocational interests of students with mild mental retardation or learning disabilities who are in grades 7 through 12. The norms need updating to reflect recent census figures. Reliability is adequate; validity is limited. The author should provide evidence of predictive validity so that users can make predictions about vocational interests and actual vocations that are pursued.

Adaptive Behavior and Life Skills

The *Responsibility and Independence Scale for Adolescents* (*RISA*; Salvia, Neisworth, & Schmidt, 1990) is a norm-referenced measure of adolescent adaptive behavior intended for use with students who are between the ages of 12 years and 19 years, 11 months. See Chapter 14 for a detailed description of this instrument.

Work Samples

Work samples assess students' skills, aptitudes, job preferences, and ability to profit from vocational training. Work sampling evaluates abilities on tasks that simulate actual job tasks. Most commercial work sample systems are based on the *Dictionary of Occupational Titles (DOT)* (U.S. Department of Labor, 1991), a system developed by the U.S. Department of Labor that classifies occupations. Work samples are also helpful in evaluating the progress a student makes in a vocational training program.

In addition to commercial systems, evaluators can construct their own work samples and job simulations. Evaluators must conduct observations of students during vocational training and while working in actual jobs, and also collect information from interviews with job supervisors and written evaluations.

Connecting Assessment with Instruction

Curriculum-Based Vocational Assessment

Curriculum-based vocational assessment (CBVA) is a type of curriculum-based assessment used in planning and developing vocational education opportunities for students with disabilities (Albright & Cobb, 1988). Conceptually, CBVA is different from traditional vocational assessment, which focuses on occupational areas and consists of formal, standardized measures.

Albright and Cobb describe CBVA as an integral aspect of the three different stages of a student's program and list the types of questions on which the assessment should focus at each stage. For example, the first stage of the assessment process occurs prior to and during the first weeks of a student's participation in a vocational program. The sample questions at this stage are: "Which vocational program is most appropriate for the student? What are the special service needs of the student in this particular program? What will be the criteria used to determine student success?" (p. 16).

The second stage of assessment is an ongoing process of evaluation as the student progresses in the vocational education program. The sample questions include: "How is the student performing in the vocational setting? What changes are needed in the student's program?" (p. 16).

The third stage of the assessment process begins when the student exits the program. The sample questions include: "What are the special services needed to help the student transition into employment and/or postsecondary education? Which adult service agencies need to be linked up to the student? How will student adjustment be monitored?" (p. 16).

Lombard, Larsen, and Westphal (1993) developed another approach to CBVA. The Teach Prep Assessment Model consists of five steps named MAGIC. The first step (M) is Making a prediction for the student's future. Informal assessment in this phase involves gathering information about the student's needs, preferences, and interests, and formal assessment consists of the evaluation of occupational interests, vocational aptitude, academic skills, and learning style. The second step (A) is Assess entry-level skills. During this step CBVA is conducted. In the third step (G), Guide skill acquisition to skill mastery, teachers and other personnel conduct a discrepancy analysis between the student's current skills and the entry-level target skills and develop goals and objectives. The fourth step (I) is Instruct for generalization, and it focuses on using skills in multiple settings. The final step (C) is Conduct maintenance checks. During this last step, there is ongoing assessment to monitor student performance as well as the curriculum and instruction. The final step includes evaluation of both student and program. Students or employees can assist in monitoring their own demonstration of work-related behaviors and skills. A simple checklist that uses icons is ideal for this purpose (Figure 19.4).

Name: _____

Observer: _____   Date: _____

I can...		Yes	No
Tell the time to go to work.	9:00 AM		
Put on an apron.			
Find the aisle that needs to be cleaned.	3 Coffee Cereal Tea Breakfast food		
Sweep the aisle. • Get the broom • Sweep the aisle and sweep dirt into dustpan • Put dirt in the trash • Put the broom away			
Mop the aisle. • Get the mop and bucket • Mop the aisle • Fill the bucket with soapy water • Rinse out the mop • Get the mop wet • Dump out the water • Wring out the mop • Put the mop and bucket away			
Straighten the shelves.			

FIGURE 19.4 • A Picture/Symbol Checklist

Performance-Based Assessment

Chapter 6 describes portfolio assessment as the deliberate collection of the products of a student's work in order to demonstrate the student's efforts, progress, and achievement. When applied to transition assessment, portfolios document the transition needs and preferences of students. Documentation of a student's transition needs can include work samples, audiotapes, videotapes, inventories, checklists, observations, and self-reports.

A portfolio that documents transition needs and preferences produces a rich, detailed portrait of the student. It depicts the student in natural work and living environments and provides continuous information, feedback, and growth toward transition needs and goals. Further, portfolio assessment can link interventions directly to the student's activities.

In addition to the assessment tools this chapter describes, the assessment of transition needs can include many of the procedures that previous chapters describe, including:

- Oral descriptions
- Written descriptions
- Checklists and questionnaires
- Interviews
- Conferences
- Student journals and notebooks
- Discussions between students, parents, and teachers.

▶ How can performance-based assessment contribute to the assessment of transition needs and preferences?

Summary

- The overall intent of transition assessment is to assist students in making a transition from school to postschool activities, including postsecondary education, vocational training, integrated employment (including supported employment), continuing and adult education, adult services, independent living, and community participation.

- Transition assessment must include the evaluation of vocational, career, academic, personal, social, and living needs.

- Transition assessment is an outcome-oriented process that begins when the child is young and takes place over a period of time.

- Transition assessment involves person-centered planning. This means that the student with the disability engages in an active meaningful way with parents, educators, community members and others during the assessment, planning, and service delivery processes. Person-centered planning focuses on self-determination and on the students' hopes, dreams, and desires.

REFERENCES

Albright, L., & Cobb, R. B. (1988). Curriculum-based vocational assessment: A concept whose time has come. *Journal for Vocational Special Needs Education 10*(2): 13–16.

Becker, R. L. (2000). *Reading-free vocational interest, inventory-2,* Lutz, FL: Psychological Assessment Resources.

Blackorby, J., & Wagner, M. (1996). Longitudinal post-school outcomes of youth with disabilities: Findings from the national longitudinal transition study. *Exceptional Children 62*: 399–413.

Clark, G. M. (1996). Transition planning assessment for secondary-level students with learning disabilities. *Journal of Learning Disabilities 29*: 79–92.

Geist, H. (1964). *Geist picture interest inventory.* Los Angeles, CA: Western Psychological Corporation.

Greene, G., & Kochbar-Bryant, C. A. (2003). *Pathways to successful transition for youth with disabilities.* Columbus, OH: Merrill Prentice-Hall.

Halpern, A. S. (1994). The transition of youth with disabilities to adult life: A position statement of the division on career development and transition, the Council for Exceptional Children. *Career Development for Exceptional Individuals 17*: 115–124.

Hutchins, M. P., & Renzaglia, A. (1998). Interviewing families for effective transition to employment. *Teaching Exceptional Children 30*: 72–78.

Lombard, R. C., Larsen, K. A., & Westphal, S. E. (1993). Validation of vocational assessment services for special populations in tech-prep: A model for translating the Perkins assurances into practice. *Journal for Vocational Special Needs Education 16*(1): 14–22.

National Council on Disability and the Social Security Administration. (2000). *Transition and post-school outcomes for youth with disabilities: Closing the gaps to post-secondary education and employment* [online]. Retrieved November 2000. Available: http://www.ncd.gov.

Rueda, R., Monzo, L., Shapiro, J., Gomez, J., & Blacher, J. (2005). Cultural models of transition: Latina mothers of young adults with developmental disabilities. *Exceptional Children 71* (4): 401–414.

Salvia, J., Neisworth, J. T., & Schmidt, M. W. (1990). *Responsibility and independence scale for adolescents*. Allen, TX: DLM.

Sitlington, P. L., Neubert, D. A., Begun, W., Lombard, R. C., & Leconte, P. J. (1996). *Assess for success*. Reston, VA: Council for Exceptional Children.

U.S. Department of Labor. (1991). *Dictionary of occupational titles* (4th ed.). Washington, DC: U.S. Government Printing Office.

Wagner, M., Newman, L., Carneto, R., & Levine, P. (2005). *Changes over time in the early postschool outcomes of youth with disabilities*. Washington, DC: U.S. Department of Education.

Wehman, P. (2001). *Life beyond the classroom* (3rd ed.). Baltimore, MD: Paul H. Brookes.

Wehman, P., Everson, J. M., & Reid, D. H. (2001). Beyond programs and placements. In P. Wehman (Ed.), *Life beyond the classroom* (pp. 91–124). Baltimore: Paul H. Brookes.

Glossary

accommodations   Changes to the education program and assessment procedures and materials that do not substantially alter the instructional level, the content of the curriculum, or the assessment criteria.

achievement testing   The assessment of past learning.

adaptive behavior   The collection of conceptual, social, and practical skills that individuals learn in order to function in their everyday lives.

adequate yearly progress (AYP)   Required by No Child Left Behind legislation, this is an annual report of a school's progress in meeting state standards.

alternate assessments   Assessments that allow students with persistent academic problems and students with severe or significant disabilities who are working toward modified or alternative achievement standards to participate in general large-scale assessments.

alternate form reliability   An estimate of the correlation of scores between two forms of the same test.

analytic scoring   A type of scoring in which an independent score is reported for each area of the scoring rubric. This type of scoring provides diagnostic information. Individual scores indicate areas of strengths and areas that need improvement.

anchor papers   Student papers that represent writing at different levels of performance.

anecdotal record   A brief narrative description of an event or events that the observer felt was important to record.

antecedents   The events that happen before the behavior occurs.

assessment   A global term for observing, collecting, recording, and interpreting information to answer questions and make legal and instructional decisions about students.

assessment approach   A term used to describe the way information is collected for making an educational decision.

assessment strategies   Individualized activities or routines that the teacher follows that assist students to demonstrate their best effort.

assistive technology   Any item, piece of equipment, or product system, whether acquired commercially off the shelf, modified, or customized, that is used to increase, maintain, or improve functional capabilities of a child with a disability.

assistive technology services   Services that assist students with disabilities in selecting, acquiring, and using assistive technology devices.

augmentative or alternative communication (AAC)   A method or device used by a person with a communication disability in order to communicate.

authentic assessment   An assessment during which the student completes or demonstrates knowledge, skills, or behavior in a real-life context.

basal level   The point below which the examiner assumes that the student could obtain all correct responses and at which the examiner begins testing.

benchmarks   Examples of student work that illustrate each scoring level on the assessment scale.

category recording   A system of recording behavior by discrete groupings.

ceiling level   The point above which the examiner assumes that the student would obtain all incorrect responses if the testing were to continue and the point at which the examiner stops testing.

checklist   A list of characteristics or behaviors arranged in a consistent manner that allows the evaluator to record the presence or absence of individual characteristics, events, or behaviors.

child find   A series of activities that increase public awareness and provide information about screening, programs, and early intervention or special education services. These services and activities help in locating children with special needs.

chronological age   The precise age of a person in years, months, and days.

collaborating   A process that involves a commitment to work cooperatively with others to address common interests and issues.

communicate   To use oral symbols, written symbols, or manuals signs or gestures to express meaning.

concurrent validity   The extent to which two different tests administered at about the same time correlate with each other.

conferencing   A process conducted by two or more individuals for the purpose of sharing information, concerns, and ideas regarding common issues.

confidence interval   The range within which the true score can be found; frequently called the band of error or confidence level.

consequences　Events that follow the behavior.

consequential validity　The extent to which an assessment instrument promotes the intended consequences.

construct validity　The extent to which a test measures a particular construct or concept.

content validity　The extent to which the test items reflect the content they are designed to cover.

correlation　The extent to which two or more scores vary together.

correlation coefficient　A statistic that measures the correlation, or relationship, between tests, test items, scoring procedures, observations, or behavior ratings. A correlation coefficient quantifies a relationship and provides information about whether there is a relationship, strength of the relationship, and the direction of the relationship. The symbol for correlation coefficient is a lowercase r.

criterion-referenced test (CRT)　A test that measures a student's test performance with respect to a well-defined content domain.

criterion-related validity　The extent that test scores obtained on one test or another measure are related to scores obtained on another test or another outcome.

critical period　An interval of time in which the child is most responsive. If the individual has little or no opportunity to develop the skill or behavior during this period, the individual may have difficulty in doing so later on.

curriculum-based assessment (CBA)　A broad approach to linking instruction with assessment.

curriculum-based measurement (CBM)　A type of curriculum-based assessment that emphasizes repeated, direct measurement of student performance.

curriculum-based vocational assessment (CBVA)　A type of curriculum-based assessment used in planning and developing vocational educational opportunities for students with disabilities.

cut scores　A prespecified score established in order to select or classify students for special education or labeling.

derived scores　The result of transforming raw scores to other types of scores.

descriptors　Written descriptions used in a rating scale or in a rubric to explain and provide more detail about each of the levels of achievement.

determining eligibility　A process used to determine if a student meets the eligibility criteria for services according to federal and state definitions.

developmental delay　A delay in one or more of the following areas of development: physical, including fine and gross motor; cognitive; communication; social or emotional; or adaptive development. The term is used to identify infants and toddlers so that they can receive early intervention services without being labeled for a specific disability. IDEA states that, at the discretion of an individual state, the term developmental delay may be used with children ages 3 through 9 so that young children can receive special education services without being labeled for a specific disability category.

developmental domains　Areas associated with the young child's general development. These areas include: physical, cognitive, communication, social, emotional, and adaptive development.

developmental score　Raw score that has been transformed to reflect the average performance at age and grade levels.

developmental quotient　An estimate of the rate of development.

deviation IQ score　A standard score with a mean of 100 and a standard deviation of 15 or 16.

due process　A set of safeguards to be followed during the assessment process and the delivery of services described in IDEA. Due process ensures that the rights of families and their children are not violated.

duration recording　A method of recording that measures the length of time a specific event or behavior persists.

early childhood team　A team that consists of the parents, the family service coordinator, and representatives of various disciplines who assess and implement early intervention services. The team makes decisions regarding eligibility and services for children birth through age 2 and, in some states, for children ages 3 to 5.

error analysis　A technique that identifies patterns of errors in students' work.

error of commission　Including information that did not actually occur.

error of omission　Leaving out information that is helpful or important to understanding a student's behavior.

error of transmission　Recording behaviors in an improper sequence.

evaluation　The process of establishing a value judgment based on the collection of actual data.

event recording　The recording of a behavior each time it occurs during an observation period; also called frequency recording.

examiner bias　Personal or professional perspectives that can interfere with the interpretation of assessment results.

expansion   A restatement of the student's verbal language that adds words or more complex phrases.

expressive language   The ability to use language to communicate information, thoughts, feelings, and ideas.

exhibition   A display of a student's work that demonstrates knowledge, abilities, skills, and attitudes.

external evaluator   A person with a background in research design, measurement, and evaluation who is hired specifically for the purpose of completing an evaluation.

externalizing behaviors   A broad array of behaviors directed outward that include disruptive and antisocial behaviors.

extrapolation   The process of estimating the performance of students outside the ages and grades of the normative sample.

false negative   The type of error that is made when a student is not referred by the screening but should have been.

false positive   The type of error that is made when a student is referred by the screening but should not have been.

family   A unit of two or more individuals who may or may not be related but who have extended commitments to each other.

family-centered philosophy   An approach to working with families that emphasizes the importance of enabling family members to mobilize their own resources in order to promote child and family functioning.

Family Educational Rights and Privacy Act (FERPA)   The Family Rights and Privacy Act (PL 93–380) states that no educational agency may release student information without written consent from the student's parents. FERPA also gives the family the right to review all records kept on its child as well as the right to challenge any of the information within the records.

focus groups   Small gatherings of individuals from similar constituencies or from different backgrounds who respond to specific questions or provide informal feedback to the group facilitator. Focus groups can be used to evaluate the overall effectiveness of a school program.

formative evaluation   An evaluation that is ongoing during the period of program implementation.

frequency distribution   A way of organizing test scores based on how often they occur.

functional behavioral assessment   A systematic process of gathering information that identifies the causes of and interventions for addressing problem behaviors.

grapheme   The written equivalent of a phoneme.

holistic scoring   A type of scoring in which the teacher assigns a single score based on a scoring rubric. This type of scoring lacks the depth of information found in analytic scoring; however, it may be easier to design and conduct than analytic scoring.

hypothesis generation   A process used in interpreting the results of testing that provides an explanation of a student's performance and behavior based on the collected assessment data.

IEP team   A multidisciplinary team consisting of the parents, school personnel, and, when possible the student, that is responsible for planning, developing, monitoring, and evaluating specialized instruction and related services for a student with a disability.

individualized education program (IEP)   IDEA mandates that all students with disabilities ages 3 through 21 have an individualized education program (IEP). This written plan specifies the special education and related services that must be provided.

individualized family service plan (IFSP)   IDEA mandates that all young children (birth through 2 years) and their families have an individualized family service plan (IFSP). Children ages 3 to 5 may receive services provided by an IFSP or an IEP. The IFSP is a written document that specifies the plan for services and is guided by the family's concerns, priorities, and resources.

Individuals with Disabilities Education Act (IDEA) of 2004   A federal law that focuses on the education of children and youth with disabilities. IDEA mandates specific requirements relating to the assessment process that teachers and test examiners must know and understand.

informant   An individual who knows a student well and who can provide information about that student.

informed consent   A process that involves: (1) presenting information so that it can be easily understood, (2) providing alternatives, (3) identifying risks and benefits, (4) accepting or consenting to the information proposed.

inner language   The language used during thinking, planning, and other mental processes.

intensity recording   A measure of the strength of a behavior.

internal consistency reliability   An estimate of the homogeneity or interrelatedness of responses to test items.

internal evaluator   A person such as a teacher or administrator employed by the school who is trained in research design, measurement, and evaluation and who conducts and completes an evaluation.

internalizing behaviors   Behaviors that are inner-directed and include social withdrawal, anxious or inhibited behaviors, or somatic problems.

interpolation   The process of estimating the scores of students within the ages and grades of the norming sample.

interscorer/interrater/interobserver reliability   An estimate of the extent to which two or more scorers, observers, or raters agree on how to score a test or how to observe behaviors.

interval recording   A recording of specific events or behaviors during a prespecified time interval.

interval scale   A scale in which the items are the same distance apart; the scale does not have an absolute zero.

item response theory (IRT).   IRT involves a statistical calculation that determines how well the instrument differentiates between individuals at various levels of measured abilities or characteristics.

language   Symbols used to communicate thoughts, feelings, ideas, and information.

language disorder   A difficulty or inability in decoding or encoding the set of symbols used in language or an inability to effectively use inner language. See also speech disorder.

language dominance   An individual's preferred language.

language probe   A diagnostic technique in which instruction is modified to elicit specific information about a student's receptive or expressive language.

language proficiency   An individual's level of expertise in a language.

language sample   A recording of a student's oral language that yields information regarding vocabulary, syntax, semantics, articulation, and the ability to use language in functional ways.

latency recording   A measure of the amount of time elapsed between a behavior or event (or request to begin the behavior) and the beginning of the prespecified behavior.

literacy   The ability to read, write, think, and communicate.

maladaptive behaviors   Behaviors that include antisocial behaviors, aggression, withdrawal behavior, delayed social skills, and difficulties with interpersonal relationships.

mean   The average score.

mean length of utterance (MLU)   The average number of individual units of meaning that the student expresses using phrases or sentences during the observation period. MLU can be used to assess amount of spoken language.

median   The point on a scale above which and below which 50 percent of the cases occur. A point or score that separates the top 50 percent of students who took the test from the bottom 50 percent of students.

mode   The score that occurs most often in a group of scores; the most commonly occurring test score.

modeling   Teaching by performing the behavior to be learned.

modifications   Changes or adaptations made to the educational program or assessment that alter the level, content, and or assessment criteria.

monitoring individual progress   A process used to determine if the student is making progress by examining the student's work, accomplishments, and achievements.

morpheme   The single unit of letters that comprise a unit of meaning. A morpheme may be a whole word, prefix, or a suffix.

morphology   The study of the single units of letters that represent a unit of meaning.

negative reinforcer   The removal of a stimulus, contingent upon a response, which increases the future probability of the response.

No Child Left Behind Act (NCLB) of 2001   A federal law that created many changes with the goals of improving academic performance for ALL students. This act stressed accountability through scientifically based research practices and regular and ongoing assessment of student progress.

nominal scale   The items on the scale represent names; the values assigned to the names do not have any innate meaning or value.

normal curve   A symmetrical bell-shaped curve.

normal curve equivalent (NCE)   A standard score with a mean of 50 and a standard deviation of 21.06.

norm-referenced test   A test that compares a student's test performance with that of similar students who have taken the same test.

observation   A systematic process of gathering information by looking at students and their environments.

observer drift   Changes in observation resulting from the observer's shifting away from the original objectives of the observation.

ordinal scale   The items on the scale are listed in rank order.

out-of-level testing   Students in one grade level are assessed with tests that are designed for students in another grade level.

percentage duration rate   The percent of time that a behavior or event occurs. To calculate the percentage duration rate, the observer divides the total duration of the behavior or event by the total time of the observation and multiplies this answer by 100 to obtain a percentage.

percentage score   The percent of test items that were answered correctly.

percentile rank   The point in a distribution at or below which the scores of a given percentage of students fall.

performance-based assessment   The demonstration of knowledge, skills, or behavior.

person-centered planning   The student with the disability engages in an active meaningful way with parents, educators, community members, and others during the assessment, planning, and service delivery processes.

phoneme   The smallest unit of sound that has meaning in a language.

phonemic awareness   The skills of recognizing separating, blending, and manipulating phonemes.

phonics   Knowledge of how specific spoken sounds relate to particular written letters.

phonology   The study of speech sounds.

population   The large group from which the sample of individuals is selected and to which individual comparisons are made regarding test performance.

portfolio   A systematic collection of a student's work, assembled over a period of time, that demonstrates the student's efforts, progress, and achievement.

positive reinforcer   A stimulus that is presented, contingent upon a response, and that increases the future probability of the response.

pragmatics   The study of the use of language in social situations.

predetermined expectation   Bias held by an examiner or educator that interferes with an accurate assessment.

probe   A diagnostic technique that modifies instruction in order to determine whether an instructional strategy is effective.

program evaluation   A process used to assess (1) the progress the student has made in the individualized education program and (2) the overall quality of the school program.

program planning   The process of determining the student's current level of functioning and planning the instructional program.

qualitative data   Information that is descriptive rather than numeric.

quantitative data   Information that can be assigned a number or score.

questionnaire   A set of questions designed to gather information.

rating scale   An instrument that measures the degree of the response.

ratio scale   A scale where the items on the scale are the same distance apart; the scale does have an absolute zero.

raw score   The number of items correct without adjustment for guessing.

reactivity   The adjustments that individuals make in behaviors during an observation.

reading comprehension   Being able to obtain meaning from a text, understand what is read, connect information within the context of a text, and relate what is being read to what is already known.

reading fluency   Being able to read letters, sounds, words, and text passages quickly, automatically, accurately, and smoothly.

receptive language   The ability to understand spoken language.

referral   A process in which questions and concerns about a student are raised and referred to the IEP team. The referral may come from a teacher, parent, or the student.

reliability   The consistency or stability of test performance. The 1999 edition of *Standards for Educational and Psychological Testing* describes reliability and provides a departure from more traditional thinking about reliability. In this edition, reliability refers to the scoring procedure that enables the examiner to quantify, evaluate, and interpret behavior or work samples and the consistency of such measurements when the testing procedure is repeated on a population of individuals or groups.

response to intervention (RTI)   A prereferral activity that occurs prior to a referral for special education services.

rubric   An assessment scale that identifies the area(s) of performance and defines various levels of achievement.

running record   A description of the events that is written as the events occur.

sample   A subgroup of a large group that is representative of the large group. This subgroup is the group that is actually tested.

scatter plot   A type of interval recording form that the observer uses to record single behaviors or a series of behaviors during the observation period.

screening   A process used to identify students who may have a disability and who will be referred for further assessment.

self-determination   When an individual's hopes, dreams, and desires influence the types of assessments that the transition team implements.

semantics   The study of word meanings.

shaping   The technique of reinforcing successive approximations of the target or goal behavior. In reference to the development of language, the verbal response is reinforced as the sound or word being produced more and more closely approximates the sound or word in the language.

skewed distribution   A curve in which most of the scores are at either the low end or the high end of the curve.

speech   The production of oral language for the purpose of expression.

speech disorder   A difficulty in articulation, such as the way words are pronounced; the fluency of speech, including rate and rhythm; or the pitch, volume, and quality of the voice.

split-half reliability   An estimate of the correlation of scores between two halves of a test.

stakeholders   Individuals who are interested in the results of the evaluation.

standard deviation (SD)   A measure of the degree to which various scores deviate from the mean, or average score.

standard error of measurement (SEM)   The amount of error associated with individual test scores, test items, item samples, and test times.

standardization sample   The individuals who are actually tested during the process of test development.

standardized test   A test in which the administration, scoring, and interpretation procedures are prescribed in the test manual and must be strictly followed. A standardized test is usually norm referenced.

standard scores   Raw scores that have been transformed so that they have the same mean and the same standard deviation.

stanine   A type of standard score that has a mean of 5 and a standard deviation of 2; a distribution of scores can be divided into 9 stanines.

stimulus   An environmental condition, event, teacher, or other individual that can affect behavior.

student assistance team   See assistance team.

summative evaluation   An evaluation that is completed at the end of a cycle or program year.

supports   Resources and strategies that aim to promote the development, education, interests, and personal well-being of a person and that enhance individual function. Services are one type of support provide by professional and agencies.

syntax   A system of rules that dictates how words are combined into meaningful phrases and sentences.

target behavior   A behavior that is acquired or eliminated by manipulating the antecedents and consequences.

task analysis   The division of a skill into small, discrete, sequential steps.

test-retest reliability   An estimate of the correlation between scores when the same test is administered two times.

transition   Moving from one system of services to another.

transition services   A coordinated set of activities for a student, designed within an outcome-oriented process, that promotes movement from school to postschool activities, including postsecondary education, vocational training, integrated employment (including supported employment), continuing and adult education, adult services, independent living, and community participation.

triangulation   Conclusions about student performance that are based on multiple sources of information.

true score   The score an individual would obtain on a test if there were no measurement errors.

universal design   " . . . a concept or philosophy for designing and delivering products and services that are usable by people with the widest possible range of functional capabilities, which include products and services that are directly usable (without requiring assistive technologies) and products and services that are made usable with assistive technologies." (20 USC Sec. 602(35); 29 USC Sec. 3002)

validity   The extent to which a test measures what it says it measures.

young children   Children ages birth through age 8.

Index